D0160438

The Seattle School of Theology & Psychology
2501 Elliott Ave.
Seattle, WA 98121
theseattleschool.edu

WITHDRAWN

SEEKING UNDERSTANDING

The Stob Lectures, 1986–1998

Henry Stob was born in Chicago on June 24, 1908. He was reared in a devout Calvinist family and educated from the beginning in the Christian day schools that are interwoven into the total religious perspective of his church and community. He graduated from Calvin College in 1932 and from Calvin Theological Seminary in 1935. He took a Master's degree from Hartford Theological Seminary in 1936, and then went to Europe to study philosophy at the University of Göttingen, taking his Ph.D. in 1938. His dissertation, written in German, was an analysis of Max Weber's sociology of religion. Stob stayed in Europe for a year of postdoctoral study to investigate the efforts then being made by Herman Dooyeweerd and D. H. Th. Vollenhoven to construct a Christian philosophical system. He returned to the United States in 1939 as the war closed in on Europe.

Dr. Stob began his academic career as a professor of philosophy at his alma mater the year he returned. In 1943 he entered the U.S. Navy and served as a lieutenant in the Pacific war zone until shortly after the war ended; he was a member of General MacArthur's occupation staff in Japan until the spring of 1946. Resuming his teaching at Calvin College on his release from the Navy, Stob remained there until 1952, when he was appointed by the Synod of the Christian Reformed Church to teach philosophical and moral theology at Calvin Seminary. There he taught, with a year's interruption as a visiting professor of ethics in the Kobe Reformed Seminary in Japan and the Hapdong Seminary in Seoul, Korea, until his retirement. He received the Calvin College Distinguished Alumni Award in 1976.

Dr. Stob died on May 27, 1996, leaving many students influenced greatly by his teaching. His wife, Hilda (De Graaf), died August 26, 1999. They are survived by their children, Ellen and Richard, and five grandchildren.

The Stob Lectures are sponsored annually by Calvin College and Calvin Theological Seminary in honor of the late Henry J. Stob. Their subject matter is normally restricted to the fields of ethics, apologetics, and philosophical theology. The Stob Lectures are funded by the Henry J. Stob Endowment and are administered by a committee including the presidents of Calvin College and Calvin Theological Seminary.

This volume contains the series of lectures delivered from 1986 to 1998. The annual sets of lectures since 1999 are being published in individual volumes by Eerdmans.

The views and opinions expressed in the Stob Lectures are those of the author only. The publication of these lectures in no way constitutes an endorsement or approval of the lecture content by Calvin College or Calvin Theological Seminary.

Henry J. Stob

SEEKING UNDERSTANDING

The Stob Lectures, 1986–1998

William B. Eerdmans Publishing Company

Grand Rapids, Michigan / Cambridge, U.K.

Collection published 2001 by Wm. B. Eerdmans Publishing Co.
255 Jefferson Ave. S.E., Grand Rapids, Michigan 49503 /
P.O. Box 163, Cambridge CB3 9PU U.K.

Printed in the United States of America

06 05 04 03 02 01   7 6 5 4 3 2 1

Library of Congress Cataloging-in-Publication Data

Seeking understanding : the Stob lectures, 1986-1998.
        p.   cm.
Contents: The making and keeping of commitments / Lewis B. Smedes —
Varieties of moral discourse / James M. Gustafson —
Two arguments from the heart for immortality / Peter Kreeft —
The twin pillars of Christian scholarship / Alvin Plantinga —
Denominations near century's end / Martin E. Marty —
The practices of piety and the practice of medicine / Allen Verhey —
What New Haven and Grand Rapids have to say to each other / Nicholas P. Wolterstorff —
Happiness, goal or gift? / Dewey J. Hoitenga, Jr. —
Conflict, its resolution and the completion of creation / John Feikens —
The ghost in the ivory tower / George I. Mavrodes —
The soul of the Christian university / Arthur F. Holmes —
Sin or sickness / J. Harold Ellens —
Faith and the problem of evil / Eleonore Stump.

ISBN 0-8028-4939-3 (alk. paper)
1. Theology. I. Title: Stob lectures, 1986-1998.
        BR50 .S39 2001
230 — dc21
                                                          2001033223

www.eerdmans.com

Contents

Contents

Contributors

J. Harold Ellens is Editor-in-Chief Emeritus of the *Journal of Psychology and Christianity*.

John Feikens was the United States District Judge for the Eastern District of Michigan (retired).

James M. Gustafson is the Woodruff Professor Emeritus of Religion at Emory University in Atlanta, Georgia.

Dewey J. Hoitenga, Jr. is Professor of Philosophy at Grand Valley State University in Allendale, Michigan.

Arthur F. Holmes is Professor Emeritus of Philosophy at Wheaton College in Wheaton, Illinois.

Peter Kreeft is Professor of Philosophy at Boston College in Boston, Massachusetts.

Martin E. Marty is the Fairfax M. Cone Professor Emeritus of the History of Christianity at the University of Chicago Divinity School in Chicago, Illinois.

George I. Mavrodes is Professor Emeritus of Philosophy at the University of Michigan in Ann Arbor, Michigan.

Alvin Plantinga is the John A. O'Brien Professor of Philosophy and director of the Center for Philosophy of Religion at Notre Dame University in Notre Dame, Indiana.

Lewis B. Smedes is Professor Emeritus of Theology and Ethics at Fuller Theological Seminary in Pasadena, California.

Contributors

Eleonore Stump is the Robert J. Henle Professor of Philosophy at St. Louis University in St. Louis, Missouri.

Allen D. Verhey is the Evert J. and Hattie E. Blekkink Professor of Religion and Chair of the Department of Religion at Hope College in Holland, Michigan.

Nicholas P. Wolterstorff is the Noah Porter Professor of Philosophical Theology at Yale University Divinity School.

The Making and Keeping of Commitments

LEWIS B. SMEDES

Contents

Introduction

Robert Bellah's much talked-about book, *Habits of the Heart*, has the subtitle *Individualism and Commitment in American Life*, and it gives strong evidence for a hunch most of us have had anyway, that individualism is winning out over commitment to other people in the struggle for the American soul. Bellah's thesis is that our individualistic ethos has given birth to what he calls a therapeutic culture whose unwritten creed is every individual's right to psychic well-being. People of the therapeutic culture relate to each other on the premise that every human association is one means for the individual to gain a bit more of the personal fulfillment that he or she has a right to have. In the individualist's life, a human relationship itself has no moral claims on the individuals who are in it; nobody has a duty to stick with a relationship he or she is stuck with if sticking does not pay off in private satisfaction.

In the Christian moral tradition, we generally assume that the Creator has lovingly intended us to make commitments to other people and to keep the commitments we make. We enter some human relationships with a commitment to stay with them, and, afterward, we have a moral obligation to keep the commitment even though keeping it does not pay off well in individual satisfaction. We are not meant to keep our bags packed, ready to take off and leave the other person to pick up the pieces whenever the grass looks greener down the street.

But this is a very general observation. Real life, in the anguish and sin of concrete situations, does not always present us with two clear options: keep one's commitments at all costs or selfishly follow one's desires. Nor does life present us with two wholly different sorts of persons: the free-wheeling uncommitted individual on one hand and the uncompromising keepers of commitments on the other.

What we have are many different sorts of human relationships, each of which needs its own sort of commitment. And what we have are people who are more or less committed and more or less given to staking their claims to personal fulfillment.

So I come to these lectures impressed with two things. The first is that commitment-making and commitment-keeping are important moral qualities, and that human communities suffer where commitments are not kept. The second is that commitment-making and commitment-keeping are very large and fuzzy moral ideals that bear some examination.

Both of these impressions persuaded me that it might be helpful to devote the Stob Lectures this year to the subject of commitment-making and commitment-keeping.

Before we get started, I want to say a quick word about the sort of commitment I will be discussing. I will be talking about a person's freely willing to keep a commitment to another person or to other people.

There are two parts to what I just said.

First, we will be talking about a freely willed determination to stick with someone whom we promised to stick with, a daily renewable commitment. We are not talking about crossing a point of no return after which we *cannot* go back.

Having just signed a purchase agreement for a new car and driven it home, I may be attacked by a severe case of buyer's remorse; I would turn the car back in, but I cannot, for the signing of the agreement commits me: I have no choice. I may be a pilot taking a 747 into the air; my engines are throttled, my wheels are off the ground, I am three hundred feet in the air, and I can no longer decide not to be airborne: I am committed, I have no choice. This is not the sort of being committed that I will be talking about. I will be talking about commitments that I can keep if I will to keep them, and I can stop keeping whenever I will to stop.

Secondly, I will be talking about personal commitment to other persons. I will not be talking about commitment to causes or careers, and not about commitment to ideas or to truth, but only about commitments to persons in human relationships.

CHAPTER 1

What Do I Do When I Make a Commitment?

What do I do when I make a commitment to someone?

I make an appointment with someone, for some unrestricted time, sometime in his tomorrows, and all the tomorrows that follow all his yesterdays, tomorrows that neither of us can predict.

I stretch myself into a future neither of us can see, and I plan a rendezvous there with him, and ask him to trust me to be there.

I reach into the unpredictable times ahead and make one thing predictable; I will be there with him.

I throw myself into the turbulent ocean of his uncertainties and create an island of certainty there for him, the certainty of my caring presence.

I create one small space for him to have when all his foundations shake, the space of my promised presence.

These are a few of the things I do when I make a commitment.

But let us stand back a bit and take a longer look.

We have a mystery on our hands, no doubt; Gabriel Marcel was right when he called it that,[1] the mystery of a will that in the face of a universe of contingencies makes one thing incontingent. But an even greater mystery is this: why should anyone do it? Why would anyone or why should anyone bond himself or herself so unconditionally to someone in the face of the unknown?

For one thing, after I commit myself, I shall change. I shall be another person one day, different from the person who makes the commitment today. Yet, when I become that other, that different person, I intend to be bound by the commitment that this present person is making today.

---

1. Gabriel Marcel, *Creative Fidelity* (New York: Crossroad, 1982), p. 152.

So, in one bold sense, I am expecting another person to keep the commitment I make today.

The same goes for you, when I commit myself to you. You will not be the same person in the future that you are today, either. But I am making a commitment to you as you are today that I will be there with you, whoever you turn out to be tomorrow.

It is the personal changes we pass through on our pilgrimage that make our willingness to make and our power to keep commitments such a mystery.

And a gamble, too. How can we promise ourselves for the future when we don't know, cannot know, what sorts of persons we will be then? Or what life will be like in the time ahead, when the commitment we made once feels like choking smoke of regretted words after the fire of intention has died?

But, looking at it another way, the fact that we change is probably why commitment was invented. Commitments are the only way for free persons to batten down their lives a little, give them some permanence, some stability in the midst of change — to keep them from being blown away by shifts in the breezes of mood and the blustery blows of passion. Commitments are one way to put some muscle into our human relationships, give them some strength to tough out the hard times, ride out the stormy times. Commitment lifts life a niche beyond impulse, whim, desire, drive, lust, and all the other natural inclinations that make human relationships so rhapsodic and so painfully unstable.

Change and uncertainty create the problem. Commitment is our surprising solution.

When we make a commitment to another person, we surrender two things vital to autonomous individuals. We surrender our freedom and we surrender our individuality.

We surrender something of our freedom, and for an undefined time. We build invisible fences around ourselves. We decide that our lives will not flow free, unattached, uncoupled, from one personal association to another. We bind ourselves with the invisible fiber of a remembered promise, a word given and a word received, not just for now, but for an undefined time to come.

We limit our individuality, too. When I commit myself to you, I stretch myself beyond my individuality and place myself at your side, to walk with you, hand in hand, into the heather of the unknown hills before

7

us. Once committed, I shall not be a mere *I* again; I shall thereafter always be an organic member of a *we*. The mirror of my private soul no longer shows the whole of me. Now I am who I am in my linkage to another.

All this we do, and more beside, when we make our commitments to other people.

Spoken this way, it all sounds so absolute, so unconditional, so categorical, so fixed. We shall have to dip the core of commitment into the solvent of ordinary persons living their ordinary lives amid many sorts of relationships calling for different sorts of commitments, and sometimes calling for reconsiderations of commitments already made.

But, before looking at the free commitments that human beings make to each other, we must look briefly at the divine model for all our making and keeping of commitments.

The Divine Model

What we experience in our making and keeping of commitments is a reflection of God's style of creating and keeping his alliance with his human family. And what we see in God's making and keeping of commitment has to be a model of ours.

The basic fact about God in his relationship to his creation is that commitment-keeping is the essence of who he is to us — his name, his character, his identity.

Recall just a few highlights in the story of God's making and keeping commitments.

He had been on leave of absence for 400 years. Now it was time to get his program on track again. So he spotted a Semitic fugitive tending sheep in the desert, flagged him down with a clump of chaparral burning strangely long, and told him that he was to be God's point man in a campaign to liberate his family and relaunch his campaign to win the world back again.

But Moses was worried, among other things, about credibility. Who would believe this story? He needed some identification from this invisible divine stranger whose only credential is that he talked through a piece of burning chaparral. A name would help.

So God told Moses his name. But as everyone knows, the later Jews hallowed it by not using it, and all we have is a set of four consonants which probably once was a form of the verb *to be* that English translators rendered with variations on the impressive "I Am Who I Am." In Philosophy 301, we learned that the name crystallized the truth that God possessed his essence and his existence in one indivisible act.

But Moses did not take Philosophy 301. Nor did the hod-carrying Semitic slaves. The question on their minds was not the question of essence and existence. It was the question of presence and absence. They asked the pragmatic question about God: Where is he when we need him? Why isn't he here for us? And will he be here tomorrow?

And it is reasonable to suppose that God identified himself in terms appropriate to their question, and said: This is my name: The One Who Will Be There With You. That is the appropriate name for the commitment-making and keeping God. He subordinates his own entitlements to the needs of his people; he is no longer free to be a fluid individual deity; now he will always be a God *of* someone.

Yahweh is the sort who sticks with what he is stuck with. Resisting every divine impulse to call it quits when the relationship soured, he stays.

At a later time when Israel had reason to suppose that he had gone on extended leave again, he came, incognito, as the God whose name was Immanuel, the "One who was with them." And in the shadows of that shining season, when it looked as if God were after all going on another leave of absence, Jesus said: I will be with you until the end of the world — the commitment of a God whose name is: The One Who Will Be With You.

And in John's vivid vision, hope in the divine commitment is reaffirmed: "I heard a loud voice call from the throne, You see this city? Here God lives among men. He will make his home among them. . . . His name is: The God who is with them" (Rev. 21:3).

From beginning to end, the Bible tells the story of a committed God . . . a God with character to stick with what he is stuck with, in the face of a thousand reasons to pack his bags and take off to greener pastures.

He is the model for human commitment-keeping. But our human commitments cannot be simply modelled after God's commitment to us. We are not gods, only something like God, and our commitment-keeping can, at best, only be something like God's commitment-keeping.

Let me point to a few likenesses and differences. First, the likenesses:

1. A free decision to make and keep commitment is the moral mortar of God's relationships with us. It is also the moral cement of our relationship with one another. At least some human relationships entail a moral

9

obligation to commitment because commitment is the moral structure of significant personal relationships.

2. God's commitment is to our shalom, and is a good commitment for that reason. Our enduring commitments are good insofar as they, too, make for other people's peace.

Now for some differences:

1. God's commitment of grace is quite unconditional; our commitments to each other cannot be quite unconditional. Commitments, unlike contracts, do have a quality of "no matter what" to them. But all our commitments are affected by the sin and finitude that affect the relationships we are committed to. And so they cannot be, at least cannot all be, unconditional.

2. God's commitment is made unilaterally. The people were not consulted; he made the move, said the Yes, and they could only respond. Most of our commitments are made and kept reciprocally; someone must accept our commitment in order for us to keep it.

3. God commits himself inclusively; he can embrace the race. We must be exclusive in some commitments, and selective in all of them.

In sum, we can say that as God's commitment-keeping character is the moral structure of his relationship to us it is a model for our commitment-keeping, to a limited extent. But in order to know how much we ought, and how consistently we can, model our commitment-keeping after God's, we shall have to poke around some in the human dynamics of human commitment-keeping.

CHAPTER 2

What Are Commitments For?

Why is it a moral good to make commitments to people? Why is it a virtue to be a person who can be counted on to keep her commitments? Or why is it good to be a self-surrendering commitment-keeper?

There is something to be said for commitment-keeping simply as a virtue, a solid building block in the edifice of character. It is a good thing to be a person of fealty: loyal, stanch, devoted. Commitment-keeping is the mark of a good character.

But I doubt that we are called to be commitment-keepers as a way of polishing our virtue, of being jaw-jutting persons who preen themselves on their moral lustre. We don't need to work at commitment-keeping simply because it makes for moral virtuosity, for its own sake, the way some people work hard to keep fit so that they can endure the exercises that keep them fit.

Commitment-keeping is not an end. It is a means. Commitments are good because life would be less good without them. Commitments are good because they create islands of security for people in their oceans of insecurity, enclaves of permanence in the jungles of change. Commitments are good because they serve human community better than does free-floating, unfettered, self-enhancing individualism.

Commitments Are for Community

Can you imagine any community where the best we could ever get from anyone was: "I'll try to be there if I can, but don't count on it"? Commitment is the moral fibre that binds a collection of individuals into a community. Everything depends on it, as Chesterton said, from a family re-

11

union to a political revolution, from the calling of a committee to the founding of a nation, from the building of a city to the coming of the Kingdom. There is no community without commitment. And community is what commitment is for.

Maybe you can have a regime, or a gang, or a crowd, or a prison full of inmates, without commitment, but you cannot have a human community.

In sum, keeping commitments is good because keeping them generally makes life better for people who live together.

On the same basis, therefore, when keeping a commitment does not make for community, the value of that commitment is in question.

I know of a man who makes a moral show of his own commitment-keeping. He reminds his wife regularly of his devotion to their marriage, of how he has been a good and faithful husband, and all of his reminders have the mucky smell of self-justification. Worse, his claim to the virtue of commitment-keeping is a thinly disguised put-down for her. He is letting her know that he sticks around, not because she is worth sticking to, but in spite of the fact that she is not worth sticking around.

So his commitment claims are a form of psychic cruelty. In fact, his commitment-keeping is a cover for all sorts of other banal brutalities.

The man's son has told me more than once that his father's righteous commitment-keeping was the cruelest cross his family had to bear. Better for everyone had he packed his bags and moved early on.

Something is wrong when the virtue of commitment becomes a burden to the person we are committed to. I recall an epitaph by C. S. Lewis:

> Erected by her sorrowing brothers
> In memory of Martha Clay.
> Here lies one who lived for others.
> Now she has peace. And so have they.

Gabriel Marcel makes a nice distinction between constancy and presence. Constancy is a kind of predictability, or dependability, or sticking-with-it-ness. Constancy is the skeleton of fidelity.

Presence turns constancy into creative commitment. When I am, with my very self, wholly involved in the dialogue of life with the other, I am committed.

When a person lets me know that he forces himself to stick, that sticking is a noble duty he does, he is being constant. When a person is with me and for me in the midst of adverse circumstances, at inconvenience to himself, but always engaged with me as if he really wanted to be, he is present.

If he lets me know that he is near me simply out of duty, I will tell him I admire his conscience, but that his constancy is of no joy to me, and we would both be served by his taking off.

Constancy plus presence: this is the equation that makes for the kind of commitment that sustains human fellowship.

Commitments Create Identity

A moral value of commitment-keeping lies in its possibilities for keeping life better for people to whom commitments are made.

But commitment-keeping also offers a crucial payoff to the commitment-keeper: it creates a lasting identity for a transient individual.

I mentioned earlier that, on the surface of it, it seems hard to make commitments for an indefinite future when we will not be the same person in the future as we were when we made the commitment. And the odd answer is: the making and keeping of commitments is a way of holding on to your identity so that, in one deep sense, you are the same in the future as you were when you made the commitment.

In a way, we are our commitments. As Paul Tournier has said: To live is to commit. And to make and keep significant commitments is to live as the particular, identifiable person one is.

One of the existence-shaping questions for each of us is: how do we manage to stay the same person while we pass through life's several stages? How can I, for instance, be the same person as the toothpick with pants on that I see in my childhood photographs?

And how do we shape an identity in the midst of the ambiguities and conflicts of our secret souls? We are all a little like that Gadarene demoniac: we are not single, we are a legion of characters struggling for control.

I, for one, have not found in myself some immutable ghost sheltered serenely in the sub-cellars of my being, the ghost I was taught to call my soul. Nor can I find my enduring identity in the feelings people are always telling me to get with, nor in the feelings I am so anxious to have other people feel about me.

How, then, do we create ourselves?

I need to create my identity in the story I am writing with the raw materials of my life. I need to create an identity by writing a continued story and not just a collection of unconnected episodes. I have got to have a thread, a story line, that ties the story into a plot.

The story line is created out of the commitments I make and keep. I cannot write a story by beginning with a new plot whenever the mood is on me. I have to accept what I have already written in my commitments as the grist for what I write today. And this is a way of saying that if I want to create a continued, single story, a real story with a beginning, a middle, and a genuine end, a story in which I can be recognized all the way through, in short if I want to have an identity, I have to find it and reveal it by a pattern of keeping commitments to people.

Alasdair MacIntyre, speaking of personal continuity, writes: "I am forever whatever I have been at any time for others . . . no matter how changed I may be now."[1] We are who we are within the narrative we are creating through our sustained relationships with people.

I was struck a long time ago by a sentence in Hannah Arendt: "Without being bound to the fulfillment of our promises, we would never be able to keep our identities; we would be condemned to wander helplessly and without direction in the darkness of each individual's lonely heart, caught in its contradictions and equivocalities."[2]

And here is Thomas More's elegant line in *A Man for All Seasons*. He is talking to his daughter, Margaret, trying to explain his suicidal bullheadedness. "When a person makes a promise, Meg, he puts himself in his hands like water. And if he opens his fingers to let it go, he need not hope to find himself again."

The other side of creating identity through commitments is that we also are created through other people's commitments to us, as we trust people to keep their commitments, and as we accept them for what they were in their commitments to us.

Who am I? I am Rena Smedes's boy. I have an identity because a certain woman committed herself to me, to me mewling and puking in her arms, committed herself without thinking about it or taking pride in it, and keeping her commitment during the times I was a very acute pain in the neck to her.

---

1. *After Virtue* (Notre Dame, Ind.: University of Notre Dame Press, 1984), p. 202.
2. *The Human Condition* (Chicago: University of Chicago Press, 1958), p. 237.

And I have an identity to the extent that I accept her as the person who gave me the basic raw materials for the story I have had to write for myself. Persons who can accept their parents, along with whatever genetic and psychological blessing or curse they laid on them, as the early grist for the story they are writing with their lives, are persons who find peace in who and what they are.

So we create our identities out of commitments in two ways: first, in accepting the commitment of others to us, and second, in committing ourselves to others.

And this is another reason why God invented commitment as a way of life for creatures who live by his grace.

CHAPTER 3

Why People Keep Commitments

I think we should not equate staying with someone with keeping one's commitment to someone.

People stay together, in marriage for instance, for reasons as many and complicated as there are people, none of them being pure devotion to the duty of keeping a commitment.

Some people just get used to each other. They don't have surprises for each other. She knows when he's coming home, what he will say when he gets in the door, what he drinks before supper and what he is likely to talk about while he eats, how he takes his clothes off and when he is likely to make love. He does not unsettle anyone with odd questions, changed opinions, or unpredicted feelings. Like the couple in the *New Yorker* cartoon: "I know what she is going to say. She knows what I'm going to say. So we just don't bother." Boring. Yes, but settling too. And boring settledness wears better than the excitement of never knowing what is coming next. Not a lot of moral grit here . . . just putting up with what you've gotten used to because it's too much nuisance to get used to somebody else.

Some people stay around because what they have is not as bad as what could be out there.

I know a woman who, after being married to him for twenty years, discovered that her husband was gay. Not a hundred percent, dyed-in-the-wool gay, but gay enough to make him ambivalent about his sexual preference. He is afraid to leave her. She is afraid to let him go. She has no job skills. He is a good person, gentle, devoutly loving, even though he cannot love her the way she desires to be loved. So she stays.

If we cannot give her much credit for commitment, and maybe even question her choice, let us at least say that she is surrendering some of her desires for the sake of some of his needs.

I know a minister who is married to a shrew who grew up as the daughter of a prima donna on the Baptist stage and thought she was marrying an even bigger star when she caught Chuck. But Chuck was not called to clerical celebrity, and their early infatuation has wilted into a tedious and tired toleration. Chuck hates the whole scene. But he has face to save, and a pension besides. If he gets a divorce, he will lose his job and his reputation for straight-line moral orthodoxy to boot.

So he sticks with what he is stuck with. Don't give him an A for commitment, but don't demand that everyone keep commitments only out of unambivalent moral motives.

Other people are simply trapped. I know a talented lady who has multiple sclerosis — and a husband who brutalizes her in various subtle fashions. I think she would leave in a minute, but she can't get away because she cannot afford to go anywhere.

Give her sympathy and some help if you can, but don't confuse her staying with commitment; give her credit for resisting a temptation to put arsenic in his coffee.

People keep real commitments, too, for many reasons.

People who keep a high quality of commitment do not do it merely out of conscious obligation to a vow they once made. It is for other, more person-directed reasons. It seems to me, in truth, that most commitment-keepers are not sticking with what they are stuck with simply because they remember that once upon a time they made a promise. They have other reasons.

Let me mention some.

People keep commitments because they care about the people they are committed to. This came to me one afternoon while I was visiting my mother in the hospital. She had broken her hip for the second time, and I, being on some business in Michigan, had my afternoons free for long talks with her just a couple of weeks, as it turned out, before she died.

My mother, I must tell you, left her home in Friesland at age twenty-one with a dreamer of a husband, to pursue the American dream with the countless other European emigrants in the early days of our century. Her husband, my father, stayed with her for eleven years and then, at age thirty-two, died and went to heaven, leaving his wife with five children and not five dollars to care for them with. She was just thirty-one, no money, no social security, no relatives, and no job skills. It was tough going. As I got older I wondered about her in a way that children seldom wonder about their parents. Did this woman, this lonely, needy woman of such intense feeling, never long for a male in her life?

So I asked her, and felt, when I did, as though I had barged into someone's sacred privacy, off-limits to sons. "Mother, you were a good looking woman, and you must have been terribly lonely. You had a right to some happiness. Didn't you ever long for a man, maybe someone who would marry you?"

She answered quickly as if she had been waiting a long time for someone to ask. "Yes," she said, "I wanted a man, but I was afraid that if I took a man he would not love my children, and I cared too much for them to take the risk."

I don't think she ever thought about having taken a vow to take care of her kids. Never prided herself, any more than a lioness would pride herself in her loyalty to her pride of cubs. She just cared for us enough to stick with what she was stuck with at considerable cost to her own desires for fulfillment.

Her commitment was the child of her care, which is a far cry from the true grit of stubborn loyalty to a vow.

People also keep commitments because they feel that they belong to the people they are committed to.

We establish relationships with some people who cleave to us like a vine twisting its branches around the trunk of a tree for so long that you cannot separate tree from vine. They belong to us, and belonging is reason enough for staying.

Albert Camus's *The Plague* is about belonging and commitment. The people of the town of Oran knew that they were in for something dreadful when the rats came out of the dark places to die in their streets and hallways and when, once the rats were all dead, the citizens began to die the same way. It was not long before a thousand persons were dying every week. So the town was quarantined; nobody could get in or out.

Dr. Bernard Rieux was caught in the plague, just like everyone else. And it never occurred to him to try to get out of town, even though he would have liked to join his wife who was a patient at a resort in another town. Dr. Rieux simply figured that he belonged to the town.

But a journalist named Raymond Rambert was caught in Oran, and he wanted to get out more than he wanted anything else. "Why should I stay?" he asked Dr. Rieux. "I'm different from the rest of the people; I don't belong here."

But he was stuck. And, for nothing better to do, he began going with Dr. Rieux on his daily rounds, as he tried to make dying a little less horrible for the people, and maybe saving some children. Raymond pitched in, doing whatever a layman could do in such chaos and death.

One day a person-smuggler offered Raymond a chance to get out — for a price. But he surprised Dr. Rieux by refusing to leave.

Stay? Why stay, Rieux asked. Your happiness is waiting for you in Paris. You have a right to be happy. And you certainly cannot be happy here.

Raymond's answer was: "Until now I always felt a stranger in this town, and that I'd no concern with you people. But now that I've seen what I have seen, I know that I belong here whether I want it or not." Raymond and Rieux were in the same boat; they were stuck because they belonged.

Most people keep commitments because they have come to feel the mystery of belonging to other people or another person.

Some people fulfill commitments because their own identity is created by the commitment.

A person makes a commitment, and lets it be a birth into a new identity. She is no longer the same person she used to be. She has a new name, God's name: The One Who Will Be There With You. And thereafter, she simply accepts whatever conditions of living God providentially creates, the way a person lives out her life the best she can once she has been born the person she is. To break the commitment is a little like taking your own life, or at least losing your identity.

There are people who accept the conditions of committed life in this fashion.

I was fascinated by this thought some months ago as I read Dale Cooper's story of his father, John Cooper. John Cooper married a sturdy, sprightly farm girl named Margie back in 1941 and settled in with Margie in high hopes of becoming the county's biggest onion grower. But four years later, with two little children in the house, Margie fell victim to polio, and was destined to spend most of the rest of her life in an iron lung. Gone were the payoffs and all the things a man is entitled to in a marriage: no house keeper, no sex partner, no child bearer, no budget balancer.

Gone, too, was the high hope of a big onion farm; you can't make it big in onion farming when you are spending big chunks of the day taking care of a paralyzed wife.

John and Margie had a fortieth wedding anniversary not too long ago; someone asked him to explain his long devotion.

"I'm a Christian," he said, "and we try to keep our promises." But I don't believe that John spent forty years gritting his teeth in legalistic bondage to a word of promise he had made to Margie. It was not as if he would have ditched her years ago had he only not been stuck to a vow he once spoke in front of a preacher. He could not have been Margie's laughing, encouraging, uplifting partner if his life was bondage to a promise.

To people like John, a promise is like being born. He did what a person born with a handicap does; he accepted his and Margie's situation as the condition of his life.

When Margie died his son Dale asked him how he had done what he had done, all those years. "I never even thought about doing anything else. You just do it, and God helps you."

You just do it. But only if you let your significant commitments be a kind of birth into a new dimension of your reality, so that sticking with what you are stuck with becomes a creative way of becoming your own self.

I have mentioned three reasons why some people keep commitments: (1) they keep commitments because they care about the people they are committed to. (2) They keep commitments because they feel that they belong to the people they are committed to. (3) They keep commitments because a commitment made is like a birth into another stage of their selfhood. In short, people who keep commitments for these reasons tend to think more about the persons they care about and belong to than about their stubborn determination to stick with what they stuck themselves with by a vow spoken in the distant past.

And yet, sometimes, when the whole thing seems to be falling apart, when a person has a lot of good reasons to pack her bags and move on, she may indeed remember that one day, ten years or a lifetime ago, she made a promise. It is as simple as that. She made a promise, and the sheer memory of words spoken before God and a few witnesses tells her that she is committed, and she has to stay. She cannot think of any hopeful reason for staying; not caring, not belonging, she stays simply because she made a promise and is bound to keeping it. This too is why some people keep commitments.

CHAPTER 4

Commitment to Friendship

There is a friend that sticketh closer than a brother. This fact may tell us as much about brothers as it does about friends. But we all do need a friend who is close to us, knows us, enjoys us, and is there with us when we need her, in ways that we do not expect or want brothers to be. And most of us consider ourselves blessed if God provides one or two in a lifetime.

But what about a friend that "sticketh," not only close, but for a long time, maybe until death doth us part?

Should we look for enduring friendship in a life where most relationships are only for the time being? Does friendship have commitment woven into it, an enduring commitment, the kind of commitment that calls us to stick with a friend without a time limit?

Alvin Toffler told us in his book *Future Shock* that in the future, which is now yesterday, friendships would be *ad hoc*, here, now, and over with when the company sends one of the friends to another plant or when the grass looks greener at another club or another church or another neighborhood.

The best friendships, C. S. Lewis reminded us, are born when two people discover that they like the same things, work for the same things, play at the same things . . . things outside of themselves . . . so that when they get together they both focus, not on each other, nor on their friendship, but on whatever it is, out there beyond themselves, that they care about and do together.

But even best friends carry on in a mobile society; they move around a lot, and get too far apart to play together at their hobbies or work together at their jobs. So they find new people to do these things with in the new place — *ad hoc* friendships, friendship for this time, this place, this club, this project. It strikes me that Lewis's ideal of friendship becomes, in an upwardly or downwardly mobile culture, a victim of mobility, just as Toffler predicted.

It is sad that it should be so. But it may be that the mobility that makes for throw-away friendship only underscores the melancholy fact that friendships are marked by the Creator for the time being only. Friendship may be tentative because it flutters with the shifting currents of personal change.

Friendship is reciprocal, rooted in mutual need, mutual affection, mutual admiration. Who would even want a friend who stuck with us only because he felt compassion for us, or only wanted to be our benefactor? My friend does not have a duty to bail me out of jail, cover a gambling debt, or pay my hospital bills. He would probably do it if he could, but coming to my rescue is not what our friendship is about. Benevolence is a Christian duty, but it can spoil a good friendship if you do too much of it, certainly if you expect too much of it.

Friends are friends, not only as they do things together that they like to do; they are friends because they like each other, and are friends only as long as they like each other. They may have agape afterward, but not friendship. There is certainly some melancholy in this. I feel just a bit cheated when I read such harsh observations as Samuel Johnson's, that "the friendship . . . practiced by common mortals must take its rise from mutual pleasure, and must end when the power ceases of delighting each other."[1] But it is true. Friends do stop pleasing each other, and when the pleasure is gone, the friends tend to become former friends.

Well, there is nothing peculiar about that; it happens all the time in a world where people change, not always for the better as far as friends are concerned. And when friends change, friendship cools. Aristotle, who valued friendliness as a noble virtue, saw the inevitability of it. "One who broke off such a friendship would not be felt to be acting oddly, because the man that he made his friend was not like that anymore; so now that he has changed . . . he gives him up" (*Nicomachaen Ethics,* IX, 3).

So, one concedes reluctantly, friendships are not bound by commitment to endure all change, abide through all changes of circumstance, or

---

1. Samuel Johnson, *Essays from the "Rambler," "Adventurer," and "Idler,"* ed. W. J. Bate (New Haven: Yale University Press, 1968), p. 283, cited by Gilbert C. Meilaender in *Friendship* (Notre Dame, Ind.: University of Notre Dame Press, 1981), p. 57.

interests, or sympathies, or feelings. If a friendship happens to last a lifetime, count it an extraordinary blessing; it did not happen because friendship obligates you to make it last.

Even the way most friendships begin hints at friendship's impermanence. Friendships do not begin with a solemn vow spoken before God and these witnesses. There is no liturgy of baptism into a friendship, or a promise to stick with our friend until death us do part.

The way Jonathan and David took an oath to friendship forever is a poetic exception. "Jonathan made a covenant with David," we read, "because he loved him. . . ." And they both banked on that sweet swearing when the time turned sour and friendship was tested in blood. Jonathan made David swear again by his love for him (1 Sam. 20:19), and David appealed, not to their mutual liking, but to his friend's loyalty. But such self-conscious swearing fits the biblical narrative and is imitated more easily by romantic children than by practical adults.

Most of us stray into friendships, almost by accident. We meet, both of us ready, needy even, maybe hungry for a friend, and we poke around delicately, discreetly, not too eagerly, as the openings come. We look each other over, see signs that we might hit it off, discover that we talk the same language, agree on what is important in life, like to do the same sorts of things when we are not at work, and we discover that we get deep satisfaction from doing them with each other. And so, we fumble into friendship.

The birth of friendship is an awkward process, unceremonial and uncontrived — and, at the beginning, uncommitted. Casual friends become best friends, not by a commitment to best friendship but by a grafting and a growing together as each learns to trust the other, understand each other, depend on each other, presume on each other, and simply expect each other to be there for them. We become best friends as we learn to feel safe in the friendship, "safe in the knowledge that we can give the other something she or he needs, something that will create a binding tie between us; somewhere inside, we may also know the friend . . . has qualities we need, qualities we envy because we cannot yet give them to ourselves."[2]

But when we don't feel safe in it anymore, can't count on it, don't envy the friend's qualities anymore, we gradually remove the life support systems and let the friendship die . . . with dignity if we are lucky, but die nonetheless.

2. Lillian Rubin, *Just Friends* (New York: Harper & Row, 1985), p. 181.

When it dies our friends and neighbors do not feel that either of us has violated a sacred commitment. There is no churchly censure on failed friendships. No guardian of the Judaeo-Christian tradition bewails the decline and fall of friendship in our culture. Friendships die and nobody lifts a moral eyebrow as when a commitment is broken and fidelity is lapsed.

Mutuality holds friends together; if two people do not feel a mutual attraction, they will not become friends, and if mutual attraction ceases, friendship will cease. But why can't friends make commitments to stay together anyway? Why can't they commit themselves to stay friends no matter what? Well, the reason is that when people stick with people they do not want to be stuck with, they are not friends. Colleagues, maybe. Married couples, maybe. But not friends.

Yet we do want more. Just because friends can be so close, closer than family, we want friendships to have commitment sewn into them. Kelly Girl friendships, *ad hoc,* as the occasion arises, are not enough. We don't want all our friendships to be like a relationship with a savvy stockbroker or a caring therapist, good people who give us care as long as we pay the fare. We want a friend like Dean Acheson, Truman's beleaguered former Secretary of State, who went to visit his friend Alger Hiss in prison, convicted traitor though he was, bad politics though it was; we want a committed friend who sticks even if sticking gets him into trouble.

Friendship does carry a need for commitment. If it does not require a commitment to permanence, it does need a commitment to loyalty or devotion.

One ought to be true to a friend. He ought to stick close to a friend when she is in trouble or sadness. She ought to listen when a friend tells of her troubles. He ought to defend his friend when he is falsely accused. She ought to give a friend preference over others, do favors to a friend that she cannot do for many others. Friendships create an inner circle where people prefer one another over outsiders.

At the very least, one ought not turn against a friend. It seems so much worse that Judas betrayed his friend than if a stranger had turned him in. It seems awesomely more wrong for Brutus to turn against Caesar than for Cassius to do the same thing. To betray a friend is a particularly grievous wrong because friendship needs loyalty, even if it does not require benefaction.

Friendship gives a friend a reason to trust a friend. Here is a cliche: If you want a friend, you must be a friend. And it must mean: If you want to be a friend, you must commit yourself to her, over others, to be with her even when being with her is a severe disadvantage to you.

And so we have a real commitment of intention even if we do not have a commitment of extension: a commitment to a quality of relationship for now even if it is not a commitment to be friends forever.

Still, having conceded so much, something in us wants more. We want a friend who sticks with us after we have moved away and we do not play tennis together anymore, or bitch about fortune and the terrors of love, or plot ways to renew the church or change the world; we want a friendship that lasts even though most of the mutually enriching ingredients of friendship are gone. We want a friend who sticketh, not only as close, but nearly as long as a brother. For when we lose a close friend, we feel a kind of death. Kierkegaard said that to lose a friend is like what happens when the second part of a hyphenated word is erased and only a dangling half-word is left, with a hyphen dangling at the end waiting for the other half to come back.

We pine for a world where long-term fidelity and friendship are compatible. And we believe that this life is worse off, that the human community forfeits its humanity when friendship is all *ad hoc,* relished today, relinquished tomorrow. The city is sad when a lonely person's best friend is his therapist, or his bartender.

Maybe our longing for lasting friendship is a hint that heaven must be real — that there must be a time and a place where nobody is a mere neighbor or brother-in-law whom you have to love because you are a Christian, but where everyone is a friend you want to love. Heaven is where friendship is both deep and enduring, and so generously, so promiscuously shared, that philia, not agape, and not eros, but philia, friendship, will be what fills the human soul.

What I suggest is that friendship, when we are all transformed, may be the essence of heaven's goodness, and that our longing for it may be a strong evidence of heaven's reality. For the time being, we accept the melancholy of transient friendships and are thankful for the gift of loyal friends as long as they last.

CHAPTER 5

Commitment in Marriage

This year about 4 million Americans will make some sort of commitment to each other in marriage. Most of them will fully expect at the time to keep their commitment. But, after a while, about half of them will decide that some private need or desire is more important than that commitment, and will get a divorce.

The shocking spread between wedding commitments and marital mortality suggests at the very least that most of us don't know what we are doing when we make a commitment for marriage. We marry the wrong person; only the very lucky ever marry exactly the right one. We change; few of us stay the same persons we were when we made the commitment. So in the nature of the case, nobody knows what he or she is doing when making the commitment of marriage.

Obviously we don't agree on what sort of commitment marriage asks of us. For some people, marriage is a special sort of friendship that entails the same sort of commitment that a friendship does: loyalty for the time being, but not necessarily forever.

We part ways in our society where the commitment to marriage intersects with commitment to friendship. We separate today on the issue of whether marriage lays on married people a moral obligation that binds them to each other permanently, even when the mutual attraction of friendship dies and the personal relationship within the marriage is unrewarding and unfulfilling. For some people, a marriage commitment has the same moral weight as a commitment to friendship: deep loyalty for the time being. For others marriage entails a different sort of commitment than friendship: deep loyalty "until death doth us part."

The Christian moral tradition teaches us that a marriage commitment is different from a friendship commitment. It is, indeed, a commitment to work at maintaining a certain quality of relationship, but to keep working on the premise that you don't quit even when the pain is larger than the pleasure.

I want to ask what there is about marriage that obligates us to stick with it even when mutual attraction is dead and when it holds no promise of personal fulfillment in it. Why does marriage pin people down with a moral duty to stay in it even when they stop liking and loving each other? Why are married people stuck forever with what they are stuck with?

Most married people don't think about commitment much until it is sorely tested. As best I remember, I never gave the word "commitment" a thought when I got married; I did have a sense that what I was doing was plopping me into a stream I was never to swim away from, but I did not think about it as a commitment.

It is obviously possible to break the commitment and dissolve the marriage by a simple act of will. If it is possible, why is it not permissible?

People who are committed don't contemplate their commitments much either. We gradually get linked; we get so used to each other that we cannot think of ourselves without thinking of the other also. We may hate each other sometimes, love each other mildly most of the time, but we gradually become each other in a way that leaves us quite crazily incomplete without the other. Being committed does not smack our minds with a moral obligation; it comes more like settling into our destiny, or blessing, as the case may be.

It is when we fear we made a mistake . . . married the wrong person . . . like somebody else a lot better . . . feel skewered into place . . . trapped, cabin'd, cribbed, confined, it is then that we ask the question of *why* we are bound to the commitment we made at the beginning.

If we want to know why we are bound to keep this special commitment, we need to ask what sort of commitment it is.

Marriage, as the Bible sees it, is a kind of social order that God created us to live in: married for good even if the marriage is not all that good. The commitment sets two people in an exclusive sexual partnership meant to last as long as both of them live. This seems to be the sort of commitment marriage requires.

Our commitment is the moral mortar that fastens people into what otherwise would be a fragile and unpredictable relationship. Our will, our

27

choice to be committed, creates of our relationship an instance of the abiding alliance God planned for sexual unions.

Some people believe that any bona fide marriage is a metaphysical entity that two people agree to enter, but that exists somehow independent of their wills. When God joins you, they suggest, you are wedlocked behind the walls of the indestructible estate called matrimony, and even if you climb the wall and get out, the estate stays behind and beckons you to come back to it.

Other people believe that marriage is only a close personal relationship — like a friendship, only more intimate. Most people want to stay in it once they begin because they believe they will be happier in it than out of it. But once the relationship breaks down, the marriage breaks down with it.

In the former view, one is obligated to keep commitment to a reality called marriage that will continue to exist, in God's sight, which means in reality, even when the two people who once lived in it are divorced, hate each other, and never look at each other. In the second view, one is obligated to a marriage pretty much as he is obligated to a friendship; the partners should be loyal to each other, but only for the time being, as long as the relationship lasts.

Speaking for myself, I cannot make any sense out of a metaphysical marriage that still exists in God's sight and summons us back to it after we break out of it.

But on the other hand I believe that marriage has more to it than a commitment to sexually intimate friendship. I believe that it has a more enduring claim on my commitment than a friendship has.

I believe that marriage as such is a social order that God wills to be permanent in each instance. I am obligated, then, by God's will for marriage to make my marriage endure.

Clear enough. But surely endurance is a grim and foreboding and unreasonable commitment when it comes to a relationship with so much potential for misery.

It seems to me that a marriage commitment is a commitment to the effort of maintaining and improving a quality of personal relationship. Commitment is not simply to the endurance of the institution, but to working at a quality of relationship.

A commitment *simply* to stick it out gets to be legalistic, oppressive, and sometimes destructive. But a commitment simply to work at the process seems too limited and conditional. One or both partners may too soon say: we've worked at it and it isn't working, so we're calling it quits. So marriage, unlike friendship, is a commitment to stick with what we are stuck with even if the relational process is stalled in the muck of mutual pain.

Now, then, we are ready to ask *why* married people should be obligated to keep their commitments to each other no matter what.

There are certainly plausible reasons why they should *not* be so bound.

One reason is the individual's autonomy, his or her sovereign right to make a choice. If individual choice is a human value, why eliminate it from marriage? If we have a free choice to marry whom and when we please, why should we not have a free choice to divorce when we please? Why should we not be free to repair mistakes? We change our jobs, we switch our political allegiances, we change our locations, and nobody clucks a moral cluck. Margaret Mead raised the question back in 1949: "If past mistakes are to be reparable in every other field of human relationships, why should marriage be the exception?"[1]

Another reason that counts against having to keep our marriage commitments is our entitlement to fulfill ourselves as individuals. It seems reasonable to suppose that individuals are entitled to some personal satisfaction in life. We don't have to buy into everyone's entitlement to self-fulfillment and satisfaction to sense that everyone has an entitlement to avoid needless misery and cruelty. Even if no one has an inalienable right to everything his or her heart yearns to be and do, it seems reasonable that everyone has some sort of right to cut his or her losses by leaving a personal relationship that denies her or him a bare minimum of satisfaction with life. If we do not have a right to be perfectly happy, it could be argued that we have a right to put a stop, if we can, to being perfectly miserable.

Why, then, should we continue to impose on married people a commitment so total, so fundamental, that it is a choice to surrender choice? And why should we impose on them a commitment to endurance that takes precedence to their entitlement to at least some satisfaction in life? Why should not marriage have some escape clauses, open windows if not revolving doors? Friendship does. Why not marriage?

Well, one may say, because God says so.

True. But why does God say so? Would he mind too much if we asked him why should he be so stubborn about this special sort of commitment?

---

1. *Male and Female* (New York: Morrow, 1949), p. 355.

I should like to suggest two old-fashioned reasons why commitment to endurance is the guts of a commitment to marriage.

The first reason is that marriage is for families. This is why commitments to marriage need to be kept in spite of persuasive reasons for breaking them. Marriage is for having and caring for children. If married people are free to pack their bags and leave when they are seriously dissatisfied with the marriage, they tend to harm their children. Whether they bring up kids in the uncertainty of a possible divorce or subject them to the pain of actual divorce, they hurt them. And children should at least not be hurt by our provisional commitments.

For me it is very hard to see why commitments to marriage should be unconditional if marriage is essentially about intimacy and love and mutual growth, and only accidentally, as a matter of personal preference, about children.

It is because marriages are about having families that homosexual people do not make commitments to marriage even when they commit themselves to each other with a solemn oath. Even if we agree that committed partnerships are better for gay people than are floating, promiscuous relationships, we only confuse things when we call their commitment partnerships marriages. A marriage and family therapist told me recently that she conducted a marriage encounter weekend for several gay men and women, and she asked me whether I thought she had done right. I told her that I thought she did right to help gay people keep commitments to each other, but that she should not call it a marriage encounter. What committed gay couples seem to have is a friendship trying to be a marriage when it cannot be — a fact which makes most gay alliances very unsteady.

I am not suggesting that people who get married and intend to have no children are not really married. Of course not. I do think people who get married need to have a persuasive reason for not having children, a reason beyond their commitments to careers and/or personal satisfaction. But my limited point here is to say that if they commit themselves to a marriage without children, their commitment lacks an important reason for being a commitment for better or for worse, till death them do part.

There is another reason for keeping commitments to marriage. It has to do with the paradox that individuals find their lasting identity in lasting commitments to others. Marriage is one of those commitments. It adds an ineradicable dimension to our identity. And if we annul this commitment, we fragmentize the stories we are writing with our lives, we let loose of our past and chisel away at who and what we are for the future. We lose a significant part of our own identity, of course, but what is worse, we rob another person of the identity that our commitment promised to her or to him. No wonder that, after a divorce, people are usually bewildered about who and what they are; they have lost or given away a segment of their stories.

I have suggested two practical reasons why commitment to marriage carries an obligation to keep it.

I think commitment-making and keeping are good because important and intrinsic goods are endangered if we do not make and keep them. Two of these goods are: the care of children and the creation of individual identities.

For this reason, it seems to me, marriage commitments are meant to be kept, for good. For good, in the sense of for quality of life. But for good, too, in the sense of for always.

Absolutely? Not quite. Not in a broken world where married persons can become abusive, incestuous, demeaning, adulterous, and generally dangerous to their partners, their children, and themselves. Not absolutely, but close enough to claim again that commitment is the one thing necessary in a culture of free-wheeling search for oneself — a search grounded in the mistaken notion that the primary way to achieve a self is through self-gratification, and that the primary self-creating gratification is gratifying sexual experience.

Our culture is in imminent danger of atomizing itself; individuals are estranged from themselves because of their surrender to the gods of choice and entitlement. We need not absolutize commitment-keeping, but we do well to dedicate ourselves to it, to teaching it, encouraging it, and nurturing it among ourselves.

CHAPTER 6

Commitment in Family

What does family life reveal about the mystery of commitment-making and commitment-keeping?

I am talking about a real family — crazed, confused, and chaotic as many real families may be. I am not talking about the "family feeling" that executives try to stimulate in their company or their schools. At my school we talk about the Fuller family, mostly at Christmas time. And it may be true that a lot of people feel more closeness and confidentiality and appreciation at the office than they feel at home. But the office is not a family, any more than the corporation is a bride, even though some executives are said to be married to it.

The difference between the family feeling at my shop and the family reality at home lies in the commitments proper to each. You can get fired from the office family. And if you plead family, and say, "You can't fire me, I'm family," you may be told: "No, you just used to be family, now you are former family." In a real family nobody gets fired, and that, for many families, is the bottom line.

Family is where we learn commitment because it is there where we learn to trust. A child learns what commitment is first of all by trusting her mother's commitment to her. She learns it by learning trust from her mother's willingness to surrender her own right to a night's sleep in order to be with her in her needs, to touch her, nourish her, warm her, cuddle her, nurse her, protect her.

In effect, we can learn something about commitment from our families because it is commitment that creates a family, not the accident of blood kinship. I am not bound by a drop of blood to any of the four other members of my immediate family. Families are created not by living under

32

one roof, but by the special sorts of commitment we make to each other. Loyalty commitments are like invisible fibers which hold together the complex network of love-hate relationships and create out of them the unique alliance of persons that we call a family.

But what are the sort of commitments that we make as families? I will talk here only of the commitment parents properly make to children:

1. Parental commitments are unilateral.

Like God, we commit ourselves to children who never had a chance to say "No thanks, I think I'll pick some other parents." When I committed myself to each of my children, I took charge of another human being's destiny. In a sense I foisted an identity upon them; forever and ever I determined that they would know themselves as my children. They were not consulted, had no veto, no consent.

2. Parental commitments are controlling.

Parents surrender their desires to a child's needs. But what control there is in this surrender! When Doris and I received a phone call from a young lady named Margaret at Bethany Home and were told that there was a girl child for us and when we took her in and committed ourselves to her, we took control of her. We decided what name she would bear, who her aunts and uncles would be, what religion she would be brought up in, what values she would be taught, the neighborhood where she would live, and thus the schools she would attend and the friends she would have, and how much money she would likely have at her disposal to make the lumps of life a little easier to swallow.

How wonderfully paradoxical: in giving ourselves to a child, we seize total control. Of course it did not last long, and there were many battles in store precisely about that control. The trick for parents is to accept the fact that this control is only for the time being, since when we take control we commit ourselves to preparing a child to take control of himself or herself.

3. Parental commitments are self-interested.

Commitments are born of desires for self-satisfaction through the child. Whether by birth or adoption, a parent is driven by a need to perpetuate himself beyond his mortal individuality, a need to nurture an infant, a need to have someone who can make parental dreams come true . . . and a bundle of other needs. But the sobering point is this: parental commitment to a child is balanced by self-interest without being any less a genuine commitment.

4. Parental commitments are unconditional.

Parents do not have freedom to unparent themselves; their commitment is forever, as long as life shall last. They put themselves at the disposal of a child no matter what. When a person commits herself as a parent, she has no escape clauses; she says, "Nothing you can ever do will make me be something other than a parent to you."

We have seen enough to note that these most fundamental of human commitments are unilateral, controlling, self-interested, and unconditional — as much like God's commitment as any human commitment gets.

Now I would like to ask: *what* sorts of things does a parent commit to a child? Not what might a particular parent legitimately commit, but what is the essential commitment appropriate to and expected of every parent?

We could agree, I suppose, that parents do not have to commit themselves to leave ninety percent of their estate to their children, to pay for their college education, or to go on backpacking trips with them.

But there are some commitments that family-making entails. Not all of us would agree on what they include. But let me mention a few that, for people with biblical roots, seem woven into parenting.

1. The parent is committed to giving the child a family memory.

A family is more than the sum of its parts: a family of five is more than five people. It is a chapter in a story. And a child in the family can know himself or herself as a person only by knowing the earlier chapters of the family story. Bellah speaks of a "community of memory": the family is, I think, the primary community of memory.

I think that children feel this intensely. The best stories a parent can tell are stories of the olden times when he or she was a child. I remember how I hung on my mother's odd stories about her childhood in Friesland. Why? I think it was because the stories told me who I was. I can recall visiting a cemetery near her home, along with Doris and my two young sons, and wondering at my son's compulsive photographing of the tombstones with my mother's maiden name on them. Why did he have this need to take pictures of old tombstones? I think it was his need, his human need, to have a family memory so that he could reassure himself that he was who he was. It is a need that belongs with the fact that children are not individuals who pop up in a particular time and occupy a particular space for a brief moment. They are characters in a family story. And to know their parts they need to know who came before them and what happened to them in the chapters that came before. Parents are committed to giving them their memories.

The enduring evil of child abuse is that it robs a child of memory. She blocks out significant passages of her story because they are too painful for her to bear. But she needs to know them if she is to come to genuine self-understanding. Paradoxically, it is the memory of the abuse that prevents her from accepting her identity as a character within the family story. Her only solution is that final, that unpredictable, that gracious act called for-giveness. But tragic indeed is the person who needs to be forgiven for rob-bing a child of her or his memory.

2. A parent is committed to giving the child a future connected to her past.
A child needs a future. I do not mean a future guaranteed by tuition at the right school. I do not mean a future assured by the promise of a well-stocked trust fund. I mean a future as a member of a family. Families are about seed, and about lines, and about chapters of the family story that still have to be written. And parents are committed to assuring their child a name and a role in that story. It is no small thing to give another human being a future.

The baseline commitment that a parent makes to a child is to the child's name and place within the family. This is part of the uncon-ditionality of parental commitment. In spite of conflicts of faith and mor-als, the child bears my name and is my child. When the child's values are not my values and her God is not my God, her story is my story, the story she is writing with her life flows with the story that I wrote with mine. The future of my story is the future of her story. I may not unparent myself.

3. A parent is committed to be the child's moral and religious authority. If you are a parent you are meant to tell your children what you believe is important and what is not important, what you believe is right and good about human existence, what is worth living for and what is worth dying for.
It does not matter whether a parent is correct or not. We cannot say that only parents with orthodox religious beliefs have the obligation to tell their children what they believe about God. Better to be wrong about what we believe to be of ultimate importance than to give the impression that

35

nothing is of ultimate importance. To be a parent entails a commitment to teach a child about one's ultimate commitment, to initiate a child into one's religious community, to tell a child over and over again the stories that created one's faith, to be one's self a model of the sort of piety that embodies the practice of faith.

4. Another commitment a parent makes is to her child's eventual freedom from the parents' authority.
The parent of a child has time limits on commitment. Both of them are committed to preparing the child for the time when he is on his own — on his own to decide whether to live by other moral values or to worship other gods. In short, the parent commits himself to prepare a child to take responsibility for his own moral life and religious faith, even if his choice conflicts with what his parents taught him.

No commitment made by a human being is as clearly like the commitment God makes as a parent's commitment to a child. It has practically no conditions, it is made unilaterally, as if by sovereign election, and it has as its object a child's authentic freedom. But the analogy is limited, and any parent who does not sense the differences is in terrible trouble. We can commit ourselves to our children somewhat as God commits himself to us. But we are not God. And if we make a child fear or love us as he or she fears and loves God, we and our children are in for trouble.

CHAPTER 7

Nurturing Commitment

Many of us are deeply concerned about the erosion of commitment in our culture. Some of us want to confront this situation directly with a chorus of moral indictments of the culture of self-gratification. These persons have a point: surely we need to preach the moral duty of putting commitment-keeping over our private pursuit of self-satisfaction.

It seems to me, however, that our culture is not divided simply between people who, like pit bull terriers, fasten their teeth in the commitments they make and never let loose of them, on the one hand, and, on the other, people who, like wandering mongrels sniffing from garbage can to garbage can, move from relationship to relationship in ceaseless search of private satisfaction. There also are a lot of people who are not devoted only to their private fulfillment, and who nonetheless are afraid to make commitments or are losing the struggle to keep the commitments they have made.

So I suggest that besides cursing the selfishness of our age, we ask how we might be able to help nurture a climate of commitment-keeping. To this end, we might do well to be a little less confronting, less indicting, and more indirect, more encouraging, and more concerned to know some of the needs people have in their struggles with commitment.

Here, I think, is a point at which Christian ethics, pastoral ministry, and psychological therapy converge, and where they can be allies in the nurturing of commitment-keepers. So let me pass along some thoughts I have about people in their struggles to make and keep commitments.

1. Some people need help to overcome understandable fears of commitment.
Not everyone who avoids abiding commitments is a moral butterfly. Some

of them are intimidated by scary aspects of life that could put long-term commitments into serious doubt.

Some people are afraid that there may not be a long-term future for any of us. The majority of younger people assume that the nuclear arms race is going to finish the human race. So why should they make commitments for a long haul?

Some people are afraid that they will be let down, deserted, dangling, the way their parents let them down early on.

Some people are afraid of themselves; they fear that they may not have the staying power for long haul commitment-keeping.

2. Some people need hope.

Some people give up on their commitments, I suspect, when they give up on hope. And most of us give up hope too soon. We catastrophize our problems prematurely; we assume that because we cannot see a solution to our problem today, there is no solution at all. And so we pronounce too soon the death of our marriages, our families, our friendships. We are like my middle son who was a histrionic hypochondriacal problem-catastrophizer. When he was a little boy he cut his cheek once and, seeing the blood drip on his shirt, screamed "I'm dying, I'm dying," and then, all hope lost, he croaked, "I'm already dead." What he needed to see was that he had a problem, not a catastrophe.

Hope nourishes commitment; commitment nourishes hope. But the cycle begins with hope. I believe that what some people need more than moralizing is a reason for hope that with God our problems need not have catastrophic endings.

3. Some people need realism about things they cannot change.

There are some things that do not change and the best we can do is cope with them. Life everywhere is difficult. Sometimes survival is a terrific success, and coping with unchangeables is a highly creative act. Pearls are made because oysters can only cope with an irritant they cannot get rid of. And coping is easier if we plug into the reality that some of the bad things in life don't go away, and that life therefore can be intractably hard.

A wife cannot change the fact that she has had a double mastectomy, and she may not be able to change the fact that her husband snores in decibel output roughly equivalent to a blasting tuba. A husband may not be able to change the fact that his wife is depressed or paranoid, and he may not be able to change her penchant for nagging. But coping can be creative, and if we know at the start that we cannot change some of the negative qualities in our spouses we will have an advantage in the coping handicap.

4. Some people need to settle for commitments sufficient unto each day.
"Do not make this commitment lightly, or ill-advisedly," the liturgy cautions, for it is forever. True enough. But for some people the very thought is paralyzing and self-defeating. The burden of forever is too heavy. They can make it for the long haul only if they commit themselves to the short haul of today, one day at a time.

They cannot make a promise for a lifetime. They could say the words, but the words would not express a commitment until death doth them part. But they can and do manage to renew a real commitment, as they are able, in their own way, each morning. And many mornings eventually become forever.

5. Some people need to believe that God is Lord of new beginnings.
A commitment failed can become a prelude to a new commitment kept. A second marriage, for instance, can be a new commitment better kept than the first, in terms of quality and duration. The most important thing about a second commitment is not that it is second, but that it is a new one.

There are moral absolutists who, for the sacredness of a first marriage, would sacrifice the second. This is something like burning down a village to save it from the enemy, the enemy here being the illegitimacy of remarriage after a divorce. I think we do better as Christian communities to support people in second commitments than to fret about the failure of their first. The Pauline style of forgetting the past and focusing on the future applies to the past of failed commitments and the future of new commitments. And people who failed the first time need to be helped to forgive themselves, and to rejoice in their second chance to make good on a new commitment.

6. Some people need to see that no one has an inalienable right to be satisfied with life.
Not everyone who fails to keep a commitment is a devotee of self-gratification. But some of us are, and for these, the cult needs to be demythologized. Two articles in the creed of personal entitlement that are crucially false are: (1) Every person has an undeniable right to private ful-

fillment, and if she doesn't get it someone must be at fault. (2) Sexual fulfillment is the key to human fulfillment.

I believe that sex is one of God's better inventions; I also believe that more people than we suppose find deep fulfillment without a voluptuous sex life. And I believe, too, that while personal fulfillment is a most human longing, it escapes precisely those who make it their ultimate concern.

To prepare the soil of commitment, we need to wean people away from the mythology of sexual satisfaction as the key to human fulfillment.

7. Some people need to remember that overcommitment is an enemy of quality commitment.

Only God has the whole world on his hands; we need to be selective in what we take on ours. To be committed to many people is to be well committed to none. In fact, people who overcommit themselves to too many people are usually not committed to the people at all; they are committed to commitment, or to their run at praise for being highly committed people.

8. Some people need to know that some commitments should be broken.

There is no value in keeping bad commitments. When Albert Speer came to the end of his wretched life as architect for the Third Reich, he wondered: How could I have given my life to this evil, this monstrous evil? And he supplied his own answer: I committed myself early on and never allowed myself to examine or criticize my commitment. Commitments are not holy; they are good if their purpose is good, and no one is morally bound by a commitment to evil.

It is also true that good commitments can be turned into bad commitments by the person we are committed to. If a woman is committed to a brutal person, her commitment feeds his brutality if she stays within his reach. Her commitment is nullified by his brutal misuse of it. She should withdraw it and leave him.

9. Some people need courage to trust.

It is good to mention trust after talking about times to break off commitments; to do so demonstrates how fragile and dynamic is the keeping of commitments.

Trust is the receptive side of commitment-keeping; trust is the reliance factor. When I make a commitment to you, I need to trust you not to abuse my commitment. And when you make a commitment to me, I need to trust you to keep it.

Trust is our only security in committed relationships. If we want the security of legal contracts, it is because we cannot trust enough. Where we live in relationships cemented by a will that can be changed, all we have to secure it is a courage to rest in trust.

But it is trust that makes us free. "Each partner trusts the other with his or her core self, trusts that that self will not be ridiculed or violated, trusts that it will be nurtured and protected — safe. And in that safety (that unsecured safety) lies a special kind of freedom."[1]

When trust is betrayed, one hardly dares give it again. Being a fool does not make one a good commitment-keeper. And yet the courage of trust must be nourished again and the gamble of trust be taken. Without trust, commitment dies. So we must find ways to enable people to trust again.

1. Francine Klagsbrun, *Married People: Staying Together in the Age of Divorce* (New York: Bantam, 1985), p. 288.

CHAPTER 8

Conclusion

The power to make and keep a commitment comes close to the mystery of being human, of being a person much as God is a person, a creature who creates a community and fashions her own identity out of a repeated choice to stick with what she is stuck with.

I do not think that the virtue of commitment is fostered by absolutizing it. I hope that I have been clear about this. We make our commitments in a broken world and we try to keep them as struggling, weak, and often terribly selfish people. Some commitments should never be made. Some commitments should not be kept. Perhaps some cannot be kept. We cannot hoist commitment abstractly to an inviolable absolute.

And I do not think that commitment in the lives of struggling people is best fostered by moralizing. There is indeed reason to wring our hands over a culture in which entitlement gets such better odds than commitment. There is indeed good reason to review the solemn proclamation of moral obligation to keep our commitments. But I do not think that our hope for a more committed society is best served by moral indictments and moral injunctions. I believe that most people really want to live committed lives. What they need is nurture, help, encouragement, and revival of hope more than the wallop of a moral judgment.

But — absolutism aside — in our time we need nothing more than this: that we help each other accept ourselves again as persons who, like God himself, can say to someone: I am the one who will be there with you, no matter what. And in so taking on his name, we may create communities of steadfast love and create ourselves as persons — persons who are what we are because of the commitments we have dared to make and cared to keep.

Varieties of Moral Discourse

Prophetic, Narrative, Ethical, and Policy

JAMES M. GUSTAFSON

Contents

Introduction

I am honored by the invitation to deliver the Stob Lectures at Calvin College and Seminary. Through the years I have benefited from the participation of graduates of this institution in my doctoral seminars. To name them would be meaningful to some faculty here, though probably not to students. They have all been not only natively intelligent, but also learned and trained to think rigorously. I have benefited from reading books and articles produced by members of this community; in their light I am often humbled and always challenged.

I know the intellectual legacy of Henry Stob both from his publications and from the work of those who have been influenced by his teaching and writing. Although my systematic work has taken a very different turn from his, I sense in his work a mind and spirit congenial to my own. I hope that the quality of these two lectures is not a dishonor to Henry Stob; more — I hope that it is worthy of the invitation.

First Lecture

Many years ago I heard a paper read by a colleague who was very philosophically astute and informed. The paper was on ethics, and it was rigorously argued, proper distinctions were made, and the critique of other points of view was cogent. Professor Stob and the Philosophy Department at Calvin would have found little to criticize in it. The occasion was a conference of a divinity school faculty. When my colleague finished his paper the man chairing the meeting said, "That's not ethics. Ethics has to do with prophecy. I learned that from Rabbi Abraham Heschel." The comment was a conversation-stopper.

That occasion was memorable for a number of reasons. One was that it expressed a situation which was rampant in Christian circles at the time — the late sixties. Prophetic discourse abounded. Its rhetoric pervaded college chapels, church pronouncements, and the rousing speeches given on many occasions. We were in the midst of the Vietnam War. Prophetic voices both for and against the war were loud and clear. The war, for those who approved it, was a war against the evils of communism which threatened the freedom of the world, and thus it was justified and the means used to pursue it were not always questioned. For those against it, it was an unjustified war being pursued in the interests of imperialism and colonialism, and other evil forces of repression of those who sought freedom. And the blessing of God was invoked, as has often been the case in wars, by both parties.

My colleague who had read the paper found much of that prophetic discourse to be emotive, logically fallacious, and lacking in *ethical* argumentation. The prophetic discourse was often symbolic; striking metaphors and images were used to arouse sentiments. Ethical discourse had to be rational, rigorous, intellectually self-critical, aware of its fundamental principles and how they functioned in coming to a judgment about the war. To the prophetic voices his mode of discourse was rationalistic; it did not get to the roots of the evil of the world, and more telling (from their point of view), it never motivated people to action in the face of the evils they saw.

Here I have introduced two varieties of moral discourse that I shall develop in these lectures: prophetic and ethical. We will look more closely at each in due course. But there are two others that I shall also discuss: narrative and policy.

There are those who defend the view that telling a story is a form of moral discourse, and of course it is. In Christian communities our outlooks on life, including our moral outlooks, are shaped and guided (at least to some extent) by the biblical stories. They become, as H. Richard Niebuhr stated, the story of our lives. The biblical materials provide us with a vision of the world of which we are a part: its idolatries and unfaithfulness to God and to the will of God, its possibilities for redemption through the grace of God, the importance of love and compassion toward those whom God loves, its struggles for liberation from oppression like that of the ancient Hebrew people under the rule of the Egyptian pharaohs.

And often stories help us decide what to do. We have the model of Jesus himself for this. When he was asked a question, he did not give his answer as a moral argument based on Kantian-like, Stoic, or other principles. He often told a story. The story provided insight; its implications were for his hearers to infer. But stories are not ethics, in the sense that my colleague's paper developed ethics. They make no precise conceptual distinctions; they may have a narrative logic, but that is not the logic of an ethical argument based on Kantian or Aristotelian or other principles. Nor will stories, which inform the Christian's visions of the world, or which shed insight in a moment of choice, be very helpful to responsible persons seeking to resolve issues in labor negotiations within a fiercely competitive international marketplace, or those seeking to negotiate a reduction of nuclear arms which has to take into account political and other complex factors. But for such persons an ethical argument is hardly decisive either. A well-argued case for distributive justice will often be poorly informed about the limiting conditions in which justice can be approximated; for example, the conditions of a highly competitive market economy.

And thus I have introduced the fourth variety of moral discourse that I will discuss in these lectures: policy discourse. There are morally conscientious persons, many of them with deep Christian convictions, whose positions of responsibility require them to make choices and engage in actions limited by economic, social, political, medical, and legal realities. For them, if not the first question, one of the first questions is, "What is possible within the circumstances, the resources, the competing claims, in which I act?" Multinational corporations may appear to be the root of much injustice to many Christian prophets, and they like to condemn such businesses. But that condemnation is of no moral assistance to a responsible executive in such a corporation, who seeks to direct its powers toward the public good.

Thus I have introduced four varieties of moral discourse that are found in the Christian community: prophetic, narrative, ethical, and policy. My purpose in these two lectures is to develop further some of the distinctions between them, to indicate the distinctive function and place of each, and to make (in the end) a plea for recognizing both the validity and the insufficiency of each of these forms. My aspiration is that readers become more conscious of different forms of moral language, or at least different kinds of language relevant to morality, and particularly relevant to the moral vocation of the Christian community.

Prophetic Discourse

The first comment of the chair to my philosophically, ethically trained and minded colleague's paper was, "Ethics has to do with prophecy." I agree in general, but would state the claim differently. One variety of moral discourse is prophetic discourse, but prophetic discourse is not an all-sufficient kind of moral discourse. That introduces the line of argument in this section of this lecture.

What do I mean by prophetic discourse? I clearly do not mean the predictive discourse of seers in some simple-minded way. I mean to refer to aspects of prophetic discourse found in the Bible. Prophecy clearly has biblical roots and biblical precedents. Persons more learned than I in technical biblical studies would no doubt criticize or refine my characterization of it. My point is not a biblically scholarly one, but to show some features of it and make a case that those features are present in a lively way in a lot of moral discourse in the Christian community in our time. And, as the commentator's remark suggests, for some Christians it is the exclusive mode of moral discourse. There are two aspects of it that I wish for us to keep in mind.

The first aspect is that prophetic discourse takes the form of moral or religious indictments. It is the word of the Lord proclaimed *against* the moral evil and apostasy of the world and societies. It shows in dramatically vivid language just how far the human community has fallen from what it ought to be.

Recall the prophetic books of the Bible: Hosea, Amos, and Jeremiah for examples. They powerfully indicted their people for unfaithfulness to God: they made clear how the people had lost the ground meaning of God's covenant with the people, the pledge of God's faithfulness to them, and their binding commitment of faithfulness to God. They demonstrated how disobedient the people were to the commandments, the divine law that the covenant shaped, formed, and authorized. Indictment leads to conviction of guilt; it issues in a call to a fundamental repentance, a radical turning from unfaithfulness to faithfulness. Our contemporary prophetic discourse is very similar to this.

I want to note two features of prophetic indictments. First, they usually, though not always, address what the prophet perceives to be the *root* of religious, moral, or social waywardness, not specific instances in which certain policies are judged to be inadequate or wrong. Detailed policy recommendations, matters of strategy and tactics are seldom the focus of a prophet's intentions. Rather, indictments usually construe the human conditions in quite deep but broad proportions. They do not analyze mediating and possible solutions to quite particular problems, but rather get to the roots of systemic evils that pervade institutions and cultures, or that pervade the actions and behavior of individual persons.

Prophets tend to be impatient with detailed analyses of particular choices made in the past — choices that determined how, month by month, we got to where we are from where we were. They tend to be equally impatient with how we can practically get from where we are today to some modest increments of improvement a month from now. To the prophet such preoccupation seems to be rearranging the deck chairs on the Titanic when the ship is sinking. The most important and real problems to the prophet are not changing the course of a line of policy or action that is assumed and underway. It is the basic line of policy, its fundamental assumptions and values, that are the real problem. Let me illustrate this with some contemporary examples.

Prophets scan many aspects of contemporary American society and see many indications of continuing racial discrimination. They find statistical indicators of this: the disproportionate degree of unemployment among Blacks and Hispanics, the disproportionate access to the best of medical care, the small proportion of Blacks and Hispanics in corporate law firms or in the upper echelons of management in large corporations, the contrast between housing conditions among minorities and the larger white population, and so on. They do various kinds of social analysis to attempt to explain these statistics, finding a variety of causal factors: economic, educational, and others. They take into account that civil rights laws and regulations, voluntary policies of affirmative action in jobs, education, and housing are endorsed and defended. They may admit some increments of benefits over the past quarter of a century.

But the root problem, the deepest cause, is still there. It is *racism*. It is deep beliefs, attitudes, and outlooks among the dominant ethnic group that affect how persons not only act and think, but also feel about Blacks and Hispanics. The prospects for greater distributive justice between ethnic groups will not be realized until the *root* of the evil, racism, is extricated from the outlooks of persons and the systems of institutions. Laws and policies are therapies that treat some symptoms of the moral disease, but they do not eradicate its cause, racism.

Or take the example of poverty. The prophet, if he is fair-minded, might agree that some amelioration of poverty would come from changes in tax laws which have small outcomes for the redistribution of income in America. Or he might labor to change welfare policies so that essential services and goods are available to the victims of poverty. But to many who use prophetic discourse, these palliatives only mask the root source of the injustice that the presence of poverty indicates. The root source for some is the profit motive; it is greed on the part of the rich and the powerful. It has institutional locations in our society. One finds it in the concentration of power in large industrial corporations and financial institutions whose apparent primary, if not sole, end is to increase profitability for their stockholders and increase incomes for their managers. To such prophetic voices the problem of poverty is *systemic;* it will not be resolved until there is a profound change in the economic arrangements and the political outlooks of the society. There has to be a change in the *system:* not merely fine tuning or modest alterations in the way in which it is currently working.

51

These indictments are based upon deeply held convictions, and not merely cogent rational theories, about the requirements of justice or about certain human values. The contrast between actual social conditions and these deeply held beliefs is vividly apparent, and the contrast itself is an indictment. Prophetic discourse generally looks for a demon, a power, or source, which presumably underlies all the numerous signs of what is wrong in society.

The second feature of prophetic indictments that I want to note is the language and symbols that are used to make them. In the biblical materials we have the language of harlotry, or infidelity. This is passionate language. The prophets in the Scriptures did not establish their indictments on the basis of statistical analyses; they did not use moral arguments of a philosophically rigorous sort. They used language, metaphors, and symbols that are directed to the "heart" as well as to the "head." The prophet usually does not make an argument; rather he demonstrates, he shows, he tells. And the media of showing and telling evoke our senses of moral indignation. They not only inform us, they move us — they move our "animal spirits," to use a term from Jonathan Edwards.

Contemporary prophets are in a biblical tradition, whether they know that or not. For example, much literature about the problem of population growth, with reference to the capacities of our planet to sustain it, is backed by statistical projections which, if accepted uncritically, have their own way of making a prophetic point. Something must be done to restrain population growth or an apocalyptic moment will surely come.

But one notes the use of analogies and metaphors that make statistical analysis more effective and *aff*ective in the reader. Garrett Hardin's famous article on "The Tragedy of the Commons" is a case in point. Human beings on earth are like domestic animals in the period of history when communities had "commons" in which animals were allowed to graze. There is only so much grass in the commons, and when there are too many cattle and sheep they all will starve to death. Or, another evocative and more contemporary symbol is "the spaceship earth." The earth is like a spaceship, and we know that those in a spaceship have very limited resources available to them.

Both the "commons" and "spaceship earth" as literary devices engender deep anxiety, if not dread; they become apocalyptic symbols. One reads the harder evidence through their lenses and the shape of the world to come is depicted through them.

I am not here judging them one way or the other; I only want to note how the choice of language in prophetic discourse has emotive or affective consequences; it is used to move us, to stir us to a deeper moral concern and to action. The more rational and rigorous discourse of ethics does not communicate the sense of urgency that prophetic discourse does.

Our modern media of communications have nonverbal prophetic powers. One will never know precisely, for example, how much television's vivid portrayals in millions of American homes of the suffering and horror of modern warfare during the period of the Vietnam War affected the development of public opinion in the direction of opposition to that war. The indictment does not need to be made explicit; seeing and hearing have their own powerful effects without verbal commentary.

My point here should be clear. The language that is characteristic of prophetic discourse is very different from that of ethical argumentation or economic and social policy. Its practical end is to evoke a deep moral response; it moves us.

The second aspect of prophetic discourse (indictment being the first) is utopian. It portrays an alluring vision of the future, of possibilities for life in the world in which the forms of strife and suffering we all experience are overcome. One thinks of many words of the prophet Isaiah, "The lion and the lamb shall lie down together." "The rough places shall be made a plain." I do not here develop the characteristics of utopian literature and its various forms: I use the term loosely in this lecture. All I wish to indicate is that prophets sometimes proclaim and depict an ideal state of affairs which is radically in contrast with the actual state of affairs in which we live together in society. The ideal may indict the actual, but it is meant to have another effect. It is an allure; it is a powerfully attractive vision of a future which positively moves us to approximate it.

Of itself, the utopian vision does not precisely show how we are to get from where and when we are to the fulfillment of the alluring ideal future. But prophets tell us that without some such vision we get trapped in detailed technicalities and become satisfied with small increments of improvement in social life. And like indicting prophecy, utopian prophecy uses symbols, analogies, similes, and metaphors that move us.

An example from our recent history is what I consider to be one of the most eloquent, moving speeches in American life, namely Martin Luther King's speech from the steps of the Lincoln Memorial in Washington, now a quarter of a century ago. Happily, modern technology preserves for us not only the written text, but the face and body of the man, the stirring qualities of his voice, and the powerful response of the throngs who heard it. It is usually called King's "I Have a Dream" speech. To hear and see it from time to time with great appreciation is not, I think, to be subject to romantic nostalgia. Rather it is a call to a vision, a dream, which not only indicts the present but attracts us, allures us to a better future. The speech is not a moral argument, nor is it a statement of policy — both of which King could engage in. The passion of the voice, the figures and cadences of speech, many drawn from the Bible, the moral authenticity of the prophet who delivered the address — all these and other matters move the hearer from indignation with the present to aspiration for the future.

The utopian allure is, we are told over and over, not only important but necessary. It provides hope in the midst of despair; it lifts the eyes and the aspirations beyond what hard realists see as possible to the possibilities that lie beyond. For Christian theology and ethics, it is grounded in deep theological convictions: the breaking of the bondage of death in the accounts of Jesus' resurrection, the assurance of the coming Kingdom of God in which peace and justice will reign forever. Proverbs 29:18 is often quoted, "Without a vision the people perish." Utopian discourse evokes aspirations, if not expectations.

I recently read through twenty years of publications by the Department of Church and Society of the World Council of Churches to write a critical analysis of it for that body. One found ample evidence of prophetic indictments; these were usually backed by somewhat apocalyptic interpretations of conditions in the world: the threat of overpopulation, the depletion of energy resources, the threat of nuclear holocaust, the spoiling of the natural environment, and so forth. I noted with interest how these indictments were supported by as hard evidences from various sciences as could be mustered. But also throughout was the proclamation of Christian hope — the conviction about the coming Kingdom of God, about the openness to future possibilities that the symbol of the Kingdom assured.

But one thing about this struck me forcefully. The indictments were backed by interpretations of present and future projected circumstances with graphs and tables. The hope was not backed by anything nearly as "empirical" as were the indictments. To sustain an allure for a better future beyond current problems, authors took recourse to the affective symbolism of quite purely religious and theological language. There was a gap there; prophetic utopian allures could not be "cashed out" in terms of policies very well — policies that would bring that vision of a future of peace, justice, and integrity of creation into significant realization.

The legitimacy of prophetic moral discourse, I believe, is without question. It is not, however, sufficient as moral discourse. It undercuts preoccupation with meager thinking about means to short-range ends in view; it locates the problems of humanity at deeper and profounder levels than do ethical and policy discourse; it stirs our moral sentiments, whether our sense of injustice or our more idealistic sense of the possibilities of a radically better world. Persons occupied with rigorous ethical discourse do not have the capacity to do this. Persons occupied with policy discourse, with the art of the possible based on involvement in existing institutions and mounds of various kinds of information, do not have the capacity to do this.

But prophetic discourse is not sufficient. It involves a necessary simplification of what are, from other perspectives, very complex problems and issues. Prophetic indictment has to locate a devil, a focal point of radical evil. It does not concern itself with incremental choices that have to be made by persons and institutions in which good and evil are intricately intermingled. In religious communities, while it deeply moves some persons it often alienates others — particularly (often, at least) those conscientious members of religious communities whose social roles require them to deal with conflicts of values and morality in which "trade-offs" are necessary; for example, those who must think not only of the radical evil of a nuclear war but also of how to negotiate a reduction in the arms race. Or, those who might be convinced that the distribution of income, goods, and services in our society is unjust but have to negotiate trade agreements, deal with international competition, and settle wage agreements with workers.

If prophetic discourse, in both its indictment and utopian form, is judged to be the sole and proper mode of moral discourse by Christian leaders, if it is not supplemented by other modes of moral discourse, a huge barrier is created between prophetic voices and those that speak in more precise and rational modes of argumentation, and between the prophets and those whose callings require them to make choices within complex institutions and in difficult policy issues. Prophets do not help responsible Christian persons who seek to gain political and economic power as a means to serve the public good within the constraints of political, economic, medical, or other institutions.

Narrative Discourse

At the time of the occasion of the anecdote I used to open this lecture, the terms "narrative theology" and "narrative ethics" were not in current usage. Since then they have become so. Certainly in North America, the United Kingdom, and perhaps in other places, the propounders of this form of discourse have wide and deep influence among both academics and the clergy and through them, I assume, the laity as well. The leading proponent of narrative ethics is Stanley Hauerwas, who was once my student, and who delights in defining his own work from time to time over against my own. As you shall hear, I agree that narrative is a significant form of religious and nonreligious moral discourse, but like prophetic discourse it is not sufficient.

This is not the place to expound the work of Hauerwas and others in any detail. I believe the central thesis can be stated fairly, though too simply, in the following terms. Narratives function to sustain the particular moral identity of a religious (or secular) community by rehearsing its history and traditional meanings, as these are portrayed in Scripture and other sources. Narratives shape and sustain the ethos of the community. Through our participation in such a community, the narratives also function to give shape to our moral characters, which in turn deeply affect the way we interpret or construe the world and events and thus affect what we determine to be appropriate action as members of the community. Narratives function to sustain and confirm the religious and moral identity of the Christian community, and evoke and sustain the faithfulness of its members to Jesus Christ. I shall return to this shortly.

I think there are two other functions of narrative, perhaps implied by, but not as fully developed as, what I have stated thus far. One of these is the prophetic function of narrative. For example, I recently heard a woman from the Marshall Islands in the South Pacific tell the story of the effects on those people, their health, their culture and society, of the use of the Bikini Atoll as the location of atomic testing and of the continued use of that area as a missile range. There was no theory of justice or injustice in the story; it eloquently portrayed the fate of a people subjected to the disastrous outcomes of decisions and actions in which they had no voice. It was clear who was to be indicted: the government of the United States. She used no biblical or theological language, but the story had a moving prophetic effect.

The second function of narratives that I want to note before returning to what I judge to be the principal claims of narrative ethics is at the point of making particular moral choices. There is evidence of this in the gospel narratives as well as in rabbinical literature. Jesus, and the rabbis, often answered a rather direct question not with a casuistical argument, i.e., not by stating general principles and applying them to the case at hand, but by telling a story. An apt parable, or story, is a mode of moral pedagogy.

How different this is from, for example, St. Augustine's treatise, "On Lying," which makes distinctions still used to this day even by the philosopher Sissela Bok in her book, *Lying,* or from St. Thomas Aquinas's deliberations about how to answer the question, "Whether one ought to love one's father more than one's mother" in the second part of the second part of his *Summa Theologica,* or the writings of medical moralists today who seek to determine the proper distinctions and arguments appropriate to determine the moral rightness of the removal of artificial nutrition from dying patients, or from the Halakic reasoning that has become so refined in rabbinic legal and moral writings.

Narratives as responses to moral inquiries about circumstances of quandary do not provide single, clear, and argued answers. Rather they can provide nuanced and subtle illumination both of what is at stake and of what conduct might be most appropriate. Ethical casuistic argument brings choice to a focus by distinctions and arguments; narrative evokes the imagination, stimulates our moral sensibilities and affections. Its conclusion is not as clearly decisive, but it enlarges one's vision of what is going on; one acts in its "light" more than in conformity to it — as one does to a casuistic moral argument. It often assumes an analogy between the story or parable and the circumstances out of which the question comes. Thus, "Go and do likewise."

Like the prophetic use of narrative, this is clearly to be commended for what it does. Indeed I have described it in rather commendable terms. But it is not sufficient. One does well to pause, to reflect on what sorts of reasons one might give to back or warrant what appears to be the illuminating effect of a story. Indeed, the more philosophically inclined person might very well abstract from such a story the human values or ethical principles implied in it, and make a case to support its effect in more precisely ethical terms.

Casuistic argument can be used to judge the adequacy of this use of narrative. I would affirm that the reverse is also the case; that is, narratives might also judge the adequacy of casuistry by showing us features of life that are somehow squeezed out by more abstract language. When one is asked, "What ought we to do?" it is often appropriate, but not always sufficient, to tell an apt story, a parable. It is not likely to resolve an issue in the reduction of arms between superpowers, nor will it be persuasive to management if it is all that the negotiator for unions in contract talks has to put on the table.

I now return to what are the principal claims for the proponents of narrative ethics: narratives shape the ethos of the moral and religious community, and, by participating in the community, they shape and direct vision and character. There is something, at least minimally, correct about this description of how outlooks, values, and moral interests of communities are shaped by stories. Not only narratives, but liturgies, rites, and other activities convey in concrete (rather than abstract) terms and symbols the living traditions of historic peoples.

This can be seen within the biblical materials themselves. The Bible, over and over, reminds the people of the deeds of Yahweh in liberating the people from their bondage in Egypt, of Yahweh's constituting them as a people through his covenant with them. This story is rehearsed, for it grounds the rights and obligations of the people; it evokes the motive of gratitude as a ground for their moral conduct and values.

Indeed, one finds the motif of the "imitation of God" explicit in many places and implied in many more. Because Yahweh showed his compassion and justice in leading the people from bondage, the people are to show compassion and justice to the widows, the orphans, and the strangers in the land. The recall of the past evokes a sense of gratitude and a sense of obligation. God has acted on behalf of the people and thus they are moved, both out of thankfulness and out of duty, to live a way of life grounded in the deeds of God, in the covenant, and in the Torah. God showed his steadfast love for them when they were oppressed; they are to show steadfastness toward God in the ordering of their common life.

Christian history provides similar examples. The Apostle Paul in places calls upon the shaping deeds of the Christian community as the form and pattern both of the knowledge of God's redemption and of the way of life that conforms to that knowledge. One thinks, for example, of the second chapter of Philippians. Faithful Christians through the ages have, quite likely, been moved by hearing the narratives of the gospels more than they have been moved by the theological discourse that explains and justifies the gospel and its meaning. The "ethos" of the Christian community is not easy to circumscribe, to "pin down," but its efficacy is shaped and nourished by the narratives of the Bible and the tradition. Values, outlooks, and visions are enforced by stories.

We see this in national communities as well as in religious ones. For my generation of Americans, much more than for that of my children, Abraham Lincoln stood as a symbol, as a historic person of mythic proportions, whose life and deeds represent the praiseworthy ethos of American democracy and justice.

The power of that was reinforced by knowing not only the historically accurate accounts, but also the legends of Lincoln. (I am sure, for instance, that I have read Carl Sandburg's multi-volume biography of Lincoln at least three times, knowing fully that there is quite another way to tell the story of Lincoln's life.) A visit to New Salem, Illinois, where Lincoln grew up, was like a pilgrimage to the shrine of a saint. To stand before his statue in the Lincoln Memorial in Washington and read the inscriptions was a moving act of devotion. Stories, myths, symbols bear the moral ethos of a community; they shape and nourish its moral convictions; they give priority to certain human values and moral principles.

And to participate in such a community is to make its story, as H. Richard Niebuhr once wrote, "the story of *our* life." The biblical narratives or the Lincoln stories are not mere "outer" history — objective "facts" learned about objective events for the sake of passing an examination. Rather they are "inner history"; they shape the meaning of life together in community and of persons who participate in it.

All this is quite plausible; indeed, in a general way it is quite true. But, I think it is not as reliable as some proponents of narrative ethics seem to believe. In our society we all belong to more than one community, and various communities to which we belong have different "narratives."

Indeed, part of our education is exposure to different stories, explanations, and symbols which relate to the same thing. What we learn in psychology classes does not cohere into one narrative or explanation of human behavior, and probably does not cohere with what we learned in church school. Perhaps some persons have sufficient confidence in the power of the Holy Spirit to be the transmitter and vivifier of the Christian story so that it determines the life of the Church and shapes the lives of persons who belong to it. But such confidence is questionable. Certain social and other conditions have to be met if the Christian story is to shape the activities of the Church and its members. Our individual lives and characters are deeply conditioned by many other forces, other loyalties to other traditions, in addition to religious ones.

A book I recently read about a cathedral parish church in Bangalore, India, St. Mark's, reminded me again of how many "stories" go into the shaping of the life of a particular congregation. I have worshiped in St. Mark's, and knew quite well one of its presbyters. Its difficulties are no doubt quite different from those found in a Norwegian Lutheran congregation or in a Dutch Reformed one, but interesting nonetheless. Ethnic loyalties, some to the Tamil communities, others to the Kannada-speaking, the Kerela, and to the Anglo-Indian had deep effects on the efforts to bring to one voice or even to a harmonious chorus of voices, all the programs and activities of St. Mark's parish. The Christian story was fractured by ethnic stories, by class loyalties, and even by caste loyalties. And certainly the characters of major and minor participants in St. Mark's were deeply conditioned by individual motives and personality traits, by no means shaped only by participation in that Christian community.

There is something correct about the claims for narrative ethics. Narratives can be prophetic. The story of the Marshall Islands people told by a member of that society is far more powerful than a batch of statistics and an analysis of the policy choices of the U.S. Government made by a political scientist. A parable can illumine our moral choices in particular circumstances; they cannot always be fully rationalized according to some ethical theory. Choices are informed and shaped not only by arguments but by images, stories, and symbols. The moral identity of the community is nourished by its stories, and our moral outlooks are shaped in part by them as well.

But narrative ethics is not sufficient. Symbolic prophetic indictments need to be checked against facts and figures and political analysis. Perceptive intuitions informed by parables need to be checked against more rational analysis. And we all belong to several communities. To live by the story of only one might impede our capacities to communicate with those with whom we share moral responsibilities who are informed by different stories and different communities. And our individual moral integrity is shaped in relation to more than the story of the Christian community; it is shaped by our social backgrounds, our roles in society, and other things. And, just as there is often a gap between prophetic discourses and particular choices made in the midst of medical, political, economic, and other situations, so narrative also leaves that gap.

Why cannot we accept prophetic and narrative moral discourse for what they do, and supplement what they do with other modes of moral discourse — each of which is also insufficient in itself? I think we can.

Second Lecture

Do you recall the anecdote with which I began the first lecture? The response to a philosophically rigorous paper by the chairman of the meeting was, "That's not ethics. Ethics has to do with prophecy. I learned that from Rabbi Abraham Heschel." Of course, not all Jewish scholars would agree with the opinion the chairman ascribed to the great and prophetic Rabbi Heschel. For that tradition, "ethics" has to do also with the kind of ethical, or even legal, discourse to which we now turn.

Ethical Discourse

The Protestant ecclesial and theological community in North America as well as Europe has learned in the last three decades to be more logically rigorous in its moral discourse. It has learned to use ethical discourse. Rigor has always characterized Roman Catholic moral theology; indeed, Pascal could, in his *Provincial Letters,* use satire to show that with clear and precise distinctions the Jesuit laxists of his time could find a way to justify almost any behavior they chose.

But logical rigor has also characterized the moral arguments of the morally stringent so-called "manuals" of moral theology. Essays from them on very particular topics came to conclusions about the rightness and wrongness of very particular actions, such as whether a Roman Catholic nurse in a Roman Catholic hospital cooperates with evil if she summons a Protestant clergyman for a patient who asks to see one.

The evidence for my historical claim about Protestantism comes from the literature. One need only compare the ethical writings of the generation of my teachers with those of the generation of my students to be convinced of this. One can look at many books on "Christian ethics" written during the first and middle decades of this century, and also many doctoral dissertations, to see how a concern for ethical discourse as that occurs in the community of moral philosophers was not taken into account, adapted, or even critically used by most Protestant moral theologians.

Now it is; I could cite many examples. One will do. Professor Harlan Beckley has published a sequence of two long articles in the *Journal of Religious Ethics* in which he brings together the theological ethics of Reinhold Niebuhr, with its concern for justice, with the argument of John Rawls, whose book, *A Theory of Justice,* has probably evoked more commentary and usage than any book by an American moral and political philosopher in my generation. Niebuhr, himself, was not as concerned to relate his idea of justice to philosophical literature.

In Europe one finds similar developments. One can compare the more theologically and historically oriented ethics dissertations and books written in Sweden, for example, in earlier decades with many currently being done. A recent Uppsala dissertation, *Risks and Human Values (Risker och Människolivets Värde),* which also uses Rawls heavily, develops principles and procedures to make quite precise moral assessments of risk. This kind of dissertation would have been unthinkable in Sweden in the 1950s. In *Zeitschrift für Evangelische Ethik* one can trace the gradual development of more concern for moral philosophy in the service of Christian ethics as well as for particular and practical moral problems.

On the whole this has been a positive achievement, though the formalist character of some of the writings seems to miss some of the point of theological ethics and more of the point of the lived experience of religious persons as they seek to express their faith and piety in their moral deeds. The influence of Anglo-American moral philosophy has been important in this development.

The effects have been these: more precise use of concepts such as justice, virtue, rights, and duties; more careful distinctions between concepts and between the classes of moral issues addressed; and stronger logical arguments in support of moral prescriptions or moral condemnations.

By "ethical discourse," then, I refer to basically philosophical modes of argument and analysis. There are several points in religious moral discourse at which ethical discourse enters and is taken into account.

One point is the issue of whether Christian ethics, or Jewish ethics also, is essentially the same in the values it supports and the principles it uses as the values and principles adduced by nonreligious, non-theological ethics. Let me put that in the form of the question that is often asked. When one is discussing morality, is one discussing principles and values that all persons can agree upon regardless of their religious beliefs and perspectives, or of their secular, agnostic, and atheistic beliefs and perspectives? Or are there specific and distinctive features of Christian ethics which back moral values and principles that cannot be supported on purely rational, nonreligious grounds?

The issue is whether the moral teachings and outlooks grounded in a particular religious faith, history, and community are thereby so strongly related to that faith that members of that community act differently from other persons, or that members of that community cannot agree with others about shared values or principles, or that members of that community cannot communicate about moral questions with persons who do not share their particular historic faith and history. Is Christian ethics so specifically Christian that at least aspects of Christian morality are obligatory only for Christians? Example: love of enemies.

This issue receives a considerable amount of attention currently, but it is not novel to our time. It gets special attention now for two reasons. In a pluralistic society, such as ours, in which Christians as persons or as church groups desire to have an impact on all sorts of public concerns, is there a common basis for such impacts shared between Christians and others? If there is a common basis, should that not be supported by arguments and groundings that all human beings can share, rather than those that make particular appeals to the Bible, to Christian theological themes, and to the faith of Christians?

Another reason it gets attention currently is that widely read literature disputes claims made on both sides of the issue. One thinks of the historical, theological, and ethical arguments made by Professor John Howard Yoder, for example, in his book, *The Priestly Kingdom.* Yoder's arguments are complex, and thus I shall not engage them much here. But one of the principal ones is that the fidelity of the Christian community to Jesus Christ and his particular significance was severely compromised in the Constantinian Era, when the Christian community allied itself with the state rather than standing over against it while participating in society. For Yoder social ethics — that enterprise that seeks to address public issues and policies — social ethics for Christians ought to be judged by the fidelity or infidelity it shows to Jesus Christ and to the biblical witness. Thus his famous book on *The Politics of Jesus*. Yoder's work is formidable and challenging, and anyone who wishes to stake out a different position has to come to grips with it.

On the other side are writings by both Catholics and Protestants who argue that current moral values and principles, and consequently correctly applied moral teachings, can and ought to be based on arguments which do not appeal to the biblical and specifically Christian theological materials for backing.

There are two principal defenses of this view among Christian writers. One appeals to the natural-law tradition in classic Christianity: while sacred doctrine and special revelation are necessary to know God, the moral order of the universe which participates in the mind of God can be known by human reason. And this moral order, this natural law, is essentially what is also given in the moral teachings of the Bible. Not only Thomas Aquinas held this general view; it was held by Calvin and one can well argue it was held by Luther in his view of the civic or political use of the Law.

The second principal defense stems from the incorporation of the language and ideas of Kant into the ethical writings of theologians. Morality is backed and grounded in the rational self-legislating wills of human beings, and not in a particular historical revelation in the Bible. Ethics is "autonomous"; to base it on a particular historic religious view would make it "heteronomous." Any morality that Christians defend has to be defensible by pure practical reason, and not by, or at least not only by, recourse to biblical and theological beliefs.

Among important Roman Catholic moral theologians, Josef Fuchs and Bruno Schuller both defend versions of this view. For Schuller, biblical moral discourse is the language of exhortation, not the language of ethics properly speaking. For Fuchs ethics deals with the *humanum,* the truly and universally human; Christianity provides a particular interior disposition and motivation to realize what is truly human. The contrast with the argument made by Yoder is clear, and it is extreme.

Clearly, different writers will relate the specifically religious, or Christian, in different ways to general or universal standards of moral conduct. My point here is only to show that every serious Christian group that makes moral proposals for the wider public must at least acknowledge and come to grips with this issue: the relation of Christian particularity to the universal in morality. What I here call "ethical discourse," carried in our culture not only by theology but also by moral philosophy, cannot be avoided as Christians seek to give reasons for the values, principles, and policies they prescribe and recommend to the various wider publics they address.

I do not hesitate to assert that most moral pronouncements made by various Protestant denominations have been seriously impervious to this issue. They neither justify adequately why they claim particular authority as Christians to speak on so many matters, nor why they think nonreligious persons ought to share and support what they say about them. In some way or other, they must use more ethical discourse.

At another point one finds the use of distinctions made, initially, by moral philosophers to sort out the philosophical structures or forms of ethics. We know these terms after our first course in moral philosophy or in theological ethics. Ethical theories are teleological, deontological, utilitarian, or consequentialist, etc.

Various persons in the history of Western ethical theory exemplify to a considerable extent each of the types I have named: Aristotle, Augustine, and Thomas Aquinas represent ethics directed toward a *telos,* an end; Kant, and in theological ethics perhaps Barth and Bultmann in different ways, represent deontic ethics, that is, ethics of obedience to moral principles or commands; Jeremy Bentham and John Stuart Mill represent utilitarian or consequentialist ethics, and in recent Protestant ethics Joseph Fletcher represents the type. My mentor, H. Richard Niebuhr, used a threefold typology which many students of Christian ethics have learned from his *The Responsible Self:* teleological, or man the maker; deontological, or man the citizen; and what he called *cathekontic,* or man the answerer or responder.

The impact of this kind of typology on the moral discourse of Christian writers takes more than one form. One form can be expressed by a question: ought Christian ethical writing, from a normative point of view, to be determined by one of these types of ethical theory? Paul Ramsey, for example, argues in his *Basic Christian Ethics* that Christian ethics ought to take the form of biblical ethics and that biblical ethics is deontological. That can surely be criticized on both exegetical and theological grounds.

Roman Catholic ethics, the heir of Augustine and Thomas Aquinas, takes principally the form of teleology: human beings are naturally oriented toward their good end, their happiness or human fulfillment; this provides the fundamental pattern of moral thought. Such a view also has to be, and is, justified. H. Richard Niebuhr argues that all life is characterized by responsiveness, and that God is acting in all actions upon us. We, then, are to respond to God's action and through the events and relationships in which we live. Thus, for him, the ethics of responsibility is more adequate and comprehensive than teleological or deontological ethics.

Raising this issue has the effect of asking for a kind of theoretical consistency in religious moral discourse. The consistency is judged in relation to an ideal type of philosophical moral theory. These types can be used in at least two different ways with reference to religious moral discourse. One is to judge its adequacy, such as Ramsey does. If religious ethical discourse does not conform to the type of deontic ethics, for him (at least in his early writings) it is at fault. This makes a philosophical ethical theory the principal criterion for judging the validity of religious ethical discourse.

The other way that the types can be used is heuristically, that is, to shed light on how we interpret religious moral discourse; the types are aids to our understanding but do not necessarily make a normative claim. If one uses a typology of ethical theories in this way, I believe one can find that most Christian discourse is mixed; there are elements of each of the types in it. The Bible, for example, is replete with evidence of teleological, deontic, consequentialist, and responsibility ethics. At least all of the first three can be found in the ethics of St. Thomas Aquinas.

Whatever the normative significance of the use of such typologies in religious moral discourse, it has at least raised the philosophical self-consciousness of many Christian writers. If, for example, Christians justify their actions or their recommendations on the basis of the good outcomes of them, thus in terms of their consequences, sophistication about types of ethical theories requires that they ask what makes good outcomes or consequences truly good. What is the relation between facts and values? The arguments of Christian writers, thus, tend to become more self-critical, and as a result more persuasive. This, I think, can only be beneficial to religious moral discourse.

You can see, by recollection of what I said about prophetic and narrative discourse, that they do not have the philosophical sophistication of what I call ethical discourse. But a solid ethical argument seldom, if ever, does for a religious community what prophetic and narrative discourse can do.

67

Another point at which ethical discourse has entered Protestantism in a fresh way is in its retrieval of casuistry, that is of applying principles to cases. This retrieval of casuistry has been stimulated not only by the kinds of questions religious moralists are seeking to answer; for example, is it morally right to withdraw artificial nutrition from a dying patient? It has also been stimulated by the study of Roman Catholic moral theology and the study of the Jewish ethical and legal materials. The Jewish and Catholic traditions, and to some extent the Anglican tradition also, have always sought to give precisely argued answers to inquiries about what is the morally right way to act in very particular circumstances. They have never been satisfied with the answers that have sometimes characterized Protestants; for example, do what love requires, or do that which makes and keeps human life more human. To the person asking how to act in complex and ambiguous situations, such counsel is vague, begs more questions than it answers, and seems to rely upon some inspiration of the Holy Spirit.

I have always enjoyed taking students of Christian ethics through some of the questions that Thomas Aquinas asks in the second part of the second part of his *Summa Theologica*. For example, he asks "whether one ought to love one's father more than one's mother?" and shows how one could go about answering that question by using certain distinctions, by basing one's judgment on principles which he states clearly. Or, Jesus said, "Love your enemies." Thomas asks, "Ought one to love his enemies?" and again with very sophisticated distinctions and the use of certain principles shows the reader in what senses and what ways one ought to love one's enemies and in what senses and what ways one ought *not* to love one's enemies. This is ethical discourse in the service of resolving quite particular issues that human beings, including Christians, face.

I will cite only one example of Protestantism's retrieval of casuistry in the past few decades, namely the way in which the theory of justifiable and unjustifiable war has been used. For this we have Paul Ramsey to thank (or to curse, if one does not like the theory) more than any other Protestant thinker. As you probably know, there are two main questions in the Just War Theory. Is there justifiable cause for engaging in war? If there is, what conditions must be met to justify it? And second, are there morally justifiable and morally unjustifiable ways of conducting warfare once it has begun?

I will amplify only the latter. One traditional distinction has been between combatants and noncombatants; in a justified war it is morally permissible to disable a combatant, a soldier, even if it takes his death to do so. But it is morally wrong to take the lives of noncombatants, for example women and children. The principle is clear at this level, but is it applicable in modern conditions of warfare, either those of atomic or nuclear warfare or those of guerrilla warfare? Is it applicable when much of the productive aspects of an economy are geared to making what is needed to conduct a modern war? The serious casuist, like Ramsey, is not daunted by these questions, but refines the application of the principles to very particular circumstances. He must answer the question of whether the traditional distinction between the combatant and noncombatant holds under all modern conditions. And he does.

It is not my purpose to go into the content of such arguments, but only to indicate that the Just War Theory is ethical discourse, and when it is used the moralist is capable of making very reasonable and sophisticated arguments about such things as appropriate weapons. This, like the other points at which ethical discourse has come into Protestantism, is fundamentally beneficial. Even if one chooses to disagree with the conclusion of an ethical argument, one is forced to make a sufficiently reasonable counter-argument.

My claim is that the more extensive use of ethical discourse in religious communities is a beneficial achievement. It may provide the ego satisfaction that religious moralists get when their work is more respectable in the eyes of their colleagues in moral philosophy. But that is a trivial benefit. It provides a basis for a critical assessment of moral pronouncements and other teachings that come from denominational and ecumenical bodies; it forces the writers of such things to provide more careful arguments for the conclusions they recommend or prescribe; it leads to greater precision in judging alternative courses of action from a moral point of view in social policies and in personal relations.

A prophet can utter, "The distribution of health care in American society is unjust." The narrator can tell stories of the effects of such injustice on deprived persons in our society. But to determine what a more just distribution would be requires sophisticated and rigorous use of the concept of distributive justice. Ethical discourse provides the concepts, the modes of appropriate argumentation, and important distinctions which lead to greater precision and stronger backing for what Christians and other religious communities think is the right thing to do, the good thing to do.

But ethical discourse is not sufficient in and of itself. It does not have the capacities that prophetic discourse has vividly to point to some devil, some root of evil that must be extricated, to some deep loyalties and beliefs that systemically distort human life and human community. Nor does its vocabulary move persons with a sense of urgency. Ethical discourse cannot shape the ethos of a community in the way that narratives can, in part because its language and symbols are abstract and do not have the evocative power to sustain and cultivate the nourishing common memories of a community. Its casuistic forms aid precision, but they can excessively delimit what ought to be taken into account in a good moral choice. A narrative, at the point of a choice, might help persons see themselves and circumstances in a broader context of time and history; it might enlarge the perception and imagination so that features are included that the concepts and procedures of casuistry conceal.

To anticipate, with reference to policy discourse, ethical discourse usually comes from the external perspective of an observer rather than the internal perspective of persons, or agents, who are responsible to make choices in quite complex and specific circumstances that constrain their possible actions. For example, I helped to lead a faculty seminar for about three years on the topic of ethics of nuclear deterrence. A paper by a moral philosopher very cogently argued that if it is immoral to use nuclear weapons it is immoral to threaten to use them. But the participants who are consultants on defense policy found the argument remote from the historical actualities which require many considerations not taken into account in the ethical argument. Or, no corporate executive can simply act on the basis of the conclusion of a purely ethical argument. His institutional context is always denser, more complex, than is usually taken into account in such an argument. This does not make ethical discourse irrelevant; it does, I believe, indicate its insufficiency. What ethical discourse does is deepen, broaden, and sharpen the responsible person's capacity to make morally better policy judgments.

To the prophet, ethical discourse is rearranging the deck chairs on the sinking Titanic; this attitude impedes constructive moral communication within the religious community. To the ethically oriented writer, prophetic discourse is "mere rhetoric": this also impedes important moral discourse. Such, alas, was the impasse I described in my opening anecdote.

Policy Discourse

I now turn to my last type or mode of moral discourse, policy discourse. Many refinements beyond what I can do in this lecture would be required to analyze policy discourse adequately. I mean by policy discourse the writings which seek to recommend or prescribe quite particular courses of action about quite specific issues.

Let me suggest one example. The Americans engaged in arms reduction negotiations with the Soviets aim at very specific ends such as the elimination of a specific number of a specific type of weapon in a very specific area, e.g., Central Europe. Think of the range of factors that enter into their considerations. There are political assessments: not only how much of a threat Soviet ideology is to American democratic ideology, but also how a reduction in arms will be responded to in the internal as well as external politics of nation states such as the Federal Republic of Germany. There are strategic and tactical military assessments: they have to think about which side has what advantages from a military point of view if the reduction is made; they have to think about the relative strength of each side in what is called conventional, non-nuclear armaments, if the deterrent effect of nuclear armaments is removed. There are economic assessments: put colloquially, how does one get the biggest bang for a buck? There are assessments of personal characteristics of leaders as well as other negotiators: is Gorbachev to be trusted? Is he sincere, or is he just a clever manipulator of propaganda? And so forth.

Examples like this could be multiplied. They would all suggest certain important features that distinguish policy discourse from the other forms I have delineated. Quite specific factual matters, hopefully accurate ones, have to be known and their significance understood. The range of things to be kept in mind is far more complex than a prophet normally keeps in mind, or even a moral philosopher takes into account. The persons responsible for policy have to be sensitive to their own positions of power: what is required to gain and retain the offices they hold that authorize them to determine policy? Choices have to be made among alternatives that are not ideal, but are circumscribed by the reality of institutions and events in which they participate.

I want to develop this by highlighting two features of policy discourse. First, in its most important form it is conducted not by external observers, but by the persons who have responsibility to make choices and to carry out the actions that are required by the choices. In other words, policy discourse is discourse by the agents who have accountability for the following actions and outcomes — not primarily by philosophers, theologians, political scientists, and economists who have at least one of their feet outside the arena of primary accountability. The second feature is the particularity of conditions within which policy is developed. These conditions both limit the possibilities of action and enable them.

The first question of the policymaker is likely to be "What is going on?" and not "What ought we to do?" Or, at least, both of these questions have to be kept in mind in a tandem and finally integrated way. The policymaker has to know what is possible, as well as what is the right thing to do, or what are the most desirable outcomes. What is desirable is always related to what is possible; it is always under the constraints of the possible. And a critical factor of judgment is precisely *what is possible.*

To develop this further, I resort to a narrative. It comes from one of several experiences in which I have been a participant in a policy-making process, though I have never had the primary responsibility for any momentous decisions.

In 1956 I was invited, together with a prominent New York lawyer and educational administrator who had long experience in both the military and in the Department of Defense, to help a multinational corporation determine what it should do about a possible cost reduction in the transportation of oil and refined oil products in the inland waterways of the United States. My particular assignment was to make recommendations about this work in the New York and Baltimore harbors.

Competitive market forces determined the problem. The corporation was Standard Oil of New Jersey, now called Exxon. Jersey Standard ran its own fleet of tugboats, barges, and self-propelled barges, in both harbors. Upon investigation it turned out that it would be cheaper for Exxon to contract out the tugboat and barge operations in New York than to continue to run its own fleet. (In today's jargon, Exxon was vertically integrated in its operations, and it would be more economical to out-source this aspect of them than to continue them.)

Two questions formed the main agenda of our investigations: (1) Were there qualitative aspects of the fleet and its operations that would justify its retention even at a somewhat higher cost? Was the fleet providing better services, though at a higher cost, than would be provided by the Moran corporation? If so, what higher cost could justify these better services? And (2) were there ways in which costs could be reduced in the operations while still retaining the qualitative advantage, if there was one, in a way which would be fair to the employees?

I will spare you a full description of this investigation, but highlight certain features. First, the relevant ethical concepts and theories were clear. On the one hand, some kind of utilitarian calculus was required; on the other hand, there was a genuine concern to be just, or fair, to the company's own employees. One could not choose to be only a deontic moralist concerned for justice, or only a utilitarian moralist weighing the costs and benefits of alternative courses of action.

But I was required to think about these ethical issues in a very specific context of economic, bureaucratic or institutional, historical, and even personal factors. I had to study the efficiency reports on each of twenty-one barges and nine tugboats. I had to know how much their labor costs were inflated in comparison to what could be known about the Moran alternative. The additional labor costs were the result of very generous, even paternalistic, wage and benefit programs, e.g., the fact that the larger Exxon crews spent less time per month on the water than Moran crews.

I spent a number of days on tugboats and barges in the New York harbor, observing the operations and interviewing the personnel. I spent time also observing and interviewing managerial personnel in the headquarters on 51st Street in Manhattan.

History was involved in an interesting way: the paternalistic wage and benefit policies, which made Exxon look like a private welfare state, could be traced back to the concern of John D. Rockefeller, Jr., and his reaction to the mining strikes in which Rockefeller interests were involved decades before in Colorado. Indeed, one veteran officer traced that one more step, whether accurately or not I cannot attest, to the influence of the liberal social gospel preacher and pastor, Harry Emerson Fosdick, on Mr. Rockefeller.

Personal factors were involved. The manager of Inland Waterways had been brought to New York from Venezuela where he had achieved a stupendous cost reduction in the transportation of oil in Lake Maracaibo and the Island of Aruba where Creole Oil Company, a totally owned subsidiary, had its refineries. He was blunt; he aspired to become a member of the board of directors of the international corporation. The interests of the workers were represented in management by an Inland Waterways employee relations officer, a pious Scot Presbyterian deeply committed to what he saw as the just and benevolent policies that were now under threat.

The basic issue could be stated as "Efficiency versus Justice," or fairness. To be sure, there had to be an ethical argument in our report, but it had to be embedded in our accounting for the various dense, complex, and interrelated matters I noted a moment ago. Our recommendations had to be within the context of the possible. One could not make a theoretical ethical argument about justice or utility and leave it at that. An ethical argument, *per se,* would have been insufficient. The ethical had to give direction to the policy but *per se* could not determine the policy. Our recommendations had to be spelled out not merely in terms of general concepts or general aims; they had to be quite specific in terms of reasonably accurate estimates and assessments of "what was going on."

Policy discourse requires more than the concepts and procedures of ethical discourse. Even conceptually, and not only with reference to types of information, more is required: sociological, economic, and other concepts have to be used to assess the possible. One could not say, "Be just" or "Be fair to your employees," any more than one could say only, "Do the most efficient thing from the standpoint of economic considerations." We had, in other words, to seek, insofar as possible, to assume the position of accountable agents with certain powers and limits of power, with certain information and limits of information. Policymakers necessarily think within the terms of the possible, within a limited framework of time and space. Even when they are thinking ethically, they have to know how to get from where their institutions are today to where they could be (and ought to be) a month, a year, a few years from now. The ethical, to the policymaker, is a *dimension* (in the case of my illustration) of the economic, the social, the personal, and even the historical.

The importance of policy discourse should be clear from this narrative. Prophets, storytellers, and moral theologians are seldom, if ever, the accountable agents for the outcomes of actions. They are usually observers, at best consultants. Policy discourse has distinctive demands in terms of knowledge, concepts, and understanding. Persons and institutions with various kinds of power to shape the course of events have a social role preachers and professors do not have. Indeed, a necessary condition for moral, conscientious policymakers is to ensure that they have and maintain sufficient power to have some effects.

But to limit moral discourse to policy discourse would be a mistake. Policy discourse necessarily works within limited visions, limited frames of reference. It accepts certain conditions which from prophetic and ethical perspectives could themselves be judged morally wrong, or at least morally inadequate.

For example, in 1956 multinational corporations were not as often described in the demonic terms used by many church people and others today. To the prophet, even at that time, however, I surely was prostituting my vocation by serving a multinational corporation whose right to that much power I did not make it a point to challenge. To the moral theologian and philosopher, our recommendations had inconsistencies when assessed in the light of various ethical theories. They were not purely deontological, though they had a deontic aspect in our concern for a just distribution of the costs to human beings in the cost-reduction program. They were not purely utilitarian, though we could not have made recommendations without engaging in utility calculus. And even narrative added to our understanding of the larger framework within which we worked: there was a history to the unusually generous wage and benefits programs. And if my old-timer was correct, they could be traced back to the religious, moral convictions of earlier generations. Without that story, we would have missed something important in this case.

Churches and Christian persons who aspire to affect the course of events with moral aims and principles need to be able to participate in policy discourse. It is not that prophets are powerless, but that their power is different from that of persons whose vocations and roles affect incremental, but important, changes in the course of events and states of affairs.

Now to conclude. I have argued that four different types of moral discourse not only exist, but have distinguishable functions in the human moral community, and particularly religious ones. I have suggested, but not fully argued, that writers who claim sufficiency for any one of them are in error.

The failure to recognize differences in these types of moral discourse leads to unnecessary confusion and to misplaced debates in Christian ethical literature and in the life of the churches. Stubborn adherence to only one type obstructs fruitful participation of morally serious persons, particularly in circumstances in which practical choices have to be made.

But there are different vocations among religious persons, and among morally serious persons. Policymakers need to have their institutions challenged by the prophet; they need to have their arguments and choices clarified, evaluated, and informed by the ethician. The prophet and narrator need to have their discourse subjected to ethical analysis: there are better and worse stories from a moral point of view. They also have to understand sympathetically the legitimate role of the accountable policy-maker in the determination of the course of events. The ethician needs to understand that the policymaker cannot simply apply the conclusion of a sound moral argument to his circumstances, but that ethical arguments deepen, broaden, and sharpen his capacities to make morally responsible choices.

There are many matters of intellectual interest that these two lectures have opened, but have not been developed. However, I think some practical inferences can be drawn. In churches, in gatherings of conscientious Christians, we need greater communication between persons who use primarily each of these forms. We need occasions in which mutual enlightenment and correction of participants can take place. We need greater openness to receiving the contributions of various participants. The Church, as a community of moral discourse, ought to include all four varieties.

Two Arguments from the Heart
for Immortality

PETER KREEFT

Contents

Introduction

Apologetics is the science of giving reasons for faith, in obedience to the apostolic command (1 Peter 3:15) to "be ready to give a reason for the hope that is in you." That hope, for Christians, essentially involves immortality, or life after death. Arguments for immortality, therefore, are essential to Christian apologetics.

Of the dozens of different arguments for immortality, the most fascinating ones to the modern mind (at least to most of my students, who are typical) are not the theoretical arguments from the mind and its understanding of the nature of the soul, but the practical and personal ones from the will, or heart, or desire, which also understands, which also has eyes.

Two very different twentieth-century Christian thinkers, the British, Anglican literary scholar and popular writer C. S. Lewis and the French Catholic existentialist philosopher Gabriel Marcel, have developed two different but equally fascinating arguments for immortality from premises or data in the heart rather than the head. Both are essentially very simple arguments, summarizable in a single paragraph, even a single sentence. Yet both open up vast vistas to explore. I shall attempt to lead a small landing party onto the shores of these two lands for a short visit to a far country, the land of life after death, "the undiscovered country from whose bourne no traveller returns."

C. S. Lewis's Argument from Desire

This essay is about a single argument. Next to Anselm's famous "ontological argument," I think it is the single most intriguing argument in the history of human thought. For one thing, it not only argues for the existence of God, but at the same time it argues for the existence of Heaven and for something of the essential nature of Heaven and of God — four conclusions, not just one. For another thing, it is far more moving, arresting, and apologetically effective than any other argument for God or for Heaven. At least it is that in my experience with students. Finally, it is more than an argument. Like Anselm's argument, it is also a meditation, an illumination, an experience, an invitation to an experiment with yourself, a pilgrimage.

I shall first state the argument as succinctly as possible. Second, I shall show how C. S. Lewis, who more than anyone else is associated with it, uses it in three different ways (autobiographical, practical-pastoral, and logical). Third, I shall trace contributions to it back into four lines of historical influence (experiential, historical, epistemological, and practical). Fourth, I shall try to answer the main objections against it.

I

The major premise of the argument is that every natural or innate desire in us bespeaks a corresponding real object that can satisfy the desire.

The minor premise is that there exists in us a desire which nothing in time, nothing on earth, no creature, can satisfy.

The conclusion is that there exists something outside of time, earth, and creatures which can satisfy this desire.

81

This something is what people call God and Heaven. Thus the argument seeks to prove the existence of God and Heaven via this one aspect of them, desirableness, just as Aquinas's five "ways" seek to prove the existence of God under five aspects, and concludes with: "And this is what people call 'God.'"

A word about each premise.

The major premise implicitly distinguishes desires into two kinds: innate and conditioned, natural and artificial. We naturally desire things like food, drink, sex, knowledge, friendship, and beauty, and naturally turn away from things like starvation, ignorance, loneliness, and ugliness. We also desire things like Rolls Royces, political offices, flying through the air like Superman, a Red Sox world championship, and lands like Oz. But there are two differences between the two lists. First, we do not always recognize corresponding states of deprivation of the second, as we do with the first. And, most important, the desires on the first list all come from within, from our nature, while the second come from without, from society, or advertising, or fiction. The first come from our spiritual heredity; the second come from our material environment.

The existence of desires of the second class does not necessarily mean that the objects desired exist. Rolls Royces do, Oz does not. But the existence of desires of the first class, in every discoverable case, *does* mean that the objects desired exist. No case has ever been found of an innate desire with a nonexistent object.

You may regard the argument as an argument from analogy: by analogy with all our other innate desires, which have real objects, the desire for God and Heaven must have a real object. Or you may regard the argument as one whose major premise is established inductively, by generalization. But it is better to regard the argument as a deductive syllogism, and the major premise as known in the same way that "all men are mortal" is known: by abstraction of a universal form or principle from individual material instances, by an insight into the universal form or principle that is met in the different instances or instantiations. As we shall see later, this apparently technically nitpicking point is essential to meet the most important objection to the argument.

The minor premise of the argument is an empirical observation, if "empirical" is extended to cover inner experience as well as outer, introspection as well as extrospection. The argument then depends on a personal appeal to introspective experience. Just as we cannot argue effectively about color with a blind man because he has no data, so we cannot argue about this desire with someone who cannot find the desire in question in himself, or who refuses to look for it, or who refuses to admit its presence once it is found. But, then, such a person cannot argue against us either. In a sense (a non-fallacious sense) the argument is an *ad hominem*, like Aristotle's argument against Protagoras's skeptical denial of the law of non-contradiction: if only the skeptic will make some simple admission, he can be refuted, for he contradicts himself by claiming to know something when he says he cannot know anything. But he cannot be compelled to make that admission — in Aristotle's case, to utter a putative meaningful sentence, in our case to recognize the existence of a desire for a perfect object, or for perfect joy, that no earthly object and no earthly pleasure can fulfill. If someone blandly says, "I am perfectly happy playing with mud pies, or fast cars, or money, or political power," we can query, "Are you, really?" but we can only try to inveigle him out of his childishness, we cannot compel him by logical force.

In a sense, the minor premise of the argument is more interesting than the argument itself. The phenomenon the Germans call *Sehnsucht* is psychologically fascinating, and when it occurs as subject rather than object, i.e., when we experience the desire rather than thinking about it, it is obsessive and imperious — in fact, even more imperious than erotic desire at its height. Faced with a choice between the perfect earthly beloved and the fulfillment of *Sehnsucht*, we choose *Sehnsucht*; for the object of *Sehnsucht* is the perfect heavenly beloved, whether we know it or not. As Lewis says, "Joy is not a substitute for sex; sex is very often a substitute for Joy."

The conclusion of the argument is not that all that is meant by God or Heaven in the Bible or in the popular imagination must exist. What the argument proves to exist is unidentifiable with any image or representation. Lewis describes it thus in *Surprised by Joy:*

> . . . something which, by refusing to identify itself with any object of the senses or anything whereof we have biological or social need, or anything imagined, or any state of our own minds, proclaims itself sheerly objective. Far more objective than bodies, for it is not, like them, clothed in our senses: the naked Other, imageless (though our imagination salutes it with a hundred images), unknown, undefined, desired.

It is the concept of an unknown x, but an unknown whose *direction* is known, so to speak. God is *more* — more beauty, more desirability, more awesomeness. God is to great beauty what great beauty is to small beauty or to a mixture of beauty and ugliness. And the same with other perfections. But the 'more' is *infinitely* more; thus the analogy is not proportionate. Twenty is to ten what ten is to five, but infinity is not to twenty what twenty is to ten, or five, or one. But it is 'in that direction,' so to speak. The argument is like a parable: it points down an infinite corridor in a finite direction. Its object is not 'God' as conceived and defined already, but a movingly mysterious x which is always more than any image, notion, or concept. It does not presuppose but supplies a definition of God, and one which reverses the normal positive notion of definition *(de-fino)* by asserting that God is the one *not* captureable in any finite terms. The definition of its 'God' is 'that which is more than any definition,' the God whom "eye has not seen, ear has not heard, neither has it entered into the heart of man." In other words, this is the real God.

II

There are especially three passages in C. S. Lewis where the argument from desire is stated at length, though *Sehnsucht* itself seeps out from many a page of Lewis, most perfectly in "The Weight of Glory," the best sermon I have ever read. (Have you ever read a better one?) But the three passages in which Lewis *argues* for God from *Sehnsucht* are in *Surprised by Joy, Mere Christianity,* and the Introduction to *The Pilgrim's Regress.* The *Surprised by Joy* passages are not primarily intended to argue but to reveal. The book is not philosophy but autobiography. Yet an argument is hinted at. The passage in *Mere Christianity* is more argumentative than *Surprised by Joy,* but it is primarily practical, a matter of pastoral guidance. Only in the early work, *The Pilgrim's Regress,* did Lewis use it as an explicit argument. I do not know why this is so. There is no reason to think it was because Lewis thought the argument a bad one, for there is no passage in Lewis's later works that even remotely suggests that.

The passage in *Surprised by Joy* first defines the desire by contradistinction from other desires as follows: "an unsatisfied desire which is itself more desirable than any other satisfaction." Lewis then implicitly argues for the existence of the object of this desire when he discovers the

fact that the desire is essentially intentional, or reaching out and pointing beyond itself to its object. He confesses and turns from his earlier
subjectivist error:

> I had smuggled in the assumption that what I wanted was a 'thrill,' a
> state of my own mind. And there lies the deadly error. Only when your
> whole attention and desire are fixed on something else . . . does the
> 'thrill' arise. It is a by-product. Its very existence presupposes that you
> desire not it but something other and outer. . . .
>
> Images or sensations . . . were merely the mental track left by the
> passage . . . not the wave but the wave's imprint in the sand. The inher-
> ent dialectic of desire itself had in a way already shown me this, for all
> images and sensations, if idolatrously mistaken for Joy itself, soon con-
> fessed themselves inadequate. All said, in the last resort, 'It is not I. I
> am only a reminder. Look! Look! What do I remind you of?'
>
> Inexorably Joy proclaimed, 'You want — I myself am your want of —
> something other, outside, not you or any state of you.'

Like Augustine, ending the autobiographical part of his *Confessions* in
Book X, Lewis, on the last page of the book, confesses his present state of
soul with regard to *Sehnsucht:*

> I now know that the experience, considered as a state of my own mind,
> had never had the kind of importance I once gave it. It was valuable
> only as a pointer to something other and outer. While that other was in
> doubt, the pointer naturally loomed large in my thoughts. When we
> are lost in the woods the sight of a signpost is a great matter. . . . But
> when we have found the road . . . we shall not stop and stare, or not
> much; not on this road. . . . "We would be at Jerusalem."

These passages describe the desire and head us off from the subjectivist error about it, but do not so much argue from it to the existence of its
object as immediately look along the desire at its mysterious object, or look
at its intentionality and see immediately that it must have an object, simply because it is thus essentially intentional. But Lewis does not (1) distinguish natural or innate desires from others, or (2) argue from the principle
that all natural desires have objects, yet, in this book.

The passage in *Mere Christianity* is also essentially practical, meant

85

to head the reader off from two popular mistakes. Lewis first calls our attention to the desire, then to two mistakes about it, then comes the argument:

> Most people, if they had really learned to look into their own hearts, would know that they do want, and want acutely, something that cannot be had in this world. There are all sorts of things in this world that offer to give it to you, but they never quite keep their promise. . . . Now there are two wrong ways of dealing with this fact, and one right way.
>
> (1) The Fool's Way — He puts the blame on the things themselves. He goes on all his life thinking that if only he tried another woman, or holiday, or whatever, then this time he would really catch the mysterious something. . . .
>
> (2) The Way of the Disillusioned 'Sensible' Man — He soon decides that the whole thing was moonshine. And so he represses the part of himself which used to cry for the moon. . . .
>
> (3) The Christian Way — The Christian says [and here is the argument]: Creatures are not born with desires unless satisfaction for these desires exists. A baby feels hunger; well, there is such a thing as food. A duckling wants to swim; well, there is such a thing as water. Men feel sexual desire; well, there is such a thing as sex. If I find in myself a desire which no experience in this world can satisfy, the most probable explanation is that I was made for another world.

Note that Lewis does not claim certainty for the conclusion here, just probability. For the conclusion here is only a hypothesis that explains the data better than any other, but this fact does not prove with certainty that this hypothesis is true.

Yet it does show the practical necessity of taking this desire seriously: "I must keep alive in myself the desire for my true country." Like Pascal's "Wager," the argument here shows that you are a fool if you turn your back on this strong clue, this strong probability that infinite happiness exists and that you are designed to enjoy it.

In the Introduction to *The Pilgrim's Regress,* Lewis does two things more clearly than he does anywhere else. First, he defines exactly how this desire differs from all others. Second, he argues from the principle that nature makes nothing in vain to the conclusion that the one who can satisfy this desire must exist.

The experience is one of intense longing. It is distinguished from other longings by two things. In the first place, though the sense of want is acute and even painful, yet the mere wanting is felt to be somehow a delight. . . . This hunger is better than any other fullness; this poverty better than all other wealth. . . . In the second place, there is a peculiar mystery about the *object* of this desire. . . . Every one of these supposed objects for the desire is inadequate to it. It appeared to me therefore that if a man diligently followed this desire, pursuing the false objects until their falsity appeared and then resolutely abandoning them, he must come out at last into the clear knowledge that the human soul was made to enjoy some object that is never fully given — nay, cannot even be imagined as given — in our present mode of subjective and spatio-temporal experience. This desire was, in the soul, as the Siege Perilous in Arthur's castle — the chair in which only one could sit. And if nature makes nothing in vain, the One who can sit in this chair must exist.

Here the conclusion is not called "the most probable explanation" but something that "must exist." If nature makes nothing in vain, if you admit the premise, the conclusion necessarily follows. Of course, one who wants to refuse to admit the conclusion at all costs will deny the premise — but at the cost of a meaningful universe, a universe in which desires and satisfactions match.

In other words, God can be avoided. All we need do is embrace "vanity of vanities" instead. It is a fool's bargain, of course: Everything is exchanged for Nothing — a trade even the Boston Red Sox are not fool enough to make.

III

I believe C. S. Lewis is the best apologist for the Christian faith in the twentieth century. Many virtues grace his work, but the one that lifts him above any other writer who has ever written, I believe, is how powerfully he writes about Joy, or *Sehnsucht,* the desire we are speaking of here. Many other writers excel him in originality. He did not mean to be original. ("Our Lord never tried to be original," he noted.) Perhaps a few modern writers excel him in clarity (though offhand I cannot name one) or grace, or beauty, or accuracy, or popular appeal. But no one has written better of Joy.

Yet he never wrote a whole book about this thing, though he admitted in his autobiography that it was the *leitmotif* of his whole life: "the central story of my life is about nothing else." Lewis says somewhere that he wrote the books he wanted to read, the books he wished someone else would write, but they didn't, so he did. That is why I originally wrote *Heaven, the Heart's Deepest Longing:* because, incredibly, no one had ever written a whole book about the deepest longing in human life.

From a historical point of view I think one of Lewis's chief claims to fame is that he pulled together, coalesced, and sharpened to a fine point a number of important strands in the history of Western religious and philosophical thought around this argument. The argument does not just float loose on the surface; it flowers from immense, deep tangles of growing things. Some of the most important names in our history are involved in this tangle: Moses, Solomon, Plato, Christ, Paul, Augustine, Bonaventure, Jung. I discern four distinct aspects of the argument, four strands of influence. One name that crops up in all four strands is Pascal, whom Lewis evidently read and admired, though he quoted him only sparsely. But lack of extensive quotation from Pascal is no proof of a lack of deep influence; such is the case with Kierkegaard, who fleshes out many of the *Pensées* but never mentions Pascal's name.

The first influence-strand is psychological, or experiential. It is a double experience, a negative and a positive. The negative experience is unhappiness, restlessness. The positive experience is longing, *Sehnsucht* itself. Let's look at the negative side first.

Solomon, or whoever wrote Ecclesiastes, knew the emptiness, vanity, and wretchedness of human life even at its best as well as anyone ever did. Pascal says,

> Solomon and Job have known and spoken best about man's wretchedness, one the most fortunate, the other the most unfortunate of men; one knowing by experience the vanity of pleasure, the other the reality of afflictions.

Herman Melville, in *Moby Dick,* and Thomas Wolfe, in *You Can't Go Home Again,* have both called Ecclesiastes the single greatest and truest book ever written about human life under the sun. Its conclusion is that life is "vanity of vanities." Why? Why call life "vanity"? I do not mean by that question: What evidence does Solomon use to prove his conclusion? That is painfully obvious: the oppressions of the poor, the endless cycles of time, the inevitability of death, the strength of evil over good, the indifference of nature to justice, the uncertainty of all our works, the near-impossibility of being both wise and content at the same time, and above all the mystery, remoteness, and invisibility of a God whose ways are past finding out. No, I mean a more mysterious "Why?" Why do we call this "vanity"? Why do we rail against these things? Why do we not obey the reasonable advice of nine out of ten of our psychologists, who in book after book tell us to accept ourselves as we are, become well-adjusted citizens of the Kingdom of This World, and even accept death as a friend, not an enemy? (Freud called it "making friends with the necessity of dying.") No one but a sheep or a scholar is fool enough to believe such inhuman nonsense. Instead, something in us thrills to the gloriously irrational passion of the poet Dylan Thomas when he says, "Do not go gentle into that good-night/Rage, rage against the dying of the light."

What is that thing in us that gloriously disobeys the advice of our comfort-mongering modern sages and rises to the dignity of despair? Death is the most natural thing in the world; why do we find it unnatural? "Do fish complain of the sea for being wet?" asks Lewis, in a letter to Sheldon Vanauken. "Or if they did, would that not indicate that they had not always been, or were not destined always to be, sea creatures?" But we complain about death and time. As Lewis says, "time is just another name for death." There is never enough time. Time makes being into non-being. Time is a river that takes away everything it brings: nations, civilizations, art, science, culture, plants, animals, our own bodies, the very stars — nothing stands outside this cosmic stream rushing headlong into the sea of death. Or does it? Something in us seems to stand outside it, for something in us protests this "nature" and asks: Is that all there is? We find this natural situation "vanity": empty, frustrating, wretched, unhappy. Our nature contradicts nature.

Thus there is a double datum: (1) the objective datum of death and time and all the other things in nature that make us unhappy; and (2) the subjective datum that they make us unhappy. The objective datum can be explained scientifically, but what of the subjective datum? That needs to be explained too.

There is a clue in Ecclesiastes 3:11, the one verse in the book that rings with hope like a bell in a swamp. Solomon says to God, "You have made everything fitting for its time, but you have also put eternity into man's heart." Time does not satisfy the restless heart. We cry out for eternity because God has put this desire into our hearts. Our hearts are restless until they rest in him because they were designed by him to rest in him alone. Resting in nature is unnatural for us. Our nature is to demand supernature.

The wretchedness and dissatisfaction and restlessness of the heart, the spirit, the image of God, the Godchild in us alienated from Home and the Father, is the negative side of the coin. The positive side is the hopeful longing, the energy and the homing pigeon's instinct that moves Augustine through the pages of the *Confessions*. It is the poignancy of E.T. looking for that magic place 'Home.' Pascal says, "an infinite abyss can be filled only with an infinite object, i.e. God Himself." We spend our lives trying to fill the Grand Canyon with marbles.

Even the pagan at his best knew this. Plato in the *Symposium* let the cat out of the bag. Eros, love, desire, climbs the steps of a hierarchy and will not rest with lesser, lower, particular, limited, and material loves, beautiful as they are. Only Beauty itself, absolute, pure, unmixed, perfect, and eternal, will satisfy the soul. Lewis says somewhere that no one should be allowed to die without having read Plato's *Symposium*. And he surely speaks for himself in the Narnia books when he has Professor Digory Kirke exclaim, "Why it's all in Plato! All in Plato! What *do* they teach them in the schools nowadays?" Plato is eminently convertible, Christianizeable. Paganism at its best is a virgin, Christianity a wife, modernity a divorcee. I love Chesterton's three-sentence summary of the history of Western thought: "Paganism was the biggest thing in the world, and Christianity was bigger, and everything since has been comparatively small."

A second ingredient in the background of our argument is the historical account of the Fall, recorded in Genesis 3. Our present wretchedness and restless search is a historical fact, not just a myth. Therefore the origin or cause of this fact cannot be a mere myth either, but must be a real event. The only two candidates are Creation or Fall. Either God or Man created our wretchedness. Did God push us, or did we fall? The story of a Fall, a Paradise Lost, a Primordial Tragedy, is a nearly universal theme in the world's myths. For our myths are infinitely wiser than our science, which knows nothing of such archaic and spiritual events. Our science comes from our conscious mind, but our myths come from our unconscious, which is much deeper and wiser. The unconscious remembers things the conscious mind has forgotten. The Priest of Glome is wiser than the Fox, the Greek philosopher in Lewis's historical novel *Till We Have Faces*.

Myths are even prophetic, pointing to the truth from afar, as Greek philosophy is prophetic. For God has not left himself without witnesses even outside Israel, though none of these other witnesses is divinely guaranteed and infallible. The human soul has intellect, will, and emotions; some knowledge of the true, the good, and the beautiful. And God sent prophets to all three areas of the soul: philosophers to enlighten the intellect, prophets to straighten out the will, and myth-makers to tease and touch the emotions with a desire for himself. The philosophers have an analogue in the soul, a philosopher within: our understanding. The prophets have an analogue in the soul too, a divine mouthpiece called conscience. And the myth-makers too have an analogue in the soul, a dreamer and poet and myth-maker within.

But the truths of the myths got terribly distorted, like the message in the party game whispered around a large circle. That's why Lewis calls myths "gleams of celestial strength and beauty falling on a jungle of filth and imbecility" — because "they are based on a far more solid reality than we think, but they are at an almost infinite distance from their base."

The biblical story of the Fall explains our present experience as a scientific hypothesis explains observed data. The data here are very strange: that we alone do not fit the world of time and death, we alone do not obey the advice of our own psychologists to accept ourselves as we are. The explanation must be equally strange. The human lock is weirdly shaped. The biblical key is also weirdly shaped: a story of a radical tragedy at our very roots. There are all sorts of difficulties with the story. But it fits — the key fits the lock. What happened in Eden may be hard to understand, but it makes everything else understandable.

Eden explains, e.g., the strange complication of our greatness and wretchedness. As Pascal says, "all these examples of wretchedness prove his greatness. It is the wretchedness of a great lord, the wretchedness of a dispossessed king." And "Man's greatness can be deduced from his wretchedness, for what is nature in animals [e.g., pain and death] we call wretchedness in man, thus recognizing that he must have fallen from some better state which was once his own. Who indeed would think himself unhappy not to be the king except one who had been dispossessed? . . . Who would think himself unhappy if he had only one mouth and who would not if he had only one eye! It has probably never occurred to anyone to be distressed at not having three eyes, but those who have none are inconsolable."

Eden even explains why music moves us. As Charles Williams wrote, "A voice went out from Eden. All music was the fallen echo of that sound."

Our longing for a home and a happiness that we do not ever experience in this world is a great mystery. And the story of the Fall is a great solution to it.

A third, epistemological strand of historical influence for our argument stems from Plato and his famous doctrine of Anamnesis, or Recollection. According to this doctrine, when we discover an eternal truth, we are really remembering a knowledge that is innate to us but which our conscious mind had forgotten. In light of what we have just said about the historical events in Eden being an explanation of our present unhappy state, in light of the Christian doctrine of the Fall, Plato's doctrine of Anamnesis makes acceptable sense. It also makes sense in light of our present experience of learning the truth. For whenever we discover an eternal truth, we experience an "aha!" — a moment of recognition (re-cognition, knowing-again). It is like the aha! experience of remembering an empirical object like a lost wallet when we meet it in a Lost and Found Department. If we had never known the wallet in the past, we would not be able to pick it out in the present. We recognize it only because there is a memory image in us, which came from our past experience of it. Similarly, when, like Meno's slave boy, we discover an eternal truth of mathematics like the Pythagorean Theorem, or an eternal truth of ethics such as the fundamental conclusion of Plato's *Republic,* that justice is always more profitable than injustice, or the definition of justice as health of soul — when we discover such eternal truths in the Lost and Found Department of ideas that is the history of Western thought, we experience a shock of recognition (re-cognition), a *deja vu,* an aha! The innate truth-detector in us buzzes like a Geiger counter — not infallibly, but nonetheless really. Knowledge need not be infallible to be knowledge. Meno's slave boy's truth-detector went off too soon. He made a mistake before he found the truth. But then, on the second attempt, he corrected his mistake. We too often aha! too soon and seize on a falsehood as a truth; or too late, and miss a truth that is under our nose. But we do aha! We do recognize.

From this aha! experience two possible lines of explanation of it lead out. Reductionism explains it away, debunks it (or tries to) as only empirical generalization, or projection of subjective expectation, or habit, or even by the wires of experience and memory being crossed in the brain, as the *deja vu* experience can be explained as a new experience being misfiled into the brain's memory category.

But suppose we do not explain it away, but explain it. Two dimensions of non-reductionistic explanation present themselves: the ontological, as in Augustine's theory of Divine Illumination, or the psychological, as in Jung's theory of the Collective Unconscious.

Augustine's idea of Divine Illumination as the source of *a priori* knowledge uses the image of *light* for truth and in so doing reveals something extremely important and usually forgotten in debates between Platonists like Augustine and Lewis and empiricists or positivists or analytic philosophers who criticize them. As I shall try to show in the last section of this paper, a Platonist always puts the truth of *"seeing the light"* above the truth of calculation; *intellectus* above *ratio;* the fourth quarter of the Divided Line in the *Republic* over the third quarter; the First Act of the Mind, or Simple Apprehension of an essence, above or prior to the Second and Third Acts of the Mind, judgment of a proposition as true or false, and reasoning or inference. Here is a more primordial notion of truth than the relational truth of a judgment, relating predicate to subject or proposition to fact. It is the absolute truth of an essence, or Platonic Form, and this is something like light, something almost substantial. Thus Lewis speaks of "edible" and "drinkable" truth in *The Great Divorce* (ch. 5), and Christ claims to *be* the truth, not just to *speak* it (John 14:6).

An alternative non-reductionistic explanation of the aha! epistemological experience is Jung's theory of the Collective Unconscious. It may be used either as a substitute for or as a supplement to the ontological explanation of Augustine. It may also be used either as a substitute for or as a supplement to the historical explanation of Eden. It presupposes first that there *is* an Unconscious, as nearly every philosophical psychologist except Sartre and Behaviorists do, and second that Christopher Columbus Freud only landed on its beach. Freud's mistake was not to overestimate its depth and complexity and innate power to inform and direct the conscious self, but to *under*estimate it, in reducing it all to the sex drive. Scott Peck has shown in a very practical, popular, and effective way in the first half of his best-seller *The Road Less Travelled* how incredibly wise our unconscious is. So impressive is this wisdom to him, in fact, that in the second half of the book he voyages far beyond the shores of scientific psychology into the hypothesis, apparently shared by Jung, that the unconscious is God. It is a heresy, of course, but every heresy is based on a truth that is bent. The heretic is mistaken, but some truth must be taken before it can be mistaken. The truth the Jungian takes is, I believe, precisely the truth of the Augustinian Divine Illumination — which, by the way, St. Thomas also teaches, but he clarifies it so that only *in* God's light do we see light. Divine illumination is not an object of consciousness; it is the sun shining behind us rather than in front of us. As Chesterton says, God is like the sun: only in the light of the one who cannot be seen (because he is too light, not too dark) can everything else be seen. Let one thing be mystical and everything else becomes rational. Let one thing be not a knowable object, and everything else becomes a knowable object. Let one thing be an *x* and everything else becomes a *y*.

The Platonic epistemology of *a priori* knowledge is not as intellectually silly as its current reputation. It is based on data, evidence: the fact that we function like homing pigeons, we know what is not our home, like E.T., and we also know what things are closer to Home, to Heaven, to God, than other things, though we do not know this infallibly and we can and do make many, many mistakes about it, even eternal mistakes. But we can and do judge that *y* is farther and *z* nearer to *x*, to Home, even though we have never been Home, never experienced God or Heaven as we have experienced *y* and *z*. In order to judge truly whether *y* is more or less perfect than *z*, we must use a standard, *x*. Even if we do not know *x* as an explicit, defined, experienced, or even experienceable object, we still *use x*, and thus *implicitly* know *x*. Knowledge of what is better implies knowledge of what is best. Knowledge of imperfection implies knowledge of perfection. Progress implies an unchanging goal — how can you make progress toward a moving goal line? How can a base runner score a run if home plate keeps moving?

The program is in our computer because our Creator has designed and programmed us. *Because* "Thou hast made us for Thyself," therefore "our hearts are restless until they rest in Thee." It is not a program that appears on our computer screen as data, as information to store and recall. Rather, it is an operational program, a procedural rule, a practical command and direction we follow. It is a program of the heart, not of the head or conscious mind.

But 'heart' does not mean sentiment, emotion, or feeling in Scripture, as it does in modern parlance. It means our center, our I. Pascal is quite correct to say "the heart has its reasons which the reason does not know." The heart has *reasons*. The heart has eyes. Love is not blind. How could love be blind? God is love. Is God blind? One of those three propositions must be false: that love is blind, that God is not blind, and that God is love.

This 'heart' that we have spoken of is the central concept of the fourth strand of influence, the practical or pastoral. It is the heart that is the organ of the unconscious knowledge of the way home that we have just explored. The heart is our guide, our homing pigeon. Though it is fallen and in need of correction by divine revelation, though it is "desperately wicked," according to Scripture, yet its very wretchedness shows its greatness, as the height from which we have fallen measures the depths of our fall. We are not simply bad, but a good thing gone bad, a sacred thing profaned.

Jesus appealed to the heart constantly, e.g., when he said, "Seek and you shall find." It is the heart that seeks. Pascal comments, with this promise of Jesus in mind,

> There are three kinds of people: those who have sought God and found Him, and these are reasonable and happy; those who seek God and have not yet found Him, and these are reasonable and unhappy; and those who neither seek God nor find Him, and these are unreasonable and unhappy.

There is no fourth class, those who find without seeking. Christ's promise that all who seek, find, is simultaneously reassuring and threatening: reassuring in that everyone in Pascal's second class eventually graduates into his first class (all seekers find, all who are reasonable and honest and intend God, intend repentance and faith, will find him and become happy); but threatening in that no one who does not seek will find. It is the seeking heart that determines our eternal destiny. In the heart Heaven or Hell is decided.

Christ presupposed the primacy of the heart in John 7:17 when he answered his critics' hermeneutical question, "How can we know your teaching, whether it is from God?" with scandalous simplicity: "If your will (or heart) were to do the will of My Father, you would know My teaching, that it is from Him." When it comes to knowing persons rather than things or concepts, the heart rightly leads the head. Who understands you best, a brilliant psychologist who has spent ten thousand hours interviewing you as a case study for his doctoral dissertation but who does not care about you personally, or your best friend, who is not terribly bright but who loves you very much?

William Law, one of Lewis's favorite writers, is as embarrassingly simple as Jesus because he too sees that the heart decides all, when he says, in *A Serious Call to the Devout Life,* "If you will honestly consult your own heart you will see that there is one and only one reason why you are not even now a saint: because you do not wholly want to be." Augustine says the same thing in the *Confessions:* that it is the divided will, the divided heart, that accounts for the astonishing introspective discovery of Paul in Romans 7 that "I do not understand my own behavior. For the good that I would do, I do not, and the evil that I would not, that I do."

Heart, will, and desire are essentially one. The Argument from Desire is the Argument from the Heart. Even in the heart whose "fundamental option," as Rahner puts it, is to run from God, to reject God, there is still, until death, a spark of the fire of desire for God, thus hope for repentance, for turning. It is to such an unbeliever that Pascal addresses *his* argument from desire, the famous "Wager."

The Wager presupposes the same heart-desire for happiness that Lewis's argument presupposes, but moves in a different direction: the practical calculation of winning or losing God rather than the theoretical insight that there must be a God. It is as if Lewis played with the blue chips of the truth sought by metaphysical argument while Pascal played with the red chips of the passion to possess God, to attain happiness. Lewis tries to prove that God exists; Pascal, skeptical of all argument for God's existence, does instead what Scripture does: inveigles us to make a leap of faith, a wager. "It is a remarkable fact," Pascal writes, "that no canonical writer ever tries to prove the existence of God. Rather, they all strive to make us believe in Him." The Wager appeals to our desire for God, our love of God, though on a very low and selfish level. Lewis begins with the implicit desire for God, the desire to leap into his arms, and concludes that therefore God must exist. Pascal begins with "You can't be certain God exists, but you can't be certain He doesn't, either" and concludes that we should leap into his arms.

The Wager works like Martin Buber's story about an atheist who came to a rabbi demanding that the rabbi prove to him God's existence or else he would never believe. When the rabbi refused, the atheist rose to leave, angrily. The rabbi's parting words were: "But can you be *sure* God does not exist?" Forty years later, that atheist told that story, and added that he was still an atheist, but that the rabbi's words continue to haunt him every day. If that man is honest and continues to seek and to let himself be haunted, he will one day leap and find.

Augustine uses a little thought-experiment to the same effect in his sermon "On the Pure Love of God." He says: imagine God appeared to you and said he would make a deal with you, that he would give you everything you wished, everything your heart desired, except one. You could have anything you imagine, nothing would be impossible for you, and nothing would be sinful or forbidden. But, God concluded, "you shall never see My face." Why, Augustine asks, did a terrible chill creep over your heart at those last words unless there is in your heart the love of God, the desire for God? In fact, if you wouldn't accept that deal, you really love God above all things, for look what you just did: you gave up the whole world, and more, for God.

Augustine's experiment can help you prove to yourself that the minor premise of Lewis's argument is true, that the strange desire exists, and that it is a desire for nothing less than God. Once again, the heart has led the head. Love has instructed understanding. The fear of the Lord has proved to be the beginning of wisdom.

IV

Finally, I want to defend the argument against five objections that have been made or could be made against it.

First, one may simply deny the minor premise, saying, "I simply do not observe any such desire for God, or Heaven, or infinite joy, or some mysterious x which is more than any earthly happiness." This denial can take two forms. First, one may say, "I am not perfectly content now, but I can imagine myself to be perfectly content if only I had a million dollars, a Lear jet, an immortality pill, and a new mistress every week." The reply to this, of course, is: "Try it. You won't like it." Billions of people have performed trillions of "if only" experiments with life, and they all had the same result: failure. The "if only" faith is the most foolish faith in the world, the stupidest wager in the world, for it has never paid off. It is like the game of predicting the end of the world: every batter who has ever approached that plate has struck out. There is very little reason to hope that the present ones will not do the same.

A second form of the denial of the minor premise is not "I would be perfectly content if only . . ." but "I am perfectly content now." This, I suggest, verges on culpable dishonesty, the sin against the Holy Spirit, and requires something more like exorcism than refutation. This is Merseuit in Camus's *The Stranger*. This is subhuman, this is vegetation, this is pop psychology. Even the hedonist utilitarian John Stuart Mill, one of the shallowest minds in the history of human thought, said that "It is better to be Socrates dissatisfied than a pig satisfied."

A second objection concerns the major premise. How can anyone know the truth that every natural desire has a real object without first knowing that this natural desire too has a real object? John Beversluis offers this objection in his book *C. S. Lewis and the Search for Rational Religion*, one of those rare books that is even worse than its title. Beversluis seems to believe that every single argument Lewis ever concocted is not only fallacious but downright foolish. In other words, we have in Lewis something like a negative Pope speaking *ex cathedra*: always infallibly wrong rather than infallibly right. Beversluis formulates his objection to this particular argument as follows:

> How could Lewis have known that every natural desire has a real object *before* knowing that Joy [*Sehnsucht*] has one? I can legitimately claim that every student in the class has failed the test *only* if I *first* know that *each* of them has individually failed it. The same is true of natural desires.

This argument is very foolish and very easy to refute. It amounts to saying that only through sense experience and induction is any knowledge possible, that there is only *a posteriori* knowledge, no *a priori* knowledge. This is Positivism, or at least Empiricism. The classical Empiricists and Positivists objected to all deductive reasoning as fake, as never really proving what the reasoning appeared to prove and claimed to prove, because there is no way, they contended, to know the truth of the major premise, the general principle, except by enumerative induction, i.e., by first knowing every example of it, including the conclusion. Thus knowledge really always works, according to them, in the opposite order from the way a syllogism claims to work: never from the universal to the particular but always only from the particular to the universal.

But surely this is simply not so. We can and do come to a knowledge of universals through abstraction, not only by induction. We know that all men must be mortal, or capable of speech, or laughter, or prayer, not in the same way that we know that all men have non-green skin, by mere sense observation, but by understanding something of human nature, which we

98

meet in, and abstract from, the individuals we experience. The objector denies the fourth quarter of Plato's Divided Line, Wisdom or Reason as distinct from reasoning, hypothetical deduction, "if . . . then" calculation, inference. He denies what Plato called *epistémé* as distinct from *dianoia*, or, what the medieval scholastics called *intellectus* as distinct from *ratio*. Descartes did this at the beginning of the *Discourse on Method* to ensure agreement among all men, for all have the same "reason" or "good sense" in the sense of logic — there is, e.g., no Protestant or Catholic logic, no French or English logic. But there *are* differences in reason in the sense of wisdom. All men are *not* equal here, and Descartes simply denies or ignores this.

The issue between ancients like Plato, Aristotle, Aquinas, and Lewis, and moderns like Descartes, Hume, the Logical Positivists, and Beversluis can be put this way: is there a third way of knowing in addition to sense perception and logical calculation? Is there a third kind of meaningful proposition in addition to empirically verifiable propositions and logical tautologies, Hume's "matters of fact," and "relations of ideas," Kant's "synthetic *a posteriori* judgments" and "analytic *a priori* judgments"? Are synthetic *a priori* judgments of objective truths possible?

The answer, surely, is: of course they are! In empirical propositions the predicate is accidental to the subject. In tautologies, the predicate is essential to the subject. But in metaphysical propositions, in synthetic *a priori* propositions, in propositions which express acts of understanding, the predicate is a *property* of the subject in Aristotle's technical sense: not the explicitly defined essence of the subject, as in "all effects need causes" or "red things are red," nor accidental to the subject, as in "some effects are red," but, as in "all men are mortal," understood as contained in and "flowing from" the essence of the subject, formally caused by the essence of the subject. (Formal causality is the one of Aristotle's four causes which drops out of the sight of the Empiricist.) *Because* man is a rational animal, he must be mortal (caused by his animality), loquacious (caused by his rationality), humorous (caused by the combination), and prayerful (caused by his rationality's awareness of God).

Thus the proposition "every natural, innate desire has a real object" is understood to be true because we understand what a natural desire is and what nature is. Nature is meaningful, teleological, full of design and purpose. It is ecological, arranging a fit between organism and environment, between desire and satisfaction, between appetite and food. "Nature makes nothing in vain."

All reasoning begins with some understanding of this type, some seeing. Seeing is not just sensory, but also intellectual. Some people just don't see things as well as others. All important disagreements in the history of philosophy come from this fact. That's why they are practically irresolvable, and why the history of philosophy does not lead to eventual general worldwide agreement as the history of science does.

A third objection against Lewis's Argument from Desire, also from Beversluis, is that its major premise, like all metaphysical propositions, confuses grammar with reality and reads grammar into reality. This is a typical Logical Positivist objection. "Lewis was correct, of course, in claiming that every desire is a desire *for* something. But from this purely conceptual observation nothing follows about what really exists. All desires must have *grammatical* objects, but they need not have *real* ones. People desire all sorts of imaginary things."

This is simply a misunderstanding, and quite inexcusable. Lewis's argument does not begin with a purely grammatical observation but with a metaphysical observation: that real desires really do have real objects. But he does not say that *all* desires do, only that all natural, innate, instinctive desires do. Desires for imaginary things, like Oz, are not innate. Desire for God is.

A fourth argument is that the major premise that an innate hunger proves a real food is simply untrue. Beversluis says, "the phenomenon of hunger simply does not prove that man inhabits a world in which food exists. . . . What proves that we inhabit a world in which food exists is the discovery that certain things are in fact eatable."

This is simply Empiricism blinding itself to the signature, the significance, of desire, as Empiricists tend to do to everything. Thus Beversluis says, "The Desire in and of itself proves nothing, points to nothing." But surely it does! My finger points to my dog's food. My dog, a true Empiricist, comes and sniffs my finger. Dr. Beversluis is doggedly Empiricistic. To this mentality nothing has a built-in, real, metaphysical significance. Only words are signs, things are not, to the Empiricist. In other words, the world is not full of the grandeur of God, and Paul must have been philosophically wrong (perhaps *mythically* right?) in saying, in effect, that the world is a sign and that we should be able to read it, that "the invisible things of God are known *through* the things that are made."

A fifth objection from Beversluis: "If Joy's object really is God, and if all desire is really desire for him, why when he was brought face to face with him did Lewis *cease* to desire him and search for a way of escape?" Lewis himself admits he did this. He was brought in "kicking and struggling, the most reluctant convert in all England." For God was "a transcendental Interferer," and "no word was more distasteful to me than the word *Interference*." Beversluis says, "either God is the ultimate object of desire or he is not. If he is, then it makes no sense to talk about shrinking from him the moment he is found."

I think this is just about the silliest and shallowest objection I have ever read. It shows an outstandingly immature understanding of human nature, fit perhaps for a merely logical mind but not for a human mind that exercises even a little of that non-empirical and nontautological kind of knowing called understanding or insight or wisdom or mental seeing. By this way of knowing, everyone knows that we often love and hate, desire and fear, the same object at different times or even at the same time, especially if that object is a person. How did a virgin feel about her wedding night in the days before the sexual revolution? Was there not often a fear of the great, the mysterious, the unknown, the "bigger than both of us," as well as a deep desire for it? Did Beversluis never have a hero, even a sports hero, when he was a child, whom he both desired and feared to approach? Did he never have a *parent*? Has he never met God in prayer?

Lewis has. The deep self-knowledge that lies behind his argument from desire comes from that experience, an experience no mere Positivist or Empiricist can understand. The argument from desire cuts to our heart. Its critics try to head Lewis off at the pass between the empirical and the logical walls of the canyon. But not only do they fail to head him off, they head themselves off, for their positivistic assumption is self-contradictory, being itself neither empirical nor tautological. Lewis's head feeds off his heart. Therefore his thought pulsates with real blood. Their bloodless formal critiques proceed from the ghostlike head already cut off from the heart. But any organ cut off from the heart atrophies and dies. Thus the critiques perish, but the argument from desire goes on beating, like Augustine's restless heart, until it rests in God.

Postscript

I began by referring to Anselm's "ontological argument." Let me end there too by asking whether the Argument from Desire is similar to Anselm's argument as its objectors usually maintain.

It seems so, for (1) *Sehnsucht* is a privileged, unusual desire, as the idea of God is a privileged idea; (2) it is the most moving desire, as the idea of God is the most moving idea; (3) and it seems that the very fact of the psychological occurrence of this desire in consciousness is claimed to prove the real, objective existence of its object, just as the idea of God is claimed to prove the real God.

But there are significant differences, so that objections to Anselm's argument are not valid against those of Lewis. For one thing, unlike the ontological argument, the Argument from Desire begins with data, facts, rather than simply the meaning of a word or concept. For another thing, Lewis does not *begin* with God, or a definition of God, as Anselm does, but *ends* with God, as Aquinas does ("and this [this thing we have proved] is what people call 'God'"). For a third thing, there is a major premise in the argument from desire, a general principle about all natural desires. Thus desires follow a general rule. But the idea of God in the ontological argument is the exception to the rule, the rule that no idea includes or proves existence.

Most importantly, the argument does not derive existence from the desire alone as the ontological argument derives existence from the idea alone. Rather, the Argument from Desire first derives a major premise from the world (that nature makes no desire in vain) and then applies that principle about the nature of the world to this desire. Thus the argument is based on observed facts, both outer (about the world) and inner (about desires).

Gabriel Marcel's Argument for Immortality from Death as the "Test of Presence"

A. The Question

One of the newest and most interesting of all arguments for immortality, or life after death, is that of the French Catholic personalist philosopher (often mislabeled an "Existentialist") Gabriel Marcel. Yet it is doubtful whether Marcel regarded it as a valid argument, or even an argument at all. It is the argument from death as "the test of presence." My aim here is to explain this notion of death as "the test of presence" and investigate the question whether or not it affords a basis for a valid argument for immortality.

B. Definitions

Obviously, we must first understand Marcel's notion of "presence." But this in turn can be done only in the context of Marcel's philosophy as a whole. For that philosophy is not composed of semi-independent parts, like Aristotle's, for instance, but is rather (to use Marcel's own description) like music. A theme can be isolated from the whole only by a kind of mental violence, and the result would be rather like an eye cut out of a living body and put on a platter. Apart from its organic whole, the organic part loses its life and its identity. So we must begin with a brief "back to basics" introduction to Marcel's main themes. Specifically, we must define eight terms: (1) being, (2) mystery, (3) problem, (4) participation, (5) presence,

103

(6) fidelity, (7) hope, and (8) charity as these themes interplay in Marcel's mental music.

(1) *Being.* Marcel is a metaphysician above all, for his basic theme, as indicated by the title of his *magnum opus,* is *The Mystery of Being.* Like Aristotle, like Aquinas, like Heidegger, Marcel centers on "the ancient and everlasting question: What is being?"

Briefly, *being* for Marcel is not mere *fact* but *value.* As for Plato, for Marcel *being* and *the good* are one. Marcel's formulation is this: "being is what withstands, or what would withstand, an exhaustive analysis bearing on the data of experience and aiming to reduce them increasingly to elements devoid of significant or intrinsic value." (He then illustrates by contrast: "An analysis of this type is attempted in the theoretical works of Freud.") Being, then, is not just "whatever is real" but "what is *really* real," i.e., what not only *appears* but *remains,* what resists all debunking, what withstands reductionistic analysis.

(2,3) *Mystery* and *Problem.* Being is a "mystery" rather than a "problem" for Marcel because I am inextricably *involved* in it, not detached from it as an observing subject from an observed object. He defines a "mystery" as "a problem which encroaches upon its own data, which invades them, as it were." In a mere problem, I *consider* the problem; in a mystery, I *am* the "problem." Examples include the union of soul and body, love, death, and evil. The reason none of these "problems" has ever been or ever will be adequately "solved" is that they are not problems to be solved by thought but mysteries to be lived through. Marcel shows himself here to be as practical (or "existential," if you wish) a mind as Jesus, who when his disciples asked him "Are many saved?" replied "Strive to enter in." Salvation is a perfect example of a mystery rather than a problem.

The popular meaning of "mystery," something not wholly clear, is based on a second meaning, which is the reason for the first: personal involvement. Because being is a mystery rather than a problem, I can therefore know being and know myself only in function of each other. "I" and "being," "I" and "am," are inseparable for me. This is because I am in the image of God, for whom they are inseparable because God's own self-proclaimed name and true nature is "I AM." There is a transcendental, ontological unity between I-ness. If we knew the one, we would know the other. Like Augustine, Marcel ultimately seeks to know "only two things [as Augustine puts it]: God and the self. Nothing more? Nothing more."

(4) *Participation.* We have "access" to being not merely by knowing it

as the object of mental activity, but by actually "participating" in being. This is a more primordial and more intimate relationship than knowing or desiring. Before we know being, we must already participate in being — not just in the sense that we exist, as a rock exists, but in the specifically human sense that being is *present* to us, and through the presence of being we are present to each other. The "participation" Marcel speaks of is neither subjective nor objective; neither psychological consciousness nor brute ontic fact. Rather, it is intersubjective, communal, I-Thou relational. The I-Thou relation (to use Buberian terms) is not something added to being, but is the primary and primordial way in which being is made present. "I" (personal presence) and "am" (being) are inseparable. The key to Marcel's ontology is really a *midrash* on Exodus 3:14!

The three most important forms of "participation" are "faith" (or "creative fidelity"), "hope," and "charity" (or *"disponibilité,"* "availability"). That is the link that explains Marcel's startling claim that the key to a true ontology is . . . sanctity!

(5) *Presence.* All three of these essential human modes of participation in being affirm presence. It is remarkable that the same word, "present," means (a) being-here, not absent; (b) being-now, not past or future; and (c) a gift being given, not withheld. In our language itself is inscribed the profound suggestion that our very here-and-now-being is a gift.

(6) *Fidelity* is "creative" because it is "the *active* perpetuation of presence" — the presence of the human other and (at least implicitly, in and through the human other) the divine Other. It is what Buber calls the fundamental relationship of an I to a Thou. It is fragile and perilous, and always debaseable into the I-it relationship, which is infidelity to the Thouness of the Thou, the presence of the person.

(7) *Hope* refers more explicitly to transcendence. It is not a wish, from either the mind or the desires, but it is a prophetic *assertion* from the heart, or the will — the assertion of the presence of the human other even in the face of death. Death is "the test of presence." Hope is "the assertion that there is at the heart of being, beyond all data, beyond all inventories and all calculations, a mysterious principle [*principium,* a real source, not a verbal statement] which is in connivance with me, which cannot but will that which I will if (a) what I will deserves to be willed and (b) is in fact willed by the whole of my being."

Hope is the alternative to Ecclesiastes' "vanity of vanities," the alternative to a universe which is fundamentally alien or indifferent to the human heart and its deepest and most ineradicable hopes, dreams, needs, longings, and values. The face of the universe seems impersonal and blank, indifferent. Hope asserts that behind the face is a heart. Hope cries an uncompromising "No!" to Stephen Crane's atheistic vision,

> A man said to the universe,
> "Sir, I exist!"
> "Nevertheless," replied the universe,
> "That fact has not created in me
> The slightest feeling of obligation."

(8) Finally, *charity* is "availability," *"disponibilité,"* openness to the other's presence and otherness and Thou-ness, yea-saying to the other. Prior to choosing, liking, desiring, or committing, charity is primordial love.

There are alternatives to each of these three "theological virtues" in Marcel. The alternatives to "creative fidelity" are (1) "sclerosis" and (2) "betrayal." Sclerosis is a hardening of the spiritual arteries, an uncreative pseudo-fidelity. It is pseudo-fidelity because it lacks presence: it is not fidelity to persons but to principles, as if I should answer my wife's question, "Why have you been faithful to me all these years?" by saying that I wanted to obey the seventh commandment. Betrayal is pseudo-creative infidelity. It is only pseudo-creative because it refuses the source of personal creativity, presence.

The alternative to hope is despair; but both hope and despair refer not to partial objects but are universal — as if I were to despair not of a student's passing a particular difficult test but of his very self: "you should never have been born. You are a living mistake."

The alternative to charity is not just hate, or even indifference, but their primordial foundation, egocentrism, the point of view from which I am the main character of the play and others are walk-ons.

Each of these three virtues conquers a deadly enemy. Fidelity conquers time (as Kierkegaard showed so memorably in Judge William's "knight of faith" in *Either-Or*). Hope conquers death (as we shall see). Charity conquers self and sin ("love covers a multitude of sins").

C. Focus on the Key Term 'Hope'

To evaluate Marcel's argument for immortality, or any argument, we must proceed in three stages. First, we must understand the *terms* and make sure they are not used ambiguously. Second, we must know the *premises* and be sure they contain no false assumptions. Third, we must examine the *logic* of the argument and be sure it contains no fallacy. We begin by focusing on the key term 'hope.' All three virtues really are related to immortality, but hope most explicitly.

The simplest illustration of hope is the best one, says Marcel, and he gives the example of hoping that someone I love will recover from a disease that all the experts assure me is incurable. This hope is not located in the emotions; it is not a wish or desire. Rather, it is a prophetic announcement, an insight into truth. It *sees* something, though "through a glass, darkly."

It does not calculate or prove. Hope is not a guessing game to try to outpredict the doomsday doctors. The doctors tell me the statistics: ten thousand out of ten thousand have died of this disease. But hope neither accepts nor rejects statistics; it ignores them. It does not count cases because what is seen is in the qualitative order, not the quantitative.

Hope is neither the passive acceptance of the statistics and the doctors' prediction, nor is it my mere desire or wish or even demand that the beloved recover. The former is not free and the latter is blind. But hope is free (thus not passive) and not blind (thus not merely active, but an insight into and a conformity with something that is real). It is the free option to assert that "it is impossible that I should be alone in willing this cure; it is impossible that reality in its inward depth should be hostile or so much as indifferent to what I assert is in itself a good."

A simple and perfect example of what Marcel means by hope occurs in Ingmar Bergman's cinematic masterpiece *The Seventh Seal* when Antonius Block, the agnostic, questing knight replies to his cynical squire's philosophy that after death there is simply emptiness. He says simply, "This cannot be." Later, Death himself, disguised as a priest, hears Block's confession. Block asks why, when he reaches out to seek God, there seems to be no one there? Death now tempts him to accept the appearance of emptiness as the final reality by saying, "Perhaps there *is* no one there." And Block replies, "Then life is an outrageous horror. No one can live in the face of death knowing that all is utter emptiness." That is the triumphant note of hope. It does not merely insist; it sees. It sees that "this *cannot* be."

I have been in just the situation that Marcel chooses to illustrate hope, when, ten years ago, the doctors gave my daughter 6-12 months to live after diagnosing a fatal brain tumor, and I can verify the amazing accuracy of Marcel's phenomenology. What I found arising in me when I first heard those fatal words was a kind of "denial of death" that was totally different from the first of the five stages made famous by Dr. Elizabeth Kübler-Ross. It was not a protective withdrawal from the truth, but an insight into the truth. I heard and believed the word of death, the diagnosis, but I also saw that this word *could* not be the last word. Somehow, somewhere, somewhen, in the end, in the last analysis, at the core of reality, death *cannot* be stronger than life, though it surely was stronger at the surface. This insight welled up in me totally independent from my religious faith in life after death. It is equally available to unbelievers and agnostics. What Marcel means by hope is not based on religious faith, though it confirms it. It is not based on anything. It is a primordial insight. Like love, it does not give reasons, for reasons are given from above downward, from the more basic to the less basic. In the terms of the currently fashionable philosophy, hope is "properly basic."

D. The Key Proposition: Death Is the Test of Presence

"Death is the test of presence" because if death succeeds in removing presence, as it seems to, then presence fails, and death wins. But if death fails to remove presence, then presence passes the test, is stronger than death, is not dissolved even by the universal solvent of death.

But what does it mean for presence to pass the test of death? Does it mean that the dead can still be present to the living?

Indeed it does, and not just in memory but in reality, according to Marcel. A memory image is only a dead effigy, like a photograph, not a living presence. Real presence does not depend on me, as memory does, to call it forth. Presence is not subjective.

But it is not objective either. Objects are not *present*. They are not *here*, they are only *there*. Stones, furniture, or corpses cannot be *present* to each other. If I accidentally bump into you in a crowd, that physical contact does not make us present to each other.

How can presence be neither subjective nor objective? The answer is commonsensical and well-known with regard to the living. Let us look at that before trying to apply it to the dead. In a word, the answer is intersubjectivity. Other minds are present to us, not as objects but as other subjects. Intersubjectivity transcends the Cartesian dualistic categories of subjective mind and objective matter, the thinking self and its objects.

Once the Cartesian gap opens up, four unacceptable philosophies appear as the apparently only options: (1) the unbridgeable Cartesian dualism itself, (2) an idealistic monism in which the object is reduced to and lost in the subject, (3) a materialistic monism in which the subject is reduced to and lost in the object, and (4) a pantheistic monism in which both are lost.

How can subject and object, like husband and wife, become one yet remain two? Is a happy marriage possible between these two fundamentally different and irreducible modes of being? Marcel answers: yes, through presence. Being manifests itself in the form of presence. Presence is neither I-I subjectivity nor I-it objectivity but I-Thou intersubjectivity.

We are now in a position to move from the less explicit proposition, "Death is the test of presence" to the more explicit proposition, "Presence reveals immortality."

If presence were merely the presence of an object, then death would remove presence, for death removes all objects. Only if we are "here" as subject can we remain "here" as subject after death removes our objective being-*there*.

Perhaps a clearer way to put this is as follows: if there is no presence after death, then there was no presence before death either. And since there is presence before death, therefore there is presence after death.

The question concerns whether there exists a subject irreducible to an object or not. C. S. Lewis saw precisely the same thing Marcel saw when he was grieving over his dead wife. He wrote, in *A Grief Observed,*

> If she is not now, then she never was. I mistook a cloud of atoms for a person. There aren't and never were any people. Death only reveals the vacuity that was always there. What we call the living are simply those who have not yet been unmasked. All equally bankrupt, but some not yet declared.

Lewis, like Marcel, like Ingmar Bergman's questing knight, like myself, sees simply that "this cannot be." The argument is thus a *reductio ad absurdum.* It shows the consequences of denial of immortality as denial of presence even before death.

E. The Two Key Arguments

I think this argument works in two different ways. Both ways are *reductio ad absurdum* arguments, both demonstrate immortality from presence and the refusal of vacuity, but one takes the path of the head and the other the heart; one explores consciousness, the other explores love.

E, 1. The Argument from Consciousness

The argument from consciousness in a nutshell is that the "intentionality" of consciousness manifests its transcendence of objecthood and thus its imperviousness to death's power over objects. If consciousness exists at all, it is not a *thing* but a *sign* of things; it is not a thing but "of" things. It is thus a different *kind* of "thing" from things like bodies.

Thus the argument is akin to the traditional Platonic and Scholastic argument that the soul is not killed by the things that kill the body because it is not the kind of thing the body is. However, Marcel does not use this language. He is dissatisfied with the traditional notions of both body and soul, and would disagree with the implied assumption that the body is an object. He says that I do not *have* a body; rather, I *am* my body. I can't take my body off, as I can my clothes! And as for the soul, Marcel does not like the Platonic notion of the soul as a Form or the Scholastic notion of the soul as a spiritual *substance,* a "suppositum," "a substance of a rational nature," like other substances in being a substance or thing or noun but with special powers, notably reason. Instead, Marcel sees the self as a different kind of being. Though he says he is not an existentialist but a 'Socratic,' he shares with the existentialists the insight into the unique *kind* of being the *I* has.

The argument from consciousness is put simply by C. S. Lewis when he continues the passage quoted above from *A Grief Observed* as follows. He has just seen that if his dead wife is not now, then death only reveals the vacuity that was always there, that is the ultimate truth. Like Antonius Block, he says, in effect, that this cannot be, but he gives a reason for it, and the reason is essentially the intentionality of consciousness:

> But surely this [vacuity] is nonsense. Vacuity declared to whom? I won't believe — strictly, I can't believe, that one set of atoms can be, or make, a mistake about another set.

110

E, 2. The Argument from the Heart

A second argument for immortality is from the heart, or deep self. ('Heart' does not mean 'feelings,' of course, but the center of the self, as the heart is the center of the circulatory system.) The heart has eyes, in fact three eyes: faith, hope, and love. The heart's word "this cannot be" at the outrage of death is an insight, not just a feeling or a desire. That death should triumph ultimately is not just tragic but impossible. The word "impossible," in the mouth of one like Antonius Block, sounds like a great castle, heavy with stubborn grandeur.

J. Paterson Smyth wrote of the same impossibility, the same outrage, that death should defeat presence:

> I was a little child when the news came of my father's death, far away. That night, as usual, I prayed for him. But my aunt stopped me. 'Darling,' she said, 'you must not pray for Father now. It is wrong.' And I can remember still how I shrank back, feeling as if someone had slammed a door and shut Father outside.

The aunt was more threatening than death itself, for death robbed only flesh, but she robbed presence. Death is tolerable, absence is not.

F. The Experiential Precondition for the Argument from the Heart

The argument cannot be fairly evaluated until it is understood, and the condition for understanding it is sharing its data in experience. That experience is essentially hope's assertion of presence, fidelity's perpetuation of presence, and love's welcoming of presence. These three antennae of presence are organically one, like the root, stem, and fruit of a plant. Fidelity is the "stick-in-the-mud" root, hope is the idealistically rising, growing stem, and love is the fruit, the flower, the plant's gift of itself to the world.

It is especially love that perceives a presence stronger than death. Marcel says, "Love only addresses itself to the eternal." That does not mean that only God can be loved, but that the human person, in being loved for his or her own sake, is implicitly perceived as being eternal. Marcel would quite agree with Pascal's famous saying, "The heart has its reasons which the reason does not know." The heart sees, not just feels. Love has eyes. Love is *not* blind. How could love be blind? God is love. Is God blind?

We need to go deeper into three aspects of the argument from love: first, the conclusion, the proposition: *what* does love see? Second, the argument as such. Third, the definition of its key term.

First, what does love see? Love sees the *being* of the beloved. Being for Marcel means intrinsic value. Love perceives the intrinsic value, the indispensability, of the beloved. If I do *not* love you, I see you as object, as an ingredient in the world, or in my world; and any object is replaceable and thus dispensable. But if I love you, I see you not as object but as co-subject, as sharing "co-esse" with me, as a co-center of my world. Marcel invents a new term here, one that we see as quite necessary once we understand his meaning; "co-esse" means not just "being with" another, but "with-being" as a mode of being. As Buber puts it, the I and the Thou are relative to each other and to the I-Thou relation. The relation is not an external relation, which arises after the I and Thou are already constituted as I and as Thou, but it is the I-Thou relation that makes the I and the Thou the I and the Thou. "In the beginning was relationship," writes Buber, thereby affirming, more profoundly than he realized, the absolute primordiality of the Trinity.

Once I see you as co-esse, as subject, in that very insight I also see you as unique, just as unique as myself (for every "I" is unique), thus irreplaceable and indispensable. Then and only then can I proceed to argue.

The argument proceeds as follows: how can the irreplaceable be replaceable? That is a contradiction, though not a merely formal, logical contradiction. The argument is a *moral "reductio ad absurdum"* rather than a logical one. Its point is that if there is no immortality, and the indispensable is thus dispensed with, like diapers, then reality does to persons what we must not do to persons. In that case, we are better than reality, reality is amoral, and our values cannot be grounded in reality, or even square with reality. In that case, *being* and *goodness* are fundamentally alienated. If you can accept *that* consequence, all meaning vanishes from our choices, our freedom, our personal communion, and our lives.

The form in which I have stated the argument is misleading in that our actual discovery of the beloved's immortality does not follow this long and torturous path, for that discovery is not an *inference* but an *insight;* not *ratio* but *intellectus. In* the act of loving, the eye of love perceives immediately the necessity of immortality. It is love, not reasoning, that says, "Thou, at least, *shalt* not die." (This is how Marcel formulates love's perception.) Love is the magic spell that calls forth the spirit of the dead. This does not mean anything occult or even mystical, but simply the affirmation of what is there, or rather of what is *here,* namely, presence.

The key to the argument is to understand the key term, "love." The insight does not emerge from just any kind of love. Puppy love, merely erotic love, vague philanthropy, and mere instinctive affection or liking all lack the power to generate this insight. Only charity, only *agape,* has it. Only the love that gives a blank check, the love that "bears all things, believes all things, hopes all things, endures all things" — only this love "never fails." This is the love which Kierkegaard calls "the works of love" (in his book by that title), and calls the only truly Christian love. It is the love Dostoyevski calls "love in action" when he says "Love in action is a harsh and dreadful thing compared with love in dreams." "Love in action" is *"disponible,"* as Marcel says: it is available to be used without limit, it is ready to work and suffer and sacrifice and die, if need be, for the beloved. Only the love that is willing to die, only the love that laughs at death, is stronger than death, and only this love calls forth the presence of the beloved from the shadow of death.

G. Love and Death

The argument is a dramatic one. In it, love and death fight it out for the heavyweight championship of life. Death seems to knock out love, but love knocks out death. The eye of death seems to see the eclipse of love, but the eye of love sees the eclipse of death. C. S. Lewis's epitaph for his beloved friend Charles Williams summarizes Marcel's point in a single sentence: "No event has so corroborated my belief in the next life as much as Charles Williams did simply by dying; for when the idea of death and the idea of Williams thus met in my mind, it was the idea of death that was changed." Substitute "presence" for "idea" and you have Marcel's point exactly.

The same epitaph, essentially, was given to Socrates by Plato in what is probably the most moving and memorable passage in all of philosophy: the death of Socrates, at the end of the *Phaedo.* Socrates' abstract arguments for immortality are not wholly convincing to most readers, but his personal example is irresistible. "What you are speaks so loud I can hardly hear what you say." The real evidence for immortality is not so much what

Socrates says as what he does, how he dies; for this manifests what he *is*, manifests his being, his essence, that is stronger than death. Death does not change the essence and meaning of Socrates; Socrates changes the meaning of death.

The supreme example of this same reversal is, of course, Jesus. In this case, the changed *meaning* of death flows over, so to speak, into a changed body and appearance too through the physical resurrection. What appears to the eye of the heart in any death, appears here also to the eye of the flesh, for this is the Word made flesh, the Truth become fact, the Meaning become visible. But it is the same Word, the same Truth, the same Meaning.

Love changes death as a flood changes a dam that fails to block it: the dam is swept along by the flood and transformed into a part of the flood. Love so conquers death that death becomes a part of love, a rendezvous of lovers.

H. Objections

This all sounds very nice and idealistic and poetic, of course, but we are asking whether it is an *argument*. How can this truth be *verified*?

Not by comparing concepts, but only by performing the relevant experiment. If you dare to look through Galileo's telescope, you will see the heavens move. If you dare to look through the eye of love, you will see the beloved's immortality.

But how do I know I am not deceived? How can love "believe all things" and yet not be deceived (as Kierkegaard asks)? If there is no external justification for this vision; if love, presence, and immortality are all "mysteries" rather than "problems," then how can we prove our vision is true? We are prejudiced; we are involved, not detached.

The weakness of the argument from love is the weakness of love itself. Love does not and cannot prove itself, nor can anything else prove it, validate it, justify it. Love is utterly helpless; it cannot be helped by being validated by anything prior to itself because there *is* nothing prior to itself. Like the sun, love casts light on the whole world, but nothing in the world can cast light on it. To try to validate or justify love is like trying to light up the sun with a flashlight. (Only essential love, or *agape*, is meant here, of course; reasons can and should be given for lesser, optional loves.)

There is, however, a way to win over the cynic: love him. *Give* him the very thing he denies. We are as free to create the datum of the argument (love) as he is to refuse it.

I. Is It a Proof or Not?

There is no way to *prove* immortality through love, but love offers a way to *know* it, in fact to know it with certainty. The way is one of involvement rather than detachment (as is appropriate to a "mystery"). It is the way Father Zossima offers to the "woman of little faith" in *The Brothers Karamazov* who comes to him asking how to regain her childlike faith, now shaken by scientific doubts: "What if when I come to die there are only the burdocks on my grave?" Zossima's answer:

> "There is no proving it. But you can be convinced of it."
> "How?"
> "By the experience of active love. Strive to love your neighbor actively and indefatigably. Insofar as you advance in love, you will grow surer of the reality of God and of the immortality of the soul. If you attain to perfect self-forgetfulness in the love of your neighbor, then you will believe without doubt and no doubt can possibly enter your soul. This has been tried. This is certain."

Notice the last two sentences: "This has been tried. This is certain." There is a road to certainty about immortality, and it has been traveled by many successfully. But the road is action, not thought. And that is Marcel's road. It is free, not compelling. If we choose to travel that road, if we actually create the datum of *agape* love for another, then and only then will the datum of immortality appear with certainty and undeniableness. If you love, you will see. If not, not.

Jesus used this epistemology of the heart, or will, when he solved the hermeneutical question (about which thousands of tons of theological ink have been spilled in the last few generations) in a single sentence. His interlocutors asked him how they could understand his teaching, how they were to interpret it, and how he came by it. His answer was startlingly, even offensively, simple: "If any man's will is to do his [God's] will, he shall know whether the teaching is from God." We do not understand nature by loving it, but we understand persons by loving them, in fact *only* by loving them. And God is a person. We know his teaching only by willing his will.

So Marcel's argument is *not* a proof, a logically compelling argument. Rather, it is something better, something stronger. It is a road, freely offered to any sincere seeker, with the promise that anyone who travels it will find not only truth but also certainty. And there is only one way to test that claim: to walk that road, to actually love.

By the way, my daughter did not die. The prayed-for miracle, or near-miracle, happened. The statistician's diagnosis was inadequate. So was his philosophy.

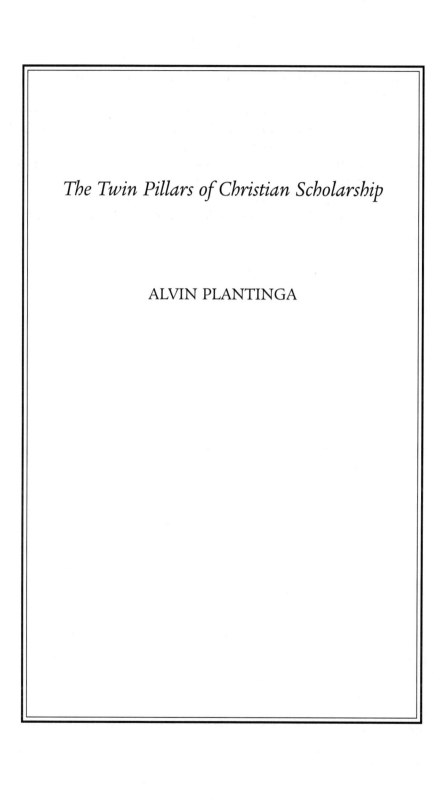

The Twin Pillars of Christian Scholarship

ALVIN PLANTINGA

Contents

Reformed Thinking: Christian Scholarship

I. The Question

When I was a student at Calvin, one of the important questions, perhaps the *main* question, was a question that has occupied Christians from the very beginning: the question of how Christianity and culture, taken broadly, should be related. Nearly all of the great thinkers of the Western world from the early days of Christianity to the 17th century devoted some of their best efforts to this question. The early Christians found themselves in a world with an ongoing culture, with art, literature, science, philosophy, history, business, the state, medicine, music, etc.; and the question was, how should the Christian approach these things? How does being a Christian make a difference to your taking part in culture or in some particular aspect of it? How does your being a Christian bear on your attitude towards it? Does it make a difference? *Should* it make a difference? That was the chief question of the early reflective Christians, including in particular the Church Fathers (Origen, for example, and Tertullian, Clement, Justin Martyr, and above all Augustine); it remains a fundamental question for us Christians today. It is of course by virtue of a quite specific view on this topic, a view held with deep resolve and commitment, that there is such a thing as Calvin College. We are here, tonight, only because those who went before us, our spiritual ancestors, took a particular view of this issue, and thought this view so important that they were prepared to expend an enormous amount of energy and resources in order to bring it into concrete expression.

So the most general question was: how shall we Christians think about, fit into, react to contemporary culture generally? But Henry Stob and the others also raised a more specific (though still very general) question: how shall we Christians fit into, think about, react to the world of contemporary scholarship? Still more specifically: what should we think about the theoretical disciplines, those disciplines that have to do with understanding ourselves and the world around us? In these two lectures I want to try to add just a bit to what I learned then on these topics; or perhaps I should say that what I want to do is repeat or report what I learned in my own way. Admittedly, this means that I may not have anything particularly original to say; but here (unlike in, say, French philosophy or liberal theology) we are less interested in novelty than in truth. So much of what I shall say I originally learned from Professors William Harry Jellema and Henry Stob and others many years ago here at Calvin College. I also recognize that here my reach vastly exceeds my grasp. To do this properly, one would need enormously more knowledge and insight than I can command; what is required is another Augustine, or perhaps another Abraham Kuyper. Still, it is of the first importance for us to think about these matters, and if we wait for another Augustine or Kuyper, we may be waiting for a long time. Accordingly, I want to say something about these topics, recognizing the risks and pitfalls. It's a nasty job, but someone has to do it. And given that the job *is* so risky, and requires so much knowledge and insight, it is obviously a good idea to try to find the right time to have your say — I mean the right time in your life. You should wait until you probably won't learn a whole lot more, but you must also make sure you say it before you are too far over the hill. Just before the onslaught of senility sounds about the right time. You'll have to judge whether I've made it in time.

Now what I learned, of course, is that we Reformed Christians do indeed think of the world of scholarship, the life of the intellect, as a place where Christianity makes a big difference. It is a basic Reformed tenet that all of life must be lived from the perspective of Christianity; in particular, then, our scholarly life must be so lived. A part of what distinguishes us from other Christian communities — from our more pietistic and fundamentalist brothers, for example — is our affirmation of all of life, and our determination to see all of it from the perspective of our faith. The genius of specifically Reformed Christianity is this effort to work out and embody our faith in our entire lives. We profess to try, and we do try, to live out our faith in our entire lives in their every aspect. Therefore we recognize this obligation in scholarship, and we often pay homage to it — particularly at the beginning of courses and on public and ceremonial occasions.

It isn't hard to see, however, that this homage is to some degree a matter of lip service with us. Or if that is too harsh a judgment, at the least it must be admitted that, when it comes to the level of detail and specificity, we often don't have much of an idea just how to do it; indeed we hardly know how to start. In a way, it is our *lack* of success here that is most striking. This whole matter of Christian scholarship is difficult, taxing, frustrating, baffling; it is easy (and tempting) to lose sight of it in the welter of everyday demands and concerns. And don't we sometimes suspect that our forefathers may have been wrong here? Is there really such a thing as Christian scholarship — or is there only scholarship *simpliciter*, which can be practiced by Christians and non-Christians, though perhaps practiced in a Christian and in a non-Christian way? Physics is physics; can we sensibly speak of Christian physics? What could that possibly be like? Where would it differ from just plain physics? History too is what it is; there isn't a Christian course of history and a non-Christian course of it: so what could specifically Christian history be? Will Christians and non-Christians differ, for example, as to whether there was such a thing as the Peloponnesian war, or as to when it occurred? Why do we need specifically Christian scholarship in areas other than theology? In what follows I want to go back to the beginning and ask what, from a Christian perspective, recommends the Reformed way of thinking about scholarship. Why do we need a place like Calvin College? Why should the Christian community concern itself with these matters? Why should it do so precisely as a *Christian community*?

There are, I think, two fundamental reasons. These reasons are at bottom both religious: but one is rooted in our nature and the other in our historical situation. Suppose we begin with the second; we'll think about the first tomorrow night.

II. The First Reason

So why do we need Christian scholarship? Here I can call on some of the great names in our tradition and wrap myself in their mantles like a politician in the flag. In particular I'd like to mention two great Reformed stalwarts here, Abraham Kuyper and St. Augustine. (Some of you might complain that St. Augustine is at best dubiously Reformed, since he displays insufficient acquaintance with the works of John Calvin. No doubt you are right; let's think of him as an early Calvinist by courtesy.) Augustine and

123

Kuyper both saw human life as involving a sort of struggle, a battle between two implacably opposed forces. Augustine spoke of the City of God and the Earthly City or City of the World: the *Civitas Dei* and the *Civitas Mundi*. The former is dedicated, in principle, to God and to his will and to his glory; but the latter is dedicated to something wholly different. Kuyper spoke of the antithesis between belief — Christian belief — and unbelief, an antithesis that is evident, in one way or another, in all the important areas of human life. Both emphasize a certain universality here: being a Christian, if done properly, involves the entire life of the *Civitas,* all the things a city or state or society does: not just private beliefs and private commitments acted on, perhaps, by way of going to church on Sunday. And of course both Augustine and Kuyper saw scholarship (taken broadly) as a central area in which the conflict in question is carried out.

I believe Kuyper and Augustine are dead right, and I want to begin by developing their insights in my own way. Indeed, we *must* do this in our own way and from our own historical perspective: the precise relationship between the City of God and the Earthly City constantly changes; the form the Earthly City itself takes constantly changes; an account of the fundamental loyalties and commitments of the Earthly City that was correct in Augustine's day, now some fifteen centuries ago, does not directly apply now. And even since the time of Kuyper (1837-1920), roughly a century ago, there has been substantial change and substantial clarification and differentiation; in some ways it is now considerably easier, I think, to see the essential contours of the modern ways of thinking that have emerged since the 17th and 18th centuries.

Augustine and Kuyper are right; and the contemporary Western intellectual world, like the worlds of their times, is a battleground or arena in which rages a battle for men's souls. This battle, I believe, is a three-way contest. There are three main contestants, in the contemporary Western intellectual world, and I want to try to characterize them. Of course an undertaking like this is at best fraught with peril (and at worst arrogantly presumptuous); the contemporary Western world is a vast and amorphous affair, including an enormous variety of people, in an enormous variety of places, with enormously different cultural backgrounds and traditions. We all know how hard it is to get a real sense of the intellectual climate of a *past* era — the Enlightenment, say, or 13th-century Europe, or 19th-century America. It is clearly much *more* difficult to come to a solid understanding of one's own time. For these general reasons, real trepidation is very much in order. There are also special less universally applicable reasons for trepidation: wouldn't it be the historians, not the philosophers, whose job it is to figure out intellectual trends, take the intellectual pulse of the time, ferret out underlying presuppositions of the whole contemporary era? So here I should defer to the historians at Calvin, who are my betters, if not my elders. I shall do my best, but I can't promise much.

As I see it, therefore, there are three main competitors vying for supremacy: three fundamental perspectives or ways of thinking about what the world is like, what we ourselves are like, what is most important about the world, what our place in it is, and what we must do to live the good life. The first of these perspectives is Christianity or Christian theism; since you all know a good bit about that, I shall say little about it. I do want to remind you, however, that despite recent successes in our part of the world, the Christian perspective has been very much on the defensive (at least in the West) ever since the Enlightenment.

In addition to the Christian perspective, then, there are, fundamentally, two others. Both of these pictures have been with us since the ancient world; but each has received much more powerful expression in modern times. According to the first perspective, there is no God, and we human beings are insignificant parts of a giant cosmic machine that proceeds in majestic indifference to us, our hopes and aspirations, our needs and desires, our sense of fairness or fittingness. This picture goes back to Epicurus, Democritus, and others in the ancient world and finds magnificent expression in Lucretius's poem, *De Rerum Natura:* call it 'Perennial Naturalism.' According to the second perspective, on the other hand, it is we ourselves — we human beings — who are responsible for the basic structure of the world. This notion goes back to Protagoras, in the ancient world, with his claim that man is the measure of all things, but finds enormously more powerful expression in Immanuel Kant's *Critique of Pure Reason:* call it 'Enlightenment Humanism,' or 'Enlightenment Subjectivism,' or maybe 'Creative Anti-Realism.' These two perspectives or pictures are very different indeed; I shall say a bit about each.

A. *Perennial Naturalism*

Perennial Naturalism ('Naturalism' for short), as I say, goes back to the ancient world; it is also to be found in the medieval world, among some of the

125

Averroists, for example. It was left to modernity, however, to display the most complete and thorough manifestations of this perspective. Hobbes, the Enlightenment Encyclopedists, and Baron D'Holbach are early modern exponents of this picture; among our contemporaries and near contemporaries there are John Dewey, Willard van Orman Quine, Wilfrid Sellars, Donald Davidson, an astounding number of liberal theologians, and a host of others in and out of academia. From this perspective, there is no God and human beings are properly seen as parts of nature. The way to understand what is most distinctive about us, our ability to love, to act, to think, to use language, our humor and playacting, our art, philosophy, literature, history, our morality, our religion, our tendency to enlist in sometimes unlikely causes and devote our lives to them — the fundamental way to understand all this is in terms of our community with (nonhuman) nature. We are best seen as parts of nature and are to be understood in terms of our place in the natural world.

A couple of examples here: first, a trivial one. Those who endorse this view often seem to think that the way to find out how we human beings should live is to see how the other animals manage things; this is the naturalistic equivalent of the biblical "Go to the ant, thou sluggard." I recently heard a TV talk show in which a scientist was belittling traditional sexual ethics and mores — "heterosexual pair bonding," he called it — on the grounds that only three percent of the other animals do things this way. He didn't say anything about plants, but no doubt even more interesting conclusions could be drawn there.

A second more serious example: a couple of years ago I heard a distinguished contemporary American philosopher reflecting on knowledge, belief, and the whole human cognitive enterprise. The way to understand this whole situation, he said — the way to see what is most basic and important about it — is not, of course, to see it as one of the manifestations of the image of God, a way in which we resemble the Lord, who is the prime knower, and who has created us in such a way as to be finite and limited mirrors of his infinite and unlimited perfection. This philosopher took quite a different line. Human beings, he said, hold beliefs; and these beliefs can cause them to act in certain ways. Put in more sophisticated if no more insightful terms, a person's beliefs can be part of a causal explanation of her actions. Now how can this be? How does it happen, how can it be that human beings are such that they can be caused to do certain things by what they believe? How does my believing there is a doughnut in the refrigerator cause

126

or partly cause this largish lumpy physical object which is my body to heave itself out of a comfortable armchair, move over to the refrigerator, and open its door? The answer: think of a thermostat: it too has beliefs — simple-minded beliefs, no doubt, but still beliefs. What it believes are such things as *it's too hot in here,* or *it's too cold in here,* or *it's just right in here;* and it is easy to see how its having those beliefs brings it about that the furnace or the air conditioning goes on. And now the basic idea: we should see human thinking as a rather more complicated case of what goes on in the thermostat. The thought was that if we think about how it goes with the thermostat, we will have the key to understanding how it goes with human beings. Of course this is just one example of a much broader project: the project of seeing *all* that is distinctive about us — literature, art, play, humor, music, morality, religion, those tendencies to enlist in improbable causes, even at serious costs to ourselves — the project is to explain *all* of these things in terms of our community with nonhuman nature.

The form this perspective takes in our own day is broadly evolutionary: we are to try to understand the above phenomena by way of their origin in genetic mutation and their perpetuation by natural selection. Consider sociobiological explanations of love, for example: love between men and women, between parents and children, love for one's friends, love of college, church, country — love in all its diverse manifestations and infinite variety. Love is a significant human phenomenon and a powerful force in our lives. On the sort of evolutionary account in question, love arose, ultimately and originally, by way of random genetic mutation; it persisted via natural selection because it has or had survival value. Male and female human beings, like male and female hippopotami, get together to have children (cubs? calves? colts? [etymologically hippopotami are river horses]) and stay together to raise them; this has survival value. Once we see that point, we understand that sort of love and see its basic significance; and the same goes for these other varieties and manifestations of love. And that, fundamentally, is what there is to say about love. From a theistic perspective, of course, this is hopelessly inadequate as an account of the significance and place of love in the world. The fact is love reflects the basic structure and nature of the universe; for God himself, the first being of the universe, is love, and we love because he has created us in his image. From the naturalistic perspective, furthermore, what goes for love goes for those other distinctively human phenomena: art, literature, music; play and humor; science, philosophy, and mathematics; our tendency to see the world

127

from a religious perspective, our inclinations towards morality, and so on. All these things are to be understood in terms of our community with non-human nature. All of these are to be seen as arising, finally, by way of the mechanisms driving evolution, and are to be understood in terms of their place in evolutionary history.

B. Enlightenment Humanism

I turn now to the other main competitor: Enlightenment Humanism, or Enlightenment Subjectivism, or Creative Anti-Realism. Here the funda-mental idea — in sharp contrast to Naturalism — is that we human beings, in some deep and important way, are ourselves responsible for the struc-ture and nature of the world; it is *we*, fundamentally, who are the architects of the universe. This view received magnificent if obscure expression in Kant's *Critique of Pure Reason*. Kant did not deny, or course, that there really are such things as mountains, horses, planets, and stars. Instead, his char-acteristic claim is that their existence and their fundamental structure have been conferred upon them by the conceptual activity of persons — not by the conceptual activity of a personal God, but by *our* conceptual activity, the conceptual activity of human beings. According to this view, the whole phenomenal world — the world of trees and planets and dinosaurs and stars — receives its basic structure from the constituting activity of mind. Such fundamental structures of the world as those of space and time, ob-ject and property, number, truth and falsehood, possibility and necessity — these are not to be found in the world as such, but are somehow consti-tuted by our own mental or conceptual activity. They are contributions from our side; they are not to be found in the things themselves. We im-pose them on the world; we do not discover them there. Were there no per-sons like ourselves engaging in noetic activities, there would be nothing in space and time, nothing displaying object-property structure, nothing that is true or false, possible or impossible, no kind of things coming in a cer-tain number — nothing like this at all.

We might think it impossible that the things we know — trees, moun-tains, plants, and animals — exist but fail to be in space-time and fail to dis-play object-property structure; indeed, we may think it impossible that there be a thing of *any* sort that doesn't have properties. If so, then Kant's view implies that there would be nothing at all if it weren't for the creative

128

structuring activity of persons like us. Of course I don't say Kant clearly *drew* this conclusion; indeed, he may have obscurely drawn the opposite conclusion: that is part of his charm. But the fundamental *thrust* of Kant's self-styled Copernican Revolution is that the things in the world owe their basic structure and perhaps their very existence to the noetic activity of our minds. Or perhaps I should say not minds but *mind;* for whether there is just one transcendental ego or several is, of course, a vexed question, as are most questions of Kantian exegesis. Indeed, this question is more than vexed; given Kant's view that quantity, number, is a human category imposed on the world, there is presumably no number *n*, finite or infinite, such that the answer to the question "how many of those transcendental egos are there?" is *n*.

Until you feel the grip of this sort of way of looking at things, it can seem a bit presumptuous, not to say preposterous. Did we structure or create the heavens and the earth? Some of us think there were animals — dinosaurs, let's say — roaming the earth before human beings had so much as put in an appearance; how could it be that those dinosaurs owed their structure to our noetic activity? What did we do to give *them* the structure they enjoyed? And what about all those stars and planets we have never so much as heard of: how have we managed to structure them? When did we do all this? Did we structure ourselves in this way too? And if the way things are is thus up to us and our structuring activity, why don't we improve things a bit?

Creative Anti-Realism can seem faintly or more than faintly ridiculous; nevertheless it is widely accepted and an extremely important force in the contemporary Western intellectual world. Vast stretches of contemporary Continental philosophy, for example, are anti-realist. There is Existentialism, according to which, at least in its Sartrian varieties, each of us structures or creates the world by way of our own decisions. There is also contemporary Heideggerian hermeneutical philosophy of various stripes; there is contemporary French philosophy, much of which beggars description, but insofar as anything at all is clear about it, is clearly anti-realist. In Anglo-American philosophy, there is the Creative Anti-Realism of Hilary Putnam and Nelson Goodman and their followers; there is the reflection of Continental Anti-Realism in such philosophers as Richard Rorty; there is the Linguistic Anti-Realism of Wittgenstein and his many followers. It is characteristic of all of these to hold that we human beings are somehow responsible for the way the world is — by way of our linguistic or more broadly symbolic activity, or by way of our decisions, or in some other way. This sort of view is to be found even in theology, for example in some of the works of Gordon Kaufmann and others heavily influenced by Kant. The same view has made its way into physics or at least philosophy of physics. It is said that there is no reality until we make the right observations; there is no such thing as reality in itself and unobserved, or if there is, it is nothing at all like the world we actually live in. In ethics, this view takes the form of the idea that no moral law can be binding on me unless I myself (or perhaps my society) issue or set that law.

Perennial Naturalism and Creative Anti-Realism are related in an interesting manner: the first vastly underestimates the place of human beings in the universe, and the second vastly overestimates it. According to the first, human beings are essentially no more than complicated machines, with no real creativity; in an important sense we can't really act at all, any more than can a spark plug, or coffee grinder, or a truck. We are not ourselves the origin of any causal chains. According to the second, by contrast, we human beings, insofar as we confer its basic structure upon the world, really take the place of God. What there is and what it is like is really up to us, and a result of our activity.

C. Relativism

So the two basic pictures or perspectives of our time, as I see it, are Naturalism and Creative Anti-Realism. But here I must call attention to some complications. First, I say that on these anti-realist views, it is we, we the speakers of language, or the users of symbols, or the thinkers of categorizing thoughts, or the makers of basic decisions, who are responsible for the fundamental lineaments of reality; in the words of Protagoras, "Man is the measure of all things." But sometimes a rather different moral is drawn from some of the same considerations. Suppose you think our world is somehow created or structured by human beings. You may then note that human beings apparently do not all construct the *same* worlds. Your *Lebenswelt* may be quite different from mine; which one, then (if either), represents the world as it really is? Here it is an easy step to another characteristically contemporary thought: the thought that there simply isn't any such thing as objective truth, or an objective way the world is, a way the world is that is the same for all of us. Rather, there is my version of reality, the way I've somehow structured things, and your version, and many other versions: and what is true in one version need not be true in another. As Marlowe's Dr. Faustus says, "Man is the measure of all things; I am a man; therefore I am the measure of all things."[1] But then there isn't any such thing as the truth *simpliciter*. There is no such thing as *the* way the world is; there is instead *my* version of reality, *your* version of it, and so on. Perhaps, then, there are as many versions as there are persons; and each at bottom is as acceptable as any other. Thus a proposition really could be true for me but false for you. I always used to think this a peculiarly sophomoric (excuse me, sophomores) confusion, but in fact it fits well with this formidable and important if lamentable way of thinking. The whole idea of an objective truth, the same for all of us, on this view, is an illusion, or a bourgeois plot, or a silly mistake. Thus does Anti-Realism breed relativism and nihilism.

In some ways this seems quite a comedown from the view that there is indeed a way the world is, and its being that way is owing to our activity. Still, there is a deep connection: on each view, whatever there is by way of truth is of our own making. The same ambiguity is to be found in Protagoras himself. "Man is the measure of all things": we can take this as the thought that there is a certain way the world is, and it is that way because of what we human beings — all human beings — do, or we can take it as the idea that each of some more limited group of persons — perhaps even each individual person — is the measure of all things. Then there would be no one way everything is, but only different versions for different individuals. This form of Enlightenment Subjectivism, like the previous ones, suffers, I think, from deep problems with self-referential incoherence; but I don't here have the time to explain why I think so.

A second complication: we have, as I said, three major perspectives, three wholly different and deeply opposed perspectives. But of course what we also have, as William James said in a different connection, is a blooming, buzzing confusion. These three main perspectives or total ways of looking at man and the world can be found in every conceivable and inconceivable sort of combination and mixture. There are many crosscurrents and eddies and halfway houses; people think and act in accordance with these basic ways of looking at things without being at all clearly aware of

---

1. Quoted in David Lyle Jeffrey, "*Caveat Lector:* Structuralism, Deconstructionism, and Ideology," *The Christian Scholar's Review,* June, 1988.

them, having at best a sort of dim apprehension of them. There is much confusion, halting between two opinions, unreflective and hasty and incongruous combinations. But what I say, I believe, is fundamentally correct. Even if it isn't, what is clear is that something *like* it is: in our culture there are deep, predominant, pervasive ways of thinking that are deeply antagonistic to a Christian way of looking at the world.

I trust it unnecessary to point out that these ways of thinking are not just *alternatives* to Christianity; they run profoundly *counter* to it. From a Christian perspective the naturalist is, of course, deeply mistaken in rejecting or ignoring God. That is bad enough; but in so doing he also cuts himself off from the possibility of properly understanding us and the world. And as for Enlightenment Subjectivism, the idea that it is really we human beings who have made or structured the world, from a Christian perspective, is no more than a piece of silly foolishness, less heroically Promethean than laughably Quixotic.[2]

III. Are Science and Scholarship Neutral?

Now the first thing to see is that scholarship and science are not neutral in this struggle for men's souls. It isn't as if there is a large neutral area of scholarship where we all agree, with disagreement rearing its ugly head only when it comes to religion and politics, perhaps. The facts are very different: the world of scholarship is intimately involved in the battle between

---

2. There are other important presuppositions of our age, and it isn't easy to see just how they fit with the above two. The Enlightenment demand for freedom and autonomy, of course, fits well with Creative Anti-Realism; indeed the latter is just the former taken, as we sometimes say, to its logical extreme. But what about such characteristically contemporary ideas as that religion is properly a private matter, and should not intrude into scholarship, politics, and the other important arenas? How does that fit in with either or both of the above two? Or is it simply another disconnected idea? And the positivistic idea that science is all there is to know: this goes, somehow, with Naturalism, but how exactly? Furthermore, there are various halfway houses between the two main views. For example, there is fact, on the one hand, and value on the other. *We* are responsible for value: for interpretation, understanding, significance, and the like. On the other hand, there is the world of fact; this owes nothing to us and our activity. The humanities, then (broadly), are the realm of value and are such that what is true or right there is our own doing; the natural sciences, broadly, go the other way. A sort of truce, an uneasy compromise.

these opposing views; contemporary scholarship is rife with projects, doctrines, and research programs that reflect these non-Christian ways of thinking. There are hundreds of examples: I shall give just a couple, and each of you can make up your own list. First, Enlightenment Humanism, with its accompanying entourage of relativism, runs rife in the humanities. Contemporary philosophy, for example, is overrun with varieties of relativism and Anti-Realism.

One widely popular version of relativism is Richard Rorty's notion that truth is what my peers will let me get away with saying. On this view what is true for me, naturally enough, might be false for you; *my* peers might let *me* get away with saying something that *your* peers won't let *you* get away with saying: for of course we may have different peers. (And even if we had the *same* peers, there is no reason why they would be obliged to let you and me get away with saying the same things.) Although this view is very much *au courant* and with-it in the contemporary intellectual world, it has consequences that are peculiar, not to say preposterous. For example, most of us think that the Chinese authorities did something monstrous in murdering those hundreds of young people in Tiananmen Square, and then compounded their wickedness by denying that they had done it. On Rorty's view, however, this is an uncharitable misunderstanding. What the authorities were really doing, in denying that they had murdered those students, was something wholly praiseworthy: they were trying to bring it about that the alleged massacre never happened. For they were trying to see to it that their peers would let them get away with saying that the massacre never happened; that is, they were trying to make it *true* that it never happened; and who can fault them for that? The same goes for those contemporary neo-Nazis who claim that there was no holocaust; from a Rortian view, they are only trying to see to it that such a terrible thing never happened; and what could be more commendable than that? This way of thinking has real possibilities for dealing with poverty and disease: if only we let each other get away with saying that there isn't any poverty and disease — no cancer or AIDS, let's say — then it would be true that there isn't any; and if it were true that there isn't any, then of course there wouldn't *be* any. That seems vastly cheaper and less cumbersome than the conventional methods of fighting poverty and disease. At a more personal level, if you have done something wrong, it is not too late: lie about it, thus bringing it about that your peers will let you get away with saying that you didn't do it, then it will be true both that you didn't do it, and, as an added bonus, that you didn't even lie about it.

Another prominent example in the humanities is presented by structuralism, post-structuralism, and deconstructionism in literary studies. All of these, at bottom, pay homage to the notion that we human beings are the source of truth, the source of the way the world is, if indeed there is any such thing as truth or the way the world is. Sometimes this is explicit and clear, as in Roland Barthes:

> Once the Author is removed, the claim to decipher a text becomes quite futile. To give a text an Author is to impose a limit on that text, to furnish it with a final signified, to close the writing. . . . In precisely this way literature (it would be better from now on to say *writing*) by refusing to assign a secret, an ultimate meaning, to the text (and to the world as text) liberates what may be called an antitheological activity, an activity that is truly revolutionary since to refuse to fix meaning is, in the end, to refuse God and his hypostases — reason, science, law.[3]

The move from structuralism to post-structuralism and deconstruction, furthermore, nicely recapitulates the move from Enlightenment Subjectivism to relativism. According to the structuralist, we human beings constitute and structure the world by language and do so *communally;* there are deep common structures involved in us all by which we structure our world. The post-structuralists and deconstructionists, noting in their incisive way that different people structure the world differently, insist that there aren't any such common structures; it is every woman for herself; each of us structures her own world her own way. Put thus baldly and held up to the clear light of day, these views may seem to be hard to take seriously. But the fact is they can be deeply seductive. First, they ordinarily aren't put clearly and usually aren't held up to the clear light of day; and second, they come in versions — Wittgensteinian Anti-Realism, for example — that are vastly more subtle and thus vastly more enticing.

My second main example is from science more narrowly so called: evolution, about which I gave a lecture at Calvin last January. Here I take evolution in the sense of universal common ancestry: it is the view according to which any two living creatures can trace their ancestry back to a common progenitor. If you go back far enough, you and the mosquitoes in

3. Roland Barthes, *Image-Music Text,* trans. Stephen Heath (New York: Hill and Wang, 1977), p. 147.

your back yard have common ancestors; indeed, the same goes for you and the weeds growing in your garden. (So perhaps herbicide is a sort of fratricide.) The experts — Francisco Ayala, Stephen Gould, Richard Dawkins, Philip Spieth, and a thousand others — tell us that this view is no mere theory; it is as solid and rock-ribbed, they say, as that the earth is round and revolves around the sun. (All of those I mentioned explicitly make the comparison with that astronomical fact.) Not only is it declared to be wholly certain; if you venture to suggest that it *isn't* absolutely certain, if you raise doubts or call it into question you are likely to be howled down; you will probably be declared an ignorant fundamentalist obscurantist or worse. In fact this isn't merely *probable;* you have already *been* so called: in a recent review in the *New York Times,* Richard Dawkins, an Oxford biologist of impeccable credentials, claims that "It is absolutely safe to say that if you meet someone who claims not to believe in evolution, that person is ignorant, stupid or insane (or wicked, but I'd rather not consider that)." (Dawkins indulgently adds that "You are probably not stupid, insane or wicked, and ignorance is not a crime. . . .")

As I argued last January, however, from a Christian perspective evolution is nowhere nearly as certain as that the earth is round. Take as evidence what the Christian knows as a Christian together with the scientific evidence — the fossil evidence, the experimental evidence, and the like: it is at best absurd exaggeration to say that, relative to that evidence, evolution is as certain as that the earth is round. My own judgment is that, relative to that evidence and leaving out of account whatever evidence is offered, if any, by the early chapters of Genesis, evolution (the thesis of universal common ancestry) is somewhat less likely than its denial. From a naturalistic perspective, on the other hand, evolution is vastly more likely and has vastly more to be said for it. First, there is the evaluation of the scientific evidence itself: some of this evidence is much stronger taken within a naturalistic context than taken within a theistic context. For example, *given* that life arose by chance, without direction by God, the fact that all living creatures employ the same genetic code strongly suggests a common origin for all living creatures. Again, given the enormous difficulty of seeing how life could have arisen even once by natural, nonteleological means, it is vastly unlikely that it arose in that way more than once; but if it arose only once, then the thesis of common ancestry follows.

But second, from a naturalistic perspective evolution is the only game in town. It is the only available answer to the question "How did it all happen? How did all of these forms of life get here? Where did this vast profusion of life come from? And what accounts for the apparent design, Hume's 'nice adjustment of means to ends' to be found throughout all of living nature?" A Christian has an easy answer to those questions: The Lord has created life in all its forms, and they got here by way of his creative activity; and as for the appearance of design, that is only to be expected since living creatures are in fact designed. But the naturalist has a vastly more difficult row to hoe. How did life get started and how did it come to assume its present multifarious forms? It is monumentally implausible to think these forms just popped into existence; that goes contrary to all our experience. So how did it happen? The evolutionary story gives the answer. Somehow life arose from nonliving matter by way of purely natural means, without the direction of God or anyone else; and once life started, all the vast profusion of contemporary plant and animal life arose from those early ancestors by way of common descent, driven by random variation and natural selection. To return to Richard Dawkins:

> All appearances to the contrary, the only watchmaker in nature is the blind forces of physics, albeit deployed in a very special way. A true watchmaker has foresight: he designs his cogs and springs, and plans their interconnections, with a future purpose in his mind's eye. Natural selection, the blind, unconscious automatic process which Darwin discovered, and which we now know is the explanation for the existence and apparently purposeful form of all life, has no purpose in mind. It has no mind and no mind's eye. It does not plan for the future. It has no vision, no foresight, no sight at all. If it can be said to play the role of watchmaker in nature, it is the *blind* watchmaker.[4]

Here we have a nice summary (complete with the obligatory bit of as-we-now-knowism) of the role played by evolution in naturalistic thought. As Dawkins once remarked to A. J. Ayer, "although atheism might have been logically tenable before Darwin," said he, "Darwin made it possible to be an intellectually fulfilled atheist."[5] And here Dawkins seems to me to be quite correct. Evolution *is* an essential part of any reasonably complete nat-

---

4. Richard Dawkins, *The Blind Watchmaker* (London and New York: W. W. Norton & Co., 1986), p. 5.

5. Dawkins, *The Blind Watchmaker,* pp. 6 and 7.

uralistic way of thinking; it plugs a very large gap in such ways of thinking; hence the pious devotion to it, the suggestions that doubts about it should not be aired in public, and the venom and abuse with which dissent is greeted. In contemporary academia, evolution has become an idol of the tribe; it serves as a shibboleth, a litmus test distinguishing the benighted fundamentalist goats from the enlightened and properly acculturated sheep. It functions as a *myth:* a widely shared way of understanding ourselves at the level of religion, a deep interpretation of ourselves to ourselves, a way of telling us why we are here, where we come from, and where we are going. And my point: the Christian community must recognize that there is vastly more to the role played by evolution in contemporary academia than a sort of straightforward science which has the same credentials viewed from any perspective.[6]

Of course many more examples could be given — from psychology, sociology, economics — across the length and breadth of the academic disciplines. And by now the moral is obvious: the Christian community as a whole must be aware of these things; it must be attuned to them, sensitive to them. We must see that intellectual culture does indeed involve a contest for basic human allegiance. It isn't enough to make the occasional ceremonial reference to world and life views or Reformed thought. We must really see that there is a battle here, and we must know what the main contestants are and how they permeate the various scholarly disciplines. These perspectives are seductive; these are widespread; they are the majority views in the universities and in intellectual culture generally in the West. We live in a world dominated by them; we imbibe them with our mother's milk; it is easy to embrace them and their projects in a sort of unthoughtful, unselfconscious way, just because they *do* dominate our intellectual culture. But these perspectives are also deeply inimical to Christianity; these ways of thinking distort our views of ourselves and the world. To the degree that we are not aware of them and do not understand their allegiances, they

---

6. Of course my point is not that you can't accept evolution without accepting naturalism. Obviously you can; evolution doesn't *entail* Naturalism; it is logically possible (obviously enough) that God should have created life in such a way that the thesis of universal common ancestry is true. My point is that the contemporary allegiance to evolution and the claims of certainty on its behalf arise out of its *mythic* function, rather than out of a sober inspection of evidence that has the same evidential bearing for a Christian as for someone committed to Naturalism.

make for confusion, and for lack of intellectual and spiritual wholeness and integrity among us Christians.

At the beginning of my talk I promised two reasons why Christian scholarship is of the first importance for the Christian community. The first reason is now obvious: clearly the Christian community needs what I shall call Christian cultural criticism. This reason is rooted in our historical situation; given its immersion in the sort of culture in which it finds itself, the Christian community sorely needs this cultural criticism, this testing of the spirits. And of course it is the Christian scholarly community on which this responsibility most directly falls. Christian scholars have an obligation to discern and analyze these perspectives, to plumb the full extent of their influence, to recognize the way in which they underlie vast stretches of contemporary intellectual life, to note how they manifest themselves in the intellectual projects and pursuits that are currently fashionable. We have an obligation to point out what we see, to react to it, to comment upon it. We must be aware of the broadly religious conflict in which scholarship is enmeshed. The Christian scholarly community must test the spirits, to see what comes ultimately from God, the source of all truth, and what comes from other sources. We need deep, penetrating, thoughtful, informed analyses of the various cultural movements and forces we encounter. To go with the crowd, to accept and take for granted what we find around us can lead us *away* from the Lord, away from an integral and unified Christian way of looking at the world.

This, therefore, is the first reason why we need Christian scholarship.

Christian Thinking: The Twin Pillars

I. Positive Christian Science

Last night I joined Reformed thinkers going all the way back to Augustine in affirming that a spiritual battle is being waged in our world. This battle has gone on for centuries. In bold and bald outline, the battle is between the *Civitas Dei*, the spiritual forces of those who enlist under Christ's banner, on the one hand, and, on the other, those who fly the flag of the Earthly City. The latter, of course, displays itself differently at different times and places. At present, and at least since the Enlightenment, its forces are divided: there are the battalions of Perennial Naturalism, but there are also the powerful forces of Enlightenment Humanism or Modern Subjectivism. Both trace their lineage back to the ancient world: the former to Lucretius and Epicurus and their bleak view of a world of atoms without God, and the latter to Protagoras with his grandiose claim that man is the measure of all things. The opposition between the *Civitas Dei* and the Earthly City is basic, fundamental, and serious; it is a battle for our very souls. I went on to draw the corollary drawn by Augustine, Kuyper, Dooyeweerd, Jellema, Stob, and many other Reformed stalwarts: scholarship and science, taken broadly, is deeply involved in this three-way battle. In a thousand ways contemporary science and scholarship displays its involvement in this struggle. Last time I gave a couple of obvious examples; they could be multiplied indefinitely. It is hard to overestimate the degree to which our own ways of thinking are likely to be shaped and molded by these visions of reality — visions that are deeply antagonistic to Christianity. These corrosive acids affect us in a thousand ways; we must recognize and combat them.

Now you may complain that this is all excessively obvious; we have learned it at our mother's knee. No doubt you are right; but these things must be recalled regularly and often; they must be kept near the forefront of our minds. And of course it is not that our only aim here is to keep ourselves pure and undefiled, unspotted from the world. We are our brothers' (and sisters') keepers, and we require this awareness also in order to witness, in a broad sense, to the rest of the world and to bring the benefits of the gospel to our fellows.

But perhaps you will go on to complain that all of this is negative; where, you say, is the positive? (Don't we need the power of positive thinking?) Tonight I do want to speak of something positive. There is much to be said here and little time to say it; so I shall have to leap lightly over large areas, areas that really require a great deal by way of investigation and discussion. (You may think this is less like leaping lightly than like skating on thin ice.)

So first: do we as Christian community need anything *more* than the cultural criticism of which I spoke last time? Do we need, not just awareness and assessment of contemporary answers to scholarly questions, but also answers of our own to those questions? Some Christians — among them many of our fundamentalist brothers and sisters — are inclined to think not. They think scholarship of this positive sort is at best unimportant and at worst spiritually dangerous. We need to cultivate the know-how needed to live well, to conquer sickness, to build condominiums, houses, and airplanes, they say; but that kind of know-how, impressive and difficult as it is, has little to do with understanding ourselves and the world and God. And as for the latter, here we have Christianity, a revelation from God himself; what more could we possibly need? In paying heed to contemporary scholarship and intellectual culture, don't we run the risk of being deeply misled? After all, St. Paul himself issues a trenchant warning: "Beware lest any man spoil you through philosophy and vain deceit, after the tradition of men, after the rudiments of the world and not after Christ" (Colossians 2, v. 8). That's the King James version: I am happy to say Paul doesn't really have *philosophy* in mind (as opposed to, e.g., history or literary criticism); here the term 'philosophy' is being used in an older and broader sense in which it applies to all the interpretative disciplines. So in another and more current translation: "Be on your guard; do not let your minds be captured by hollow and delusive speculations, based on traditions of man-made teaching and centered on the elemental spirits of the universe and not in Christ" *(New English Bible).* Is there not here a warning against trying to go beyond what we learn from the Lord himself?

This attitude is widespread in contemporary Christianity; it under-lies some of the anti-intellectualism to be found in fundamentalist circles. Sometimes it is also attributed to the church father Tertullian (160 AD), who explicitly adverts to Paul's advice:

> From philosophy come those fables and endless genealogies and fruit-less questionings, those "words that creep like as doth a canker." To hold us back from such things, the Apostle testifies expressly in his let-ter to the Colossians that we should beware of philosophy. . . . He had been at Athens where he had come to grips with the human wisdom which attacks and perverts the truth, being itself divided up into its own swarm of heresies by the variety of its mutually antagonistic sects. What has Jerusalem to do with Athens, the Church with the Academy, the Christian with the heretic? Our principles come from the porch of Solomon, who had himself taught that the Lord is to be sought in sim-plicity of heart. I have no use for a stoic or a Platonic or a dialectic Christianity. After Jesus Christ we have no need of speculation, after the gospel, no need of research. When we come to believe, we have no desire to believe anything else; for we begin by believing that there is nothing else which we have to believe.

You probably know Tertullian as the author of that dubious aphorism, *Credo quia absurdum est:* I believe because it is absurd. Many have ridiculed Tertullian for this suggestion. Sigmund Freud, for example, taking it to represent a fundamental Christian attitude, asks whether I am to try to be-lieve every absurdity (that would be pretty hard to accomplish, given the long list of absurdities); and if not why should I believe *this* one, as opposed to the others?

I very much doubt that Tertullian ever said any such thing as *Credo quia absurdum est;* I think he suffers from a bad press. Of course, great rheto-rician that he was, he sometimes exaggerates for effect; but his main point, so far as I can see, is eminently sensible. "After Jesus Christ we have no need of speculation, after the gospel, no need of research. When we come to be-lieve, we have no desire to believe anything else; for we begin by believing that there is nothing else which we have to believe." Tertullian wasn't a fool, after all; he doesn't mean literally that there is nothing else at all that

141

we have to believe. I need to have beliefs about what my name is, where I live, how to get to my office, and whether pizza is more nourishing than mud; and those things are not, so far as I know, revealed in the Scripture. What Tertullian meant is something different and very much worth thinking about. In pursuing the theoretical or interpretative disciplines, our aim is to understand ourselves and our world and the relations between us and it; but doesn't Christianity already give us what we need to know along those lines? What is the world fundamentally like, and what is our place in it? Christianity gives us the answer: the world is fundamentally God's creation. The same God who created the world also created us human beings in his image. We human beings, however, have fallen into sin, thus bringing ruin upon ourselves and our world; we require rescue and salvation. God has graciously offered a means for restoring us to health and wholeness; this is accomplished through the death and resurrection of the man Jesus Christ, who is also the second person of the Trinity. Through him we can have justification and eternal life.

And now Tertullian's point: there are some who keep trying to do research into the questions whether the fundamental lineaments and contours of Christianity are indeed true. Often they wind up convinced that these basic Christian claims cannot be true, as they stand; so they offer various substitutes of their own invention. Among the prime examples in our own day, oddly enough, are theologians, 'liberal' theologians who have given up the gospel and its claims and who propose various pale and ghostly substitutes. A century ago absolute idealism was a popular substitute; now it is considerably harder to figure out what these theologians propose, but certain brands of Heideggerian existentialism seem to be popular. For the serious Christian, however, this is wholly anomalous; as a Christian she already knows the answer to those questions; she doesn't need further research on them, and she doesn't need any of those sickly and lifeless substitutes.[1]

So here Tertullian is correct, and what he says is important. But can we properly conclude that we Christians don't need those theoretical and interpretative disciplines — philosophy, psychology, literary studies, history, economics, sociology, the natural sciences? Here the Reformed tradition is nearly unanimous: certainly not. So I shall not waste valuable time

1. Even Paul, after all, warns against those who "are always learning but never arrive at a knowledge of the truth" (2 Tim. 3:7).

arguing the point; that would be like carrying coals to Newcastle, or perhaps *banket* to Friesland.

Instead, I shall pass on to the next question: given that we *do* need these disciplines, how, exactly, shall we pursue them? Shall we work at them in the same way as the rest of the academic world, or shall we pursue them in a way that is specifically Christian? Take a given area of scholarship: philosophy, let's say, or history, or psychology, or anthropology, or economics, or sociology; should we take for granted the Christian answer to the large questions about God and creation, and then go on from that perspective to address the narrower questions of that discipline? Or is that somehow illicit or ill-advised? Put it another way: to what sort of premises can we properly appeal in working out the answers to the questions raised in a given area of scholarly or scientific inquiry? Can we properly appeal to what we know as Christians? In psychology (which I mention because it is an area in which I am unencumbered by a knowledge of the relevant facts): must the Christian community accept the basic structure and presuppositions of the contemporary practice of that discipline in trying to come to an understanding of its subject matter? Must Christian psychologists appeal only to premises accepted by all parties to the discussion, whether Christian or not?

Last time I mentioned the striking phenomenon of human love. There is love between man and woman, between parents and children, among friends; there is love of country, love for institutions such as Calvin College and the Christian Reformed Church and the broader Christian church of which the former is a small but in our estimation important part: how shall we understand this phenomenon? When a Christian psychologist addresses this question, can she properly take into account what she knows as a Christian — that, for example, we are created in God's image, that God himself *is* love, that our loving is something like a reflection of his? How shall we understand the sense of beauty we human beings share? We exulted in those marvelous, golden, luminous days of autumn of a couple of weeks ago; and a Mozart concerto can bring tears to our eyes. How must we think about this sensitivity to beauty on our part? How shall we understand this phenomenon? No doubt some will tell us that it arose, somehow, by way of genetic mutation; its significance is to be seen in the fact that it turned out, somehow, to be adaptive, or to be somehow connected with something that is adaptive. But if we take for granted a Christian explanatory background, we might come up with an entirely different view. To turn to still another example, can a Christian psychologist take account of the reality of sin in order to understand aggression and hate in all their forms?

When a Christian philosopher addresses a given philosophical question — e.g., what is the nature of knowledge, or of moral obligation, or of natural law? — can she properly appeal to what she knows as a Christian? Can a Christian economist properly take account of what he knows about human nature in trying to understand the phenomena addressed by economics? Should someone who aims to think scientifically, in a scholarly way, about the origin of the human race, appeal to the premise that God has created life generally, and us specifically? That will make a difference, as I argued last time, as to the way in which one estimates the probability or likelihood of the theory of universal common ancestry, not to mention claims to the effect that life arose in the first place by way of nothing more than the workings of the laws of physics and chemistry. Similar questions arise, of all places, even in theology. It is widely argued, for example, that a Christian Scripture scholar should not appeal to her theological beliefs — that Jesus was the divine son of God, for example — in working at Scripture scholarship; to do so would be to sacrifice detachment and objectivity.[2]

II. The Argument

Now most Reformed thinkers have held that the Christian scholar may indeed appeal to what she knows as a Christian. In fact she must. For the Christian community needs answers to these questions, and needs answers, naturally enough, that take into account *all* that we know, *everything* that is relevant to the question at hand. Take Scripture scholarship for example: here there are questions to which we need answers. There are apparent eyewitness accounts of the appearance of the risen Lord; are these really what they seem to be, or were they slipped in by the early church intent on making a theological or political point? Here, clearly enough, what you

2. See, for example, Barnabas Lindars: "The religious literature of the ancient world is full of miracle stories, and we cannot believe them all. It is not open to a scholar to decide that, just because he is a believing Christian, he will accept all the Gospel miracles at their face value, but at the same time he will repudiate miracles attributed to Isis. All such accounts have to be scrutinized with equal detachment" (*Theology*, March, 1986, p. 91).

think of Christ will be crucially relevant. Christians think that he was in fact the incarnate second person of the Trinity. If so, however, principles that may be quite acceptable in trying to decide what some merely human person would have said and done may be wholly off the mark when it is Christ of whom we speak. So if we do Scripture scholarship 'from below,' as they say, then we might get wildly wrong answers. Here what the Christian community needs is scholarship that takes into account *all* that we know, including what we know as Christians. Perhaps it might be sort of an interesting exercise or puzzle to try to see what we would think about Scripture, if we *didn't* think that Jesus Christ was divine. But in the first place it isn't necessary for us *Christians* to do that; there are plenty of others who don't think Jesus was divine, and they are only too happy to tell us what they think about Scripture. And second, the interest of the project, surely, is limited at best. It would be a bit like painting your house with a toothbrush, or mowing your lawn with a nail scissors, or emptying Reeds Lake with a coffee cup: challenging, no doubt, but hardly worth the effort.

So here we need scholarship that starts from all that we know, including what we know as Christians. But the same goes for the Christian scholar in other areas. If we need to understand love, or knowledge, or aggression, or our sense of beauty, or humor, or our moral sense, or our origins, or a thousand other things — if it is important to our intellectual and spiritual health to understand these things, then what we must do, obviously enough, is use *all* that we know, not just some limited segment of it. Why should we be buffaloed (or cowed) into trying to understand these things from a naturalistic perspective? So the central argument here is simplicity itself: as Christians we need and want answers to the sorts of questions that arise in the theoretical and interpretative disciplines; in an enormous number of such cases, what we know as Christians is crucially relevant to coming to a proper understanding; therefore we Christians should pursue these disciplines from a specifically Christian perspective.

III. Two Objections

This line of argument seems obvious and uncontroversial. Oddly enough, however, it has been widely controverted, even among Christians; and even those who endorse it often seem to pay it little more than lip service. Why should that be so? In what follows I want to address two objections to or

145

reservations about this project of Christian scholarship. First, there is the idea that what we believe as Christians is something we *believe,* and believe by faith. But then it is a matter of faith, not knowledge. On the other hand, scholarship, science, *Wissenschaft* (*Wetenschap,* if you like), is clearly a matter of knowledge; here faith is not relevant. We have science only if we have knowledge; but if in our practice of the discipline in question we rely essentially upon what we accept by faith, then the result will be faith rather than knowledge. And second, even if the first objection is mistaken — even if specifically Christian scholarship achieves knowledge rather than faith — the result of such an enterprise will be *theology* — theology rather than psychology, economics, sociology, philosophy, or whatever. This sort of suggestion is often made by our Catholic and Thomist colleagues: it is a fine thing to understand knowledge or love or aggression from a Christian perspective, but to do so is to do theology rather than philosophy or psychology. No doubt a good thing, but no substitute for the scientific understanding in question.

A. Faith vs. Knowledge

Suppose we take up these objections one at a time and in order. Is it true that if we use the deliverances of the faith in a cognitive enterprise — if, for example, we appeal to them as premises or accept them as explanatory background conditions — then the result is not knowledge but faith? How can we answer this question? Clearly, what we need first of all is some idea of what knowledge is; here we need a brief course in epistemology. So let's begin. First, everyone agrees that what is known must be true; you can't sensibly claim that Paul knows something but then go on to add that what he knows is false. (Of course we sometimes say something like "As any good liberal theologian knows, there is no such thing as absolute truth"; but that is an ironic use of the term.) So if you know something, it follows that it's true. But truth is not enough for knowledge: you can have a true belief that does not constitute knowledge. Perhaps you make a lucky guess as to which way the stock market will go tomorrow; if it really *is* just a guess, then it isn't knowledge, even if it turns out to be true. What *else* is needed for knowledge? Call this 'the problem of the *Theaetetus*'; it first appears in Plato's dialogue by that name and has been with us ever since. (Here we have another confirmation of Whitehead's remark that philosophy is a series of footnotes to Plato.) Suppose we use the term 'warrant' to refer to whatever it is that is needed in addition to true belief to have knowledge, whatever it is that distinguishes knowledge from mere true belief. Then our question is: what is warrant?

There are three views on this topic nowadays (and in our part of the world). First, there is the view dominant since the beginnings of modern philosophy. It is hard to think of a good name for this view: 'Classical Deontologism' (from the Greek word 'deon' for duty or obligation) is accurate but too forbidding. I'll use it anyway. This view goes back all the way to Descartes and Locke; its principal contemporary representative is Professor Roderick Chisholm (the dean of American epistemologists) from Brown University. The view starts from the idea that there are intellectual duties or obligations; duties to regulate our beliefs in such a way as to come into the right relationship to truth. Thus Locke:

> Faith is nothing but a firm assent of the mind: which if it be regulated, as is our duty, cannot be afforded to anything, but upon good reason; and so cannot be opposite to it. He that believes, without having any reason for believing, may be in love with his own fancies; but neither seeks truth as he ought, nor pays the obedience due his maker, who would have him use those discerning faculties he has given him, to keep him out of mistake and error. He that does not this to the best of his power, however he sometimes lights on truth, is in the right but by chance; and I know not whether the luckiness of the accident will excuse the irregularity of his proceeding. This at least is certain, that he must be accountable for whatever mistakes he runs into: whereas he that makes use of the light and faculties God has given him, and seeks sincerely to discover truth, by those helps and abilities he has, may have this satisfaction in doing his duty as a rational creature, that though he should miss truth, he will not miss the reward of it. For he governs his assent right, and places it as he should, who in any case or matter whatsoever, believes or disbelieves, according as reason directs him. He that does otherwise, transgresses against his own light, and misuses those faculties, which were given him. . . . (*Essay* IV, xvii, 24)

This passage calls for much by way of comment; I call your attention only to the repeated suggestion that we have *duties* and *obligations* with respect to the regulation of our belief or assent. "He that does not believe in accord with reason," says Locke, "transgresses against his own light and misuses those faculties that were given him by God." And now the first idea as to what warrant is: warrant essentially involves conforming to intellectual duties. A belief has warrant for you if in accepting it you go contrary to no intellectual obligations. More broadly, your duty, as a rational being, a being capable of understanding and belief, is to try to get into the right relation with the truth; and a proposition has warrant for you if believing it is a good way to satisfy those intellectual duties.

But this is clearly unacceptable; satisfying your duty is surely not enough, together with truth, for knowledge. A person may be doing his level best, may be satisfying his intellectual obligations *in excelsis,* but his beliefs may still have very little by way of warrant. Descartes mentions "certain persons, devoid of sense, whose cerebella are so troubled and clouded by the violent vapors of black bile, that they . . . imagine that they have an earthenware head or are nothing but pumpkins or are made of glass." But even a madman may be trying his best to get into the right relation to the truth; it's just that, by virtue of cognitive malfunction, he can't manage much success. He may be conforming to all his intellectual obligations; his problem is disorder or sickness rather than dereliction of duty. If I am mad, intellectually disordered, then no matter how conscientious I am about my intellectual duties in forming my beliefs, those beliefs may still have no warrant for me. Imagine that Paul suffers from a rare but interesting disorder: whenever his visual experience is like ours when we see a tree, he forms the belief that what he sees is an elephant in disguise. That belief under those circumstances seems as obvious to him as that 2 + 1 = 3. He doesn't know that he is abnormal, and his lack of awareness is in no way due to flouting his epistemic duty. Indeed, Paul is unusually dutiful, unusually concerned about fulfilling his epistemic duties; fulfilling these duties is the main passion of his life. Then, surely, Paul may be doing his epistemic duty *in excelsis* in believing as he does; but the proposition in question has little by way of warrant for him. Paul is beyond reproach; he does his duty as he sees it. He is deontologically justified, and more; for in working as hard as he does to achieve epistemic excellence, he performs works of epistemic supererogation. But that is not sufficient for warrant. Paul can be ever so conscientious about his epistemic duties, and still, because of cognitive malfunction, be such that his beliefs have very little warrant. So this view is clearly mistaken.

The second view: what makes for warrant is your belief's being *coherent* with some other body of beliefs — the rest of what you believe, for example. No doubt you believe that London, England, is larger than London, Ontario; if this belief fits in well enough, coheres well enough with the rest of what you know, then it has warrant for you; and if it is true as well, then you know it. This view, naturally enough, is called coherentism. It has always been bedeviled by a tough problem: what *is* this coherence, this fitting in? Mere logical consistency isn't sufficient for coherence, but then what more is required? I think we can easily see, however, that coherence isn't enough for warrant no matter *how* you think of it. For coherence is a relation just among beliefs; but even if your *beliefs* are related to each other in the right way, even if they are splendidly coherent, you might still fail to have knowledge; your beliefs might not be related in the right way to your *experience*. Consider the Case of the Epistemically Inflexible Climber. Rick is climbing Guide's Wall, on Storm Point in the Grand Tetons; having just led the difficult next to last pitch, he is seated on a comfortable ledge, bringing his partner up. He believes that Cascade Canyon is down to his left, that the cliffs of Mt. Owen are directly in front of him, that there is a hawk gliding in lazy circles 200 feet below his feet, that he is wearing his new *Fire* rock shoes, and so on. His beliefs, we may add, are coherent. Now imagine that Rick is struck by a wayward burst of high energy cosmic radiation. This causes his beliefs to become fixed, no longer responsive to changes in experience. At the cost of considerable effort his partner gets him down the Wall, and, in a desperate last ditch attempt at therapy, takes him to the opera in Jackson, where the New York Metropolitan Opera on tour is performing "La Bohème" (with Pavarotti singing the tenor lead). Rick is appeared to in the same way as everyone else there; he is inundated by wave after wave of golden sound. Sadly enough, this effort at therapy fails; his beliefs remain fixed and wholly unresponsive to his experience; he still believes that he is on the belay ledge at the top of the next to last pitch of Guide's Wall, that Cascade Canyon is down to his left, that there is a hawk sailing in lazy circles 200 feet below him, that he is wearing his new *Fire* rock shoes, and so on. Furthermore, since he believes the very same things he believed when seated on the ledge, his beliefs are coherent. But surely they have little or no warrant for him. The reason is cognitive malfunction; his beliefs are not appropriately responsive to experience. Clearly, then, coherence is not sufficient for positive epistemic status.

According to the third view, warrant is a matter of *reliability*. If your belief is produced by a reliable faculty, or cognitive process, or belief producing mechanism, then you have warrant; if it is also true, then it constitutes knowledge. I believe that this account of warrant is closer to the truth than the other two: nevertheless it is still mistaken. Return to Rick on Guide's Wall; perhaps the burst of high energy radiation causes the following sort of malfunction: whenever he hears the word 'prime' — as in 'The prime rate has gone down,' or 'you must prime the pump before it will work,' or 'that is certainly a piece of prime real estate,' or 'the prime minister of Great Britain is no friend of the universities' — whenever he hears the word 'prime,' he forms the belief, about some randomly selected number greater than 100, that it is not prime (i.e., that it is divisible by some number other than 1 and itself). He can't *see* that the number in question isn't prime; he simply finds himself believing it. Then his views, arising in malfunction as they do, have little by way of warrant for him. Nonetheless, since the vast majority of numbers greater than 100 are indeed nonprime, the belief is produced by a reliable cognitive process.

So none of the three current views seems right. I wish to suggest a fourth, one that fits in well with the fact that we have been created by God, but also seems correct in its own right. And the first thing to see is that (on any Christian or theistic view of the matter) we human beings, like automobiles and linear accelerators, have indeed been created and designed — by God. Further, we have been created by him *in his own image;* in certain crucial respects we resemble him. Now God is an actor, an agent, a creator: one who chooses certain ends and takes action to accomplish them. God is therefore a *practical* being. But he is also an *intellectual* or *intellecting* being. He holds beliefs; he has knowledge. Indeed, he has the maximal degree of knowledge; he knows every truth and believes no falsehoods.

In setting out to create human beings in his image, then, God set out to create them in such a way that they could reflect something of his capacity to grasp concepts and hold beliefs. Furthermore, as the whole of the Christian tradition suggests, his aim was to create them in such a way that they could reflect something of his capacity for holding *true* beliefs, for attaining *knowledge.* This has been the nearly unanimous consensus of the Christian tradition.[3] The great bulk of the tradition has seen our imaging

3. It is worth noting, however, that it isn't inevitable. God's aim in creating us with the complicated, highly articulated establishment of faculties we have could have been something quite different; in creating us with these faculties he could have been aiming us, not at truth, but at something of some other sort — survival, for example, or a

God in terms (among other things) of *knowledge:* knowledge of ourselves, of God himself, and of the world in which he has placed us; and here I shall take for granted this traditional understanding of the *imago dei.*

God has therefore created us with cognitive faculties designed to enable us to achieve true beliefs with respect to a wide variety of propositions — propositions about our immediate environment, about our own interior lives, about the thoughts and experiences of other persons, about our universe at large, about right and wrong — and about himself. These faculties are enormously complex and articulate; they work with great subtlety. They function in such a way that under the appropriate circumstances we form the appropriate belief. More exactly, the appropriate belief is *formed in us;* in the typical case we do not *decide* to hold or form the belief in question, but simply find ourselves with it. Upon being appeared to in the familiar way, I find myself holding the belief that there is a large tree before me; upon being asked what I had for breakfast, I reflect for a moment and then find myself with the belief that what I had was eggs on toast. In these and other cases I do not decide what to believe; I don't total up the evidence (I'm being appeared to redly; on most occasions when thus appeared to I am in the presence of something red; so most probably in this case I am) and make a decision as to what seems best supported; I simply find myself believing. Of course in *some* cases I may go through such a procedure. For example, I may try to assess the alleged evidence in favor of the theory that human life evolved by means of the mechanisms of random genetic mutation and natural selection from unicellular life (which itself arose by substantially similar random mechanical processes from nonliving material); I may try to determine whether the evidence is in fact compelling or, more modestly, such as to make the theory plausible. Then I may go through a procedure of that sort. Even in this sort of case I still don't really *decide* anything: I simply call the relevant evidence to mind, try in some way to weigh it up, and find myself with the appropriate belief. But in more typical and less theoretical cases of belief formation nothing like this is involved.

God has therefore created us with an astonishingly complex and subtle establishment of cognitive faculties. These faculties produce beliefs on

---

capacity to appreciate art, poetry, beauty in nature, or an ability to stand in certain relationships with each other and with him. In C. S. Lewis's novel *Out of the Silent Planet* the creatures on Mars are of several different types displaying several different kinds of cognitive excellences: some are particularly suited to scientific endeavors, some to poetry and art, and some to interpersonal sensitivity.

an enormously wide variety of topics — our everyday external environment, the thoughts and feelings of others, our own internal life (someone's internal musings and soliloquies can occupy an entire novel), the past, mathematics, science, right and wrong, what is necessary and possible, our relationships with God himself, and a host of other topics. They work with great subtlety to produce beliefs of many different degrees of strength — ranging from the merest inclination to believe to absolute dead certainty. Our beliefs and the strength with which we hold them, furthermore, are delicately responsive to changes in experience — to what people tell us, to perceptual experience, to what we read, to further reflection, and so on.

Now: how shall we think of warrant from this point of view? Note first that the problems with the other views could be brought out by considering the possibility of cognitive malfunction, of things not working right, not working the way they ought to. So here is a natural first approximation to a better view of warrant: a belief has warrant for a person only if his faculties are *working properly,* working the way they ought to work, working the way they were designed to work (working the way God designed them to work), in producing and sustaining the belief in question. I therefore suggest that a necessary condition of warrant is that one's cognitive equipment, one's belief forming and belief sustaining apparatus, be free of cognitive malfunction. It must be functioning in the way it was designed to function by the being who designed and created us — God himself. Initially, then, a belief has warrant, for me, to the degree that my faculties are functioning properly in producing and sustaining that belief; and my faculties are working properly if they are working in the way they were designed to work by God. And suppose we add that under these conditions of proper function, the more firmly you believe a proposition, the more warrant it has for you; and if you believe it firmly enough, it will have enough warrant for knowledge.

B. The Twin Pillars

There is much more to be said here: many qualifications and additions to the simple original picture are needed.[4] Nonetheless I think it is the *right*

4. For fuller accounts, see my "Justification and Theism," *Faith and Philosophy,* October, 1987; "Positive Epistemic Status and Proper Function," in *Philosophical Perspectives,*

basic picture; it is a better picture, I think, than any of its rivals, and it grows naturally out of the Christian conviction that we have been created by God. And now suppose we return to the objection that precipitated this entire epistemological excursus. That claim, you will recall, is that what we believe by faith, we *believe* rather than know. But then a discipline that essentially employs the deliverances of faith will itself deliver faith rather than knowledge. Science and scholarship, on the other hand (so the objection goes), involve knowledge, not faith; so if we pursue the scholarly disciplines in a way that essentially depends upon faith, we may have something valuable, but we won't have science or scholarship.

From our present perspective on knowledge and warrant, however, there is a prior question: why suppose that what I believe by faith cannot also constitute knowledge? That isn't just obvious or self-evident, after all. There are two important points here. First, the objector simply assumes without argument, that belief in God — belief that there *is* such a person as God — is a matter of faith rather than reason. But is he right? The difference between faith and reason, briefly put, is that reason is part of our original created noetic endowment, the cognitive powers and faculties we have just by way of being human beings. Faith, on the other hand, is a special cognitive response to a special revelation on the part of God; what we believe by faith is what the Lord teaches (in Scripture and through the church) about himself and his plan for our salvation. But then what about the belief that there really *is* such a person as God? Is that a matter of faith or a matter of reason? Well, what is the Reformed view on this matter? According to John Calvin, as good a Calvinist as any, there is a knowledge of God that is part of our original created endowment. As he says,

> There is within the human mind, and indeed by natural instinct, an awareness of divinity. This we take to be beyond controversy. To prevent anyone from taking refuge in the pretense of ignorance, God himself has implanted in all men a certain understanding of his divine majesty. Ever renewing its memory, he repeatedly sheds fresh drops. Since, therefore, men one and all perceived that there is a God and that he is their Maker, they are condemned by their own testimony because they have failed to honor him and to consecrate their lives to his

---

2; *Epistemology, 1988,* ed. James Tomberlin (Atascadero, California: Ridgeview Publishing Co., 1988); and *Warrant* (not yet committed for publication).

will. . . . therefore, since from the beginning of the world there has been no region, no city, in short, no household, that could do without religion, there lies in this a tacit confession of a sense of deity inscribed in the hearts of all.

Indeed, the perversity of the impious, who though they struggle furiously are unable to extricate themselves from the fear of God, is abundant testimony that this conviction, namely, that there is some God, is naturally inborn in all, and is fixed deep within, as it were in the very marrow. . . . From this we conclude that it is not a doctrine that must first be learned in school, but one of which each of us is master from his mother's womb and which nature itself permits no one to forget. . . .

Lest anyone, then, be excluded from access to happiness, he not only sowed in men's minds that seed of religion of which we have spoken but revealed himself and daily discloses himself in the whole workmanship of the universe. As a consequence, men cannot open their eyes without being compelled to see him.[5]

So according to Calvin, there is a natural knowledge of God. In a wide variety of circumstances — upon beholding the starry heavens above, when in danger, upon seeing that we have done something deeply wrong — we human beings find ourselves aware of God's presence, realizing that we owe him obedience and allegiance. We praise him for his glory, or ask for his help, or see him as disapproving. This is not a knowledge of God that depends upon regeneration or faith; it is a knowledge we have by virtue of our created nature. Of course it has been spoiled, suppressed, damaged by sin. We don't know God the way we would if there were no sin; if it weren't for sin, Calvin thinks, we would all believe in God with the same spontaneous and simple trust with which we believe in other human persons, our own existence, the past, and so on. Still, we do have this natural knowledge.

So the first point is that belief in God is not necessarily a matter of faith; there is a natural apprehension of God, and belief in God produced by that mechanism or cognitive process — suppose we follow Calvin and call it the *Sensus Divinitatis* — is produced by reason, not by faith. Of course this natural knowledge isn't nearly sufficient for salvation. In the believer,

5. *Institutes of the Christian Religion,* trans. Ford Lewis Battles (Philadelphia: Westminster Press, 1960), Book I, ch. iii, sec. i.

154

furthermore (and it is presumably the believer who will be engaged in the project of Christian scholarship), it isn't a *merely* natural knowledge; it is a natural knowledge qualified and corrected by faith, absorbed by and taken up into faith. The believer accepts God's promises; she therefore knows vastly more about God than is to be had by the workings of the *Sensus Divinitatis* alone. But then (and here I come to the second important point) how does the believer come to believe those things? According to Calvin, once more showing his Reformed colors, it is by virtue of the internal testimony of the Holy Spirit. The believer doesn't just *guess* at these matters, and it isn't just by accident that she holds the views she does. Rather, there is a cognitive process of a quite different sort occurring in her:

> Since for unbelieving men religion seems to stand by opinion alone, they, in order not to believe anything foolishly or lightly, both wish and demand rational proof that Moses and the prophets spoke divinely. But I reply: the testimony of the Spirit is more excellent than all reason. For as God alone is a fit witness of himself in his Word, so also the Word will not find acceptance in men's hearts before it is sealed by the inward testimony of the Spirit. The same Spirit, therefore, who has spoken through the mouths of the prophets must penetrate into our hearts to persuade us that they faithfully proclaimed what had been divinely commanded.[6]

So says John Calvin; and so says any Reformed Christian and most other Christians as well. There is such a thing as the testimony of the Holy Spirit; by virtue of that testimony we come to believe what the Scriptures teach. So to recapitulate, there is an original, increated, natural knowledge of God. That knowledge has been spoiled and distorted, overlaid and suppressed by sin; it has been obscured by the smoke of our wrongdoing, as Anselm said. In the believer, it is restored, deepened, broadened by virtue of the testimony of the Holy Spirit.

And now return, once more, to the objection: the claim that if we employ what we believe as Christians in doing scholarship, then the result won't be knowledge but only faith. Clearly the objector is jumping to conclusions. For why suppose that if a belief of mine is a deliverance of faith, it

6. Book I, ch. vii, sec. iv.

can't also be something I know, a case of knowledge? Why suppose that faith and knowledge are mutually exclusive? Calvin, again, does not:

> . . . faith consists in the knowledge of God and Christ.[7]

> Now we shall possess a right definition of faith if we call it a firm and certain knowledge of God's benevolence toward us, founded upon the truth of the freely given promise in Christ, both revealed to our minds and sealed upon our hearts through the Holy Spirit.[8]

> In understanding faith it is not merely a question of knowing that God exists, but also — and this especially — of knowing what is his will toward us. For it is not so much our concern to know who he is in himself, as what he wills to be toward us.[9]

> Now therefore, we hold faith to be a knowledge of God's will toward us, perceived from his Word.[10]

According to Calvin, faith is a kind or variety of knowledge; faith and knowledge are not opposed, for faith itself *is* knowledge. It is essentially a knowledge of God's will towards us, that is, of his hatred of sin and his plan of salvation for us.

Calvin's claims here fit nicely into the perspective on knowledge I outlined a moment ago. The *Sensus Divinitatis* and the testimony of the Holy Spirit are, of course, sources of belief, belief producing processes or mechanisms, as we might say; in this regard they are just like memory, perception, and other belief producing systems. Their purpose is to enable us to form true beliefs we wouldn't otherwise form. God provides them in order to enable us to have true beliefs on these extremely important topics. The beliefs they produce, furthermore, are in fact true, and they are often held with very considerable firmness. But then it follows, on the above account of knowledge, that they do indeed sometimes constitute knowledge. If so, however, reasoning from them in doing scholarship won't have the

---

7. Book III, ch. II, sec. iii.
8. Book III, ch. II, sec. vii.
9. Book III, ch. II, sec. vi.
10. Book III, ch. II, sec. vi.

slightest tendency to bring it about that the result of doing scholarship in that way is not knowledge. This objection, therefore, fails.

I turn to the other objection: the complaint that if as a scholar you start from what you know by way of faith, then your results will really be *theology* rather than philosophy or psychology or sociology or whatever. If you start from theological convictions in a given area — in understanding love, or humor, or aggression, for example — then any conclusions you come to will be dependent upon theological convictions and will themselves, in consequence, be theology. Theology in, theology out, as we may say, drawing on the computer *literati*. And while a theological understanding of these phenomena may indeed be desirable or necessary, it is still theology; it isn't psychology, or sociology or whatever. To have the latter, we must keep ourselves pure and unspotted from theology.

This is a common view; I have heard it urged at Calvin, and it is perhaps something like a semi-official position of our Catholic brothers and sisters. But here we must note that there are two quite different Christian traditions on this point: call them the Augustinian and Thomist traditions. According to the latter, there is theology, and there are the other sciences. The nontheological sciences are the province of reason; they contain what we can know by natural reason unaided by faith or special revelation. They concern general revelation as opposed to special revelation; and in pursuing them it is illegitimate to appeal to theology or to what one knows by way of faith. Of course the reason isn't that we don't need to know what we know by faith; theology is both important and necessary. But we also need the nontheological disciplines. According to the Augustinian tradition, by contrast, what we need and want, in studying a given area, is the best total understanding we can get: the question whether that best understanding should be called 'theology' on the one hand, or 'sociology' or 'psychology' or 'philosophy' on the other, is of secondary interest.

Well, *why* does the Thomist think it is important to have a psychology, for example, that is unspotted by theology? What is the value of such science, and why should we expend a portion of our intellectual resources on it? (After all, it is not as if the latter are unlimited.) The Thomist will answer that what we know by way of reason has for us an epistemic or epistemological or cognitive *advantage* over what we know by way of faith. What we grasp by faith, we know by way of *testimony;* we take it on the authority of someone else. If that someone else is God, then the belief in question is backed up by high authority indeed; objectively speaking, furthermore, it is also maximally certain. Still, we don't really *know* what we take on trust, what we take someone else's word for, even if that someone else is God himself. Or, if we say that we *do* know it, we don't have the highest and best form of knowledge of it. Consider, for example, the Pythagorean Theorem, or the proposition that there is no set of all sets, or Gödel's Theorem on the incompleteness of arithmetic, and consider two ways of believing it. In the first way, you believe it on the authority of your favorite mathematician, for example, who, however confused and unreliable he may be on other topics, is authoritative on ones like these. Then compare believing it by way of grasping, understanding the proof, and seeing for yourself that the theorem is not only true, but couldn't possibly be false. It makes good sense to say, with the Thomist, that in the second case the knowledge you have of that truth is better, more valuable, a higher kind of knowledge than in the first case. It is more like God's knowledge — God, after all, never has to take anybody's word for anything.

This reply has a sort of appeal; but I think the appeal is limited. For in most of the sciences we don't at all have the sort of knowledge we have of the Pythagorean Theorem or the Fundamental Theorem of the Calculus; we don't have anything like the sort of certainty we have in elementary logic and mathematics. Consider physics, for example. First, most of us who know anything about physics know what we know by way of taking someone else's word for it. How do I know that the velocity of light in a vacuum is 186,000 miles per second? I read it in a physics text, or heard it in a physics class, or saw it in an article in *Scientific American*. I certainly didn't measure the velocity of light myself, and I daresay the same is true for you. How do I know that there are experiments that favor relativity theory over Newtonian mechanics? The same way; I learned it in a physics class. I didn't myself perform those experiments involving muon decay or the rapid transport of cesium clocks. Indeed, the same goes for the physicists at Calvin: so far as I know, they haven't performed those experiments either; no doubt they read about them in a physics journal, and took the author's word for what he said. As a matter of fact, even those who *did* perform the experiments had to take a great deal on the authority of others: that the velocity of the plane transporting the cesium clock was in fact so and so, that the plane flew the relevant distance and the right course, and so on. Anyone who makes an advance in physics and discovers something new obviously takes an enormous amount on the say so of others — for example, how the earlier experiments relevant to his project turned out. According to the Thomist, the difference in noetic value between theology and the nontheological sciences is said to be that in the former we must rely on the testimony of others (even if on such an other as God himself), while in the latter we have the level of knowledge that goes with simply seeing that some proposition is true. This difference, however, is a difference that applies very narrowly — only to elementary mathematics and logic, and perhaps to such obvious perceptual beliefs as that, e.g., the pointer is now between the 4 and the 5 on the dial.

My sympathies, therefore, lie with the Augustinian view; I am at best suspicious of the epistemic benefits claimed on behalf of science untainted by theology. But perhaps there is less separation here than meets the eye: I wish to make an irenic proposal. Think again about those theoretical or interpretative sciences: philosophy, anthropology, psychology, sociology, economics, and others. The best way to do these sciences, says the Augustinian, is to use all that we know, including what we know by way of faith or revelation; according to the Thomist the way to proceed is to bracket what we know by faith and appeal only to premises we know by reason. But Thomist and Augustinian agree that the Christian community badly needs that fuller understanding of these phenomena. So suppose we think of the matter as follows. There are the deliverances of faith: call them 'F'; there is also the result of thinking about the subject matter of science, appealing to the deliverances of faith as well as to the deliverances of reason: call that 'FS.' Thomist and Augustinian concur that we need FS; but the Thomist adds that FS is really theology rather than sociology or psychology or whatever. But now consider the conditional or hypothetical proposition *if F then FS:* the proposition that says what the implications of the faith *are* for the discipline in question. Perhaps this proposition *if F then FS* is best thought of as a large number of propositions, each explicating the bearing of the faith on some part of the discipline in question — or perhaps we should think of it as one enormously long proposition. Either way, both parties to the discussion will agree that this proposition is not *itself* among the deliverances of faith; we learn it, or know it, by reason, not by faith. It is by reason rather than faith that we see what the bearing of the faith is on psychology; it is by reason rather than faith that we see how the scriptural teaching on love, or sin, or morality bears on what we study in psychology or anthropology or sociology.

So both sides agree, in fact, insist that we, the Christian community, need to know how the faith bears on these areas. And both agree that working at these conditionals is a matter, not of faith and theology, but of reason and the relevant science. Further, both agree that we Christians will *assert* the consequents of these conditionals; that is, we will assert the result of seeing how faith applies to the domain in question. The two sides differ only in this: according to the Thomist, but not the Augustinian, when you assert the consequent of the conditional you are really doing theology rather than the science in question. Well, why shouldn't the Augustinian peaceably concede the point, at least for present purposes? Perhaps it doesn't greatly matter whether we say that asserting those consequents is theology, on the one hand, or philosophy, psychology or economics or whatever on the other. What *is* of great importance, at present, is that we work at discovering the conditionals. And working at those conditionals is not doing theology: it clearly falls within the domain of the nontheological disciplines involved. It is not the theologian who is most appropriately trained and qualified for work on these conditionals; it is instead the psychologist, historian, biologist, economist, sociologist, literary critic, and so on. Here Augustinian and Thomist can agree. They can agree on the importance, the enormous importance of this work for the spiritual and intellectual health of the Christian community, and they can agree that in working at these conditionals we are doing nontheological science rather than theology.

By way of conclusion, then: I wish to add my voice to the voices of those who call for Christian scholarship. This scholarship has at least two important parts: the criticism I mentioned last time, but also the positive application of what we know by faith to the central areas of science and scholarship. We all realize, of course, that both of these, but in particular the second, are matters of uncommon difficulty. We Christians who go on to become professional scientists and scholars attend 20th-century graduate schools and universities (we don't have much by way of an alternative). But the kind of scholarship of which I speak gets short shrift at these universities. Questions about the bearing of Christianity on economics or psychology or literary theory are not high on the agenda there. At the major universities, these topics are not given pride of place; they are given no place at all. There are no courses in psychology or sociology at Oxford entitled "Aggression and the Christian View of Man." At Yale they don't teach a course called "Deconstruction from a Christian Perspective" (and not because they aren't interested in deconstruction). It is very difficult to write a dissertation on topics such as these. They don't form a part of the ordinary day to day work done in these disciplines in the major universities; the entire structure of contemporary university life is such as to discourage serious work on them. A student who wants to think seriously about these topics is very much on her own; more than that, she is likely to be thought weird, peculiar, marginal, out of the mainstream. Scholarship is an intensely social activity; we learn our craft from our elders and mentors; but we can't learn how to do Christian scholarship from our mentors at these universities. That is why it is of first importance that there be Christian universities, institutions where these questions do take pride of place, and where a student can think about the bearing of Christianity on her disciplines in a regular and institutionally sanctioned way.

So the Christian community needs to work on these questions. *We* need to work on them; for the Reformed community is perhaps uniquely well-equipped by way of tradition and training to offer leadership here. That means that a genuinely serious responsibility falls squarely on our shoulders. I say we must get on with it. I commend to you this task of Christian scholarship.

Denominations Near Century's End

MARTIN E. MARTY

Contents

Introduction

The opportunity to deliver lectures with the honoree present is rare, but I was able to take advantage of one with the Henry Stob Lectures. As a long-time reader of journals emanating from Calvin College and Seminary and from the Reformed orbit at Grand Rapids, and a teacher of alumni of the Calvin schools, I of course had long known the name and work of Professor Stob. But there was special warmth in this occasion with its richly personal dimension.

I like to lecture on assigned topics, and accepted the request that I deal with denominationalism today. In one sense, historians of American religion, or theologians who deal with the American religious experience, are always dealing with denominations and denominationalism. But for some years we have not isolated them as topics, and they were being pushed off to the margins. It will be clear at once that in these lectures I picture that they are not going away, but are assuming new roles. Let me keep you in suspense for just a page or two, where, after this introduction, I get to elaborate on the pros and the cons, the yeses and the nos of this modern and durable form of religious life. It is a pleasure to foresee the possibility of the lectures having an influence beyond the immediate occasion of their delivery.

It is my practice not to read a manuscript or transcribe from a tape; this is instead an original elaboration of the lecture themes, but one which tries to keep some sense of the informal and oral style.

FIRST LECTURE

Denominations:
We Cannot Get Along with Them

In a secular culture, religion may not count for much. In the religious sub-cultures Christianity may not mean everything. Within Christian cultural circles, "the organized church" receives criticism and suffers neglect. In the maze of organizations which make up the church the denomination is per-haps the most scorned.

On the other hand, to the believing and practicing Christian, the de-nomination presents itself as an almost inescapable and pervasive reality. Second to the local congregation, it is the most manifest form of the orga-nized church. Taken together, denominations remain vivid to any who own a phone book with Yellow Pages or who want to choose which clustering of congregations, which more-than-local part of the organized church should serve as an instrument for expressing their faith. And the mix of denomina-tions confronts the secular culture and demands that it be reconceived as a pluralist culture, in which religious and non-religious elements mix.

Denominations somehow matter.

The scholar who accepts an invitation to help Christians update their thinking about the denomination will not run out of subject matter. The *World Christian Encyclopedia* presses this reality with statistics. Despite eight decades of ecumenical activity designed to bring denominations into concord or even to lead to mergers, the growth in numbers of denomina-tions is so rapid that, to the eye of the self-styled ecumaniac, it has to look cancerous. In 1900 there were 1,900 denominations, but in 1980 there were 20,780 and the encyclopedists projected 22,190 by 1985. "The present nett [*sic*] increase is 270 new denominations each year (5 new ones a week)."

The encyclopedia editors, who like to tabulate growth in Christian statistics, are uneasy about this part of the growth. They continue: "In many countries [denominational growth] produces serious overlapping, competition, rivalries, clashes, violence, and even lawsuits and protracted litigation. The confusion and even scandal that this vast fragmentation generates in non-Christian lands, or in the minds of non-Christians anywhere," said the authors, was best illustrated in a reproduced cartoon in which the cartoon figure contrasted Jesus' "most important message," "love one another," with the reality of 20,780 distinct denominations: "and they all hate each other."

The *World Christian Encyclopedia,* whose editors are marvellous categorizers, do some classifying to diminish the scandal somewhat. For example, they find that the 20,780 distinct denominations can be conceived in "156 major ecclesiastical traditions." The four largest of these, for example, are Latin-rite Roman Catholics, Slavonic-rite Orthodox, Protestants in united churches formed as unions of several older Protestant traditions, and Pentecostals in Pentecostal denominations. To illustrate further what is meant by "ecclesiastical traditions," the editors break Protestant into "united," "Lutheran," "Reformed," "Baptist," "Methodist," "Pentecostal," Disciples," "Holiness," and the like. And they make one further effort at reducing the maze of denominationalism by speaking of "seven major blocs" of organized Christianity. Here alongside "Protestant" and "Orthodox" and others are "Non-White Indigenous," "Anglican," "Marginal Protestant," and more.[1]

One cannot do away with denominations by clustering and classifying them into traditions and blocs. Theirs remain the names by which Christians are called and they do seem to organize much of extra-parochial life. But if they grow in numbers and seem vital, in the United States at least it is possible for responsible scholars also to speak of "The Declining Significance of Denominationalism." The most noted sociologist of religion in the middle generation, Robert Wuthnow, does that in a worthily influential book on the restructuring of American religion. His fifth chapter is entirely devoted to this theme of declining denominational significance. So consistent and cogent is his comment on the evidence that one does best to convince readers that they must familiarize themselves with

1. David B. Barrett, ed., *World Christian Encyclopedia* (New York: Oxford, 1982), pp. 15-17.

Wuthnow's analysis. But we owe the present reader at least a broad outline of his argument.

First Wuthnow pointed to the decline of "satanic ideologies." That is, a half century ago, believers fought other believers across denominational lines, using biblical vocabularies to identify those of other denominations in demonic terms. That kind of pointing and naming is rare, meaningless, and without effect in America today. Second, while there have been few mergers across the lines of "traditions" (in the encyclopedists' designation), mergers have occurred and the rhetoric supporting the merging impulse has undercut old ideologies of support for denominationalism. Third, "denominational switching" occurs with increasing frequency, and that practice undercuts the loyalties people once showed to denominations. Pollsters also turn up evidence that Christians value denominations less today than they did decades ago. Wuthnow then cites "the growth of special purpose groups" as an agency of rivalry to denominations. The issue before us will be not only what the "decline" means, but whether we might not as well speak of "change," since denominations thrive even if they do not mean to people what they did decades ago.[2]

Denomination: it is and was intended to be a "nothing" word, designed to express social realities having little to do with anything in biblical or Christian traditional witness. The money in one's pocket comes in different "denominations," but that fact means much less than whether it says "one" or "twenty" or "one hundred" on each bill. You have said little when you merely announce that money or religion comes in denominations. What one does with that concept and reality makes all the difference.

Why care about denominations now? The historian has no choice. Again, this caring takes on a different character than once it did. There was a time when denominationalism provided the most convenient and perhaps most helpful way of accounting for religious trends through American history. But that is no longer the case, as I have tried to demonstrate in earlier work. The denominational was only second in a sequence of modes available for mapping American religion. The first reflected territorial and theological situations in predenominational colonial America. Then followed the prevalent denominational form. One no longer by

2. Robert Wuthnow, *The Restructuring of American Religion: Society and Faith Since World War II* (Princeton: Princeton University Press, 1988), chaps. 5 and 6, pp. 71-99, 100-132.

then would answer "Who am I?" so much by reference to Plymouth or Virginia and its single religious matrix. One then answered, say, "I am a Presbyterian," or "I am a Cumberland Presbyterian." Today, however, different behavioral patterns provide different clusterings. Increasingly people identify themselves as "mainline," "evangelical and fundamentalist," "pentecostal-charismatic," or by various civil, ethnic, or "new" religious references. Denominationalism therefore has declined as an identifying factor. But, still, denominations remained in numbers as before, if not greater than before, and one could not not reckon without them in any historical or sociological accountings.[3]

The presence of the denomination represents part of Christianity's centuries-long struggle for forms. In today's culture that struggle occurs under a shadow of anti-institutionalism. Many religious seekers ignore or are indifferent to denominations, or find them dysfunctional. The denomination, among all the major Christian forms, probably has the fewest defenders. One can always speak up for the local church or the parachurch — Wuthnow's "special purpose groups" — with some measure of confidence. To advocate denominations and denominationalism always carries with it some stigma, some need for justification.

This is not the place to present full evidence for this observation, but it is valid to do some pointing for the sake of the do-it-yourself discerner of trends. One does well to note how in the culture at large the denomination, along with the rest of institutional religion, is seen as a kind of kindergarten of the faith. In accountings of the life of celebrities who are perceived to be religious, one expects to see near the end of conventional biographical sketches a line something like: "Of course, Ms. Christian no longer attends a denominational church . . ." or "Of course, Mr. Christian, brought up in the Suchandsuch denomination, is now on a pilgrimage of his own and does not find it useful." Again, however: despite such dismissals of their potency and promise, denominations remain. We address ourselves to their meaning.

A strange word, this "nothing" term "denomination." Church, sect, cult: these have weight and fiber. They demand further inquiry and become fighting words. There lies, there *merely* lies, "denomination." Analyses of biblical metaphors and images for the church run into the dozens

3. Martin E. Marty, *A Nation of Behavers* (Chicago: University of Chicago, 1976), pp. 3ff.

and scores; they tend to be dynamic: the vine, the people of God, the new Israel, the citizens of heaven, the pilgrims. Again, there, extrabiblically, lies the denomination. In the classic dictionaries denomination means first "naming" and "designation." Far down the page of listings there is at last reference to denomination as a "class": thus, "a collection of individuals classed together under some name; now almost always *spec.* a religious sect or body having a common faith and organization, and designated by a distinctive name." Even in the dictionary, among all the "ert" words, it is inert. There it lies.

Scholars argue over the origination of the religious usage. While the Oxford English Dictionary, as the first modern identification, cites Benjamin Franklin in 1788, historian Winthrop Hudson has traced the roots of the term and its usefulness to seventeenth-century England and its free church Independent divines. Hudson's classic essay shows that the earliest users had ecumenical intentions and that they did not intend, with it, to be more divisive than were earlier devisers of concepts of Christian polity.[4]

The United States was the natural environment for the development of the denominational concept. No historian has dealt with the context as creatively as did Sidney E. Mead in another essay that has to be called classic. Mead pointed to several features that went into denominationalism. First — and here he countered Hudson — was a "sectarian" tendency in which each denomination tried to justify its peculiar interpretations and practices. Next, denominations grew in response to voluntaryism, the system of churching based on "choice" as a corollary and result of religious freedom. Third, denominations were channels for mission. The Protestant dimension was evident in Mead's fourth element in the impulse: revivalism, which fed denominations and which they used to extend and enliven themselves. Fifth, and here a Meadian bias came into play: denominations became enemies of the reasoned Enlightenment and made their case for a "flight from 'Reason'" by religious people through this form. Finally, denominations legitimated competition. In sum: denominations were purposive — far cries from the theological no-

---

4. Winthrop Hudson, "Denominationalism as a Basis for Ecumenicity: A Seventeenth Century Conception," in Russell E. Richey, ed., *Denominationalism* (Nashville: Abingdon, 1977), pp. 21-44; the essay first appeared in *Church History* #24 (1955), pp. 32-50. The Richey book collects important essays on denominationalism.

tion that they were mutually complementary elements in the Body of Christ.[5]

It is time to give my own accounting. First, the concept of the denomination makes possible the "bracketing," the "suspending of judgment" about theological verity and quality while speaking of religious organizations. It allows for the committed believer, the bystander, and the enemy of religion alike to see all religious partisans on the same level playing field. Without such a concept all analyses would be inclined to be judgmental. The typical accounting in the contest of theological biases would classify religion in two categories: *our* truth and all the *other* falsehoods. With denominations, however, one can speak without bias and while withholding judgment. The term has achieved a splendid neutrality. True, some Roman or Anglican Catholics have always protested the term, arguing that they are not denominations with all the rest. But common sense, common usage, common people, common sociologists, and common lexicographers take care of that: they say that everyone in a religious organization of a certain sort is in a denomination.

Despite occasional "high ch rch" grumblings, most denominationalists have accepted denominationalism, even if it does not represent ideal circumstances or by itself make room for theological weight. However grudgingly, even "Churches of Christ" have to appear among the denominations in the *Yearbook of American and Canadian Churches*. They may describe themselves as made up of "autonomous congregations" without "central offices or officers"; the statisticians and classifiers pay no attention to their claim. They become a denomination among the denominations, albeit with an idiosyncrasy. So must and does the "Community Churches, International Council of . . ."[6] When bodies apply for 501 (c) 3 status for purposes of tax exemption, they know that the I.R.S. or state licensing bodies will list their Churches of Christ or Community Church, their Catholic or Anglican cluster, under "denominations."

Now we should elaborate on the general motifs which Mead summarized, and set them in a new context for present purposes. The grand reason behind the invention of the denomination was part of the eighteenth-

5. Sidney E. Mead, "Denominationalism: The Shape of Protestantism in America," in Richey, pp. 70-105; the essay first appeared in *Church History* #23 (1954), pp. 291-320.

6. See Constant H. Jacquet, ed., *Yearbook of American and Canadian Churches* (Nashville: Abingdon, dated annually).

century revolution in America (and elsewhere) which set churches on courses *independent* of the state. It was, in other words, an innovation of early post-Constantinian Christianity. From the fourth to the eighteenth century, wherever there were Christians they tended to "run the show," to be established, to dominate. As such the dominator was not a denomination. Others could possibly survive as dissidents or dissenters, though some were killed and many were driven to the hills. It was always clear that one group was "in" and the others were "out." With separation of church and state and religious freedom, this situation changed. No one was to be more "in" or "out" than any other in a legal sense. Hence: denomination.

Second, the grand corollary: in Constantinian Christianity believers were ordinarily seen as fated to be in the body which dominated. Religion "went with the territory." Orthodox, Catholic, and then established Protestants deprived people of *choice*. But with modernity came "the freedom to choose." Capitalism meant just that: rational choice should come into play. Less important than predestiny of class — whether of landholder, peasant, noble, or bourgeois — now choice was more determinative. Shall I invest in rum or shipping or land or slaves? So with religion: I am free to choose. Shall I stay with establishment or sign up with the person on horseback who has excited me revivalistically and is setting up competitive shop?

Competitive: that is the next key. In a sense modernity compels believers to see themselves and others, converted or not, in a market situation. Denominations developed distinctive patterns to reach various elements in the markets. Ecumenists argued that evangelism and mission would be speeded along if the offense of denominational competition were minimized. Antiecumenicals had statistics on their side: denominationalists who repudiated others or who willingly accepted the terms of competition prospered because they tailored their products for the market needs. They could not do this only locally, and the denomination provided a larger structure.

Denominations, next, were and are *purposive*. They may have organized for revivalist purposes, or to send missionaries, publish, train seminarians. They might even be creedal and confessional, but they are likely to advertise their creedal integrity as a basis for their continuing statement of purpose.

Integrity: locked into that paragraph is the seed of the next. The concept of the denomination allowed for the assertion and experience of integrity. The outsider might say that the presence of so many denominations simply promoted relativism and indifference. The denominationalist, however, in good faith could say that whatever others thought of them, they could use the denominational exoskeleton as a form into which they could grow independently and on their own terms.

Often I have used the past tense in these paragraphs while describing how and why denominations formed and what their functions were. That tense plays into the theme of "declining significance" or it certainly reinforces the notion of change — as it was intended to. To speak thus can be liberating. Denominations, now going through change, may some day be replaced by another form. It is good to be reminded that the Church of Jesus Christ does not depend upon them. From the year thirty until about 1788 it did not have them to depend upon. The denomination, like the competitive congregation-system, the Sunday School, the mission movement, the voluntary society pattern, and even early ecumenism, is an invention of early industrial and democratic Western life. All these social forms, now troubled, were invented between around 1750 and 1850. They can come and go with their age. The point, however, is that denominations are not "going." They are simply changing.

Denominations: there they are. And our first judgment, to be apparently at least partly contradicted by our second one is that "we" — society, culture, religious people, Christians in the church — cannot get along *with* them. First comes what we might call the culture critique. The word announced in the culture is that denominations are sectarian and thus to be seen as malign, as representative of atrophied imaginations. To be sectarian is to be self-centered, petty, self-seeking. Denominations by and large may have left this aspect behind, but not in public perception. Philanthropic foundations, for example, devote only about one percent of their grants to religious institutions in the broadest sense — even if these command the loyalties of three out of five Americans and keep two out of five Americans very busy, often in basic human service realms. Ask executives of foundations why they are so wary of granting anything to religion and they will cite sectarian competition. "If we do something for Baptists, we will win the disdain of Methodists." Little empirical warrant for such a claim is available; it belongs to folklore or the language of evasion. Grant a million dollars to Baptists and they will faint, as will the Methodists. But those left out by a foundation, it turns out, will not put energy into attacking the grantor. The denomination as such has had poor public relations. It may *not* be sectarian but is often dismissed as such.

A corollary to that first perception is that one sees the denomination representing a very delicate zone which wise and civil people must avoid. Citizens of the United States may hold favorable attitudes toward spirituality — the current vogue word — or religion, the enduring vague word. Spirituality may be important in their personal searches or as part of their private lives. But they resent or are cautious about encroaching on the territorial zones of anything so "thick" as a denomination. They may misunderstand or misrepresent the denomination and thus suffer for having evoked it.

Third, the denomination looks simply irrelevant. After the time of disestablishment and the separation of church and state, Americans came to keep formal religion at a distance: religion, after all, "is a private affair," in such language and practice. Some constitutional scholars argue that the way the founders of the nation solved the religious problem was *not* to solve it, but to keep it at a distance, to push it aside, to place it in safe channels where it could have neither positive or negative effects on what really mattered in politics, economics, or social life. But there, in that scene of private religion, the denomination does take up public space and make public claims. It deals with taxing bodies, selective service for the military, advertisers, public relations, and the like, and thus somehow looks less "pure" than is the religion that cannot make it into the Yellow Pages because it is individualized and private.

If such criticisms as those three categorical ones come from the public, the church catholic has theological reasons for finding it difficult to get along with denominations. If the church ever had a clear, positive, theological rationale for them, such an apologia has largely been unheard or forgotten and maybe even displaced. For example, there is no biblical warrant or base, none at all, for an emergence like the denomination. There are plenty of depictions of and injunctions toward local fellowships, which are analogues to today's congregations. There is also a deep grounding for the *una sancta,* the one, holy, catholic, and apostolic church as witnessed to in the creeds and as chartered in Pauline and other New Testament writings. But there is no trace of a clear biblical charter for the denomination.

Still, Christians have developed any number of legitimacies, on theological grounds, for realities that have no explicit biblical base — including the fundamental depiction of God as Trinity. Where, then, is the denomination? The church is designed to be one and whole, and here are differences, hardened into organizational forms. Classifications enter: the

175

church at Ephesus, Laodicea, and Corinth; or Jew versus Greek, male versus female, bond versus free — but all one in Christ. The ecumenical vision gets all the biblical points. In the Fourth Gospel Jesus is overheard praying (John 17:23 NRSV) "that they may become completely one." In the letters of Paul anything that anticipates the denomination would have to be seen as "of the flesh." One side of denominational existence has to be seen as an expression of what 1 Corinthians 3:3-4 (NRSV) talked about: "you are still of the flesh. For as long as there is jealousy and quarreling among you, are you not of the flesh, and behaving according to human inclinations . . . [Are you] not merely human?" Of course, all forms of the church are "earthen vessels," but the root of denominationalism lies in the structuring of difference and, originally, of division.

The churches by and large have acknowledged that between 1910 and 1965 the vast majority of them, Catholic, Orthodox, and Protestant, turned toward ecumenical rationales. Even the evangelical-pentecostal and sometimes the fundamentalist flanks move toward the ecumenical rationale, if sometimes on grounds impossible for others to grasp. Some began to favor organic union and others moved toward federation. This latter, the conciliar form, permitted denominational autonomy, but still indicated that common activity or the transcendence of autonomy was a higher value. It has been almost a century since serious people tried to come up with fresh theological rationales for the denomination in an ecumenical age.

If rationales were voiced, they may have been legitimate but tended to be subtheological. Thus there can be a case for denominations on grounds of efficiency: that is, they can do some things that other agencies cannot, and they can do them with a minimum of fuss (publishing, running of theological schools, and the like). Or one can make a case that parallels the one for religious freedom in general: the denomination allows people to make a choice. At best, there can be argument for the denomination as a protector of integrity: even though no one outside my group may agree with its theology, the denomination assures that we in it are not second class religious citizens, since others will recognize through our adherence that we take faith and practice seriously. All that is probably true, but still the denomination seems to be a vestige, like the vermiform appendix in humans or the electoral college in politics.

The churches local get the energies and the rationales in our own time. They too suffer and merit critiques of all sorts. But they are so vivid and rich in impulse that most Christians will put their commitments to work through such gatherings. G. K. Chesterton has said somewhere that to be real something must be local. The congregation is thus real while the denomination is less so.

On local congregational grounds, the denomination looks remote and secondary. This does not mean that members reject it; they simply give priority to something else. A personal illustration will speak to and for most congregational members. A couple of years ago a religious magazine wanted to feature my own ecclesiastical tradition (I am using Barrett's term), the Lutheran, along with several denominations of Lutherans, to one of which I belong. Would I be interviewed? Yes, I agreed, if my pastor could be there to provide a reality check. Why that? Because most surveys depend upon theologians, sociologists, bureaucrats, and the like. Fine. We sat on a porch and the interview began.

First: "I understand that there is a $15.9 million shortfall in your denomination's intake this year. The reason I have been given for this is that the lay people are up in arms. They give money to the denomination, for example, for its hunger program. They want to feed the hungry. But some of those funds go into advocacy, into lobbying for certain laws that have to deal with hunger. And they don't want the church to be in politics." I turned to my pastor, who showed an expression of bemusement and amusement: not at all! He is not only pastor of a typical parish but dean of thirty-six churches, from inner city to outer suburb, in the Chicago Metropolitan Synod slicing of the pie. True the congregations had not "come through" for the denomination. Why?

Local realism: inflation increased by, say, 6%; member giving in these parishes went up by 9%. But medical insurance for staffs rose by, say again, 20% in a year. Heating and lighting costs rose higher than inflation or increased giving levels. The churches in this zone are aging. One congregation needed thousands for a roof and another some thousands for a boiler. All may have liked to do more for benevolences and all could have and should have. But in the scale of present stewardship and its boundaries, the local prevailed.

What about the notion of protest against the denomination? It would have been wonderful, my pastor implied, if one lay person or one pastor somewhere had made a point of that. Probably not one of them had heard of it; most of them simply cared that feeding and advocacy were going on; that the church cared about the hungry, as did they. But they did not follow the details of denominational life and did not listen to the theopolitical advocates on either side who fought these battles. This is not to say that there was no potential for criticism or reason to make it: denominational people can on occasion be reached positively and negatively. But when trying to account for religious response, it always pays to look to the local, first.

Criticism does come. Conventionally it takes patterns like these: the denomination *is* remote and can be impervious. Curiously, people in many denominations refer to their headquarters as numbers: "475"; in our case, "8765," indicating the mailing addresses. People care about whether their Jetta or Honda or Chevrolet works. Only an elite of dealers and editors of auto magazines or financial reviews care about how auto plants in Germany, Japan, or Detroit run their daily affairs. The denomination is often rightly seen as unresponsive. It includes many voices, many interests, many elites, and they cannot respond equally to everything that an interest group sets forth.

Denominations appear to be demanding. Most of all, they seem to want money to run their programs, and their demands are more vivid and visible than are the services performed for each congregation and each congregant. And there are also legitimate expressions of concern over the inevitable bureaucratization of the denomination, which was born as a bureaucracy and born to be bureaucratic. Max Weber spoke of the "iron cage" that developed in the world of modern organizations where rationalities of purposive-instrumental sorts prevailed. The denomination can hardly be organized on other than bureaucratic principles, and must suffer categorically with other bureaucracies.

Over against bureaucratic rationality, most practicing Christians today seek personal, responsive, emotionally rich agencies, which their congregation or certain parachurch forms embody. They want I-Thou relations and the denomination seems to present them only with I-It patterns. This is, as Arnold Gehlen speaks of it, "the age of the person," and the denomination makes it "the age of the organization." It cannot be flexible enough to meet changing needs, whereas the parachurch is poised to shift constantly, because it has a single focus and is free to be market conscious.

If the culture, the church catholic, and the church local are critical of the denomination, so is the church personal: what does the denomination accomplish to enhance *my* pilgrimage? it is asked. In the iron caged modern (or postmodern, if we must) situation, people have chosen a spiritual route which is often devoted to interior life. It is hard for the denomination to enrich this devotion. Charismatic individuals, television figures, retreat leaders, bestselling authors, and pastors can contribute, but denominations rarely do.

Today the metaphor for this personal search is often "pilgrimage," a notion rich in imagery for the seekers. But the denomination just lies there, static, unbudging. Today a kind of "pick and choose" cafeteria Christianity is popular, but the denomination presents itself in a kind of "take it all" way. Today many serious Christians want to be challenged to find higher, if personalized, norms for their Christian life. The denomination must make such a broad appeal that its challenges will look *pro forma*, generalized, incapable of being rendered dramatic.

On all these terms — and each reader can personalize the critique — it becomes clear that "we cannot live *with* the denomination." It is declining, dysfunctional, and maybe should be superseded. A great theological relativization has gone into the subject, so it is harder than ever to give one's heart to it. Some Christians stand in a prophetic, Amos-like stance: the denomination is the unbudging, vulnerable form that qualifies for being scorned as an agent for the "solemn assemblies" that God despises. Most of us, however, are not prophets, but critics. We lack charisma or credentials for being prophetic, but we are asked to make judgments.

At best, it would seem, we have to accept the denomination grudgingly and live with it. The best deal possible, we might be counselled, is to live with this version of the "earthen vessel" following the lines of the apostle Paul's famed "as if not" *(hoos mee)* dialectic of 1 Corinthians 7:29-31. In this unsettled, temporary time, the counsel is in place: "the appointed time has grown short." Let "those who mourn [live] as though they were not mourning, and those who rejoice as though they were not rejoicing, and those who buy as though they had no possessions, and those who deal with the world as though they had no dealings with it. For the present form of this world is passing away."

Let those who live in the denomination live "as if not." That is good theological advice, so far as it goes. But more can be said.

SECOND LECTURE

Denominations: We Cannot
Get Along without Them

While denominations merit and receive criticism to such an extent that we might say "we cannot get along with them," it is also true that to the serious Christian of today, "we cannot get along *without* them" — or their equivalent. There is no reason here to insist that the name or exactly the present form must survive; that would represent an out of place "morphological fundamentalism." But we have pictured a kind of structural or functional place in Christianity which the denomination has filled. That place substantially remains, however much improvisation or innovation goes on, thanks to the pressures of modernity and the calls for adaptation. So some partly new form might come along; one is tempted to say, it *must* come along, if there is to be the creation of instrumentalities to address new needs. But this something, I will argue, would be in many respects like the denomination.

To the Platonist or the purist, to spend so much energy on the *morphee*, the form this or that Christian expression takes, may seem to be a departure from high and holy things. Yet Christianity is an incarnational faith, with physical expressions. One needs, it has been said, at least "a loaf of bread, a bottle of wine, and a river" for celebrating its mysteries. Its vessel may be earthen, but it needs a vessel and is not ashamed of its earthenness. So we see the denomination as a physical form with which Christians reckon.

The denomination will turn out to be part of a very complex ecosystem in the culture and the faith. This struck me as I wrote a history of America between the two World Wars. I had intended to contribute to the

180

school of thought which saw the denomination to be irrelevant and dysfunctional. One could write on the high dramas of religious conflict without focusing on the denomination. The battles of that time had to do with birth control, woman suffrage, the Red Scare, immigration restriction, the Al Smith campaign, creating an international order of peace, the Ku Klux Klan, religious rationales for and against the New Deal, Father Coughlin, Huey Long, the American Communist Party, pacifism, and the like.

In that set of interests, where did denominations fit? Protestants fought Catholics, Christians fought Jews, believers fought secularists, but without much denominational passion. Then finally I noticed that most of these battles did divide the denominations, or pit them against each other. And there were also more explicitly theological battles, as between fundamentalists and modernists and then between liberals and realists in Protestantism. People fought for control of the Baptist, Presbyterian, Disciples, Episcopalian and — it came to me later — Mennonite and Lutheran and other denominations. It was easy to take lightly these battles over evolution and biblical criticism, over the bobbing of hair and the carrying of hip flasks, to see them as tempests in small teapots, as bubblings up in meandering streamlets alongside the great torrents of national life.

Yet what the people of 1925 fought over in denominations was part of that complex ecosystem. Sooner or later their concerns became a part of other elements in the political and social system. By the time of the American election campaigns of the 1970s, great political parties mobilized around issues raised precisely by fundamentalists years before. American fundamentalism had a patent on dispensationalism and premillennialism, on views of the second coming of Christ and the part political Israel would play. There were in the late 1970s some efforts to bomb the Temple Mount in Israel, efforts encouraged by Texas Baptists and enacted by Jewish denominationalists in Jerusalem. World War III could have ensued. The roots of this lay in denominational battles waged more than a half century earlier in America. One could provide many illustrations of this process.

So the cynic in me who would have dismissed denominations as dysfunctional was taught instead to look for their new functions. It is in that spirit that I turn from the "we cannot live *with* them" approach to a set of discernments of why "we" — America at large and the believing and practicing believers within it — cannot get along *without* denominations.

First, the "something like denominations" motif needs addressing. There will be "something like" denominations in the unfolding of society in immediate futures. This projection implies that there will *be* institutions, organized religion. We might define an institution as anything that two people would like to have endure for two seconds. It is possible for a solitary person to have an instantaneous experience of what William James would call "religion." But any perpetuation beyond that single individual in a single moment demands an institution of some sort. What shall it be?

We argue, second, that while any number of institutions can and will develop, they will not fill out the ecosystem unless these emergences make some room for the denomination or its equivalent. Curiously, one reason for this envisionment is that most of the denomination's competitors or accompaniments are naturally *too* functional to fulfill all the messy purposes of Christianity. Some will cater too much to the momentary needs of consumers, shoppers, and pick-and-choose Christians, to survive their fads and eccentricities. Others may lack the synoptic aspect of denominations, however undramatic they seem. I recall once reading a critique of books on theologies of hope, defined as theologies of politics and revolution. The reviewer said that these books represented but limited interest. They were written by middle class men with at least *some* measure of power, tenured people with some security. The authors could afford to hope. But the reviewer was interested in this writing only if the theological hope turned out to be Christian in an expansive sense. It dared not depend only on human inventiveness and rationality or purpose. Such hope must give expression to God's intervention in history, as in the work of Jesus Christ — and thus be able to address needs of people in the nursing home, the cancer ward, the chamber of the despairing. Alternatives to denominations embody the neatness that goes with ministering to some needs and talents, but are likely to lack the inclusiveness to which Christian hope calls people.

In this sense, one function of the denomination is to blunt or diffuse the particularities of parachurches and other emergent rivals to denominations. Those who share the lecturers' circuit often compare notes. A common complaint is that after a lecture on an announced topic in which the speaker has some expertise, questioners will respond with a theme that the speaker has overlooked. "Why did you not apply this to the Koreans or Native Americans?" "Why did you devote yourself only to the sexually straight world?" Why were you Euroamerican?" The parachurches are asked specific questions about the fulfillments of their narrow, focused, however vital functions. The denomination is committed "across the board," if in a more diffuse way. One does not leave out so much when dealing with the denominations.

The third thing to say about the denominations in an incarnational world, about such denominations which serve because they *are* messy, is that support of them is a good distraction from triumphalism. Some experiments in the church "work," if at the expense of other loyalties. Charismatic movements work. Church growth movements work. Televangelism empires work(ed). Best-selling authors' tours work. Gimmicks work. Many of them draw people off existing frameworks into newly promoted ones. In most cases, apologists are tempted to say, and do say, that one can tell the truth of what they are about because the movements are successful. If they were not successful, God would not be blessing them and the reading of manifest needs would have been wrong. Never mind that the argument about growth also works in the cases of demonic powers or the forces of trivia and kitsch. One would not likely say that the enormously popular soap opera is a "true" and God-pleasing portrait of reality simply because it draws well. Yet in the Christian world the triumphalist spirit keeps appearing and reappearing.

In America, however, triumphalism seldom gets put to work in the denominational framework. It is true that now and then a denomination will have its inning. Not many years ago Christian Science was "fast growing," but then experienced decline. The Southern Baptist Convention still prospers, but also at enormous internal cost and with public scandal. The Assemblies of God have their decades, much as Methodism had its own around the turn of the century. But if one reckons with the more than two hundred denominations in the *Yearbook,* not more than twenty could draw the public relations experts to make a credible case that they are "winning" against the world, death, devil, and the flesh. In other words, the denomination with its mix of health and unhealth represents realism appropriate to the Christian norms. The existence of the denomination is a bracing reminder of finitude, contingency, and transience, characterizations of mortal life and all human productions, though these are often forgotten in moments of Christian triumphalism.

If the denomination cannot be easily used for bragging or for promoting distorted views of Christian success, it can serve as a reminder that the church needs constant experiment. Alternatives to it are not always so reformable. In the 1950s there were many claims that "viable emerging structures" were developing to replace congregations and denominations.

Most of them, as we said then, were not viable, never fully emerged, and were structurally unsound. They rarely outlasted the charismatic founders for whom such extravagant claims were made. They have disappeared with the snows of yesteryear. Yet congregations and denominations keep surviving and adapting, never with enough experimental display but, on this bleak landscape, some is better than none.

The next contribution to a rationale for the denomination is the manifest need for *some* form smaller than the ecumenical church, as we shall say at more length later. The local congregation can be so demanding, exacting, and promising that it can become a subject of idolatry and obsession. The local congregation is not simply a microcosm of the whole church in its whole mission. It rarely permits the development of empathy for Christians in situations which differ vastly from those of each congregation. Denominations come in here: they can serve as reminders and agents of something larger.

In a still underattended-to essay and theme, Catholic theologian Gregory Baum proposed almost thirty years ago an ecumenical model which I believe has room in it for the denomination. Baum advocated that we see the church catholic neither on the pattern of autonomy and chaos, as in pure congregationalism and individualism, nor on the opposite pattern of hierarchy and authoritarian order, as in traditional Catholicism. Instead the catholic church, he says, is and is to be seen as "a family of apostolic churches." He wrote: "The unity in a family is not oppressive; precisely because it is inseparable, a family permits tensions and a variety of different views. Calling the church a family therefore emphasizes that the bond of cohesion is not law but charity and that its unity is alive with Christian diversity."

Baum continued: "Conceiving the Catholic Church as a family of apostolic churches opens the way for a greater decentralization than she possesses at the moment, and offers a theological foundation for a greater diversity in life and piety within the unity of faith and obedience."[1] In this model, all Christian denominations, from Catholic to the (undenominational!) Churches of Christ are churches within the family of apostolic churches. Each of them enlarges the scope of the parishes, local churches and congregations, yet each serves as mediator or (to use Father Divine's term) a "tangibilificator" of something smaller than the professed one,

---

1. In William S. Morris, ed., *The Unity We Seek* (New York: Oxford, 1963), pp. 1ff.

holy, catholic, and apostolic church, which can in the imagination often drift into invisibility, impalpability, and Platonic idealism.

As such, the denomination can be a contributor to the identity of Christians who might otherwise be lost in diffusion. Many modern thinkers and poets have pointed to the need for such fabricators of identity, networks in which trust can develop. José Ortega y Gasset pictured humans who lack communal bonds like drops in an undifferentiated fog or cloud; William Butler Yeats said that we cannot grasp the universe barehanded. We need a glove, which something like an ethnic group or nation can provide; in the Christian case, the denomination may.

Through the denomination Christians experience something of the color, the thickness of the cultures that give them a grasp on Christianity. Yet they are not simply tribal because they aspire to and often do transcend the local or the single racial or national or ethnic group. Today it is tribalism that threatens civil and ecclesiastical order. In its arguments, only women can belong to womanchurch, African-Americans to some black churches; WASPs have long had waspish enclaves; only people of a certain experience on a side of a river are allowed to bond with their kind. Now the church growth people have taken an observation about sinful human nature — that we have a hard time giving embodiment to diversity in Christ in intimate circles — and legitimated it as a norm called the Homogeneous Unit Principle. Their observation is certainly exact; their technique is masterful; their results are impresssive; they must be taken into account over against romantic theories of inclusiveness. But as a theological legitimation this principle denies much of that to which Christians ought to aspire. It is successful precisely for the reasons all tribalisms tend to be successful in our time of eroded personal and social identities. But the denomination aspires and claims to be more and other than tribal.

Again, let me illustrate what I would call this "cross-cutting" principle that goes with denominational life by reference to the communion I know best, my own, Lutheranism. In the United States it is a 98% and more white (non-African, non-Asian, non-Native American, non-Hispanic) group which, for reasons of historical accident can lead its members to think that Christ died for Scandinavioid-Germanic types. Christian Reformed and Reformed Church in America people may have a similar negative vision and counter it with the positive hunch that it was for the Netherlands that Christ's atoning work proceeded. The Presbyterians are tempted to think thus of Scotland and Scotch-Irishdom, the Anglicans of

England, and so on. (Fortunately for Baptists and Methodists, among others, this temptation is less strong, thanks to the African-American presences in the "eccesiastical traditions" if not often in the denominations.)

My denomination, however, also hooks me up into world Lutheranism. There I learn that the Lutheran World Federation ejected the Lutheran churches of South Africa because, for all their letter of the law observance of Lutheran confessionalism, they seemed to be in fundamental disagreement with Christian norms, professed also by Lutherans, through their support of apartheid. Meanwhile, across a boundary in Namibia, as of 1960, the census showed that 60.9% of the population was Protestant, 40% of the whole population being Lutheran. (Tribal religionists, with 15.1% and Catholics with 13.6% of the population were next largest).[2]

Most American Lutherans would have been hard pressed in 1960 (and many might still be thirty years later) to point to Namibia (a.k.a., formerly and alas, Southwest Africa) on a map. But as it was pointed out to them in denominational journals, they might now find new reasons for curiosity and identification to know that their fellow confessionalists were involved in the long struggle for independence from South Africa. These co-believers helped remind Lutherans that not all their kin and kind looked like the 98% majority in the United States. Under gifted leadership, such an insight could lead to new empathy and action. One can work out negative and positive analogues for any number of denominations which have spiritual cousins in different cultures.

The denomination, conversely, can provide specialties which the local manifestations of community cannot. The suburban church cannot envision all the interests and needs of the inner city, nor can the ghetto Christians impart their gifts to the suburbs if only the local church and the one, holy, catholic, and apostolic churches exist. True, parachurches often efficiently connect Christians across local boundaries. To take one example out of tens of thousands: Bread for the World addresses hunger on a more than local, less than universal, other than denominational ground. Yet it too reaches people through the network of loyalties stimulated and encouraged by denominations. "Let's get the United Methodist mailing list," is a natural way for parachurch leaders to express their designs.

The local church, for example, cannot effectively train ministers, engage in publishing across the spectrum of possibilities, or mobilize many

---

2. Barrett, ed., *World Christian Encyclopedia*, p. 503.

people for refugee and relief services. Denominations may and do combine in Church World Service and similar agencies. But such agencies tend to be inefficient and powerless if they do not, from the other direction, recognize the organization of life that consistently goes on in the denominations.

The denomination, where it is effective, provides a center for hospitality. Not everyone is so congenial and anticipatory as the Moravians are or used to be. My library includes in its curio corner a 1952 *Moravian Travel Guide* listing the denomination's congregations for its "ever-enlarging fellowship." The guide was designed for glove compartments of automobiles. The book includes descriptions of all the congregations in the denomination, with a careful listing of their addresses. The implication is that wherever Moravians go, if there is a Moravian congregation, they should expect hospitality. I have no idea whether such books are still being published by Moravians; the world is less hospitable than it was in 1952, and Moravianism may have joined others in experiencing the decline of neighborliness. But many a Presbyterian youth group stranded with a broken-down bus on the way to the mountains has been rescued through the simple act of looking at Yellow Pages and finding local Presbyterians. Of course, Christian should always be ready to take in Christian, and the believer should adopt the unbeliever. But the denominational network allows for intermediate zones of hospitality and some measure of trusted encounter with the Other; the system has not wholly broken down.

The denomination thus provides also for a larger framework of imaginative identity. It was often an inadequate form for presenting the fulness of faith life, to be sure. For example, I have often compared notes with adults who were once children in various conservative denominations, and the experiences tended to be similar to each other. We children would be shown a map with the nations of the world colored gray and dark. Then a sudden bright spot might appear. *That* year "our" denomination sent its first missionary couple into, say, Nigeria. Suddenly "Christ" had come to Nigeria. As if no other Christian witness had been there, the children were taught to pray for those who now first were bringing the light to that dark place. The notion today looks as sectarian and narrow as it really was. Yet the experience was larger than that of worlds unknown, unrecognized, where a particular family in Christ went unrepresented. Ecumenical understanding was still to come, but localism was already transcended. For all the limits of the experiment, children began to know something more than before about the map, about other kinds of people, about new kinds of Christians.

Next in the sequence of possibilities toward the development of a rationale for denominations, another "we can't get along without them" apologia, is the fact that one apparently needs some sort of "family" experience to help traditions become alive. This is not the place to set forth a full defense of tradition. For the moment we need think only of the root of the term itself: *traditum*, that which is handed down, or the act of handing down or over. The heart of the Christian tradition is God's act of "handing down" God's self in Jesus Christ. The Christian tradition is the handed down scriptural story as embodied in successive generations.

Tradition in print, in book and library, may satisfy intellectual and esthetic quests. But living tradition demands active response and participation. Here the denomination also plays its part. Those of us who write about denominations, even in a time of mixed marriages and switching, of diffusion and loss of identity and decline, know that denominations possess and evidence different colors, textures, and smells. People who cannot easily define cognitively, for example, what it is to be a Presbyterian, emit signals which make it possible to locate them as Presbyterian. This would be bad in the eyes of an ecumenist who believes that there can and should be only a single form of manifestation of Christian expression. But those who are committed to the notion of thickness and vividness know that a tradition disembodied is a contradiction in terms. The denomination may not well perpetuate the story, but without it, the story of a particular experience would be lost entirely.

A close relative to that apologetic note is the sense that just as "tradition" needs the denomination for expression, so does "confession," which here means the creedal and doctrinal life. This form of embodiment will vary greatly across the spectrum of denominations, and may not even be acknowledged in many cases. Yet, paradoxically, some sort of cognitive framework appears even where members of a denomination deny its existence. Baptists in the American South boasted that they were a noncreedal church, but their blend of hermeneutics and exegesis — say all non-Baptists, at least — turns into predictable and coherent forms of witness. How else could Southern Baptists make heresy charges or experience near-schism over "doctrine"? To carry the case to its furthest point: the Unitarian Universalist Association is an anti-confessional denomination. Its members pride themselves on complete rejection of creeds. Does that mean they have none? Sidney E. Mead, himself a Unitarian, years ago posed the issue: what if, following purely rational forms of skeptical inquiry, a member of the UUA came to the conclusion that Athanasian Trinitarian Orthodoxy were to be the only pure expression of UUA life? Would he or she be seen as still welcome in the denomination? Perhaps in mental institutions or counselling centers of the church she might find a home; otherwise, she would be seen as violating what the denomination is all about. Confession here is not a heteronomous instance, as in, "This you must believe." Instead it has to do with identity and voluntary life: "If you want to understand us, you should know that this is what we believe."

Confessions do not automatically propagate themselves, get refined, or become troves from which people can selectively retrieve that which gives witness to their faith, in disembodied forms. They live instead because seminaries, pastors, theologians, conventions, task forces, and celebrations reflect on them. In a world of nondescriptness about religion, the denomination can help give vitality by contributing to "descriptness."

Finally, the denomination gives expression to some dimensions of what we have called the "public church." The public church is that clustering of denominational expressions in which some positive view of what God is doing, or *that* God is doing something, in the spheres beyond the church, finds open expression. In local communities congregations can demonstrate this, but their witness can easily be thus limited and isolated. The whole Christian church may give general expression to the public thing *(res publica)*, but it will not have practical expression. It is the denomination which allows for the voice and the ear, the speaking and the listening, the participating in the public order. By "public," be it noted, we do not mean simply "politics." "Public" includes the mall and the clinic, the university and the gallery, the concert hall and the market, the political order and the sphere of family activities. Denominations set some boundaries on public church activity, but they also legitimate it and provide channels for it in the first place.

In these two chapters I have not set out to do what historians usually do: to visit the career of an institution through history. We have made occasional references to, say, 1788 and 1910 and 1965 as turning points. Some might be disappointed that we neither attacked nor defended, indeed that we did not even begin to evaluate, the present leadership of denominations. Often they get attacked as being "politicians" if elected and "bureaucrats" if appointed. Most of us who cover the denominational circuit find reason to be impressed by the individual talent of many who are elected and employed, and find that at least they do not represent *lower* levels of commitment and expertise than one finds in ecumenical or local spheres. But such an evaluation would be beside the point here. The current focus has been on the essentials of criticism and the rudiments of apology which go into the double-sidedness of appraisal.

The denomination is an earthen vessel, full of cracks and holes. But the church in the present day unfolding of history needs such vessels, or something like them. Built into those denominations that stand the best chance of enduring and serving are mechanisms and impulses for reform and renewal. Their significance is less one that can be marked by "decline" and more by something that sounds much simpler but is deliciously more complex: "change."

*The Practices of Piety
and the Practice of Medicine*

Prayer, Scripture, and Medical Ethics

ALLEN D. VERHEY

Contents

A Tribute to Henry Stob

The Stob Lectures are given annually in honor of Henry Stob.

The lecturers frequently begin with some small acknowledgement of Henry Stob's enormous contributions to Calvin College and Seminary and to the Christian Reformed Church, to the Christian academy, and to the larger Church of Christ.

It would be unfitting and ungrateful if I were to begin in any other way. Henry Stob was my teacher, and he remains my model of what a good teacher should be.

I remember with appreciation being patiently tutored through passages of Augustine and Aquinas, Barth and Bonhoeffer, and, of course, Calvin. I remember with admiration the finely crafted lectures written in pencil on half-sheets of paper. I remember with affection that my sophomoric questions were transformed somehow into intelligent inquiry. And I remember with awe being in the presence of one who combined precision with piety.

Henry Stob was a teacher whose passion for the truth was joined to faith in the one who is the Truth. He was a scholar whose work was done in hope, in the happy and humble confidence that the Truth would one day be revealed. He was a theologian for whom ethics was a work of love, a labor of loving God with all one's mind and of learning to love the neighbor in each one's life.

If I am worthy of the honor of the invitation to give these lectures, it is due in no small measure to what I learned from Henry Stob — not only about Aquinas and Barth and Calvin, but also about faith and hope and love as virtues not only for the Christian life but also for the theological task.

These lectures hope to honor Henry Stob by stealing one of his ideas, the significance of simple acts of piety for the Christian life, and by examining the value of this stolen notion for medical ethics, a field in which Henry Stob wrote some of his finest essays.[1]

The stolen idea comes from an essay entitled "Justification and Sanctification: Liturgy and Ethics."[2] There Henry Stob argues (stealing an idea from John Calvin) that human beings are inalienably religious, that there is deep in human experience what Calvin called a *sensus divinitatis*, a sense of the presence and power of a transcendent and inscrutable Other who bears down on us and sustains us in our strength and in our weakness, in the midst of our powers and at the limit of our powers. Human beings, therefore, in their whole being, and in all their doing, are religious. Worship, then, is not the whole of religion, but it serves to orient the whole of one's being and all of one's doing toward God in praise of God's glory. And in the simplest acts of Christian piety, offering prayer and reading scripture, we not only commune with God but we find new strength — new virtue — for daily life.[3]

That is the stolen notion I want to take to medicine and to medical ethics.

1. See, for example, "Christian Ethics and Scientific Control," in Charles Hatfield, ed., *The Scientist and Ethical Decision* (Downers Grove: Inter-Varsity Press, 1973), pp. 3-24, reprinted in Henry Stob, *Ethical Reflections: Essays on Moral Themes* (Grand Rapids: Wm. B. Eerdmans Publishing Co., 1978), pp. 209-22, and "Toward a Human Medicine," in Henry Stob, *Ethical Reflections*, pp. 223-27.

2. Henry Stob, "Justification and Sanctification: Liturgy and Ethics," in Paul C. Empie and James I. McCord, eds., *Marburg Revisited* (Minneapolis: Augsburg Publishing House, 1966), pp. 105-17; reprinted as "God and Man," in Henry Stob, *Ethical Reflections*, pp. 50-61.

3. Henry Stob, "Justification and Sanctification: Liturgy and Ethics," in Paul C. Empie and James I. McCord, eds., *Marburg Revisited*, p. 116.

CHAPTER ONE

Piety in a "World Come of Age"

Through prayer and scriptural meditation, we hold communion with
our God and find new strength for daily tasks.[1]

I want to take this reminder of the significance of prayer and scripture to
the hospital, to the nursing home, to all the places we endure and care in the
face of pain and sickness and death. That may seem a daunting task and an
unpromising project, for modern medicine seems thoroughly "religionless," and much of contemporary medical ethics is self-consciously secular.

Modern medicine seems thoroughly "religionless" and a technologi-
cally well-equipped hospital is emblematic of a "world come of age."[2] The
practices of piety — and indeed "God" — seem to have been pushed to the
margins of medical care, retreating more and more as the knowledge and
powers of medicine advance more and more, surviving in a bad joke now
and then — as when the doctor told her patient that the only thing left to
do was to pray and the patient replied, "Is it that bad, then?"

1. Henry Stob, "Justification and Sanctification: Liturgy and Ethics," in Paul C.
Empie and James I. McCord, eds., *Marburg Revisited,* p. 116.
2. These phrases, of course, are from Dietrich Bonhoeffer, *Letters and Papers from
Prison* (New York: Macmillan, 1953). On a "world come of age" see especially the letters
of June 8, 1944 (pp. 194-200), June 30, 1944 (pp. 206-10), and July 16, 1944 (pp. 215-20).
There is an enormous secondary literature on Bonhoeffer, but the recent chapter by
Larry Rasmussen, "Worship in a World Come of Age," in his *Dietrich Bonhoeffer — His Sig-
nificance for North Americans* (Minneapolis: Fortress Press, 1990), pp. 57-71, is especially
relevant to the issue of prayer in "a world come of age." Henry Stob taught a course on
Bonhoeffer at Calvin Seminary that I remember with great appreciation.

I have no stake in these lectures in the sort of poisonous religiosity which regards "God" as a working hypothesis to explain whatever is (or seems to be) beyond the reach of human knowing. I do not mean to defend the sort of contemptible piety which regards "God" as a divine last resort, a *deus ex machina,* to rescue us from dangers which are (or are thought to be) beyond the reach of human powers.[3] Such piety can only retreat to the margins while medical knowledge and power advance.

But I take courage in Henry Stob's point that human beings — including those who give and receive medical care — are ineluctably religious beings.[4] I take courage in the fact that many physicians and nurses, even if they invoke no god by name, still enter and practice their professions with a lively sense of gratitude for the givenness (the gifts) of life and health, with a humble sense of dependence upon some dimly known but reliable order, with a sad sense of a tragic flaw that runs through our world and through our embodied selves, with a hopeful sense of new possibilities on the horizon, and with a keen sense of responsibility to some inscrutable power who gives the gifts, sustains the order, judges the flaw, and provides the new possibilities.[5]

I take courage in the fact that there are many others, patients in the "religionless" world of medicine, who are not members of any community of faith, for whom the events of birth or suffering or death are surrounded not only by technology but by a *sensus divinitatis* as well, by a sense of their dependence upon and their indebtedness to a transcendent Other that bears down on human life and human powers and sustains them as well.

I take courage in the simple fact that these simple acts of piety, prayer and reading scripture, are as common in hospitals as in churches. Think of that: as noisily secular as modern medicine is, these practices of piety are commonplace. When people hurt and suffer, or when they are about to give birth or to die, we are likely to find them under the care of a physician, and in a hospital, *and* praying or reading the Bible.

---

3. Both Larry Rasmussen in the article cited above and Henry Stob in the course mentioned above identified such piety as the object of Bonhoeffer's scorn in calling for a "religionless Christianity."

4. See, for example, "Justification and Sanctification: Liturgy and Ethics," in Paul C. Empie and James I. McCord, eds., *Marburg Revisited,* p. 111.

5. This account of a "natural piety" is dependent upon James Gustafson, *Ethics from a Theocentric Perspective: Theology and Ethics* (Chicago: University of Chicago Press, 1981), pp. 129-36.

To be sure, sometimes those acts of piety seem to regard God as a divine last resort, as a heavenly pharmacopoeia. But the simple fact that such acts of piety are commonplace suggests that it is not unreasonable — and may be important — to ask how the practice of prayer can and does and should nurture and sustain and qualify the practice of medicine, or how the practice of attending to scripture can and does and should illumine and challenge our endurance of pain and suffering and our attentiveness to the sick and dying.

Medical ethics, however, has paid very little attention to these practices of piety — in spite of their frequency in hospitals. I hope in these lectures to remedy that a little, for medical ethics has neglected these acts of piety to its great loss. At the very least ethicists should find it curious that large numbers of patients (and large numbers of doctors and nurses, too) keep calling on God for guidance rather than on the experts in medical ethics.

It remains a daunting task, however, not only because of what medicine has become but even more because of what medical ethics has become. It is true that much of contemporary medical ethics is self-consciously secular, deliberately "religionless."

I take some courage for the task of these lectures in the fact that there are long and worthy traditions of theological reflection about sickness and healing, about death and dying, about care and respect for the suffering, and about meeting the needs of the sick poor. Long before medical ethics became a distinct field of inquiry, let alone the growth industry of the academy, Christians and others with religious convictions were engaged with moral questions posed by medical care and were trying to answer them in ways appropriate to the ways they talked of God and *to* God.

Prayer and scripture were at home in these traditions. There was plenty of foolishness mixed in with those traditions, to be sure, but there were traditions. There were resources for the doctor and the nurse who tried conscientiously to bring their practice into line with their religious profession. There were resources for the patient who longed to live and to die in ways that were faithful and full of faith. There were resources for religious leaders who struggled to find a word of God that would appropriately admonish and encourage a medical professional or patient.

It is not surprising, therefore, that theologians played such an important role in the development of this new field twenty-five years ago, in what one scholar called the "renaissance" of medical ethics.[6] Paul Ramsey, for example, who is usually credited with opening up this new field of inquiry with his "explorations into medical ethics,"[7] always wrote, he said, "as a Christian ethicist and not as some hypothetical common denominator."[8] And so, it may be said, did Henry Stob when he wrote on medical ethics.

After the "renaissance," however, came the "enlightenment" of medical ethics. It did not come, of course, by any inexorable design of history, nor even by the design of the philosophers who entered the field twenty years ago; but it came.

The moral dilemmas to which medical ethics gave attention seemed to demand the application of principles concerning which one could (and would) presume consensus, even in the context of American pluralism. Public conversation about such quandaries seemed to require that we all learn to speak "moral esperanto"[9] instead of the natural tongue of our particular moral and religious traditions. And the regulatory questions, the questions of public policy, seemed to call for an appreciation of pluralism and the application of the minimal requirements necessary for people with different convictions to live — and die — together peaceably.[10]

The discipline undertook the enlightenment project, sometimes to justify but always to identify and apply the generic moral principles that all people could (and should) hold independently of their particular communities and particular histories, quite apart from their specific loyalties and specific identities, unbiased by any peculiar narrative or story which they might own and which would sustain their moral identity and their moral

---

6. LeRoy Walters, "Religion and the Renaissance of Medical Ethics," in Earl E. Shelp, ed., *Theology and Bioethics: Exploring the Foundations and Frontiers,* Philosophy and Medicine, 20 (Dordrecht: D. Reidel Publishing Company, 1985), pp. 3-16.

7. The Lyman Beecher lectures at Yale in 1969, later published as Paul Ramsey, *The Patient as Person: Explorations in Medical Ethics* (New Haven: Yale University Press, 1970).

8. Paul Ramsey, "The Indignity of 'Death with Dignity,'" *Hastings Center Studies* 2:2 (1974), pp. 47-62, p. 56.

9. Jeffrey Stout, *Ethics after Babel: The Languages of Morals and Their Discontents* (Boston: Beacon Press, 1988), p. 294, defines "moral esperanto" as "what optimistic modernism strives for in ethics; an artificial moral language invented in the (unrealistic) hope that everyone will want to speak it."

10. See further Daniel Callahan, "Religion and the Secularization of Bioethics," in *The Hastings Center Report* 20:4 (July-August, 1990), Special Supplement, "Theology, Religious Traditions, and Bioethics," pp. 2-4.

passion. Medical ethics, longing to stand above traditions, found itself standing squarely in the enlightenment tradition — with an enlightenment suspicion of (other) particular traditions, an enlightenment confidence in the progress of science and unqualified reason, and an enlightenment celebration of individual autonomy over the "authority" of priest and politician and that new figure of arbitrary dominance, the physician.

The importance of an arena of "privacy" was typically underscored, a space for autonomy and preference; and it was also underscored that what matters publicly is simply that there be such a space, not how it is filled. Talk of God — and talk *to* God — was assigned to this private space, and so to the margins of public discourse.

People trained as theologians still wrote on medical ethics and still contributed to public discourse about the new powers of medicine, but — for a time at least — they muted their theological voice. They were more easily identified as followers of Mill or Kant than as followers of Jesus. They learned to speak moral "esperanto," but they began to stutter in the native tongue of Christian piety.

The language of prayer and scripture will seem alien and strange to such a "religionless" medical ethic, a foreign tongue in a moral world "come of age."

Still, I take courage from the public lament by Jim Gustafson[11] that so little of the commentary on medical ethics written by people trained as theologians makes any explicit appeal to religious convictions or theological traditions. He admitted that the task of theological reflection about medical ethics would not be an easy one, and he did not claim that quandaries or public policy problems would go away if only some people would talk of God and other people would listen. He acknowledged that there are sometimes good reasons for silence about one's religious convictions. But he more vigorously pointed out reasons to lament that silence, and chief among them was the simple fact that faithful members of Christian communities want to live and die — and give birth and suffer and care for the suffering — with Christian integrity, not just with impartial rationality.

And I take courage from the fact that Gustafson's lament was echoed by others, and that it signaled renewed attention to theological traditions and to religious congregations as communities of moral discourse and dis-

11. James Gustafson, "Theology Confronts Technology and the Life Sciences," *Commonweal*, 16 June 1978, pp. 386-92.

cernment with respect to medical care.[12] To this point the retrieval of religious traditions has focused on theological convictions and confessional formulations, asking what relevance particular beliefs about creation or providence or redemption have for medical ethics. There has not yet been significant attention to the practices of piety,[13] to prayer and scripture reading (or to the Lord's Supper and Baptism), and to how such acts of piety might form and inform the imagination and the deliberation of persons practicing or using medicine.

That brings us back to the beginning: to the notion stolen from Henry Stob that in the simplest acts of piety we find new virtue for daily life and to the task of asking what that means for medicine and for medical ethics.

12. Among those echoing Gustafson's lament were the voices of Stanley Hauerwas, "Can Ethics Be Theological?" *Hastings Center Report* 8:5 (1978), pp. 47-49, and Richard A. McCormick, "Notes on Moral Theology," *Theological Studies* 40 (1979), pp. 98-99. The signs of renewed attention to religious traditions have appeared in many places in the last decade. They include the Park Ridge Center and its publications, including its journal *Second Opinion,* the volume *Theology and Bioethics: Exploring the Foundations and Frontiers* in the Philosophy and Medicine series published by D. Reidel, the fact that a parallel series Theology and Medicine has been undertaken, and a number of important books. Even so, the field still seems to belong to those who speak "esperanto," and "most religious ethicists entering the public practice of ethics leave their special religious insights at the door." So at least Leon Kass said in his recent important criticism of contemporary bioethics, "Practicing Ethics: Where's the Action?" *Hastings Center Report* 20:1 (Jan./Feb., 1990), pp. S-12.

13. Timothy Sedgwick, "A Moral Matrix: Religious Practices and Medical Care," unpublished manuscript.

CHAPTER TWO

The Case of Coles's Friend

It is conventional that lectures in medical ethics consider a case. So, consider this:

In his *Harvard Diary* Robert Coles tells the story of a Catholic friend of his, a physician who knows his cancer is not likely to be beaten back, a Christian who knows the final triumph belongs to the risen Christ.[1]

The dying man was visited by a hospital chaplain, who asked how he was "coping." "Fine," he said, in the fashion of all those replies by which people indicate that they are doing reasonably well given their circumstances and that they would rather not elaborate just now on what those circumstances are.

But this chaplain was unwilling to accept such a reply. He inquired again about how the man was feeling, how he was managing, how he was dealing with the stress. Relentlessly he pressed on to questions about denial and anger and acceptance. But finally he gave up with the suggestion that when the man was ready to discuss things he should not hesitate to call the chaplain.

After the chaplain left, Coles's friend did get angry, not so much about his circumstances or his dying, but about the chaplain. The chaplain, he said, was a psycho-babbling fool. And Robert Coles, the eminent Harvard psychiatrist, agreed. What his friend needed and wanted, Coles says, was someone with whom to attend to God and to God's word, not someone who dwelt upon the stages of dying as though they were "Stations of the Cross."

1. Robert Coles, "Psychiatric Stations of the Cross," *Harvard Diary: Reflections on the Sacred and the Profane* (New York: Crossroad Publishing Company, 1990), pp. 10-12. See also pp. 92-94.

Coles's friend was not finished with the chaplain. He called for the chaplain to return; there were some ideas, he said, that he wanted to bring up "for discussion." When the chaplain returned, Coles's friend had his Bible out, with the bookmark set to Psalm 69, and he simply asked the chaplain to read.

Coles quotes the opening words of Psalm 69. It is a prayer, a lament: "Save me, O God, for the waters have come up to my neck. . . . I have come into the deep waters. . . ." Coles might have read a little farther. The chaplain, at least, was probably instructed to continue. It is an imprecatory psalm, after all, and the curse on the enemy may be no small part of the reason this dying man chose this passage for this particular representative of the church. "I looked for sympathy," it says, "but there was none; for comforters, but I found none. They put gall in my food, and gave me vinegar for my thirst. May the table set before them become a snare; may it become retribution and a trap."[2]

Coles's friend, with his complaint about gall in his food and vinegar for his thirst, was not, of course, complaining about hospital food. He was complaining about a chaplain who had emptied his role of the practice of piety, who neglected prayer and scripture, and who filled his visits to the sick with the practices of psychotherapy. And his curse upon the table set before him, I suppose, was not intended to suggest that the skills and language of psychology are useless, but rather to remind the chaplain that at the table set before us we may eat and drink judgment to ourselves if we forget or ignore the gifts of God for the people of God, which surely include not only bread and wine, but prayer and scripture and the presence of a suffering and risen Christ.

Our concern tonight, however, is not that the church or its representatives will forfeit their inheritance for a mess of psychology. Our concern is rather with medical ethics and with the possibility that Christians will ignore or neglect the practices of piety for the sake of an impartial point of view and the generic moral principles favored by medical ethicists.

Just imagine for a moment that the chaplain who visited Coles's friend had been enlisted on the hospital ethics committee and there taught a little Mill and a little Kant, taught to respect and protect a patient's autonomy, taught to regard human relationships as contracts between self-

---

2. These citations of Psalm 69:1, 2, 20-22 are from the NIV. All other references are to the RSV.

interested and autonomous individuals, taught to speak a universal moral language, a form of moral "esperanto."

Then perhaps you can imagine Coles's friend being visited by this chaplain again, now trained as an ethicist rather than psychological counselor. The chaplain turned ethicist might still be just trying to be tactful and helpful, still be struggling to find work and words appropriate to his role in that "world come of age" called a hospital, still be embracing perhaps some notion of a "religionless Christianity" and "religionless" work and words in that secular world called medicine.[3] But the chaplain turned ethicist would now be anxious not so much with psychological states and stages as with not interfering with the patient's rights, including, of course, the right to be left alone.

This visit might begin with an inquiry about whether the patient understood the consent form he had refused to sign and continue with a question about whether he had signed a living will or assigned durable power of attorney for medical decisions. The chaplain turned ethicist might be no less relentless than before, but now pressing toward the goal of respecting and protecting the so-called autonomy of this patient. Indeed, the chaplain turned ethicist might now resist with still more resolve praying and reading scripture with the patient, for such activities come dangerously close to a violation of privacy and surely substitute a particular vision of human flourishing for the impartial and universal perspective regarded as important by philosophers and ethics committees.

His enthusiasm for a common moral language, for the kind of "esperanto" ethicists like to speak, will make him hesitate to speak in a distinctively Christian voice, hesitate to use and to offer the gifts of prayer and scripture when people are dying or suffering and face hard medical and moral decisions.

If you can imagine all of that, then you can also imagine that after this visit of the chaplain turned ethicist Coles's friend might complain no less bitterly about gall in his food and curse the ethicist no less legitimately. He might call this ethicist back with the bookmark set at Psalm 69. Again the point would not be that philosophical skills or generic moral principles are

---

3. The celebrations of secularism in the sixties were based in part on a misreading of Bonhoeffer's *Letters and Papers from Prison,* a reading which did not have the advantage of being tutored by Henry Stob, a reading that has been corrected by Larry Rasmussen. (See footnotes 2 and 3 in Chapter One.)

useless. But Coles's friend still needs and wants hard praying, not just to have his "autonomy" respected and protected. He still needs and wants someone to talk of God and the ways of God, not a conversation in moral "esperanto," a language he little understands and doesn't really care to learn, not now as he lies dying at any rate. He has decisions to make, to be sure, hard medical and moral decisions about what should be done and what left undone but he wants to make them oriented to God by the gifts of God; by the practices of piety, and not just with impartial rationality.

Now imagine something more: Imagine that this chaplain turned ethicist returns to his office after reading Psalm 69. Imagine that he wonders there whether there had been some test of his theological and religious integrity in that hospital room. And imagine that he decides he did not pass this test.

He sees that he was not altogether faithful to his identity as a Christian pastor and Christian ethicist. His agenda as a medical ethicist had left no room for the possible contribution of activities central to Christian piety. He had presumed that the practices of piety were irrelevant to discernment. He had condescendingly interpreted the disposition to pray either as a slothful refusal to do the hard intellectual work necessary for discernment or as a proud claim to have some magical access to the right answers.[4]

"A patient might legitimately expect more from a representative of the church, even in this secular world of medicine and medical ethics," he says to himself, and he resolves to make one more visit to the room of Coles's friend, there perhaps to learn something from the pious sick that he had forgotten under the instruction of medical ethicists, something of how the practices of piety might still form and inform the practice of medicine.

4. See further Allen Verhey, "Praying with Dirty Hands," *Reformed Journal,* July, 1989, pp. 11-14.

CHAPTER THREE

Prayer as a Practice

The ethicist makes his way to the room of Coles's friend. Let's go with him.

"We have come to pray," we say, "for we know 'the Lord hears the needy'" (Psalm 69:33), hoping he will recognize the citation of Psalm 69. He welcomes us, and the hint of a smile suggests that he did in fact recognize that we had continued to read the psalm that contained his complaint and his curse. Before we begin to pray, however, we ask why prayer is so important to him.

His reply, I imagine, would go something like this: "It is important because I am a Christian and because I long to live the Christian life, even in the dying of it, and prayer is part of the Christian life. Indeed, it is, as John Calvin (the theologian you so much admire) said, the most important part, 'the chief exercise of faith.'[1] Moreover, it is a part of the whole Christian life which cannot be left out without the whole ceasing to be the Christian life. The Christian life is a life of prayer. It is, as Karl Barth (that student of Calvin's) said, a life of 'humble and resolute, frightened and joyful invocation of the gracious God in gratitude, praise, and above all, petition.'"[2]

---

1. John Calvin, *Institutes of the Christian Religion,* ed. John T. McNeill, trans. Ford Lewis Battles (Philadelphia: Westminster Press, 1960), III.xx.1. In *Nisi Domino Frustra,* a Calvin Seminary club which Henry Stob led, we read and discussed Calvin's *Institutes.* The most intellectually stimulating and satisfying times of my tenure at Calvin as a student were spent in that little group with Henry Stob as mentor.

2. Karl Barth, *The Christian Life: Church Dogmatics* IV, 4, trans. Geoffrey Bromiley (Grand Rapids: Wm. B. Eerdmans Publishing Company, 1981), p. 43. On the ethics of Barth see Henry Stob, "Themes in Barth's Ethics," *Ethical Reflections: Essays on Moral Themes,* pp. 103-10.

Well, perhaps his response would not go exactly like that. Not very many people quote Calvin and Barth in their hospital rooms.

Perhaps his reply would rather go something like this: "Prayer is important because it is a practice of piety. As you know, chaplain, the philosopher Alasdair MacIntyre defined a practice as a

> form of socially established cooperative human activity through which goods internal to that form of activity are realized in the course of trying to achieve those standards of excellence which are appropriate to, and partially definitive of, that form of activity with the result that human powers to achieve excellence and human conceptions of the ends and goods involved are systematically extended.[3]

Well, okay, probably not.

But even if he has not memorized an important and difficult passage from MacIntyre's *After Virtue,* even if he has never read a philosopher or a theologian, he may still make a reply to which John Calvin, Karl Barth, and Alasdair MacIntyre would nod their heads and say, "Yes, that's what I meant."

He is a Christian. He has learned to pray in the Christian community. And in learning to pray, he has learned as well the good that is intrinsic to prayer. He has learned, that is, to attend to God, to look to God.[4] And he has learned it not just intellectually, not just as an idea.

---

3. Alasdair MacIntyre, *After Virtue: A Study in Moral Theory* (Notre Dame: University of Notre Dame Press, 1981), p. 175. On the notion of a "Practice" see also Jeffrey Stout, *Ethics After Babel: The Languages of Morals and Their Discontents,* pp. 267-76.

4. On prayer as attention see especially Iris Murdoch, "On 'God' and 'Good,'" in Stanley Hauerwas and Alasdair MacIntyre, eds., *Revisions: Changing Perspectives in Moral Philosophy* (Notre Dame: University of Notre Dame Press, 1983), pp. 68-91. See also Craig Dykstra, *Vision and Character* (New York: Paulist Press, 1981), pp. 45-98; Simone Weil, *Waiting on God,* trans. E. Craufurd (London: Routledge and Kegan Paul, Ltd., 1951), p. 51. I am sympathetic to the definitions of prayer as "communion" (e.g., Henry Stob, "Prayer and Providence," *Theological Reflections* [Grand Rapids: Wm. B. Eerdmans Publishing Company, 1981], p. 91) and as "intimate conversation of the pious with God" (John Calvin, *Institutes,* IV. xx.16). And I am confident that attention to God is both evoked and met by the presence of God. Nevertheless, I have chosen to focus on the human side of the practice of prayer, the human disposition and action in the practice of prayer, simple attention to God. I would not establish extravagant expectations of "mystic communion," and I would not have attention to God be regarded as a "means" even to such religious experience.

In learning to pray, he has learned a human activity which engages his body as well as his mind, his affections and passions and loyalty as well as his rationality, and which focuses his whole self on God.

To attend to God is not easy to learn — or painless. And given our inveterate attention to ourselves and to our own needs and wants, we frequently corrupt it. We corrupt prayer whenever we turn it to a means to accomplish some other good than the good of prayer, whenever we make of it an instrument to achieve wealth or happiness or life or health or moral improvement. In learning to pray, Coles's friend has learned to look to God, and, after the blinding vision, to begin to look at all else in a new light.

In prayer he does not attend to something beyond God, which God — or prayer — might be used in order to reach; he attends to God. That is the good intrinsic to prayer, the good "internal to that form of activity."

In learning to pray, he has learned as well certain standards of excellence[5] that belong to prayer and its attention to God, that are "appropriate to" prayer and "partially definitive" of prayer.

He has learned *reverence,* the readiness to attend to God as God and to attend to all else in his life as related to God.

He has learned *humility,* the readiness to acknowledge that we are not gods, but the creatures of God, cherished by God but finite and mortal and, yes, sinful creatures in need finally of God's grace and God's future.

He has learned *gratitude,* a disposition of thankfulness for the opportunities within the limits of our finiteness and mortality to delight in God and in the gifts of God.

Attentive to God, he has learned *care.* Attentive to God, he grows attentive to the neighbor as related to God. He has learned to care even for those who are least, to care especially for those who hurt and cry out to high heaven in anguish.

Looking to God, he has learned *hope,* a disposition of confidence and courage that comes not from trusting oneself and the little truth one knows well or the little good one does well, but from trusting the grace and power of God.

These standards of excellence form virtues not only for prayer but for daily life. The prayer-formed person — in the whole of her being and in all

---

5. Consider John Calvin's attention to the "rules" of prayer in *Institutes,* III.xx.4-16. Calvin's "rules" are reverence, a sincere sense of want (i.e., to pray earnestly), humility, and confident hope.

of her doing — will be reverent, humble, grateful, caring, and hopeful.[6] One does not pray *in order to* achieve those virtues. They are not formed when we use prayer as a technique. But they are formed in simple attentiveness to God, and they spill over into new virtues for daily life.

"That's why prayer is so important to me," Coles's friend might conclude.

"That's why I called it the 'chief exercise of faith,'" Calvin might say.

"That's why I said the Christian life was 'invocation,'" Barth might say.

"That's what I meant by a 'practice,'" MacIntyre might add.

And if I may add my own word here, that's how we can begin to see the links between this practice of piety and the practice of medicine. We can try to envision the prayer-formed physician and the prayer-formed patient and the prayer-formed community that supports and sustains them both.

---

6. Proper prayer is characterized by these standards of excellence, and because prayer is itself a "characterizing activity" (Donald Saliers, "Liturgy and Ethics: Some New Beginnings," *Journal of Religious Ethics* 7 [Fall, 1979], pp. 173-89, at p. 175), these standards of excellence are formed in those who practice prayer.

CHAPTER FOUR

A Prayer-Formed Practice of Medicine

We are ready at last to offer prayer with Coles's friend. "And how shall we begin?" we ask; and Coles's friend replies, "With *invocation,* of course, for prayer is to call upon God and to adore God as the one on whom we depend."[1]

To call upon God is to re-call who God is and what God has done.[2] We invoke not just any old god, not some nameless god of philosophical theism, not some idolatrous object of someone's "ultimate concern," but the God remembered in religious community and in other practices of piety.

Invocation is remembrance, and remembrance is not just recollection but the way identity and community are constituted. So we invoke the God made known in mighty works and great promises, and as we do we are oriented to that God and to all things in relation to God.

We invoke God as *creator;* and as we do, we learn to make neither life nor choice an idol; for nothing God made is god. That is a good and simple gift to medical ethics, when talk of "the sanctity of life" would require our friend to make every effort to preserve his life and when "respect for autonomy" would prohibit every moral question besides "Who should decide?"

---

1. I take as my guide for the components of prayer the acronym I learned in Sunday School and learned to appreciate in the congregational prayers of Rev. Ren Broekhuizen: ACTS, adoration, confession, thanksgiving, and supplication. William F. May, "Images That Shape the Public Obligations of the Minister," *Bulletin of the Park Ridge Center* 4:1 (January, 1989), pp. 20-37, considers the same set of components.

2. On prayer as an act of remembrance see Nicholas Wolterstorff, "Justice and Worship: The Tragedy of Liturgy in Protestantism," in his *Until Justice and Peace Embrace* (Grand Rapids: Wm. B. Eerdmans Publishing Company, 1983), pp. 146-61, especially 152, 154-56. Donald Saliers, "Liturgy and Ethics: Some New Beginnings," also emphasizes that "the shape and substance of prayer is *anamnetic,*" p. 178.

211

We invoke God as creator; and as we do, we learn as well not to turn our back to life or to choice; for all that God made is good. That, too, is a good and simple gift to medical ethics, when Dr. Kevorkian kills or when another would exercise some arbitrary power to keep Coles's friend alive.

We invoke God as creator; and as we do, we learn to refuse to reduce the embodied selves God made either to mere organisms or merely to their capacities for agency. And resistance to both forms of reductionism is a gift to medical ethics both at the beginnings and at the endings of life, and in all the care between, as well.

Then we invoke God as *provider.* We do so in remembrance that God has heard the cries of those who hurt, that God has cared. We do so in remembrance of one who suffered and died, and we attend to that cross as the place the truth about our world was nailed.

The truth about our world is the horrible reality of suffering and death. The truth about our world is the power of evil in the story of a cross and in the myriads of sad stories others tell with and of their bodies. The truth about our world is dripping with blood and hanging on a cross, but the same cross that points to the reality and power of evil also points to the real presence of God and to the constant care of God.

So, in invocation and remembrance we learn again that in spite of sickness, in spite of cancer, in spite of death's apparent triumph, God's care is the world's constant companion and our friend's constant companion. Invocation and remembrance do not deny the sad truth about our world or about our friend; they do not provide any magic charm against death or sickness; they do not provide a tidy theodicy to "justify" God and the ways of God.[3] But by attention to this God we may learn that God cares, that God suffers with those who hurt, even in places no medicine can touch.

Then our friend — and every patient — may be permitted to cry out, "God, why?" and still be assured he is not abandoned by God. And the rest of us — including physicians — may be formed by such prayer to embody care even when medicine cannot cure, to be present to the sick even when our powers to heal have failed, and to resist the temptation to abandon the one who reminds us of our weakness — and the great weakness of our great medical powers.

Such prayer is not an alternative to medicine, "not a supplement to

---

3. See Stanley Hauerwas, *Naming the Silences: God, Medicine, and the Problem of Suffering* (Grand Rapids: Wm. B. Eerdmans Publishing Co., 1990).

the insufficiency of our medical knowledge"[4] and skills; rather, it forms and sustains as a standard of excellence in medical practice simple presence — to the sick and a simple refusal to abandon them to their hurt. Such invocation and such a prayer-formed medicine will not always triumph over disease or death, but it will always gesture care in the midst of them and in spite of them.

We invoke God, too, as *redeemer* and as healer. We make such invocation, too, of course, in remembrance of Jesus, and in the hope of the good future that he made real and present by his works of healing and his words of blessing, and that God made sure by raising him from the dead.

As we invoke this God, as we attend to the redeemer, as we orient ourselves to the healer in prayer, we orient all of life and our medicine — along with our prayers — to God's promise and claim. So, a prayerful people and a prayer-formed medicine will celebrate and toast life, not death, but be able to endure even dying with hope. A prayerful people and a prayer-formed medicine will delight in human flourishing, including the human flourishing we call health. They will not welcome the dwindling of human strength to be human, including the loss of strength called sickness; yet they can endure even that in the confidence that God's grace is sufficient.

A prayer-formed community will not despise medicine, as if to turn to medicine were to turn against God and God's grace. Medicine is a good gift of God the creator, and a gracious provision of God the provider, and a reflection and servant of God the redeemer. To condemn medicine because God is the healer would be like condemning government because God is the ruler, or condemning families because God is "Abba."

Or course, if medicine presumes for itself the role of faithful savior or ultimate healer, then its arrogance may be and must be condemned. One cannot invoke the one true God and take a presumptuous medicine too seriously (or a presumptuous state or a presumptuous parent).[5]

Perhaps Coles's friend, like other good and honest doctors, is less tempted to this sort of idolatrous and extravagant expectation of medicine than are many other patients who sometimes enter the hospital speaking some version of the line from W. H. Auden: "We who must die demand a

---

4. Stanley Hauerwas, *Suffering Presence* (Notre Dame: University of Notre Dame Press, 1986), p. 81.

5. I am reminded of one of Henry Stob's favorite quotes, the line from T. B. Macauley's *Essays on Milton:* "He prostrates himself in the dust before his Maker; but he sets his foot on the neck of his king." See, e.g., Henry Stob, *Ethical Reflections,* p. 107.

miracle."[6] But when we invoke God as redeemer, we are freed from the vanity and illusion of wielding human power to defeat mortality or to eliminate the human vulnerability to suffering. An honest prayer could "let the air out of inflationary"[7] medical promises and restore a modest medicine to its rightful place alongside other measures that protect and promote life and health, like good nutrition, public sanitation, a clean environment, and the like.

One more thing here: A prayer-formed people, celebrating life and health as the good gifts and wonderful promises of God, will acknowledge that a life oriented to the kingdom may be shorter and harder, for there are goods more important than our own survival, and there are duties more overriding than our ease.

Having made invocation, we pause to ask whether we should continue. Coles's friends says, "Yes," and we ask, "How?" "With prayers of *confession,* of course," he says, "for those who have invoked God can make no pretense to be worthy of God's care and presence. Those oriented to God are reoriented to all else; it is called, I think, *metanoia,* a turning, repentance."

It seems clear to us that we have no major league sinner here, but we humor him.

"What would you confess?" we ask. "Are you a smoker?"

"That, too," he says. "But I see a reflection of my life in my doctor, and I don't like it. I have been where she is, angry at the patient who refuses another round of therapy, angry at my own powerlessness to save him, eager to use my authority as a physician to convince him to try again, and eager to avoid him when he refuses to try again or dies before we can. It is no great callousness I confess; it is the failure to acknowledge the fallibility and limits of medical care.[8]

"And now I find myself where my patients have been; and I don't like

6. W. H. Auden, "For the Time Being," in Marvin Halversin, ed., *Religious Drama/1* (Cleveland: Meridian Books, The World Publishing Company, 1957), p. 17.

7. William F. May, "Images That Shape the Public Obligations of the Minister," p. 25, on prayers of invocation and adoration and their effect on political rhetoric.

8. See Douglas Anderson, "The Physician's Experience: Witnessing Numinous Reality," *Second Opinion,* 13 (March, 1990), pp. 111-22. Pp. 117-22 focus on confession, the freedom it gives from being "blinded by the utopian images arising from uncritical overestimations of technology's power" (pp. 121-122) and the freedom it gives for presence to those who hurt or grieve.

it much better, angry at the doctor who cannot deliver a miracle, judging her much too quickly and severely, angrier still that she would try to tell me how to live while I am dying, and eager to render her still more powerless and optionless. It is no great callousness I confess here either; it is the failure to acknowledge the fallibility and limits of my own autonomy."

Confession is good for the soul, of course, but it's also good for medical ethics. It helps us see the fallibility of both medicine and patients. It helps us recognize the evil we sometimes do in resisting evil, the suffering we sometimes inflict in the effort to banish suffering and those who remind us of it.[9]

A prayer of confession, this form of attention to God, may help the dying to turn from despising the doctor because the doctor is a reminder of his sickness and mortality. And it may help the doctor to turn from both the disposition to abandon the patient because the patient is a reminder of her powerlessness to save him and from any readiness to eliminate suffering by eliminating the sufferer.

A prayer of confession may form the possibility of a continuing conversation. When the assertion of authority by a physician would ordinarily have put a stop to an argument and reduced the patient to manipulable nature, a prayer of confession may enable the conversation to continue. And when the assertion of autonomy by a patient would ordinarily have put a stop to a discussion and reduced the physician to an animated tool, a prayer of confession may enable the conversation to continue.[10] We may at least talk together longer and listen to each other better if in confession we turn from the pretense of being either final judge or final savior, for we are formed by prayers of confession to be critical without condescension and helpful without conceit. And that is a good and simple gift to medical practice and to medical ethics.

"There are prayers of *thanksgiving* to be made as well," our friend says and he begins to mention gifts great and small.

And not the least among the gifts for which he gives thanks are opportunities to fulfill some tasks, great and small. He thanks God for a little time to be reconciled with an enemy and for enough relief from pain for

9. See Stanley Hauerwas, *Suffering Presence.*

10. See further Allen Verhey, "Christian Community and Identity: What Difference Do They Make to Patients and Physicians Finally?" *Linacre Quarterly* 52 (May, 1985), pp. 149-69.

the tasks of fun with the family. He gives thanks for the opportunity and the task of being a witness, a "martyr," he says, to demonstrate even in his dying that some things are more important than mere survival, and that many things are more to be feared than death.

There is a gift here to medicine and to medical ethics in the simple and joyful acknowledgement that the sick and dying are still living, that they may not be reduced to the passivity of their sick role, and that their choices may not be regarded simply in terms of the arbitrary self-assertiveness of their autonomy. The sick and dying have tasks and opportunities which must be considered both by themselves and by their caregivers.

Gratitude forms us not to count what is given as "ours to dispose of as if we created it nor ours to serve only our own interests."[11] Thankfulness, this form of attention to God, is the reminder that God has been good to us, and that in gratitude to God we have reason enough to do good to others. Prayers of thankfulness form us and move us to seek the neighbor's good.

Prayers of thankfulness can form medical practice, too. The ideal of much medical practice is philanthropy; the virtue of much medical practice is beneficence. This is not to be despised, for it commends to the physician a love for humankind that issues in deeds of service. But it divides the human race — and a hospital — into two groups: the relatively self-sufficient benefactors and the needy beneficiaries.

Prayers of thanksgiving provide a different picture and different relations, a world — and a hospital — in which each is the recipient of gifts, in which human giving is put "in the context of primordial receiving."[12] Prayers of thanksgiving also commend and form deeds of love and service, but not as a self-important conceit of philanthropy — rather as little deeds of kindness which are no less a response to gifts than the prayers of thanksgiving themselves.

Prayers of thanksgiving can form in the medical practitioner the simple and joyful acknowledgement that those who care for the sick are themselves "gifted" (the recipients of gifts) and not only gifted with their powers but gifted with their patients. Medical practice might be formed to see the

---

11. James M. Gustafson, "Spiritual Life and Moral Life," *Theology and Christian Ethics* (Philadelphia: Pilgrim Press, 1974), pp. 161-76, at p. 170.

12. William F. May, "Images That Shape the Public Obligations of the Minister," p. 28.

opportunities to respond to the Lord in their opportunities to respond to the sick, opportunities gratefully to see and to serve the Lord in their opportunities to see and to serve "the least of these."

There is very little time when we turn finally to *petition,* and we apologize a little, but our friend will have no apologies.

"Prayer is not magic," he says. "It is not a way to put God at my disposal. It is the way to put myself at God's disposal. It is not a technique to get what I want,[13] whether a fortune or fourteen more healthy years.[14] It is not a spiritual technology to be pulled out as a last resort when medical technologies have failed. What was that bad joke you told earlier? Prayer is not a means, not even a 'means to make God present.'[15] It attends to God; and as it does, it discovers in memory and hope that God *is* present. To treat prayer as a means to some other good than the good that belongs to prayer makes prayer a superstition — and trivializes God into some 'great scalpel in the sky.'"[16]

"May we not then make petition together?" we ask, a little shocked.

"Of course we can," he says, "but carefully; for here it is easy to attend to ourselves rather than to God, and to our wishes rather than to God's cause."

So we form our petitions on the model of the one to whom we attend. We pray — and pray boldly — that God's name and power may be hallowed, that God's kingdom may come, that God's good future will be established "speedily and soon" — in this man's own lifetime.[17]

---

13. Henry Stob, "Prayer and Providence," in his *Theological Reflections* (Grand Rapids: Wm. B. Eerdmans Publishing Company, 1981), p. 91: "[At] the bottom, and in its purest state, prayer is not a way to get things out of God, but rather to receive what he freely offers — fellowship with himself. At the heart of prayer is *communion.* . . ."

14. See Courtney S. Campbell, "Haven't Got a Prayer," *Hastings Center Report* 19:3 (May/June, 1989), pp. 2-3, who reviews the ambiguous results of efforts to test the healing effectiveness of intercessory prayer. He concludes with a "health care version of Pascal's wager: Prayer doesn't appear to hurt, and it may help, recovery."

15. Against Stanley Hauerwas, *Suffering Presence,* p. 81.

16. William F. May, *The Physician's Covenant: Images of the Healer in Medical Ethics* (Philadelphia: Westminster Press, 1983), p. 60.

17. The Lord's Prayer was modeled after the Kaddish, which was (and is — in an expanded form) used in synagogue services. Joachim Jeremias, *The Prayers of Jesus,* Studies in Biblical Theology, Second Series, 6 (London: SCM Press, 1967), p. 98, offers this reconstruction of the oldest form of this prayer: Exalted and hallowed be his great name in the world which he created according to his will. May he let his kingdom rule in

217

And because that good future is *already* established, we pray — and pray boldly — as the Lord taught us, for a taste of that future, for a taste of it in such ordinary things as everyday bread and everyday forgiveness, in such ordinary things as tonight's rest and tomorrow's life, in such mundane stuff as the workings of mortal flesh, and the healing of our embodied selves.

But because that good future is *not yet* — still sadly not yet — we pray no less boldly for the presence of the one who suffers with us, the one who hurts in our pain. We pray no less boldly for that than for the power of the one who promises in God's good future to raise us up and heal us: "the redemption of our bodies" (Rom. 8:23).

We do not, and I think we may not, pray for death. Death is not the cause of God. In the good future of God death will be no more. Attending to God rather than to ourselves, to God's cause rather than to our own wishes, we are unlikely to bring a petition for death to our lips. Until that good future comes, however, there will sometimes be good reasons to cease praying for a patient's survival. Attending to God in confident hope of God's final triumph frees us from desperately holding onto this life, frees us to let go of it, leaving it in the hands of the one who can be trusted.

Incidentally, these questions of what we may pray for are interesting and illuminating moral questions. They are found in the Talmud[18] and in the church fathers, but they are not found in the recent literature on medical ethics. I suppose medical ethics does not really need any additional interesting questions right now, but it is poorer for its failure to attend to prayer. It is poorer for its failure to attend by prayer to God.

---

your lifetime and in your days and in the lifetime of the whole house of Israel, speedily and soon.

18. For example, there is the wonderful story and subsequent debates about the behavior of Rabbi Judah's maid in Babylonian Talmud, tractate Kethuboth 104A. The maid saw Rabbi Judah's unrelieved suffering and, in fact, "prayed that it should be God's will that the immortals [angels, who wanted his death] should win over the mortals [humans, who did not]." When the rabbi's colleagues continued to pray for his survival, she dropped a jar from the roof. When it shattered, the rabbis stopped praying, and Rabbi Judah died. Did this woman, noted for her wisdom in other places in the Talmud, do right? Did she violate the teaching of the rabbis that death not be hastened? On this story and the debate see Baruch A. Brody, "An Historical Introduction to Jewish Casuistry on Suicide and Euthanasia," in Baruch A. Brody, ed., *Suicide and Euthanasia: Historical and Contemporary Themes*, Philosophy and Medicine, 35 (Dordrecht: Kluwer Academic Publishers, 1989), pp. 39-75, at pp. 63-64.

Perhaps only a prayer-formed person will see so clearly that there is an important moral difference not only between praying for someone's death and ceasing to pray for someone's life but also between killing and allowing to die, between intending death and letting go a desperate hold on life. At least it seems increasingly difficult to make that distinction in moral "esperanto," whether the language chosen is one of utility or autonomy.

Doctors and nurses make intercession, too, of course — as well as patients. They make petition for those for whom they care, and over whom they exercise responsibility. The conscientious doctor and nurse, especially the ones who take themselves too seriously and regard themselves messianically, will be tempted to make prayer a means again, a supplementary technology, to insure the effectiveness of their own work. But such a prayer is no less corrupted into superstition because the petitioner is medical practitioner, and "God" is no less trivialized as the great scalpel in the sky because the bloody hands of a surgeon are lifted up in such a prayer.

Prayers of intercession and petition, this form of attention to God, not ourselves, can and sometimes do and should form an altered sense of responsibility (and an *altared* sense of responsibility). In petition the doctor or the nurse hands the one under their care over to the hands of God,[19] remembering and hoping that the God to whom they attend is abounding in steadfast love and able to heal the hurt no medicine can touch.

In making petition medical practitioners let go of the anxious control they have conscientiously assumed. The doctor who prays seriously for a patient can take herself a little less seriously. In making petition the medical practitioner learns again that she is not Messiah, and she is freed from the intolerable burden of inaugurating God's good future for the patient. She can freely acknowledge the limits of the art and her own limits. The doctor who prays seriously for a patient will be formed to provide the best care she can, of course; but she no longer anxiously substitutes for an absent God. In making petition the medical practitioner learns again a care-free care. And in that "altared" sense of responsibility we lay the best medical skills and the worst medical cases before God with bloody hands and lift them up in prayer.

19. William F. May, *The Physician's Covenant*, p. 60. See also Craig Dykstra, *Vision and Character* (New York: Paulist Press, 1981), p. 94, who describes repentance as a "letting go": "So repentance is a 'letting go,' in trust and humility, of our striving to control everything in order to establish and sustain ourselves."

"One final word," Coles's friend says. "We said before that a prayer-formed people will not despise medicine. It may also be said that a prayer-formed people will not despise medical ethics either. Only let them pray now and then. Prayer is not magic for decisions either, of course. It is not a technique to get what I want, even when what I want is an answer or a solution to a dilemma rather than a fortune or fourteen more healthy years. It is not a technology to be pulled out as a last resort when medical ethics has failed to tell us clearly what we ought to do. It does not rescue us from moral ambiguity. Part of what we know to be God's cause may still conflict with another part of what we know to be God's cause. You will still have to work hard, attending to cases, sorting out principles, identifying the various goods at stake, listening carefully to different accounts of the situation. Prayer does not rescue you from all that, but it does permit you to do all that in ways that are attentive to God and attentive, as well, to the relations of all that to God."

"In prayer," he says, "we not only commune with God but find new strength — new virtue — for daily life. A wise ethicist once told me that."

CHAPTER FIVE

Coles's Friend Revisited

I admitted at the very beginning that the idea for these lectures was stolen from the man they are intended to honor. The idea is this: that a faithful Christian life depends finally on simple acts of piety, on the practices of offering prayer and reading scripture. "Through prayer and scripture," Henry Stob said, "we not only commune with God but find new strength — new virtue — for daily life."

These lectures attempt to honor Henry Stob by taking that idea to the hospital, to the nursing home, to all the places where we endure and care in the face of pain and sickness and death. The task undertaken in these lectures is to take Henry Stob's reminder of the significance of prayer and scripture to medicine and to medical ethics.

We began with prayer, and we asked how that practice of piety might support and challenge the practice of medicine.

Since every lecture in medical ethics needs a case, we retold a story Robert Coles tells in his *Harvard Diary.* It is the story of a Catholic friend of his, a physician who became a patient who knew his cancer would not likely be beaten back, a Christian who knew the final triumph belongs to the risen Christ. The eminent Harvard psychiatrist said of his friend that he wanted and needed "some good hard praying." He wanted and needed someone with whom to talk of God and someone with whom to talk to God. What he got instead, as Coles tells the story, was a visit from a chaplain who neglected the practices of piety for the sake of the "religionless" and generic language of psychology. The chaplain spoke "psychobabble" and dwelt upon the stages of dying as though they were "Stations of the Cross." So, at least, Coles and his friend complained.

In our retelling of the story the chaplain turned medical ethicist. He

221

still ignored the practices of piety, now for the sake of an impartial moral point of view and universal principles. He still spoke a "religionless" and generic language, now a form of moral "esperanto," the universal moral language that is no one's natural moral tongue. The chaplain turned ethicist now dwelt upon the principles of autonomy and privacy as though they were the first and great and only commandments.

And Coles's friend still got angry. He invited this chaplain turned ethicist back to his hospital room, set his bookmark at Psalm 69, and told his visitor to read.

As Coles points out, Psalm 69 is a prayer, a lament actually, a cry of anguish and a call for help: "Save me, O God, for the waters have come up to my neck." But the chaplain turned ethicist surely discovered, as he continued to read, what Coles did not mention, that Psalm 69 is an imprecatory psalm, a cry of anguish that vents its anger in curses on those who fail to comfort, a cry for help that asks not just for rescue but for revenge.

In our retelling of Coles's story the chaplain turned ethicist was stung by this psalm, chastened by this angry rebuke; and he resolved to visit Coles's friend one more time. We went with him then and found in Coles's friend one of a great number who still call on God, not some medical ethicist, for guidance.

We went to his room and learned something (I hope) about the ways in which the practice of prayer might nurture and sustain — and qualify and challenge — the practice of medicine. We discovered (I hope) that Henry Stob was right, that attention to God in the forms of invocation and confession and gratitude and petition could, sometimes did, and surely should form new virtue for the daily tasks of both those who are sick and those who care for them.

Now we turn to scripture, to the practice of piety in reading scripture. Perhaps we can also learn from Coles's friend something of how the practice of reading the Bible might illumine — and reform — medical practice and medical ethics.

Let's go back to the room of Coles's friend again, this time to offer to read some scripture. We hope, of course, that we do not end up reading another imprecatory psalm, calling curses upon our own heads again. Before we even reach the elevator, however, we grow a little anxious about reading scripture as normative for medicine and medical ethics. We remember some stories of the use of scripture, and we are anxious not to repeat them.

There is the story of the heart patient who opened his Bible to Psalm 51 and laid his finger on verse 10: "Create in me a clean heart, O God." He told his physician of this remarkable event, and insisted it was a sign that he should receive a Jarvik VII, an artificial heart. The physician tried to explain that a Jarvik VII is probably not what the psalmist had in mind, at least the FDA seems not to think so. The physician refused to take Psalm 51:10 as an indication of a need for a Jarvik VII or any other artificial heart transplant; and as he left, he put his finger on the still open Bible, on the page before Psalm 51, on Psalm 50 verse 9; and he read the words, "I will accept no bull from your house."

That sort of "bull" is probably not what the psalmist had in mind either, we think to ourselves as the elevator arrives to pick us up; but the problem is whether we can read scripture as relevant to sickness and to the care of the sick without falling into it.

On the elevator we remember other stories. There is a story told of Dr. Tiemersma, the retired English professor at Calvin College, and one of the pre-sem students he delighted in humbling. It was the beginning of class; and when he had gathered everyone's attention, he looked to this student and said, "Verhey, I understand you're going to be a pastor some day." Verhey nodded, worried about what would come next. "Well," he said, "one day you will probably find yourself counseling a married couple. Suppose the issue is whether to have more children. The wife says she is worn out with the three they already have and would like to return to her work when the youngest gets to school. The husband, however, wants more children; and he says to you, 'But pastor, it says in scripture, "Happy is the man who has his quiver full." And what would you say, Verhey?" Verhey responded quickly, "um . . . well . . . um." The class was silent; and with the little part of his mind that he could spare just then, Verhey wondered whether it was silent sympathy or silent glee at his embarrassment. Tiemersma meanwhile was counting the "ums" and judging the blush of rising embarrassment; and when they had reached full measure, he said, "Verhey, has it never occurred to you that quivers come in different sizes?"

There is the story of every Dutch Calvinist's great-great grandfather in the Netherlands. He was famous for his piety and especially for his ability to recite a scripture verse for any occasion. He was, however, infamous as a horse trader. None of the villagers who so respected him for his ability to quote scripture would deal with him when they needed a horse. One day a stranger's horse went lame, and great-great grampa sold the stranger an old nag to get home for about four times its value. Great-great gramma complained about the sale, calling attention to her husband's reputation among the villagers. Great-great grampa retorted quickly, "But great-great gramma, I did it by the command of the Lord: I saw a stranger, and I took him in."

The elevator arrives, and so does a serious case of anxiety concerning what we are about to do. Reading scripture as relevant to the moral life in general or to medical ethics in particular — it seems — can get scripture, the moral life, and medicine in a good deal of trouble.

So, as we come near the room of Coles's friend, we resolve to point out some problems in reading scripture as relevant to medicine and medical ethics and to ask him just why reading scripture is so important to him.

We enter his room and are glad to be greeted warmly. At least we need not worry about imprecatory psalms. "We have come to read some scripture," we say, "but let's admit there are some problems reading scripture in this 'world come of age' called a hospital." "Problems?" he says, "I don't know what you mean." "Then let us explain," we say, and begin to list some.

"One problem is the silence of scripture. Scripture simply does not deal with new powers of medicine or with the new moral problems they pose. No law code of Israel attempted a statutory definition of death in response to technology that could keep the heart beating and the lungs pumping. No sage ever commented on the wisdom of *in vitro* fertilization or on the prudence of another round of chemotherapy and radiation in what looks like a losing battle against the cancer of Coles's friend. The prophets who beat against injustice with their words never mentioned the allocation of scarce medical resources. No scribe ever asked Jesus about withholding artificial nutrition and hydration. Nor did any early Christian community ask Paul about medical experimentation. The creatures of Revelation may seem to a contemporary reader the result of a failed adventure in genetic modification, but the author does not address the issue of genetic control.

"The Bible simply does not answer many of the questions which new medical powers have forced us to ask; the authors, even the most visionary of them, never dreamt of these new powers of medicine. To use *any* passage of scripture to answer directly any of the particular problems posed by these new powers is likely to be no less anachronistic and no more plausible than to use Psalm 51:10 to support a Jarvik VII."

Coles's friend is clearly perplexed by this last reference, and we remember he wasn't on the elevator with us. But we do not pause to tell the story again; we press on to the next problem.

"The silence of scripture is not the only reason — or the main reason — to be reticent about relating the practice of reading scripture and the practice of medicine. Besides the silence of scripture, there is the strangeness of scripture. When scripture does speak about sickness and the power to heal, its words are, well, quaint.

"The world of sickness in scripture is strange and alien to us. When King Asa is chided by the Chronicler, for example, for consulting physicians about his diseased feet (2 Chron. 16:12), it is a strange world of sickness of which we read. When the sick cry out in anguish and join to their lament a confession of their sins, as though their sicknesses are divine punishment for their sins: 'There is no soundness in my flesh because of thy indignation; there is no health in my bones because of my sins' (Ps. 38:3), then it is a strange world of sickness of which we read. And when a person with a chronic skin disease, characterized by red patches covered with white scales, is declared ritually impure by the priests and instructed to cry 'Unclean, Unclean,' to any who pass by (Lev. 13:45), it is a strange world of sickness of which we read. I mean, talk about the 'heartbreak of psoriasis.'[1]

"It is not difficult to multiply examples; much of what we read in scripture about sickness and healing is alien to us, and honest Christians are driven to admit that the words of scripture are human words, words we may not simply identify with timeless truths dropped from heaven or repeat without qualification as Christian counsel for providing or utilizing medical care today."

Coles's friend is nodding in agreement. We hasten on.

"Scripture is sometimes silent, sometimes strange — and usually diverse. That's the third problem. Scripture does not speak with one voice about sickness and healing. The Chronicler evidently rejected physicians and their medicines, but in Ecclesiasticus the sage Jesus ben Sirach effortlessly integrated physicians and medicines into Jewish faith in God" (Ecclesiasticus 38:1-15). (Coles's friend, a Catholic, smiles at our reference

---

1. The disease was probably not modern leprosy, or Hansen's bacillus. See Klaus Seybold and Ulrich B. Mueller, *Sickness and Healing,* trans. Douglas W. Stott (Nashville: Abingdon, 1981), pp. 67-74. The identification of the disorder called *sara'at* as psoriasis is given at p. 69.

to Ecclesiasticus, a book of the apocrypha; but we explain that the Belgic Confession lets us learn from those books, too.)

"The lament of the psalmist and the curse of Psalm 69 clearly assume that sickness and suffering are God's punishment for sins; but Job raised his voice against that assumption, rejecting the conventional wisdom of his friends. In the midst of suffering and in *spite* of it, he insisted upon his own innocence and brought suit against the Lord (for divine malpractice, presumably). The Philistines learned at Ashdod, where Dagon fell before the ark, that their tumors (which according to one scholar were probably hemorrhoids)[2] did not happen 'by chance,' that it was God's 'hand that struck us' (1 Sam. 6:9). But other voices could tell of natural causes at work in sickness and in healing (Ecclesiasticus 31:20-22, 37:27-31), and still other voices spoke of demons or the dominion of death as the cause of sickness.[3]

"The diversity of scripture on these matters might give us pause before we attempt to relate the practice of reading scripture and the practice of medicine today."

Coles's friend is patient with us. "Is there anything else?" he asks.

"Yes," we say, "as a matter of fact there is. It must simply be admitted that appeals to scripture have sometimes done a great deal of harm. When Genesis 3:16, 'in pain you shall bring forth children,' was quoted to oppose pain relief for women in labor,[4] a great deal of harm was done. When the Bible was pointed to by those who said that AIDS was God's punishment for homosexual behavior,[5] a great deal of harm was done. When children are denied transfusions because of a curious reading of a curious set of texts about blood,[6] a great deal of harm is done. When some Dutch Calvin-

---

2. D. W. Amundsen and G. B. Ferngren, "Medicine and Religion: Pre-Christian Antiquity," in Martin Marty and Kenneth Vaux, eds., *Health/Medicine and the Faith Traditions* (Philadelphia: Fortress Press, 1982), pp. 53-92, at p. 62.

3. See Klaus Seybold and Ulrich Mueller, *Sickness and Healing,* pp. 112-14.

4. See Ronald L. Numbers and Ronald C. Sawyer, "Medicine and Christianity in the Modern World," in Martin Marty and Kenneth Vaux, eds., *Health/Medicine and the Faith Traditions,* pp. 133-60, at p. 134. Numbers and Sawyer also observe, however, that scripture was also cited to justify the use of anesthetics, notably Gen. 2:21, where God mercifully caused "a deep sleep to fall upon Adam" before removing his rib.

5. According to a 1988 Gallup poll of registered voters, 42.5 percent of those surveyed agreed with the statement that AIDS is God's punishment for immoral behaviors (*Newsweek,* 1 Feb. 1988, p. 7).

6. On the Jehovah's Witness' position prohibiting blood transfusions on the basis

ists, the 'Old Reformed,' refused to have their children immunized against polio because Jesus said, 'those who are well have no need of a physician' (Matt. 9:12), then a great deal of harm was done.[7] It may be said — and I think rightly said — that these uses of scripture are all abuses of scripture; but patients have nevertheless been harmed, usually women and children and marginalized patients, seldom 'righteous' adult males who need care.

"Episodes of the abuse of scripture and episodes of the abuse of patients by reading scripture should make us hesitate before we attempt to connect this 'infallible rule' to medical ethics."

Coles's friend is evidently collecting his thoughts to make response. The moment's quiet is interrupted by our words summarizing the problems and attempting to clench the argument.

"The silence of scripture, the strangeness of scripture, the diversity of scripture, and the abuse of scripture all seem to hint that there might be wisdom in simply rejecting an attempt to relate the practice of reading scripture to the practice of medicine. And if there are things about scripture which seem to hint that such is wisdom, there are things about medical practice and medical ethics which seem to shout it.

"Modern medicine is a thoroughly secular enterprise. It attends to the body, not the spirit; to cells, not the soul. It focuses on the presence of natural causes of disease and discomfort, not on the presence of divine powers who smite with sickness those who are sinners or make whole those to whom Asclepius or Jesus elect to be gracious.

"And it is a pluralistic society, after all. When the professional group one wants to persuade is composed of both Christians and those who are not, or when the public policy makers one hopes to convince have been sworn to protect freedom of religion and not to establish a peculiarly Christian policy, or when the society within which one tries to form a con-

---

of Genesis 9:4, Leviticus 17:13-14, Acts 15:29, etc., see W. H. Cumberland, "The Jehovah's Witness Tradition," in R. L. Numbers and D. W. Amundsen, eds., *Caring and Curing: Health and Medicine in the Western Religious Traditions* (New York: Macmillan, 1986), pp. 468-85.

7. See Richard Mouw, "Biblical Revelation and Medical Decisions," in Stanley Hauerwas and Alasdair MacIntyre, eds., *Revisions: Changing Perspectives in Moral Philosophy* (Notre Dame: University of Notre Dame Press, 1983), pp. 182-202, at pp. 197-98. Mouw puts the best possible face on this foolishness, construing it as resistance against the tendency to reduce the human struggle with suffering to the medical model for that struggle.

sensus is — or seems to be — overwhelmingly secular, then arguments based on scripture may well be regarded as, at best, insufficient and probably irrelevant. Such contexts for public discourse about medical practice seem to require arguments based on universal and generic moral principles or on legal precedents within a society and on an impartial and objective point of view, and such are the arguments one typically finds in the literature on medical ethics.

"It is little wonder that in medical ethics even those trained as theologians sound more like followers of Mill or Kant or John Rawls than like disciples of Jesus. It is little wonder that even those who know scripture hesitate to quote it."

Coles's friend can restrain himself no longer. "It is little wonder," he says, "but it is nevertheless lamentable."[8]

"It is lamentable," he says, "because a genuinely pluralistic society presumably profits from the candid articulation and vigorous defense of particular points of view. The particular views of identifiable communities serve to remind pluralistic societies not only of the moral necessity of some minimal moral requirements for people to live together and die together peaceably,[9] but also that such requirements are, indeed, *minimal.* If society ignores or denies the richer voices of particular moral traditions, it will be finally unable to nurture any character besides the rational self-interested individual, unable to sustain any community other than that based on the contracts entered by such individuals, and unable even to ask seriously 'what should be decided?' and not just 'who should decide?'

"The failure to attend to scripture is lamentable, moreover," he says, "because the practice of medicine is not 'religionless.' The extraordinary human events to which medicine ordinarily attends, giving birth and suffering and dying, have an inalienably religious character. And the care with which we attend to them is no less ineluctably religious.

"Even those who invoke no God by name have a *sensus divinitatis,* a sense of the presence and power of an Other (or Others) who bears down on us or sustains us in our weakness and in our power. Sometimes it is a sense of dependence; sometimes, a sense of gratitude; sometimes it is a

8. See further Allen Verhey, "Talking of God — But with Whom?" *Hastings Center Report* 20:4, Special Supplement, "Theology, Religious Traditions, and Bioethics," pp. 21-24.

9. H. Tristram Engelhardt, "Bioethics in Pluralist Societies," *Perspectives in Biology and Medicine* 26:1 (1982), pp. 64-77.

sense of remorse; sometimes, a sense of hope; sometimes it is a sense of responsibility; often, it is a curious mixture, but always it is a sense of the presence and power of an inscrutable Other in and through all else on which we depend and for which we give thanks, in and through all else which brings regret or gives hope or calls us toward the right and good. To deny or ignore these senses and this Other is lamentable, both for patient and practitioner. Candid and public attention to particular religious traditions may serve to nurture and sustain such senses and to orient both such 'natural piety' and such medicine.

"It must be said, as well," he says, "that sometimes such 'natural piety' and such medicine need prophetic correction. When, for example, some presumably 'religionless' patient has idolatrous expectations of medical technology, when such a patient petitions a doctor as wizard or priest to provide a medical miracle with technological grace that will rescue the patient from finitude and deliver the patient to flourishing, then candid attention to the one God of scripture and to scripture's warnings against idolatry can make a public contribution.

"Finally, however," Coles's friend says, "it is lamentable for me. When people who know scripture fail to consider its bearing on medical care, it is lamentable for me — and for people like me.

"Faithful members of Christian community long to live and to die faithfully. If we must suffer while we live or as we die, we want to suffer with Christian integrity — not just impartial rationality. If we are called to care for the suffering (and we are), we want to care with integrity — not just with impartial rationality.

"This longing of faith and of the faithful for Christian integrity is not served by ignoring the resources of the tradition or by silencing the peculiar voices of scripture. It is served by talking together and thinking together and praying together about the ways in which the story that Christians love to tell and long to live can form and inform a response to the ancient human events of giving birth and suffering and dying and about how the same story can guide and limit the uses of the new medical powers.

"In Christian community the tradition, including scripture, does not merely exist as an archaic relic in an age of science and reason. In Christian community scripture exists as that which continues to evoke loyalties and to form and reform character and conduct into dispositions and deeds 'worthy of the gospel'" (Phil. 1:27).

"I take it then," we say rather lamely, "that scripture is important to you."

I'll delete the expletive of his response. He gets a little excited. When he calms down a little, he says, "'Important' hardly covers it. It is the Word of God, after all, and 'profitable for teaching, for reproof, for correction, and for training in righteousness'" (2 Tim. 3:16).

10. See, for example, the wonderful essay by William F. May, "The Sacral Power of Death in Contemporary Experience," *Social Research* 39 (1972), pp. 463-88.

CHAPTER SIX

Reading Scripture as a Practice

All scripture is inspired by God and profitable for teaching, for reproof, for correction, for training in righteousness, that the man of God may be complete, equipped for every good work. (2 Tim. 3:16-17)

Coles's friend evidently knows the passage that runs down the centuries of the church's attention to scripture. "'Important' hardly covers it," he says.

"That seems a long way from where we began," we say and remind him that he was nodding in agreement when we talked about the silence and strangeness of scripture.

"I do not deny that these words are human words," he says, "and I do not claim that we may simply repeat them as Christian counsel about medical practice and medical ethics today. But these words are also the Word of God, our faith reminds us, and they may not simply be discredited at our convenience."

There is a pause; and then he says to us, "You like problems evidently. Let me give you one: There is no Christian life that is not tied *somehow* to scripture. There is no Christian ethic that is not formed and informed *somehow* by scripture. Yet, as you say, the world of sickness and healing in scripture is sometimes strange and alien, and a Christian medical ethic will not simply be identical with it, but *somehow* informed by it.[1] The problem is

1. See the "important two-part consensus" identified by Bruce Birch and Larry Rasmussen that "Christian ethics is not synonymous with biblical ethics" and that "for Christian ethics the Bible is somehow normative." Bruce Birch and Larry Rasmussen, *Bible and Ethics in the Christian Life* (Minneapolis: Augsburg, 1976), pp. 45-46. The same

not whether to relate scripture and medicine, for there is no Christian moral reflection which is not tied *somehow* to scripture. The problem is not *whether* — but *how* — to relate them."

There is another pause, but finally we agree and ask the question we had earlier resolved to ask, "So why — or how — is scripture so important to you?"

"Scripture is important to me," he says, "because Article Seven of the Belgic Confession calls it an 'infallible rule.'" Well, okay, probably not; he is a Catholic after all, but he is no more likely to have said, "Scripture is important to me because the Second Vatican Council calls it 'the supreme rule of faith.'"[2] He has not learned of scripture and its significance from a confession or a creed but from participation in the practice of reading it with the people of God.

This is what he says: "Scripture is important to me because reading scripture is what Alasdair MacIntyre called a 'practice.'" Okay, he probably doesn't say that either. He has probably never read *After Virtue;* and if he had, he would be no more likely to remember MacIntyre's definition of a practice than you would if you heard it last night. He is not a philosopher, after all.

But he is a Christian, and he has learned in Christian community the practice of reading scripture, even if he has never learned MacIntyre's account of what a practice is. He is a Christian. He has learned to read scripture in Christian community. And in learning to read scripture, he has learned as well the good that belongs to reading scripture, the good "internal to that form of activity." He has learned, that is, to remember.[3]

And he has learned it not only intellectually. That is to say, he has learned not just a mental process of recollection, not just disinterested recall of objective historical facts. He has learned to own a past as his own,

---

claims are found in the revised edition (Minneapolis: Augsburg, 1989), p. 189. See also Allen Verhey, *The Great Reversal: Ethics and the New Testament* (Grand Rapids: Wm. B. Eerdmans Publishing Company, 1984), pp. 153-97.

2. "Dogmatic Constitution on Divine Revelation," in Walter M. Abbott, S.J., ed., *The Documents of Vatican II* (New York: Guild Press, 1966), pp. 111-28, at p. 125.

3. For the notion of remembrance as "the good" of reading scripture (and for much besides), I am indebted to Stanley Hauerwas. See his essay "The Moral Authority of Scripture: The Politics and Ethics of Remembering," *A Community of Character* (Notre Dame: University of Notre Dame Press, 1981), pp. 53-71. See also Hans Frei, *The Eclipse of Biblical Narrative* (New Haven: Yale University Press, 1974).

and to own it as constitutive of identity and determinative for discernment. Without remembering there is no identity. In amnesia one loses oneself. In memory one finds an identity. And without common remembering there is no community. It is little wonder that the church sustains this practice of piety, and is herself sustained by it and again and again made new by reading scripture and remembering.

Coles's friend may never have read MacIntyre, but he has read John Bunyan's wonderful allegory *Pilgrim's Progress,* and he knows what Great Heart knew. He knows what that marvelous helper and guide said to the son of Christian as he pointed ahead to a place called "Forgetful Green." "That place," he said, "is the most dangerous place in all these parts."[4] Coles's friend knows that a pilgrim's progress comes by remembering. "That's why scripture is important to me," he says.

He may never have read MacIntyre, but he has read scripture, and he knows what Moses said to a bunch of slaves looking across the Jordan to their future. "Remember the Lord your God," he said (Deut. 8:18). "Take heed lest you forget the Lord your God," he said (Deut. 8:11). "Good times may come, and you may find yourself on Forgetful Green, and that is the most dangerous place in all those parts" (cf. Deut. 8:12-18). Moses might have said as well, of course, as many prophets after him did, "Take heed lest you forget. Bad times may come. You may find yourself in Forgetful Straits. And that is a dangerous place across this river, too." He knows that again and again and yet again Moses and Joshua and Nathan and Amos and all the prophets and all the psalmists called the people to remember. "Remember that you were slaves in Egypt" (cf. Deut. 5:15). "Remember the ways the Lord your God led you in the wilderness" (cf. Deut. 8:2). "Remember the days of old" (Deut. 32:7). "Remember the wonderful works the Lord has done" (Ps. 105:5). "Remember." He knows that the gospels are written in remembrance and that Paul writes "by way of reminder" (Rom. 15:15). "That's why scripture is important to me," he says.

In learning to read scripture in Christian community he has learned that the art of remembering among God's people has always involved story-telling. The remedy for forgetfulness has always been a wonderful and lively story. Story after story was told generation after generation. Sometimes on Forgetful Greens the people forgot the stories — or forgot to

---

4. John Bunyan, *The Pilgrim's Progress* (New York: Washington Square Press, 1957), p. 234. (It was originally published in 1678.)

tell them. And sometimes in Forgetful Straits the people nearly lost their memory — and their identity. But the remedy for forgetfulness was always to tell the old, old story, and a new generation would remember and own the story as their story and God as their God.

In learning to read scripture in Christian community he has learned as well not only that remembering involved story-telling but also that remembering took the shape of obedience. To remember the Lord your God, to own the stories of God's glories, of God's works of power and grace, always meant among God's people to live them, to shape one's life and character and conduct into something fitting to them. To remember that God rescued you from Pharaoh's oppression took the shape of freeing a hired hand from your own oppression, no longer cheating him of a living or of rest. To remember that God gave manna, enough for all to share, took the shape of leaving the edge of the field unharvested for the poor. To remember Jesus took the shape of discipleship.

Coles's friend has learned no theory of memory from reading scripture,[5] but he has learned to remember. "That's why — and how — scripture is important to me," he says. "I know the temptation to forgetfulness in the Forgetful Green of health and in the great medical powers to heal. I know the temptation to forgetfulness in the Forgetful Straits of pain and suffering and in the final powerlessness of medicine. I fear amnesia in this 'world come of age' called a hospital and in this 'religionless' world called medicine. That's why I lament so deeply the failure of some medical ethicists who know scripture to remind me of it. That's why I long so deeply to connect the remembrance that belongs to the practice of reading scripture with the suffering and care for the suffering that belong to medicine."

"There are problems," we say, ready to rehearse again the silence and strangeness and diversity and abuse of scripture. But they do not seem quite so overwhelming now, for we recognize that in learning to read scripture he has learned not only the good that belongs to this practice — remembrance — but also some standards of excellence "appropriate to" reading scripture and "partially definitive of" this practice of piety.

He has learned, that is, both holiness and sanctification, both fidelity and creativity, both discipline and discernment — three pairs of virtues for reading scripture. *Holiness* is the standard of excellence in reading scripture

---

5. There is nothing in scripture to compare, for example, with Aristotle's treatise *De Memoria*.

that not only sets these writings apart from others but that is ready to set apart a time and a place to read them and to remember, ready to set aside a time and a place and to protect that time and place from the tendencies of "the world" and from our obligations within the world to render our lives "profane," to reduce them to something "religionless."[6]

Sanctification is the standard of excellence in reading scripture that is ready to set the remembered story alongside all the stories of our suffering and our dying, alongside the stories of our healing and our caring,[7] until *all* the times and *all* the spaces of our lives are made new by the power of God, made to fit remembrance, made worthy of the gospel.

Our practice here is frequently better than our theology. Our theology tends to construe God's relation to scripture and to us through scripture simply as "revealer." Then the content of scripture can simply be identified with revelation, and the theological task becomes simply to systematize and republish timeless biblical ideas or doctrines or principles or rules.

In the practice of reading scripture in Christian community, however, we learn, I think, to construe God's relation to scripture and surely to us through scripture as "sanctifier."[8] Then what one understands when one understands scripture in remembrance is the creative and re-creative power of God to renew life, to transform identities, to create a people and a world for God's own glory and for their flourishing.

Remembrance takes place in holiness and calls for sanctification. It takes place in a context set aside and set apart, and it makes place for the grace and power of God to touch all of life with remembrance and to orient all of life to God's cause, hoped for because remembered, and present now in memory and in hope.

Besides both holiness and sanctification the practice of reading scripture also requires both fidelity and creativity.

Remembrance provides identity, and *fidelity* is simply the standard of

6. Stephen E. Fowl and L. Gregory Jones, *Reading in Communion: Scripture and Ethics in Christian Life* (Grand Rapids: Wm. B. Eerdmans Publishing Company, 1991), pp. 31-33.

7. See, for example, Stanley Hauerwas, *Naming the Silences: God, Medicine, and the Problem of Suffering* (Grand Rapids: Wm. B. Eerdmans Publishing Company, 1990), pp. 34-147.

8. See further Allen Verhey, *The Great Reversal*, pp. 180-81, and David Kelsey, "The Bible and Christian Theology," *The Journal of the American Academy of Religion* 68:3 (1980), pp. 385-402.

excellence that is ready to live with integrity in that identity, ready to be faithful to the memory the church has owned as her own. But fidelity requires a process of continual change, of *creativity*.[9] Remembrance requires creativity, for the past is past, and we do not live in it even if we remember it. We do not live in Asa's court or in the Jerusalem of Pontius Pilate. And creativity is the standard of excellence in reading scripture that refuses to reduce fidelity to an anachronistic, if amiable, eccentricity.

Nicholas Lash makes the point quite nicely with respect to the traditions and ecclesiastical dress of the Franciscans. "If, in thirteenth-century Italy, you wandered around in a coarse brown gown," he said, ". . . your dress said you were one of the poor. If, in twentieth-century Cambridge, you wander around in a coarse brown gown, . . . your dress now says, not that you are one of the poor, but that you are some kind of oddity in the business of 'religion.'"[10] Fidelity to a tradition of solidarity with the poor requires creativity and change.

Fidelity to the identity provided by remembrance must never be confused with anachronistic, if amiable, eccentricity. The practice of reading scripture and the good of remembrance that belongs to it require both fidelity and creativity.

Again the practice of reading scripture is sometimes better than our theology for it. There are some theologians who insist on continuity, who are suspicious of creativity, and who think of themselves as embattled defenders of a tradition threatened by change. These stand ready to accuse others of "accommodation."[11] There are other theologians (or philosophical theists) who insist on change, who minimize the significance of continuity, and who stand ready to accuse others of "irrational conservativism."[12]

---

9. Continuity and change are marks of any living tradition. They mark scripture itself, and they mark the tradition and practice of reading scripture as a guide for faith and life in the church. See Nicholas Lash, *Theology on the Way to Emmaus* (London: SCM Press, 1986); at p. 55 Lash says, "Fidelity to tradition, in action and speech, is a risky business because it entails active engagement in a process of continual change."

10. Nicholas Lash, *Theology on the Way to Emmaus,* p. 54.

11. Franklin E. Payne, *Biblical/Medical Ethics* (Milford, Mich., Mott Media, 1985), an unnumbered page in the Introduction. Similarly John M. Frame, *Medical Ethics: Principles, Persons, and Problems* (Phillipsburg, N.J.: Presbyterian and Reformed, 1988), p. 2, says "Scripture says it, we believe it, and that settles it."

12. For example, Charles Hartshorne, "Scientific and Religious Aspects of Bioethics," in E. E. Shelp, ed., *Theology and Bioethics: Exploring the Foundations and the Frontiers,* pp. 27-44, at p. 28.

But the practice of reading scripture rejects both extremes; it insists on both fidelity and creativity, on both continuity and change.

Then to treat scripture as a revealed medical text or as a timeless moral code for medicine is a corruption of the practice of reading scripture. It confuses fidelity with an anachronistic — and sometimes less than amiable — eccentricity. And to treat scripture as simply dated and as irrelevant to contemporary medical practice and medical ethics is also a corruption of the practice. It turns remembrance to an archivist's recollection and runs the risk of alienating the Christian community from its own moral tradition and from its own moral identity. It invites amnesia.

A pilgrim's progress still comes by way of remembering, by the practice of reading scripture — whether the pilgrim is a physician or a patient; and the narrow path between anachronism and amnesia requires both discipline and discernment.

Discipline is the standard of excellence for reading scripture that marks one as being ready to be a disciple, ready to follow the one of whom the story is told, ready to order one's life and one's common life to fit the story. It is the readiness to read scripture "over-against ourselves" and not just "for ourselves,"[13] "over-against" our lives, in judgment upon them and not just in self-serving defense of them, "over-against" even our conventional reading of biblical texts, subverting our own efforts to use scripture to boast about our own righteousness or to protect our own status and power. It is the humility of submission. The remedy for forgetfulness is still to tell the old, old story; and remembrance still takes the shape of obedience. A costly discipleship tests character and conduct by the truth of the story we love to tell.

But the shape of that story and of lives formed to it requires discernment. *Discernment* is the ability to recognize "fittingness."[14] In reading

---

13. Dietrich Bonhoeffer, *No Rusty Swords,* trans. E. H. Robertson and John Bowden (New York: Harper and Row, 1965), p. 185; see also pp. 308-25. One might regard Rich Mouw's contrast between a "priestly" reading of scripture and a "prophetic" reading of scripture to be analogous to Bonhoeffer's contrast; see "Biblical Revelation and Medical Decisions," p. 196.

14. On discernment see especially the work of James Gustafson, "Moral Discernment in the Christian Life," in Gene H. Outka and Paul Ramsey, eds., *Norm and Context in Christian Ethics* (New York: Charles Scribner's Sons, 1968), pp. 17-36; and William C. Spohn, S.J., "The Reasoning Heart: An American Approach to Christian Discernment," in *Theological Studies* 44 (March, 1983), pp. 30-52.

scripture, discernment is the ability to recognize the plot of the story, to see the wholeness of scripture, and to order the interpretation of any part toward that whole. It is to recognize how a statute or a psalm or a story "fits" the whole. And in reading scripture as "profitable . . . for training in righteousness," discernment is the ability to plot our lives to "fit" the whole of scripture, to order every part of our lives — including our medicine — toward that whole. It is to recognize how doing one thing rather than another or doing nothing rather than something may "fit" the story we love to hear and long to live.

Moral discernment is a complex but practical wisdom. It does not rely on spontaneous intuition nor on the simple application of general principles (whether of hermeneutics or of ethics) to particular cases by neutral and rational agents. As there is no theory of memory in scripture, neither is there any theory of discernment. There is no checklist, no flow chart for decisions. But as there is remembering in scripture and in the community that reads it, so there is discernment in scripture and in the community that struggles to live it.

Discernment regards decision as the recognition of what is fitting, coherent, to the kind of person one is and hopes to become. It asks not just "What should a rational person do in a case like this one?" but "What should *I* do in this case?" It recognizes that serious moral questions are always asked in the first person, and it insists on the moral significance of the question "Who am I?" The practice of reading scripture and the good of remembrance that belongs to it give us identity and form character and conduct into something fitting to it.

Discernment regards decision as the recognition of what is fitting or coherent to the circumstances, to what is going on. It recognizes that the meaning of circumstances is not exhausted by objective observation or public inspection. There is no label for life like the label on a can of peas that tells us what the ingredients are. But reading scripture trains us to see the religious significance of events, to read the signs of the times in the things that are happening about us,[15] and to locate events and circum-

---

15. H. Richard Niebuhr, *The Meaning of Revelation* (New York: Macmillan, 1974), p. 109: "What concerns us at this point is not the fact that the revelatory moment shines by its own light but rather that it illumines other events and enables us to understand them. Whatever else revelation means it does mean an event in our history which brings rationality and wholeness into the confused joys and sorrows of personal existence and allows us to discern order in the brawl of communal histories."

stances — as well as our selves — in a story of God's power and grace. Reading scripture trains us to answer the question "What is going on?" with reference to the remembered story, fitting the parts of our lives into the whole of scripture.

Discernment is learned and tested in the community gathered around the scripture, and it involves the diversity of gifts present in the congregation. Some are gifted with the scholarly tools of historical and literary and social scientific investigation. Some are gifted with moral imagination and sensitivity. Some are gifted with a passion for justice, some with a sweet reasonableness. Some are gifted with intellectual clarity, some with simple purity. Some are gifted with courage, some with patience. But all are gifted with their own experience, and each is gifted with the Spirit that brings remembrance (John 14:26).

To be sure, in the community some are blinded by fear, and some are blinded by duty, and the perception of each is abridged by investments in their culture or in their class. To be sure, sometimes whole communities are blinded by idolatrous loyalties to their race or to their social standing or to their power. Witness, for example, the "German Christians" or the Dutch Reformed Church of South Africa. And to be sure, the practice of reading scripture is then corrupted. Such communities stand at risk of forgetfulness, even if they treat scripture as an icon.[16]

The remedy for forgetfulness is still to hear and to tell the old, old story, but to hear it now and then from saints[17] and now and then from strangers for whom Christ also died.[18] Remembrance is served in a community of discernment, reading scripture with those whose experience is

16. Witness the report of the Dutch Reformed Church's 1974 General Synod, *Human Relations and the South African Scene in the Light of Scripture* (Cape Town-Pretoria: Dutch Reformed Church Publishers, 1974). It appeals to scripture to justify apartheid. It has been properly subjected to strong criticism in John de Gruchy and Charles Villa-Vicencio, eds., *Apartheid Is a Heresy* (Grand Rapids: Wm. B. Eerdmans Publishing Company, 1983); see especially pp. 94-143. Witness also the appeals to scripture in Margaret Atwood's powerful novel *The Handmaid's Tale* (New York: Fawcett Crest, 1985).

17. Stephen E. Fowl and L. Gregory Jones, *Reading in Communion: Scripture and Ethics in the Christian Life*, pp. 62-63. They quote Athanasius, *The Incarnation of the Word of God* (New York: Macmillan, 1946), p. 96: "Anyone who wishes to understand the mind of the sacred writers must first cleanse his own life, and approach the saints by copying their deeds."

18. See further Stephen E. Fowl and L. Gregory Jones, *Reading in Communion: Scripture and Ethics in the Christian Life*, pp. 110-34.

different from ours and whose experience of scripture is different from ours. We may learn in such discourse with saints and strangers that our reading of scripture does not yet "fit" scripture itself, and that our lives and our communities do not yet "fit" the story we love to tell and long to live. Then discernment is joined to discipline again, and the recognition of a more fitting way to tell the story and to live it prepares the way for humble submission and discipleship. Once again, the practice is sometimes better than our theology for it. The slogan "sola scriptura" is sometimes used to deny or ignore the relevance of other voices and other sources, to discount natural science or "natural" morality.[19] And talk of the "authority" of scripture is sometimes used to end discussion as though we could beat those who speak from some other experience or for some other source into silence and submission.

The practice can become corrupt, we said, but it can also sometimes be better than our theology. Discernment, or the perception of what is fitting, cannot demand that people violate what they know they know in other ways. It cannot demand that they violate either the experience of oppression or the assured results of science or the rational standards of justice. Of course, there can be disagreements — and discussion — about how to read and interpret one's experience or the "assured results" of science or some minimal notion of justice, as there can be disagreements — and discussion — about how to read and interpret scripture.

Where remembrance takes the shape of obedience, the practice of reading scripture engages the community in discernment. Together they plot the story of scripture. Together they talk and argue about how to interpret and shape their lives in remembrance. In that dialogue people must listen to scripture and to each other — and to what each has experienced or knows — muting neither each other nor scripture. In that communal discernment and mutual discipline, the authority of scripture is "nonviolent."[20] The moment of recognition of scripture's wholeness and truthfulness comes before the moment of submission to any part of it and prepares the way for it.

19. On the relevance of other sources see further Allen Verhey, *The Great Reversal*, pp. 187-96.

20. Paul Ricoeur, *Essays on Biblical Interpretation*, ed. L. S. Mudge (Philadelphia: Fortress Press, 1980), p. 95. See also Margaret Farley, "Feminist Consciousness and the Interpretation of Scripture," in Letty M. Russell, ed., *Feminist Interpretation of the Bible* (Philadelphia: Westminster Press, 1985), pp. 41-51, at pp. 42-44.

In the struggle against forgetfulness both holiness and sanctification, both fidelity and creativity, both discipline and discernment are required. "That's why — and how — scripture is important to me," Coles's friend says. So we prepare to read a little scripture together.

CHAPTER SEVEN

A Scripture-Formed Practice of Medicine

We are ready at last to read some scripture with Coles's friend.

Just then, however, our friend's doctor comes in the room. "She's still trying to talk me into another round of chemotherapy," our friend says to us with more than a hint of impatience.

We politely offer to return another time, but each seems eager to enlist us as an ally in the struggle with the other. The doctor expects us to define our role (as chaplain or as ethicist) in terms of the therapeutic ambitions of the medical establishment, and Coles's friend hopes we will be an advocate of the patient's perspective. We are happy enough to be able to report that we came to read scripture, to remember the story, and not simply to be defenders of either the authority of physicians or the autonomy of patients.

Coles's friend tells his doctor to sit down for a moment, and she does. He hands us his Bible. It is still marked at Psalm 69 with its curses on the enemy.

We suggest a different text, perhaps the word of Jesus: "Love your enemies . . . , bless those who curse you, pray for those who abuse you" (Luke 6:27-28).

Coles's friend insists that he did not intend that we read Psalm 69 again. But he has been reminded by our words — by Jesus' word, actually — of the story of an Armenian Christian woman. The woman, it seems, was kept for a time by a Turkish officer who had raided her home and killed her aged parents. After she escaped, she trained to be a nurse. Some time later, when this officer became gravely ill, she happened to be his nurse. Exceptional nursing care was required, and exceptional care was given. When finally the officer recovered, his doctor pointed to the nurse and told the man that the credit for his recovery belonged to her. When he looked at her, he said, "We have met before, haven't we?" And when he recognized her, he asked, "Why did you provide such care for me?" Her reply was simply this: "I am a follower of the one who said, 'Love your enemies.'"[1]

Our friend's doctor is evidently touched by the story. "It makes me a little ashamed," she says, "of the way I treated the patient I just left. I think I'll look in on him again in a few minutes."

Our friend smiles at that, thinking, perhaps, that there may be hope for this physician yet. And then he says, "That woman was a saint, one of the company of those to whom we must listen when we would read scripture for the moral life and the medical life. How do you think she read scripture? She appeals to a command, to be sure, but not as though scripture were to be regarded as 'a system of divine laws.'[2] She describes herself as a 'follower' of Christ. The command to 'love the enemy' coheres with a story, not with some eternal code. Scripture does not give us a moral handbook; it gives us a story we own as our own. It is a story we may love to remember and tell and must struggle to practice and live even when we are dying or caring for the dying. And the plot of the story climaxes in the resurrection of Jesus of Nazareth. There was the *final* revelation, and the reading of scripture and the practice of medicine must both be made to fit with that final disclosure of God's cause and purpose.[3]

"Jesus came announcing that the good future of God was 'at hand' and already made its power felt in his works of healing and in his words of

1. The story is told in Geoffrey Wainwright, *Doxology* (London: Epworth Press, 1980), p. 434, and in Stephen E. Fowl and L. Gregory Jones, *Reading in Communion*, pp. 79-80.

2. Against John M. Frame, *Medical Ethics: Principles, Persons, and Problems*, p. 10. By this judgment about the wholeness of scripture Frame provides backing for his appeals to scripture as a moral code to answer directly questions about conduct. But many theologians, no less convinced of the authority of scripture, would argue that such an account of the wholeness of scripture is not a discerning reading of scripture, that it is wrong, and that, therefore, the use of scripture in ways coherent with it (as moral code) is flawed. I count myself among that number.

3. For resurrection as the key to scripture see Allen Verhey, *The Great Reversal*, pp. 181-83; David Kelsey, "The Bible and Christian Theology," *Journal of the American Academy of Religion* 68:3 (1980), pp. 385-402, especially pp. 398-402; and the essay by Oliver O'Donovan, "Keeping Body and Soul Together," in Kenneth Vaux, ed., *Covenants of Life: Contemporary Medical Ethics in Light of the Thought of Paul Ramsey* (Champaign: University of Illinois Press, 1991).

blessing. He suffered for the sake of God's cause in the world, but when death and doom had done their damnedest, God raised him up. So, we read all scripture in remembrance of Jesus and in hope of God's final triumph. And reading scripture, we learn to practice medicine in remembrance of the same Jesus and in the same hope."

It was a discerning judgment, we think to ourselves, and we begin to see for ourselves how — and why — the practice of reading scripture (in spite of the problems) might form and inform the practice of medicine.

"Let's read of Jesus," we say and turn to a story of Jesus' healing. In all those stories Jesus makes known God's cause against death and Satan and sin, and in the resurrection God establishes God's own future sovereignty against that triumvirate of this age.

Reading such a story might point to the victory over death and sickness. Jesus raised the dead and those who were thought in the first century to be "like dead" or under the power of death: the blind, the lame, the lepers (Luke 7:22-23).[4] "There God's cause is disclosed," we say, "and in the resurrection that cause is assured. God's cause is life, not death; health, not sickness. Then physicians and nurses may think of their profession as a calling, indeed, as a 'holy' calling, and of themselves as 'disciples of the saving Christ.'[5] Medicine is a way God's future may still be given token." The doctor eagerly nods her head in agreement — so eagerly that we quickly add, "Of course, the victory is God's victory. Our hope for the future is God, not some technological defeat of mortality."

Reading such a story might also point to the victory over Satan and his hosts: "If I by the finger of God cast out demons, then the kingdom of God has come upon you," Jesus says (Luke 11:20). The doctor cringes a little. The exorcisms seem a strange and alien world of sickness in the hospital room of Coles's friend.[6] The stories do not provide answers to the questions an objective clinical practitioner like this physician is likely to ask, and they may not be used to prescribe a way to diagnose suffering or to

4. See Klaus Seybold and Ulrich B. Mueller, *Sickness and Healing*, p. 123.
5. Walter Rauschenbusch, "For Doctors and Nurses," in Stephen Lammers and Allen Verhey, eds., *On Moral Medicine* (Grand Rapids: Wm. B. Eerdmans Publishing Company, 1987), p. 5.
6. The demonological understanding of sickness and psychosis was widespread in the ancient Mediterranean world. See Klaus Seybold and Ulrich B. Mueller, *Sickness and Healing*, p. 116.

provide therapy for Coles's friend. But they remain part of the Word of God to us and to them, and they disclose something of the cause of God.

One decisive feature of "possession" was precisely *possession.* The "possessed" did not have control of themselves; their speech and action had no genuine connection with who they were. And a second feature of "possession" was *isolation.* The sick were separated from community, alienated from the very ones who would help if they could. The strong man of Mark 5, for example, "lived among the tombs, and no one could bind him anymore, even with a chain" (Mark 5:3). But Jesus healed him, restored him to self-control (Mark 5:15) and to community: "Go home to your friends," he said (Mark 5:19).

"The exorcisms freed people to be themselves and to be with others," we say. "The cause of God made known in them is human flourishing, and the human flourishing revealed in the exorcisms involves integrity and community. Physicians may and must use their best medical skills and knowledge to explain what is happening in and to their patients, but a scripture-formed medical practice must use that knowledge in ways that still honor God and serve God's cause, including not only life and health but also the integrity of patients and their community with those who are well.

"Sometimes sickness threatens that embodied integrity and community, and medicine then can serve God's cause by using its powers. But sometimes medicine itself — with its great powers — threatens the power of patients to live (or die) with integrity or within community, and then medicine can only serve God's cause by *not* using its powers. When, for example, medicine can only prolong a person's dying, or when by its technological interventions it can only rob the dying of their dignity and separate the dying from the human companionship of family and friends, then a scripture-formed medicine must acknowledge that the moral limits to its powers come long before the technological limit to its powers." It is Coles's friend's turn now to nod a little too eagerly.

Reading such a story might also point to the victory over sin. In the ministry of Jesus sins were forgiven in token of God's good future on the far side of the last judgment. And in his healing ministry Jesus broke both the power of sin and the traditional assumption that sickness and death were consequences of sin. In John 9, for example, Jesus rejected the assumption that the man's blindness must be caused by either his sin or the sin of his parents. Instead, he simply pointed to the power of God to heal and made that power felt.

To remember Jesus, to read this scripture, is to disown any putative connection between sin and sickness whenever it is used to distance ourselves from the sick, whenever it is used to renege on our obligations of solidarity with the suffering, whenever it is used self-righteously to justify segregating the "sinful" sick from the "righteous" well. When, for example, a person with AIDS is abandoned or neglected or shunned or condemned, then Jesus is not remembered or the scripture honored. That is not a scripture-formed practice of medicine.

On the other hand, Jesus replies to a request for healing, "My son, your sins are forgiven" (Mark 2:5). In this text the connection of sin and sickness is apparently accepted, but it is not used to isolate, segregate, judge, or condemn the sick. On the contrary, the whole person was renewed as an earnest of God's good future.

To remember this remark and to hope for the good future of God it signals is not to disown a duty to care and a desire to cure, but to recognize and to deal with the whole person, refusing to reduce a person's suffering to its physical manifestations or its clinical symptoms. Persons with AIDS, for example, sometimes hurt in places no medicine can touch; they have needs which are not just medical but psychological and social and spiritual. Sometimes they need relief from a sense of isolation and abandonment; always they need to restore and maintain not only certain physiological processes but also certain relationships with others. A scripture-formed practice of medicine must not reduce patients to their pathologies — "the heart attack in room 515," for example — nor reduce the practice of medicine to a collection of skills and tools.

Neither Coles's friend nor his doctor nods in enthusiastic agreement at this point, but we may hope both acknowledge its relevance. Each had been a little too ready to condemn and to blame; the doctor thought it would be her patient's *fault* if he died, and Coles's friend thought the doctor's passion for his life impertinent. The doctor had been ready to reduce Coles's friend to his disease and then to combat it (and to combat him). And Coles's friend had been ready to reduce the doctor to an "animated tool"[7] and then to put it down (and put her down). Forgiveness might heal their relation a little, at least enable them to listen to each other a little longer and a little better.

---

7. "Animated tool" is Aristotle's definition of a slave. See Paul Ramsey, *Ethics at the Edges of Life* (New Haven: Yale University Press, 1978), pp. 45, 158.

A scripture-formed practice of medicine will not render the patient optionless and choiceless by insisting on a physician's authority nor be rendered optionless and choiceless itself by appeal to a patient's autonomy.

"Let's read of Jesus," we say; but it is not just to stories of healing to which we must turn. This Jesus who was raised was not only a healer but a preacher of "good news to the poor" (Luke 4:18).

The physician Luke elegantly says so. We might read, for example, the story of the Rich Man and Lazarus (Luke 16:19-31) and ask how medical practice and hospital administrations and, yes, public policy might be formed and informed to "fit" such a story. We might ask how remembrance and hope might shape the sharing of scarce resources, including medical resources. But time is also a scarce resource, and we decide to leave that story and that question for another day and for a different room, perhaps the board room.

There is no remembrance of Jesus, however, if we neglect the story of his death. The Jesus who was raised was a *wounded* healer, and his wounds were raised with him. He "suffered under Pontius Pilate, was crucified, dead, and buried." The story of his passion is remembered by each of the evangelists. Indeed, the gospels decisively tie the memories of Jesus as healer and as teacher to the story of his cross.

Apart from it the church is always at risk of distorting the good news of the gospel into a pollyanna triumphalism and then of self-deceptively ignoring or denying the sad truth about our world — and the sad truth about Coles's friend. Apart from the story of the cross our culture is always at risk of distorting the good news of some medical breakthrough into a pollyanna medical triumphalism and then of self-deceptively ignoring or denying the sad truth that there is no medical technology to rescue the human condition from finitude or mortality or its vulnerability to suffering.

Jesus has been raised. God has established God's own good future when "death shall be no more, neither will there be mourning nor crying nor pain any more" (Rev. 21:4). But we live under the sign of the cross, and that promised age of God's unchallenged sovereignty is not yet, *still not yet*.

Yet, already, the story of the wounded healer sheds its light on our sicknesses and on our care for the sick.

To those who suffer, the story of Jesus is a glad story indeed, but a glad story which does not deny the sad truth about our world. The gospel of Jesus and his suffering and his way to death does not announce here and now an end to our pains or an avoidance of our death but it does provide an unshakable assurance that we do not suffer alone, that we are not and will not be abandoned, that Jesus suffers with us, that God cares. The glad story of Jesus is indeed a hard reminder that in a world like this one, however righteous and repentant we are, we cannot expect to be spared pain and sorrow. Certainly health and life are goods which I may and must seek, but they are not the greatest goods, and if "a disciple is not above his teacher" (Matt. 10:24), then one's own survival and one's own ease may not become the law of one's own being. In our sad stories we keep good company. That's a part of the good news — and this: that beyond the cross is the resurrection, the triumph of God over diseases and death.

The stories of Jesus and his cross do not "fit" the story sometimes told by medical practice to patients (and sometimes told by patients to medical practice) that death is the ultimate enemy and the worst evil, to be put off by any means. And if people then sometimes blame the physicians for keeping them alive beyond all reason, the stories of Jesus and his cross do not "fit" the story told by Jack Kevorkian and the Hemlock Society that life is the enemy, and that physicians may become killers.

The story of a wounded healer can form not only the dispositions of those who suffer but also the practice of those who would care for them. It is a call to those who would follow Jesus to minister to the sick as though to care for them were to care for Christ. He said as much, of course: inasmuch "as you did it to one of the least of these . . . , you did it unto me" (Matt. 25:40).

Reading scripture is like putting on glasses ("spectacles," Calvin said) which correct our vision, enabling the physician to see in those who hurt not only manipulable nature but the very image of Christ the Lord.

Called by a story of a wounded healer to minister to the sick, the physician may delight in her tools as gifts of God, celebrating scientific advances and technological breakthroughs for the powers they give to intervene in the sad stories people tell with and of their bodies.

But the glasses of scripture also correct her vision if she regards her technology as the faithful savior and relies on it to remedy the human condition, to provide the happy ending or to sustain either her patients or her care for them in the face of their suffering.

It is God who will bring in the good future when pain and death will be no more, not technology. With corrected vision the physician may use technology to give some small token of God's good future without extravagant expectations of her tools.

It is God who suffers with us and for us, not technology. And with corrected vision the physician will be less tempted by the techno-logic of "If we can, we must," and may instead be enabled to give some small token of God's presence to the patient by her own presence, listening to the patient's sighs as well as to his chest, touching the patient in a way that signals simple human compassion and not just medical probing, talking with a patient to share some wisdom about life in a mortal body.

The glasses of scripture can form the vision of physicians until they learn to see even themselves in a new way — as followers of a wounded healer, as disciples of one who shared the lament of the sick and dying, as imitators of one who knew our pain and did not abandon us to our hurt.

That new vision might nurture and sustain an old vision of medicine, that medical practice has at its heart and center the extraordinary commitment to *care* for the sick. That old vision seeks and celebrates the competence to cure if one can; but it also insists, when one cannot cure, on practicing presence to those in pain, on being the "good company" even the dying may keep, and on never abandoning the one who hurts even when it cannot heal. It will refuse to eliminate suffering by eliminating the sufferer.

That old vision of medical practice may not be sustainable in our culture. The tendency to reduce the practice to a technological control over manipulable nature may not be turned back. The tendency in another direction — to reduce the practice to skills available on the marketplace to be purchased by presumably autonomous consumers — may be irresistible.

But in our culture some Christians still gather to remember Jesus and to attend to God. They read scripture and pray, and those practices of piety form virtues and visions for both the sick and those who care for them. They form character and finally conduct into something fitting to the gospel.

It is not my claim that the practice of reading scripture will settle the dispute between Coles's friend and his doctor — or between any patient and any physician. I am not suggesting that the right text will magically resolve medical and moral dilemmas — which are, after all, sometimes the genuine conflict of genuine goods.

I am saying that for Christian patients these decisions are not merely "private" decisions and that for Christian physicians these decisions are not merely "professional" decisions. They ought to be made with Christian integrity. That is to say, they can and sometimes are and surely should be made in the context of the Christian community's attention to God and common memory. That is to say, they can and sometimes are and surely should be made in performance of the story we love to tell.

Attention to God and remembrance can support both the art of dying and the practice of medicine. The church which practices piety may never abandon care for the sick and dying to the medical profession, but neither may it abandon the physician or the nurse to science or to the marketplace.

The practices of piety are not undertaken for the sake of medicine, but the best hope for a morally worthy practice of medicine may finally be the practices of piety. That is my claim.

At least I hope to have shown this: that Henry Stob was right, that the practices of prayer and reading scripture have contributions to make to medicine and to medical ethics. If the church attends to God in prayer and remembers Jesus in reading scripture, then perhaps our own strange world of medicine can be healed a little.

In prayer and reading scripture we not only commune with God but find new strength — new virtue — for daily life.

Thanks be to God for the wise ethicist who once taught me that.

8. See further Hessel Bouma III et al., *Christian Faith, Health, and Medical Practice* (Grand Rapids: Wm. B. Eerdmans Publishing Company, 1989), pp. 21-23, 144-75; John Kilner, "A Needy World — A Needed Word: Scarce Medical Resources and the Christian Story," *Asbury Theological Journal* 41:2 (1986), pp. 23-58; and Richard Mouw, "Biblical Revelation and Medical Decisions," pp. 200-201.

*What New Haven and Grand Rapids
Have to Say to Each Other*

NICHOLAS P. WOLTERSTORFF

Contents

First Lecture

I live and work today at the intersection of two traditions. One is the tradition of so-called "neo-Calvinism" to which I was introduced when a student here at Calvin College — by, among others, the person in whose honor this lecture series was founded, Henry Stob — and which has continued to shape my thought and sensibilities ever since. In this tradition philosophy has always occupied a prominent place, perhaps, indeed, *the* prominent place. Its great founding figure was the turn-of-the-century Dutchman, Abraham Kuyper. The other tradition is that of so-called "Yale theology." Its two principal figures are the late Hans Frei and George Lindbeck; but the great grey eminence behind them is Karl Barth. Grand Rapids and New Haven; Amsterdam and Basel.

I propose in these lectures to reflect on the relationship between these two traditions. Each will prove to have some critical remarks to make about the other. Much more important than that, however, will be the remarkable similarity of concern, and the even more remarkable similarity of strategy for dealing with that concern, which come to light when we compare them. If some of you, not surmising that the names in my title were metaphors, came expecting me to discuss what the city of New Haven and the city of Grand Rapids have to say to each other — to you I must say, sorry to disappoint you!

In a recent essay of his entitled "Scripture, Consensus, and Community," George Lindbeck analyzes and laments the decline in the formative role of Scripture in the life of the Church. Once upon a time, he says, "Narrative and typological interpretation enabled the Bible to speak with its own voice in new situations. Scripture, in Calvin's phrase, could serve as the spectacles, the lens, through which faith views all reality; and, to change the figure, the world of the reader could be absorbed into the biblical world."[1] Lindbeck then goes on to remark that "Now, however, the interpretive direction is reversed: the biblical message is translated into contemporary conceptualities. This always happens unconsciously in varying degrees (subtly in Luther and Calvin, and more blatantly in much Christian Platonism), but from Schleiermacher through Karl Rahner and to liberation theologies, translation into nonbiblical idioms has been done deliberately and systematically."[2] Lindbeck's response to this situation is a plea for the recovery of the tradition by reversing the modern reversal of direction of interpretation.

I submit that anyone reared in the tradition of neo-Calvinism, upon reading these words, will feel at once that he has met a blood brother! The call to *reverse the direction of conformation:* that, at bottom, is what unites these two traditions of twentieth-century Christian thought. The call of the Yale theologians for reversing the direction has focussed on theology and biblical interpretation — though from Lindbeck's words it's clear that reversing the reversal in biblical interpretation and theology will, in his view, have consequences throughout the life of the Christian community. The call of the neo-Calvinists for reversing the direction has explicitly been more wide-flung in its scope. In a wide variety of different areas of culture and society they have called for reversing the direction — while at the same time their call for reversal in the areas of theology and biblical interpretation has been curiously low-voiced, both when compared to the volume of their own call for reversal in such areas as philosophy and politics, and when compared to the volume of the call by the Yale theologians for reversal in theology and biblical interpretation. So there are differences of emphasis, and we will try to understand those. But I suggest that in the thought of both there is no deeper guiding metaphor than this: *reversing the direction of conformation.*

Though the call for reversing the direction has application far beyond academia — implicitly so in the case of the Yale theologians, explicitly so in the case of the neo-Calvinists — nonetheless, extraordinarily prominent in both have been reflections on the relation of Christianity to academic learning. I see the predominant concern of each as having a sort of

---

1. George Lindbeck, "Scripture, Consensus, and Community," in R. J. Neuhaus, ed., *Biblical Interpretation in Crisis* (Grand Rapids: Eerdmans Publishing Co., 1989), p. 86.

2. Lindbeck, "Scripture, Consensus, and Community," p. 87.

elliptical structure, one focus of the ellipse being the Christian religion and the other being academic learning. Over and over one sees in the texts of these two traditions the attempt to understand these two phenomena, and the attempt to understand how they have been related. And over and over, when it comes time to speak of how they *should be* related, one hears the call to reverse the direction — remarkably so, since both between and within these traditions one finds significant differences in how the Christian religion is understood.

I think it will be helpful, before I set out to articulate for you the pattern of thought of these two traditions, to try to say what I think is most important in their shared understanding of academic learning. Suppose we distinguish between the actual way in which the social practice of academic learning is conducted in the modern world, and the *self-image* of the practice held by those who engage in it. Both traditions will on occasion use the same word to describe what they regard as prominent in the regnant self-image of academic learning, the word "autonomy." The regnant self-image of science is that it is an autonomous enterprise — provided it's conducted properly.

What do they mean by that? Well, coming from the Greek, "autonomous" means *self-normed*. Part of what goes into the formation of an academic discipline is the certification of certain methods for arriving at data and conclusions as acceptable methods in that discipline. Presumably then an autonomous or self-normed discipline would be one which never at any point made use of convictions not arrived at by practitioners of the discipline using methods deemed proper within that discipline.

Now there's a good deal that one could say about that. But for our purposes, notice that it remains a purely formal characterization. Do the Yale theologians and the neo-Calvinists also think that the regnant self-image of academic learning includes some view as to what in general a method must be like to be deemed acceptable within the disciplines? Yes, I think so. The guiding thought is that the academic disciplines are to be a *purely human* enterprise, so that, over the long haul if not immediately, the results of applying the methods will enjoy consensus among all knowledgeable human beings. Perhaps a pictorial way of expressing the thought will be helpful: Before entering the halls of learning we are to strip off all our particularities, particularities of gender, of race, of nationality, of religion, of social class, of age, and enter purely as human beings. If it turns out that we have failed to strip off some particularity and the others in the hall notice this, they are to order us back into the entry, there to strip off the particularity which, unintentionally or not, we kept on. Thus, on the regnant understanding of science, black history, feminist sociology, Muslim political theory, and liberation theology are *bad* history, *bad* sociology, *bad* political theory, *bad* theology. In the practice of science we are to make use of only such belief-forming dispositions as are shared among all human beings, and we are to accept only the deliverances of such shared human dispositions.

To this general characterization a few qualifications must be added, however, if we are to have a fully accurate picture of the regnant self-understanding of academic learning. In the first place, if we bring infants into the picture along with those adults whose belief-forming capacities are in one way or another malformed — the color blind, the schizophrenic, etc. — then it's not clear that we're going to find much at all by way of belief-forming dispositions truly common to all human beings. The response of those who hold to the regnant self-understanding of science is clear: Only adults are to be allowed into the halls of science, and, within the halls, malformed adults are to concern themselves exclusively with those parts of science in which their particular malformation plays no role. Don't let the color blind develop theories of color vision!

But, second, we human beings are not autonomic information-processing mechanisms. We always put our belief-forming dispositions to use in certain ways. And we learn these ways. In part we are taught them by others; in part we learn them from our own experience. A fundamental determinant is what is judged to be a more reliable and a less reliable way of using one's indigenous dispositions. For example, each of us learned early in life that in general one can get more reliable beliefs about the size and shape of objects by looking at them from a distance appropriate to their size: close up if they are small, farther off if they are big. Here then is the question: Which learned uses of indigenous capacities are allowable within the halls of science? Obviously not any old learned use whatsoever; not the learned use which consists of reading tea leaves to predict fortunes. On the other hand, we obviously allow more than those learned uses of indigenous capacities which are engaged in by all normal adults; we allow our scientists to engage in all sorts of sophisticated uses of their indigenous capacities which non-scientists may never have heard of. So how do we pick and choose? I think the fundamental idea is probably to allow those learned uses whose reliability can be defended by reference solely to the indigenous capacities of normal adults.

This has been rather complex! So let me summarize (a bit loosely) what we have learned so far: Fundamental in the regnant self-image of academic learning has been the conviction that one is to practice academic learning just qua normal adult human being — not qua American, not qua black, not qua Christian, not qua female, not qua proletarian, not *qua* any particularity whatsoever. We can expect that the results of learning so practiced will eventually gain consensus among all normal adult human beings knowledgeable in the discipline. When academic learning is rightly conducted, pluralism in the academy is an accidental and temporary phenomenon. Particularist learning — learning practiced not *qua* human being but *qua* some particular kind of human being — is misbegotten learning. This seems to me the understanding of the regnant self-image of academic learning which the Yale theologians and the neo-Calvinists both operate with. It is, in my judgment, an accurate understanding of that image.

Let me now, more quickly, single out two other aspects of the regnant self-image on which there is probably less consensus than on the conviction that acceptable scholarship is generically human, but which nonetheless are widely accepted. It has been widely held that acceptable scholarship will be foundational in structure. (What is meant by that will become clear in my second lecture; we can make do with the metaphor until then.) And it has been widely held that it is the business of philosophers to offer a general account of things, with the other disciplines then filling in the specifics, that it is the business of philosophers to construct or display foundations for all the disciplines, and that it is the business of philosophers to uncover the necessary conditions, in human nature, of theoretical activity; and that philosophers do all this in a way which is itself autonomous, generically human, and foundational in structure.

Common to Yale theology and neo-Calvinism is their rejection of this self-image of acceptable learning as an autonomous, generically human, foundationally structured practice which is grounded and situated within universal structures by philosophers. The Yale theologians reject it by arguing that Christian theologians and biblical scholars have no obligation to conform their thought to that image. The neo-Calvinists reject it by arguing that this self-image is itself a piece of ideological illusion: It neither fits the actuality of reputable learning, nor is it inherently defensible. They then go on to join the Yale theologians in arguing that Christian academics should feel no obligation to conform their thought to this image — neither Christian theologians, nor Christians in any other discipline.

The tradition of Yale theology will be less familiar to most of you here than the tradition of neo-Calvinism. Let me for that reason begin with it. Rehearsal of the familiar has a decidedly soporific effect on most people. Sometimes, though, when the familiar is seen against the background of the unfamiliar, it doesn't seem quite so familiar. So, perhaps, by considering things in this order, there's a chance of not just postponing but forestalling the soporific effects of dwelling on the familiar!

The hedgehog, so I am told, thinks long about few things; the fox, briefly about many things. I can believe it. If my information about hedgehogs is correct, Hans Frei was a hedgehog in his thought. He thought long and deep — whether the long thought of hedgehogs is also deep, we are not told — he thought long and deep about just two matters: How the Christian community could recover the practice of interpreting Scripture as realist narrative, and how its theology should be related to the academy in general. Furthermore, he saw the positions that he took on these two issues as intimately connected — though I myself doubt that they are in fact as intimately connected as he thought they were. Be that as it may, given his own view as to the intimate connection, it doesn't make much difference where we begin; either way, we'll be led from one to the other. Let me begin with his reflections on the proper relation of Christian theology to the non-theological learning of the general academy. And when I speak henceforth of the general academy, I mean all those working within the academy or some branch thereof, regardless of their religious or ideological convictions.

Frei was of the conviction that the founding of the University of Berlin in 1809 starkly confronted Christian theologians with an issue which had been brewing for some time but never decisively faced, and which has remained on the agenda ever since. The issue is this: What is the place of Christian theology in the academy? By which is not so much meant, Where is Christian theology to be located in the organizational structure of the university? but more important, Where does Christian theology fit among the sciences, the academic disciplines, the *Wissenschaften,* of the general academy?

For Frei, answering this question required getting clear first of all on what we take Christianity to be; this in turn required getting clear on what we take a religion to be. Frei was well aware of the traditional view that a religion is a complex of beliefs about the transcendent. The dominant view in his own environment was not that, however, but the *phenomenological* view, according to which "religion is a component of human experience and . . . this experience is a primordial element in the human constitution. It is not something that can be ferreted out by ordinary examination for information, but rather it is part of the structure of the human psyche with which we come to grips when we come to grips with the things that are actually given to the human psyche."[3] In short, the *essence* of religion, according to the phenomenologist, is a certain structure of the experiencing self. As to what makes one religion different from another, there have been different views. But whatever view was held on that matter, it was held that the universal *essence* always gets *expressed* in such *manifestations* as rituals, ethical prescriptions, theologies, etc. Religion is located in "a whole-making capacity in the structure of the psyche that does the experiencing. The religion is constituted by an experienced unity, or essence, of which all these external, social aspects are signs and manifestations rather than being the religion as such."[4] Those who have held this view have typically thought it the business of philosophers to describe for us the essence of religion in general, the business of theologians to describe for us the essence of some particular religion, and the business of historians, social scientists, art critics, etc., to illuminate us concerning the manifestations of the various particular religions.

One can see in Frei's career a pattern of more and more firmly and explicitly rejecting this phenomenological approach to Christianity, and more and more firmly and explicitly embracing the alternative view that the most fundamental reality of the Christian religion is *the Church*. Christianity, he says, is

> a social organism. . . . It is a community held together by constantly changing, yet enduring structures, practices, and institutions, as other religious communities are: for example, a sacred text, regulated relations between an elite . . . and more general body of adherents, a set of rituals — preaching, baptism, the celebration of communion, common beliefs and attitudes — all of which are linked (again typical of a religion) with a set of narratives connected with each other in the sacred text and its interpretive traditions. [These are] not the *signs* or *manifesta-*

3. Hans W. Frei, *Types of Christian Theology* (New Haven: Yale Univ. Press, 1992), p. 22.

4. Frei, *Types of Christian Theology,* p. 22.

tions of the religion; they constitute it in complex and changing coherence."[5]

He adds that on this view "the social scientific description of Christianity" will come closer to "a self-description of Christianity" than does a phenomenological description composed by philosophers and by theologians engaging in a "philosophical kind of theologizing. . . ."[6]

When we think of Christianity along these lines, namely, as "a religious community called after its founder, whose name, Jesus of Nazareth, is linked to the title embodying the claim his followers made on his behalf, that he was the Christ," then we will notice that theology has emerged as an aspect of the Church's life, specifically, as an aspect of the Church's self-description. "It is an inquiry into the internal logic of the Christian community's language — the rules, largely implicit rather than explicit, that are exhibited in its use in worship and Christian life, as well as in the confessions of Christian belief."[7] Christian theology, thus understood, is "critical or normed Christian self-description."[8] On one side of it is to be found "Christian witness, including the confession of specific beliefs (for example, the creeds) that seem on the face of them to be talking about acknowledging a state of affairs that holds true whether one believes it or not." Theology itself is the attempt to elucidate what may be called, metaphorically, the logic or grammar of that first-order witness — "an endeavor to bring out the rules implicit in first-order statements." And on the other side is to be found the activity, philosophical or quasi-philosophical in character, of "trying to tell others . . . how these rules compare and contrast with their kinds of ruled discourse."[9]

We can now state the issue which occupied so much of Frei's attention and which he spied haunting modern theologians in general: What is the relation of theology, thus understood, to the non-theological learning of the general academy and to the regnant self-image of such learning? Frei distinguished five types of answers that he found his fellow theologians in the modern world giving to this question — five types of theology; I think it will be helpful, for understanding Frei's own position, if we look ever so

5. Frei, *Types of Christian Theology*, p. 22.
6. Frei, *Types of Christian Theology*, p. 22.
7. Frei, *Types of Christian Theology*, p. 20.
8. Frei, *Types of Christian Theology*, p. 21.
9. Frei, *Types of Christian Theology*, pp. 20-21.

briefly at those five types. For the benefit of the theologians among you, I will in each case cite a theologian whose work Frei regards as exemplifying that type more than any other.

Type I pays no explicit attention whatsoever to the theological self-description of the Christian community. It sees good and proper theology as entirely a project of the general academy, to be conducted by the rules of the academy. It is located in the general academy as a branch of academic philosophy. In so far as the theologizing that takes place in the Christian community diverges in its methods and conclusions from academic theology, it's just *bad* theology. Frei's example of a Type I theologian is the Harvard theologian Gordon Kaufmann.

Type II theology always works with some sort of distinction between *the general* and *the specific*. The philosopher in the general academy uncovers the nature of humanity's openness to the transcendent, or the nature of the religious dimension of human existence — an impulse to transcendence, an ultimate concern, a need for ultimate meaning, a capacity for revelatory experience, a feeling of ultimate dependence, a longing for ultimate security — the list goes on and on. Christianity is then regarded as a definite and distinct species of this generality; and Christian theology is to be developed within the academy as the elucidation of this species of the generality. Frei's example of a Type II theologian is the Chicago theologian David Tracy.

Type III theology is Church theology. Church theology is that aspect of the Church's life in which it aims at achieving theological self-understanding; as such, it has its own integrity, its own goals, its own methods, its own standards. However, the general academy, following its own agenda, discusses a large number of issues which overlap with the endeavors and results of the Church theologian. Church theologians must see to it that their own methods and results do not conflict with the well established methods and results of the historians and philosophers, the sociologists and scientists, of the general academy. Frei formulated this third type of theology with Friedrich Schleiermacher in mind.

Type IV theology is also Church theology. What makes it different from Type III theology is that it does not regard itself as beholden to the methods and results of the general academy. It follows its own drummer.

Theology as specific and critical Christian self-description and self-examination by the Church of its language takes absolute priority over theology as an academic discipline. Philosophy as conceptual system describing and referring to 'reality' is not a basis on which to build theology, and even philosophy as a set of formal, universal rules or criteria for what may count as coherent and true in Christian discourse as in every other kind of conceptual practice is not basic to or foundational of Christian theology.[10]

Theology "arises because the Church is accountable to God for its discourse about God. To the best of its lights . . . the Church must undertake a critique and correction of her discourse in the light of the norm she sees as the presence of God to the Church, in obedience to God's grace."[11] Nonetheless, theology of Type IV does not ignore the endeavors and results of the non-theological disciplines in the general academy. It eclectically picks and chooses whatever it finds of use there, adapting its gleanings to its own purposes. As you will have guessed, Karl Barth is Frei's paradigmatic example of a Type IV theologian.

Type V theology is like Types III and IV in being Church theology, but unlike them in making no use whatsoever of what goes on in the non-theological disciplines. The Wittgensteinian philosopher of religion D. Z. Phillips is cited by Frei as a Type V theologian — or, more accurately, as a philosopher who, while not himself doing theology, argues that Christian theology should be of Type V.

Frei allied himself openly and explicitly with Karl Barth under Type IV, tirelessly advocating what in recent years has come to be called *Anselmian* theology. The Church theologian of Type IV does not articulate Christian theology so that it offers an answer to what philosophy has first told us is the universally human religious question, for the Scriptures which norm the thought of the community and its theologians present us with God's question as well as God's answer. Neither does the Church theologian of Type IV articulate Christian theology so that it presents us with one way of attaining what philosophers have already told us is the universally human quest for meaning; in the course of telling us how to achieve meaning for our lives, the Scriptures tell us also what is the meaning thereby achieved. Nor does the Church theologian of Type IV articulate Christian theology so that it sets before us the grace which saves us from what philosophers have already told us we all need saving from; in telling

10. Frei, *Types of Christian Theology*, p. 40.
11. Frei, *Types of Christian Theology*, p. 39.

us of the grace which saves, the Scriptures tell us of our plight from which grace saves us. And so forth.

It was Frei's reading of the historical situation that the great majority of culturally influential theologians over the past two centuries have been theologians of one or the other of the first three types, advocating that Christian theology conform itself, in one way or another, and to one degree or another, to the results and the self-image of the general academy. The Anselmian theologian, by contrast, after picking and choosing from the results and self-image of the general academy, modifies the pickings so that they conform to, and serve, his or her own agenda of developing Christian theology as Church theology. The direction of conformation is reversed. And since Frei regards modern theology of the first three types as itself a reversal of the direction of conformation dominant until two or three centuries ago, his call for reversing the direction of conformation is a call for reversing the reversal.

Even those of us who accept the call are left with a number of questions, however. Once the theologians of the Church have seen the issue and resolutely renounced any general obligation to conform their endeavors to the results and self-image of the general academy, what then is the attitude of the Church toward the general academy? What advice does it give those academics in its midst who are not theologians; how should their work be related to that of the general academy? And what is it about the general academy which yields the result that Christian theologians cannot simply build on its reputable results and adopt its self-perceived standards and methods? Clement of Alexandria, who flourished around 200 A.D., was of the view that the relation of Christianity to pagan learning, at its best, is that it fulfills it rather than contradicts it. Down through the ages, the Clementine model has probably been the Church's favorite model for understanding the relation of its own theology to the reputable results and self-image of the non-theological general academy. Obviously the Yale theologians are rejecting the Clementine model. But why? And in favor of what alternative model? Further, is it true that Church theologians cannot *learn* from the general academy, that they can only steal from it? These questions have been discussed with extraordinary intensity by the neo-Calvinists; they have not, so far as I can tell, been seriously discussed by the Yale theologians or their mentor, Karl Barth. Their defense would probably be that these are philosophical issues, not theological; and that their concern has been theological. Fair enough. But the questions nag.

Let us move on to Frei's reflections on Scripture interpretation. Before actually presenting Frei's line of thought, let me set the stage by quoting a brief passage from his response to some questions posed to him by Carl Henry:

> When I wrote *The Eclipse of Biblical Narrative*, what I had in mind was the fact that if something didn't seem to fit the world view of the day, then liberals quickly reinterpreted it, or as we say today, 'revised' it. And my sense of the matter, though I'm not antiliberal, was that you can revise the text to suit yourself only just so far. There really is an analogy between the Bible and a novel writer who says something like this: I mean what I say whether or not anything took place. I mean what I say. It's as simple as that: the text means what it says.[12]

In reading this passage I am reminded of a vivid passage from John Locke in which the same point is made: "So that the scripture serves but, like a nose of wax, to be turned and bent, just as may fit the contrary orthodoxies of different societies. For it is these several systems, that to each party are the just standards of truth, and the meaning of the scripture is to be measured only by them."[13]

The Church, like most if not all religious communities, has a sacred Scripture, a canonical text. But texts have to be interpreted. And Frei saw, or thought he saw, not only a common canonical text in the Christian community but, amidst all the different ways in which Christians have interpreted this text, a few fundamental points of near-consensus on interpretation. There has been near-consensus around the conviction that, somehow or other, the Bible must be interpreted as one book. There has been near-consensus around the conviction that, in interpreting the Bible as one book, the Gospels must be given priority. And there has been near-consensus around the conviction that the Gospels as a whole must be interpreted literally. Parts of them, indeed, all of them, may be interpreted in other ways as well; some parts, such as the parables, *must be* interpreted in other ways. But as a whole, they must *at least* be interpreted literally.

12. Hans W. Frei, "Response to 'Narrative Theology: An Evangelical Appraisal,'" in *Trinity Journal* 8 NS (1987), pp. 21-22.

13. John Locke, *A Second Vindication of the Reasonableness of Christianity*, in *Works* (12th ed., 1824), vol. 6, p. 295.

What did Frei mean in speaking of *literal* interpretation? It's my impression that he never fully succeeded, and felt that he had never fully succeeded, in saying what he meant. He struggled, over and over. Let me say what I think he was trying to get at. Suppose I write a narrative setting forth the so-called "winning of the American West" — a description of the phenomenon which is, as I trust we all recognize today, highly Eurocentric. The point of my narrative, its meaning, its subject, what it's about, what I want to get across to my readers, what I want to communicate to them, present to them, is just the narrated events in the narrated pattern. For exactly those events in that sequence is what I take *to be* "the winning of the American West." Like the snake curling back on itself, the point of my story is the story, the meaning of my narrative is the narrated events in their narrated structure. As Frei put it in the passage I quoted, "I mean what I say." By those words Frei did not mean, "I said what I intended to say." He meant rather, "The point of my story is the significant enacted sequence which is my story." If I'm a historian, I naturally hope and claim that my story fits what actually happened; but even if I got things seriously wrong, the winning of the American West remains both the point and the stuff of my story. Admittedly there are ambiguities here. Suppose someone asks me what my story is about. So far I have been taking such a person to be asking about the theme enacted in my story. But the person might instead be asking, What are the events in reality whose overarching significance I purport to have captured?

Now when Frei talks about a near-consensus in the church concerning the primacy of the literal interpretation of the Gospels, he has in mind interpreting the Gospels along the lines I have just indicated; viz., interpreting the meaning of the Gospel narratives as the theme enacted in those narratives. It's possible to tell other kinds of stories, or to tell stories in other kinds of ways, so that the point of the story is not the theme enacted in the story. Aesop's fables, for example, are stories, all right; but the point is not to set before us a significant enacted sequence. The point is to propound an abstract moral. Once again, though, it is Frei's view that it has been a near-consensus within the Church that the Gospels are to be interpreted, first of all, as stories whose point is to present to us a significant enacted sequence.

What is the significant enacted sequence which the Gospels present to us? We should beware of thinking we can capture it in any one formula; we should even beware of thinking we can capture it in all of our formulas together. But one approach is this: The Gospels present to us Jesus' enactment of his identity as Messiah. Having said this, I can now state one more facet of the near-consensus of interpretation which Frei sees pervading the history of the Church: The Gospels are to be interpreted as being about a specific person's enactment of his identity. Jesus, in the Gospels, is not a personification of some abstract Platonic idea. Jesus is a person enacting his identity. And it was Frei's view that the Chalcedonian formula does a very good job of expressing, in the conceptuality of Greek philosophy, what that identity was.

Let me now use Frei's terminology and call this way of interpreting a story the realistic narrative way. Some narratives we interpret as parables, some as allegories, some as myths; and some we interpret as realistic narratives. The Church has enjoyed a near-consensus that the Gospels are to be interpreted as realistic narratives, presenting to us Jesus' enactment of his Messiahship; and it has done its best to interpret the rest of the Bible in the light of this.

But now, says Frei, a curious thing has happened in the modern Church. In spite of the long-enduring near-consensus on primarily interpreting the Gospels as realistic narratives, that in the narratives which invites them to be interpreted in this way has been lost from view by biblical scholars. Biblical scholars in the Church have taken to giving all sorts of other answers to the question of what these Gospels are about. Instead of saying some such thing as that they are about Jesus' enactment of his Messiahship, they have said that they are about the Kingdom of God, or about authentic existence, or about reconciliation, or about a charismatic first-century Jewish peasant filled with God consciousness.

How, asks Frei, have biblical scholars in the modern Church been led into saying such curious things as these? If I write a narrative about the winning of the American West, nobody is going to put out of mind that it is a narrative of the winning of the American West and describe it as a cautionary tale about the disadvantages of disarmament. Why is it that though the Gospels seem so obviously narratives of Jesus' enactment of his identity as Messiah, and for millennia have primarily been so interpreted, nonetheless Christian biblical scholars in the modern world have taken to saying such strange oblivious things as that they are about authentic existence?

Well, look once again at my story of the winning of the American West. We agreed that it is an example of a realistic narrative — or, at least, an example of a narrative which begs to be interpreted as a realistic narrative. And to interpret it as a realistic narrative is to regard its point, its meaning, as being the significant enacted sequence which it presents to us. The point of the story is the story. And that, we said, is quite a different matter from whether I got things right in my story — whether things transpired out there on the prairies as they do in my story. Frei's way of putting this last point is this: The history-likeness of a realistic narrative is distinct from its historicity, though easily confused with it.

This confusion, so Frei suggests, is what modern biblical scholars fell into in their interpretation of the Gospels. For centuries and centuries, Christians unquestioningly took the Gospel narratives to be historically accurate; in fact, they made no distinction between their history-likeness and their historicity. Neither did the early moderns. They took the meaning of these narratives to be events in first-century Palestine. But then the moderns, unlike their predecessors in the Church, became historical sceptics. They began to doubt that anybody had stilled the waves there in first-century Palestine, that anybody had healed blind persons, that anybody had risen from the dead. That meant that a good deal of what earlier readers had taken to be the meaning of these narratives was slipping away from them. But for the most part they remained members of the Church and so refused to conclude that these texts are meaningless. Accordingly, they searched for other meanings, the yield of their search typically being abstractions such as the Kingdom of God, authentic existence, and reconciliation.

We must put an axe to the tree at its root, said Frei, and stop making our interpretation of the Gospels conform to our scientifically and philosophically shaped convictions as to what is true. Whether or not we find it believable that a person rose from the dead, the Gospel narratives of Jesus' enactment of his identity as Messiah include, as their decisive episode, Jesus rising from the dead. Issues of interpretation must be kept separate from the issue of whether to believe. If they are kept separate, then, though the Church's interpretation of the Gospel narratives will no doubt diverge from purely literary interpretations, nonetheless it will prove much more like such interpretations than like the historico-critical interpretations which have dominated the scene in the modern liberal Church. "I am persuaded," writes Frei, "that historical inquiry is a useful and necessary procedure but that theological reading is the reading of the text, and not the reading of a source, which is how historians read it. Historical inquiry, while telling us many useful things, does not tell us how we are to understand the texts as texts."[14]

All of this is about interpreting the Gospel narrative. What about believing it? What about faith? At a certain point I understand what I read; then I face the question: Is it true? Is it true that the Jesus of Nazareth who walked the roads of first-century Palestine enacted the identity which the Jesus-character of the Gospel narratives is depicted as enacting? To put it more abstractly: Is it true that the Chalcedonian formula fits that first-century Palestinian Jew?

Some of us do believe. There is no explaining that, says Frei; it is a mystery, the work of the Spirit. For most of us, "belief in the resurrection is a matter of faith and not of arguments from possibility or evidence."[15] But neither can we cite laws of nature discovered by our scientists which adequately explain such non-evidence-based faith. It's true that there could in principle be historical evidence which counts against the truth of our belief — evidence to the effect that Jesus of Nazareth did not go to his death obediently, evidence to the effect that there was no resurrection. But Frei was of the view that historical evidence, in the nature of the case, always falls short of rendering it probable that the historical Jesus had the identity ascribed to the character Jesus in the Gospels. On what sort of historical evidence, he asks, would it be probable that some particular person satisfied the Chalcedonian formula: two natures in one person, divine and human, inseparable but not confused?

I would guess that your response to this line of thought is rather like mine: I find it fascinating and provocative; but before I buy it as a total package I want to reflect on the many issues which it raises. On this occasion, however, I must forgo such reflection and close this lecture by returning to my major theme in these lectures: that Yale theology and neo-Calvinism are united in following the strategy of reversing the direction. When Hans Frei surveyed the pattern of biblical interpretation in the modern Church, he found it more and more common for interpreters to require of their interpretation of the Gospels' message that that message conform to what the non-theological academy in its generality has determined is true. The effect has been to eclipse the long-enduring consensus of the

---

14. Frei, *Types of Christian Theology*, p. 11.

15. Hans W. Frei, *The Identity of Jesus Christ* (Philadelphia: Fortress Press, 1975), p. 152.

Church, that the Gospels are to be read primarily as realistic narratives of Jesus' enactment of his identity as Messiah. But the project of Anselmian theology, theology of Type IV, is just to elucidate for us the normed discourse of the Church, borrowing and adapting from the *Wissenschaften* whatever is useful for such elucidation, but never feeling an obligation to "buckle under" to them. It follows that the modern pattern of so interpreting the Gospels that their message conforms to the deliverances of the general academy must be rejected. Church theology of Type IV will consist fundamentally of exegesis of, meditation on, and application of the Gospel narrative of God's enactment of our redemption in Jesus Christ. Anselmian theology will, in that way, be *narrative* theology. And it will be unabashedly particularist, making no pretense of being generically human. For, in Frei's words, "it is the Christian community's second-order appraisal of its own language and actions under a norm or norms internal to the community itself," rather than a branch of inquiry "to be subsumed under general criteria of intelligibility, coherence, and truth that it must share with other academic disciplines."[16]

A final point: Suppose the Anselmian theologian is pressed as to why he, personally, chooses to practice theology as he does; what would he say? Granted that the practice of Church theology requires reversing the direction; why has he personally opted for Church theology? I think Frei and Lindbeck would be inclined to answer that they felt called (or inclined) to practice theology; and since they were committed members of the Church, thus subject in their theologizing to its norms, it followed for them that it was Church theology they had to practice.

That response invites us to pose a new question: Why are they members of the Church? My sense is that Lindbeck would be inclined to give a somewhat different answer at this point than Frei. Lindbeck would say, I think, that when he interprets the Bible along the lines of the consensus traditional within the Church and then, from there, seeks to conform his own interpretation of reality to that of the biblical text — in short, when he reverses the reversal — what he discovers is that the text is "followable," its world, "habitable." What more could one ask than that? A followable text, says Lindbeck,

> must supply followable directions for coherent patterns of life in new situations. If it does this, it can be considered rational to dwell within it:

16. Frei, *Types of Christian Theology*, p. 2.

no other foundations are necessary or, in the contemporary climate of opinion, possible. Much contemporary intellectual life can be understood as a search for such texts. Contemporary Marxists and Freudians, for example, now rarely seek to ground their favorite authors' writings scientifically or philosophically. They simply ask that they be followable, that they be construable in such a way as to provide guidance for society, in the one case, and for individual life, in the other. Thus it is that Enlightenment systems which once claimed rational foundations have now turned into foundationless hermeneutical enterprises. . . . Ours is again an age when old foundations and legitimating structures have crumbled. Even the defenders of reason think it unreasonable to ask anything more than that they be followable of philosophies and religions, or of the texts which give them richness, comprehensiveness, and stability. There are fewer and fewer intellectual objections to the legitimacy or possibility of treating a classic, whether religious or nonreligious, as a perspicuous guide to life and thought. The only question is whether one is interested and can make it work.[17]

That is why Lindbeck is a member of the Church. And he is an Anselmian theologian because Anselmian theology, better than any other type, honors his experience that the Gospels, read as realistic narratives, are a followable text that works.

Frei's answer to our question would, I think, go along the following lines: Upon reading the Gospels in the mode of realistic narrative, he finds himself believing that their narrative of Jesus' enactment of his identity as Messiah fits the historical person Jesus of Nazareth — finds himself believing that they make Jesus the Christ present to us. When he now looks back on the dynamics of faith — the dynamics of interpreting the Gospels in narrative fashion and finding himself believing — when he now looks back on those dynamics, he finds himself convinced that this is not only our *best* access to Jesus the Christ but that it is adequate access. We don't need more. That's why Frei is a member of the Church. And he is an Anselmian theologian because Anselmian theology, better than any other type, honors that conviction. Rather than regretting the fact that the Gospels are not biographies of a twentieth-century sort, we should celebrate it. Biographies of that sort could never substitute for what these Gospels are: "loosely

17. Lindbeck, "Scripture, Consensus, and Community," p. 97.

structured nonfictional novels"[18] depicting Jesus as God among us, thus making the Word of God present to us.

The answers are different. But notice that in both cases Anselmian theology is theology without foundations because Christian faith is not based on evidence. I ask you to keep this point in mind; it will turn up again at the end of our second lecture.

18. Words of David Kelsey, cited by Frei in *Types of Christian Theology*, p. 135.

Second Lecture

I mentioned in the introduction to my first lecture that I now live and work at the intersection of two traditions. One is the tradition of so-called "neo-Calvinism," into which I was inducted as a student at Calvin College and which continues to shape and nourish my thought. The other is the tradition which surrounds me in my present work at Yale, so-called "Yale theology." My project in these lectures is to probe the affinities between these two traditions, while also taking note of their differences.

The affinities, as I suggested, go deep. A looming presence in the thought of both is the practice of academic learning in the modern world, along with the regnant self-image of that practice as an autonomous, generically human, foundationally structured enterprise, whose final foundations and universal language are developed, and necessary conditions in human nature uncovered, by philosophers whose work is itself autonomous, generically human, and foundationally structured. The two traditions offer narratives concerning the relation of Christian thinkers in the modern world to this practice and its self-image. The basic theme of the two narratives is the same: Over and over, Christian thinkers in the modern world have felt a general obligation to conform their thought to the results of reputable non-theological learning and to the academy's self-image of its standards and methods. To this pattern of conformation, the two traditions urge the same response, namely, that the pattern of conformation be broken, that it be reversed. Since the Yale theologians think that the direction of conformation characteristic of Christian thinkers in the modern world is itself a reversal of that characteristic of Christian thinkers in the premodern world, their call for reversing the direction of conformation is a call for reversing the reversal.

Let me briefly review what we saw in my first lecture to be the line of thought of the Yale theologians. In its worship and practice the Church exhibits a normed way of thinking and speaking about God, humanity, and the world. Down through the centuries the Church has found it important that certain of its members elucidate that normed way of thinking and speaking, and point out where the thought and speech of the Church fail to satisfy its own norms. Such elucidation and critique is theology; *Church* theology we may call it, since it is a project by and for the church. As such, it is itself subject to the norms of the Church for the thought and speech of its members. Church theologians practice theology as *insiders* to the Church, not as outsiders; though it is part of their calling to subject the Church's actual thought and speech to critique, their project is more a project of *retrieval* than of *suspicion*. The Yale theologians are Church theologians.

Now when Church theologians survey the history of Christian theology in the modern world, they notice that a good many Christian theologians have felt a general obligation to conform their endeavors to the results of the non-theological disciplines as practiced by the general academy, and to the academy's self-image of its methods and standards. Church theologians, out of fidelity to the norms of the Church, urge that this direction of conformation be reversed. The academy need not be, *should not be*, ignored. But let Church theologians, following the norms implicit in their own project, pick and choose in eclectic fashion from the standards, methods, and results of the general academy whatever promises, upon adaptation, to be useful for their project. And as for the attempt of philosophers to construct foundations for all the disciplines, to develop an account of things in general, and to uncover the necessary conditions of theorizing in human nature: Church theology has no need of such foundations, it will offer its own account of things in general, and from its own subject matter it will discern what makes it possible.

We saw that there was a second point at which the Yale theologians urge reversing the direction of conformation. The Scriptures play a fundamental role in norming the thought and speech of the members of the Church. But of course texts have to be interpreted. Looking over the history of the Church, the Yale theologians spy, amidst the bewildering variety of scriptural interpretation, certain points of near-consensus. One such point is that the Gospels are to be interpreted as narratives of Jesus enacting his identity as Messiah. They also notice, however, that in the modern

Church this normative consensus has been weakened and endangered. Their diagnosis of this development is that it is a consequence of *biblical scholars* in the modern Church feeling a general obligation to conform *their* thought to the general academy. Specifically, biblical scholars have felt obligated to interpret Scripture in such a way that *what it says* does not conflict with the well-established results of the general academy. Christian fidelity requires that also this pattern of conformation be repudiated and its direction reversed. Instead of requiring of our interpretations of what Scripture says that they conform to what science claims is true, we should, as interpreters, take the meaning of the Gospel narratives to be the narratives themselves, narratives of Jesus enacting his identity as Messiah, and then, as faithful members of the Church, seek to conform our lives, and our interpretation of our world, to that narrative.

When Christian theology is practiced as *Church* theology, it becomes, unabashedly, a particularist enterprise. If, in spite of making no pretense of being generically human, it is nonetheless allowed into the academy, the consequence is pluralization of the academy.

Let us now see how these themes get played out in the neo-Calvinist tradition. The neo-Calvinist finds it as obvious as does the Yale theologian that in the modern world the normed thought and speech of the Church frequently come into conflict, or appear to come into conflict, with reputable results of the non-theological disciplines. The Clementine model doesn't seem at all plausible as a description. Further, the neo-Calvinist spies in the response of Christian academics in general the same pattern that the Yale theologians spy in the response of Christian theologians and biblical scholars: Christian thinkers have felt a general obligation to conform their thought to the reputable results of the general academy and to the standards and methods in the regnant self-image of the academy. Now though neo-Calvinist rhetoric often suggests otherwise, the neo-Calvinist is not of the view that conformation to the results of the general academy is always mistaken. There aren't any flat-earthers among neo-Calvinists, nor any geo centrists. But what about the *general pattern?* What about the operating assumption that Christian thinkers have a *general* obligation to see to it that their thought conforms to the academy?

First, one more point about the general pattern. It would be possible for Christian thinkers to conform their thought to the results of the academy in thoroughly ad hoc fashion: Whenever a conflict arises between Christian conviction and some reputable result of academic learning, alter one's Christian conviction so as to bring it into conformity. Few have been content with such ad hoc-ism, however. So the view has arisen, and become popular in the contemporary Church, that Christian thought and speech should be understood to be, or should be revised to become, about something else than what non-theological learning is about: about something beyond the reach of such learning — about a way of valuing facts rather than about the facts valued, about a way of orienting oneself within the whole world rather than about the world as a whole, about the transcendent rather than about the immanent, or whatever. The goal, you see, is to so interpret or revise Christianity as to make it impossible that any conflicts arise in the future.

The neo-Calvinists, like the Yale theologians, take the different tack of rejecting the pattern of conformation and urging its reversal. In cases of conflict, let those academics who are members of the Christian community norm their thought and speech by the norms of that community rather than by those of the general academy. Where neo-Calvinists differ from Yale theologians is, first, in urging this reversal for Christian thinkers generally and not just for theologians and biblical scholars. From this a second difference follows: In seeking to work out the reversal, Christian thinkers in general will not be able to confine themselves to eclectically picking and choosing from the general academy but will sometimes have to engage in alternative theorizing. Perhaps it's possible for the theologians of the Christian community to pick and choose eclectically from, for example, the philosophy produced by the general academy — though the dangers in their doing so are surely considerable. But it's not possible for the *philosophers* of the Christian community to just pick and choose from their fellow philosophers. They will have to become constructive philosophers. Thus reversing the direction of conformation takes on a quite different character in the neo-Calvinist tradition from that in the tradition of Yale theology: Rather than reversing the direction of conformation by eclectically picking and choosing from other disciplines in accord with the norms of the Christian community, one reverses the direction of conformation by alternative theorizing in one's own discipline in accord with those norms.

The major root of these two differences between neo-Calvinism and Yale theology is to be found in yet a third difference. The neo-Calvinist poses to the general academy a fundamental question which the Yale theologians do not explicitly pose (though one surmises that the answer they would give would be the same). The question is this: Is the regnant self-image of the modern academy tenable? The neo-Calvinist contends that it is not — that it is in fact a piece of self-delusion. Academic learning is not and *could not be* an autonomous, generically human, foundationally structured enterprise whose final foundations, universal theory, and necessary conditions are developed by philosophers. It is my judgment that this question and this answer have been the generating impulse of the neo-Calvinist line of thought.

The question was already posed and answered with stark clarity by Abraham Kuyper in the 1880s. I have long thought, and I continue to think, that that was remarkable. It's remarkable that Karl Barth should have arrived in the 1920s at the views which I characterized as those of the Yale theologians, views which we can now recognize to be — I stifle my dislike for modish language — *postmodern* views. But it's even more remarkable that Abraham Kuyper should have arrived at postmodern views of academic learning fifty years before that, more than a hundred years ago.

A prominent component in that loosely unified movement which began at the end of the eighteenth century and which we now call "Romanticism" was dislike for the new science. Science "unweaves the rainbow," said John Keats, takes the mystery out of things. But never, to the best of my knowledge, did the Romantics question the accuracy of the regnant self-image of modern science. They lamented its consequences, they rejected its pretension of being the sole reliable access to truth; but the Romantics tacitly conceded that modern science was what it said it was — an autonomous, generically human, foundationally structured enterprise. Today that once-regnant self-image is widely rejected, such rejection figuring prominently in what those who call our present-day culture "postmodern" have in mind. But no one in Kuyper's day was questioning the accuracy of the self-image. Except, I suppose, Marx and Nietzsche; they too did not concede that the scholarship of the academy is what its practitioners profess it to be.

It was especially the pretension of academic learning to being autonomous and generically human that Kuyper zeroed in on; later thinkers in the neo-Calvinist tradition, as we will see, have zeroed in on the pretension to being foundational in structure. I judge Kuyper's best statement of his line of thought to occur in the second volume of his *Encyclopedia of Sacred Theology,* in the chapters entitled "Science Impaired by Sin" and "The Two-fold Development of Science." Perhaps it will be easier to follow the general drift of Kuyper's thought if I say at the beginning that it was his deep conviction that to be a Christian is not just to have convictions about the transcendent but to operate with a highly general hermeneutic of reality.

Consider that among the dispositions characteristic of us human beings are what might be called *belief-dispositions* — dispositions which, upon being activated, produce beliefs. Now if we try to account for the particular belief-dispositions present in an adult at a given time, no doubt we will have to appeal both to the indigenous constitution of the person and to what the person has learned. Kuyper's argument in the chapters I mentioned is, in effect, that a full accounting will require appealing to a third factor as well: sin. Our belief-dispositions are formed not only by nature and nurture, but also by sin. Or better: Sin results in their *malformation*. And we bring these malformed dispositions with us to our practice of science, unavoidably so.

Kuyper calls attention to a number of such malformations, the point of so doing being to cast doubt on the claim of the academy that its learning is generically human. Here is just one example; he is talking about the effects of sympathy and antipathy:

> The darkening of the understanding . . . would be better understood if we called it the *darkening of our consciousness*. Over against sin stands love, the sympathy of existence, and even in our present sinful conditions the fact is noteworthy, that where this sympathy is active you understand much better and more accurately than where this sympathy is wanting. A friend of children understands the child and the child's life. A lover of animals understands the life of the animal. In order to study nature in its material operations, you must love her. Without this inclination and this desire toward the object of your study, you do not advance an inch. . . . And this is significant in every department of study.[1]

We all know how defenders of the accuracy of the academy's regnant self-image would try to defend themselves against Kuyper's observations: It's true, they would say, that you can point to cases in which one and another kind of malformation has influenced someone's work in the academy. But remember: It is only properly formed adults who are to be allowed

---

1. Abraham Kuyper, *Principles of Sacred Theology* (Grand Rapids: Baker Book House, 1980 repr.), p. 111.

to do the work of the academy. Or to put the point more strictly: Scholars are each to work only on those branches of learning for which their own particular malformations are irrelevant — those who are color-blind are not to develop theories of color-vision, those who are hostile to the English are not to research the role of England in the modern world, etc. And if a person's work in the academy does prove at some point to be influenced by one of his or her malformations, it is the duty of the other members of the academy to call attention to the misdeed.

I think some cogent responses can be made to this rejoinder. For example, discriminations between the well formed and the malformed will themselves have to be made in a generically human way; but can they be so made for the sorts of phenomena that Kuyper cites as malformations? And can the malformations always be eliminated? Here is another of Kuyper's observations, this one on the effects of persons' social background on their thought:

> He who has had his bringing-up in the midst of want and neglect will entertain entirely different views of jural relationships and social regulations from him who from his youth has been bathed in prosperity.[2]

Suppose we accept the accuracy of this observation and resolve, accordingly, not to have social theory developed by persons whose perspectives on social structure and dynamics have been skewed by their occupying a particular rung on the social ladder. Where are we to find impartial observers who occupy no rung?

But Kuyper doesn't stop to consider either the rejoinder mentioned above or these responses to the rejoinder; he is after bigger game. He is going to argue that the failure of academic learning to satisfy its regnant self-image is not accidental; learning, even in the non-theological disciplines, *cannot be* generically human. The twentieth-century Dutch philosopher Herman Dooyeweerd followed Kuyper on this point; some of us Americans have been content to argue a more modest case, which shortly I will describe. But let us try to get hold of the main lines of Kuyper's argument. It will help to keep in mind that Kuyper is here engaged in what the Yale theologians would call Church theology. He is explicating what he takes to be Christian belief, not engaging in what purports to be autonomous philosophy.

2. Kuyper, *Principles of Sacred Theology*, p. 109.

Consider what the Christian regards as the most important malformation worked by sin, namely, malformation of our capacity

> for obtaining the knowledge of God, and thus for obtaining the conception of the whole. Without the sense of God in the heart no one shall ever attain unto a knowledge of God, and without love, or, if you please, a holy sympathy for God, that knowledge shall never be rich in content.[3]

With the words "obtaining the conception of the whole," Kuyper was hinting at his view that someone who knows and loves God apprehends thereby a fundamental aspect of what reality is like as a whole — an apprehension unattainable by the person who lacks such knowledge and love. Thus sin, which in this case inhibits the knowledge and love of God, produces once again a cognitive malformation. Allow Kuyper to make the point in his own words:

> Suppose that you had succeeded in attaining an adequate knowledge of all the parts of the cosmos, the product of these results would not yet give you the adequate knowledge of the whole. The whole is always something different from the combination of its parts. First because of the organic relation which holds the parts together; but much more because of the entirely new questions which the combination of the whole presents: questions as to the origin and end of the whole; questions as to the categories which govern the object in its reflection in your consciousness; questions as to absolute being, and as to what non-cosmos is. In order to answer these questions, you must subject the whole cosmos to yourself, your own self included; in order to do this in your consciousness you must step out from the cosmos, and you must have a starting-point in the *non*-cosmos; and this is altogether impossible as long as sin confines you with your consciousness to the cosmos.[4]

In summary: It is the conviction of the Christian community that by faith, and the second birth of which faith is the expression, we gain knowl-

---

3. Kuyper, *Principles of Sacred Theology*, p. 113.
4. Kuyper, *Principles of Sacred Theology*, p. 113.

edge and love of God; thereby we also apprehend fundamental aspects of the totality of things which formerly were inaccessible to us. But, now, the acquisition of such apprehension of totality is far from merely *adding* to our consciousness; it fundamentally alters our consciousness and gives us a new hermeneutic of reality. Thus there are, at a most fundamental level, two kinds of people: those who, by second birth and faith, have the rudiments of an accurate apprehension of the totality of things, and those who, remaining in a state of malformation, lack such apprehension. Both, of course, are human;

> but one is inwardly different from the other, and consequently feels a different content rising from his consciousness; thus they face the cosmos from different points of view, and are impelled by different impulses. And the fact that there are two kinds of *people* occasions of necessity the fact of two kinds of human *life* and *consciousness* of life, and of two kinds of *science.* . . .[5]

Two kinds of science! Having said that there *must be* two kinds of science, given that there are these two kinds of people with their different hermeneutics of reality in general, Kuyper at once goes on to say that there are nonetheless commonalities between these two kinds of people in their practice of science. To follow Kuyper in his line of thought here, we must realize that what he was doing was insistently probing the contribution of the theorizer, in all his or her particularity, to the practice of science. The theorist is not a blotter soaking up the facts of the world; the theorist is a dynamic, structured, believing and, feeling self. These aspects of the self unavoidably come to expression in the person's practice of academic learning and, thereby, in the results at which the person arrives. In particular, the subject unavoidably brings to the practice of science either that apprehension of the whole of things which faith makes possible or the lack of that apprehension. But faith, new birth, and that apprehension of totality do not touch everything in the human self; in Kuyper's view they work "no change in the senses," nor in "the formal process of thought." So there will be commonality amidst the diversity — at these points and others.

Nonetheless, "a universally compulsory science, that shall be com-

5. Kuyper, *Principles of Sacred Theology,* p. 154.

pulsory upon all men is inconceivable."[6] There comes a point in the dialogue between Christian thinkers and others where it proves "impossible to settle the difference of insight."[7] At that point, "No polemics . . . can ever serve any purpose."[8] All each party can do is explain to the other why it thinks as it does. It's important to offer such explanations. Yet they must be seen for what, at bottom, they are: "the confession of the reason why one refuses to follow the tendency of the other. . . ."[9] It was clearly Kuyper's view that this standoff in persuasion may well leave each party entitled to its views and entitled to pursue academic learning in accord with its views. Pluralism within the academy is unavoidable in our religiously divided world.

In our first lecture we noted that a standard part of the regnant self-image of the academy is that malformations are to be kept out; though academic learning will be spoken of as properly a generically human enterprise, that is not to be understood as meaning that everyone whatsoever is entitled to engage in it, but rather, that adults whose belief-dispositions are properly formed are so entitled. But in spite of the fact that Kuyper thought the belief-dispositions of the unbeliever to be malformed in a fundamental way, he was certainly not of the view that only learning which conforms to Christian convictions is reputable learning. And that implies that he has rejected not only the claim of the modern academy that its practice fits its self-image, but he has rejected also the very criteria for acceptable learning embodied in that self-image. That leaves us wondering what Kuyper would himself propose as the criteria for acceptable theorizing. The following, quite unsatisfactory, comment is the most he ever says on the matter:

> both parts of humanity . . . feel the impulse to investigate the object, and, by doing this in a scientific way, to obtain a scientific systematization of that which exists. The effort and activity of both bear the same character; they are both impelled by the same purpose; both devote their strength to the same kind of labor; and this kind of labor is in each case called the prosecution of science.[10]

6. Kuyper, *Principles of Sacred Theology*, p. 182.
7. Kuyper, *Principles of Sacred Theology*, p. 160.
8. Kuyper, *Principles of Sacred Theology*, p. 160.
9. Kuyper, *Principles of Sacred Theology*, p. 161.
10. Kuyper, *Principles of Sacred Theology*, p. 155.

Let us stop our forward progress for a moment now to reflect a bit on Kuyper's line of thought. I am, for one thing, dissatisfied with Kuyper's setting the Christian thinker off from everybody else in the practice of academic learning. That may be appropriate on a few matters; but on many issues which arise in the non-theological disciplines, the relevant distinction proves not to be that between Christians and everyone else, but between adherents to the three "religions of the book" and everyone else. And on other issues, yet different distinctions will be the relevant ones. The relevant distinctions are far more contextual than Kuyper thought.

Second, though it surely is part of Christian conviction that the Christian has an apprehension of an aspect of the totality of things which others do not have, and though it seems a priori plausible that this totality-apprehension has wide-flung ramifications in the life and thought of the person who enjoys it, we would like to know a good deal more about the *what* and the *how* of these ramifications in the practice of academic learning. Kant, for example, gave an elaborate argument in support of his denial of such ramifications. But Kuyper lets us down here, contenting himself with such remarks as "their activities run in opposite directions, because they have different starting points" and "because they themselves are differently constituted, they see a corresponding difference in the constitution of all things."[11]

Part of Dooyeweerd's project was to improve on Kuyper at this very point. The improvement he proffered went along the following lines. Begin with the "functions" of things, as Dooyeweerd calls them — the properties, the qualities, the actions, and so forth. These come objectively differentiated into fourteen or fifteen distinct *modalities*. One such grouping of functions constitutes the *physical* modality; another, the *psychic* modality; yet a third, the *aesthetic* modality; and so forth. It was furthermore Dooyeweerd's claim that the subject, the *Gegenstand*, of the theorist's endeavors in the various special sciences, that is, the entity on which the theorist focuses his or her inquiries, is always one such abstract modality. The goal of the theorist in a specific discipline is to formulate laws concerning the interrelationship of the functions belonging to the modality proper to that discipline — or, perhaps, laws concerning the interrelationship of entities with respect to the functions they possess within that modality. Dooyeweerd completes his picture of academic learning by asserting that

11. Kuyper, *Principles of Sacred Theology*, p. 155.

it is the business of philosophy to give a synoptic account of the interrelation of the modalities.

From here, Dooyeweerd went on to argue that it is inherent in the structure of the special sciences that they make philosophical commitments, and, in turn, that it is inherent in the structure of philosophical theorizing to take something as absolute, as ultimate interpretive clue for the construction of a general theory of reality. What a given philosopher takes as absolute, as ultimate interpretive clue, may be either one of the modalities — in which case his or her thought will acquire a reductionist character — or what lies outside the modalities — namely, God — in which case there is the possibility, at least, of escaping reductionism. But when we speak of taking something as absolute, we are, in Dooyeweerd's view, perforce in the realm of religion. Thus, religious commitment is unavoidable in the practice of theorizing. In truth, it is unavoidable for human beings. The structure of being human is such that we all strive to bring unity into our lives by taking something as absolute; we all have and must have an ultimate concern. Ideally, what functions as absolute in a person's practice of scholarship will be identical with that person's ultimate life-concern. As a matter of fact, it often is not.

This argument can be seen as, and was no doubt intended to be, a fleshing out of Kuyper's argument; nonetheless it diverges from Kuyper's argument in a most important way. Kuyper's line of thought begins unambiguously from what the Yale theologians would call *Church theology*. Part of Christian conviction is that faith, and the new birth of which faith is the expression, open up to us a certain apprehension of the totality of things; these call forth a new life and a new way of thinking. When Kuyper came to the last step of his argument, the link between the Christian's totality-apprehension and his or her practice of academic learning in the non-theological disciplines, he became hasty and vague. I suppose one might say, in extenuation, that clarification of this relationship is not a matter of Church theology, but rather of philosophy. Be that as it may: Dooyeweerd, by contrast, starts not from an elucidation of Christian conviction but from a philosophical analysis of the nature of theorizing, arguing that theorizing in its very nature is such that it must be pursued in some specific religious direction, and that all but one such direction results in reductionism.

Given this way of proceeding, a question concerning reflexivity is obviously in order for Dooyeweerd. The argument of Dooyeweerd, which we have just reviewed, to the effect that philosophizing is always perspectival, that it always consists of saying how reality looks when viewed from the perspective of some specific absolute, and that all but one of such perspectives are distortedly reductionistic: Is this argument itself specific to one such perspective, namely, the Christian, or more generally, the theistic one? I think Dooyeweerd never really made up his mind how to answer this question. One can see why: There are strong considerations pulling in opposite directions. To concede that this very argument for the perspectival character of philosophizing is itself specific to the Christian, or theistic, perspective would be to break off from the very beginning the possibility of serious dialogue with representatives of other perspectives; yet Dooyeweerd was intensely interested in persuading his peers in the academy of the religiously perspectival character of all theorizing, their own included. On the other hand, to say that this argument itself is not specific to any perspective but a prolegomenon to all would be to exempt a large and very important piece of philosophizing from the thesis that philosophizing is always perspectival. My own exploration of an alternative way of articulating the basic insights of the neo-Calvinist tradition was in part motivated by the fact that the alternative answers to this reflexivity question are equally unpalatable.

One last point about the strategies of Kuyper and Dooyeweerd can serve at the same time as an entry to my own way of thinking about these matters.

You will recall that in my first lecture I rehearsed some of the reflections of the Yale theologians on how we should think of Christianity when we discuss the relation of Christianity to academic learning. Frei, following Barth, took the fundamental reality to be the Church. But Frei observed that it has been common among his fellow theologians to treat Christianity instead as a specific version of some general structure of consciousness and then to look to philosophers for descriptions of that general structure; this is the *phenomenological* approach. Now if one reads Dooyeweerd with these points fresh in mind, one is immediately struck by the similarity between Dooyeweerd's approach and that of the phenomenologists. If Frei were to learn of that similarity, and if he were to to learn, in addition, that Dooyeweerd leaves it unclear whether his phenomenological prolegomena are intended as a neutral preface to Christian philosophy or as a proper part thereof, he would be as suspicious of Dooyeweerd as he was of Type II theologians in general!

Though Kuyper's thought about these matters was probably the same as Dooyeweerd's, his emphasis, as I have mentioned, was different. Though he probably thought that everyone operates with a totality-conception structurally similar to that of the Christian, all that he explicitly argued was that Christians have a certain totality-apprehension which non-Christians lack. But notice that, in spite of this difference, both Kuyper and Dooyeweerd begin not from the Church and the norms pertaining to its members but from the reborn Christian self. I have come to think that it is in good measure on account of beginning here that neo-Calvinism, especially in its Dutch manifestations, has so often erupted into triumphalist expectations expressed in the language of transformation. One who starts not from the reborn self but from the all-too-defective, though normed, life of members of the Church will tend to expect something less from the endeavors of Christian scholars than *transformation* of their discipline.

Harry Jellema, the philosopher who taught both Henry Stob and me, thought of Christianity as one of a number of objective "minds," as he called them, which find their expression in society and culture and which individuals become members of; his approach was thus quasi-Hegelian, rather than phenomenological. When I now look back on my own work, I see that my inclination has been to think of Christianity in a different way yet, namely, as a way of being in the world; and though early on I too worked with the genus/species distinction, arguing that everybody exhibits a way of being in the world which is structurally similar to that of the Christian, in more recent years I have been content to forgo that argument and simply explore how those committed to the Christian way of being in the world should think and live. I now realize that in that way my more recent thought has been like that of the Yale theologians and Karl Barth, who also forgo arguing, indeed, *resist* arguing, that Christianity is a species of some inescapable structure. Furthermore, in recent years I have come to think that fundamental to the Christian's way of being in the world is membership in the Church. I am now inclined to complete the process and begin, as do Barth and the Yale theologians, with the Church rather than the individual — which also brings me close once again to the thought of Harry Jellema, deleted of its Hegelian overtones.

It has seemed to me, as it does to everyone in these two traditions, that those who are members of the Church should break the grip of that general pattern of conformation so characteristic of Christian thinkers in the modern world. Rather than feeling some general obligation to conform, we should reflect, case by case, what the direction of conformation should be. You will recognize, I'm sure, that the alternative as I have just stated it is more measured and qualified than that urged by those we have considered so far. They all say: Reverse the direction of conformation. I say: Reflect, case by case, whether the direction of conformation should be reversed. I think the Church did the right thing when it conformed its thought to the new science by surrendering its commitment to geocentrism; thus it is my judgment that not all conformation in that direction is wrong. On the other hand, there are plenty of examples of Christian thinkers conforming their thought to modern academia when, in my judgment, Christian fidelity required resolving the tension in the other direction. And while avoiding the language of one-directional conformation, this is the point to which I have given primary emphasis in my writings, since this seems to me the point which most needs making to most audiences in the present-day context.

I went on to ask why it is that the general pattern of conformation, in the direction *Church to academia,* has seemed so compellingly right to so many Christian thinkers in the modern world. My conclusion was that they had imbibed part of the self-image of the academy. They had accepted the thesis that academic learning, properly conducted, is foundational in structure; and they had furthermore accepted the claim of the general academy that its own reputable results do in fact exhibit that foundational structure. So it seemed to me that, if the general pattern of conformation was to be broken, the spell of foundationalism, specifically now of classical foundationalism, had to be broken.

Let me briefly explain what I mean by classical foundationalism as a theory of the proper structure of theorizing. Foundationalists, be they classical or non-classical, always begin by distinguishing between those of our beliefs which we hold on the basis of other beliefs of ours, and those of our beliefs which we do not so hold; let us call these, respectively, mediated beliefs and immediate beliefs. Having made this distinction, classical foundationalists interested in offering a theory of theorizing then ask: Under what conditions is it proper in the practice of science to hold a certain belief *immediately,* and under what conditions is it proper to hold a certain belief *mediately?* Their answer — and here we see why the metaphor of foundation is appropriate — their answer is that it is proper to hold a belief *mediately* if it is held on the basis of beliefs that it is proper to hold *immedi-*

ately, and if, in addition, the mediate belief is probable on the evidence of all one's properly held immediate beliefs. (There are variations with respect to this last clause.) And their answer is that it is proper to hold a belief *immediately* if it is certain for one. (On this, too, there are variations.) I trust you see the basic thrust of this: Good science is founded on certitude.

Now if you, a Christian, accept the thesis of the modern academy that acceptable academic learning is foundational in structure, and if you furthermore believe the claim of the modern academy that its own practice of academic learning satisfies its self-image in this respect, then you are more than likely to be intimidated by the results of the academy. Apart from quibbles here and there, you will do your best to conform your thought to those results. After all, beliefs probable with respect to what is certain for some person appear to have a lot going for them.

What I argued, however, was that almost no specimens of learning accepted as reputable in the modern academy do satisfy the criteria of the classical foundationalist; and that this is not accidental, but in the nature of the thing. Thus are the fangs pulled from what has so intimidated Christian scholars in the modern world. I went on to propose a model for the "logic" of science alternative to the classical foundationalist model. In the academic disciplines we do not work with just data and theories, assessing the probability of the data on the theories. We also work with what I called "control beliefs" — general convictions as to the sorts of theories acceptable to us, this to be understood as including convictions as to how our theories must be related to our data. Given some data, we try to devise theories which satisfy those control beliefs with respect to those data. Sometimes we find it impossible to come up with such theories. Then we start juggling things. We work back and ask whether perhaps we were mistaken in some of what we accepted as data. Or we work ahead and consider whether perhaps we have to change some of our control beliefs. What we try to achieve by such juggling back and forth is equilibrium. The deep reason, then, why large stretches of reputable learning in the modern academy prove to be incompatible with Christianity is that the control beliefs operating in much learning are incompatible with Christianity. It's pretty obvious what the goal should be of those academics who are members of the Church: We should allow what is normative for the thought of the Church to function, whenever relevant, as control beliefs in our practice of academic learning.

You see, I trust, the relative theoretical modesty of this way of thinking as compared, for example, to Dooyeweerd's; in thinking along these lines, we take just enough theoretical hay onto our forks for the task at hand. I did not argue that all academic learning is religiously perspectival in character. I did not argue that everyone unavoidably has an ultimate concern. I argued just that the control beliefs operative in much learning are alien to Christianity, that what is normative for the thought of the Church's members should be allowed by them to function as control beliefs in their practice of academic learning, and that classical foundationalism should no longer be offered as an objection to this last thesis but should instead be rejected as an unacceptable account of either the actual or proper structure of theorizing.

Modest though it may be in its theoretical commitments, however, the proposal cries out for elaboration, support, and defense at many different points. I shall ignore all but one, one which enables me to bring the work of my friend, erstwhile colleague, and former Stob Lecturer, Alvin Plantinga, into the picture. It will be said by some that Christians are not *entitled* to let their religious convictions function as control beliefs in their practice of academic learning, because they are not even entitled to *hold* those convictions, let alone entitled to let them function as control beliefs. They are not entitled to hold them because they hold them on inadequate evidence — or worse, because they do not hold them on any evidence at all, instead believing them immediately. Alvin Plantinga has powerfully undercut this objection, and stirred up a lot of discussion among philosophers in the process. There is no way in which I can here give you a feeling for the power of his undercutting; all I can do is sketch with quick strokes its general character.

Probably most intellectuals in the modern world have accepted the thesis coming out of the Enlightenment that a person is entitled to hold his or her religious beliefs only if the person holds them on the basis of evidence — satisfactory evidence, of course. The response of most Christian intellectuals has been to scurry about trying to find satisfactory evidence and to revise Christian belief until it fits such evidence as we appear to have; the response of non-Christians has been to point out where the proffered evidence is unsatisfactory. To this farrago Plantinga posed the simple but unsettling question: Why should the assumption be accepted that evidence is always required? Who says that we may only *reason to* our convictions about God, never simply *reason from* them? If one wants to think along foundational lines, who says that beliefs about God may never be in *the foundation?* I trust you will recognize a striking similarity between Plantinga's contention at this point, and what at the end of my last lecture I cited Hans Frei as saying. There's this large difference, though: Frei, as he would be the first to admit, was just expressing his intuition, that one's faith that Jesus is the Messiah doesn't have to be based on evidence and arguments. Plantinga, by contrast, is developing an epistemology which honors this intuition.

Let me close by briefly summarizing what we have learned, and then posing a question for reflection. You will have surmised that the preparation of these lectures has been for me a journey into self-understanding. Reared in the tradition of neo-Calvinism, I now find myself working in the ambience of Yale theology. I have used the occasion of these lectures to come to some understanding of how these two traditions are related. I hope I haven't abused the occasion!

The conclusion I have been led to is that there is a deep affinity between these two traditions which intersect in my person. That affinity is captured in the metaphor of reversing the direction of conformation. Looking at the course of Christian theology in the modern world, the Yale theologian is struck by the pervasiveness of the conviction that Christian theologians are obligated to conform their thought to the reputable results of the non-theological general academy and to what the academy perceives to be its standards and methods. Now as a matter of fact, the Yale theologians occupy university positions. Nonetheless, they see their calling to be that of filling the ecclesiastical office of theologian. As such, their task is to elucidate the structure of the Church's normed thought and speech, and to hold the actual thought and speech of the Church up to critique by its own norms. Since their calling is that of Church theologian, their own theological thought and speech is subject to those same norms of the Church. Accordingly, if there is conforming to be done, it must go in the other direction. The direction of conformation must be reversed — as it must, for similar reasons, be reversed by the biblical scholars of the Church.

The neo-Calvinists cast their glance more widely, though let me say, once again, that this wider glance comes perilously close to overlooking theologians and biblical scholars. They cast their glance over Christian scholars generally; and when they survey the work of Christian scholars in the modern world, they notice the very same pattern of conformation that the Yale theologians noticed with respect to theologians and biblical scholars. Their response to noticing the pattern is also the same: They urge that the direction of conformation be reversed. And their reason is the same: Fidelity to the witness of the Bible to God in Jesus Christ requires the reversal. They go beyond their Yale-theologian compatriots in launching a counter-attack: Consider that self-image of the general academy, as engaged in autonomous, generically human, foundationally structured learning: Not only is it impossible to defend the picture of acceptable theorizing embodied in the image, but the practice of the academy doesn't come anywhere near fitting its own self-image, nor could it. The academy has been living in self-delusion.

Lastly, the question for reflection. You will have guessed from some of the things I have said that I am myself not entirely happy with this metaphor of reversing the direction of conformation. I'm all for Church theology. But is the relation of the Church theologian to the non-theological disciplines exclusively that of melting down gold taken from the Egyptians? Isn't some of the statuary of the Egyptians quite OK as it is? Does it all reek of idolatry? Isn't there something for the Church theologian to *learn* from the non-theological disciplines? So too for the biblical scholars of the Church. The Yale theologians are not flat-earthers or geocentrists; they interpret their Bibles so that Christian fidelity does not require joining the Flat Earth Society. So it is misleading to use exclusively one-directional metaphors. It's true that, instead of making the world of the Bible fit into our world, we ought to fit our world into its world. But in some respects, even in *many* respects; not in all. What you and I know as human beings of the twentieth century does and should enter into the mix from which Church theology and Church biblical interpretation emerge. And not all that we know as human beings of the twentieth century comes from our life within the Church. Some of it comes from academia — and from many other places as well. Comments of exactly the same sort apply to members of the neo-Calvinist tradition; they too, many of them if not most of them, have thought much too one-directionally.

Anyone who has absorbed the thought pattern of either of these two traditions will react to this point with a mixture of concession and worry. Yes, of course, we in the Church did the right thing when we conformed our thought and biblical interpretation to the heliocentric theory. But if we concede that this is just one of a number of similar examples rather than a flukey exception, then how do we avoid Scripture's becoming once again a wax nose, molded by each as he or she wishes? How do we avoid sliding into Type II theology? How do we prevent the project of Christian learning from slipping irrevocably away from us?

I have some vague ideas as to how these questions should be answered; but at present, no more than that, no more than vague ideas. What I want is a place to stand between Karl Barth and Friedrich Schleiermacher. I think there is such a place; I think I'm already standing there.

Schleiermacher, while resisting the suggestion that Church theology is just a species of academic learning, nonetheless believed that we had to struggle to fit them together into some sort of whole. I admire him for that. But he seems to have accepted the self-image of the non-theological academy that it is engaged in an autonomous, generically human, foundationally structured enterprise. And so of course he thought that equilibrium has to be achieved by making Church theology conform to the academy. And since Church theology is the Church's organ of self-critique, that implies that the thought and life and speech of the Church itself must be brought into conformity. The neo-Calvinists can be seen as agreeing with Schleiermacher, that we must struggle toward equilibrium; they recommend, however, that it be achieved in just the opposite way, making the academy conform to the normed thought of the Church. That, at least, is how they often speak, as do the Yale theologians when they move beyond theology proper and begin to speak more generally of incorporating our world into the biblical world. My own position is to affirm the struggle toward equilibrium but then to insist that the conformation must sometimes be allowed to go in one direction and sometimes in the other. Three positions within the middle type, Type III; I occupy the middle position within the middle type. What could be more evenhanded than that?

But I don't mean to be fundamentally evenhanded. Though sometimes the Church must revise its thought in the light of what transpires in the sciences — I see that as one implication of a healthy doctrine of God as Creator — nonetheless, it is God's Word in Jesus Christ which is final and decisive for us. Our difficulty is that sometimes we misinterpret that Word, and sometimes it is the academy which persuades us that we have done so. No doubt that fact sometimes seems threatening; but I suggest that a person in the middle position in the middle type will finally and ultimately feel more thankful for it than threatened by it.

Happiness: Goal or Gift?

Two Lectures on the Relationship
between Knowledge, Goodness, and
Happiness in Plato and Calvin

DEWEY J. HOITENGA, JR.

Contents

Introduction

I am pleased and greatly honored to be here tonight to pay tribute to Henry Stob. Professor Stob was my first teacher in Philosophy at Calvin College. Then it was my good fortune to study three more years with him at Calvin Seminary, which we entered in the same year, 1952 — he as the newly appointed Professor of Ethics and Apologetics, I as a student eager to study Reformed theology. I owe more to him than any other teacher during those seven splendid years of study. He became my mentor and friend, and I am thankful for this special opportunity to acknowledge my intellectual and spiritual debt to him.

I am also grateful to God for my Christian parents, to whom I owe both my Christian faith and my love of learning. My father is a retired minister in the Christian Reformed Church; my mother taught in several Christian schools. God has given them many years; he is 91, she is 90. They, too, are admirers of Henry Stob, and I am glad they can be with us tonight to share this happy occasion.

Goodness for the Sake of Happiness:
Plato's Problem

"For the Greek, salvation was an achievement; for the Christian it was a gift."
— Henry Stob

I. The Issue: Happiness, Goodness, or Knowledge?

If I were to ask, would you rather be happy or good, what would you say?

While you're considering this choice, let me say that it reminds me of a game I used to play with one of my boyhood friends. We took turns asking, what would you rather be, this or that? The questioner had to fill in the *this* and the *that*; but each of us had to give his answer. We took turns being questioner, posing the choice. One question I still remember was, What would you rather be, a sidewalk or a utility pole? I remember my friend choosing to be a sidewalk and myself, the utility pole. Now we couldn't just give our answers; we also had to give our reasons for our choices, especially if we disagreed. My friend's reason for being a sidewalk was that he could then be in many places at once. My reason for choosing to be a utility pole was that, even though I was stuck in one place, I could from my top see all over; I could see many more places than a sidewalk could ever manage either to be or to see. The game led to some long and interesting discussions, even debates; sometimes even to one of us persuading the other to change his mind.

So what would you rather be, happy or good? This choice is certainly more important than any that occurred to my boyish mind, playing my boyish game, many years ago. Did you perhaps choose goodness, because you thought it might lead to happiness? If so, do you know that it does? That, of course, is another large question, which the original choice invites you to ask. What must you know, both about goodness and happiness, and about anything else, in order to be either good, or happy, or both?

Knowledge, Goodness, and Happiness

It is the relationship between these three things, knowledge, goodness, and happiness, that I want to examine in these lectures. In particular, I want to examine their relationship in Plato and John Calvin. Plato is the first Western thinker to discuss it. He relates these three things so closely that his view has often been summarized in two statements: Knowledge is virtue and Virtue is its own reward. *Virtue* is the term Plato uses for what I have been calling *goodness,* because it conveys better to us what Plato meant by virtue. I will continue to prefer the term *goodness,* but when I use *virtue,* I will mean the same thing. Either term refers to what we mean when we say that someone is *not* just a good musician or good carpenter, as the case may be, but a morally good person, a morally good human being.

Now Calvin also relates knowledge, goodness, and happiness very closely to each other, but no one (so far as I know) has either examined his view of their relationship or compared his view with Plato's. These two goals constitute my project.

Reformed Epistemology

The project first occurred to me when I was studying Plato and Calvin for my book on the theory of knowledge, more particularly, on what is now called *Reformed epistemology.*[1] The heart of Reformed epistemology, as I see it, consists of two claims about our knowledge of God: its immediacy and its vitality. By *immediacy* I refer to Calvin's claim that our knowledge of God is originally experiential and direct, not inferential or the result of reasoning. It is a thesis that Alvin Plantinga and other Calvinist philosophers have recently revived, restating it in a way that addresses the general issues

---

1. *Faith and Reason from Plato to Plantinga: An Introduction to Reformed Epistemology* (Grand Rapids: Eerdmans, 1991).

about the nature of knowledge as they are being discussed by contemporary philosophers. In fact, it is Plantinga who first used the new term *Reformed epistemology* to identify this thesis.[2]

But Calvin has a second important thesis about our knowledge of God, which I call its *vitality*. I discuss it briefly in my chapter on Calvin but saw that it was too large a topic to explore there. By *vitality* I refer to Calvin's claim that the knowledge of God is always characterized by a moral response. Thus he writes, in a famous passage in his *Institutes:* "We shall not say that, properly speaking, God is known where there is no religion or piety" (I.ii.1). In these words Calvin lays down a condition for knowing God, namely piety; piety, of course, is one of the most important virtues in the Christian concept of moral goodness. Where there is no piety, says Calvin, there is no knowledge of God, properly speaking.

Calvin's own theology, indeed, has often been regarded as a model of "pious theology," exemplifying his own prescription for what the knowledge of God should be like. John T. McNeill writes, in his "Introduction" to the Battles translation of the *Institutes:* "The whole work is suffused with an awed sense of God's ineffable majesty, sovereign power, and immediate presence with us men" (li).

The sense of awe and reverence is not totally absent, however, from ancient Greek philosophy. Indeed, in another striking passage, Calvin appeals to Plato as the prime analogue among these philosophers of his own view:

> It is clear, that all those who do not direct every thought and action in their lives to this goal [the knowledge of God] degenerate from the law of their creation. This was not unknown to the philosophers. Plato meant nothing but this when he often taught that the highest good of the soul is likeness to God, where, when the soul has grasped the knowledge of God, it is wholly transformed into his likeness. (I.iii.3)

Thus Plato, too, affirms the close connection between our knowledge of God and our love of God (which may be taken as the meaning of "being transformed into his likeness"). Of course, Calvin here reads into Plato the Christian language of God and of love. Still, the affinity between Plato's ul-

2. In "The Reformed Objection to Natural Theology," *Proceedings of the American Catholic Philosophical Association*, 1980.

timate principle of the Good and the biblical concept of God has often been noted.[3]

In any case, what Calvin alludes to here is Plato's famous teaching that knowledge and virtue are one. To know the Good is to follow it. Now I propose that, when Calvin teaches that the soul, having "grasped the knowledge of God, . . . is wholly transformed into his likeness," he is stating a Christian version of the Platonic doctrine that knowledge and virtue are one. To know God, who is the Christian's highest Good, is to love him; the knowledge of God and loving him are inseparably linked.

The Unity of Knowledge and Virtue

Now this unity of knowledge and virtue, on either version, Platonic or Calvinian, is highly paradoxical. For it implies that whoever knows the good will do it, and also, that whoever does evil does it from ignorance. These two implications are often called the "Socratic paradoxes," *Socratic* because Socrates was the first to teach them, and *paradoxes* because they conflict with one of the elemental teachings of human experience. This

---

3. H. D. Lewis identifies Plato's idea of the Good as "the first formulation in Western thought of the idea of transcendence as it came to dominate much subsequent thinking" ("History of Philosophy of Religion," in *Encyclopedia of Philosophy*, ed. P. Edwards [New York: Macmillan, 1967], p. 278). And Etienne Gilson: "Nothing more closely resembles the definition of the Christian God than [Plato's] definition of the Good" (*God and Philosophy* [New Haven: Yale University Press, 1951], p. 25).

For a thorough discussion of the issues involved and references to the opposed interpretations, see C. G. Rutenber, *The Doctrine of the Imitation of God in Plato* (New York: King's Crown Press, 1969). Rutenber focusses his study upon the significance of Plato's increasing tendency, in his later dialogues, to formulate the human ethical ideal as the imitation of God (godlikeness). He concludes, however, that "Plato fell short in his effort to build a metaphysic which would give mind its proper place in the scheme of things. It remained for Christian philosophy to play Plato to his Anaxagoras (*Phaedo* 97) and make mind absolutely central, through the doctrine of a personal God who creates *ex nihilo*" (p. 108).

Still, notes Rutenber, if "the forms are the ground of the life and goodness of God" (p. 15), and if God (and the lesser gods which Plato frequently invokes) approximates the moral ideal of Goodness more closely than human beings, it explains why Plato can formulate the ethical ideal "not in terms of man's likeness to his form but in terms of his likeness to God" (p. 38). It is thus no wonder that Christian thinkers have found support in this aspect of Plato's thought for their own religious approach to ethics.

teaching is that we can sometimes know what is good, yet do what is evil; so that some evil-doing, at least, is not due to ignorance.

Calvin, as we shall see next time, resolves this paradox with his concept of the human will. His view differs from Plato's not only on the origin and nature of evil-doing but also on the relationship of goodness to happiness, as this affects our motive for the pursuit of goodness. Still, the two thinkers agree on the intimate relationship between knowledge, goodness, and happiness, and even further, as I will argue, on the primacy of knowledge in that relationship. All of this, the agreements and the disagreements, will have to wait until the second lecture. In this lecture I will focus on Plato.

II. Happiness as Harmony

Plato on Happiness

Plato's ethics is an ethics of happiness. As such, it is appealing and even correct, in a certain way. For any theory of ethics must take account of both happiness and goodness, as well as knowledge. Plato's concept of happiness is also appealing and, I think, profoundly correct as far as it goes; and it goes far, indeed. Of course, Plato reached his idea of happiness only after considering other possibilities, such as pleasure, power, health, and wealth, even life itself, only to find them all inadequate. He does not deny that such things may be components of happiness, but happiness itself cannot be reduced to them. Moreover, he teaches, it must be connected to knowledge and virtue.

Happiness, for Plato, is a special kind of harmony. The word *harmony* stands for a complex idea, viz., the fitting together of several different parts into a unified whole. In music, it signifies at least two different notes that sound well together. In carpentry, it means joining together two or more pieces of wood so that they interlock neatly into one piece. There can be no harmony where there is only one thing; there must be at least two different things that can be brought together in such a way that they are one, without, however, obliterating the distinction between them. To produce the harmony of music and buildings requires the different skills of the composer and the carpenter. Since such skills are forms of knowledge, they are an early sign that knowledge, for Plato, will also be necessary for the harmony that constitutes human happiness.

The special kind of harmony that constitutes happiness, for Plato, consists of the parts of human nature working together as a unified whole. The Greek word that captures the result of such working together is *eudaimonia,* or well-being.[4] Plato begins his moral inquiry, therefore, with a study of human nature itself. For this study he was inspired, doubtless, by his mentor, Socrates, who followed the Delphic oracle; the oracle summed up the beginning of wisdom in the command, "Know yourself!" Plato gives us his most complete account of human nature in his *Republic.* In this dialogue, Plato analyzes human nature on three levels: what we are as individuals, as social beings, and as part of the universe. Thus happiness is not just a private, individual matter; no one can be happy all by himself, giving no thought to one's place in society and, finally, to one's place in the universe itself.

The First Level

On the first and most immediate level is the individual self that constitutes each of us as human beings. What distinguishes us as human beings from the material universe is that we are alive. This means that each of us has a soul, which is the principle of life. What distinguishes us from other living things is our reason, which is the ability to think and to know. Our souls have two other powers: a spirited element, which we may refer to as "heart," since it is the source of emotion and ambition,[5] and finally, appetite, which is the source of our bodily desires. Our emotions, ambitions, and desires

---

4. *Eudaimonia* differs from the English *happiness,* which tends to denote only the subjective state of pleasure, contentment, and satisfaction, by denoting also an objective state of well-being, flourishing, prosperity, or success. Gregory Vlastos gives a useful account of the problems in translation and concludes that there "is ample reason for sticking to the traditional translation, provided only that we bear in mind that in its pre-theoretical uses *eudaimonia* puts a heavier loading on the objective factor in 'happiness' than does the English word" (*Socrates: Ironist and Moral Philosopher* [Ithaca, N.Y.: Cornell University Press, 1991], p. 203).

5. Gr. *thumos.* Liddell and Scott actually give as its first meaning: *soul, life, breath,* corresponding to L. *anima.* Second meaning: *heart,* L. *animus,* any *vehement passion* such as anger or, in a good sense, *spirit.* Third meaning: *mind, will, purpose.* Cornford and Grube both translate it *the spirited element* of the soul. This multiplicity of meanings is clear evidence that the effort of the Greek philosophers to distinguish different powers of the soul never quite overcame the vagueness and overlap of such powers in the earlier conceptions of the Greek poets. (This fact bears especially on the problem of moral weakness; see n. 12 below.)

are many and diverse and thus potentially in conflict (and actually, as experience often teaches us), not only with each other but also with what our reason tells us is right and good.

Underlying these three "parts of the soul" and expressing itself though all of them is the deepest motivating force of all, the love called *eros*. *Eros* is the source of our deep and pervasive desire for happiness (thus, for harmony); but it does not know in what this happiness or harmony consists. Reason alone can find out, if it seeks the truth about ourselves.

On this first level, the harmony that makes for happiness comes only when our emotions and appetites follow the rule of reason. And the rule of reason consists in its knowing not only itself and the other powers of the soul but also the proper function of each, when they function together in harmony. Reason thus organizes and governs our individual lives. It will do this correctly, however, only when it really knows the truth about our nature.[6] When reason really does show us this truth about ourselves, we will naturally submit to it; for to know our own true well-being, happiness itself, and not pursue it would be irrational — going against reason itself. For Plato, that is psychologically inconceivable, for it would imply that we deliberately avoid what we most deeply want when we discover what it is and how to obtain it. Hence the close connection between knowledge and happiness.

The Second Level

It is not sufficient, however, to know ourselves as individuals. We must also discover that as individuals we are inseparably connected with other human individuals, whose make-up is just like our own. We must come to know ourselves as social beings. The most obvious sign of this connectedness is that we depend on other human beings for the satisfaction of many, if not all, of our own individual needs. The proper satisfaction of these needs is essential to our happiness. For example, we cannot even come to

---

6. Plato does not deny that true opinion or belief can guide the moral life correctly. However, he sharply distinguishes true belief from knowledge, precisely in terms of its inability to withstand the pressures of emotion and appetite because it is not, like knowledge, "fastened like a chain" to reality (*Meno* 98A). "Have you not noticed that opinions not based on knowledge are ugly things? The best of them are blind . . ." (*Republic* 506c).

know ourselves as individuals, let alone anything else, without the help of those who are our teachers. We also need food, clothing, homes, and many other things, which we can't even begin to produce all by ourselves. So there needs to be a division of labor among human beings, each one of us doing or making something that is useful to others.

This economic aspect of human nature bears on everyone's individual happiness, not only one's own. If I am not working for others and others are not working for me, everyone's happiness will be diminished. There must therefore be a harmony in the working together of all the individuals that make up society. Societies, like individuals, can be happy societies or not, depending on the harmony of their individuals living and working together.

The Parts of Society

To achieve such harmony Plato shows that society, like the individual, requires by its nature three different elements: rulers, who must know in what the harmony of society consists in order to make its laws; their assistants, the police and military, who must enforce the laws; and producers, who must make the goods and provide the services that everyone needs. A happy society exists when its rulers, their assistants, and all its workers are performing their special functions properly. Like the individuals who constitute it, a society must organize the functioning of its different parts if it wants happiness; and that requires, above all, knowledge in those who rule, but also obedience of everyone else to the laws they make. In short, every society must be a state. It is an inspiring ideal that Plato describes, as everyone knows who reads the *Republic.*

Of course, it is too good to be true, and Plato is the first to admit it. And why is it too good to be true? Plato's answer is that our social, economic, and political disorders are caused by the same ignorance that accounts for the disorder in our individual lives. If human beings really knew themselves and what could make them happy, not only in their individual nature but also in the nature of the society they constitute together, they would not only pursue such harmony in themselves but also in their dealings with each other. For again, it is psychologically inconceivable, according to Plato, to know what happiness is and how to get it, yet not pursue it.

III. Justice in the *Republic*

Those familiar with Plato's *Republic* may wonder why I have said nothing to this point about justice, which is generally taken to be the main topic of the dialogue. By contrast with knowledge and happiness, which have preoccupied us so far, justice is very clearly a *moral* concept. For Plato, in fact, it is identical with goodness, the term I have been using as a synonym for moral virtue. It is Plato's broadest moral concept; whoever has the virtue of justice has every other virtue as well. Thus it functions for Plato as the virtue of love does for Christians; it denotes the essence of human goodness.

The reason I have not yet discussed Plato's idea of justice is to highlight Plato's strategy in the *Republic*. Plato fully realizes that the desire for happiness is not matched by an equal desire for virtue or goodness; indeed, that realization underlies his strategy.[7] This strategy is to define justice, the sum of moral goodness, as the *very same harmony* that constitutes happiness. A human being is just whenever each of the powers of the soul is functioning properly. These powers function properly when reason rules the heart and the appetites. For reason to rule properly, it must acquire wisdom, which is then its special virtue. When by its wisdom reason shows the heart what is rightly to be feared and what not, a person will be brave, which is the heart's special virtue; and when reason discovers the mean between the extremes of over- and under-indulgence of the appetites, a person will be temperate or self-controlled, which is the special virtue of the appetites. Thus justice in the individual is the sum of the proper functions of the three parts of the soul, of their three respective virtues. Similarly, justice in the state is achieved when its rulers — Plato's famous philosopher-kings — are wise, their assistants brave, and the producers, temperate and given to self-control, both in their production and consumption of the things necessary for human life.

We can see now what virtue or goodness is. It is, as the Greek term *arete* suggests, an excellence in the way we function as human beings, both individually and together in society. Two of the specific excellences or virtues, courage and temperance, are moral, one, wisdom, intellectual; although it would be misleading to draw a rigid line. That is especially evident if we ask whether justice is mainly a moral or intellectual virtue. It is clearly both.

---

7. Here I follow the line of interpretation defended by H. A. Prichard in *Moral Obligation* [Oxford: Oxford University Press, 1949], pp. 103-11, and David Sachs, "A Fallacy in Plato's *Republic*," *The Philosophical Review*, LXXII (1963), pp. 141-58.

IV. The Special Role of Knowledge (Wisdom)

Wisdom

Still, the intellectual virtue of wisdom is particularly important, for it is the source of all the other virtues and the happiness that attends them. The love of such wisdom is just what makes the true philosopher, which is the special sense, long since lost sight of, that Plato gives to that term. The philosopher and the philosopher alone, for Plato, because of his love of knowledge and wisdom, is on the right road to goodness and happiness.

Two Kinds of Knowledge

There is an important link between the knowledge required for the harmony that is goodness and happiness and the knowledge required for the multitudinous occupations any complex society requires. Both are knowledge, both are skills: one tells us how to live, the other how to make or do something in particular. The latter is the expertise we can acquire by developing our particular talents and abilities. Unlike the knowledge of virtue that everyone should share *(arete),* this knowledge is a specialized skill-knowledge *(techne* or *poiesis)* that will differ according to the differences between those talents and abilities that individual human beings possess. Some will be carpenters, others musicians; some physicians, others — relatively few — rulers.

The difference between the two knowledges signifies the difference between a good human being and a good worker, whatever that work may be. Everyone should be a good human being to be happy, but not everyone should be a carpenter. Still, according to Plato, everyone should develop some special ability, for in that way one repays one's fellow human beings for what they do for one. So every human being should not only be *good,* but also good *at* something; both are required by justice. Plato here outlines the first work ethic; being productive, like being morally good, is a question of justice: whoever eats ought to work. It is also, therefore, a question of happiness, for being productive is essential to an individual's proper function as a part of the larger society to which he naturally belongs.

Thus the *Republic* is not only about the virtue of justice but also, and equally, about knowledge and happiness. Plato's overall argument, actually, is to show us that we cannot have one of these without the other two. So it is a mistake to think that the *Republic* is only, or even centrally, about justice or goodness. If we insist on formulating its thesis as one about justice, it is the thesis that we cannot have justice without knowledge as its necessary condition and without happiness as its necessary consequence. So the thesis is that knowledge, goodness, and happiness are three things in one, themselves an example of the harmony of different things that governs Plato's analysis of goodness and happiness. Knowledge is virtue and virtue is its own reward.

Similarly, ignorance, vice (or badness), and unhappiness go together, but instead of producing a harmony, they produce the disharmony and disorder that characterize the life of non-philosophers who live, and are content to live, in ignorance of what it is to be a human being. We who are non-philosophers may think we know ourselves, may even think we are good and happy; but Plato teaches that we can be mistaken in our beliefs about these things, and most likely are until we become philosophers. That is why for him, as for his mentor, Socrates, the unexamined life is not worth living; there is always the possibility one will be mistaken in one's most important beliefs, and thereby miss not only virtue but true happiness as well. Ignorance is not bliss.

V. Plato's Appeal

We can now review several points that explain the perennial appeal of Plato's account.

1. Objective Basis

First is the objective basis he provides for both goodness and happiness, two things the nature of which we are (as were many of Plato's contemporaries) sorely tempted to regard as relative to individual opinions about them. But such opinions vary widely, so that if goodness and happiness are only what people think they are, there is no point in looking, by reason or any other way, for any truth about them that applies universally to all human beings. In particular, there is no point in studying human nature as such, to find out how we ought to live. But if the harmony that is goodness and happiness is like the harmony that the musician discovers in the nature of the notes themselves that are required to compose a symphony, or the carpenter finds or makes between the shapes of the pieces of wood required to make a house, human goodness and happiness may not be a matter of subjective opinion at all but of solid fact.[8]

2. Motive

Second, if virtue or goodness is closely related to happiness, we have a motive for pursuing it that we won't have so long as we think goodness and happiness are quite different and unrelated things. But once we believe they are intimately connected, we will have the strongest possible motive for virtue, namely, our deep and persistent desire for happiness.

3. Experience

Third, a great amount of our experience supports Plato's claim that virtue brings happiness, both on the individual and the social level. If we do not moderate our appetites by what we know from past experience of over (or under) indulgence of them, we will be both intemperate and unhappy. Likewise, in the state, if the rulers legislate unjustly, or their assistants fail for lack of courage to enforce just laws, a disorderly and unhappy society will follow. Much of our experience, then, reinforces the link that Plato wants to forge between goodness (virtue) and happiness. A good society has to be a happy one; a happy one has to be morally good. Isn't that something everyone who thinks about it really knows?

4. Unity of the Virtues

Another appealing feature of Plato's account is its suggestion that the virtues are one. What look like disparate ways of being good — justice, cour-

---

8. The relativist alternative is as ancient as Protagoras, who taught that "man is the measure of all things," and as modern as the typical contemporary university student of whom Allan Bloom reminds us in a widely quoted passage in *The Closing of the American Mind*. Plato argues against it in the *Protagoras* and the *Theaetetus*.

age, and temperance — are ultimately united in the knowledge or wisdom that each requires. Thus wisdom, the intellectual virtue of reason, is especially important, since it is essential to all the moral virtues.

5. A Comprehensive View

Finally, Plato's account of knowledge, goodness, and happiness is appealing in the comprehensive way in which Plato discusses them. In pointing out their integrated relationship to all aspects of human life, Plato's thought is an antidote to a culture like ours in which human life has become exceptionally fragmented. Indeed, these three things no longer seem closely connected at all. Happiness is taken by many to be winning a million dollars in a state lottery, which has no apparent connection with the winner's knowledge or goodness (or the state's). Knowledge is produced in superabundance by the modern university, the heir of Plato's Academy, but who is the wiser for it, or more virtuous? To study the *Republic*, however, is to catch a vision of the integration of all knowledge, both moral and scientific, and of all arts, useful, liberal, and fine, within a comprehensive view of the universe as a whole.

We are ready now to turn to this last topic, as we look at the third level of what it means, for Plato, to know ourselves as the human beings we are.

The Third Level

Plato's account of human nature on this level is perhaps the most important aspect of the three. For one thing, he here develops his answer to the very important question, What is the source of our moral ignorance? According to Plato, we cannot discover the source of our ignorance until we discover more than our nature as individuals and our connectedness to one another in society. We must also come to know that we are connected to something beyond both ourselves and other people. To be ignorant of our place in the universe is the sorriest ignorance of all. It is to be ignorant of our origin and destiny.

The Soul and Its Immortality

The most immediate and conspicuous evidence of such a connection is our existence in bodily form. That we exist in bodies is palpable fact. But Plato's first question is whether material existence is the only kind of existence there is. His answer is, it isn't. The very immaterial nature of our reason and its ideas, he thinks, is a clue to the existence of an immaterial world of goodness and perfection, to which our souls are akin. Moreover, in the soul, it is our reason alone that finally constitutes its essence, not our heart or our appetites; for these are rooted in our bodies and as such, as we have seen, are properly subject to reason during our bodily existence. Our bodies, of course, are changing, transient things. They did not always exist, nor will they exist after we die.

But not so our souls. They are immortal. For Plato, immortality means not only that our souls survive death but also that they existed prior to our birth. We are therefore, in our true nature, akin to the gods, who are likewise immortal. Ignorance of this radical difference between our bodies and our souls will be a fundamental ignorance, because we will not even be able to discover the cause of our ignorance nor, then, its remedy. And if we cannot find the cause of our ignorance, neither will we find the cause of our wrongdoing and unhappiness, nor their remedy. The cause of ignorance in the soul, according to Plato, is precisely that it is now attached to bodily existence. Just as the emotions of the heart and the carnal desires of the appetites can overwhelm reason, so that it fails to find knowledge and wisdom, so the senses of the body are likely to lead reason away from its true world, to focus on the material world instead. We are then very likely to think that our happiness consists in satisfying the needs of the body alone, not the needs of the soul. We may even be led to think that this life in the body is the only life there is and that the material world is the only reality we need to confront. If so, we will make the biggest mistake we can ever make, which is to miss not only our true nature as immortal souls but also the nature of true goodness and happiness.

Human Destiny

For such happiness consists, finally, not in the harmony among the parts of an individual as a body-soul and the harmony of individuals in society;

such harmony is only earthly happiness. Ultimate happiness, for Plato, consists rather in a deliverance of the soul from this bodily existence and from the cycle of reincarnation of which present bodily existence is a single phase.[9] For to live in a body is just what prevents the soul's attaining perfect harmony with itself, other souls, and that part of the universe itself from which it came and to which it is destined to return. That part of the universe is the perfect, eternal, invisible reality which Plato calls the realm of the Forms, and sometimes the realm of the gods. The highest Form is the Form of the Good itself, the source of the harmony among all the Forms and among all the souls that exist in the universe.

On this highest level of self-knowledge, to know ourselves is, then, to know the kinship between our souls and this highest Good, or, as Plato also puts it, the kinship between our souls and the gods. Ignorance of this kinship, this likeness, is ignorance of both ourselves and the ultimate Good; but to know ourselves and the Good is, in Calvin's language quoted earlier, to be transformed by that Good. For the Good is the source of all goodness, including the moral goodness that brings us happiness. To seek the goodness of the gods is to seek the happiness of the gods, the perfect happiness that we never find in our earthly existence. That happiness is the deepest desire of the soul.

VI. Difficulties in Plato's Thought

Plato's picture of human life and its aspiration for the perfection of an ideal world has its enduring appeal. It contains a number of difficulties, however; here are five:

9. The doctrine of reincarnation is contained in many of the myths Plato recounts. It is a mistake, I think, not to incorporate Plato's myths into his moral and metaphysical philosophy. It undermines the full religious and philosophical force and substance of his thought in the same way as modern theological attempts (Bultmann, Tillich) to demythologize the Bible undermine the Christian view of morality and human destiny. Plato himself suggests that the issue is not how to get rid of myth, but how to decide which myth to follow: "It is not a tale of Alcinous [in Homer's *Odyssey*] that I shall tell you, but that of a brave man, Er the son of Armenias . . ." (*Republic* 614b).

Needless to say, the significance of myth in religion has been poisoned by the term's having become synonymous with *fictitious or false*. A definition that leaves open the question of which myth is preferable to another is simply: "any narrative story of supernatural beings, places, and events."

1. The Problem of Matter

First, the existence of matter creates an unaccountable crack in the harmony of Plato's universe. If Goodness produces the harmony of the Forms and of the souls that return to this invisible realm of their origin, whence arises material existence? It is matter that is the source of evil, discord, and disharmony in the universe. Matter is evil in that it requires all individual objects made of it to come into and go out of existence, so that the value these objects possess while they exist does not endure in them nor save them from perishing.

In particular, some of these objects, the bodies of human beings, become the prisons (Plato's own metaphor) that confine their souls, forcing them to forget the knowledge of the Good they originally enjoyed when they were still in the realm of the gods. Why should rational souls find themselves enmeshed in such bodily existence? If matter in itself is irrational and evil, and thus at odds with Reason and Goodness which are ultimate, why does it exist at all? Plato has no answer to this question.[10]

2. The Difficulty of Salvation

In every description Plato gives of philosophy, it is immensely difficult. As the way of salvation from the cycle of reincarnation, it can be followed seriously only by very few human beings — those who are born into fortunate circumstances and whose rational powers are strong enough to overcome the wiles of bodily temptations. Socrates escaped reincarnation, so Plato may have thought; but it is clear from Plato's eschatological myths that he believes most human beings, including the great heroes of the Greek past, face many more cycles of death and reincarnation before they eventually return to the realm of the gods. Plato's religion — for that is clearly what he takes philosophy to be — is a religion of the elite.[11]

10. "Plato . . . does not hold to the Orphic-Pythagorean doctrine of a 'fall' of the soul, and never explains clearly why it has to be embodied" (A. H. Armstrong, *An Introduction to Ancient Philosophy* [Totowa, N.J.: Rowman and Allanheld, 1983], p. 40).

11. There is perhaps no better evidence that philosophy is religion, for Plato, than one of his definitions of it as "preparation for death" (*Phaedo* 64a). Later in the dialogue he refers to "those who have purified themselves sufficiently by philosophy" (114c). Rites of purification have been associated with religion from time immemorial.

3. The Problem of Guilt

Plato takes no account of guilt, except in the minimal sense of identifying the wrongdoer. Scan every index to Plato's writings and to the commentaries on them for an entry on guilt; you will come up empty-handed. But this should come as no surprise; for, given Plato's view that wrongdoing is owing to ignorance, he has to deny the reality of guilt, in its maximal sense of one's internalizing an objective disapproval of oneself for the wrong one has done.

Plato's denial of guilt in this sense has exactly the consequences we might expect. Here are four:

First is Plato's denial of moral weakness. By moral weakness is meant the performance of an action in spite of one's knowledge that it is wrong. But moral weakness had been recognized, along with the guilt that attends it, by the Greek poets from Homer to Euripides.[12] They recognized it because, of course, it is a conspicuous feature of human moral experience. Plato explains moral weakness as the overcoming of reason by emotion or desire. This may sound like an explanation for a fact that Plato recognizes; actually, however, it explains the fact away. Like Socrates, his mentor, Plato finds it inconceivable that we should *know* what is good and therefore conducive to our happiness, *yet do* what is bad. As he states clearly in the *Protagoras:* "Knowledge is a noble thing and fit to command in man, which cannot be overcome and will not allow a man, if he only knows the good and the evil, to do anything which is contrary to what his knowledge bids him do."[13]

---

12. Achilles knowingly does evil when he refuses to return to the Achaeans; he says to Ajax: "All that you have said seems spoken after my own mind./Yet still the heart in me swells up in anger . . ." (*Iliad* 9.645f). Medea, planning to slay her sons to avenge herself against Jason, says: "I know indeed what evil I intend to do,/But stronger than all my afterthoughts is my fury,/Fury that brings upon mortals the greatest evils" (*Medea* 1078-1080).

13. *Protagoras* 352c. Says Grube: "Plato maintained [the Socratic] paradox throughout; it is asserted in almost every one of his works" (*Plato's Thought* [Indianapolis: Hackett, 1980], p. 216).

Jon Moline argues that Plato's denial of moral weakness is paradoxical only if we translate *episteme* with the English *knowledge*, a term which has no necessary motivational connotations. By contrast, the "Platonic *episteme* was plainly a state which was conceived of as if it had both articulate intellectual characteristics and powerful motivational ones" (*Plato's Theory of Understanding* [Madison, Wis., University of Wisconsin Press, 1981], pp. 27-28).

Moreover, says Moline, "we discover not just that pre-Socratic writers [likewise]

Another consequence of Plato's denial of guilt is the excessive confidence he has in education to achieve human goodness; it is, he says, "the one great thing" (*Republic* 423e). No wonder, then, that Plato devotes two of the ten books of his *Republic* to this topic; for if wrong doing is due to ignorance, education — the right education, a search for knowledge and wisdom — must be the only possible answer to our moral ills.

A third consequence of Plato's denial of guilt is his reformative theory of punishment. No wonder here, either; for as Socrates argues so pointedly in the *Apology*, if he corrupts the youth, it has to be quite unintentional; and if it is unintentional, he should not be brought to court for public condemnation but taken aside privately to be instructed and exhorted; whereupon, if he learns better, he will certainly cease to do what he has been doing.[14]

The fourth consequence — or is it a premise? — of Plato's denial of human guilt is his rejection of the possibility of divine expiation for it. There is no pardon or forgiveness, divine or human.[15] Our salvation from wrongdoing lies exclusively in the efforts that we put forth to discover what is good; upon this discovery, we will follow the good naturally.

This is not the place to discuss further these four consequences of

---

thought *episteme* a potent state motivationally but that some thought it motivated one to do the *right* thing" (p. 20). Thus Moline recommends translating *episteme* as *understanding,* which, if one has it, one is expected to *do* the appropriate thing in the circumstances one is in. This is because *understanding* implies not only the knowledge required to act in the circumstances but also the right feelings and motives that make the knowledge properly effective (pp. 29-30).

That the Greeks really did affirm the virtuous implications of knowledge in some sense is clear from Aristotle, the most analytic inquirer into the issue. Though some regard Aristotle as affirming the possibility of moral weakness against Socrates (and therefore also Plato), Moline shows that even Aristotle makes distinctions that reveal his basic agreement with them (pp. 26-27).

I will argue in the next lecture that Calvin accounts for both possibilities: the sufficiency *and* the insufficiency of knowledge for virtue, the difference being accounted for less by the nature of knowledge than by the condition of the will, which Calvin adds to the Greek account of the powers of the soul.

14. For a detailed argument against a retributive interpretation of Plato's theory of punishment, see M. M. Mackenzie, *Plato on Punishment* (Berkeley: University of California Press, 1991).

15. *Laws* 905-908. Mark Moes pointed out to me that there is perhaps a hint of human forgiveness, at least, in *Phaedo* 114b, where some of the "curable" wrongdoers are relieved of their suffering upon a successful petition to their victims "to receive them."

Plato's denial of guilt; it is enough to say that they are far-reaching indeed, and that they are all in direct conflict with the teachings of Christianity.

4. Justice as Obligation

Closely related to Plato's denial of guilt is Plato's failure to take due account of that feature of justice in which it presents itself to us, not as an ideal to be pursued, but as an obligation unfulfilled and unfulfillable. Plato is familiar enough with the language of obligation and duty, of course; he frequently speaks (quoting Simonides, for example) of justice as giving everyone their due (*Republic* 332a). So what is the problem? The problem is a deep complexity in the concept of justice — and in every moral concept. Justice indeed signifies an ideal good, which may attract and inspire us, especially when we consider the happiness it implies; this sense governs Plato's discussion of justice. But this sense of justice has an implication, the full impact of which Plato overlooks, which is to reprove us for our failure to live up to the ideal. Of course, if this moral failure is due to our ignorance, as Plato teaches, we cannot be held guilty for it or need expiation. We need only to discover what justice is and mend our ways.

Duty and Interest

A related issue that Plato ignores is the common experience of a conflict between duty and interest. As social beings, we are often duty-bound to do things for others that conflict with seeking our own interests. In these situations, the good of others, their happiness, overrides our own. Sometimes the pursuit of justice does not appear to be a harmony between our own interests and those of other people; it appears instead to involve a conflict between them. Thrasymachus vividly lays out this conflict in Book I of the *Republic*. Glaucon and Adeimantus refurbish the conflict at the beginning of Book II and request Socrates to show, what he has earlier claimed, that, contrary to our experience, it always pays to be just.

That justice always pays is the thesis Plato has Socrates pursue in the remaining eight and one-half books of the *Republic*. But the fact that our duties sometimes conflict with our legitimate interests suggests that the source of our moral ills, individual and social, is something deeper than ignorance. Plato does not ask what this might be; instead, he goes on to argue at length that it isn't real.

5. Motive

The last difficulty stems from one of the advantages of Plato's ethics. Since happiness is our deepest desire, it offers the strongest motive for pursuing moral goodness. But this motive opens the door to our seeking goodness not for its own sake, but because it conduces to, or is an essential ingredient in, our happiness. That seems to corrupt our motive for morality. For if we seek virtue because it makes us happy and avoid vice because it makes us unhappy, then our happiness, not our virtue, becomes our highest value, our ultimate goal. But this strategy anchors our motive for moral goodness in a self-interest that flies in the face of what we expect such goodness to be.

Yet that is precisely Plato's strategy in his *Republic*, namely, to convince us that it pays to be good, and hurts to be bad. Having defined justice as the very harmony that also defines happiness, Socrates says to Glaucon: "So now it only remains to consider which is the more profitable course: to do right and live honorably and be just . . . or to do wrong and be unjust. . . ." Glaucon's reply says it all: "But really, Socrates, it seems to me ridiculous to ask that question now that the nature of justice and injustice has been brought to light" (445a).

VII. Conclusion

In summary, Plato's ethics is an ethics built around our deepest desire, which is for happiness. We fail to find happiness because of our ignorance — of ourselves, our social nature, and the nature of the universe to which we are linked. In particular, we are ignorant of the Good, of the goodness of moral virtue, and of the intimate connection (perhaps even their identity) between moral virtue and happiness. We do not know the potential harmony that exists within ourselves, between us as individuals and other individuals, and ultimately between us and the universe itself. What we most need, then, for goodness and happiness is knowledge; all evil-doing is due to ignorance. Indeed, every human being begins life on earth in ignorance. The soul once possessed the knowledge it requires, but has now "forgotten" this knowledge because of its plunge into bodily existence. If, however, we seek and begin again to discover ourselves and the Good to which our souls are akin, we cannot help but pursue it, for it brings us happiness, our deepest desire.

In contrast to Plato's ethics of happiness, Calvin's ethics is centered on goodness as defined by the moral law. As a moral law ethics, it begins not with our deepest desire (the love of eros) for happiness but with our obligations to God and our fellow human beings. It requires not only certain actions of us but also certain virtues, chiefly the virtue of *agape* love. Likewise it forbids not only certain actions of us but also certain vices, chiefly the vice of pride or self-conceit, which lead to an indifference to others and even hatred. Moreover, for Calvin, the moral law is something everyone knows, so that we do not begin the moral life in ignorance, in any way comparable to Plato's claim.

In these respects and in others, the two approaches to ethics seem deeply opposed. One is egoistic, focussed on our own good; the other is altruistic, focussed on the good of others. One absorbs the ideal of justice into the ideal of harmony and happiness; the other seems to ignore our happiness by focussing on what we ought to do and to be. One appeals to a world of perfect harmony beyond the one in which we live, a world of perfect harmony between the true, the good, and the beautiful, a world attainable by reason alone — the reason of a fortunate few. The other teaches that this world is not essentially evil but good, being a creation of God himself. This God reveals himself to us as our sovereign Lord, he writes the moral law in our hearts, and he holds us responsible to keep it even though we are, in ourselves, tragic moral failures.

In the light of these contrasts, is it possible that Calvin's appeal to Plato for the unity of knowledge, virtue, and happiness, which I cited at the beginning, is simply a passing fancy? Does Plato's glimpse of this unity suggest only a misguided, rationalistic pagan mind, with which Calvin's biblical ethics is altogether in conflict and should, therefore, have nothing to do? Or is there a credible Reformed version of the unity of knowledge, goodness, and happiness, one that can both take into account the appealing features of Plato's approach and resolve its difficulties? Those are the questions I will take up in Lecture Two.

SECOND LECTURE

Happiness for the Sake of Goodness: Calvin's Solution

I. Two Kinds of Ethics

Last time we saw that there are two kinds of ethics, an ethics of happiness and an ethics of moral law. Following Plato, we saw that his ethics of happiness works back from our desire for happiness as a goal to what moral goodness is as a means for reaching that goal. After noting some appealing aspects of Plato's approach and some difficulties in it, we concluded with a brief sketch of a quite different approach: Calvin's ethics of the moral law. You may find the move from Plato's happiness ethics to Calvin's moral law ethics a rude awakening. The move is nicely captured in a little poem printed on a yellow satin pillow that graced our living room couch in my boyhood home. Flanked by a picture of a child peacefully asleep at the top and another of the same child awake and busily sweeping the house at the bottom, the poem read:

> I slept and dreamt that life is beauty;
> I woke and found that life is duty.[1]

Going from Plato to Calvin is something like that, for it is going from an ideal goal of happiness as a harmony of all good things to the stern call of duty.

For, at first sight, Calvin's ethics of the moral law is just that; it is not

1. Ellen Sturgis Hooper, 1816-1841.

320

about the happiness we desire but the duties God imposes on us. If this sounds like the ethics of the Bible, so, of course, it is. Calvin's ethics is inspired by the Bible, its rediscovery in the Reformation, and its theological interpretation during the 1000-some years preceding him.

II. The Problems of a Moral Law Ethics

1. The Happiness Problem

An ethics of the moral law confronts us, at first sight, with what I have called the stern call of duty. By that phrase I refer to at least two closely related features that characterize Calvin's moral law ethics: first, that it subordinates our happiness to the happiness of others and second, that it intensifies any unhappiness we already experience with the conviction of guilt.

First, the moral law seems to ignore the question of our own happiness by focussing our attention on the happiness of others. For that is what its duties and obligations concern: the welfare and, therefore, the happiness of others. We ought to honor our father and mother and all in authority over us, preserve and promote the lives and property of others, tell the truth and keep our promises; and maintain the integrity of marriage. We may not dishonor those in authority, kill anyone, steal, commit adultery, lie, or covet our neighbor's possessions. The moral law also prescribes our obligations to God and forbids the things we may not do to him. We must have him alone as God; worship him without images; hallow his name; and keep the sabbath day holy.

Further, we are to fulfill these duties not for what we can get out of it, even if doing so is sometimes to our advantage, but out of love for others and for God himself. In other words, we must do our duty for duty's sake, which really means for the sake of others, not ourselves.[2] Even our restraint from wrongdoing is to be motivated not by "ambition or self-love" (which is nicely concealed in the slogan, "honesty is the best policy") but for the end of serving our neighbors and God himself (III.xiv.3).

In other words, the moral law requires of us not only that we do cer-

---

2. For Calvin's exposition of the Ten Commandments, see the *Institutes* II.iii. The abstract Kantian locution, "duty for duty's sake," is not to be found in Calvin, as far as I know; his focus is always upon duty for the sake of God and neighbor.

tain actions, forbidding their opposites, but also that we be certain kinds of persons, viz., persons inwardly disposed towards doing the actions the law requires and avoiding those it forbids. Says Calvin: "First, let us agree that through the law man's life is molded not only to outward honesty but to inward and spiritual righteousness" (II.viii.6). This "inward righteousness" is the Christian virtue of love, the sum of moral goodness. We are not only to keep our promises but to do so out of love for those to whom we make them. We are not only to worship God but to do so out of love for him. Right acts without loving agents are bare.

The moral law thus insists on our goodness without obviously providing for our happiness. Often its duties go against the grain of our desires, even when those desires express the legitimate needs of our nature. Indeed, the Ten Commandments do not appeal in any immediate way to our desire for happiness nor are we typically given to think of performing its duties as satisfying our deepest desire.

Guilt

The moral law seems not only to ignore our happiness by focussing our attention on the happiness of others, but also to place us under judgment; and this judgment adds to any unhappiness we already experience in life. Indeed, says Calvin, rightly understood, such judgment is the very "first use" or function of the moral law: "Of itself the law can only accuse, condemn, and destroy" (II.vii.7). It accuses us by laying down duties we have not fulfilled and cannot fulfil. As a result, to think of the law is to think of our moral failure; and to think of moral failure is to experience guilt.[3]

How different from Plato, who says that once we discover what justice is, we will follow it as an ideal, because it is the way to happiness. Calvin thinks, however, that we do not begin the moral life in ignorance of justice; for we know the moral law, and its duties are obligations of justice itself.

---

3. Here Calvin picks up the biblical teaching, stated succinctly by St. Paul: "Through the law is the knowledge of sin" (Rom. 3:20). Calvin's comments on these words are illuminating:

> It is therefore a memorable truth of the first importance that no one can obtain righteousness by keeping the law. Paul has given his reason for this, and he will presently repeat it — all men without exception are guilty of transgression and condemned of unrighteousness by the law. *(Com. in loco)*

But it defines justice, then, not in terms of our own happiness but in terms of the happiness of others. Its justice is an ideal, but not one that inspires us so much as condemns us because we fail to measure up. So Plato and Calvin differ in how they view justice: Plato assimilates it to happiness, in order to make it an object of desire; Calvin regards it as a set of duties, which are not obviously an object of our desires.

The Powers of the Soul

This contrast between justice as an attractive ideal and as an unfullfilled obligation must be related to a contrast between how the two thinkers understand the soul. Like Plato, Calvin affirms our reason as "the leader and governor of the soul" (I.xv.7; II.ii.22).[4] Calvin also agrees that reason sometimes fails to exercise this leadership. He differs, however, on the explanation for this. Whereas Plato attributes reason's failure to an ignorance brought on by its association with the body (because of which it is subject to being misled by the bodily senses, emotions, and appetites), Calvin attributes the failure of reason to its being subject to a corrupted will (which sometimes leads us to disobey the moral law in spite of knowing the justice of its demands). So Calvin adds the power of will to Plato's three powers of the soul (I.xv.6, 8).[5] Instead of causing deception and ignorance (although it can do this, as we will see in a moment), as do the senses, emotions, and

4. It should be noted that Calvin also affirms the deep aspiration for happiness that Plato identifies as *eros:* Speaking of happiness, he says: "Thus, also, the chief activity of the soul is to aspire thither." He goes on to link this aspiration especially with reason: "The more anyone endeavors to approach God, the more he proves himself endowed with reason" (I.xv.6).

5. The addition of will to the powers of the soul is not original with Calvin, of course; it stems from the biblical view of human beings. In that view human beings are created in the image of God, who, according to the Bible, is a being of will. Indeed, it can be easily argued that the central theme of the Bible is precisely the will of God. In one of its senses, the will of God signifies the way in which he requires us to live, which is expressed in the moral law. (Two other senses: the free decision by which God wills to create the world and the plan he has for its destiny.)

For an illuminating account of the development of a theory of will in the moral law tradition, see Albrecht Dihle, *The Theory of Will in Classical Antiquity* (Berkeley: University of California Press, 1982), ch. 4. Dihle argues that there is an important correlation between a theistic moral law ethics and the role of will in the theory of human action. The

appetites for Plato, the will gives us freedom to act against our better knowledge. Thus Calvin's theory of our human powers can explain not only actions done from moral weakness and even moral perversity, but also the guilt that results from each. That is its great advantage over Plato's account. For, although it paints a darker picture of our moral powers, it accords better with human experience than Plato's more optimistic view.

Interestingly, Calvin also accounts for the denial of guilt. Because moral guilt is so painful, one of our tendencies is to become so "indulgent" towards ourselves (as he puts it) that we avert our attention from our responsibility and guilt. Calvin even suggests that such self-deception (for that is what it is) underlies Plato's attempt to account for evil-doing by ignorance (II.ii.22).

2. The Motive Problem

We noted earlier that the moral law seems to ignore our happiness by focussing our attention on the happiness of others. That is, of course, not quite correct. Upon more careful analysis, the moral law can be seen to involve happiness after all. It does this differently from Plato's account, however. Whereas Plato defines justice as happiness, according to Calvin

---

moral law takes the form of a set of commands. But God can command a being what to do only if such a being is capable of acting freely. Therefore, if God wanted a creature to whom he could issue commands, he had to give him a free will analogous to his own. For God can command a being what to do only if such a being is capable of acting freely in the world God made, even as God acted freely in his own environment of nothing outside himself when he created such a world. To command a person to do the only thing he can do would be pointless. A moral law ethics presupposes, then, that we are not only creatures of reason, with the capacity to know and understand what the moral law requires, but also of will, with the capacity of deliberately doing the opposite.

There are actually two kinds of biblical commands. Besides the moral law, there is the "cultural mandate" of Genesis 1:28. This mandate addresses us as beings capable of productivity *(techne* or *poesis),* by which we freely make things that help us subdue the earth for our own welfare (Gen. 1:28-29). This mandate compares with Plato's analysis of the economic nature of human beings. The moral law addresses us as social beings, governing our moral relationships to one another and to him, which compares with Plato's justice. (Plato divides justice into the same two parts as the "two tables" of the moral law: piety to the gods and harmony with our fellow human beings [*Euthyphro* 12e].)

In Calvin, this social dimension of human nature is more richly conceived, since it reflects our being created in the image of one God, who is nevertheless a community of three persons that have different functions organized into the harmony of one being.

(II.vii.4), the moral law contains a promise of happiness for fulfilling its requirements (and also, a promise of punishment, for failure).

This promise is actually implied by the very same justice that underwrites the duties of the moral law. Here we can distinguish the justice of performing its duties from the justice by which we deserve happiness for performing those duties — the justice of a due reward for goodness. Doing our duty sometimes coincides with happiness, as we noted earlier. Our moral intuition tells us that this is the way it *should* be. But precisely that intuition invites the motive problem. For according to this second sense of justice as due reward, promised by God himself, doing our duty *ought* to be followed by happiness even in those cases where it isn't. An intuition of this moral connection between justice and happiness may be what leads Plato to his thesis that virtue is its own reward, vice its own punishment, and thus to his defining virtue in terms of the very harmony that is happiness. If so, his strategy reveals his conviction that the universe is ultimately a moral universe.[6]

In the biblical picture, the morality of the universe is underwritten not by a definition but by a fact: the existence of God, who not only gives us the moral law but rewards those who keep it and punishes those who do not. "The Lord loves the righteous" but "the way of the wicked he brings to ruin" (Psalm 146:8, 9). The Ten Commandments themselves include two references to such sanctions: one command (honor your father and mother) promises a reward; another (do not take God's name in vain) threatens a punishment.

But this feature of Calvin's moral law ethics clearly threatens to corrupt the very motive it requires, viz., doing our duty for duty's sake, i.e., for our neighbor's sake. For it invites us to do our duty for the sake of the reward God promises for keeping it and in order to avoid the punishment he threatens for failure. Worse, it may even tempt us to think we are able to fulfil the moral law, thus joining Plato in his optimism, when, of course, the truth is that we cannot.

Thus Calvin's moral law ethics seems to threaten the purity of our motivation for virtue no less than Plato's happiness ethics. How, then, can the thought of our own happiness and self-interest not contaminate our motive for goodness? Will not our natural self-love, corrupted by an inordinate preference for self, corrupt our motive for serving others and even

---

6. The belief in a moral universe manifests itself in all times and places. Calvin Van Reken offers a lively discussion of it as involving the concept of reciprocity in "Wisdom and the Moral Life," *Perspectives*, December 1992, pp. 22-25.

God himself, both when duty and advantage coincide and even when they don't? Does Job serve God for nothing? Satan asks, observing Job's prosperity. Does Job also serve God for nothing in his adversity? The wonder is that Job does not ask this question about himself.

III. Calvin on Happiness

I turn now to Calvin's answer to these problems, which seem inherent in his moral law ethics — the happiness problem and the motive problem. Not that Calvin faces the two problems in just the way I have formulated them, but that there are answers to them in other parts of his thought which we have so far ignored. Actually, as we have so far considered it, an ethics of the moral law is flawed, no less than Plato's ethics of happiness. As I hope to show, Calvin relates goodness to happiness in a way that avoids the two problems I have identified.

The Primacy of Knowledge

He does this by beginning, as Plato does, with the role that knowledge plays in the moral life; and by following this point, we shall finally discover Calvin's version of the Platonic teaching that knowledge really is the key to both goodness and happiness and their proper relationship.

I was surprised to find that Calvin addresses both problems already in the two opening chapters of his *Institutes*. Indeed, it has not been duly noticed that Calvin begins his *Institutes* by focusing upon the intimate relationship between knowledge, virtue, and happiness — the Platonic theme of these lectures.[7] I shall restrict my focus here to these chapters, taking

7. Perhaps this oversight has occurred because other important themes are also conspicuous in these opening chapters, such as the two-fold knowledge of God; creation, fall and redemption; and God as Father, Son, and Holy Spirit.

The importance of the opening chapters of the *Institutes* as an introduction to the entire work has often been noted. For example, in his recent, widely acclaimed study of Calvin, John Bouwsma says: "The first nine chapters of Book I constitute a kind of epistemological introduction to the work as a whole, as they consider the possibility and the processes of the knowledge of God before proceeding to its con-time only in passing to indicate how Calvin elaborates upon this theme at a few important points later in the *Institutes*.

Calvin begins his book with the idea of knowledge itself. In its first sentence he analyzes the intellectual virtue of human wisdom: "True and sound wisdom consists of two parts: the knowledge of God and of ourselves." And the first thing Calvin says about these two knowledges is that, "while joined by many bonds, which one precedes and brings forth the other is not easy to discern" (I.i.1). His own opinion is that both are true: each knowledge leads to the other, so that we can't have one without having the other. This twofold claim provides the first two arguments of the *Institutes*.[8]

The Necessity of Self-Knowledge

Calvin's first argument in the *Institutes* is that we must begin the moral life with the knowledge of ourselves. The parallel with Socrates and Plato is obvious and Calvin acknowledges it later, at the beginning of Book II. There

---

tent" (*John Calvin: A Sixteenth Century Portrait* [New York: Oxford University Press, 1988], p. 153).

Calvin even entitles the first two books, "The Knowledge of God the Creator" and "The Knowledge of God the Redeemer." He thus joins the throng of early modern philosophers, whose preoccupation with the problem of knowledge is evident from the titles of the main works that have made them famous.

But just as the philosophers' investigation of knowledge has inevitable implications for ethics and metaphysics, so does Calvin's. As I show below, Calvin does far more at the beginning of his *Institutes* than Bouwsma claims, and in far less space — namely, in the first two chapters alone. He there provides not only an epistemological but also an ethical and metaphysical introduction to his entire work.

It is important to point out that Calvin thinks of "philosophy" in the classical sense as a "way of life." He even regards his entire project, which we tend to identify as "theology," as "the Christian philosophy" ("Subject Matter of the Present Work," p. 6, Battles edition; see n. 8 there for an important review of the meaning of "philosophy" in ancient and medieval thinkers).

8. And sets the stage for a paradox. For if we can't have one of two things without the other, it means that one depends on the other. If this mutual dependence is merely logical, there is no difficulty in understanding it; for example, no one can become a husband without making someone else a wife, and vice versa. But if this mutual dependence is causal (if each of two things "precedes and brings forth the other"), a difficulty arises. For how can two things precede and cause one another? But that is exactly what Calvin claims. I have no space here to show how the paradox can be resolved.

he refers to the Delphic oracle, "Know yourself," and exclaims that ignorance of ourselves is "detestable" when it concerns the questions that matter most (II.i.1).

What is it, then, about ourselves that is so important to know? Two
things: The "mighty gifts with which we are endowed" and "the world of
miseries" we experience in spite of these gifts. By "mighty gifts," Calvin almost certainly alludes to the natural powers of the soul that Plato discusses, and to which, as we have seen, he adds the will. Indeed, these gifts
constitute the image of God himself, who created us. Does Calvin also allude to the gift of divine salvation? Perhaps not, but he will shortly, as we
will see. By "the world of miseries" he refers to the miseries that we suffer
and to their cause, which lies in our moral "depravity and corruption"; this
corruption stems, of course, from the willful "rebellion" that led to our fall
from a state of original goodness (I.i.1.).

Knowing these two things about ourselves — our gifts and our miseries — is necessary for knowing God in two ways: first, like Plato, Calvin regards the good things of life as a necessary component of our happiness,
the bad things, of our unhappiness; and second, both good and bad things
motivate us to find God, since he is the source of all good things. First, the
good things: They lead us to God when we recognize that the "mighty gifts
. . . are hardly from ourselves." These gifts lead us to wonder not only about
their source, but even about the source of our very existence. Calvin's discussion parallels Plato's, who likewise teaches that reflection on ourselves
and the good things in this world leads us to seek the knowledge of their
transcendent source. Thus Calvin writes: "By these benefits shed like dew
from heaven upon us, we are led as by rivulets to the spring itself" (I.i.1).

But even bad things, which make us unhappy, lead us to God. Says Calvin: "The miserable ruin, into which the rebellion of the first man cast us, especially compels us to look upward." Why "especially"? Simply because the
good things of God must be the antidote to the bad things that make us unhappy, so that to seek to know the source of the good things that will relieve
our unhappiness is to seek the same source of the good things we already enjoy. So Calvin writes: "Each of us must, then, be so stung by the consciousness of his own unhappiness as to attain at least some knowledge of God."
And again, "To this extent we are prompted by our own ills to contemplate
the good things of God; and we cannot seriously aspire to him before we begin to become displeased with ourselves" (I.i.1). Thus both happiness and
unhappiness motivate us, but to the same end: to know God.

Indeed, of the two, our unhappiness proves a better guide than our happiness. We just heard Calvin say that our miserable ruin "especially compels us to look upward." Before that he writes, "Indeed, our poverty better discloses the infinitude of benefits reposing in God." Why does Calvin think so? Here is his answer: "Not only will we, in fasting and hungering, seek thence [from God] what we lack; but, in being aroused by fear, we shall learn humility" (I.i.1). His mention of "fear" alludes to the sense of guilt that results from our being the very cause, in our disobedience, of our miserable ruin; perhaps it also suggests our vague recognition that we cannot undo our ruin without God's help. Calvin's mention of humility here is significant, for it is his first mention of moral goodness in the *Institutes*. Humility is connected to the greater value of unhappiness over happiness as a motive in seeking God. For without the unhappiness of pondering our "miserable ruin" and the humility it occasions, we might celebrate our "mighty gifts" with a pride and self-confidence that tempt us to think we do not need divine help.

Thus Calvin plunges us, in his very opening paragraph of the *Institutes*, into thinking about knowledge, happiness, and moral goodness and their intimate relationship. Not only does Calvin not ignore happiness, he even affirms its motivational role, as part of the self-knowledge that leads us to the knowledge of God.

Thus he concludes his first argument:

> For what man in all the world would not gladly remain as he is — what man does not remain as he is — so long as he does not know himself, that is, while content with his own gifts, and either ignorant or unmindful of his own misery? Accordingly, the knowledge of ourselves not only arouses us to seek God, but also, as it were, leads us by the hand to find him. (I.i.1)

The Necessity of Knowing God

Calvin's second argument in his opening chapter is that, unless we begin with the knowledge of God, we will not come to know ourselves. The God Calvin focusses upon here, however, is not, as in the previous argument, the God who is the author of all good but the God who is the author of the moral law.

This is not surprising, perhaps, in view of what he has just said, viz., that knowing our unhappiness, a crucial aspect of which is our guilt, is a better guide to God than knowing our happiness. Indeed, he immediately returns to the point he has just made about pride and humility: "For we always seem to ourselves righteous and upright and wise and holy — this pride is innate in all of us — unless by clear proofs we stand convinced of our own unrighteousness, foulness, folly, and impurity" (I.i.2). And God is "the sole standard by which this judgment [of our moral worth] must be measured." Indeed, ignorance of the divine standard of moral perfection contained in the moral law will have the same result Calvin attached earlier to ignorance of ourselves, viz., complacency: "As long as we do not look beyond the earth, being quite content with our own righteousness, wisdom, and virtue, we flatter ourselves most sweetly, and fancy ourselves all but demigods" (I.i.2).[9]

At this point, we need to acknowledge what has often been noted by readers of Calvin, both sympathetic and otherwise, that Calvin is preoccupied in his thinking with the transcendent majesty of God and with the devastating effects that a clear and deep sense of this majesty has upon human beings. Calvin's preoccupation with divine majesty is evident throughout his writings generally; it appears here also, in the very opening chapter of the *Institutes*. Calvin continues:

> Suppose we but once begin to raise our thoughts to God, and to ponder his nature, and how completely perfect are his righteousness, wisdom, and power — the straightedge to which we must be shaped. Then, what masquerading earlier as righteousness was pleasing in us will soon grow filthy in its consummate wickedness. (I.i.2)

9. As an example of such over-confidence in human powers, Calvin refers, later on, to "certain philosophers, who, while urging man to know himself, propose the goal of recognizing his own worth and excellence" (II.i.1). When this happens, "man seems to know himself very well when, confident in his understanding and uprightness, he becomes bold and urges himself to the duties of virtue, and, declaring war on vices, endeavors to exert himself with all his ardor toward the excellent and the honorable" (II.i.3).

Was Calvin also thinking of Plato in this allusion to "certain philosophers"? It could be, for Plato certainly had confidence that by reason alone human beings can, if not sooner then later, attain virtue and happiness. (By "later" I refer to his myths of reincarnation, which suggest that eventually the vast majority of souls attain virtue and happiness.)

That is pretty strong language with which to describe the human moral condition, knowledge of which arises from a recognition of God's transcendent holiness; it translates, of course, into a tremendous sense of guilt. Still, Calvin suggests that such a knowledge can only intensify the strength of our motive to know God as the source of whatever good he offers, if any, that will rescue us from such great unhappiness. The question whether there is another side to God that provides just such relief, however, Calvin leaves not only unanswered in Chapter One, but unasked.

The Proper Knowledge of God

For the first hint of Calvin's answer, that there is another side to God, we need to proceed to Chapter Two, in which he directly begins the elaboration of the knowledge of God he promises at the close of Chapter One. The answer is a happy one: the other side to God is that he is a gracious Redeemer. But here Calvin introduces a qualification of utmost importance, which, following the language of his qualifying phrase, may be called the *proper* knowledge of God. This is how he defines it: "that by which we not only conceive that there is a God but also grasp what befits us and is proper to his glory, in fine, what is to our advantage to know him. Indeed, we shall not say that, properly speaking, God is known where there is no religion or piety" (I.ii.1). Notice that he defines such "proper knowledge of God" both in terms of "what is to our advantage" and "piety." Our "advantage" certainly suggests our happiness and "piety" is his second reference to moral goodness. So once again, Calvin, like Plato, connects the knowledge we need very closely with both happiness and goodness. To know God properly is both pious and advantageous; somehow, to know God makes us both good and happy.

What is the *improper knowledge* of God that Calvin's important distinction suggests? It can only be a knowledge of God accompanied not by virtue and happiness but by vice and unhappiness. Calvin describes it in the next two chapters. It is the natural knowledge of God (the famous *sensus divinitatis*) implanted in every human mind, which has been "either smothered or corrupted, partly by ignorance, partly by malice" (I.iv).[10]

---

10. This knowledge is also the "seed of religion in all men. But scarcely one man in a hundred is met with who fosters it, once received, in his heart, and none in whom it ripens" (I.iv.1). It manifests itself in many forms — "idle speculations" (I.ii.2), supersti-

Again, there is a parallel in Plato, for whom the knowledge of the Good is likewise innate in human minds; but the parallel breaks down on the issue of ignorance. For Plato, we can only recover our knowledge of the transcendent Good, which is "forgotten" at birth, by a life-long rational search for it. For Calvin, we do not begin the moral life in ignorance but with an awareness of God that we naturally develop as we grow up, which we also, however, tend to suppress because of the adverse judgment it makes on our lives. For Calvin, then, human beings differ from each other not by their knowledge or ignorance of God, but by whether their knowledge of God is accompanied by virtue or vice, happiness or unhappiness.

Although Calvin does not introduce this distinction between proper and improper knowledge of God until Chapter Two, it is clear that the knowledge of God Calvin has been discussing in Chapter One is the same thing as the "proper knowledge" of Chapter Two.[11] The close connection between knowledge, goodness, and happiness is exemplified only in those who possess the proper knowledge, for they are the only ones who possess the piety this knowledge requires.

Faith

I should point out, in passing, that the proper knowledge with which Calvin begins the *Institutes*, and which we have been discussing as the counterpart to Plato's highest knowledge of the Good, is none other than the knowledge of biblical faith itself. Although Calvin does not discuss this faith until Book III,[12] and when he does, he does not relate it explicitly to

---

tions (I.iv.3), even hypocrisy (I.iii.4), and just ignorance (I.iv.1). But every manifestation, even (paradoxically) a protestation of ignorance, is characterized by a deliberateness, a willfulness, that leaves it inexcusable (I.iv.1, 2). Such deliberateness, of course, only adds to the guilt we have already discussed.

11. This is proved as follows: In the opening sentence Calvin sets out to define "true and sound wisdom." Moreover, Calvin characterizes such wisdom, as we saw earlier, by virtue — the virtue of humility, which opposes the pride of those who fail to recognize God as the sole standard by which to measure their goodness. Finally, Calvin illustrates this wisdom with the saintly examples of Abraham, Job, Elijah, Isaiah, and the Psalmist (I.i.3).

12. With a few exceptions: When he argues that it is grounded in God himself speaking in Scripture, not in the authority of the church (I.v.14; vi.1, 2; vii.3); and when he argues that it has Christ as its object even for the Old Testament saints, of whom Abraham is "the best model" (II.vi.2-4; x.11).

his opening discussion of proper knowledge, they are easily shown to be one and the same thing. For they share important characteristics. Both involve trust (I.ii.2; III.ii.15, 36). Neither is possible by reason alone, that is, by reason in its fallen condition. Their most important shared feature for our purpose is that each one is virtuous knowledge. Faith as knowledge is the chief Christian intellectual virtue and it motivates love, the essence of Christian moral virtue. Similarly, proper knowledge is pious knowledge, and piety is the essence of religious virtue. The similarity of either one to Plato's intimate relationship between true knowledge and virtue is evident.

Union with God

We can also find a striking parallel between Calvin's and Plato's concept of happiness, when we look deeper into the *Institutes*. At its beginning, Calvin discusses happiness largely as the enjoyment of the good things that come from God. Later on, however, he defines it more precisely as our union with God himself (I.xv.6). Interestingly he offers this definition of happiness while he is discussing the soul and its faculties. The first point he makes is that to be ignorant of this meaning of happiness is "to be bereft of the principal use of [our] understanding." In language reminiscent of Plato, whom he has just praised as having an opinion on such matters that is "more correct" than the other philosophers, he says: "Thus also the chief activity of the soul is to aspire thither. Hence the more anyone endeavors to approach to God, the more he proves himself endowed with reason" (I.xv.6).[13]

Not only is Calvin's aspirational language here Platonic, so is the concept of happiness itself. For if happiness is union with God, it is a harmony between us and our transcendent source. For Plato, this harmony is intellectual and aspirational, consisting as it does in the knowledge of Goodness combined with *eros* as our deepest desire. For Calvin, on the other hand, though the harmony includes the exercise of reason and satisfies the deepest human desire, it is originally and primarily a harmony of the human will with the divine will.[14] For both Calvin and Plato, however, a

---

13. See note 4 above.

14. It is important to emphasize that Calvin's concept of union with God is a moral one, a unity between our will and God's will. It is not an ontological absorption of

proper knowledge entails the pursuit of moral virtue, which brings us into harmony with the ultimate moral principle of the universe; for Plato, this ultimate reality is only a principle, for Calvin it is also a person.

---

the human soul into the divine substance. Only rarely does Calvin speak of the union as a "mystical" one, and on one of these occasions, he is arguing against the view of Osiander that sharing God's holiness requires sharing God's substance (III.xi.10).

By contrast, Plato approaches a view that our souls, being themselves divine, eventually return to an identity with the divine reality that is their origin (*Phaedo* 79; *Philebus* 30; *Timaeus* 30, 34). Though Plato's language on this point is obscure, he clearly has no doctrine of divine creation *ex nihilo* to head off his suggestions that our souls eventually rejoin the divine substance from which they come.

But Calvin does. Hence he generally describes the union in terms that do not imply the union of our being and God's. Thus, there are moral terms, such as the harmony of our wills with God's will, social terms, such as our fellowship and communion with him, and there are metaphors. These metaphors are the biblical ones, drawn mostly from the organic unity of living things. Referring to Christ, the origin and basis of our reunion with God, he speaks of our "being engrafted into him," "being made members of his body," and entering into a "sacred wedlock through which we are made flesh of his flesh and bone of his bone." One metaphor is architectural: the Holy Spirit dedicates us as temples to God (III.i.1; vi.3).

But the language of living in harmony with God's will, i.e., his moral law, and enjoying his fellowship is more common. The whole purpose of redemption, says Calvin, "is to manifest in the life of believers a harmony and agreement between God's righteousness and their obedience" (III.vi.1). And again, "When we hear mention of our union with God, let us remember that holiness must be its bond; not because we come into communion with him by virtue of our holiness! Rather we ought first to cleave unto him so that, infused with his holiness, we may follow whither he calls" (III.vi.2). These quotations are found in the "Golden Booklet of the Christian Life" (III.vi-x), a section of the *Institutes* devoted to the Christian virtues, the good works that "follow from" faith, and to the proper motives for them.

It is important to emphasize the moral nature of our union with God also because it contrasts with the Incarnation of Christ (Book II.ix-xvii), which provides the basis for it. For the Incarnation is a metaphysical union of God with humanity, though of a very special kind, in which the divine and human natures are not confused with one another. Christ provides for our moral reunion with God by the moral character of his life and death, which constitutes an atonement for our sin. As Calvin conceives the atonement, it constitutes an expiation for sin.

The term *at-one-ment* also signifies harmony; and it is our will that Christ's expiation for sin makes one with God's will. On this point, of course, Calvin differs sharply from Plato, who rejects the possibility of divine expiation for sin. That is because, as we saw last time, Plato knows only the justice of God, not his love. Still, Plato could only applaud Calvin's belief that the fulfillment of divine justice is a necessary corollary to the expression of divine love and mercy.

IV. Happiness as the Motive for Goodness

The Solution to the Motive Problem

How, then, does Calvin bring knowledge, virtue, and happiness together in such a way that happiness remains a motive for pursuing virtue without corrupting that pursuit with the thought of reward? At long last, we are ready for Calvin's answer. It is simple and surprising, but ultimately paradoxical. The problem with Plato's definition of justice as happiness, it will be recalled, is that it invites the pursuit of justice for the sake of happiness as its goal; similarly, a moral law ethics invites the pursuit of duty for the sake of happiness as its just reward.

Simple

Calvin rescues the motive of happiness by proposing, simply, that happiness is a gift, not a goal. He announces this idea in the very opening paragraph of the *Institutes*, in a sentence quoted earlier: "For, quite clearly, the mighty gifts with which we are endowed are hardly from ourselves" (I.i.1). The key word here is *gifts*. Every good thing we enjoy in life is a gift from God. These gifts are of two kinds, natural and moral; gifts of creation and of redemption. The former include, as Calvin says, "our very being" itself (I.i.1), plus, of course the splendid powers we possess, especially reason and will, with which God created us in his own image. The latter, the moral and redemptive gifts, refer to "the grace of reconciliation offered to us in Christ" (I.ii.1). The heart of this reconciliation is the forgiveness of our sins, which are the central obstacle to our reunion with God.

Knowledge a Necessary Condition

But, of course, it is necessary for us to know that these good things are gifts of God before they can function as motives for virtue. As Calvin says, "For until men recognize that they owe everything to God, that they are nourished by his fatherly care, that he is the Author of their every good, that they should seek nothing beyond him — they will never yield him willing service" (I.ii.1).

Knowledge a Sufficient Condition

Once we do know God as the author of all good things, the happiness accompanying this knowledge will lead to virtue. As Calvin puts it: "This sense of the powers of God is for us a fit teacher of piety, from which religion is born. I call piety that reverence joined with love of God which the knowledge of his benefits induces" (I.ii.1). Notice his language. Piety, that is, "reverence joined with love of God," which is the highest virtue, is "induced" by "the knowledge of his benefits." In other words, such knowledge is sufficient to motivate virtue. Calvin repeats the point later on in a particularly eloquent passage about faith, the equivalent of the knowledge he is here discussing:

> But how can the mind be aroused [by faith] to taste the divine goodness without at the same time being wholly kindled to love God in return? For truly, that abundant sweetness which God has stored up for those who fear him cannot be known without at the same time powerfully moving us. And once anyone has been moved by it, it utterly ravishes him and draws him to itself. (III.ii.41)

Thus Calvin brings together all three things: knowledge, happiness, and goodness, in that significant order: knowledge that all good things are gifts of God; the happiness which these good things give us; and the goodness of piety itself. So Calvin does not ignore happiness, as we first may have thought, but actually places it ahead of moral goodness and virtue. He claims, indeed, that by this approach he "establishes" human happiness in God: "Unless they establish their complete happiness in him, they will never give themselves truly and sincerely to him" (I.ii.1).[15]

Thus happiness — more exactly, knowing that our happiness is "established" in God as his gift — becomes the motive for virtue. The proper knowledge of God, in short, becomes, by way of the happiness it brings, the motive for virtue. This has the all-important effect of placing happiness before the moral life of virtue instead of after it, as a goal. It is Calvin's simple solution to the motive problem.

15. The language of this quotation resembles the language that appears on the Calvin College and Seminary symbol: "My heart I offer you, Lord, eagerly and sincerely." (I have found no more complete passage in Calvin's writings from which the motto may have been derived.)

Gratitude

But one more piece is required to complete the picture of just how the thought of such happiness motivates virtue, without its becoming an ulterior, self-interested motive in the process. Calvin suggests this missing piece in the following passage from the very same paragraph: "Thus we may learn to await and seek all these things from him, and thankfully to ascribe them, once received, to him" (I.ii.1). That is, good things — the things that make us happy — motivate gratitude to God, but only after they are "once received." We cannot be grateful for what we want but do not yet have; but once we have it, and see it as a gift, we can.

So the little word *gift* and the larger one *gratitude* may be taken as two keys, linked together, in resolving the motive problem. If the good things we enjoy in life, which make us happy, are gifts of God, they are not rewards for any virtue we have nor do they need to include any virtue we may pursue. Even our union with God, his greatest gift and the essence of happiness, is not a reward for our goodness but a precondition for it.[16] Where there is gratitude for gifts already received and for happiness already enjoyed, all thoughts of our obeying God's law in order to get something good as a reward or to avoid being punished if we don't obey — all such thoughts are undercut. Although Calvin does not say it here, that is, for him, what it must mean to live by grace.[17]

16. More exactly, we should distinguish two senses of our union with God, which reflect Calvin's distinction between justification and sanctification. The former refers to that aspect of our union with God which God first secures for us by imputing Christ's goodness to us; the latter to that aspect of our union with God in which we are called actually to achieve in ourselves the life of virtue itself, to align our wills with God's will. Knowing the former is the motivating condition for the latter.

17. As the etymology of *grace* and *gratitude* shows, it is no accident that the concepts are tightly linked. *Gratia* (L.) means both *favor* and *thanks,* each of which suggests pleasure, a component of happiness. Compare *charis* (Gr.) for the same connection. The "Three Graces" of Greek mythology were the goddesses that conferred the favor of victory in the games; thus the idea of divine favor is present even in ancient Greek religion, though it seems to be associated more with success than with moral goodness.

Surprising

With our happiness secure as a gift from God, we no longer need to pursue it as a goal. The thought that we already possess it motivates us, by way of expressing our gratitude, to pursue the the happiness of others, which is just what the moral law requires. The surprising thing about gratitude is that it takes full account of our self-interest and desire for happiness but puts them both behind us; that is the motivational miracle wrought by putting happiness before virtue. We love God because he has given us happiness, especially the happiness of being reunited with him after being at odds with him; not because we expect his love as a reward for anything we try to do to impress him with our goodness. In other words, we are not good in order to be happy, but happy in order to be good. Happiness is for the sake of goodness, which reverses Plato's order of goodness for the sake of happiness.[18]

Paradoxical

It may be objected that gratitude is itself a virtue, and not quite the natural response to gifts received that it may first appear to be. That is, of course, correct. Indeed, Calvin regards "ungratefulness" as an important ingredient in the Fall itself (II.i.4). But then gratitude is in the same trouble as all the other virtues, itself hindered by the same moral corruption that threatens our pursuit of the others. Indeed, gratitude, too, is a duty, a veritable requirement of justice. So how can gratitude be part of the solution to the motivational problem?[19]

Calvin, moral realist and anti-perfectionist that he is, accepts this

18. In an early dialogue Plato entertains the possibility that virtue might be a gift of the gods beyond our understanding (*Meno* 99e; 100b). But the word translated *gift* (*moira*) means *what is meet or right or due* (Liddell and Scott) more than *gift*, so the parallel with Calvin's concept of divine grace is weak, if not altogether misleading. Plato's word, however, also connotes destiny, one's assigned lot in life; this sense suggests a better parallel in Calvin's doctrine of predestination, which he connects with salvation by grace. That happiness, too, was anciently regarded as something beyond our understanding (and perhaps control) is suggested by its derivation from M.E. *hap*, meaning *fortune, chance*.

19. I once argued that, from a certain point of view, the distinction between natural and moral motives breaks down ("Motives and Obligations," in *Faith and Philosophy*, ed. Alvin Plantinga [Grand Rapids: Eerdmans, 1964], pp. 161-78; esp. pp. 169-77).

ness and happiness? Calvin disagrees with Plato over what that knowledge is, what it is of, and how to get it. Plato says it is a knowledge of the Good, and that we can get such knowledge by a life devoted to reason and reasoning. Calvin says it is the pious knowledge of God, and in particular, of his love as he reveals it to us in Christ, and that we can get this knowledge as a gift from God himself, by believing the gospel that declares his love for us.

So there is the Reformed version of the Platonic unity of knowledge, goodness, and happiness. I have argued that it is implicit in Calvin's *Institutes,* and I have tried to make it explicit. Though, like Plato's version, it harbors a paradox — the paradox of gratitude — unlike Plato's version, it solves the problem of how happiness can motivate the moral life without corrupting that motivation.

That is the significant Genevan transformation of Athens. For the original unity of knowledge, goodness, and happiness, we must turn to Plato; for the Christian version, let Calvin be our guide.

*Conflict: Its Resolution
and the Completion of Creation*

JOHN FEIKENS

Contents

First Lecture

The Stob Lectures provide a prestigious platform for a discussion of important ideas. Coupled as these lectures are with a great person, whose name they bear, they connect us, because of his wide-ranging philosophical inquiries, teachings, and writings, in a continuing exploration and discussion of perspectives of substance.

I am pleased to be a part of this pursuit and I thank you for inviting me to this platform.

I came to the selection of the topic of these lectures — "Conflict: Its Resolution and the Completion of Creation" — because of my training in law. I am acquainted with the types of conflict with which lawyers and judges deal. I am familiar with confrontation and the legal procedures that are used to resolve conflicts. As a judge I have been an active participant in the adversarial system, the bedrock legal structure in our country, for conflict confrontation and resolution.

I do not intend to discuss legal conflict, such as civil and criminal disputes, which are handled in the law courts. While I will allude to the adversarial system used in law to resolve disputes, I will do so in the context of a broader perspective.

There are more immediate reasons for my choice of this topic. For example, I wonder how, in our democratic society, free speech, which is one of our prime freedoms, has now, in some of its forms, become politically incorrect. There are those in our society who want to limit speech. They do so, they say, because words may be hurtful and cause injury.

While the source is not entirely clear, there is in our country a radical elite who wish to control expression of thought in speech. And they argue that if those claimed correct ways are not followed, then such speech should be banned and the speaker held up to ridicule, opprobrium, and potential litigation.

Political correctness manifests itself in strange ways: recently, a student at The University of Michigan was forced to write a confession of political error because in a classroom discussion he questioned the morality of homosexuality.

The aim of this elite group is to stifle speech and to regulate thought; their aim is to prevent conflict and the confrontation of conflict by substituting thought control.

This phenomenon — I wish I could call it only a fad — now rivets the attention of many people. To them it is a buffer for avoiding the difficult realities of discussion and choice. In the name of sensitivity, they say they will not use hurtful words, and they avoid conflict and confrontation on tough issues so that feelings will not be bruised.

A prime exponent of this new thought control is Catharine Mac-Kinnon, a professor of law at The University of Michigan. She believes that free speech fosters the social inferiority of women and minorities. She claims that it supports social dominance. To that the editors of *The Defender* (of the Center for the Study of Popular Culture) respond that MacKinnon's view of the First Amendment is that it "is nothing but a pillar of patriarchal privilege and the oppression of women."[1]

Words, to Professor MacKinnon, are the equivalent of acts. Thoughts become behavior and thought control becomes as important as behavior modification, leading thereby to the erosion of the First Amendment.

I have another concern. The evidence is overwhelming that, either individually or as groups, we avoid the truth that conflict is inevitable. We avoid conflict because of a misunderstanding of its nature and necessity. We misunderstand its nature when we define conflict as a necessary evil. To test this in a small group, before presenting my definition of conflict, I asked if they thought of conflict as a necessary evil. Most of them did. We misunderstand its necessity because we do not link our God-given ability to think, to reason, to discern, and to choose, which is inherent in our natures, to a search for truth and a quest for justice. What troubles our society is the need for instant gratification and short-term solutions.

While these are my immediate reasons, I base my fundamental argument on five irrefutable, self-evident characteristics which our planet and

---

1. "The First Freedom Under the Gun," *The Defender* (March 1994), p. 8.

all human beings within it possess. These characteristics are bedrock to my assertion that, as partners with God in the completion of creation, we must confront conflict and undertake its resolution, for it is only in confrontation and free discussion that we find truth and attain justice.

1. Our planet is a part of a universe which exists and functions according to demonstrable rules of order.
2. Human beings on this planet have the God-given ability to think, to reason, to discern, and to make choices. That ability may even make them a little higher than the angels. While there may be some cognitive ability in species of life forms other than human beings, the ability of human beings to reason and to make choices clearly distinguishes them from animals, birds, reptiles, or plants. It is this God-given ability to think, to reason, to discern, and to make choices that is his greatest creation.
3. Throughout our planet, human beings share certain common moral principles, irrespective of differences in cultural and religious beliefs. One common moral principle is the aversion to and condemnation of murder. Another common ideal that is overarchingly shared is the universal struggle to attain justice.
4. Conflict exists and is inherent in our planet and in creation. Conflict is caused by our God-given natures. Since we have the ability to think, to reason, to discern, and to make choices, we stake out moral claims as individuals or as societies, claims which differ markedly from those held by other individuals or societies. Conflict stems from a search for truth amid a clash of legitimate claims, philosophies, cultures, and religions.
5. Human beings and all that exists on our planet and universe are part of a creation which is not yet complete and is in the dynamic unfolding process of completing itself.

This having been said, I return to a full discussion of the nature of conflict and the need to confront it.

Conflict breeds vitality; it involves the application of the intellect to the social, religious, and ethical realities of our world; conflict which envelops us, surrounding us as the air we breathe, must be faced; indeed, in facing conflict we involve the force of life; it is in this facing, this confrontation, with all of its difficulty and ambiguity, that we experience not only the weariness and frustration but also the richness of living and achieving.

This richness and satisfaction are felt particularly in the function or operation of a system of ethics, which seeks to resolve conflict between differing moral approaches in the achievement of justice.

A towering figure who has spoken at length on this subject is Dr. Reinhold Niebuhr. He was an ordained minister in the Evangelical Synod of North America. A graduate of Eden Theological Seminary in St. Louis, he took his advanced degrees at Yale Divinity School. By the way, he was a pastor in Detroit before World War II. His major work was undertaken at Union Theological Seminary; he was pre-eminent there, both as a theologian and as a philosopher. In two books, *The Nature and Destiny of Man* and *Moral Man and Immoral Society,* he argues forcefully for a need to rethink conflict and its inevitability in human society.

Niebuhr recognized the existence of group conflict but saw no good in it. He railed against social Darwinists, liberal theologians, and Marxists, whom he called moralists. He said their aims were doomed; they could not overcome conflict. He wrote that conflict is an inevitability in human history, and it will continue probably to the very end of history. Then, warming to his subject, he said:

> What is lacking among all these moralists, whether religious or rational, is an understanding of the brutal character of the behavior of all human collectives and the power of self-interest and collective egoism in all inter-group relations. Failure to recognize the stubborn resistance of group egoism to all moral and inclusive social objectives inevitably involves them in unrealistic and confused political thought. They regard social conflict either as an impossible method of achieving morally approved ends or as a momentary expedient which a more perfect education or a purer religion will make unnecessary. *They do not see that the limitations of the human imagination, the easy subservience of reason to prejudice and passion, and the consequent persistence of irrational egoism, particularly in group behavior, make social conflict an inevitability in human history, probably to its very end.*[2] (Emphasis added)

---

2. Reinhold Niebuhr, *Moral Man and Immoral Society* (New York: Charles Scribner's Sons, 1932), p. xx.

He concludes with this thought:

> *Whatever increase in social intelligence and moral goodwill may be achieved in human history, may serve to mitigate the brutalities of social conflict, but they cannot abolish the conflict itself.* That could be accomplished only if human groups, whether racial, national, or economic, could achieve a degree of reason and sympathy which would permit them to see and to understand the interests of others as vividly as they understand their own, and a moral goodwill which would prompt them to affirm the rights of others as vigorously as they affirm their own. *Given the inevitable limitations of human nature and the limits of the human imagination and intelligence, this is an ideal which individuals may approximate but which is beyond the capacities of human societies.*[3] (Emphasis added)

Joseph L. Allen, Professor of Christian Ethics at Southern Methodist University, does not agree with Niebuhr. In his work *Love and Conflict,* he writes:

> Sin enormously intensifies conflict, to be sure. People come to any situation with somewhat conflicting and somewhat harmonious interests, and then through unfaith toward God and untrustworthiness toward one another they bring about unnecessary harm in one relationship after another, from intrafamily conflict to war. So much is this the case that it is understandable that one would oversimplify the source of conflict by ascribing it solely to sin, especially since we have never encountered any human relationship in which created nature and its sinful distortions were not thoroughly interwoven. Logically, though, the human creation entails conflict, however much sin exacerbates it.[4]

Niebuhr maintains that one may be obligated to enter into social conflict for the sake of another's interests, but he judges that doing so is a moral compromise. Allen is critical of that. Niebuhr, he says, demands that one do the impossible: not enter into social conflict. Allen states his position:

3. Niebuhr, pp. xxiii-xxiv.
4. Joseph L. Allen, *Love and Conflict: A Covenantal Model of Christian Ethics* (Nashville: Abingdon Press, 1984), p. 93.

How can one ever not? To withdraw from struggle is still to decide about the use of one's potential power and to have a different effect on the struggle from what one might have had. The only way not to be involved in power struggles is to be dead. And if Niebuhr replies that he indeed wishes to require the impossible of us, we must reject that requirement. Regarding what we should outwardly do, Kant's dictum, "Ought implies can," is irrefutable. It is never our duty, or at least never our *actual* duty (as contrasted with our prima facie duties), to perform an act that we cannot possibly perform, externally speaking. Our actual duty must lie somewhere within the array of possible alternatives. And among those possibilities, at least one act must be right (and not merely a moral compromise), in the sense that considering all the prima facie duties upon us, this act (and possibly some others) responds to them as well as possible under the circumstances.[5]

Allen concludes, rather, that "the question is *how* to enter into conflict in ways that contribute to a mutually affirming and faithful community, conflict that does not unjustifiably harm one another, but always seeks the enhancement of the life of each within the community of all."[6]

But Niebuhr may have had some lingering doubt about his strong conclusion that conflict, though inevitable, is evil. While he said that conflict is inevitable in human history and would *probably* continue to its very end, he recognized some need for human involvement in conflict. He said, "We will know we cannot purge ourselves of the sin and guilt in which we are involved by the moral ambiguities of politics without also disavowing responsibility for the creative possibilities of justice."[7] Even here, Niebuhr concedes only grudgingly the necessity and usefulness of conflict, implying, however, that it is still a moral compromise.

I argue, on the other hand, for the objective good in conflict and the need for its resolution in order to complete creation.

To demonstrate this good, I point, first to conflict that is perverted. Examples are abundant: unjust war, conflict driven by the desire of conquest, or conflict caused by greed or by sin.

---

5. Allen, pp. 96-97.

6. Allen, p. 99.

7. Reinhold Niebuhr, *The Nature and Destiny of Man* (New York: Charles Scribner's Sons, 1949), p. 284.

But because such conflict is perverted, I cannot, and do not, conclude that conflict is inherently bad. For example, conflict within an already framed moral consensus, when it is addressed and resolved, enriches and strengthens that moral consensus. It is this process within our ethical system that broadens and develops an understanding and acceptance of moral values.

Conflict and its resolution are also of imperative importance in the development and growth of social, ethical, political, and religious systems.

I contend that:

1. Conflict is a good.
2. Conflict must be confronted.
3. Conflict should be resolved.
4. The goals of conflict confrontation and resolution are to secure justice.
5. This process is imperative in the attainment of justice in social, ethical, political, and religious systems.
6. Through this process we are involved in the completion of creation.
7. The law's adversarial system is a model for conflict, confrontation, and resolution.

I use, as a source to explain the good in conflict, Kurt Wolff's translation of Georg Simmel's massive work, *Der Streit*.[8] The German word "streit" is usually translated as "quarrel," but it has a broader meaning for Simmel; "conflict" seems better. In defining conflict, he asserts eight propositions:

1. Individuals do not attain the unity of their personalities exclusively by an exhaustive harmonization according to logical, objective, religious, or ethical norms of the contents of their personalities. On the contrary, contradiction and conflict not only precede this unity but are operative in it at *every moment of its existence.*
2. Conflict sets boundaries between groups within a social system by strengthening group consciousness and awareness of separateness, thus establishing the identity of groups within the system. Reciprocal repulsions maintain a total social system by creating balance between its various groups.

8. Georg Simmel, *Conflict*, trans. Kurt H. Wolff (Glencoe, Ill.: The Free Press, 1955).

3. Conflict with other groups contributes to the establishment and re-affirmation of the identity of the group and maintains its boundaries against the surrounding social world.

4. Conflict performs group-maintaining functions. It clears the air; that is, it eliminates the accumulation of balked hostile dispositions by allowing their free behavioral expression.

5. Conflict serves as an outlet for the release of hostilities which, were no such outlet provided, would sunder the relation between the antagonists.

6. The need for a safety valve increases with the rigidity of the social structure. Oppression usually increases if it is suffered calmly and without protest.

7. Conflict is not necessarily dysfunctional for the relationship within which it occurs. Often, conflict is necessary to maintain such a relationship. Without ways to vent hostility toward each other and to express dissent, group members might feel completely crushed and might react by withdrawal. By setting free pent-up feelings of hostility, conflicts serve to maintain a relationship. Antagonism is a central part of intimate social relations.

8. The absence of conflict cannot be taken as an index of the strength and stability of a relationship. In fact, stable relationships may be characterized by conflict. But closeness gives rise to frequent occasions for conflict. If the participants feel that their relationship is tenuous, they will avoid conflict, fearing that it might endanger the continuance of the relationship.

Lewis Coser, in *The Functions of Social Conflict,* argues that "Conflict as struggle over . . . values and claims has positive functions for social groups. . . . A certain degree of conflict is an essential element in group formation and the persistence of group life."[9] He claims that whether conflict is harmful or helpful depends on two conditions. First, conflicts in which the contending parties no longer share the basic values upon which the legitimacy of the social system rests threaten to disrupt the structure. Second, social conflict which does not undermine the basic assumptions upon which the societal relationship is founded tends to be positively functional.

Human nature has a love-hate relationship with conflict. Because we

9. Lewis Coser, *The Functions of Social Conflict* (New York: The Free Press, 1964).

have the ability to think, to reason, to discern, and to choose, it is inevitable that we have differing points of view. This human condition is self-evident. We are surrounded by disagreement and conflict, not only between individuals but also between groups of people, societies, and states.

Conflict exists in creation because moral, social, and religious claims continue to be made by human beings who think, who reason, who discern, and who make choices. Conflict exists because of competing interests of various peoples and groups of people. It is evidenced by the struggle of those interests.

Nonetheless, conflict is feared. It is regarded as an unhappy state. Avoidance of conflict is a human reaction. Harmony is craved. Conflict is considered an evil. It is defined as a product of sin. Such reactions to conflict cause continued societal difficulties and, frequently, almost chaotic conditions.

It is perplexing to confront the reality that conflict is inherent in creation, that it exists as a purposeful characteristic of our human condition, that it is God-ordained and since conflict is inherent in creation and that whatever God creates is good, conflict then must be viewed as good.

Those who dislike or fear conflict, or who believe it is engulfed in sin, cannot deny that conflict is inherent in creation. Faced with their fears and dislikes of conflict, they want to limit the reality of conflict by claiming that it is a process to be endured, such as illness or extreme heat or cold. But, as soon as such conflict results in some form of accommodation, usually at any price, they dismiss conflict from that context. They are thankful that, though they had to endure it, they can now relegate its happening to the category of dysfunction or sin. Niebuhr comes close to this erroneous attitude.

Because the art of dealing with conflict is central to the practice of politics, many people deliberately downgrade its importance. They dismiss politics as corrupt or evil. This makes it easy for them to live in a society in which they can avoid responsibility for political decisions while, at the same time, claiming the full right to be critical of such decisions. Such views are either cynical or naive. They rest upon a self-serving excuse that there are conflicts that ought not to be entrusted to the political process. Such a view is cynical because those who hold to it know full well that in a democracy such process is vital. Such a view is naive if those who hold to it think democracy can survive without conflict.

The words of Walter Lippmann, in his essay *The Indispensable Opposition,* are easily forgotten. He said:

We must protect the right of our opponents to speak because we must hear what they have to say. This is the creative principle of freedom of speech, not that it is a system for the tolerating of error, but that it is a system for finding the truth.[10]

What is tragic about this abject fear of conflict is that it breeds accommodations which cause more difficulty, more hurt, and more pain than the conflict itself. Make no mistake about this. Unless one has a healthy, mature view as to the necessity of conflict, the outcome forged by those who view conflict only as sinful or dysfunctional will likely be some sort of questionable solution, a soft love approach that jeopardizes resolution and causes failure.

Disputes and controversies are not considered to be joyful experiences when they occur in the human condition. Most people shun confrontation. This is so both for individuals and groups of individuals. In religious communities, conflict most often is viewed as an evil to be avoided. Even societies often regard conflict as dysfunctional.

Earlier I referred to Dr. Niebuhr's book *Moral Man and Immoral Society*. In it he distinguishes the conflicts that exist in individual relationships from those that exist in societies or states. Because nations, unlike individuals, cannot love, they cannot be selfless, he says. Thus they cannot succeed in conflict confrontation and resolution. I know of only one instance in recorded history in which a state was capable of love. In 1943, Denmark, already under the occupation of Nazi Germany, transported more than 7,000 Jews into the safety of neutral Sweden. The Danish king, Christian X, openly opposed the cult of the *Fuhrer*.

Totalitarian states or societies also hate conflict.

Stephen Carter, Cromwell Professor of Law at Yale University, says in his book *The Culture of Disbelief: How American Law and Politics Trivialize Religious Devotion* that:

A pervasive, totalitarian state will of course find these conflicts threatening [conflicts between the visions imagined by the state and visions imposed by the religions], which is why religious liberty is among the first freedoms to go when statist dictators take firm hold. A state that

10. Walter Lippmann, "The Indispensable Opposition," in *Atlantic Essays* (Boston: D. C. Heath, 1958), pp. 363-69.

loves liberty and cherishes its diversity, however, should revel in these conflicts, welcoming them as a sign of political and spiritual health.[11]

Conflict tends to be dysfunctional in a social structure in which there is no, or insufficient, tolerance; that is, the loss of a consensus of basic moral values. What threatens that structure is not conflict, as such, but rigidity — which permits hostilities to accumulate but permits them to be channeled only along one major line of cleavage.

Consider the major institutions in our society. Conflicts exist both within and between religious groups. In the Christian Reformed Church, a major conflict exists as to the ordination of women into the ministry. There are also major differences between religious groups as to the status of homosexuals; these differences are certainly conflicts. In public education, perennial conflict recurs as to the content of educational programs — what studies should or should not be taught; how education should be financed; the problems of integration and segregation of public school students.

At our country's national level there are deep divisions in welfare, health care, education, and crime policies.

In international affairs, constant turmoil exists between Israel and the PLO, as well as the conflict between Israel and the Arab countries, and between the Serbs and the Muslims in Bosnia. South Africa, as it rids itself of apartheid and labors to install a new form of democracy, is rife with conflict.

It is clearly evident that these conflicts that confront us today are similar to conflicts that have occurred throughout history. These conflicts throughout history have a common characteristic. They stem from power, the power to choose.

Pre-eminent in the current assertions of conflicting moral, social, and religious claims by groups within our society is the power of each to choose. Unfortunately, such groups often make choices without adequate study, discussion, reflection, or appreciation of the consequences of choice.

Difficulty also results from a current phenomenon that holds that choice is not free. Henry Hart in his treatise *Law, Liberty and Morality* makes

11. Stephen Carter, *The Culture of Disbelief: How American Law and Politics Trivialize Religious Devotion* (New York: Basic Books, 1993), p. 274.

that point. He writes: "There is a general decline in the belief that individuals know their own interests best and to an increased awareness of a great range of factors which diminish the significance to be attached to an apparently free choice. . . ."[12]

However we view these difficulties, it does not do away with the need to choose. I repeat Joseph Allen's argument: "How can one ever not [choose]? . . . The only way not to be involved . . . is to be dead."[13]

It is clear that malaise or chaos results in any group or society when it refuses or neglects to confront conflict. That refusal or neglect itself is corrosive. To remain vital, democratic society needs to confront conflict, to discuss and to decide issues that constantly surface as a part of its being. A society such as ours would not function at all well were no challenges mounted to issues in conflict and, because of fear, inertia, neglect, or refusal, were such challenges not developed. Such a society will not retain its vitality since its basic underpinning is being denied, *i.e.,* the right of its members to be free, to think, to discern, and to choose. Recall Edmund Burke's admonition: "The only thing necessary for the triumph of evil is for good men to do nothing."

Indeed the touchstone of an open society is its avid willingness to confront, engage in the process of, and resolve conflict; the dominant characteristic of a closed society is its refusal to permit the process of conflict, confrontation, and conflict resolution.

We cannot, as a society, refuse to make choices because we do not know or care about the likely consequences of choice. To not choose is still to choose. To not think, to not discuss, to not act on conflicting moral claims, to not work toward a just result because of a lack of concern, or because of a misplaced view of an issue in conflict, will not deter a result.

I leave the extension of this thought to another time, but I add that wherever this lack of concern occurs there is a strong need for society to address it.

What is even more critical is the pervasive negative attitude toward conflict and conflict resolution. Dominant in this attitude is the trivializing view of conflict which a consideration of the *dynamic* of conflict induces. That attitude only infrequently reveals a positive view of conflict

---

12. Henry Hart, *Law, Liberty and Morality* (Stanford, Calif.: Stanford University Press, 1963).

13. Allen, p. 96.

and then only when it is seen in competitive terms, as in sports, in litera- ture, or in the dramatic arts.

Such negative attitudes characteristically cause denial and evasion and are a root cause of much of human dissension. In religious institu- tions, fear of conflict is endemic. Themes that pervade discussion, writing, dialogue, and ministry veer away from difficult moral, social, religious, and political issues which are deeply rooted in the fabric of the human condi- tion. In religious discussions one hears, instead, a fervent evangelicalism which invites attention to a life hereafter and which deliberately ignores the difficulties of this life.

Dr. Billy Graham in his Crusades undoubtedly provides great com- fort through his messages to people who desperately need to be comforted. That part of his ministry is sound. But he does not use his vast influence to take on the deep social, moral, and political issues we face.

Far too many religious groups shun this conflict. Their evasion stems from a misplaced belief that "we are in this world but not of it."

I will not be misunderstood.

Faith, belief, salvation, and God's limitless grace are vital in Christian societies. But these concepts have far more relevance and deeper meaning when they are related to conflict and its resolution in this life. Even more is this so when one considers conflict between competing moral claims in so- ciety, conflicts within and between religious denominations, conflicts in tough social issues, conflicts regarding political issues — all of which come about because of the capacities and choices of thinking, discerning, and choosing human beings within those groups. Much of what seems, in the human condition, to be a seething, roiling, meaningless ferment, accord- ing to those who fear conflict and desire peace or harmony at almost any price, really is the working out of God's purposes in creation.

I do not deny the existence of evil.

I know that conflict is often perverted by sin.

But I contend that the avoidance of conflicts caused by the choices or demands that are legitimately made as to moral claims, social and religious issues, and political disputes is a denial of God's purposes in this creation. This avoidance cannot be explained as a failure to clearly understand God's will. It is more than that; it is a refusal to understand and to accept God's purposes in creation.

I will be explicit.

In much of religious discussion as to eternal life, there is the dominant thought that this life is only a rite of passage. The hope is not for what may be attained in this life but for the joyous release which comes with death and, ultimately, with the end of time.

I contend that in substantial part many religious denominations are not addressing significant conflicts caused by our human condition. I contend that if such conflict issues are avoided or addressed only with "soft love" approaches, *i.e.*, sentimental and romantic ideas of non-conflicted love, rather than an attempt to reach just results, many parishioners will continue to be turned off and conclude that the Church is piously irrelevant. Why do our religious leaders shun controversial issues? In substantial part, many are not and do not keep themselves informed. Many do not read widely in other disciplines. Many are complacent. To take on tough social, political, and religious issues is thought by such folk to run counter to the need to be loved.

A rebuttal may be made to this. It will be said that confrontation in any group will cause irreparable harm, that it will result in discord and dissension and be counterproductive. I reply that while the handling of conflict and confrontation, in many instances, will be difficult, it does call for skill, wisdom, constructive style, and good judgment. That it is difficult is no excuse for not undertaking the challenge.

Another rebuttal is phrased in this way: "[R]eligious participation in resolving issues of public concern is inconsistent with our national commitment to free, open-minded debate and inquiry."[14]

Elizabeth Mensch and Alan Freeman, in their book *The Politics of Virtue: Is Abortion Debatable?*, make this response:

> Religion in the United States provides both an incentive to act responsibly in the world, and it also offers that "pause" which makes complete allegiance to any political order impossible. This is why religion provides a counterforce to totalizing secular ideologies, whether of the right or left — so long, that is, as churches resist the temptation to identify themselves too fully with the state.[15]

14. Michael W. McConnell, "Religion and the Search for a Middle Ground on Abortion," *Michigan Law Review* 92 (1994), p. 1896.

15. Elizabeth Mensch and Alan Freeman, *The Politics of Virtue: Is Abortion Debatable?* (Durham: Duke University Press, 1993), p. 140.

To early Calvinists, it would seem most strange to see their descendants avoid conflict. The early Calvinists and their leader took on conflict with robust zeal. Their impact, as reformers, on world society was enormous. Indeed, history teaches that through the movement of Calvinism in Western Europe and the English colonies in the New World, the birth of the United States was profoundly affected.

In an extract from *Conflict and Harmony,* a part of the Andrew B. Cecil Lectures on "Moral Values in a Free Society," Donald Shriver writes that the Puritan revolution in England had its largest continuation in the next 150 years of European settlement of America. Lord Acton called John Calvin the virtual founder of the United States of America.

In that article, Shriver continues: What Calvinists did for the Protestant notion of the supremacy of God was to take it out of the static structure of medieval society and out of the equally static boxes of Luther and to understand that divine will as restlessly at work in the whole human and nonhuman world. Calvinists, said A. S. P. Woodhouse, "lived in a world of particular providences."[16] To them the whole world was "the theater of God's glory," which could never be tamed or institutionalized. Human beings are obliged, by this vision, to be constantly at the work of seeing, obeying, institutionalizing, and reinstitutionalizing the ever-transcending intentions of their divine ruler. That rule aims at unceasing *transformation* of all things human in the direction toward which God impels the world.[17]

A parallel, hostile position — parallel, in the sense that here the emphasis is to prevent involvement in conflict — has been developing with the entry into active political involvement of what is called the Religious Right. I refer to the criticism being directed by those "who denounce the Christian Right because it is Christian and who see religious activism in politics as a threat to 'the American Way.'"[18]

Stephen Carter, whom I quoted earlier, a black law professor at Yale, is "alarmed at the open animosity many liberals . . . direct at the Religious Right."[19]

16. A. S. P. Woodhouse, *Puritanism and Liberty* (Chicago: The University of Chicago Press, 1951), p. 42.

17. Donald Shriver, "Collision and Community: Church and State in a Humane Society," in *Conflict and Harmony,* ed. Andrew R. Cecil (Dallas: University of Texas, 1982), p. 80.

18. Glenn C. Loury, "Spiritual Politics," *The Public Interest* 114 (1994), p. 111.

19. Loury, p. 111.

Glenn Loury, commenting on Carter's views, writes:

The most interesting and persuasive aspect of his argument that conservative Christians should be received as legitimate (if, to his mind,
mistaken) participants in political debates is his recollection of an earlier movement of religious activists with political ambitions — a movement that marches under the banner of civil rights. When Christians
and Jews openly invoked the Almighty in their effort to overturn segregation, they enjoyed enthusiastic support on the Left. They were not
criticized for seeking to impose on the country a moral vision
grounded in their particular interpretation of Scripture, though that is
clearly what many of them sought to do. Mr. Carter asks why, if Martin
Luther King, Jr., could legitimately call on God's name and His word
when addressing matters political, should not Pat Robertson also be
able to do so?[20]

I am not at all supportive of some of the Reverend Pat Robertson's
views. Putting that aside, however, I accept the efforts that the so-called Religious Right are making in the taking on of conflict and its resolution in
moral, social, and political arenas.

Robertson and his followers can be challenged on theological
grounds, but they have the right to make choices in the plethora of competing moral and social claims.

I conclude this portion of my lecture with a statement as to what is
still to come. I will discuss:

1. The goals of conflict confrontation and conflict resolution; these
   goals are to secure justice.
2. This process is imperative in the attainment of social, ethical, political, and religious systems grounded on justice.
3. The law's adversarial system is a model for conflict confrontation
   and resolution.

20. Loury, p. 112.

Second Lecture

So far I have argued that conflict is a good, that it must be confronted, and that it should be resolved.

Why?

There are two dominant, interrelated reasons.

1. Creation is incomplete, and it is our transcendent task to assist God in its enhancement and completion; and
2. In that effort our goal in conflict confrontation and resolution is to attain justice.

We must understand the reality of our human condition. In a world in which that human condition is largely driven by choices that are made either randomly, blindly, sinfully or without realistic confrontation, we stumble and stagger in our participation in the completion of creation.

That human condition needs no exhaustive definition. It exists in history and is currently experienced. It is how humanity lives, and moves, and is.

Niebuhr claims that these goals of justice cannot be achieved in this temporal creation and that it is futile to try.

To accept that claim is to acknowledge the defeat of God's purposes in creation. I cannot accept the claim that this creation, with all of its wonder and beauty, cannot be enhanced because we feel it is futile to exercise the will to act. Niebuhr was troubled by that; in the concluding paragraph of his book *Moral Man and Immoral Society*, he writes:

> In the task of that redemption the most effective agents will be men who have substituted some new illusions for the abandoned ones. The most important of these illusions is that the collective life of mankind

can achieve perfect justice. It is a very valuable illusion for the moment; for justice cannot be approximated if the hope of its perfect realization does not generate a sublime madness in the soul. Nothing but such madness will do battle with malignant power and "spiritual wickedness in high places." The illusion is dangerous because it encourages terrible fanaticisms. It must therefore be brought under the control of reason. One can only hope that reason will not destroy it before its work is done.[1]

What must be grasped is God's purpose in this creation. He did not give human beings the ability to think, to reason, to discern, and to make choices so that they could destroy this creation. He did not decree that when the human condition had completely deteriorated, he would intervene, declare time at an end, and proclaim his work a failure. To accept such a view of the end of this temporal creation is to marginalize God.

This is not my belief.

I believe that God's purpose was, and is, to people his creation so that people can assist in its enhancement and completion. Faced as they have been throughout human history with conflict stemming from a search for truth amid a clash of legitimate claims, philosophies, cultures, and religions, human beings are required to confront and resolve these competing claims to secure justice.

To explain my belief, I take up the concept of justice. I prefer not to get into a debate whether love is a part of justice or justice is a part of love. Dr. Stob puts the question appropriately:

> Is this relation a relation of identity? Is justice but one of the many forms or qualities of love, and should it therefore be defined in terms of love, *i.e.,* in terms of love's most basic meaning; or is justice something quite distinct from love, something which while it does not contradict love, must, in order to be understood, be given independent status, and contrasted with love?[2]

Since I quote Dr. Stob's question, I give his answer. He says:

---

1. Niebuhr, *Moral Man and Immoral Society,* p. 277.
2. Henry Stob, *Ethical Reflections: Essays on Moral Themes* (Grand Rapids: Eerdmans, 1978), p. 123.

In considering this relation I took, and now take, my position on the side of love. That is, I construe the relation of love and justice from the side of love. I do this because love, in my judgment, is the greater and higher of the two.[3]

It is with some trepidation that I differ from my beloved friend, as I differ also with Dr. Niebuhr.

Niebuhr claims that groups of collective individuals, *i.e.,* societies or states, are not capable of love. He argues that this is an ideal which individuals may approximate but which is beyond the capacities of human societies.

As to Dr. Stob's position, perhaps I read more into his description of the relation between love and justice than he intends; but I take his statement "that love goes beyond, exceeds justice"[4] to mean that groups of Christians have as their ultimate goal demonstrable love, not necessarily justice. I think his point is misplaced. While individuals may demonstrate selflessness and love in the resolution of conflict, and demonstrate love both as to the means and the goal of their endeavors, "groups of collectives," to use Niebuhr's terms, cannot do so.

I see it differently.

When Stob endows love as a higher goal than justice, he places a burden on human society which is not realistic.

Niebuhr has it right when he says that human societies cannot show love; he does not have it right when he says that conflict resolution, therefore, is futile.

Justice is the goal toward which the striving to complete this creation should be directed. Julian Bond once said in a lecture in Detroit that the only way that institutions can exercise love is by insuring justice.[5]

Throughout this planet, human beings crave justice. In recorded history that desperate need has been amply documented. Coupled with an ability to think and to make choices, human beings possess an innate sense of justice. This sense is present in the quest for justice and drives it relentlessly.

The constitutions on which democratic governments are based, the

3. Stob, p. 135.
4. Stob, p. 143.
5. When asked personally about this quotation from his Detroit lecture, Bond said that the original author of this thought may be Andrew Young.

books of the great religions, the diverse cultures, all have at their core this overarching moral quest: Justice.

Beyond this, it is not my purpose to analyze further the technical, legal meanings of justice. Both as a concept and as a result, it is elusive, ambiguous, difficult, harsh, sometimes unloving, and not always final.

Yet it is recognizable.

It is recognizable by *finite* human beings, *i.e.,* finite in the sense that when compared to the long sweeps of time in history, an eighty- or ninety-year-old person, attuned to that history and to his or her place in it, may nonetheless conclude that justice was attained when what is due a society, a country, or an individual has been granted.

I quote Dr. Stob: "The formula [of justice]: to each what is coming to him. . . . Justice is concerned with moral symmetry, the symbol for it being a balanced scale."[6]

Put another way, Stob says: "Justice is served when each man is given both the freedom and the opportunity to attain the level of personal achievement of which he is capable."[7]

Justice is administered through the establishment or determination of rights according to rules of law.

I believe that a "soft love" approach, when used as a substitute for the securing of a just result in the resolution of social conflicts, is often misplaced. No matter how well-intentioned that soft love approach may be, the result is often skewed. It is skewed because what should be considered is a just result — not a loving result. For example, the welfare system "as we know it" is based on the good intention of society to provide for those who are in need of assistance. But the welfare system often stifles self-respect and may curtail initiative on the part of those individuals whom it seeks to assist.

Another example: A social conflict exists in education caused by a policy that pushes students into higher grades and graduation, even students who have not demonstrated the ability to be promoted or to graduate. Accommodation to that difficulty is then made by a soft love approach that lowers academic standards; and this is a significant cause of mediocrity in our educational system.

In Christian religion, a soft love approach spawns pious irrelevance. For example, if the only challenge to a parishioner is "What must I do to be

6. Stob, p. 124.
7. Stob, p. 133.

saved?" then the equally relevant question "Now that I am saved, how and what should I do to complete creation?" is avoided.

As much as a group or a society may be directed or inspired by its leaders to be motivated by love in a resolution of its conflicts, such admonition is not only not realistic, but it is also misdirected. This is so because what motivates most groups is not love but power. The resolution of conflict can come only from a balancing of that power between those groups.

Consider examples in recent history.

The fragile accord that has been reached in South Africa has at its core the balancing of power between the races. While in the struggle, Bishop Tutu talked occasionally about the love command; he wisely avoided overstatement while he vigorously demanded power-sharing.

Niebuhr, a pacifist until he realized what the horrors of Hitlerism meant, thereafter no longer countenanced non-violence.

Gandhi is often misrepresented as the champion of the non-violent approach to conflict resolution. His success was otherwise achieved. He knew that he could make the British back down because their culture and their law would not permit the slaughter of his people to defeat the rebellion.

In our country the slow and steady effort of black people to achieve a balance of their rights with white people is based on power-sharing and not on love.

It is this reality that Niebuhr conceptually could not face. He wanted justice as a balancing mechanism to be obtained through love. When he realized that that could not succeed, he criticized the brutal character of the behavior of all human collectives and the power of self-interest and collective egoism in all inter-group relations.

By stating that conflict resolution may, in many instances, involve a struggle for power, I do not mean to indicate that these struggles are sinful or evil. To brand all such struggles as such would be totally unrealistic. These struggles, which we may also describe as efforts to achieve just balances in society, are the day-in, day-out, year-in, year-out, century-in, century-out ways in and through which creation is enhanced and completed.

In the words of Professor Waldo Beach, "It means only that life's real choices are inevitably compromises . . . the highest attainable quality of life for the greatest number of persons."[8]

---

8. Waldo Beach, *Christian Ethics in the Protestant Tradition* (Atlanta: John Knox Press, 1988), p. 52.

In these struggles I assert that God is involved in ways that we cannot comprehend. I view with wonder the founding of our country. There converged in Philadelphia in 1776 a group of great men — Washington, Hamilton, Jefferson, Madison, Hancock, and others — who, openly and avowedly led by God, declared that under his guidance we are one nation dedicated to the proposition that we are created equal and endowed by our Creator with certain inalienable rights.

The Old Testament is the supreme document testifying to the partnership that God has with his people in the completion of creation. Repeatedly he led the Israelites, his chosen people, and with them their leaders, until they came to that point in history when the world stood still and God became man.

The humanity which he created and which he sustains in its efforts to seek justice does, in indefinable ways, have his subtle guidance and support and reflects his nature and image. Even though it is impossible for our finite minds to comprehend the workings of our infinite God, there is a guidepost along the way which we can recognize as his handiwork.

This guidepost is our system of justice which, I believe, it is not arrogant or pietistic to claim is a product of the patient, subtle providence of God in history, accomplished through debate, conflict negotiation, compromise, and resolution. These are its characteristics:

1. An open, democratic society;
2. A government based on a constitution that safeguards and nurtures individual human rights, such as the freedom of speech and religion, and contains built-in check-and-balance mechanisms;
3. The encouragement of full discussion of conflict issues and a necessary free press to inform as to the parameters of the debate;
4. Due process, the right to speak and to be heard, according to *now* deeply ingrained rules of law, based on fairness principles and an unquestioned acceptance of those rules. Due process is the heart of the law's adversarial system.

This system of justice, which is embodied in the principles of our Common Law and Western legal tradition, and exercised through the law's adversarial system, furnishes us, in our time and place in history, with a solid methodology for the resolution of conflict and the attainment of justice.

Professor Alice-Erh-Soon Tay describes this system as "a continuing sense of justice." She writes: "This sense of justice which is involved but is not exhausted by principles of fairness, equality, respect for persons, a concern with social adjustment and well-being, a capacity to recognize wrongs and make room for rights . . . is a constant pursuit."[9]

It is the pursuit of justice which many groups find difficult, if not impossible, to undertake. Here again the love-hate relationship with conflict reappears. Groups in an empowered position on an issue, whether societies or states, are reluctant to allow other groups which disagree with them to oppose their position.

Those groups do not want to encourage a full discussion of conflict issues conducted on fairness principles, particularly the right that the opposing group has to speak, to be heard, and to have its views considered.

This difficulty also blocks the resolution of conflicts between individuals.

Think about this: Groups and individuals in positions of power often take short-cuts in conflict resolution.

The pursuit of justice in the confrontation and resolution of conflict requires a relentless persistence, toughness, and fairness.

Throughout history, two methods that non-government and government groups have used to resolve conflict are violent and non-violent actions.

There is a third method toward which history has been pointing and which clearly indicates a path for the pursuit and attainment of justice and the work of completing creation.

That path is democracy in action, groups and states ascribing to democratic values.

That path leads toward a consortium of nations whose governments ascribe to democratic values, imperfect though some of them may be.

That path is a reasoned check-and-balance system through the use of parleys, discussion, understanding, and persuasion in which peaceful coercion may be used. Non-violent coercion, too, has an important place in democratic governmental systems.

It is becoming clear that the strong movement toward the formation of democratic societies continues.

---

9. Tay Alice-Erh-Soon, ed., *Justice* (New York: St. Martin's Press, 1980), p. 79.

But even more to the point: This process is deeply involved in the continuing completion of creation.

Two quotations are the predicate for a discussion of this concept. Dr. Niebuhr, in his book *The Nature and Destiny of Man*, writes: "Eternity will fufill and not annul the richness and the variety which the temporal process has elaborated."[10]

And in a lecture at Calvin Seminary in 1966 (I am indebted to Dr. J. Harold Ellens, who attended that lecture and furnished the quotation), Dr. Jellema said:

> I believe that the purpose of life is the development of our rationality in thinking God's thoughts after him. I believe that heaven is a continuation of the development of that rationality. I do not mean rationalism nor rationalistic cognition. And I believe that that continuing growth in rationality starts in heaven at the point at which it left off in this life. Therefore, the enterprise of inquiry and growth in understanding which we achieve in this life is of immense importance to our eternal destiny.[11]

These ideas are fascinating. They speak eloquently to the relationship between our actions here and in eternity. When Niebuhr refers to the "richness and variety of the temporal process," and when Jellema speaks of "the enterprise of inquiry and growth in understanding which we achieve in this life," each strongly implicates the work involved in the completion of creation.

On a day in the summer of 1994, I think and write about this idea: the Completion of Creation. Surrounding me is the verdancy of nature. From 30,000 feet comes the drone of a 747. A hot, sticky day in Michigan. Not an ideal time to tackle this lofty theme.

Yet I know that it is a day like all days before it in this temporal creation, a day that is part of history.

From the first day of creation until this day, each day has been involved in and used, for better or worse, in the development and completion of creation.

10. Niebuhr, *Nature and Destiny of Man*, p. 284.
11. Letter from Dr. J. Harold Ellens, April 7, 1994.

I think of it as an unbroken span in time from this day in the summer of 1994 back to the first day of creation.

In each of those days — whether it was Adam naming the animals in Eden, Abraham moving to Canaan, Moses leading the Israelites out of Egypt, Solomon building the temple, the great prophets inveighing against evil, the conquest of the then-known world by the Romans, the birth of Jesus Christ, the spread of Christianity and the growth of other great religions, the development of the rule of law, the Renaissance, the Reformation, the growth and development of nation-states and the concomitant emergence of democracy — God's creation is in the process of being completed.

Not one of these events is capricious or accidental. The thread, the weave in all, was and is God's grand design in which his greatest creation — thinking, choosing, discerning human beings — were, are, or should have been actively involved with him in these events and their unfolding.

Václav Havel, President of the Czech Republic, in an address on July 4 of this year, when he received the Philadelphia Liberty Medal, spoke of our need to be aware of our relation to creation. He said:

> [We must revive this] awareness of our being anchored in the Earth and the universe, the awareness that we are not here alone nor for ourselves alone but that we are an integral part of higher, mysterious entities against whom it is not advisable to blaspheme.
>
> This forgotten awareness is encoded in all religions.
>
> All cultures anticipate it in various forms. . . .
>
> The only real hope of people today is probably a renewal of our certainty that we are rooted in the Earth and, at the same time, the cosmos. This awareness endows us with the capacity for self-transcendence. . . .
>
> Only someone who submits to the authority of the universal order and of creation, who values the right to be a part of it, and a participant in it, can genuinely value himself and his neighbors and thus honor their rights as well.[12]

At the heart of this awareness of and this activity in the completion of creation are *two* great parallel efforts:

12. Václav Havel, "The New Measure of Man," *New York Times* (8 July 1994, late ed.), A:27.

371

1. The redemptive process of salvation working in history, led by Jesus Christ and manifested by God's limitless grace and love. This redemptive process also goes forward through the belief and work of the other great religions; and
2. The *equally important effort* to complete creation through the day-in, day-out, year-in, year-out, century-in, century-out redemptive process in the quest for justice.

It is this other effort which is so often ignored, not because it is not happening, but because its burdensome tasks are so often avoided.

Niebuhr's magnificent thought that "eternity will fulfill and not annul the richness and the variety which the temporal process has elaborated" crystallizes with heart-stopping impact what this other effort must be. Jellema's equally astounding thought that the "understanding which we achieve in this life is of immense importance to our eternal destiny" links this other effort to the need to be involved in the completion of creation.

But even more than that, the work of completing creation will continue into eternity. Neither Niebuhr nor Jellema says that the effort of completing creation will stop when time ends. The exhilarating thought that each expresses speaks to the ongoing completion of creation in eternity.

What is fascinating to contemplate is what the role of thinking, reasoning, discerning, and choosing human beings will be in eternity. It is my belief that the process which begins in this life will continue to unfold and to re-create again and again forever.

The Ghost in the Ivory Tower

Can a Philosopher Find Happiness
in a Haunted House?

GEORGE I. MAVRODES

Contents

First Lecture

I begin this lecture with a story. The title of the lecture might suggest that this should be a ghost story. Unfortunately, the story itself is more prosaic. The ghost comes in later on.

Some forty years ago, more or less, I was a student in a theological seminary. (I hasten to add that, for better or worse, it was not Calvin Seminary.) I had already decided that I would try to make a career in philosophy, and I had been reading some philosophy on my own hook, along with books on Christian apologetics. But, since my principal interest was already in the philosophy of religion and I wanted to come to the field in a way that was faithful to my own Christian commitment, I thought it would be a good thing to do some preliminary study in fields such as Christian theology, the Bible and church history, before taking up graduate work in philosophy. So I went to a seminary. One of my fellow students there knew about my interest in philosophy, apologetics, proofs of the existence of God, and things like that; and this student had a friend who was an atheist. My student colleague put two and two together, and invited me and that friend to have dinner with him and his wife one evening.

Well, I came to the dinner eager to make a rational conversion and was primed with an argument for the existence of God. The atheist, of course, probably also had some idea of what he was getting into. He knew, after all, that his host was a seminary student, and that I was one too. So I suppose he was not all that surprised when we maneuvered the conversation to the topic of God. And thus it was not on an entirely unsuspecting fellow guest that I proceeded to unload my argument.

Well, we talked back and forth for a while. I don't now remember just what I said or just what he said. What I do recall is that it eventually became clear to me that my argument had no bite at all with the atheist. When the evening came to an end, he was, so far as I could see, no closer to being a Christian, or indeed to being a theist of any sort, than when he had come to the dinner. I never did hear of his coming to believe in God. That attempt at philosophical apologetics struck me as a dismal failure.

I've remembered that incident throughout my whole philosophical career. I have thought many times about how that episode, and other philosophical attempts, might be usefully evaluated. I thought that evening, and I continue to think now, that my foray into the field of philosophical apologetics was a failure. In a way, of course, that is comparatively unproblematic. I have no doubt that there was a failure there, and I have failed many times since then both in philosophy and in other endeavors. But I'm not satisfied with leaving it at that.

To classify the incident as a failure is to make a negative evaluation of it. But "failure" is a rather general negative term. It is something like going to a doctor, and hearing him say after his examination, "Well, you're sick." We might wish that he had some more specific idea of what the trouble is because in that case he might also have some idea of a specific course of action which could improve matters. I too wanted to have a terminology and a way of using that terminology — some criteria if possible, which would enable me to say more specifically what went wrong that evening and what might be done in a better way on some other occasion.

This problem, indeed, is not all that far removed from the questions which are often asked by beginning students in philosophy. What is philosophy after all and what is its project? What good is philosophy? What is the difference between good philosophy and bad philosophy? Does just anything go in philosophy? If not, what are the standards for what goes and what doesn't go? And what is the rationale for accepting those standards rather than others?

These are evaluative questions. They ask about the worth of philosophy, how that worth can be recognized and how it can be achieved. They are asked, it seems to me, against the background assumption that philosophy is an enterprise in which one might succeed or fail — succeed or fail, that is, in achieving some appreciable value. Or perhaps one might have a partial success and a partial failure — an achievement which was a matter of degree.

Well, some of us here have been studying philosophical works now for many years, and we have been trying to do some philosophy too. Maybe

378

there are others here who have not made a professional and academic career in this field, but who nevertheless have some real interest in it as thoughtful observers. Maybe those outside observers feel, as I do myself, that philosophy may be too important to be left entirely to the academic philosophers. And so, have *we* learned what philosophy is, we who have had this long association with it? Do we now know what the value of philosophy is and what the properties which make philosophical work worthwhile are? If we do have some understanding of these things, then can we now make some stab at articulating what we have learned by saying what it is we aim to achieve in our philosophical work?

I just now asked what we aim for in our work. Let me emphasize that point a little. Evaluative criteria enable us to judge the worth of something after it has been done. Academicians are accustomed to doing that, because the grade sheets have to be filled out at the end of every semester and filed in the appropriate administrative office. All of those are grades for work that has been done — work that has been "turned in." That is certainly one use of evaluative criteria, but it is not the only one.

More important for our thinking here in these two sessions, in my opinion at least, is the fact that evaluative criteria also provide us with a guide for choosing what work to do or attempt and a guide for doing the work while it is yet in progress. The girl who asks her grade-school teacher whether "neatness counts" in her book report is taking that prospective view. If the teacher assures her that neatness does indeed count, then the girl will probably devote some care and effort to making her report look neat. The teacher may use that criterion in assigning a grade after the work is done, but the student uses the criterion as a guide in the doing of the work. I am thinking primarily of the prospective, forward-looking use of criteria, though occasionally also of their retrospective use.[1]

Let me plunge in, then, by making an initial stab — putting forward a thesis about the evaluation of philosophical work. The thesis here has two parts. The first part is the background assumption that philosophical

---

1. But might there be a value which a work could have, and which could even be recognized retrospectively, but which it would be improper to aim for? Perhaps. A Christian friend, a Catholic philosopher, told me once that he wished that he could be a great theologian. But if not, then he hoped that he would be a great heretic. For, he said, the great heretics force the Church to define orthodoxy more clearly. If he was right, then heresy might have a value after all, a kind of serendipity. But it would probably not be right for a Christian to aim at being a heretic.

work is an enterprise which has an aim and that the most general form of that aim is effecting some improvement in human intellectual life.[2] The second part of the thesis is that no piece of philosophical work — no finished, rounded-off, argument, analysis, explanation, refutation, etc. — is a success unless it does make some significant and positive difference in the intellectual life of some actual human being.

Some of you are probably already thinking that this thesis is such a commonplace one that it hardly deserves notice. But this thesis involves some costs which, I think, many philosophers have been reluctant to pay. Much of the second lecture is devoted to exploring some ways in which philosophers have attempted to evade, or at least reduce, those costs.

Maybe there are some others here who are skeptical about this initial thesis. I have put it as a universal generalization. Universal generalizations or "blanket statements" as they are sometimes called profess to cover *everything* within a specified domain. They are therefore vulnerable to refutation through the use of a counter-example. One looks, that is, for something in the specified domain that does not fit under "the blanket." If you are skeptical about my thesis, then I invite you, as things go along, to try to think of a counter-example to it.

But let me not forget to invite also the ghost whom I have promised to you. This ghost has his own name, but I will leave that name unspoken for the moment. For now I will simply call him the ghost who haunts the grave of Protagoras, an early Greek philosopher. We know of Protagoras's views from brief references in the works of other writers. I call on Protagoras to share with us only a single memorable sentence which Plato attributes to him. According to Plato, Protagoras said that "Man is the measure of all things."[3] I call on Protagoras for the sake of this one sentence. But the ghost who haunts Protagoras's grave is always listening and, if it suits his purposes, he too responds to the call.

First, however, is a little more about what I want from Protagoras. I do not issue my call to him as a scholar of the history of philosophy, for I am not. I must leave serious historical work on the philosophy of Protagoras to others, some of whom may well be here today. Instead, I pro-

---

2. I have no objection to anyone who wants to expand this aim beyond the realm of the human, to include other (possible) rational and cognitive agents, such as angels, devils, Martians, etc. But here I restrict my own speculations to the realm of the human.

3. Plato, *Theaetetus,* 152.

pose to use Protagoras, shamelessly, for my own purposes. I will take the sentence Plato quotes, the *Homo Mensura* as it is sometimes called, as a peg on which to hang a philosophical reflection. I give his sentence an interpretation which suits my own intention, an interpretation which may or may not be what Protagoras himself intended. If Protagoras himself is somewhere reading this, then perhaps there will be a time (as Socrates once speculated) when we will have occasion to discuss it together.

The first connection which I made, a couple of years ago, between Protagoras's sentence and my remembered incident, is attached to the word "measure." It occurred to me that we can interpret this word to refer not to just any old sort of measure, but specifically to an *evaluative* measure, which is fitted to enter into judgments of good and bad, right and wrong, success and failure. That is how I propose to read the word "measure."

Having said that, I can go on to state briefly how I intend to interpret the other significant terms in this sentence. Protagoras said "man *is* the measure." One way of reading that is to think that man is the agent who measures all things, man is the *measurer*. But it can also be read as meaning that man is himself the *measuring rod,* so to speak, regardless of whether he is the measuring agent. On this interpretation, man or, more cautiously, something human is the evaluative standard against which something is to be measured and evaluated. So we can read Protagoras — my Protagoras, that is, whether historical or fictional — as saying that even if it is God who in the end measures the worth of something, nevertheless, he measures it against a standard which includes something human. It is this latter sense which I intend to give to Protagoras's sentence.

Protagoras said "*man* is the measure." I propose to understand the reference to man, initially, at least, as a way of referring to individual, particular human beings, rather than as a reference to humanity, the human species or any other such abstraction or generalization. (Nor, of course, do I read "man" in this sentence as restricted to males.) In the way in which I understand this saying, then, it could perhaps be better expressed now by putting the reference in the plural form, saying that men and women are the measures. And, as I suggested in the preceding paragraph, I intend to broaden the reference here to include the idea of *something* human, something which pertains to individual human beings.

Protagoras said "man is *the* measure." The definite article there makes it sound as though there is only one evaluative standard, the one which is constituted by man. However, I want to explore a somewhat weaker claim, namely that man is *a* standard, one standard (perhaps one of several) for the evaluation of things. Or perhaps it will turn out that man (or, more properly, something human) is one element in a complex standard which also includes other elements. Weakening the apparent Protagorean claim in this way might, of course, lead to a thesis so weak as to be of little interest; I will argue, however, that the man-standard, though perhaps only one of several, or only one element in a complex combination, is a crucial and irreplaceable measure.

Finally, Protagoras says here "man is the measure of *all things*." I am not going to defend the universality of that claim. Instead, here too I want to assert a somewhat weaker thesis — that the man-standard is a crucial and irreplaceable measure of the worth of *some* things; in particular, it is crucial in the measurement of philosophical work.

Combining these interpretive glosses, we can recast Protagoras's brief and punchy sentence into the more cumbersome form: "There is a crucial human element, an element which relates to particular men and women, in the proper measure, the evaluative standard, for philosophical work."

Now, the rustling of the ghost from Protagoras's grave has become somewhat more evident. We may as well call him by his own name now; I suppose he is already so provoked that nothing will rouse him much further. The true name of this ghost is "Relativism."

The ghost comes, as I understand it, to ask whether we are willing to pay him his due. His name, he says, represents his birthright. He is the guardian of relativistic judgments. He sees that we are encroaching on his territory when we think of adopting my thesis, my interpretation of Protagoras's provocative sentence. He sees, that is, that if we accept the Protagorean *dictum,* the *Homo Mensura,* in the way in which I have interpreted it, then we are saying that the worth of philosophical work and what makes it good or bad is relative to individual men and women, and that consequently the aims of philosophical endeavor should be adjusted to those individuals. We relativize philosophy to a human standard and to human limitations.

This cold ghost, I know, is in bad repute among Christians and perhaps particularly among Christian philosophers; but I have come to appreciate him more than I used to. I hope to make him somewhat more welcome among us generally. I suggest that we should indeed pay him his due.

Let me say a little here about the notion attached to the word "relative." I intend an idea which is close to that which we have in mind when we ask someone whether she has any relatives living in The Netherlands. We think of special ways in which the woman might be linked to some other person. The usual links for these "familial" relations are genetic and biological (e.g., being born of the same parents) or socio-legal (e.g., being married to someone) or some combination of biological and legal factors (e.g., being the brother of one's spouse). The people, if any, who have these links to this woman are her relatives. She is related to them, and they to her. In a similar way when I say that the measure of philosophy is relative, I mean to say that this measure provides an evaluation of philosophy on the basis of whether the philosophical work has certain kinds of links with particular human beings. One example of such a link is that of *belief.* There will be an evaluative criterion, I suggest, which depends on whether there is a suitable person who believes a suitable element in the philosophical work.

There are at least two further ways in which the evaluative relativism which I intend to defend is analogous to ordinary familial relationships. First, we may notice that when someone is an aunt, for example, the interrogative pronoun, "Who" and its cognates, is relevant and applicable. Whose aunt is she and who is the nephew or niece to whom she is related? We may not know the answer to that question, of course, and, for that matter, the aunt herself may not know it either. But there has to *be* an answer for it, in the sense that there has to be someone to whom she is related in that way. Being an aunt is a relation, and it requires someone on the other end of the relational link. She cannot be an aunt all by herself. In an analogous way, the Protagorean relations with which I am concerned all require the involvement of some particular human person. If there is no such person, then the Protagorean relation does not hold.

Second, a woman may be an aunt without being everybody's aunt. Being an aunt is not a universal relation. It can be (and among us it always is) highly particularistic. In an analogous way, the Protagorean relations with which I am concerned seem also to be particularistic. Thus, the virtues with which they are associated will attach to philosophic work only in relation to certain specific persons and not in relation to others. This particularity is, I think, probably the most disturbing feature of the ghost whom I have invited here this evening. For some people, it is the most troubling part of the price for his services. This price will be discussed somewhat further in the second lecture.

For now, however, we can at least see that a *belief,* which I have suggested as our initial example of a Protagorean evaluative criterion, readily exhibits these two analogues of the aunt relation. If something is believed, then there must be someone who believes it. And something may be believed by one person without thereby being believed by everyone else or perhaps even by anyone else.

Now we can often get a better grip on a notion if we have an idea of with what it is to be contrasted. We might ask, therefore, whether there are any non-Protagorean evaluative categories for philosophical work, categories that are not relativistic. Certainly there are, though maybe not as many as we might initially think. Perhaps the most prominent and most important among them is truth. Since these lectures are primarily about the more neglected Protagorean categories, I won't say all that much about truth. However, it may be useful to think about it briefly here, as a useful contrast with the Protagorean categories.

Some of you will recall a story about Calvin Coolidge, noted for his taciturn manner of speech. According to this story, Mr. Coolidge went to church alone one Sunday morning while Mrs. Coolidge, perhaps feeling indisposed, remained at home. When Mr. Coolidge returned, his wife pressed him for an account of the church service.

"What did the minister preach about?" she asked.

"He preached about sin," Mr. Coolidge replied and offered no further elaboration. But his wife was not satisfied with that.

"And what did he say about it?" she asked again.

Mr. Coolidge replied, "He is against it."

Well, that minister was perhaps a man who had a clear and concise point to make, and he got it across to his congregation. A preacher like that is someone to be emulated. Let me say bluntly, therefore, that I am in favor of truth. It seems to me that in our philosophical work we should aim at saying the truth, especially in the philosophy of religion where we deal with matters of high import and if we are Christians who profess to serve the God of truth.[4]

Normally, then, I would take it to be a serious defect in a piece of philosophical work if a false conclusion were drawn in it or if a falsehood were propounded and defended. Even if the conclusion drawn in an argu-

4. But might there be some occasions when falsehood is more appropriate than truth in the service of God? Some Christian philosophers have occasionally made some provocative suggestions to that effect. See, e.g.: Nicholas Wolterstorff, *Reason within the Bounds of Religion Alone,* 2nd ed. (Grand Rapids: Wm. B. Eerdmans Publishing Company, 1984), p. 156, n. 38.

ment were true, the argument might nevertheless depend upon a false premise, and I would take that to be a defect.

Taking the prospective view, I think that we should aim at deriving true conclusions in the course of our philosophical reflections, and we should aim at defending or recommending those conclusions by deriving them from true premises rather than from falsehoods and by deducing them validly rather than invalidly.

I do not intend, then, to deny the relevance or importance of non-relativistic evaluative categories such as truth. I do not deny that they are necessary elements in our evaluative arsenal. What I deny is that these non-relativistic criteria are *sufficient* for measuring philosophy.[5]

For the time being, at least, truth can serve as our example of a non-Protagorean category. What about the Protagorean categories, those which do involve an essential relation to human persons? Because philosophy is so directed toward cognitive concerns, one of the most prominent of such categories is that of *belief,* which I already mentioned. Perhaps, indeed, it is the most important of the Protagorean criteria for philosophy.

Initially I said that I made a negative evaluation of my attempt at philosophical apologetics in my friend's apartment some forty years ago. What constituted that attempt as a failure? It is quite possible, of course, that it fell short of more than one standard. At that dinner, I tried to formulate and defend an argument which concluded to the existence of God. I still suppose that this conclusion is true, so I am unwilling, even now, to fault my argument with respect to the truth of its conclusion. However, it is quite possible that I made some mistake with respect to truth elsewhere

---

5. Some of you may think of suggesting at this point that perhaps truth is itself a relativistic category after all. And others, no doubt, would bristle at any such suggestion. There is more than one version of the claim that truth is relative. I mention one briefly here to get it out of the way. There is a metaphysical view, perhaps traceable to Plato, to the effect that many of the properties which we ordinarily do not think of as relations — maybe all properties — really are relations after all. All properties really are relations between some substance and an ideal and abstract form. So, for example, on this view a tomato is green if and only if it bears a certain relation, sometimes called "participation," to the form of greenness. So a true proposition would be true in virtue of a certain relation, its participation of truth.

I don't want to say anything for or against this way of construing properties. This is not the sort of relation which I am considering here. The Protagorean relations are "man-relations," relations to human beings, not to ideal forms. And truth does not seem, to me anyway, to be constituted by a relation of that sort.

in the argument, in appealing to some premise or to some principle. I may have blundered somewhere in the logic and thus have made an invalid inference. Since I don't now remember the course of the conversation that evening in any useful detail, I cannot now identify those non-Protagorean faults, if there were any. But what I do seem to recall clearly about the evening is that my attempt failed according to the standard of belief. It did not generate the desired alteration of belief in the mind of my atheistic fellow guest. So far as I could tell, it did not even tend in that direction. To all appearances, at least, my argument had no cognitive effect at all.[6] And even if it had no defect of truth or logic, that failure with respect to belief — a Protagorean, relativistic failure — would, in my view at least, constitute a serious shortcoming in that enterprise.

I say "even if it had no defect of truth or logic." Of course, the failure in belief might have been due to a failure with respect to some non-relativistic ideal. Maybe I made a mistake in logic, for example, and the atheist saw through it. That would certainly have given him a plausible reason for rejecting my argument. In that case, maybe I would have done better with respect to belief if I had done better with respect to logic. It is also possible, however, that the failure of belief may have been independent of any non-relativistic failure. Perhaps the atheist did not end by believing my conclusion because he did not begin by believing my premises but that fact may have been independent of the truth of my premises. All of us human beings, atheists and theists alike, are finite knowers and finite believers. None of us believes every truth. The mere fact that some proposition is true does not guarantee that any particular person believes it, and it does not, in any useful sense, give anyone a reason for believing it.

Well, maybe it is clear enough that if we adopt a Protagorean category of belief as part of our evaluative machinery, then we have a ready way of saying something about what went wrong at the dinner party. Why should we build Protagoreanism into our evaluative machinery in the first place though? Why should we not make do with the absolutistic, non-Protagorean criteria — principally the criterion of *truth*, which perhaps has the widest applicability, adding for the case of arguments the criterion of

6. It is possible, of course, that it had some hidden effect about which I never heard. Perhaps it did eventually play a role in the conversion of that man to some theistic view of reality. That would be just one more example of the general fact that our actions often have effects which are hidden from us, and so our judgments about those actions are always subject to error.

logical validity (or something like *strength* for inductive arguments), and perhaps some other criteria of a similar non-relativistic sort? Why should these admirable properties be merely prominent elements in our evaluative criteria? Why should they not constitute the *whole* of our criterion?

The short answer is that the non-Protagorean criteria are simply not rigorous enough to generate a significant value in philosophy. A corollary is that they are so easily satisfied that they make philosophy into a trivial enterprise.

These answers seem to be crucial to my project of making the ghost welcome among us. We will welcome him, I think, only if we understand that we actually need him, only if we understand that what we can have in his absence is not enough. So I say that truth is a fine thing, but truth is not enough.

It is often suggested, I think, that belief is cheap while truth is a high and noble virtue, a pearl of great price. Going along with that is the view that belief is easy — anyone can have an opinion — but truth is hard, something which demands a rigorous discipline and represents an elevated level of intellectual achievement. These common reactions seem to me now to be, at best, misleading.

Whatever may be the case with belief, it is not an unambiguous fact that truth is hard. Truth is, in fact, a commonplace and easy to come by. It is very easy to speak the truth, and it is easy to hear the truth — and I don't mean merely the truth about trivial matters. It is easy to speak the truth about high and noble matters, about matters of profound importance. It is, for example, easy to speak the truth and to hear the truth too about the most profound elements of Christian theology. In fact, there are systematic strategies for easily achieving this result.

One can adopt, for example, what I call "The Dominican Strategy." I give it that name because it is so well-illustrated in the *Summa Theologica* of Thomas Aquinas, the great Dominican theologian and philosopher of the high Middle Ages. This work is divided into a large number of sections, called in the English translation "Questions," each of which identifies a moderately large topic for investigation. Question 30 of Part I, for example, is given the title, "The plurality of persons in God," and it is part of Thomas's exploration of the doctrine of the Trinity. These sections in turn are further divided into smaller units, each of which deals with a single, carefully formulated and limited point. All of the substantive claims, arguments, refutations, etc., are contained in these smallest sub-divisions of the

Summa. These smallest sub-divisions are called "Articles," but in fact in almost every one of them the point to be discussed is put in the form of a question.[7] For example, the topic of Article 1 of Question 30 is "Whether there are several persons in God?" Article 2 is given to "Whether there are more than three persons in God?" In Question 31, Article 1 deals with "Whether there is Trinity in God?" and Article 2 concerns "Whether the Son is other than the Father?"

These questions share a common format which will perhaps become evident when we notice that there is no article whose question is "How many persons are there in God?" The questions around which the arguments and discussions of the *Summa* are organized are all "yes or no" questions. They admit of only two candidate answers. We do not find here the large, open-ended questions which admit an indefinite range, or even a large range, of possible answers. I recall reading somewhere that this format reflects the practice of the live disputations in the Medieval Dominican houses of study. Apparently, in those schools a topic was not considered really suitable for a scholarly disputation until it had been put in the form of a yes or no question. Then it could be engaged by two disputants, each of whom would try to establish and defend one of the two possible answers to the question.

This format for a discussion has a consequence which, I suppose, would not have escaped notice by the Dominican scholars. The format guarantees that in every discussion of a well-formulated Dominican question one of the parties will be defending a truth. He may possibly give a poor defense of it, but, at the very worst, the conclusion which he tries to draw will be a truth. Suppose that you paid three dollars to sit in the balcony for an afternoon where you could listen to six Dominican disputations — the discussion, that is, of six Dominican questions. You would be guaranteed a minimum of six theological truths, and this guarantee would hold good regardless of the theological competence of the discussants. That is fifty cents per truth — perhaps not a bad bargain.

Would you not also be guaranteed at least six theological falsehoods? Indeed you would. The format has that consequence also. Perhaps you are worried that you might not be able to tell the truths from the falsehoods reliably, and that even the master of the disputation may not be competent enough to sort them out for you with perfect accuracy. You may well worry

---

7. A rare exception is Article 1 of Question 29, whose topic is given as "The definition of 'person.'"

about those things when you are about to lay down your three dollars for a seat in the balcony. It is only fifty cents or less per truth. But will you recognize the truth when it comes along? To engage in that sort of worry, however, and to think about it, you will need categories in addition to that of truth and falsehood. You need Protagorean categories of belief and recognition, relativistic categories which express and report some relation between the truths which are uttered in the disputation and yourself as a finite, human, cognitive agent.

Some of you will remember the story of Cassandra, mentioned briefly by Homer and then developed further by Aeschylus in his drama, *Agamemnon.* According to the story, Cassandra was a Trojan woman who had a remarkable gift of prophecy given to her by the god Apollo. But soon after the giving and receiving of this gift, Cassandra and Apollo had a falling out, and he then gave her a curse to go along with the gift. The curse was that no one would believe her prophecies.

When we hear about Cassandra and her gift, we may initially suppose that Cassandra must have been of great benefit to her community. Would it not be very valuable to have a citizen who could foresee impending invasions, earthquakes, and bountiful harvests? The curse shows that this judgment is somewhat rash. Apollo's curse did not interfere with the clarity of Cassandra's foresight; it did not introduce any element of falsehood into her predictions, it did not reduce the importance of the matters on which she offered her prophecies. The divine curse sapped the value from them entirely by cutting off a relation which was essential to that value. It seems that a prophecy which is not believed, regardless of what high truth it may contain, is of no more value than no prophecy at all. Cassandra retained the gift of prophecy, but Apollo robbed her of the *value* of that gift by depriving her of the services of that ghost who would later haunt Protagoras's tomb. Without his ghostly touch, the truths she uttered made no contact with human life. She might as well have remained silent.

We who attempt philosophy need the service of that ghost just as much as Cassandra needed it. If any modern-day Apollo succeeds in barring him from ivory towers, lecture rooms, or computer terminals, then our words shall be as futile as hers. I began with a story about a dinner party forty years ago in which my philosophical argumentation was as futile as Cassandra's prophesying. Like hers, my speech was futile in that it gathered no belief. So far as I could tell, I might as well have remained silent throughout the evening.

Of course, it may strike you that this was an attempt at positive apologetics, and belief is the avowed aim of that enterprise.[8] You might suggest that this example is too specialized to support a general thesis. There are, however, any number of other examples. The same can be said of a study in the history of philosophy, say on the philosophy of Immanuel Kant. Regardless of what virtues of truth and logic it may have, if in the end I understand the thought of Kant no better than before, then it has done me no good. Of course, the failure might be largely my fault. Wherever the fault lies, however, the fact remains that the author failed to do me any good.

Now, for a "worst-case" scenario, suppose that the same thing happens with every reader, so that in the end there is no one at all who actually benefits from that scholarly study. In what way is it better that the study was published than if it had not been published? In what way is it better that the study was done than if it had not been done?

Did I forget the author himself? May not the author have derived some benefit from his study even though none of his readers did? Certainly that is a possibility, and I do not mean to ignore it. *He* may now understand Kant better than he did, even if I do not. If that is so, then that piece of philosophical work was not entirely a failure. It has some success, perhaps a modest amount of success. But this virtue of his work is a relative virtue, a Protagorean virtue. His work was a success relative to him, but it was a failure relative to me. It improved his understanding, but it did not improve mine. The particularity of the relation which is relevant to this success is just as evident as is the fact that the author's aunt may not be my aunt.

However, the reminder that the one who does a piece of philosophical work may benefit from it himself or herself is valuable and we should not let it slip. The philosopher is himself or herself a "man," in the Protagorean aphorism, and is as well-suited to be a "measure" of philosophical worth as is any other human person. The worth of the work may derive from its relation to the doer as well as from its relation to the audience. And some philosophers at least profess that they work primarily for

8. At an earlier presentation of this thesis, a critic suggested that apologetics is not a properly philosophical enterprise at all. That seems to me implausible, but I will not argue it here, since the point at issue can be illustrated by many examples of other sorts of philosophical work.

some improvement in themselves. Anselm, for example, says in his preface to the *Proslogium* that he writes it "in the person of one who strives to lift his mind to the contemplation of God, and seeks to understand what he believes," adding that his first title for the book was "Faith Seeking Understanding." The first chapter ends with the prayer, "I long to understand in some degree thy truth, which my heart believes and loves. For I do not seek to understand that I may believe, but I believe in order to understand." And the second chapter opens with a continuation of the prayer, "And so, Lord, do thou, who dost give understanding to faith, give me, so far as thou knowest it to be profitable, to understand that thou art as we believe; and that thou art that which we believe."[9]

This suggests that Anselm himself did not think of the *Proslogium* as a work of apologetics, even though it contains what is probably the most celebrated argument for the existence of God in the history of western philosophy. Anselm apparently did not construe his book as one which was addressed to the project of bringing unbelievers into the Christian faith or even into some more general form of theism. He undertakes this reflection as someone who is already a Christian believer and one who expresses no doubt about the truth of that faith. He wishes to deepen his own spiritual life in some way. He prays that God will give him something — understanding, as he calls it — which will result in or will be a part of such a deepening. Perhaps Anselm's project is continued today by some of those who reflect upon what is sometimes called "philosophical theology."

Even if Anselm is not here an apologist, is he not engaged in an enterprise in which he might succeed or might fail? And must not the measure of his success or failure be in the end a Protagorean measure? Anselm said that he longed "to understand in some degree thy truth." It seems, then, that if his philosophical reflection actually did contribute to some deepening of his understanding of the divine truth, then it had some success. But if, in fact, Anselm understood the truth no better after writing this book than he did before, would that not be a failure?[10]

I hope to have convinced you that we should welcome this ghost, the ghost who answers to the name of "Relativism," into the study, the lecture

9. Anselm, *Proslogium*, trans. Sidney Norton Deane (La Salle, Ill.: The Open Court Publishing Company, 1951), preface, chs. 1 and 2 (pp. 2, 7).

10. It might be a noble failure. We need not dread failure, especially in undertaking a high and difficult project. But we should not *aim* at failure. To undertake a project seriously is to try to succeed in it.

room, the publishing house of philosophy. I have argued that we need him, that without him philosophical reflection, philosophical argument, philosophical analysis cannot achieve a value which is relevant to human life. The ghost cannot do it by himself, but the non-relativistic virtues, such as truth, cannot do it without the ghost. Nevertheless, I think that some of you still fear that this ghost will demand, in the end, too high a price for his assistance. Next, I will try to address that fear, and I will consider some proposed strategies for bargaining with the ghost, in an effort to reduce his price.

Second Lecture

In the first of this two-part series, I argued that we cannot properly evaluate philosophical work unless we can appeal to Protagorean, relativistic categories. I did not argue that the relativistic categories are sufficient measures of philosophy, and in fact I do not believe that. I think that a proper measure of philosophy must also appeal to non-relativistic criteria, such as *truth* and *logical validity*. But I did argue that these non-relativistic criteria are not sufficient measures of philosophy; they do not sufficiently represent the worth, the value of philosophical work and its contribution to the bettering of human intellectual life. So I proposed that we invite and welcome the ghost in whose domain those other criteria belong, the ghost whose name is "Relativism."

Some of you will remember that there is an old saying, "He who sups with the devil needs a long spoon." There is truth in that, although supping with the devil is probably not the worst thing that can happen to a philosopher. Supping with a devil's advocate, for example, may be worse, a dreary and fruitless enterprise. One needs for that not only a long spoon but also a dash of jalapeño salsa to enliven the meal. At any rate, here we are for the second course of our dinner with the ghost. Let us arm ourselves with whatever length of spoon will make us feel comfortable and start on the soup.

I propose that we begin now by agreeing (even if tentatively) that a successful piece of philosophical work must have some virtue besides that of truth, valid reasoning, and the like. What else might it have of a more Protagorean nature? I suggested that *belief* is one of the most important of the Protagorean criteria. If a successful piece of philosophy must make some positive contribution to human intellectual life, then a plausible place to look for such a benefit is in making a difference with respect to

393

our beliefs. Philosophical reasoning might enable us to have a true belief which we would not otherwise have had, to retain a true belief which we would otherwise have lost, or to abandon a false belief which we would otherwise have retained. Perhaps there are other ways in which philosophy might, and sometimes does, deepen and nourish our intellectual lives, but for the purposes of this lecture I will focus on belief.

Suppose we take the prospective view which I mentioned in part one, and use this criterion of *belief* not just to evaluate some philosophy already done but rather to guide us in doing some piece of philosophy. What might such a prospective approach amount to in practice? We can try our hands at a comparatively easy sort of case which, in fact, is fairly common in philosophy. This is the situation in which I already have some conviction of my own, one about which I am not much troubled, for the present at least. I know that there are some other people who do not share this conviction or at least seem not to share it. So I think of recommending my conviction to them. I will try to give them a reason to believe what I believe. How would that go?

If I think of doing this by means of some piece of philosophical work, then almost surely the idea of formulating an argument in support of my conviction will occur to me. That may not be the only way in which I can recommend my belief, but this strategy has loomed so large in the history of western philosophy that it is now almost sure that I will consider using it. To follow up on the story with which I began part one, and at the same time to choose an example which is likely to be of some interest (though now the project becomes far from easy), I will suppose that the belief which I want to recommend and for which I propose to supply a reason is the belief that God exists. Where can we go from there?

We want an argument which has "God exists" for its conclusion. So far, that's not hard. We can begin by taking a sheet of paper, leaving some blank lines at the top for the premises, and then writing in, "Therefore, God exists" at the bottom. That's not the whole argument, of course, since we haven't yet put in the premises, but it is a start.

You may recall that I said I was in favor of truth — not merely truth in advertising, but truth in philosophy. Well, so far as I can see, this beginning fragment of an argument satisfies that ambition, that criterion. It has truth in its conclusion. I also professed to accept the criterion of truth in the premises of the argument and logical validity in the derivation of the conclusion from the premises? Can we now find a set of premises which are true and which validly entail the conclusion which we have already written in? Some philosophers and logicians use the word "sound" as a technical term to identify an argument of this sort, and I will follow that usage here. If we can think of a sound argument for our desired conclusion, then we will have an argument which satisfies at least the major non-Protagorean criteria for a successful piece of philosophical reasoning.

So far, our desired argument is described entirely in non-Protagorean terms, just in the non-relativistic terms of truth and validity. At this point, therefore, the ghost has no claim upon us — he will leave us in peace, and we need have no truck with him. We need not worry, so far, about the length of our spoons.

Can we, then, produce a sound argument for the existence of God? Some people apparently think that is a very difficult thing to do — but that can't be right. Either the desired argument, as it has been described so far, is very easy to produce — so easy that I can do it myself without breaking a sweat — or else it is absolutely impossible, beyond even the power of God to achieve. It cannot just be hard. There is nothing special about the existence of God in this. These consequences follow from the concept of a sound argument, regardless of its conclusion.

Now, if it is impossible to produce a sound argument for the existence of God, then it is false that God exists. That's what would make the desired argument impossible. However, I think that God does exist, and I suppose that some others also think so. Therefore, I propose to go along the other track, at least for a while, exploring what we might need to do after we do what's easy.

Let's suppose, therefore, that we have a theistic argument which satisfies the criteria of truth and logic. I said that I would like to recommend theistic belief to someone. How could my argument connect with the "unbeliever" to whom I am making this recommendation? Recently I saw a cartoon in the *Ann Arbor News*. It shows a man, apparently a job applicant, being interviewed. On the wall behind the interviewer there is a sign which says "Security Clearance Required." The applicant is saying, "Oh, I'm very good at keeping secrets. Nobody pays any attention to me." Well, in this case I'm presumably not trying to keep my conclusion secret. It's just the opposite. I want to share it; I would like to have my hearers accept my conclusion. But what if I have a problem like Rodney Dangerfield, and (as he often says) "I can't get no respect"? Or more specifically, maybe my argument doesn't get any respect.

Let me put forward still another conjecture which seems plausible to me. Some arguments for the existence of God don't get much respect, from some hearers anyway, because the premises from which those arguments begin don't appeal to those hearers. Those premises don't strike the hearers as being true. They don't find those premises among the stock of beliefs which they already hold. In fact, they may positively think that one or another of those premises is false. Since they don't accept the truth of the premises, it is not surprising that they do not find in that argument a reason to accept the truth of the conclusion. So it may well turn out that our argument, so far, is a miserable failure along this line — worse than a replacement baseball player.

If that is so, then we have our work cut out for us. We need to recast our argument or maybe find a completely new argument so that without losing the virtues of truth and validity the new argument makes contact with already existing and functioning intellectual life of the hearers. While the project of constructing a sound argument for the existence of God is really easy, this latter task — that of constructing a sound *and intellectually effective argument* — may not be easy at all. It may turn out to be an utterly daunting task.

If we try it, however, we will be engaged in a search for what has sometimes been called "common ground" — a starting point which is shared between ourselves and the unbeliever. Let me, in passing, call your attention to the word "common" in that phrase. It suggests that what we are seeking is something which we share with the unbeliever, something which belongs to both of us. It is quite possible for me to construct a valid argument for the existence of God beginning with premises which I do not believe. Some of those arguments may, by accident, turn out to be sound as well as valid. I might even, by a second lucky accident, hit on an argument of that sort which has premises that the unbeliever accepts, and which, therefore, may be attractive to him or her. That argument, though it might be effective, would not begin from *common* ground. It would begin from my interlocutor's ground, but not from mine, even though it led to my conclusion. It would be *insincere*. In asserting the premises, even if they happened to be true, I would not be asserting what I really believed.

Sincerity and *insincerity* are Protagorean categories. The very same argument put forward by someone who had beliefs different from mine might be perfectly sincere. One and the same argument would be insincere relative to me and sincere relative to her. I'm inclined to think that sincerity is an important virtue in philosophical work, and we should aim for it.

We would be looking for something which is common to us and our interlocutors. That certainly looks, initially at least, like a Protagorean project. My success in that project must be measured against the "man-standard," measured by whether I and my interlocutors really do stand on the ground which I allege to be common. If we do, then well and good. If we do not have those shared beliefs, then so far I have failed in my project.

It seems pretty clear to me that theists do have some common ground with many people who are not theists. It is hard to see how theists and non-theists could cooperate to the extent that they do in work, in games, in schools, in commerce, sometimes even in a single nuclear family, unless they characteristically shared many beliefs. All of you can think of your own examples of that. Of course, I don't share all of the beliefs of my non-Christian friends. Then again, I don't share all of the beliefs of my Christian friends either. All of us have a lot of beliefs, and probably we share a different subset of them with each of the various people with whom we come in contact. Whatever I do share with some other person, however, is the common ground between us.

So I have common ground with my non-Christian friends. It does not follow, however, that this common ground could supply the premises of a sound and effective theistic argument — a reason for belief in God. What is common between us might not be rich enough to support a valid inference to the theistic conclusion.

Such a failure, however, does not imply that I have no true beliefs which entail the divine existence. It does not even imply that the atheist has no true beliefs which entail the divine existence. All it implies is that the beliefs which we share do not have that entailment. If that is so, then there is no sound argument for God *from our common ground*.

That is a sort of worst-case scenario for our project. Of course, it is a worst-case scenario only relative to that particular friend.[1] There could be some other non-believing friend with whom I share a rather different common ground which does in fact provide suitable premises.

This situation exhibits again, of course, the stock features of relativ-

---

1. It may also be a worst-case scenario only relative to me. Some other Christian theist may share with that same atheist a common ground which does entail the divine existence.

ism which make it seem so distressing to many of us. I may possibly hit on an argument which is successful with the second of these friends, but that argument will not be successful with the first one. The success is relative to this person and to that one and is not an independent property of the argument considered in isolation.

There may be people who are suspicious of this second scenario, and there are two versions of this suspicion or objection.

The first version holds that there is no common ground at all between Christians and others; they live in totally disparate intellectual worlds. I have already said almost all that I can say about this version, when I said that it seems pretty hard to see how we could get along as well as we do if this theory were true. I might add, however, that if Christian theism is true, then the atheist is, just like the Christian, a person whom God has created, and the atheist, just like the Christian, lives in a world which God has created. There is, after all, no other world for him or her to live in. Is it not straining things to suppose that such a person could not have some true beliefs about the world, beliefs which they might share with some Christians?

The second version of this objection is more modest, but it would be equally damaging to my second scenario. It does not deny that there may be *some* common ground here, but it denies that there could be common ground sufficient for a sound theistic argument. Atheists, just because they are atheists, do not have the basis for theistic belief. This may be put forward as a thesis in logic. Would it not be flatly and logically inconsistent for an atheist to accept premises which entail that God exists?

It may be useful here to notice that there could be two somewhat different kinds of atheism, sometimes called positive and negative atheism.[2] Positive atheists do not have the belief that God exists; instead they believe that there is no God. Negative atheists also do not have the belief that God exists, but neither do they believe that there is no God. They have no belief either way about God. Perhaps, for example, they have just been too busy and preoccupied with other things ever to give any thought to the question of God, and so they have never formed any belief at all on this subject.

A negative atheist who had some beliefs which entailed that God exists would not thereby be involved in a logical inconsistency for she does not have the belief that there is no God. The worst that we could say of

2. See, e.g., Michael Martin, *Atheism* (Philadelphia: Temple University Press, 1990), p. 26.

such people would be that they do not believe everything which is entailed by the things they believe. That is perhaps an imperfection in an intellectual life, but if it is, then it is an imperfection which all of us as Christians have also. None of us believes all of the things which are entailed by the beliefs which we actually have. Perhaps, indeed, it would be impossible for any finite believer to achieve that ideal.

The situation of positive atheists is somewhat different. These people, by definition, have the positive belief that there is no God. If they also have some beliefs which entail that there is a God, then they do have a logically inconsistent set of beliefs. Why should that fact be taken as an objection to the second scenario? Are we to suppose that atheists cannot be inconsistent in this way? Must every atheist be a walking handbook of logic? It hardly seems so. For that matter, must we suppose that every Christian is a textbook of that sort? Or even that any of us are? For myself, I think that it is practically certain that I have inconsistent beliefs: it is so likely to be true that I have no heart at all for denying it. It seems to me, indeed, that this failing is likely to be part of the common human condition in this present world, at least as common as tooth decay. I cannot see why we should not avail ourselves of each other's true beliefs to help each other to be rid of some false beliefs. In this way we would, in fact, help each other to be rid of some inconsistencies also.

If I could actualize the second scenario, then I might have (in my opinion, at least) a successful piece of philosophical work. I might have succeeded in recommending theistic belief in such a way as actually to contribute something which made a difference in someone's belief — an improvement in belief. I say "might" here, however, because even the sort of argument which I have described would not *guarantee* that my interlocutor would adopt a theistic belief. People to whom such an argument is presented have at least three options. They might adopt the conclusion of the argument, since they now see that it is entailed by premises which they believe to be true. That is, presumably, the happy outcome for which I was hoping. They may also decide to reject the conclusion, while continuing to retain their former beliefs. They would, that is, simply resolve to live with a recognized inconsistent set of beliefs.[3]

---

3. We should not be quick to scoff at this choice, for there may be a kind of sense in it. Logical inconsistency may not be the worst thing that can happen to a person, and the cost of removing the inconsistency may strike the person as one which is too high

The third option for the atheist would be to invert my argument, take atheism as a premise, and infer (as a conclusion) that at least one of my premises is false. This inverted argument will have essentially the same logic as my own argument had, so one cannot choose between them on the basis of logic alone. It too will have premises which the atheist believes. Perhaps that argument will be more attractive to him or her than my argument was. The net result of my formulating a sound argument for theism may turn out to be that the atheist remains an atheist and gives up one or more true beliefs to boot.

Because there will always be these other options, no argument can fully guarantee an improvement in intellectual life. But if any argument has a shot at it, then it would seem that one of the sort we have been describing would be a good candidate — an argument whose premises are true, whose logic is valid, and which links up with beliefs which the hearer already acknowledges. That last factor, of course, is the Protagorean element. The ghost from Protagoras's grave is no doubt here. He is here to ask that we acknowledge the characteristic features of relativism, the ways in which the value of our argument is vulnerable to the idiosyncrasies and differences in the various human persons in which the "man-standard" is to be found.

I said previously that some of us may think that this is too high a price to pay, and we might cast about for some way to bargain with the ghost over this cost. Let me quote for you a striking example of such an attempt by Ralph McInerny, a contemporary admirer of the work of Thomas Aquinas. McInerny is speaking of the project of natural theology as it was attempted by Thomas and other theologian-philosophers of the Medieval period, and he says the following:

> The notion of philosophizing that emerges from such discussions is this. No matter how arcane and sophisticated a philosophical discussion becomes, it is in principle possible for the philosopher to lead the discussion back to starting points which are available to any man in virtue of his being human. Philosophical doctrines do not appeal to some special knowledge or insight had by the few, though only a few

---

for him or her to pay. Nicholas Wolterstorff, for example, has suggested that Christians may have a duty to retain their belief in God even in the face of contrary arguments in which they can find no flaw. See his "Can Belief in God be Rational If It Has No Foundations?" in Alvin Plantinga and Nicholas Wolterstorff, eds., *Faith and Rationality* (Notre Dame, Ind.: University of Notre Dame Press, 1983), pp. 176, 177.

may succeed in arriving at these doctrines. However chancy arrival at the *terminus ad quem* may be, the *terminus a quo* is where each and everyone of us already is. That is why a theology based on natural reason must be able to show how truths about God are derived from truths about the world and depend ultimately on truths no man can gainsay.[4]

Regardless of whether McInerny is here representing the Medieval project of natural theology accurately, it seems pretty clear that he is stating his own ideal for that project. You will realize, of course, that he and I share some of that ideal. Like me, McInerny recognizes that not any old argument with true premises will achieve the value at which philosophy aims. He recognizes the need for premises which catch us where we are, some common ground as the launching place for the philosophical endeavor. Unlike me, however, McInerny seems unwilling to pay his dues to the ghost. He is not content to have his natural theologian find some common ground with some unbeliever and thus to find a starting point for an argument which might have a limited, though real, range of success. McInerny insists on a *universal* common ground, a ground which is common not just to you and me or to me and some atheist friend. According to McInerny the ground must be common to *all* of us, "available to any man in virtue of his being human." To satisfy him, we must begin from a point "where each and everyone of us already is," appealing to "truths which no man can gainsay."

This is the notion of common ground with a vengeance. If it is satisfied, however, then I suppose we can have relativism without particularism which is something like finding an uncle who is everyone's uncle. The success of a theistic argument will still depend upon its relation to actual human beings. We will have a relation which is such that, if an argument has that relation to any one person, then it must have that relation to every person. If any one of us is standing on McInerny's common ground then everyone is standing there. Arguments which satisfy McInerny's criterion will not be vulnerable to the idiosyncrasies and differences among human beings. They will be grounded, instead, at a level beneath all the idiosyncrasies, a level at which there are no differences. Here, indeed, is a philosopher who has a really high ambition for philosophy or at least for natural theology and theistic argumentation.

4. Ralph McInerny, "On Behalf of Natural Theology," in *Proceedings of the American Catholic Philosophical Association*, vol. LIV (1980), p. 64.

McInerny does not have this merely as an ideal, however. He apparently thinks that this ideal has actually been achieved by the great Medieval philosopher-theologians, such as Thomas, and perhaps even before them by Aristotle. I think of the joke which begins by asking "What is a philosopher?" The reply is that "A philosopher is a blind man, in a dark basement, looking for a black cat that isn't there." Then a cynic adds that "A theologian is just like a philosopher, except that he comes up with the cat." If Thomas, or anyone else, really has come up with this cat, which is a theistic argument which satisfies the McInerny criterion, then we have at hand not merely a high ambition but also a really high achievement in philosophy. For that argument would appear to have the virtue which I envisioned for my second scenario only multiplied a million-fold.

Where is that argument? Evidently it is not in the *Summa Theologica*. Thomas's formulation there of five lines of world-based argument for the existence of God has been enormously provocative and suggestive, an inspiration to hopeful natural theologians from his own time down to the present. Is it not also evident in the history of philosophy from then to now that those arguments have also been the source of intense controversy? Are the Thomistic arguments really based on "truths no man can gainsay"? I'm not asking whether they are based on truths, but rather whether their bases, true or not, are such that no man can gainsay them. It seems to me that the claim that Thomas used premises of that sort must be among the very best examples of an empirically refuted historical claim about philosophy.

We need not go very far into history to refute it, because contemporary philosophy is full of people who gainsay the Thomistic premises. Of course, the first sentence of some of the Thomistic arguments states a commonplace as a premise — "some things are in motion," for example. It may be a little difficult to find someone to deny *those* premises. However, the Thomistic arguments cannot get going on the basis of such premises alone. For example, Michael Martin, a contemporary critic, points out that the argument from contingency and necessity appeals to the principle that "there could not be something brought into existence by nothing."[5] Martin then observes that this "is by no means self-evident. At least, given the

5. Michael Martin, *Atheism*, p. 99. Thomas's own formulation of the principle is "that which does not exist begins to exist only through something already existing." *Summa Theologica*, Part I, Q. 2, Art. 3.

biblical authority of the book of Genesis, where God created the world out of nothing, it should not have seemed so to Aquinas. For if God could create the world out of nothing, one might suppose that something could be spontaneously generated out of nothing without God's help."[6] He goes on to add that speculations about the spontaneous generation of the universe from nothing are now being taken seriously by some scientific cosmologists and philosophers of science.

Martin is a professed atheist. Alvin Plantinga, who is not an atheist however, expresses a somewhat similar reservation about this principle, saying that "there are reasons for doubting that [this principle] is self-evident or necessarily true. Is it not logically possible that an elementary particle (or for that matter a full-grown horse) should just pop into existence, uncaused by anything else? It is certainly hard to detect any inconsistency in that notion."[7]

It seems unlikely, to say the least, that any argument about which such opinions are expressed should be taken as satisfying the McInerny criterion. We need not deny the nobility of the ambition which is incorporated in that ideal. However, I have no confidence at all in its feasibility. I should like to see some reason for supposing that there is any common ground of the sort which McInerny envisages, any substantial body of belief which is shared universally in the human race.[8]

The quotations which I have just cited from Martin and Plantinga make use of the term "self-evident." That suggests another, though perhaps related, way in which we might attempt to escape from the demands of the ghost. We might escape from relativism, or at least alleviate the demands it makes, by basing our theistic arguments not merely on truths but on *self-evident* truths.

What is self-evidence? The definition suggested by Thomas Reid in the 18th century contains elements which are often repeated in later formulations, and it is worth quoting:

6. Martin, *Atheism,* p. 100.

7. Alvin Plantinga, *God and Other Minds* (Ithaca, N.Y.: Cornell University Press, 1967), p. 13.

8. That there is no common ground of the sort McInerny needs does not entail that there are some people who have no beliefs which entail the existence of God. For it might be the case that everyone has some set or other of true beliefs which have the theistic entailment, but there is no *one* such set which is shared by everyone.

In propositions that are submitted to our judgment, there is this great difference; some are of such a nature that a man of ripe understanding may apprehend them distinctly, and perfectly understand their meaning without finding himself under any necessity of believing them to be true or false, probable or improbable. The judgment remains in suspense, until it is inclined to one side or another by reasons or arguments.

But there are other propositions which are no sooner understood than they are believed. The judgment follows the apprehension of them necessarily, and both are equally the work of nature, and the result of our original powers. There is no searching for evidence; no weighing of arguments; the proposition is not deduced or inferred from another; it has the light of truth in itself, and has no occasion to borrow it from another.

Propositions of the last kind, when they are used in matters of science, have commonly been called *axioms;* and on whatever occasion they are used, are called *first principles, principles of common sense, common notions, self-evident truths.*[9]

There are two separable elements in Reid's characterization of a self-evident truth. One is that these truths "are no sooner understood than they are believed." Apparently, then, for these propositions understanding them is immediately sufficient for believing them — immediately sufficient, that is, in the temporal sense.

The other element in Reid's description of self-evidence is that belief in self-evident propositions is not generated by a consideration of evidence or by induction or deduction from other beliefs. This element makes a self-evident belief sound very much like a "basic" belief, as that notion has figured in philosophical speculation and controversy over the past couple of decades.

Reid may have taken these two characterizations to be equivalent, but they are not. Imagine that I come upon some proposition which I have never considered before — perhaps the claim that a full-grown horse could not spring into existence spontaneously without the action of some already existing agent. Suppose that I think about that proposition until I

9. Thomas Reid, *Essays on the Intellectual Powers of Man* (1785) (Cambridge, Mass.: The M.I.T. Press, 1969), p. 593 (Essay VI, Chap. IV).

understand it as well as can be. Suppose further that I am still puzzled as to whether it is true. It would seem, then, that this proposition is not self-evident according to the first element of Reid's criterion.

Suppose that as I think about this proposition I find a conviction about it growing in me, so that at the end of a fortnight I have a firm assurance that it is true. Suppose also that I have not come to that conviction by considering any evidence, nor by inferring or deducing that proposition from anything else which I believe. Perhaps, indeed, I have no idea of what kind of thing would constitute evidence for the impossibility which is alleged in that proposition, and I don't think of any other beliefs of mine which seem to be relevant to it. Nevertheless, at the end of the two weeks I am firmly convinced that it is true. That would seem to make the proposition self-evident according to Reid's second element.

This second part of Reid's criterion identifies an epistemologically interesting fact about some beliefs, namely that they are not based on any external evidence. They would, therefore, seem to be held on no evidence whatsoever, or else they somehow generate or constitute evidence for themselves.[10] On the other hand, I fail to see what difference is made by the presence or absence of Reid's first element, that of the temporal immediacy of belief following understanding. I will, therefore, not say much more about that first element.

Reid's definition, however, may invite us to choose between another pair of alternatives and this choice may be more important. We might understand Reid's account in a thoroughly Protagorean way, as providing us with a notion which belongs squarely within the domain of the ghost — the idea, that is, of a proposition which is self-evident to you or to me or to someone else. We would take Reid to be saying that if there is some proposition which I believe without appealing to any evidence, without inferring it, then that proposition is self-evident to me.[11] That would leave open the possibility that some other people might not believe that proposition at all, even though they understood it. Still others might believe it on the ba-

---

10. In the following discussion I will continue to refer to "self-evident" propositions, in deference to Reid. But I do not know why that description of them should be thought better than simply saying that they are believed without evidence at all and the latter may in the end be more straightforward.

11. Reid seems to want to include the notion of *truth* in that of *self-evidence*. If we want to follow him in this we could insert "true" as a qualifier for the propositions involved here.

sis of some evidence or inference. To people of both these latter classes the proposition would not be self-evident.

The other way to understand Reid is in a thoroughly universalistic way. It construes him as saying that some propositions have a property ("the light of truth in itself"?) whose effect is that everyone who understands them must believe them and must believe them independently of evidence and inference. Understood in this way, self-evidence turns out to be a universal relation. If a proposition has that relation at all, then it has that relation to every human being. Self-evidence of this sort would provide an escape at least from the particularism which is, for some of us, so repellent a feature of relativism.

Most of what Reid says about self-evident propositions suggests to me that he thinks about self-evidence in the second, universalistic way and not in the Protagorean way. However, not everything in Reid points in that direction, and maybe he did not clearly consider these two alternatives. In any case, we can pursue the matter a little further ourselves by recurring to the sort of question which I asked in connection with McInerny. Is there any reason for supposing that there are any self-evident propositions or any which have any interesting logical consequences?

Reid himself says, "I take it for granted, that there are self-evident principles. Nobody, I think, denies it."[12] Well, there certainly seem to me to be self-evident propositions *in the Protagorean sense*. There seem to me to be a lot of propositions which I now believe, but for which I would not now say (with a straight face) that I believe on the basis of some evidence or because I infer them from some other belief of mine. Maybe there are even some propositions which I believed as soon as I understood them.[13] On the Protagorean reading, these propositions (or at least the true ones) would be self-evident to me. I think there is a good argument for the claim that every finite knower is related to some propositions in this way. I will come to that argument very shortly.

Read in the universalistic way, however, I myself am inclined to deny that there are any self-evident propositions. To put it somewhat more cautiously, I have very little confidence in the claim that there are such propo-

12. Reid, *Essays on Intellectual Powers*, p. 594.

13. I once wrote a short story about someone who made just such a claim about a surprising proposition. "The Stranger" in Alvin Plantinga and Nicholas Wolterstorff, eds., *Faith and Rationality*, pp. 94-102.

sitions. That claim seems to me to be itself in need of considerable evidence.

Now, it is a curious fact that Reid, though he says that no one denies the existence of self-evident propositions, soon proposes an argument in support of them. I quote Reid's argument:

> I hold it to be certain, and even demonstrable, that all knowledge got by reasoning must be built upon first principles.
>
> This is as certain as that every house must have a foundation. The power of reasoning, in this respect, resembles the mechanical powers of engines; it must have a fixed point to rest upon, otherwise it spends its force in the air, and produces no effect.
>
> When we examine, in the way of analysis, the evidence of any proposition, either we find it self-evident, or it rests upon one or more propositions that support it. The same thing may be said of the propositions that support it; and of those that support them, as far back as we can go. But we cannot go back in this track to infinity. Where then must this analysis stop? It is evident that it must stop only when we come to propositions, which support all that are built upon them, but are themselves supported by none, that is, to self-evident propositions.[14]

There is something curious about this argument in the context of Reid's claim. This is a very strong argument in support of the claim that every finite reasoner must begin with propositions which are self-evident to him or to her — self-evident, that is, in the Protagorean sense. However, it is a very weak argument if it is applied to the claim that there are propositions which are self-evident in the universalistic sense.

Reid's argument is analogous to an argument which shows that if I now own a car then I must sometime have owned a first car — a car, that is, such that I owned no other car before that one. The line of argument is simple and powerful. I own a car now. Perhaps I did not own any car prior to this one. In that case, my present car is my first car, and the argument comes quickly to the desired end. On the other hand, perhaps I did own a previous car, and maybe one before that and so on. But I am only a finite owner. I cannot have owned an infinite series of cars. So that back-tracking series must come somewhere to an end, in a car which was not preceded, in

14. Reid, *Essays on Intellectual Powers*, p. 596.

my ownership, by any other car. That was my first car. In fact I did have a first car, a Pontiac which I inherited upon the death of my father.

The same line of argument will, of course, show that anyone here who now owns a car must sometime have owned a first car. It does not tend to show that my first car is the same car as your first car. It does not even tend to show that my first car was the same make, model, or style as your first car. It does not tend to show that there is some particular car or even some style or model of car which is uniquely suited to be a first car or better suited than other cars.

Assuming that the evidence relation is linear and not circular and that we are finite believers who do not have an infinite set of evidentially ordered beliefs, Reid's argument shows that anyone who has any beliefs at all has some beliefs which are not evidentially based on his or her other beliefs.[15] Those unbased beliefs seem to satisfy the second part of Reid's definition of self-evidence, *if that definition is read in the Protagorean sense.* However, nothing in Reid's argument tends to show that these believers need to have the same proposition as their starting point. It does not support the universalistic reading of Reid's claim. The fact that Reid gives this argument in support of what seems otherwise to be a universalistic notion of self-evidence suggests to me that Reid may never have clearly distinguished these senses.

However that may be, I do not know of any strong reason to suppose that there are any self-evident beliefs in the universalistic sense, especially any which have any interesting logical consequences. The fact that I do not know such a reason, of course, is not very strong evidence that there is no such reason. Maybe someone will propose such a reason, and I can consider it. For now, however, I speak for myself, from where I stand. I am inclined to think that if we are to engage in theistic argumentation at all — indeed, if we are to engage in any serious enterprise in philosophy — then we must be prepared to pay the ghost his due. We cannot measure the positive worth of philosophy, either retrospectively or more importantly prospectively, without making use of relativistic, "man-measure," notions and criteria. So we must be prepared to accept a relativistic and particularistic

---

15. It is essential to this line of argument that we be finite believers. The argument will not apply to an infinite knower, so it cannot be used to show that some things are self-evident to God. I discuss this further in "How Does God Know the Things He Knows?" in Thomas V. Morris, ed., *Divine & Human Action* (Ithaca, N.Y.: Cornell University Press, 1988), pp. 345-61.

idea of success, and to value modest achievements, even if we continue to aim higher. The ghost from Protagoras's tomb does not seem to me to be so fearsome as he once did. He has indeed sometimes been recruited for an unworthy cause — that of eating away the truth. In that cause he is rightly resisted. However, this ghost survives a thousand exorcisms, a thousand denunciations and refutations, because there is also in him some life blood of truth. I hope that I have made him somewhat more welcome here. Let us see how far we can make him our friend, and even our teacher, in the intellectual life which may be our particular part of the divine calling.

The Soul of the Christian University

ARTHUR F. HOLMES

Contents

What Has Jerusalem to Do with Alexandria?

Over the past few years, we have been treated to a variety of books lamenting the state of higher education in America. You probably recall some of the titles: *The Closing of the American Mind, Exiles from Eden,* George Marsden's much-discussed work, *The Soul of the American University,* and, more recently, *The Abandoned Generation.* For laments about Christian higher education and intellectual life, including seminaries, we have *No Place for Truth, The Scandal of the Evangelical Mind,* and Douglas Sloan's insightful study of mainline Protestant institutions, *Faith and Knowledge.* The criticisms are outspoken: today's students are nihilists who claim there are no such things as truth and falsity, or right and wrong; they have no ethic to give life meaning; or, secularization has gutted the university of its Christian heritage; or, the academic vocation has been narrowed to scholarly research to the neglect of moral and spiritual formation; or, Christian colleges have narrowed that vocation to teaching undergraduates to the neglect of scholarly research; or, we have replaced theology with therapy; or, church-related colleges settle for a two-realm theory of truth.

Jeremiads of this sort need to be heard; after all, the original Jeremiah made it into the biblical canon. And like Old Testament prophets our authors propose remedies: get back to the Great Books tradition of the University of Chicago, or restore academic freedom to Christian scholars in secular universities, or develop community, nurture religious values in specially designed Christian academic communities, or find new ways of relating faith to knowledge. All of this no doubt merits consideration, but I want to probe the underlying problem further. What was higher education like before the Enlightenment when, as Marsden implies, it lost its soul? What in reality was the soul of the earlier Christian university, that gave it

415

vitality and distinctive purpose? What were its driving concerns, its essential goals, and, even more crucial, its theological bases? And what happened to Christian learning in the course of history that made it vulnerable to losing its soul? And what does this soul from the past say to academia today, in a postmodern age when the notion of unchanging truth, and even the existence of truth, is in question? This first lecture, then, will be historical, an attempt to identify the soul of the Christian university. The second will be more analytic, probing the changes that made it vulnerable and applying these lessons of history for Christian academics today.

We need to go back to the beginnings of Christian involvement in what we call higher education, back in fact to second-century Alexandria. But remember that, in patristic times, Christians frequently attended pagan schools. Hellenistic education had developed from early Greek *paideia,* an attempt to transmit the heritage of the culture through familiarity with its literature. So young people were immersed in Homer: they identified with the exploits of heroes, reciting their speeches, capturing their emotions and imitating their deeds until the underlying values became their own. Literature was taught in ancient Greek schools for its historical and moral importance, and its mythical features became allegories that justified their continuance as *paideia* — hence the threefold interpretation (literal, moral, and allegorical) that church fathers like Origen later adopted. But in addition to these schools, wealthy parents would commit the guidance of their youth to a trusted slave, a *paidagogos,* who became a constant companion, adviser, and disciplinarian, not an instructor but a mentor who initiated his charge into the ethos of Greek society. So moral development, what Plato called the "improvement of the soul," was the original purpose of Greek education both in school and without.

A so-called "circle of learning" developed, the *enkuklios paideia* (from which our term "encyclopedia" derives): it embraced the seven liberal arts, three verbal (grammar, rhetoric, dialectic) and four mathematical (arithmetic, geometry, astronomy, and music). This was the "way" (Latin *via*) to wisdom, a threefold way *(trivium),* and a fourfold way *(quadrivium).* Grammar meant language and literature, reading Homer and the poets; music could both soothe the emotions and contribute to civic and religious ceremonies; astronomy taught the need for an order in which everything has its place; geometry instilled the values of equality and proportion, the seeds of justice. Thus liberal learning led to the love of wisdom, *philosophia,* and became the preparation needed for engaging in law and, in Rome at

416

least, in politics; rhetoric especially was valued for its practical uses although, to avoid Sophist abuses and keep it from being reduced to pedantic rules, Isocrates and, later, Cicero insisted on combining it with philosophy. By Hellenistic times, *paideia* came to mean not just moral formation, but the development of a whole person — the humanist ideal. Excellence or virtue *(arete)* meant human flourishing.

This, then, was the kind of education and the kind of educational ideal to which early Christians were exposed: its original purposes were moral development and preparation for civic responsibilities. Tertullian objected to Christians teaching in pagan schools, because by teaching about pagan gods and festivals they would seem to countenance idolatry. Being a student was allowed, however: students need intellectual discipline, and need not agree with all they read and hear.[1] Christians were also concerned about the moral influence of pagan literature. Basil of Caesarea, for instance, wrote "An Address to Young Men on Reading Greek Literature," advising that, while many Greek poets teach virtue and philosophy can point us away from bodily passions to the contemplation of eternal truths, yet we should not leave the entire guidance of our lives to heathen teachers. So Christians combined Hellenistic schooling with biblical and catechetical instruction, and the uses of liberal learning grew to include preparation for biblical study and theology.

So it was in Alexandria, one of the leading intellectual centers of antiquity. Ptolemy's famous Museum (literally, "the place of the Muses"), with its library and botanical and zoological gardens, attracted poets and scholars from across the Roman world. Here the Christian community established a catechetical school that was led in turn by Clement and then Origen. Origen, in fact, grew up in Alexandria, the son of Christian parents who supplemented Hellenistic schooling with a close knowledge of Scripture. When his father died, a martyr, Origen went to work teaching grammar, which meant language and literature — including its moral application and its allegories about human life and destiny. When at the age of eighteen he moved to the catechetical school he extended his studies to Hebrew and philosophy, and began a career of textual, exegetical, and apologetic writing with a grammarian's attention to moral and allegorical meanings. Origen reportedly taught the so-called "circle of learning" in such a way that astronomy revealed "the sacred economy of the universe," while

1. Tertullian, *On Idolatry*, x.

417

dialectic disciplined the mind to protect it against deception. He added Christian ethics, and students who lived in his home saw him as a kind of *paidagogos* who confirmed his moral advice by his own actions.

Origen recognized that Alexandrian believers needed a thorough education if they were to match their pagan peers' understanding; he saw that learning which satisfies the understanding would also equip them to understand and explain the Scriptures. As liberal learning prepares the mind for philosophy, so philosophy prepares it for theology. Plato was helpful, particularly in the face of Gnosticism, because he wrote of one God, the artificer who ordered everything for good, and because he taught that we must love the good. Of course, Greek literature extolled heroes with vices as well as virtues, and it cannot itself make us virtuous, but it can ready us for the law of Moses and the teaching of Christ.[2]

Philo, the Alexandrian Jew, had made the point in a little piece entitled "On Mating with Hagar the Egyptian." Abraham was unable to have a child with Sarah, until after she gave him her Egyptian *(sic!)* servant. So, too, we cannot be productive in studying divine wisdom until we have been faithful in Alexandrian learning. Clement adopted this same allegorical reading of the Hagar story, but cautioned against being so absorbed with the handmaiden as to forsake your true spouse.[3] Origen, ever the grammar teacher, had an allegory of his own that Augustine was to pick up later: as the Israelites took from the Egyptians the riches needed for the worship of God, so Christians are free to bring the treasures of pagan learning to the word and service of God.[4] We may not think this kind of allegorical interpretation the treasure Clement and Origen supposed, but it made their point: what the law was for the Jews the love of wisdom (*i.e.,* philosophy) was for the Greeks — a *paidagogos* (Paul uses that term in Galatians 3:24) leading them to Christ. And that was at the heart and soul of their involvement in education.

But how could these pagans know so much? How could it happen that pagan learning comports so well with what Christians believe? The Alexandrian answer, of course, was the Logos doctrine, as it had also been for Justin Martyr and others of the fathers. Clement had in mind the personi-

---

2. Origen, *Contra Celsum,* VI.xiii-xiv, liv-lviii. See also J. W. Trigg, *Origen: The Bible and Philosophy in the Third Century Church* (Atlanta: John Knox, 1983).

3. Clement, *Stromata,* I.V.

4. Origen, *Letter to Gregory,* I.

fication of wisdom in the Old Testament book of Proverbs and the apocryphal Wisdom of Solomon — itself a product of Alexandrian Judaism — where the wisdom that pervades nature and orders our lives was with God from the beginning. In his *Exhortation to the Greeks*, Clement says the divine Logos made this great world in harmonious order, and "the little world of man" too, creating us in his own rational image. So Christianity is the true *gnosis*, the wisdom of God himself. Greek wisdom, he adds in his *Stromata*, is a fruit of the rational image of God in a Logos-ordered world. Clement, in fact, presents a threefold Logos: the Logos of creation who orders the world he makes in harmonious fashion; the Logos of wisdom and reason who made us in his own rational image; and the Logos of the incarnation. The first two together imply the unity of truth, the harmony of the Greek circle of human learning with divine revelation in an integrally related whole. The third, the Logos of the incarnation, Clement presents in his *Paidagogos* (notice that title) in relation to moral formation: Jesus Christ is our moral mentor and guide to eternal life. The Logos therefore speaks to both the intellectual and the moral dimensions of education.

Now pause for a moment and see what is at the heart and soul of Alexandrian Christian higher education. Three major concerns have emerged: the improvement of the soul (Gregory of Nyssa called it *morphosis*, formation), the unity of truth whether gained by natural means or from biblical revelation, and the usefulness of liberal learning as preparation for service to church and society. The theological basis for this kind of education is a threefold Logos doctrine. And this soul of Christian learning is what Alexandria has to do with Jerusalem.

Clement, of course, was not alone in appealing to the divine Logos. Justin Martyr, for instance, had a similar explanation of pagan wisdom, and even Tertullian invoked the Stoic Logos in affirming the goodness of creation against the Gnostics.[5] Origen developed the theology in more Platonic fashion. The Middle Platonists had identified the Stoic Logos with Plato's Demiurge as God's intermediary in dealing with the creation. Origen therefore sees Plato's forms as archetypal ideas, the wisdom of the Creator-Logos, a view followed by Christian learning for centuries to come.

Consider Augustine. His *Confessions* tells of his own Hellenistic education, his reading of Vergil and Homer, for example, and the advanced work in rhetoric that prepared him for his chosen profession. But he became dis-

---

5. Justin Martyr, *Second Apology*, viii-xiii; Tertullian, *Apology*, xxi.10.

illusioned with rhetoric: public contests feed pride not virtue, and aim at success not truth. Cicero's *Hortensius* persuaded him to combine wisdom with eloquence, and the love of wisdom took over. Liberal learning had prepared him for philosophy, and Platonic philosophy now prepared him for theology — just as the Alexandrians had found.

But the substance of Augustine's educational thought comes out in discussions with his students at the Cassiciacum retreat shortly after his conversion. The dialog *De Ordine,* unfortunately translated as *On Divine Providence and the Problem of Evil,* highlights the order of nature, without which nothing can be good or beautiful or even exist. Within that order every particular is distinguished from other particulars by its form, so that everything obeys the eternal law of God. Augustine accordingly works his way through the seven liberal arts, showing how each in turn presupposes that God ordered his creation by forms. He intended to write an entire book on each of the liberal arts, but in fact only wrote half of one: his *De Musica* is on rhythm, the other half — on melody — remained undone. But *De Musica* distinguishes five kinds of numbers inherent in rhythm: one is heard as present sounds, another occurs in remembered past sounds, a third in reacting to sounds, a fourth in anticipating future sounds. All four of these are temporal and pass away, but a fifth kind of number never dies away but is eternal: judicial numbers, as he calls them, are unchanging forms. So music depends ultimately on judicial numbers, the archetypal exemplars of order in musical rhythm *(rationes aeternae)* in the mind of God. This kind of exemplarism Augustine applies to everything in creation, to every art and every science.

It therefore affects teaching and learning. At first we learn by authority, until we see the wisdom in what we are told and follow the line of reasoning. Then we can learn by reason and begin to see the form of things as a whole. Following authority alone can lead to right living, but not to liberal learning. The authority of a teacher's words cannot make one see the truth, for the student must take thought within herself about what is said. Neither can sense experience, unless we think inwardly about the changeless order of things. Then the light of eternal truth, the archetypal truth, can illumine the mind. So our real teacher is always the eternal wisdom of God, the Logos who enlightens everyone who comes into the world. The Logos of creation is also the Logos of reason.

But Augustine was concerned about more than the liberal arts, more than intellectual development and even the unity of truth. He was also concerned for his students' moral and spiritual development. God's purpose in giving us the arts and sciences reaches beyond our enjoyment and intellectual satisfaction. They point us to what is eternal, to God himself, and so Augustine declares he desires only to know God and the soul.[6] Since learning of that sort has moral prerequisites, he urges disciplined attitudes and lifestyle: vices like sleepiness, gluttony, jealousy, and pride must be shunned; so too must idle curiosity, because it violates the divine order for the use and enjoyment of things in this world. It is a kind of *cupiditas,* a disordered love that desires things of this world for their own sake rather than out of love for God. Later he spells out what we would now call seven developmental stages for the improvement of the soul. So the Logos of creation and reason is also the Logos who leads us to eternal life.

Yet Augustine's best-known work on education was written when, as a bishop, he was more involved with training clergy and catechetical instructors. *On Christian Teaching* addresses the utility of the liberal arts for understanding and teaching the Scriptures. He apparently expects seminarians to know both the trivium and the quadrivium, but he specifically applies his own field of rhetoric to their teaching ministry: eloquence can serve either truth or falsity, right or wrong, so clarity of meaning must take precedence over style. He quotes Cicero: "To teach is a necessity, to please is sweetness, to persuade is victory." Yet the life of the speaker carries even greater weight than eloquence. Augustine also wrote a piece *On Catechizing the Uninstructed,* making the point that while liberally educated catechumens will need to probe all sorts of questions, with the uneducated we must keep it simple, clear, and direct. The purpose of teaching must govern both content and style.

So Augustine's educational concerns, like his underlying Logos theology, follow the Alexandrians: moral and spiritual development, the unity of truth and preparation for life's service, all of which place Christ the Logos at the heart and soul of the whole endeavor.

The same pattern reappears in medieval times. With the revival of learning under Charlemagne, monastery and cathedral schools continued to emphasize liberal learning and to explore the underlying order that makes it possible. Like Augustine, Boethius, who also delineated the issues involved in the theory of universals, wrote about music, claiming that its mathematical order helps "harmonize" the soul. Cassiodorus remarked

6. *Soliloquies,* I.7.

that it can lift the soul to heavenly things and calm the emotions. Hugh of St. Victor maintained that while physical sensations and bodily forms obscure eternal truth, the pursuit of wisdom is itself medicine for the soul. Liberal learning helps us discern the God-given order of things, but it requires humility: with meditation and prayer, it leads us to contemplate the eternal.[7] Augustine's exemplarism again is taken for granted.

Implicit in Hugh's account is a further educational concern that became explicit in monastery schools: learning becomes an act of worship. Monastery education was dominantly literary. "Grammar" was primarily preparation for reading the Bible, and the Bible was read in a liturgical context, aloud. So both literature and the Bible were studied contemplatively, pondering themes, tracing style, reflecting on images, meditating out loud on quotations, and praising God along the way. Anselm was a monastery teacher, and so his writings reflect that practice when he addresses his ontological argument to God. This doxological note, while less direct and overt previously, dominated the monastery school and its efforts at moral and spiritual development. Cathedral schools, on the other hand, reflected the more active life of the cities, studying the arts in preparation for more intellectually rigorous theology and emphasizing civic virtues.[8] Tensions between these two views of education arose over Abelard's teaching of theology. To begin, he had taken issue with the sacred cow of Platonism that the medievals had inherited from Augustine and the Alexandrians, and adopted a kind of conceptualism on the theory of universals. So, rather than teaching students to contemplate eternal forms and so rise to the contemplation of God, he taught dialectical skills as the way to avoid error and ensure truth. He collected biblical texts *pro* and *con* theological positions, as source material for disputations. *Sic et Non* was the title of that book, hardly calculated to reassure people of piety, but quite certain to engage students in the detached analysis his teaching required. Peter Lombard wrote a similar book with quotations from the church fathers in his *Sentences,* a work that became the standard theology text for centuries. But it was Abelard who provoked the antagonism of monastic teachers: they saw in him a lack of moral and spiritual concern for students, no car-

7. Boethius in *De Institutione Musica;* Cassiodorus in his *Institutiones,* II.v; Hugh of St. Victor, *Didascalion.*

8. On monastery schools, see Jean LeClerq, *The Love of Learning and the Desire for God* (New York: Fordham Univ. Press, 1960). On cathedral schools, see *The Envy of Angels* (Philadelphia: Univ. of Pennsylvania Press, 1994).

ing for the soul, no real mysteries of the faith and, to top it off, they accused him of doctrinal error. For twenty years the dispute dragged on, until Abelard was forbidden to teach, and shortly died.

I will come back to this kind of tension in the second lecture, but I introduce it now to provide some sense of both the medieval university and monastery education. Like Abelard, the University of Paris when it emerged laid emphasis on logic and disputations, and Thomas Aquinas taught at the university while a short distance away Bonaventure taught Franciscan monks and headed the entire Franciscan order with its Augustinian tradition. To get at their differing educational concerns, compare the religious significance they gave to studying the creation order — which in practice, of course, meant studying the quadrivium.

Aquinas finds it edifying to admire the wisdom, power, and goodness of God attested by his works and to reflect on our bearing God's image. He thinks that familiarity with the creation has apologetic uses in refuting mistaken concepts of God; and he observes that the Christian studies creatures from the standpoint of their relation to God, their First Cause, rather than just in terms of natural processes.[9] Bonaventure spells out his approach in his book *The Mind's Road to God*. He agrees with Aquinas that nature proclaims God's wisdom, power, and goodness, but then adds that God himself is present in nature as Light, as Logos, as Beauty. He agrees with Aquinas that the human mind is made in the image of God, but reiterates Augustine's psychological analogy for the divine trinity and then adds that God himself is present in the believing mind in a divine trinity of virtues — faith, hope, and love. Nature proclaims its maker, but God's actual presence is revealed by nature's symbolism. Its light reveals God the Eternal Light; its logos-structure reveals God the Eternal Truth; its harmonies reveal God, Eternal Beauty. The laws of nature that the liberal arts show us are God-given lights that lighten everyone who comes into the world.

How should we characterize the difference between these two scholars? Both of them see liberal learning in Christian perspective. Bonaventure is oriented to the literary, Aquinas to logic. But Bonaventure's sense of the presence of God in his creation, the mystery and wonder of it all, is far stronger. His imaginative symbols revealing God's presence may seem neo-Platonic: some, like "light," seem at first to confuse physical with

9. *Summa Contra Gentiles,* II.2-4.

423

intellectual experience. But whereas Aquinas acknowledges the witness of nature to its Creator, Bonaventure holds his readers in awe at God's actual presence. Liberal learning for him is theology, meditation, doxology. Aquinas, without disparaging the contemplative life, sees teaching as a more active involvement with people.

Compare also the format of their writings. Bonaventure's *The Mind's Road to God* is a meditation leading by divine illumination to a mystical vision that transcends both sensory experience and intellectual activity: it emphasizes grace, not learning; desire, not understanding; the Bridegroom, not the teacher; darkness, not clarity. Aquinas's writing, on the other hand, reflects Scholastic teaching and its concern to demonstrate the unity of truth, truths of faith and truths of reason. So we find a question for debate, different views to examine, objections and responses and logically well-formed arguments. One such question concerns teaching: "Can a man or only God teach and be called Teacher?"[10] Aquinas addresses this question to both moral education and scientific knowledge (the quadrivium), arguing that every finite being has its natural potency from God, its First Cause. Teaching activates a natural potency by showing how we do something and then providing the student with practice in doing it herself. So learning is a natural process of active discovery by the natural light of reason, rather than by Bonaventure's mysterious effluence of divine light upon our path.

These differences showed up in the famous dispute over Averroism. Averroes, the Moslem philosopher, had interpreted Aristotle in ways that seemed incompatible with either Moslem or Christian theology: prime matter, for example, is an uncreated potency from which God drew the forms of things he created, so something in addition to God (namely prime matter) is uncreated and eternal. The Latin Averroists talked of two-fold truth, truths of faith and truths of reason in opposition, as if that were possible. Bonaventure responded by rejecting Aristotelian philosophy altogether: unbelievers like Aristotle and Averroes could not philosophize in the light of the faith, and without that divine illumination one cannot find truth. Aquinas was not prepared to write Aristotle off that readily, for even a pagan philosopher attains some truth by the light of reason in which we all participate. So Aquinas opted to retain Aristotle's view of natural potencies, explaining creation in terms of Aristotle's four kinds of cause with the

10. *Truth,* q. 11.

help of Augustine's archetypal ideas in the mind of God. *Ex nihilo* means there is no uncreated potency in material causes. God himself is then not only efficient cause, but also formal cause (he is the Logos of creation) and final cause (the one for whom as well as by whom all things exist),[11] and the unity of truth is restored.

That, for now, is the important point. Aquinas, despite his differences philosophically and educationally from Bonaventure, retained the basic Logos theology that had undergirded Christian educational thought since Alexandria. The Creator Logos ordered the world by means of natural potencies he created; the Logos of reason endowed us with the light of rational powers that finitely image his own, and the incarnate Logos leads us in grace to life eternal.

But, you might ask, what about Calvin and the Reformation? Calvin had no sympathy with Scholastic metaphysics and medieval theories about real universals. Where does this leave him on the foundations of higher learning? I agree that the philosophical picture changes, and so does the university, and I plan to talk about those changes in the second lecture. But for now, let me remind you of what Calvin says in his *Institutes,* book II, chapter 2, in discussing our natural talents in the light of human sin. He says we still see some desire for investigating truth, some perspicuity of understanding, some love of truth. Civil polity, domestic economy, the seeds of which are innate in all mankind, without any instruction or legislator, afford a powerful argument "that in the constitution of this life no man is destitute of *the light of reason.*" Notice that phrase.

He then turns to the liberal and manual arts, where people display aptitude and ingenuity in inventing something new, and in improving on what they were taught. This plainly proves "that men are endowed with a general apprehension of reason and understanding." He turns to heathen writers where "the light of truth" is admirably displayed in philosophy, logic, medicine, mathematics. God, he claims, "replenishes, actuates and quickens all creatures, according to the property of each species which he has given it by the law of creation." This is partly Aristotelian language he uses to spell out his own belief in an orderly, law-governed creation. And then he cites Augustine, with whom "the Master of the *Sentences*" (Peter Lombard) and the "Schoolmen" agreed, that our natural talents, though corrupted, still remain. These remaining marks of the divine image distin-

11. *Summa Theologica,* I. q. 44.

guish the human race from all other creatures, and attest our God-given capacity for knowledge and righteousness and dominion over the earth.

Consider also Calvin's comments on the divine Logos in his commentary on John's Gospel. John calls Jesus the Word because he is the eternal wisdom and will of God, the express image of his purpose. That "all things were made by him" (vs. 3) shows that God had in mind a concept of the whole of creation — not quite Augustine's exemplarism but approaching it. The life that was the light of men (vs. 4) was the light of reason common to the whole human race (vs. 10). So Calvin, too, appeals to both the Logos of creation and the Logos of reason and, of course, the Logos of the incarnation; and he recognizes this as agreeing with the Scholastics, despite his disinterest in metaphysical Scholastic arguments.

There are disagreements, too, of course, as we shall see, but it is now clear why Jerusalem has so much to do with Alexandria. It is because, at the heart and soul of the Christian university are four basic concerns (the improvement of the soul, the unity of truth, the usefulness of liberal learning, and a doxological emphasis), and underlying all four is the divine Logos, Jesus Christ. The question remains, however, as to how this vision eroded, and what Alexandria has to do with academia today.

What Has Alexandria to Do with Academia Today?

In the first lecture we saw that, beginning in Alexandria and extending throughout the Middle Ages, four basic concerns gave vitality and purpose to Christian higher education: the improvement of the soul — what we call faith development and character formation, the unity of truth whether known by natural reason or by divine revelation, liberal learning as preparation for service to the church and society, and a pervasive doxological spirit. These concerns were also evident in Calvin, along with the underlying threefold Logos theology that developed in Alexandria: the Logos of creation by whom and for whom all things exist in their intended order, the Logos of reason who made us in his own image, and the Logos of the incarnation, full of grace as well as truth.

The question before us now is what happened to this vision of Christian higher education? George Marsden and his compatriots blame the Enlightenment, and they have carefully documented the process of secularization in American institutions of learning. I am interested in what led up to the Enlightenment. If the soul of the Christian college and university was as I have proposed, what about it was so vulnerable, so susceptible to erosion? How did we get from the medieval university or the Puritan college to Enlightenment secularism? What happened to those four basic concerns, and to the Logos theology?

I want to propose that the answer can be found, at least to a significant extent, in changes that occurred in Christian learning itself. I see these changes, first, in the opposition of humanist learning to Scholasticism, then in the relationship between contemplative and active learning and, in the third place, in a growing emphasis first on objectivity and then on subjectivity.

1. The distinctive feature of the Scholastic university was its method of teaching. You recall the influence of Abelard and his *Sic et Non,* with the listing of biblical texts on both sides of a theological issue as grist for student debates. Or think of the format Aquinas adopted in writing his *Summa Theologica:* state the question to be debated, list your opponent's objections, pose a contrary position, develop your overall answer, and then respond systematically to each of the initial objections. Teaching consisted largely of disputations about such questions, pressing arguments pro and con, citing Christian and heathen authorities alike in order to train students in logic.

Nor was this logic the dialectic that was part of the traditional trivium of liberal arts. It was the Aristotelian logic rediscovered in the twelfth century, and it excelled at exploring logical connections between universals and providing rigorous logical proofs: an excellent tool for working out interconnections within the unity of truth. This the Scholastics endeavored to do, with universals both as exemplars in God's mind, and as ordering principles within the particulars of creation, and as abstract ideas in human thought, with the result that the entire furniture of heaven and earth formed one magnificent hierarchy of being and goodness, like a cosmic choreographed dance to the glory of God. The intellectual development that resulted from such pedagogy, along with detailed attention to the unity of truth and the inherent doxology to God, addressed at least in some measure three of the educational essentials we have identified, and prepared theological students for the fourth; namely, service to the church or, in the case of law students, to society.

But as this kind of Scholastic university developed, grammar lost its ties to literature and moral development, becoming just a branch of logic, while rhetoric was increasingly ignored. In a commentary on Boethius, for example, Thomas Aquinas divided the liberal arts into natural philosophy, mathematics, and natural theology, ignoring the trivium altogether. And, by shortly before the Reformation, the German university of Erfurt listed twenty-two books to be studied for the BA degree, seventeen of them in logic and none in rhetoric.

That kind of lopsidedness was sure to produce a reaction. Augustine and the early medievals had emphasized the traditional trivium of grammar, rhetoric, and dialectic, and Bonaventure's imaginative symbolism of liberal learning was the mind's road to mystical union with God. So it is not surprising that Renaissance humanists sought to replace Scholastic with traditional humanist approaches to learning, enriched with the study of history. By the fifteenth century, the liberal arts were again identified with the trivium. Classical rhetoric revived, supported in the course of time by the "natural logic" of Peter Ramus, who rejected the Aristotelian emphasis on metaphysical proofs in favor of the more informal dialectic of ordinary discourse. Peter Ramus, incidentally, converted to Calvinism and eleven years later was killed in the St. Bartholomew's Day massacre of 1572. But over a period of seven years, the enrollment at the Scholastic university in Erfurt dropped from 311 to only 14 students. Where schools under church control failed to change their Scholastic approach, the nobility and the merchants took the initiative and founded colleges for humanistic studies that also taught the natural logic of Ramus.

Martin Luther, you may recall, was educated at Erfurt in the Scholastic tradition, studying Aristotle's metaphysics, and as a professor at Wittenberg he lectured on Aristotle's physics and ethics and on Peter Lombard's *Sentences* — the traditional Scholastic agenda. In 1517, however, in his "Disputation Against Scholastic Theology" he denounced Aristotle's intrusion into theology, and three years later he urged the German nobility to reform the university in the humanistic direction. Classical literature and rhetoric would provide the mastery of ancient languages needed for extended biblical study, in contrast to Scholastic disputations about isolated biblical texts. Logic may be useful, not so much syllogisms as dialectic, but rhetoric pleases and persuades, history reinforces human wisdom, while music calms and refreshes the heart.

The purposes behind this shift from Scholasticism to humanistic learning are plain: the care of the soul, the utility of classical languages for the study of Scripture, and of liberal learning in ordinary life — the very things deemed lacking in Scholasticism. But notice that the connection between natural knowledge and revealed truth or between faith and learning is no longer intrinsic but extrinsic. The emphasis is not on the unity of truth but on the utility of learning.

Luther, of course, was not the only Reformer who preferred humanistic education. Melanchthon was even more actively involved in reform at Wittenberg. Calvin was educated under French Renaissance scholars, and, for his Academy at Geneva, adopted as his aim "wise and eloquent piety" — a phrase that combines virtue, religion, and rhetoric. He wanted education to change people's values. Classical languages and rhetoric were essential, natural philosophy (primarily doxological) exalted God's power and goodness, and, according to his associate, Beza, all the arts were to make orderly sense within one comprehensive philosophy.[1] Calvin, in fact, had himself traced similarities between Christianity and Stoicism in his early commentary on Seneca's *De Clementia*, while still complaining about Stoic indifference to human need. So his goals were much like Luther's, but with more explicit attention to the underlying unity of truth.

In England, too, the humanist trend took over. A royal decree limited the number of Scholastic textbooks to make room for ancient languages and the humanist curriculum. In 1550, Duns Scotus's books were burned in public at Oxford. New humanist colleges were founded to better educate clergy and later, under Cromwell, to educate the children of merchants who appreciated the practical uses of Ramist logic and aspired to be "English gentlemen." Milton gave voice to these humanist goals: a complete education fits one "to perform justly, skillfully and magnanimously all the offices, both private and public, of peace and war." But notice also his Puritan care for the soul:

> The end, then, of learning is to repair the ruins of our first parents by regaining to know God aright, and out of that knowledge to love him, to imitate him, to be like him, as we may the nearest, by possessing our souls of true virtue, which, being united to the heavenly grace of faith, makes up the highest perfection.[2]

Noble goals that compensate for any Scholastic imbalance. But what about the unity of truth and Logos theology? The Scholastics emphasized this without as much attention as the humanists gave to our earthly "offices." But by and large, the humanists are not as clear about it as they are about the care of the soul or the usefulness of classical languages and literature for biblical study. Calvin seems to be: he has no interest in Scholastic metaphysics, but his early work on Seneca would have familiarized him with the Stoic Logos and its ordered unity of nature.

1. W. Stanford Reid, "Calvin and the Founding of the Academy of Geneva," in *Articles on Calvin and Calvinism*, ed. R. Gamble (New York: Garland Publishing Co., 1992), vol. 3, pp. 237-70; Gillian Lewis, "The Geneva Academy," in *Calvin in Europe, 1540-1620*, ed. A. Petegree *et al.* (Cambridge: Cambridge Univ. Press, 1994), ch. 3.

2. John Milton, *On Education*, in *Paradise Lost and Selected Poetry and Prose*, ed. Northrop Frye (New York: Rinehart Press, 1951), p. 439.

Luther, however, studied under nominalist teachers, and even called William of Occam "my dear teacher." Understandably, then, instead of tracing the order of nature to universal exemplars in the mind of God, as the medievals had done and Calvin also implies, Luther's sermon on John's Logos simply affirms that God created, governs, and preserves this world. The Logos of John 1:4 enlightens everyone with the light of reason, so that wisdom and the arts are not restricted to the faithful. In temporal affairs people are rational enough that God doesn't teach us in Scripture how to milk cows or build houses. The image of God gives promise of *useful* knowledge, but not a *true* knowledge of God; that depends on the "true light" of John 1:9. So Luther warns against the falsehoods of philosophers and sophists.[3] He values liberal learning for its utility both in earthly matters and in preparation for interpreting Scripture, rather than for contemplating eternal truth or tracing the unity of truth, a crucial change from what had gone before in both monastic and Scholastic learning. Scholastic education highlighted the unity of truth and the Logos theology, with less emphasis on moral formation, while humanistic learning highlighted moral education without as consistent an emphasis on the unity of truth and the divine Logos. The dilemma could not be avoided.

2. This included a change in the relationship between the contemplative and the active life. The contemplative life sought eternal truths and thereby contemplated the archetypal wisdom and goodness of God, while the active life was involved with temporal affairs. In a monastery school, where the abbot directed studies with a view to the spiritual growth of each monk, the contemplative life prevailed. So, for Bonaventure, liberal learning was a path to the contemplation of God. In the university, Aquinas debated whether teaching was part of the contemplative or the active life, pointing out that the verb "to teach" has two objects. If we stress teaching subject matter, uncreated truth, then teaching is part of the contemplative life; but if we stress teaching students, then it is part of the active life.[4]

This distinction, however, assumes that the university teaches eternal truth, namely archetypal exemplars as distinct from the temporal particulars of everyday affairs. The rise of nominalism challenged this practice. If

3. *Luther's Works,* ed. Jaroslav Pelikan (Saint Louis: Concordia, 1957), vol. 22, pp. 30f.; *What Luther Says,* comp. E. M. Plass (Saint Louis: Concordia, 1959), vol. 2, p. 1158; B. A. Garrish, "Luther," in *Encyclopedia of Philosophy* (New York: Macmillan, 1967), vol. V, p. 112.

4. *Truth,* q. 11, art. 4.

there are no universals and no abstract universal ideas, but only general terms that name similar particulars, then Aquinas's distinction between teaching as contemplation of the eternal and teaching as this-worldly action collapses. Nominalism encouraged the rise of empirical science, and empirical science produced useful worldly knowledge. So the liberal arts increasingly became useful arts. Classical languages and literature, in the idiom of one college, became just "Greek for Testament." The Protestant Reformers themselves contributed to this increased attention to the active life: Luther with his emphasis on this-worldly tasks as God-given vocations, and Calvin by his attention to the creation mandate, both underscored the importance of service to society as well as the church.

But Francis Bacon best represents the change. A Reformed Christian, he was also a Renaissance man, a typical humanist who claimed that studying history makes us wise, poetry witty, and mathematics subtle. He complained that humanist rhetoric had degenerated into ornamentation, that Scholastic debates were unrelated to the realities of life, and that Scholastic methods ignored both the word of God and God's works, the creation. But the greatest error had been in mistaking the ultimate end of knowledge: it should be a rich storehouse for the glory of the Creator and the relief of the human condition. On the one hand, the dignity of knowledge rests first in its archetype, for in the workings of creation we observe the attributes and acts of God. But on the other hand contemplation and action, he said, must be more united. At the time, in 1605, he did not say how except to affirm that learning should both glorify God and preserve the faith.[5]

Fifteen years later he returned to the subject. At the fall, we lost both our innocence and the dominion over nature entrusted to us by God. Both can be partly recovered in this life, our innocence by religion and faith, control over nature by the arts and by sciences that follow new inductive methods. So his *Novum Organum* sought to replace Aristotle's logic and reform education in order to relieve the human condition. Active learning can glorify God by creating a society that is improved and governed, as Bacon is careful to say, in love.

How does he then "reunite contemplation and action"? In ethics, like other nominalists, he appeals to "religion and right reason." Religion tells

5. F. Bacon, *Essays, Advancement of Learning, New Atlantis and Other Pieces,* ed. R. F. Jones (New York: Odyssey Press, 1937), pp. 214ff.

him to seek God's glory and exercise dominion in his creation, while "right reason" seeks means to that end, hence inductive methods for discovering the causal forces in nature. If we can control those forces, we can then remedy many of the problems from which we suffer. This is instrumental thinking: religion defines the ends, science finds the means. That is how he connects contemplation with action.

But the end, this telos, is something faith adds to knowledge, not something intrinsic to the subject matter and to learning itself. Since nominalism forfeits any intrinsic connection between fact and value, Bacon favors Democritus's mechanistic view of nature over Aristotle's teleology: but matter and causal forces are things so blind that, as Tennyson says, they are not to be trusted with our "mortal good."

So Bacon is a kind of Christian utilitarian directing blind causal forces to active ends that religious contemplation requires. The change is radical and, as secularization increases, who will determine the ends, or who define the good? Moreover, the discovery of new knowledge is now more important than the transmission of truth we inherit from the past. Discovery requires specialization, so that all that remains of the unity of knowledge is the methodological unity of science. Hence the slogan "religion and right reason" becomes in the Enlightenment "reason alone," the rule of natural science. The unity of truth no longer seems important.

3. The third change was a growing emphasis on objectivity. Francis Bacon intended his inductive methods to free science from philosophical influences and place it beyond such futile disputes. Descartes, for his part, suspended judgment on everything that could even in principle be doubted, so as to ensure that knowledge be clear, distinct, and certain. The Scholastics, on the other hand, for all of their Aristotelian logic and natural theology, still acknowledged the Augustinian principle of faith seeking understanding: in the Averroist controversy, for instance, remember that it was Aquinas's theology that led him to introduce Augustine's exemplarism into Aristotle's philosophy. But Bacon wanted no religious intrusions into science: religious disputes were politically dangerous at that juncture in English history. So he unwittingly fed the coming Enlightenment appetite for an objectivity free from all authority and tradition. The rule of reason was to be the rule of objective science.

A further factor was his nominalism. When William of Occam rejected the possibility of thinking in abstract ideas, he had concluded that our awareness of particular objects is direct rather than mediated through ideas. The mental act by which we give common terms to similar objects does not involve mental representations, so there is no room for ideas to shape perceptions. Direct awareness ensures objective knowledge. Bacon agrees. He rejects "idols of the tribe" because the human understanding distorts and discolors the nature of things by mingling its own nature with those things, and "idols of the cave" because we refract and discolor the light of nature with our own chance impressions. So objectivity prevails.

But this assumption of direct perception which is so crucial to objective knowledge proved to be the Achilles' heel of the Enlightenment. As every beginning philosophy student knows, Descartes held that perception is indirect rather than direct: objects and their properties are represented in our minds by subjective ideas, so what I am directly aware of is not this room itself but my ideas of it. I think, therefore I exist, but it is ideas that I think. Ideas are subjective mental states produced by multiple causal influences, rather than Xerox copies of objective things. So the door was opened to subjectivity, and you know the story. Berkeley refuted materialism by showing that, since the physical properties we perceive are all subjective, matter itself — the supposed substratum — is an abstract term devoid of any empirical reference. Hume in his turn was skeptical about knowing anything beyond our present ideas — whether matter, mind itself, or God. Kant argued that the entire Newtonian space-time world is a subjective mental construct.

On the one hand, the demand for objectivity implied that knowledge will be universally the same, neutral with regards to matters like religion where people disagree. So the Augustinian view of faith that seeks and shapes understanding was gone. Even ethics became a religiously neutral science in utilitarian hands (as Alasdair MacIntyre points out in his Gifford Lectures, *Three Rival Versions of Moral Enquiry*). But if knowledge is religiously neutral, then the distinctive concerns of a Christian college move from what transpires within the lab or library or classroom to outside it: to student development and occasional doxological activities, rather than disciplinary content. The Logos of creation and reason was no longer fundamental to education: only the incarnate Logos who cares for the soul remained, and even that did not last.

On the other hand, subjectivity became increasingly a problem as it was historicized in the nineteenth century. Historical and cultural relativism increased, and led in time to the kind of postmodern pluralism we now face. Enlightenment expectations for a universal and neutral knowledge now seem a thing of the past, as seemingly incommensurable perspectives vie for a hearing. But this is not all. The postmodern problem is not just the plurality of points of view in a multicultural society. That is enough of a problem for epistemological subjectivity to have created. But we now face the additional problem of what I call "metaphysical subjectivity": the claim that truth itself is just a subjective mental construct, that no such thing as truth exists objectively at all. As Richard Rorty points out, if historicism and nominalism reject beliefs that refer to something beyond the reach of time and chance, then they will reject belief in objective truth. It was the legacy of an age that believed in God.[6] Without archetypal truth in the mind of God, truth has no objective locus. Without the Logos of reason knowledge of truth is impossible, but without the Logos of creation there can be no such thing as truth. The theological erosion is complete.

You now have my overall thesis. Let me summarize. The soul of the Christian university, its essential concerns and its Logos theology, was vulnerable to secularization because of changes within Christian learning. The opposition of humanistic to Scholastic learning, for all its advantages, weakened the emphasis on the unity of truth and the underlying Logos doctrine; the Baconian turn from contemplation to active or instrumental learning likewise, for it turned from archetypal and eternal truth in the mind of God to the utility of new discoveries; the Baconian emphasis on epistemological objectivity separated faith from learning, but also produced that creeping subjectivism which now throws into question the existence of truth itself. At stake throughout is Logos theology. Calvin held to both Logos theology and the usefulness of liberal learning, but nominalists like Bacon and Luther appealed only to the latter, stressing the creation mandate and our earthly vocations. Fading attention to the unity of truth, and the concurrent loss of Logos theology, dissipated the very soul of what had been the Christian university.

But what has this analysis to say to us in academia today? Plainly all four educational concerns I have identified remain relevant, and a case could be made that liberal learning is basic to all four — to student formation, to preparation for life's responsibilities in church and society, to the unity of truth, and to glorifying God in the contemplative as well as the active life. Plainly, too, there are dangers in an active, utilitarian view of learn-

6. Richard Rorty, *Contingency, Irony and Solidarity* (Cambridge and New York: Cambridge Univ. Press, 1989), pp. xv, 5.

ing without a more wholistic contemplative understanding. But of the four, the critical concern both historically and, I believe, today is the unity of truth. Douglas Sloan, in the book I mentioned last evening, complains that mainline Protestant colleges have settled for a two-realm theory of truth. Evangelical colleges too easily do the same, having drunk too deeply at the wellspring of the Enlightenment and by adopting a too-utilitarian view of learning. The soul of the Christian university, historically, was more Logos-centered than that.

So what does the threefold Logos doctrine say to academia today? In the first place, *the Logos of creation* affirms the objectivity of truth. Years ago, before the term "postmodern" had been coined, I ran into a former student whose husband was involved in the realism debate in philosophy of language. As we talked, she said, "At least theism gives you a locus for truth." She was so right. For theism, the ultimate locus of truth is not our propositions, nor our thought, but the mind of God: the tacit reference of all our truth claims is to God's archetypal knowledge. Rorty is right: the idea of truth is a carryover from belief in God, or some philosophically equivalent Logos.

Keep in mind that the Logos concept arose from considering the orderedness of nature that is evident in the arts and sciences. The divine Logos is *the Logos of creation* so that, as Augustine put it, *rationes aeternae* in God's mind are the source of *rationes seminales* immanent in the creation. Does this mean that Logos theology commits us to real universals and to Scholastic metaphysics? We could do a lot worse. Neither nominalism nor conceptualism provide any insight into the natural order other than saying "there it is!" and "God did it!" as if the archetypal wisdom of God is a needless abstraction. But metaphysical issues cannot be avoided. Nick Wolterstorff, for instance, argues for universals as objectively real logical possibilities from which God chose what to actually create. That's a kind of exemplarism about the Logos of creation, and it affirms both the theistic reference of truth and a theocentric unity of truth.[7]

In the second place, *the Logos of reason* underscores what I call the "perspectival" nature of finite and historically situated human knowledge, and that reveals an affinity with postmodern rather than Enlightenment ideals. Today's pluralism has, of course, legitimized different perspectives: black theology, feminist theology, gay perspectives, and so on: whatever de-

---

7. Nicholas Wolterstorff, *On Universals* (Chicago: Univ. of Chicago Press, 1970).

fines your self-identity shapes your thinking. But by the same token if "creatureliness" and "Christian" define my self-identity, then I will think from a creaturely and Christian perspective. Augustine said "faith is understanding's step" because he knew how his restless mind was drawn towards God, and "understanding is faith's reward" because it opened up new horizons of learning. He knew that Christian learning and all human learning is perspectival.

But is the ideal of a universal knowledge entirely a will o' the wisp? Human perspectives differ, but they can never be wholly different, entirely relative. Postmodern relativism, like other kinds of cultural and historical relativism, seems to assume that the diversity of human beliefs and perspectives is so determined by biographical and cultural factors as to be beyond criticism and beyond control. But even if that sort of determinism were true — which I'm convinced it is not — even then it would not imply that different perspectives have nothing in common. No human perspective is wholly idiosyncratic, no cultural perspectives devoid of all similarity, nor is Christian perspective unrelated to our generic humanness. We share a somewhat common world, and the Logos enlightens *everyone* who comes into this world, for we all also share his image. In principle, then, different perspectives cannot be entirely incommensurable: some points of contact, some similarities and agreements occur. Pluralism? Yes. Total relativism? No — thanks to the Logos of reason enlightening all who come into this world. Calvin makes the point (*Inst.* II.2.xii) that even sin has not deprived us of the love of truth or perspicuity of understanding. The light of truth, he claims, is "admirably displayed" in the works of heathen writers, philosophers as well as mathematicians and lawyers, for God is the only fountain of truth wherever it is found.

Finally, *the Logos incarnate* who nurtured faith and character by embodying himself in a community of disciples reminds us that faith and moral values are a heritage transmitted within earthly communities. By contrast, Descartes regarded belief as an act of the will that could be freely withheld or freely given. It is a wholly individual affair. Consider what the university would be like that is shaped by that view. It would provide a neutral marketplace of ideas with full academic freedom, in which rational choices can be made by each individual independently on an evidentialist basis. Tradition and authority, religious or political, are disregarded. That is the essence of Enlightenment learning. Compare a postmodern view: knowledge and belief come loaded with the perspectives of race and gender, or some other group identity. Roots matter, for perspectives are forged in history. Beliefs and values are shaped and nurtured by participating in the life of that community of which one is part. Surely in this regard also the history of Christian learning is closer to the postmodern.

It began in the Christian community in Alexandria, where Clement introduced the Logos incarnate as a *paidagogos* who nurtures faith and morality and improves the soul. Origen played the *paidagogos* role: his students lived in his home, and found that his life reinforced the faith and morality he taught. Augustine's Cassiciacum writings record not only what he taught, but also that he did so in a small community, with group expectations about a disciplined lifestyle, and with pastoral concern for the improvement of their souls. Monastery schools were designed to that end, with faith nurtured by learning as well as prayer under the pastoral direction of an abbot. And later John Milton, in his essay *On Education,* called for a small residential community designed for holistic student growth — a far cry from a "Descartes University."

This concern for a Christian learning community reflects the biblical story of a heritage of faith transmitted through Abraham to his seed, on and on forever, or of Israel as a community of faith, learning through both law (promulgated and enforced) and grace. It is the sort of thing Stanley Hauerwas and Parker Palmer write about and, of course, Alasdair MacIntyre: if human knowing and moral belief are perspectival then this corollary follows, that faith and moral formation are acquired usually and best, not by force of argument or weight of objective evidence, but by entering into the life of a community and making its heritage one's own. The Christian university is closer here to the postmodern university than to the University of Descartes. It is itself, of course, pre-modern, and that is why it is out of kilter with both. A Christian university is one where Christ himself is present, the *paidagogos* at work in his church.

We hear the phrase, "Christ-centered education." We can see now what it should really mean. At the heart and soul of the Christian university is Christ, the Logos of creation, reason, and incarnation. This is what makes it Christian, gives it theological basis and educational purpose. This is what was lost sight of historically, and so fell prey to Enlightenment influences, and this is what Christian higher education must recover and reaffirm for the future.

Sin or Sickness

The Problem of Human Dysfunction

J. HAROLD ELLENS

Contents

FIRST LECTURE

Theology and Ethics: Posing a Problem

I. Introduction

Henry Stob, even though he is now in God's eternal kingdom, is still with us tonight. These lectures which memorialize his name, his life, and his work, enable us to recall vivid memories of him and to feel his presence among us. I thank God again and again that he was my friend. Thus, as I present these lectures, I have a clear sense of Henry Stob's longing for insight regarding the knotty enigma of God, our humanity, and how we carry ourselves before God's face. This quest for understanding God and ourselves is also my deep longing. It is basic to my discussion of Sin or Sickness: The Problem of Human Dysfunction.

I have a sense of being "surrounded by a great cloud of witnesses," the heroes of faith from twenty centuries of Christian quest, and the inquiring spirits from every spiritual pilgrimage who have longed throughout history to understand themselves, the meaning of their own natures, the perplexity of their dysfunction, and in Augustine's classic lines,[1] sought diligently to find their restless soul's true home, in the face of what Barbara Mertz has called "our common human terror and our common hope."[2]

I am greatly honored by the invitation to present The Henry J. Stob Lectures in Ethics for the 1997-1998 academic year. My primary objective in these two lectures is to set before you a number of questions, within the

1. Aurelius Augustine, "Confessions," in *A Select Library of the Nicene and Post-Nicene Fathers of the Christian Church,* ed. Philip Schaff (Grand Rapids: Eerdmans, 1956), vol. 1, pp. 45-208.
2. Barbara Mertz, *Red Land, Black Land* (New York: Coward, McCann, and Geoghegan, 1966).

443

construct of a psycho-spiritual model, which will stimulate some dialogue between us over the coming years. The intent of raising these questions about sin and salvation is to provoke, if possible, a fresh look at God and the human predicament. This is more important to me tonight than attempting, in two short lectures, to give definitive and final answers.

God has always been an enigma to us in our quest for truth, and God remains so; but no greater a riddle than our own natures. Rare is the person who has not sensed that the two are related and interactive. It is my desire to wrestle somewhat with those essential enigmas as they arise from the perplexity of the central human predicament, a *psycho-spiritual* predicament. We have an infinite capacity to imagine ideal worlds. We do it constantly to our great advantage and challenge. We differ considerably in the worlds we idealize and we tend to idolize our own and turn them into oppressive task-masters for ourselves and others. On the other hand, we have only limited capacity to create those ideal worlds: intellectual, psychological, spiritual, emotional, sexual, and material. The distance we experience between our ideal worlds and our real worlds is the dimension of our pain and loss. We call that sin and misery: evil.

This is the great ambiguity: the magnificence and malignance inherent in God's created universe. It is grounded in the empirically demonstrable fact that all human beings are fraught with personal and communal dysfunction. That problem is enlarged by the limitation of our knowledge, the unknown of our future, the fragile quality of our hope, and our perception of the danger of the dissolution of our selves in meaninglessness or death.[3] The Psalmist expressed such desperation in Psalm 88:1-4: "O Lord . . . I cry out in your presence . . . my soul is full of troubles and my life draws near to She'ol. I am counted among those who go down to the Pit; I am like those who have no help." In Kohut's Self Psychology the key to human dysfunction is the chaotic turbulence of the dissolving self.[4] In

3. For a treatment of anxiety regarding dissolution of the self in the Psalmists' use of nephesh and Kohut's use of the concept of self, see Jeffrey H. Boyd, "Reclaiming the Soul: A Psychological and Biblical-Critical Enterprise," a paper read at the Society of Biblical Literature annual convention, San Francisco, November, 1997.

4. Heinz Kohut, *The Analysis of the Self: A Systematic Approach to the Psychoanalytic Treatment of Narcissistic Personality Disorders* (New York: International Universities Press, 1971). See also Heinz Kohut, *The Restoration of the Self* (New York: International Universities Press, 1977), and "Summarizing Reflections," in A. Goldberg, ed., *Advances in Self Psychology* (New York: International Universities Press, 1980).

ethical and theological terms it comes down to the question of sin or sickness.

Whether one considers the story of the Fall in Genesis 3 to be paradigmatic myth which serves the spiritual purpose of theological confession or whether one thinks of that narrative as a graphic historical report, it is nonetheless the case that all of us spontaneously acknowledge that the story fits our predicament. We are flawed, orphaned, lost souls. We have been cast out of our mother's womb and on our own we cannot catch hold of our Father's hand.

Professor Rolf Knierim declares at the outset of his superb chapter on sin that "It may be characteristic of our time that the subject of sin and guilt has come to elude intelligibility while the reality of evil pervades this planet at least as intensively as ever before. Everyone stares into the face of evil daily. Evil affects every human being in one way or another. This reality may defy rational explanation, but it can certainly be recognized. One need not be a pessimist to say that the idea of the perfectly good human being, or of progress toward that end, is unrealistically utopian."[5]

However, is the essential human difficulty a matter of pilot error or structural defect? (1) Are we flawed because we are corrupted by insidious moral perfidy? (2) Are we flawed by an early alienation which leaves us orphaned and desperate, thus fraught with defensive and aggressive needs to reduce our pain by self-inflicted wounds or by wounding others? (3) Are we flawed by reason of our incompleteness as immature creatures designed for growth and self-actualization and thus always possessed of inadequate information, foreshortened vision, incomplete wisdom, and uninformed judgment? (4) Are we creatures set upon a trajectory of development which always involves anxiety-inducing change and thus the destabilizing reach beyond our grasp, with which we are inevitably inadequate to cope? (5) Are we in the process of an evolution in which our genetics and biochemistry have not yet worked out all of their kinks and imbalances and thus leave us fretfully and frightfully short of our true destiny? Are we sinful or sick? Are we totally depraved or as yet too primal and under-actualized?[6]

5. Rolf P. Knierim, "On the Contours of Old Testament and Biblical Hamartiology," in his *The Task of Old Testament Theology: Method and Cases* (Grand Rapids: Eerdmans, 1995), p. 416.

6. For interesting data and commentary on these issues see "Targeting the Brain," *Time Magazine, Special Issue on The Frontiers of Medicine*, vol. 148, no. 14, Fall 1996, pp. 46-50.

With rare exception, human beings intend to do the right thing if they can. When that is not the case, the person or situation is pathological, by definition, psychologically or spiritually or both. Such concepts as original sin or total depravity are terms with which we attempted in the past to describe the observable fact that everything human tends to fall short of that which is ideal. "All have sinned and come short of the glory of God," is Paul's way of putting it.[7] That ideal, of course, is a human conception, conjured up by human minds which are always able to imagine or fantasize perfect worlds while being able to create only human and apparently flawed ones. The distance between what we can imagine or idealize and what we can create marks out the area and dimension of our pain, shame, guilt, and fear. Therefore, we take the measure of the nature and size of that discrepancy, between our ideal and actual states, and call it evil: sin and misery. Is it more sin or more misery? Is it sin or sickness?

II. Exposition

Whatever Became of Sin?

Twenty-five years ago secular and religious America alike were surprised and delighted when a noted psychiatrist published *Whatever Became of Sin?* for the book urged our society to recover a significant sense of human sinfulness and to motivate good behavior by increasing guilt levels. For those of us who were born in the depression and by sheer force of disciplined will defeated it and all our enemies in the great war that followed and then, in the '50s went on to build the most magnificent world which this planet had ever known, Menninger's book seemed to give us some sense of hope and stability when, in the late '60s, our world began to go out of control. Menninger claimed that sin is an alienation from our true selves, each other, and the universe, resulting from inattention to responsible relationship. With illustrations drawn mainly from the politics of ecology, poverty, and waste of national resources, he reduced the issue of sin and guilt to willful disobedience and thus to a matter of morality.

Unfortunately, this simplistic formula played directly into the secular notion that human dysfunction is simply a failure to keep the law and

7. Romans 3:23.

the Evangelical notion that it is merely a moralistic aberration. He thought that the pain of guilt would produce moral behavior, though there is no evidence that it ever has. He was calling for a return to the emphasis upon sin for its utilitarian value, a thing he thought the social sciences had psychologized away. The net effect was to reinforce the equation in which both secular and religious America are entrenched with great psychological investment: (anxiety/shame/guilt/blame) + (justice/penalty/punishment/expiation) = (justification/forgiveness/restoration/equilibrium).[8]

Not many voices were raised to counter this outlook. To many people in many ways it sounded good, a return to the foundations. After all, does the Bible not speak this way of the human predicament? Robin C. Cover tells us in the *Anchor Bible Dictionary*[9] that "The elaborate conception of sin in the Hebrew Bible reflects the influence of Semitic culture and the strongly ethical-moralistic character of ancient Israelite religion." What is easily overlooked by the general reader of the Bible in English, of course, is what Cover next asserts, "The complexity of sin as a doctrine in the Hebrew Bible is heightened because different literary genres depict sin in various ways." The subtleties, nuances, and complexities of the biblical message about what we in English call sin has been streamlined by the believing community for twenty centuries, and too easily reduced to mere moralism. Thus Menninger's brief was popular and continues to be.

What in the World Is Sin?

In *Counseling and the Human Predicament, A Study of Sin, Guilt, and Forgiveness,* I suggested that the "term we use to describe the nature of human failure must express three things. It must describe the brokenness of those relationships which are essential to our achievement of our true destiny. It must describe our proclivity to break the rules of moral responsibility. It must describe the systemic disorder which casts us inevitably into those first two dysfunctions and prevents us from lifting ourselves out of our

8. For secularists expiation must be made by the guilty person, for Fundamentalists and Evangelicals it can be made by God. For the latter, also, equilibrium must be restored in both the wrathful God and the dysfunctional human.

9. Robin C. Cover, "Sin, Sinners (Old Testament)," in David Noel Freedman *et alii,* eds., *The Anchor Bible Dictionary* (New York: Doubleday, 1992), vol. 6, p. 31.

forlorn predicament."[10] Implied in the term, *sin,* whether employed in a secular or sacred way, there must also be some reflection of the possibility of a resolution of the problem described. In religious perspective the term must imply the restoration of some kind of equilibrium within God, between God and humans, and within human beings. In biblical religion it should include notions of reconciliation of broken relationships, the forgiveness of transgressions and of our proclivity to commit them, the healing of the systemic disorder that prevents us from either avoiding our tragedy or healing it ourselves, and a restoration of the soul of the sinner (Ps. 19:14) and of our relationship with God.

Is the term *sin,* as the Bible uses it in our translations, or as people popularly use it, the best term to describe what ails us? Given our understanding of human dynamics, is it possible that the term *sickness* might express the biblical message about our dysfunction even better. The answer is *not* self-evident or a foregone conclusion. Whichever is the more adequate construct to carry the biblical revelation about the nature and implied cure of our problem, is obviously the one we are called upon to employ. Unfortunately, it *is* self-evident that when we use the term *sin* we have a 2,500-year history of reducing the concept to the (anxiety/shame/guilt/blame) + (justice/penalty/punishment/expiation) = (justification/forgiveness/restoration/equilibrium) equation, that is, to merely a juridical matter. This equation implies that our failure is moral turpitude and God's posture toward us is merely one of praise or blame. Then human disorder can be treated merely by the regimens of punishment or expiation. That does not handle adequately the complexities of the biblical message, and even more obviously, does not fit what we now know works psycho-spiritually for life change and growth in real persons.

Is it possible that the term *sin* has become a stereotyped and culture-bound notion, entrenched either in the Semitic or Hellenistic cultures of the biblical era or in the postures and predilections of the ancient or medieval church? It would be unbiblical to import post-biblical content into the biblical terms for sin, thus giving them different meaning freight than the biblical authors intended them to carry. Likewise, it is erroneous to import from the Bible a culture-bound or time-bound term which in

10. J. Harold Ellens, "Sin and Sickness: The Nature of Human Failure," in Leroy Aden and David G. Benner, eds., *Counseling and the Human Predicament: A Study of Sin, Guilt, and Forgiveness* (Grand Rapids: Baker, 1989), p. 58.

our century and thought-frames fails to describe adequately the human predicament of psycho-spiritual dysfunction upon which the Bible intends to speak to us. "This is particularly true of concepts that describe our humanness, since these often do not communicate with our sociological and psychological understanding of humanness and personhood."[11] We are morally and hermeneutically bound to employ for our culture, terms that accurately express the notion of human failure and its remedy, thereby preserving the biblical intent and the contemporary understanding. Are we talking about sin or sickness? Which one tells our story best?

Of course, this question has within it other questions. What is the Bible's message about human dysfunction and what is crucial in its intent? Did the church historically have those real issues clearly in mind in its use of the term *sin?* Do we know more about ourselves, about the dynamics of our function and dysfunction, today than did the biblical authors or the historic church? As we approach the new millennium we bring with us a well-developed science of the human psyche and spirit, Evangelical iconoclasts such as Paul Vitz and Mary Stewart Van Leeuwen to the contrary notwithstanding. That science provides us with an enormous empirical and phenomenological data base, thanks to such scholars as H. Newton Malony, Richard Gorsuch, Bernard Spilka, and others. Excellent models have been floated for understanding the disorder in persons and society, and we know a lot about its repair. Should this say anything definitive about how we hear the biblical message and act upon it? I think so. Both of God's books, in creation and Scripture, must be understood in the light of each other if either is to be taken seriously. The truth in each is God's truth and neither has higher priority or greater valence, as truth, than the other. God does not speak with a forked tongue. So any theologian who does not take seriously the light of psychology is not serious about doing sound theology; just as any psychologist who does not invite the illuminations of theology is not serious about scientifically sound psychology. Both psychology and theology have the same subject and data base: the living human document.[12] They must be compelled to speak to and illumine each other.[13]

11. Ibid., p. 59.

12. Charles V. Gerkin, *The Living Human Document, Re-Visioning Pastoral Counseling in a Hermeneutical Mode* (Nashville: Abingdon, 1984).

13. For various treatments of this issue of the interface of Psychology and Theology as sciences, see the following publications:

What Does the Bible Say?

The Bible has no word which is exactly equivalent to the English word *sin*. At least since the King James Version was published, *sin* is the English word used to translate at least thirteen biblical words, six Hebrew and seven Greek, the latter duplicating the constructs of the former. Cover states that "Like Hittite, Sumerian, and Akkadian literature, Israelite literature draws upon a rich thesaurus of terminology relating to sin. One may count over fifty words for 'sin' in biblical Hebrew. . . . The plethora of Hebrew terms and their ubiquitous presence in the Hebrew Bible testify to the fact that sin was a dominant concern of the Israelite theologians. Indeed, their high-lighting of human failure, deficiency, or offense in the cultic, ethical, and moral spheres constitutes a central theme of OT theology."[14] E. P. Sanders, in his treatment of sin in the New Testament, confirms this claim and emphasizes the dependence of the New Testament concept upon its Semitic precursors.[15] Simon John De Vries, in his definitive article in the *Interpreter's Dictionary of the Bible,* observes that "It is no accident that the Bible, with its keen sense of moral and spiritual values, is particularly rich in the vocabulary of sin. This is especially true of the OT. Not being interested in offering a theoretical definition, the Hebrew writers only strove to reflect in their rich and vivid terminology the profundity and the widespread effects of sin as they experienced it."[16]

Please notice that Cover emphasizes that the biblical authors were concerned with the broad spectrum of "human failure, deficiency, or offense" and De Vries points out that they were not interested in the theo-

---

J. Harold Ellens, *God's Grace and Human Health* (Nashville: Abingdon, 1982);

J. Harold Ellens, *Psychotheology: Key Issues* (Pretoria: UNISA, 1987);

J. Harold Ellens, "Guest Editorial: Psychology and the Bible: The Interface of Corollary Disciplines," and "The Bible and Psychology, an Interdisciplinary Pilgrimage," in *Pastoral Psychology,* vol. 45, no. 3, January 1997;

J. Harold Ellens, "The Interface of Psychology and Theology," in the *Journal of Psychology and Christianity,* vol. 16, no. 1, Spring 1997;

J. Harold Ellens, "Christian Humanistic Psychology," in Don Moss, ed., *Humanistic Psychology,* forthcoming from Greenwood Press, 1998.

14. Cover, "Sin, Sinners (Old Testament)," p. 31.

15. E. P. Sanders, "Sin, Sinners (New Testament)," in David Noel Freedman *et alii,* eds., *The Anchor Bible Dictionary* (New York: Doubleday, 1992), vol. 6, pp. 40-47.

16. Simon John De Vries, "Sin, Sinners," in *The Interpreter's Dictionary of the Bible* (Nashville: Abingdon, 1972), vol. IV, p. 361.

retical definition of sin so much as in wrestling with its operational manifestations. This strongly suggests that if the biblical authors were writing in our day they would be very much concerned to enunciate the scope and complexity of human dysfunction as they saw it, far beyond the range of mere moral failure. They were wrestling with the generalized predicament of humans falling short in every area of potential growth, development, and actualization — short of our own possibilities and God's expectations. Those authors, therefore, would be most interested in taking into consideration, in their conceptual models, the entire empirical and phenomenological data base we now have available to us regarding function and dysfunction in the human person, psyche, and spirit. Indeed, it seems an inevitable conclusion that they would consider their constructs grossly deficient without it.

The biblical terms that we render *sin* in English all call our attention to relational dysfunction or inappropriateness of some kind. Behind these biblical terms and concepts lies the root idea that by nature our proper destiny is in relationship. By virtue of our existence we are in covenant with ourselves, others, creation, and God. These covenantal relationships, essential as they are to our self-actualization as persons made in God's image, imply responsibility. The human dysfunction at stake in the notion we call sin, is a failure to attend properly to this responsibility. This notion has many subsidiary aspects, one of which is the *moral* component of the biblical concept of sin, that is, willful failure to be responsible in a setting in which we have the capacity to be responsible.

But the biblical terminology weaves a basket which carries a much larger load than this one subsidiary notion. Indeed, the moral component is by no means the primary problem in the human predicament as seen by the biblical authors. Paul's greatest concern was about "the good that I would which I do not, and the evil which I would not, but I do." The weightiest perplexity in the biblical concept of sin concerns that wide scope of human dysfunction which is not chosen by the perpetrator, over which he seemingly has little or no control, and which seems a systemic affliction of persons and societies. Already fifteen years ago Martin Seligman published his extensive study on what can and cannot be changed in human disorders. He made the conservative estimate, on the basis of the data then available, that less than 50 percent of all human psycho-spiritual dysfunction can be changed by moral-spiritual and psycho-social strategies or by therapeutic intervention that does not address the issues of chemistry. Since then the overwhelming data available has moved that number closer to 20 percent, in the judgment of most clinicians and research psychologists.[17]

The biblical words are very interesting.[18] They tell us of the inherent human inclination to miss the mark, to fall short of expectations, to veer from the standard, to be inadequate to requirements, to evidence a nasty disposition, to be perverted in character, to be insensitive and situationally inappropriate, particularly as compatriots of God living before God's face. In sum, they speak of our failure to reflect, do, or achieve the ideal design for us; a failure to achieve our ideal potential actualization as persons filled with all the possibilities of God's creative image in us. There is a distortion, fracture, or deficiency in God's nature in us. These dysfunctions are occasionally characterized as impiety or even rebellion, more frequently, in the New Testament at least, unrighteousness and depravity. However, the general pattern which these terms describe is a dynamic operational program that would fall clearly within the contemporary diagnosis of Borderline Personality Syndrome (Borderline Psychosis).

This syndrome generally has five characteristics or symptoms: a high degree of narcissism, a schizoid model of reality which does not calibrate with the real world, lack of impulse control, situationally inappropriate behavior, and a combination of anxiety and depression.[19] It tends to show up during the biochemical turbulence of puberty. It falls into categories of mild, moderate, and severe. We now know that this condition is inherited, that it is biochemically mediated in a person's character and personality function, and that it is almost certainly gene-linked. It is estimated that 40 percent of any given human community suffer from one of the three degrees of this disorder. The manifestations of this condition are now relatively effectively eliminated by the application of brain chemistry supplements which provide those which are deficient in a person's inherited biochemistry.

Most studies of the biblical theology of sin have tended to read the data primarily through the distorted lens that focuses mainly upon the

17. Martin E. P. Seligman, *What You Can Change . . . And What You Can't* (New York: Fawcett Columbine, 1993) (original clothbound edition published by Alfred A. Knopf).

18. Ellens, "Sin and Sickness: The Nature of Human Failure," in Leroy Aden and David G. Benner, eds., *Counseling and the Human Predicament: A Study of Sin, Guilt, and Forgiveness* (Grand Rapids: Baker, 1989), pp. 60-65.

19. DSM IV.

moral component of human dysfunction. However, even the biblical concern with unrighteousness, depravity, and rebellion is largely a focus upon a state or condition of disorder rather than upon the consequence of willful choices. The Bible seems overwhelmingly concerned with the pathetic predicament of humans being abjectly out of joint with, or off the track of, the true destiny of appropriate human actualization, a perplexing state from which only external healing intervention can deliver. Legalistic models of sin, guilt, and blame, whether secular or Evangelical, which are oriented upon juridical solutions of atonement and justification are far too simplistic. They do not begin to comprehend the extent of the human tragedy. Our state and condition is far worse than that. Without an external healer and an unconditional altruistic healing intervention, we are lost.

Our information is inadequate, our experience too limited, our vision too blurred, our inherent qualities insufficient, and our maturity incomplete. We are cast out of the womb of Eden without a vote. We cannot catch hold of our Father's hand unless he reaches out and clasps ours in his. We long mystically and confusingly for home. Meanwhile, we stumble often, ever struggle, and blindly stagger, looking for the light. Some of us lose hope, convert the pain to neurotic guilt and slowly die of myriad forms of dis-ease. Others convert the pain to rage and aggressive destruction of others and self-defeat. Are we sinful or are we sick? Both! But more the latter than the former. If we are to take the biblical terminology seriously, with the chastening caution which James Barr lays upon us,[20] we are forced to the conclusion that the Bible is saying more about our pathology than our moral perfidy, more about our lostness than our chosen lousiness. It is imperative that the believing community comes to terms with this and rewrites the corpus of theology to reflect its implications for a sound theology of sin and salvation.

What Are We Really up Against?

If we are to be true to the biblical notions about human dysfunction we must shift the valence of our concept of sin somewhat away from the equation of (anxiety/shame/guilt/blame) + (justice/ penalty/punishment/expi-

---

20. James Barr, *The Semantics of Biblical Language* (Oxford: Oxford, 1961; third impression (pb), Philadelphia: Trinity Press International, 1991).

ation) = (justification/forgiveness/restoration/equilibrium) which has dominated that concept for twenty centuries. We must move more radically toward a formula which gets us out of the blame process into a category in which the real force of grace is the dominant consideration. Such a healing-oriented model would recognize the proportional degree to which the Bible emphasizes a compassionate sense of the psychopathological nature of the human problem. That equation would probably look more like the following: (pain/shame/guilt/anxiety) + (passion/compassion/mercy/grace) = (forgiveness [and other therapies]/affirmation/healing/actualization).[21]

To continue to use the first model, which we might call the blame-justification model and which continues to have great appeal to the secular and religious worlds, runs obviously unacceptable risks, as we have seen. It authorizes the excessive moralization of human dysfunction. It does not take the human predicament seriously enough. It biases the issue toward legalism, prompting self-demeanment or defensive-aggressive self-justification strategies instead of true spirituality and psychological

21. Paolo Sacchi, *Jewish Apocalyptic and Its History* (Sheffield: Sheffield Academic Press, 1990), pp. 72-87. Sacchi informs us that this set of equations for the relationship between God and humans was already solidly in place in the two kingdoms of Israel in the eighth century BCE. The Northern Kingdom generally represented the legalistic model with its salvation by obedience to the covenant laws. The Southern Kingdom represented the grace model with its salvation by trusting God's unconditional promise. The Josiah reform included the attempt to conflate the two as a concession to the northern priests deported to Jerusalem as Josiah spread southern theology and its Jerusalem-centered worship to the north, destroying the northern worship centers. Sacchi suggests that the deportation to Babylon included these northern priests whose ideology triumphed during the captivity. The exiles returned under Zerubbabel with northern theology and encountered southern grace theology among the remnant in the land of Judea. They attempted to integrate the two as had Josiah. When the exiles who returned later under Nehemiah arrived they uncompromisingly imposed northern theology upon the inhabitants of Judea and Jerusalem. This later manifested itself in the tradition of the Pharisees and subsequently the Rabbis and the *Talmudim*. Deuteronomy and related literature are northern documents. The southern documentary tradition was repressed, but is now somewhat preserved in the unofficial tradition of such extra-canonical books as *I Enoch* (an alternate Pentateuch), *Apocalypse of Zephaniah, Syriac Apocalypse of Baruch,* and *4 Ezra*. Jesus was a northerner from Nazareth in Galilee but he seems to have opposed the southern Pharisees from Jerusalem for their "northern" legalistic theology while he held out for a "southern" grace theology. Both are in the Bible. Which is the word of God?

wholeness. It increases psychospiritual and social dysfunction. It makes the concept and experience of grace difficult to receive. It alienates us further from our own natures and from others by implying that relief and repair can be acquired through achievement or atonement: paying the fee.

Six Case Illustrations

This perspective becomes particularly malignant and complex in view of the increasingly evident data of recent research which suggests that up to 80 percent of the psychopathology distorting the function of human character and personality operations derives from genetic and biochemical sources which the subject did not choose and over which the person has no significant control. A few illustrations will suffice, so I offer them as follows.

First, whereas I do not consider homosexual orientation to be sinful, many believers do, and in any case there seems reason to consider it a departure from the norm. From this variance has devolved much suffering and dysfunction for many persons. Recent brain tissue studies, biological studies, psycho-social analyses, twin studies,[22] and longitudinal assessments indicate that homosexual orientation is an inborn sexual posture, neither chosen nor changeable by the homosexual person, alone or through therapy.[23] You may wish to examine an extended study of this

---

22. For a critical assessment of this issue see R. L. Suddath, G. W. Christison, E. F. Torrey, M. F. Casanova, and D. R. Weinberger, "Anatomical Abnormalities in the Brains of Monozygotic Twins Discordant for Schizophrenia, *New England Journal of Medicine*, vol. 332, p. 793. See also "Kids with Schizophrenia Yield Brain Clues," in *Science News*, vol. 152, no. 17, October 25, 1997, p. 261; Glenn Weisfeld and Donald M. Aytch, "Biological Factors in Family Violence," in *Michigan Faculty Review, Attacking Violence: Prevention and Intervention*, vol. 2, no. 1, Spring 1996, pp. 25-39; and Thomas H. Maugh II, "Scientists Identify Gene That May Raise Schizophrenia Risk," *Los Angeles Times*, October 31, 1997, pp. 3ff.

23. See, for example, the following:

Anthony Kosnik *et alii, Human Sexuality* (New York: Paulist, 1977).

"Brain Feature Linked to Sexual Orientation," *Science News*, vol. 140, Aug. 31, 1991, p. 134.

"Genetic Clue to Male Homosexuality Emerges," *Science News*, vol. 144, July 17, 1993, p. 37.

"Genetic Influence Tied to Male Sexual Orientation," *Science News*, vol. 141, Jan. 4, 1992, p. 6.

matter which I published as "Homosexuality in Biblical Perspective" in the September 1997 issue of *Pastoral Psychology*.[24]

Second, the familial patterns so apparent in the syndrome of alcoholism and other addictive behaviors such as drug abuse, gambling, and true forms of sexual addiction have long been observed. Now a genetic source for predilection toward alcoholism seems already to have appeared over the horizon and the typical addictive personality is generally most readily accounted for as a form of Borderline Syndrome.

Third, the inherited and biochemical sources for many psychoses, particularly the various schizophrenias, have been suspected for a half century and understood more clearly for three decades. Now we have empirical and heuristic evidence that most psychoses are associated with chemical deficiencies or disturbances and that Borderline Personality Syndrome is likewise inherited and biochemical in root. These data are confirmed by the significant positive results which derive from appropriate brain chemistry supplements, versus the mere mood manipulators which we needed to use two decades ago, for want of anything better. Formerly we referred to people suffering with Borderline Syndrome as Psychopaths and Sociopaths, terms which implied a capacity to behave more appropriately and a moral decision to behave destructively. Now we know that the patient neither chooses nor can change this condition on his or her own. This might well be considered the most pervasive and destructive of all human dysfunctions.

Fourth, it is increasingly evident to most clinicians that the enormous number of children being diagnosed by school psychologists and social workers as ADD and ADHD today, is largely a function of the need for the schools to achieve the maximum income from the state by keeping the maximum number of students, namely 27 percent of the school population, in special categories. There is now strong evidence that most of these children are really Borderline Syndrome.

Four decades ago those in the severe category were diagnosed as Schizophrenics and treated in adolescence with anti-psychotic medication, with some degree of success. The most recent reports indicate that 600,000

"Homosexual Parents: All in the Family," *Science News*, vol. 147, Jan. 21, 1995, p. 42.

"X Chromosome Again Linked to Sexuality," *Science News*, vol. 148, Nov. 4, 1995, p. 295.

24. J. Harold Ellens, "Homosexuality in Biblical Perspective," in *Pastoral Psychology*, vol. 46, no. 1, September 1997.

American children are now being successfully treated for Borderline Syndrome with the current medication of choice, one of the five or six Prozacs available for modulating the serotonin production in the brain, and/or the dopamine levels.[25] This is a very rewarding state of affairs. Finally, we are treating these unfortunate persons in a way which can normalize them rather than moralize their dysfunction and blame them. These are the people with the pattern of characteristics which most accurately fit the comprehensive biblical paradigm or taxonomy of disorders identified by the six Hebrew and seven Greek words we translate as *sin*.

Fifth, 80 percent of the women in the world are afflicted with PMS. Twenty percent fall into the severe category of this disorder, experiencing enormous suffering, psychotic-like symptoms with serious psychologically and socially destructive behavior. This is, of course, derived exclusively from periodic biochemical changes.[26] If this chronic Borderline-like suffering had been the burden of men instead of women, it would have been definitively addressed a few thousand years ago, rather than only in the last decade. Both the analysis and medical treatment of this disorder confirms its biochemical source and its tendency to appear in familial patterns.

Sixth, similar data can be adduced regarding panic disorders, most depression and anxiety disorders, seasonal affective disorder, and obsessive-compulsive disorders. Most of the diagnosable disorders mentioned have in common at least three of the following five factors: familial patterns, relative ineffectiveness of psychotherapy by itself, effectiveness of medical intervention, empirically assessable chemistry deficiencies or aberrations, and strong confirmation of inherited roots by such research as the twin studies, and the like. Some are now directly linked to specific aberrant genes or brain tissue variants.

Theological Implications

This state of affairs has two significant theological implications which the church must take as its main theological task for the 21st century. The first

25. News Report on CNN Headline News, 10 Aug. 1997, 7:30 P.M.
26. Norbert O. Anderson and J. Harold Ellens, "Endocrine Chemistry and Psychological States," in the *Journal of Psychology and Christianity*, vol. 8, no. 2, Summer 1989.

element of this task is to address the rather awesome problem that the ancient issue of determinism has once again reared its ugly head. This time it is less the philosophical problem of divine determinism in some kind of intentional predestination. Now we face the problem of biological determinism.[27] The church did not deal well or honestly with this issue when Darwin raised it 150 years ago, despite his massive data base, but now we cannot avoid dealing with it directly, since the empirical biochemical data driving it is overwhelming and unavoidable. Inherent in the data is the clear picture that a great deal of the spiritual, psychological, and social function and dysfunction characteristic of humans is preset to a large extent by the operations of and disturbances in the endocrine/chemistry/psychological/states equation.

This difficulty has two perplexing problems within it. It asks us to what extent humans can be held accountable, and, therefore, in what ways we must rewrite our theology of sin. And it asks us what salvation can possibly mean in the face of the real data about the extent of our helplessness and hopelessness. Henry Stob often said that our wills are free only within the bounds of that to which our hearts are committed. Now we know that our hearts' capacity for commitments is frequently preset by our biochemistry. We must rewrite our theology of sin and of salvation in new and *operationally responsive* terms that take this seriously or we will continue to be guilty of being abusive of suffering humankind.

What can sin mean and what must grace mean, in view of what we now know about the real state of our humanness and our inherently flawed nature? How can we start to talk about the human condition in operational terms that are not other worldly and mythic but rather grounded in our experience and our earthly pilgrimage, seen starkly for what it is? How can we learn to speak of salvation in a language which describes the operations of grace in a human being and in human social process in experiential terms? How can we make that into language which reflects empirical and heuristic evidence for actual human change, its sources, character, components, trajectories, and drivers, rather than language which speaks in grand historic terms about mythic interpretations of ancient events? How can we speak of the cross as operational in the healing of what we

---

27. For a rather popularized critique of this position see "Born Bad? How the Politics of Biology Shapes Opinion, Policy, and our Self Image," *U.S. News and World Report*, August 21, 1997.

know is wrong with us, rather than representing it as the center of an abstract myth about divine equilibrium, the foundation of a theoretical model of remote divine juridical intervention on our behalf, and religious symbology conveyed in mystically spiritualized constructs, languaged in metaphors of ancient and alien cultures?

Can grace speak to the psychologized world of our time and explain in our language how, operationally, it changes things for us? If so, what does that sound like? Only religious poetry? Only churchy words and confessional creeds? Only spiritualized rubrics? Only mythic models of thought?

In his poetic and marvelously readable piece, *A Breviary of Sin,* Cornelius Plantinga worries on page 103 that asking these questions in a way which implies high priority to psychological models runs the risk of reductionism.[28] I too am worried about reductionism, but then the Pauline model of the cross is already a theological reductionism, as is a worse case, the Chalcedonian Creed, filled as it is with Alexandrian Hellenistic Neo-Platonism. Every human attempt to ask the crucial questions about what the Bible can possibly mean for us in operationally redemptive terms heads us inevitably into reductionism of some sort. That is how we get hold of things, try to understand things, attempt to control the data with hypotheses that might help us perceive better and work more honestly. Is psychological reductionism worse than theological reductionism?

It is not inherently reductionistic to pursue the quest for truth down unusual or untraditional roads if that pursuit is done with integrity, its presuppositions and limitations acknowledged up front. To ask the Bible to speak to our 20th-century understanding of the human psyche and spirit, and to do it in our language, looks like reductionism only from the perspective of an insufficiently critical and perhaps too traditional theological model. *Any* perspective one takes constitutes a lens through which to look at a matter and its relevant data. The language and models we use shape the focus of our vision and inherently constrain us from seeing reality, data, or any question, in a new way. Using a new paradigm, such as a psychological or psycho-spiritual perspective, to look at issues which have generally been handled in a theological perspective may not be reductionist at all. That may have just the opposite effect, namely,

28. Cornelius Plantinga, Jr., *Not the Way It's Supposed to Be: A Breviary of Sin* (Grand Rapids: Eerdmans, 1995).

to expand the way we see the matter — and hence to expand our grasp of the truth. That would enlarge the picture rather than reduce it. My assumption in these lectures is that if we can look at sin and grace theologically and psychologically, without trying to fix a line or chasm between the two, we shall finally be able to construct our questions and answers in usefully operational terms.

The second major theological issue which the church must address is the question as to whether it really can overcome its historic popular predilection toward the blame-justification model and shift its view to the radical grace equation which is so obviously the central truth of the gospel.[29] Can the church claim the truth that the state of affairs is better described in the (pain/shame/guilt/anxiety) + (passion/compassion/mercy/grace) = (forgiveness [and other therapies]/affirmation/healing/actualization) equation? Can the church then rewrite its theology of salvation in the kind of operational terms which make it articulate to every suffering soul out there who is hungering for home in his or her own personal pathological way? What does it mean to be saved? Can we answer that in terms of the rubrics of psychological, spiritual, social, and political wholeness? If we cannot, we do not know what we are talking about and the world will never be able to figure it out either.

In his provocative Stob Lectures of October 1994, John Feikens attempted to do what I am talking about. He spoke on *Conflict: Its Resolution and the Completion of Creation.* His brief was a claim that salvation takes the operational social form of working through the violence of conflict to the representation of everyone's legitimate claims and on to a negotiated resolution in which social process and human growth and healing can go forward at the personal and communal levels. In this matter, he asserted, the adversarial process is part of God's ordained technique for working through us to complete his work of insuring that the needs and wants of individual persons and groups are adequately attended and taken seriously, individuality is certified in the context of communal life, and freedom is enhanced. It can be seen clearly how this expresses the socio-political operations of salvation process.[30] Karl Popper made much the same point in his

29. J. Harold Ellens, "God's Grace, The Radical Option," in *Perspectives: A Journal of Reformed Thought*, vol. 4, no. 9, November 1989.

30. John Feikens, *Conflict: Its Resolution and the Completion of Creation* (Grand Rapids: The Stob Lectures Endowment at Calvin College and Calvin Theological Seminary, 1995).

autobiography, *Unended Quest,* when he said that criticism and conflict are essential to growth, progress, and healing. Truth, like organic species, evolves through contest and competition, conjecture and refutation. "The human society without conflict would be a society not of friends but of ants."[31] Kathleen J. Greider, Assistant Professor of Pastoral Care and Counseling at the School of Theology at Claremont following Howard Clinebell's retirement, agrees as she attempts to bring psychological and pastoral theological insights to bear on our strategies of justice, a thing she considers one of the crucial operational dimensions of salvation.[32]

Is it possible to make similar claims for the salvation which comes in the forms of psychological healing and the restoration of social function? Can we create operational models for that which adequately reflect what the Bible intends to tell us about salvation? Can we go further than that and create operational models for the healing of the inner spiritual self in its capacity for the transcendent reach for God and ultimate meaning? Can we do more than poetry and metaphor to describe the actual operational steps which take place in the soul to accomplish what David claims happened to him salvifically (Psalm 19:7-8):

> The law of the Lord is perfect, reviving the soul;
> The decrees of the Lord are sure, making wise the simple;
> The precepts of the Lord are right, rejoicing the heart;
> The commandments of the Lord are clear,
> > enlightening the eyes.

Can David's experiential report in Psalm 23:2-4 be translated into operational models, terms, and steps?

> God makes me lie down in green pastures;
> He leads me beside still waters;
> He restores my soul.
> Though I walk through the darkest valley, I fear not
> For you are with me.

31. Karl Popper, *Unended Quest* (La Salle, Ill.: Open Court, 1974; revised edition, 1982), p. 116.

32. Kathleen J. Greider, "'Too Militant?': Aggression, Gender, and the Construction of Justice," Inaugural Lecture, School of Theology at Claremont, March 9, 1993, published as *Occasional Paper, No. 10,* vol. 3, no. 2, School of Theology at Claremont.

I do not wish to destroy poetry or devalue the stimulating delight of metaphor. I am simply asking, What is David, the man like me, describing as happening inside of him? Can we give it concrete language? Can we convey to a suffering soul what he or she is in for or what he or she can get to in psycho-spiritual steps along David's trajectory? Is John 3:16-17 translatable into operational categories? Something like that was attempted thirty years ago in the Love of God Controversy, as it was then styled. What destroyed the endeavor was the management of the discussion at Synod in such a manner that the debate was forced back upon the language terrain of medieval theological categories. As long as the hermeneutical process was forced into that construct, no new questions could be asked and no new ways of answering the old questions could be found. The proponents of this endeavor could not achieve a footing upon which to get the church to talk about the truths at stake in contemporary operational language that made practical sense. Synod was happy, of course. The Imperial Church was safe and victorious. But the believing community lost out in its quest for self-understanding and God's redemptive way with it in something other than medieval idiom.

Seward Hiltner, likewise wrote his *Theological Dynamics* in an effort to translate the language of sin and salvation into operational terms.[33] To the extent that he succeeded it is a result of his agile mind. But he largely failed in the task because he was, himself, so constrained by the traditional language and rubrics of historic theology that he was limited in his ability to ask the questions in a new and fresh way. Similarly, the Pastoral Care movement and the Clinical Pastoral Education movement made efforts to develop operational models which took with adequate seriousness what we know about human dysfunction and healing from both theology and psychology. In the case of the former, as with Hiltner himself, the enterprise floundered because it could not escape the mythic language and images of the ancient church's constructs. The CPE movement failed because it so aggressively avoided those mythic models that it resorted exclusively to psychological, or more accurately, pop-psych models, which, in the end, held no water, conveyed no meaning, and could not restore the soul.

Can we not do better than that? Is it so difficult to write a creed in which we can say in operational terms, in 20th-century language, that the passionate positive regard of God and God's people toward us is radical,

33. Seward Hiltner, *Theological Dynamics* (Nashville: Abingdon, 1972).

unconditional, and universal; and say it or enact it in such a way that the least informed and most desperate person can see the practical way in which that truth saves him or her from fear, guilt, shame, anxiety, defeating strategies of self-justification, destructive aggression, and alienation from self-actualization? Can we hook that up with the action of intervening medically and psychologically in his or her life so as to free that spirit and psyche from inherent pathologies, to experience life whole — to be saved?

Ethical Implications

I have stated that 80 percent of everything we see of human dysfunction is genetic and biochemical in origin and must be treated by some form of brain chemistry supplement in order to restore the capacity to function. I have contended that 40 percent of any human community suffers from a mild, moderate, or severe form of Borderline Personality Syndrome. This is at least the case for North Americans who derive from North European genetic roots. One-third of these, or 13.5 percent of the population, are mildly afflicted. These are the folks who seem very bright, creative, engaging, seductive, imaginative, and expressive, from whom you expect great things, but they have little or no ability to focus upon long-term goals, follow through on opportunities, or build upon their own achievements. They do not learn from experience. They seem to manage rather normally step-by-step day-by-day but when you see them ten years later you are surprised that they have not gotten anywhere, so to speak.

Another third, or 13.5 percent of the total population, is moderately afflicted. These folks function from day to day about the same as the mildly affected, but under any type of crisis or unexpected development they seriously dysfunction, reacting in a situationally inappropriate manner: fear, insensitivity, rage, neurotic anxiety, hopelessness, paranoia, aggression, or the like. The final third fall into the category of severe Borderline Syndrome. Most of these people are in psychiatric hospitals or prisons or probably should be. Now we must remind ourselves that Borderline Syndrome is an inherited disorder which the person suffering with it did not choose and cannot change or control.

A high percentage of prisoners apparently fall into the category of severe Borderline.

A recent report of a ten-year longitudinal study of the population of Women's Correctional Facilities in Texas, reported by Anderson, indicated that 80 percent were diagnosable as Borderline Psychotic.[34] Felicity de Zulueta, in *From Pain to Violence,* confirms this picture for men as well as women.[35] In 1985 two Harvard research scholars, Wilson and Herrnstein, studied biology, gender, race, age, personality, intelligence, and culture as correlates of crime. Both have numerous publications in quantitative and qualitative analysis of human criminality and related psycho-social dysfunction. This present study, *Crime and Human Nature,* drew similar conclusions to those of Anderson and Zulueta, emphasizing in addition that crime is often a matter of a person's choice but the choice is usually forced by internal rather than external factors and biology ranks high in those causes.[36] It is of at least incidental interest that men prisoners tend to manifest Borderline symptoms in the form of unstable ego structures, narcissism, schizoid perceptions of reality, and the consequent situationally inappropriate behavior, usually in destructively aggressive form. Women tend to manifest higher levels of paranoia, schizoid perceptions of reality, depression and anxiety, and the consequent situationally inappropriate behavior, often passive-aggressive and more directly self-destructive.

Is it any wonder, then, that measured by the government's own statistical reports, the $40 billion the US has spent on prison rehabilitation programs over the last forty years shows so little outcome success? If an overwhelming percentage of persons, in and out of prison, who dysfunction severely in our society, are Borderlines, they are incapable of projecting themselves into other persons' feeling worlds, incapable of viewing themselves from afar with any objectivity, and incapable of learning from experience or building upon prior achievement. They are not cerebrally wired, so to speak, for constructive relational function unless they are medicated. The key ethical issue for the 21st century is, Who is going to assume the responsibility for medicating the severely dysfunctional in our society so as to save these suffering souls from their enormous pain and dysfunction,

34. A. J. Williams, Ph.D., in a personal conversation with J. Harold Ellens, Ph.D., 28 July 1997.

35. Felicity de Zulueta, *From Pain to Violence: The Traumatic Roots of Destructiveness* (New York: Jason Aronson, 1994).

36. James Q. Wilson and Richard J. Herrnstein, *Crime and Human Nature* (New York: Simon and Schuster, a Touchstone Book, 1985).

and save society billions of dollars from the destruction they wreak, the public support they require, and the loss of productivity they represent; billions we could really use elsewhere?

III. Conclusion

The church, the believing community, and the Christian helping professions must take the lead in answering these weighty theological and ethical questions because no one else is equipped to do so. To do this we must either get rid of our moralistic concept of sin altogether and recognize that the overwhelming problem for humans is diagnosable pathology, or we must infuse our theology of sin with the biblical meanings of dysfunction and illness, thus shifting the process from the (anxiety/shame/guilt/blame) + (justice/penalty/punishment/expiation) = (justification/forgiveness/restoration/equilibrium) equation to the (pain/shame/guilt/anxiety) + (passion/compassion/mercy/grace) = (forgiveness [and other therapies]/affirmation/healing/actualization) formula. To do this we will need to disabuse both the Christian and secular communities of their enormous investment in preserving the moralistic notion of sin; and of legalistic, mechanical, materialistic, or merely mythical notions of both sin and salvation.

If the church does not equip itself to lead the way in developing a theological world view and an operational ethical proposal for society in the matter of biological determinism and of medicating the seriously dysfunctional, no one will. No other institution or community in our society is equipped to give the kind of ideological leadership grounded in operational data required in this matter. These kinds of issues require a redemptive idea that gives sufficient meaning and focus to the perplexing practical issues involved, that people can believe in a redemptive course of action that will work. Then, as a society, we will do it. In case the church does not rise to the occasion, society will blunder into horrible pitfalls of ethical, political, and spiritual abuse of its needy citizens and the church will find itself increasingly distanced from the real issues of human dysfunction and suffering.

If we can undertake this enterprise successfully it will be possible to empower our society with a sound theological-philosophical basis and rationale for making the awesome imperative ethical decisions we will face in the next century and millennium. A crucial consequence of this will be to shift the focus from denigrating the dysfunctional person as inherently an aberration, to a compassionate concern to affirm the person in his or her suffering and intervene with definitive empowerment for healing. Then we can challenge him or her to disciplined management of his or her symptoms, in so far as possible, by cooperation with the healing interventions provided. Grace and healing will thus lead to compassionate tough love, providing the appropriate limits on the pathology, and creating useful boundaries for behavior. This should normalize such persons so that the inner illumination of faith, trust, and hope can bring spiritual salvation, as well. Surely, all of these factors are important contours on the terrain of the experience of divine redemption.

Theology and Ethics: From the Bottom Up

I. Introduction

Throughout the history of the church, with rare exception, we have done theology and ethics from the top down. We have taken the ancient constructs, metaphors, and language of scriptures formulated during the 1200 years from David to the Apostle John and deduced from those the philosophical formulations of historic theology. From these philosophical formulas we have deduced Christian ethics. In this process we have forced contemporary language, metaphor, data, and idiom to stand aside while we endeavored to make the ancient words make modern sense. As a result, the church has constantly created a message and meanings which speak only to the in-crowd and sound to the wide world of suffering humanity like gibberish which does not plug in to real life.

While the Imperial Church lasted, its rubrics could be imposed upon society whether folks understood the message or not.[1] Since then orthodox theology has really been mainly a theodicy. Like that of Job's three friends, orthodox theology has been largely an enterprise designed to justify God in the face of the brokenness of God's world. It has not been a reach into the human and cosmic brokenness with the primary ambition of discerning the language of healing. Now that, during the last two centuries, Constantine's Imperial Church has eroded and decayed under the impact of the Enlightenment and its aftermath, the church's message is no

---

1. Douglas Hall, *The End of Christendom and the Future of Christianity* (Philadelphia: Trinity Press International, 1995).

more possible to hear today than it ever was and the church's power to impose it upon society has significantly lessened.

But hungry hearts still long for home and transcendent meaning everywhere. As a result we live in an age in which humanity has gone *en masse* after other spiritual experiences. Some have embraced the spirituality of cynicism and hopelessness, some New Age theological mythology, still others Eastern mysticism and Indian Gurus, while others are flying back into the mystic mythology and magical thinking of American Fundamentalism. Moreover, this is not just happening in those who have left the church. It is happening to those who are still within the church as well — within your churches.

Of course, there have been some exceptions to the church doing its theology only in terms of the ancient metaphors and from the top down. In the first lecture I mentioned the efforts of Seward Hiltner in his *Theological Dynamics* to restate Christian theology from the perspective of Pastoral Care and its claims. I also mentioned the Pastoral Care movement and the Clinical Pastoral Education movement, both of which, incidently, were initiated under Hiltner's influence, and which made some attempt to create theological constructs sensitive to the dynamics of psycho-spiritual function and dysfunction. I note, too, the attempts by Jürgen Moltmann in his development of a theology of hope,[2] as well as the Liberation Theologies[3] which attempted to start in the experience of the barrios of Latin America and discern what the biblical metaphors could be made to mean in modern idiom. These attempts should be seen as beginning efforts to do precisely what most needs to be done for the gospel of grace in our time.

We are in our time in possession of an enormous data base about the function and dysfunction of human personality and character. We should

2. Jürgen Moltmann, *Religion, Revolution, and the Future* (New York: Scribners, 1969). See also by the same author, *Theology of Hope* (New York: Harper, 1967); *Creating a Just Future* (Philadelphia: Trinity Press International, 1989); *The Way of Jesus Christ: Christology in Messianic Dimensions* (San Francisco: Harper, 1990); *The Church in the Power of the Spirit* (New York: Harper, 1977); *The Experiment Hope* (Philadelphia: Fortress, 1975). See also M. Douglas Meeks, *Origins of the Theology of Hope* (Philadelphia: Fortress, 1974).

3. Jürgen Moltmann, *The Power of the Powerless: The Word of Liberation for Today* (San Francisco: Harper, 1983). See also Scott Mainwaring and Alexander Wilde, eds., *The Progressive Church in Latin America* (Notre Dame: Univ. of Notre Dame Press, 1989), and Phillip Berryman, *The Religious Roots of Rebellion: Christians in Central American Revolutions* (Maryknoll, N.Y.: Orbis, 1984).

be able to formulate with confidence, clear and comprehensive constructs descriptive of what ails us and what, expressed in operational terms, saves us. It should be possible for us to express this concern for what saves us in concrete language and idiom. Moreover, that expression should include the entire range of human dysfunction which needs redemption: a salvation which deals specifically with human spirituality and its reach for the transcendent, human psychology and its reach for our inner selves and the other, human sociology and our need for community, human politics and our quest for order and the redeemed use of power, human economics and the godly use of the material creation, and the like. To excessively spiritualize what salvation means is as erroneous as over-psychologizing it.

In the first lecture I urged that we construct a comprehensive theology of salvation from the bottom up by rethinking our theological framework and content in terms of operational models. Let me try to set forth in some graphic detail what I mean by an operational model. I mean that we should construct a model of human dysfunction and of God's intervention in it, in which we are able to describe in concrete language the specific elements of human psycho-spiritual operations in a person and/or community, which go wrong in our sin or sickness, and the palpable ways in which they fail. The model must also be able to describe in similar concreteness the elements inherent in God's intervention of grace which can be identified as the tangible factors that effect change spiritually, psychologically, and socio-politically. The model must assume and describe the specific ways in which dysfunction and salvation are comprehensive operations that involve the entire life of the individual and his or her communal set. That is, sin or sickness and salvation have to do with failure and re-normalization of a person's sense of being cherished, hopeful, secure, purposeful, focused, joyful, employed, relationally fulfilled, empowered, creative, in communion with God, praise-filled, generative, and communally significant.

Such an operational model must identify those specific social, chemical, psychological, and spiritual components which effect change in humans for ill or good. These include internal and external factors. It must also describe precisely the way in which each is positively or negatively modified when we fail or when healing intervention is applied. It must define the specific forces which effect dysfunction or salvation and describe on empirical grounds just how they work.

I might take an illustration from my childhood. In my home church a sixty-year-old man began to report that he had committed the unforgivable sin. He had been a life-long saint and generative leader in the church and community. Now he could not come to worship because he was filled with shame and guilt. He went about his life in enormous sadness. His behavior became bizarre. He wandered the fields day and night. Like a mad man, in his wanderings he cried out to God for mercy. He said he could not pray because heaven seemed like a lead vault his petitions could not penetrate. God had cast him off. He was bound for eternal damnation. His appearance deteriorated. His clothes were filthy and disheveled. He was constantly hostile and abusive to his wife who tried to corral him into more situation-appropriate behavior. He became increasingly alienated from the community. He developed exotic ideas of theological mythology, saw demons regularly, and generally harangued the world of heaven and earth with his vastly distorted notions of reality. He was spiritually, theologically, psychologically, socially, and emotionally dysfunctional and treated other humans inappropriately while being wholly irresponsible about managing those affairs of his life for which he was expected to be accountable. He seemed prepared to curse God and die.

Was he sick or sinful? By common definitions, he was both. But what was the real problem.

It turned out that he suffered from a frequently seen though not exactly common malady for men between fifty-seven and sixty-three years of age. He had male menopause. In those days, six decades ago, it was called involutional melancholia. It was produced by a dysfunction of his testosterone production system. Today it is diagnosed as Major Depressive Disorder, Melancholic Type.

What can salvation mean in such a case? It means assessing the syndrome of symptoms in evidence, identifying the chemical agent responsible, providing a proper prescription of chemistry supplement, counseling him regarding the damage done to himself and those around him by the disorder, guiding him through the shame, guilt, fear, depression, and sense of defeat, and encouraging him and those around him to grace-filled restoration of his relationships. A crucial part of this would be getting across to him that his relationship with God and God's people does not depend upon the quality of his character and behavior but upon the character and behavior of God and God's people in the radical, unconditional, and universal acceptance of him as he was and is, not as they or he might think he should be. That would assist him to recover the relief of grace with its attendant joy, peace, communion with God, worshipful life, and heartfelt praise.

Under the rubrics of a correct operational model it is possible to identify each of his symptoms, perceive the specific breakdown of function behind each one, ascertain exactly what intervention is required to restore physiological, psychological, social, and spiritual normalcy, and afford this suffering soul the consolations of that comprehensive grace and redemption which is surely the intent of our loving God.

What prevents us from getting on with the formulation of such a comprehensive operational and systematic theology? As I implied in the first lecture, I believe three things get in the way. First, our addiction to ancient biblical constructs, language, and metaphor prevents us from thinking about the old spiritual insights in new ways. Second, we are afraid to get the radical character of the theology of grace solidly in focus and work from that position to make sense out of theology and life without tempering it with all kinds of conditionalism and moralism, which one unfortunately can also find in the Bible. Third, we have made such an idolatrous object of our concept of Christ that we have been unable to see clearly and deal directly with God. Since the dominating enterprise of the Imperial Church in its councils from Nicea to Chalcedon, Christology has functioned as an idol which has obstructed the achievement of a profound theology of God as the God of radical grace.

We have been doing theology and ethics from the top down and we must start doing both from the bottom up. It is my purpose this evening to say some things about how we could go about that and what that would look like. Let me do that by addressing a number of hypothetical cases.

II. Exposition

Case One: The Cross of Christ

Every serious theologian and pastor should now be informed of the fact that Paul's language and metaphors about the cross are a product of his Enochian Apocalyptic Judaism as a Pharisee with a predilection for that tradition. This perspective Paul translated into messianic apocalyptic constructs as a way to interpret the cataclysmic event of Jesus' crucifixion.[4]

---

4. Gabriele Boccaccini, *Beyond the Essene Hypothesis: The Parting of the Ways Between Qumran and Enochic Judaism* (Grand Rapids: Eerdmans, 1998).

Thus Paul uses such terminology as substitution, expiation, atonement, and the like. These are all ancient metaphors ringing with the sounds of the Great Day of Atonement from Post Exilic Judaism and the juridical constructs of Pharisaic legalism, cast in the apocalyptic world view of an Enochian Essene. We have fixed upon this ancient language and it is not readily apparent to the average citizen of this world that those images have anything whatsoever to do with his heart's hunger or his perplexing and painful predicament of such persistent and pervasive dysfunction that the good he would he doesn't and the evil he wouldn't he does.

However, the important question here is a different one. It is this. Is that set of metaphors and images the message Paul really wanted to send about God to suffering humanity? Is that set of ancient idioms merely a handy framework for him with the audience he had at that time or is it inherent to the content of his message? If we started in Romans 8, for example, or if we had only Romans 8, which has nothing of an atoning or expiatory crucifixion in it, could we confidently count on having the essence of the salvific gospel? Is that statement about God's radical, unconditional, and universal grace in Romans 8 really the content of the message about how God embraces and heals us, or is the juridical atonement language crucial? If our theology of Scripture allowed us to claim that the message of radical grace is the essence of the redemptive gospel and that biblical metaphors about atonement and satisfaction for sin and settling the score or balancing the scales are peripheral, then would we not have set the stage to start from the bottom in our data about human dysfunction and work up to an operational perception about how unconditional, radical, and universal acceptance and forgiveness enters into the life of a suffering human who is not part of the theological in-crowd, and saves him or her? Would it not be possible, then, for that person to read the language gratifyingly because it is his or her daily language?

After all, where is there in Scripture a more profound and comprehensive declaration of redeeming grace than in Micah 7:18-20, and what is there of an atonement day or an atoning crucifixion there?

Who is a God like our God
Who pardons iniquity, passes over transgression,
Will not keep his anger forever,
And delights in steadfast love?
He will have compassion upon us.

He treads our iniquities under his foot.
He will cast all our sins into the depths of the sea.
He will be faithful to us with unswerving loyalty.
He has guaranteed this to us
Through our fathers and mothers
From the days of old.

There is much more in the Bible which would represent the cross of Christ as the source of Demonstration Theology than Atonement Theology: namely, the cross as an expression of how far God will go to get across to us the message that God embraces us in our sins and miseries, in spite of ourselves, no strings attached, no conditions set, no guarantees withheld. But we have been hooked on the metaphors of juridical divine action, patently absurd to a non-imperial world where negotiation and democracy more-or-less prevail.

I do not mean that we should change the Bible, if atonement metaphors are central to the message rather than merely to the framework. But I do mean to take seriously the work of René Girard and others, who have demonstrated not only the absurdity of such juridical constructs to the present day suffering humanity, but of much greater concern, they have urged us to consider how incomparably destructive it has been for the last twenty centuries to have such a metaphor of violence right at the center of our theology, thought, and Western culture.[5] Is that really what God had in mind in articulating the message of radical grace to and through the Psalmists, the Prophets, and Apostles? Did God really intend to represent himself as a character who, enraged by human dysfunctions, cannot re-achieve divine equilibrium except by someone's death: Canaanites, Moabites, Israelites, Jesus? Should it trouble us at all that, whereas Abraham learned that child-sacrifice should be terminated among the people of Yahweh, in the atonement theology Yahweh sacrificed his own son?

What if we started with the problem of human suffering in the life of the average person out there who has not been part of the in-crowd because he or she has never been infused with the sounds, images, and language of

5. René Girard, *The Scapegoat* (Baltimore: Johns Hopkins Univ. Press, 1989). See also Erika Bourguignon's review of this volume in the *Journal of Psychoanalytic Anthropology*, December 1987, and Christopher Candland, ed., *The Spirit of Violence: An Interdisciplinary Bibliography of Religion and Violence*, Occasional Papers of the Frank Guggenheim Foundation, no. 6 (New York: H. F. Guggenheim Foundation, 1992).

the ancient metaphors and has never gone through the painful mystic process of rationalizing them into an acceptable personal mythology. Let us take such a man and identify his pain. Such a person is afraid that he will not be loved or cherished by anyone to the extent of his inner feeling of need for it. Yet he does not know how to express that. He is angry that one has to work so hard at getting anyone to notice or esteem him. He is sad that his parents both died in their fifties and he was an orphan at twenty-five. Worse than that, secretly he believes he will also die in his fifties, ten years from now. Moreover, his father died young because he was an alcoholic and this young man is fighting addiction himself. Moreover, the alcohol served his father as a medication to damp down his obsessive-compulsive perfectionism which caused him occasionally, even when sober, to physically abuse his mother because, though she was a great lover, she was a little slow, a slob, and could never focus enough to keep a decent house. Of course, she was constantly in a depressive quiet rage over the still-birth of her two daughters.

Now, can we build a theology of grace out of this man's stuff? Can we talk about salvation as a thing which first gets him into therapy for his grief and despair, then gets him medicated for the inherited obsessive-compulsive disorder which drives his addiction, then speak to him of God's passion and compassion for him, and perhaps even suggest at some point how this is demonstrated in the way Jesus of Nazareth handled people long ago and died for it? Can we work from the bottom up and all the while believe and convey that every aspect of this process is the action and mediation of God's grace right now saving this man through *our* acceptance and love of him? When that is achieved and he is praising God for his deliverance, is there anything else one needs to say? Do we really need to load him up with the conundrums of medieval argument or ancient Jewish apocalyptic metaphor?

Clearly the church is facing the need to construct a new theological paradigm which acknowledges the following factors:

A. The psychopathological roots of human dysfunction.
B. The biochemical roots of most psychopathology.
C. The spiritual consequences of this etiology of human dysfunction.
D. The dynamic, operational manner in which grace relates to and is mediated into this dysfunction.
E. The impact and modes by which grace becomes a dynamic opera-

tional agent in this dysfunction, in actually implementing the redemption and healing action in persons, behaviorally described.

F. The relevant new definitions required for our understanding of sin, misery, confession, salvation, redemption, and redeemed life with God.

G. The psycho-spiritual and socio-political implications of these new and more biblical perceptions of human failure, divine salvific sufficiency, human wholeness, and holiness.

This must be our theological charter for the 21st century.

Case Two: Original Sin

I am aware of the fact that the language of original sin is not at the forefront of our thought systems these days, but it lurks behind the scenes in our world view, nonetheless. It is part of the orthodox juridical theological framework, and until this day it has had significant shaping effect upon our thought about God, ourselves, and our brokenness. Whether the language is the Roman Catholic term, original sin, or the Reformation term, total depravity, or other constructs about inherent perversity, it is questionable whether these notions which are really medieval metaphors lurking around the backsides of our subconscious, contribute anything to our self-understanding; or whether their implied blame-quality makes them obstacles to our salvation.

Is it not the case that what we want to talk about in the employment of these old terms is the empirically demonstrable fact that almost anything human falls a little or a lot short of our ideal possibilities — and for many of us, short of what we think God wants for us? Well, if that is what we are talking about, can we not talk about that in operational terms, on the basis of the psychological, sociological, and spiritual data we have, and make more sense of it for suffering humanity than with those ancient metaphors from an essentially alien imperial or feudal culture?

We might, for example, meet a young lady on the street who is obviously suffering from malnutrition and discover that it is because she is white, uneducated, unskilled, and lives downtown on a subsistence diet which she picks from garbage cans when she cannot get work. She has been a prostitute but found it too demeaning a way to make a living. She has been fired from the local McDonald's because they reduced their staff and kept the blacks because the manager is black. Besides she had dark marks under her fingernails which the manager thought were from shooting heroin. She is uneducated because, though she is the daughter of a minister from the rural provinces, her parents and two siblings were killed in a house fire from which she alone escaped. Having no relatives, she has made her way as best she could, but thinking she found love and companionship with a crowd of young people in town she tried drugs, and found that they knocked out the headache she had regularly for the previous four years. She became addicted and her meager existence, marginal health, depressed spirit, loneliness, sexual obsession, sense of abandonment by God and humankind, and helpless hopelessness all followed from that.

Can we start in her pain and perplexity and make sense out of building a theology of grace from there? She was once a part of the in-crowd but is probably worse off than our first case because she cannot figure out any longer what all that apparently useless and irrelevant religious language, word pictures, and abstract ideas from such ancient times was about or why it ever made any sense to her. Can we talk about, can we incarnate, can we formulate the message of grace so that it becomes an operationally useful comprehensive salvation of her life?

Can we believe that it is grace that gets her a bath, grace that warms her body in a clean place, grace that affirms her tenuous escape from the self-demeanment of prostitution, grace that takes the risk to give her a job when we did not really need to hire an extra person, grace that helps her hope that there is something out there ahead for her, grace that teases out the traces of beauty in her character and her body so she can start to recover self-esteem, grace that counsels her to self-understanding, grace that interprets our love as a mode of God's grace that saves her? Don't you think that kind of operational theology can make sense to *anyone* and requires none of the ancient theological metaphors except those of Romans 8 or Micah 7? Is her problem sin or sickness, psycho-socially and spiritually? Does it make a difference which it is or what we name it? Is atonement imagery or intervention really the salvific issue, or is it simply a tangible operationally healing grace incarnated by caring people of God?

Is it really true that her problem is original sin or total depravity, or is it merely that she is a human being who was inadequate, immature, and incomplete in her formation in the cocoon of life when she was blasted out into the wasteland of our social culture and lived out the raw operational brokenness of *all of us* in her life, exploited along the way by others, each broken in his or her own manner? Is her salvation a matter of mysterious metaphors of ancient worlds and alien cultures or is it simply a matter of distilling into her real psychological, social, and spiritual struggle the essences of that acceptance which is greater than all our dysfunction, that grace we cannot sin ourselves out of, that long embrace out of which we cannot squirm; made operationally real by my embrace, my intervention, my care, and my practical strategies to help her set her life upon a hope-filled trajectory toward genuine actualization of her potentials, interpreted in the light of God's perpetual providence and grace, and which leads her to practical joy and profound praise? Does more really need to be said than that, to be true to the message of the Bible and the needs of God's children?

But it is not only the down and out for whom grace is operationally important and redeeming. It is as much for the up and out — and the up and in! It is as crucial for you and me. What about the man who has wrestled with life creatively and aggressively and at fifty years of age knows that he never really needs to earn another dollar. His bank account is adequate for a luxurious retirement. He has interesting work to keep him focused for the rest of his life, if he wishes. But he feels profoundly empty. His wife has been on an alternate track for the last ten years. She seems to manage to be busy when he is free for relaxation or travel. Just when he is heavily preoccupied with urgent responsibilities for a few weeks, that is when she wants him to take her to her favorite spa or to visit the children.

He wants to visit the children but it gives him unbearable grief that when he is away from them his heart aches for them. He longs for an intimate relationship with them. When he visits them they seem to have no interest in his ideas and he cannot seem to connect with their agendas of life or thought. They seem trivial in their preoccupations and alienated from him. When he points this out to them, the best they seem able to offer is that they are from a different generation and never could figure him out anyway. He secretly believes that they do not know him at all nor like him very much. He feels silently guilty about it. He suspects it is because when they were children and teenagers he was so committed to his work and "supporting the family" that he hardly had time for them. He realizes that he does not really know who they are. It makes him ashamed and fearful. Sometimes he hates that. Sometimes he hates them. He has never admitted it but he hates his wife because she does not seem to even think about having a shared life with him since the children have been grown and gone.

477

The moments of hate make him feel more guilty, angry, and depressed. Who is there to tell his anger to? He always thought that his job was to work hard, have integrity, devote himself to building a good business with satisfied employees, pour plenty of time and energy into the church, generously support the Christian school with leadership and money, and be a force for good in the community. He had really believed that if he took care of those responsibilities and built a significant estate for his family, making sure his children got good educations, that God would look after the children's spiritual growth and psychological health. They would grow up well in God's favor and providence. But it did not work. Three of his kids will not darken a church door.

The other two seem to be so busy with getting degrees and following their own rather selfish interests that they have no time for him. All the kids seem to associate with their mother, phoning her, remembering her birthdays, and he feels on the outside looking in.

So now he is a multimillionaire. He considers himself a loving father, a faithful husband, and a responsible man. But God did not keep up his end of the bargain. His wife has betrayed him by wandering off on an alien track socially and spiritually. His kids seem like creatures from another world. He doesn't really know anymore what to believe. Perhaps his religious traditions are really fiction. Maybe this business of relationships is not really worth the effort. Should he look for new friends, new worlds, a new life, a new wife? He is fifty. He has everything. He feels like he has nothing. He probably ought to talk to the preacher but the preacher seems lost in some wild-eyed world of ancient myth and does not seem able to plug into the realities of this world — at least his world. The preacher seems to be great with the derelicts and dropouts of the inner city mission but he cannot imagine the guy would understand what he is up against. Better have another martini and see if he can get a good night's sleep for once. If he does not get better rest the doctor says he is a prime candidate for a heart attack.

What does salvation mean for this man? What concrete steps should we be able to prescribe for his healing? How shall we get at his depression? How shall we restore hope? Is there a redemptive intervention which will make it possible for him to believe that he can have a really cherishing and zesty relationship with his wife again? Does saving him have something to do with whether he can ever find his kids back? What does God have to say and do, presumably through his people, so this man can honestly believe in

God again? More than that, what is it about salvation, operationally, that can give the old hymns their deep reassurances to him again? Can he transcend his depression, alienation, rage, hate, fear, shame, guilt, and emptiness? What will it take for prayer to mean anything again? How does salvation work in that, complicated as it is by spiritual, psychological, social, and material factors woven in and through each other in an unsortable confusion? Should he go to those new charismatic meetings the preacher is promoting on Wednesday and shout "Jesus saves!" with his hands in the air? Will some lightning strike him there?

Our operational model can work for this man. Some caring person needs to intuit his lostness and take the time to sit down with him and listen. The first thing to do to save him is to help him believe that he is worth caring for and therefore that he can trust his listener to know how to listen and to care enough to hang in there. If he is going to experience God's salvation, true redemption, that is the beginning of it. The second step will be to discern carefully how much of his depression is the rage internalized and how much is biochemical. The third step is to insure that any of the latter is medicated and any of the former is catharted. The rage must be dug out and articulated, with all its sources and reasons. The fourth step will be helping him envision what his heart's hunger really is, what his long-term goals are, what deficiencies are the palpable reasons for his feeling so empty, that is, what conscious or unconscious expectations and longings he has which have been frustrated and left him emotionally deprived. The fifth step must be to discern to what extent his desire for relationship with his wife and children is real or just a fictional side effect of his cultural conditioning that such relationships are the right thing to have. Has he excessively sentimentalized ideas of home and family or are his notions about these authentic and realistic?

The sixth step in our model will be to encourage and facilitate a communication process with his wife and children, guiding it into deep emotional and intellectual connection, thereby coming to an understanding where the brokenness is in his relationships, in their lives and function, and who needs what kind of intervention. It is important at this stage to help him to see clearly whether he really is motivated to put significant energy into this exploration and rebuilding — and if so, how much he can give; how much they can give. The seventh step will be a substantive engagement with the fact that acceptance and forgiveness, grace, from each member of this family to every other member is the key redemptive move. This grace-filled investment in each other must be carried out in terms of each knowing exactly how things got the way they have and what it is they are forgiving, the extent to which they really want to or are ready to do this, and how they envision the outcome. The eighth step will have to do with each member experiencing a profound sense of their grace to each other being an illustration of God's grace to us all, not just ordinary everyday human graciousness, but acceptance and cherishing so unconditional that nothing can obstruct it, so radical that it gets around behind all our defenses and self-justifications and conditional notions of relationship and penetrates our central problem of orphaned empty lostness, so universal that Paul can shout, "Every eye shall see, every knee bow, every tongue confess to the glory of God." That does not say, to the vindication of God or the justification of God. It speaks of the glory and glorying God experiences when the broken one is healed. The ninth step is to coach this man and his family to the life of relief, freedom, joy, and praise that their sin or dysfunction does not count, has been ruled out of the equation, and that all that counts is their growth together. The Heidelberg Catechism has in it a couple of superb psycho-theological perceptions.[6] The most important one is that our only comfort is that we belong. The second is that the life of growth is all about gratitude. The more we live out of fear of ourselves or God, the sicker we get. The more we live out of gratitude, the healthier we get.

This man's original problem began with bad theology. He really believed in a conditional grace theology — the one that reigns almost everywhere in the church today. He believed that if he did his duty, as he saw it, God would take care of everything else in a reciprocal equation. That failed because it is a pagan lie. It failed because life is a dynamic operation which does not depend upon divine magic but upon chemistry, biology, sociology, psychology, spirituality, and the like. Life is a growth and unfolding process and if it is not fed in a certain way it goes awry. Indeed, since all of us are inadequately informed, experienced, matured, and whole, it inevitably goes awry. What this man needs for his salvation is the realization that God is not a God of magic but rather of grace; grace that accepts him as a fractured human exactly where he is in his odyssey, exactly as he is, with all his dysfunction, fear, guilt, shame, and alienation from himself and his

6. Zacharius Ursinus and Caspar Olevianus, *The Heidelberg Catechism,* published in the *Psalter Hymnal* (Grand Rapids: CRC Publications, 1987), pp. 860-925.

family. God's kind of grace is the kind that he cannot acquire by doing his duty, but that comes to him in his sins and miseries, to turn the wreckage and waste in his life into the very stuff of which burgeoning growth springs.

The problem of the human predicament is a great deal worse than merely an original sin or even total depravity in which everything is to some degree impaired and falls short of its best possibilities. The problem of humanity is that there is a structural brokenness that pervades the whole of the human experience. It is a brokenness which derives from the fact that we are incompletely evolved. Every generation must start over where the last one started in all the things that really count: educationally, morally, spiritually, and in all the other issues of maturation. We can stand upon the shoulders of previous generations in mechanical and technological advances, and those are important. We can make better cars and refrigerators than our ancestors could, so fewer babies die of bad food or windy, cold carriages, but we are not born better people, more equipped or complete. We must all start over and grow, through the pain of change and development, through the mystification of life and death, through the unknown of the present and the future, through the anxiety about inadequate or evil pasts; and we only get about a half century to figure it out. Moreover, the enigma of life is in the fact that we must do it right in the middle of it. Parents do not get to use the first child as a throw-away. We do not get a dry run or a second chance. We must do it right the first time though no one can, or we must suffer the consequences of fear, shame, guilt, loss, and grief. To these grace must speak in passionate and compassionate ways not in juridical and blame-oriented ways. Our problem is bad enough without it being complicated by a threatening God or blaming theologies.

The church has had a persisting problem with the biblical concept of grace because "the idea is so radical in both the Hebrew Bible and the New Testament. God's grace is represented as an arbitrary intervention on behalf of humankind. It is announced and not negotiated, covenanted by God from his side and guaranteed. It is guaranteed to us in spite of ourselves. Furthermore, it does not merely treat our symptoms of disobedience, ignorance, or unbelief but moves past those symptoms to our sickness. That root sickness is a deficit and disorder in our very nature whereby we are alienated from God without consciously choosing to be, without comprehending the full tragic import of it, and without any ability to remedy it. It is a sickness in that it is a condition of our nature, not merely a malfunction of our intent or behavior. Moreover, it is a sickness in that it infects every aspect of our personhood and all facets of the cosmos. It is a disease in us that leaves everything about us fractured, limited, and infectious. . . . And we infect each other, our children, our community, and our world with an infection that becomes a disposition of our hearts, an orientation of our intellects, a pattern of our emotions, and a response of our spirits. The infection pervades our entire organism, individual and communal."

This sickness is mediated by the distortions and incompleteness in our organism: physical, psychological, and spiritual. It gives rise to "all manner of psychological and spiritual reaction formation, defensiveness, and secondary distortions and symptomology. This development complicates our situation, making it difficult for us to see the real problem from which we suffer. It is a fulminating infection until the grace of God enters into our psycho-spiritual (and socio-political) process and reduces the infection" by assuring us that we are OK to God just as we are. This grace comes in all the forms that treatment and healing need to take. It includes, particularly, the psycho-spiritual medicine of God's declaration that the sickness does not count, so far as he is concerned. "A superficial concept of sin is too optimistic about the human condition and too pessimistic about the redeeming intent and function of God's grace. God intends not merely judgment and forgiveness but the healing of our generic disease and craziness." He frees us from our fear, guilt, and shame by his arbitrary declaration of grace so that we need not invest any more of our psychic energy in those wasteful experiences and can apply those energies instead to growth. He intends and invites us to grow, not merely to shape up. "The biblical concept of sickness can help us to appropriate these truths, making our concept of human sin and our understanding of God's grace more profoundly adequate to the healing of human failure."[7]

7. The quotations in this section are taken from J. Harold Ellens, "Sin and Sickness: The Nature of Human Failure," in LeRoy Aden and David G. Benner, eds., *Counseling and the Human Predicament: A Study of Sin, Guilt, and Forgiveness* (Grand Rapids: Baker, 1989), pp. 71-75.

Case Three: The Bible as Sacred Scripture

It seems to me to be the case that accomplishing what I have urged in Cases One and Two will become much easier and more readily actualized if we can resolve the problem of Case Three, that is, our notion of the nature of the authority of Scripture. It seems to me that a serious revision of our theology of Scripture has been long overdue. Brief attempts with fits and starts have marked the history of the Reformed community for a long time; but it has never really been true to its own superscription, *Reformans Reformanda,* in this matter of a theology of the Word.

In the late '50s the question was raised with a significant article in *Stromata,* the seminary paper. Some at the Calvin Seminary initially supported this position but later abandoned the cause. Others remained silent. The thing died. At the time of the Love of God Controversy the one thing that was urgently needed to allow the real debate to go forward generatively regarding the exegesis of John 3:16-17 and all the theology we had hung on that, was for the issue of the theology of Scripture to be raised so that the text of the Bible could have been allowed to speak for itself in the operational terms the proponents of the endeavor had set for the debate. That would have prevented those who opposed the matter from pushing the Bible back under the rubrics of medieval theology and forcing proponents to argue the case on medieval terms rather than on contemporary operational terms.

The real issue at stake was less that of the love of God and more that of the nature of the authority of Scripture. I think the opponents intuited that and thus insisted upon a systematic theology debate which raged mainly in philosophical terms, rather than allowing a biblical theological debate in terms of the operational experience of the people on the street and the pastors in the provinces. However, once again, the church and its ancient constructs of theological philosophy prevailed, instead of either the Bible or suffering humanity.

If we would be true to the message in the Bible we will be required to revise our notions of the authority of Scripture. Our notions of biblical authority have been based upon mythological foundations that are shaped and contoured by magical thinking about unique divine interventions which gave to the pens of prophets and apostles special messages directly from the divine mind. These are confessional theological claims which were held simply because it was thought that they had always been held. I know that there are many among you who would testify to more enlightened notions of scriptural authority than that. I am sure many of you even remember what organic inspiration was originally supposed to mean in Reformed theology. But I am concerned that the people who fill your congregations and mine operate with a magical notion about the nature and authority of Scripture which is completely out of touch with reality.

The Christian Reformed Church and the Presbyterian Church are today, in this and other regards, more fraught with American Fundamentalism and more filled with simplistic Evangelicalism, than they were thirty years ago. The most obvious place at which that is evident is in the average parishioner's theology of Scripture. So far as I can tell, little is being done to disabuse the church of that. Much is being done by omission and commission to reinforce it because it keeps the natives quiet. There is nothing like a magical world view and a certainty that God speaks and deals directly with us to keep people under control. When God is allowed his real and actual operational subtleness, people may get restless.

We must jettison all notions of scriptural authority which are based merely upon mythic theological-philosophical foundations or confessional grounds, that are held because they are entrenched in the historic theology of the church. Every thoughtful biblical scholar knows that the Bible is a set of cultural-historical documents which record in sometimes religious expressions the perceptions of human beings like you and me regarding what they experienced in the mindfulness of creation, the benevolence of providence, the urge in all things toward the aesthetic ideal, and the incredible operational relevance of the insight and experience of grace. In that process, sometimes they saw clearly and sometimes through a fog. They got some things right and some wrong, just as we do. The launching of an egregious and exploitive Israel foreign policy and lust for power in the extermination of the Canaanites, men, women, children, dogs, cats, and pet skunks, as though it was the will and command of God, was a serious mistake in perception. Micah's perception of God, not as a threat but as a lover of infinite grace, was right on. Paul's notions about women were wrong, about ultimate universal salvation correct.

The authority of Scripture is not just the result of its being the witness of the prophets and apostles. Any responsible notion of the authority of Scripture must be based upon demonstrable operational grounds, rooted in empirical data, warranted by longitudinal studies regarding the manner in which its message effects genuine and measurable psycho-spiritually constructive change. It is, for example, operationally demonstrable that singing and identifying with some of the Psalms of David over a lifetime produces a redemptive shift in a person's perspective on self, purpose, destiny, God, our transcendent hunger and irrepressible reach for God, our sense of the congenial companionship of God and his people; as well as in the levels of psychoactive joy, fear-reduction, shame and guilt reduction, and the channeling of rage which prevail in fractured humans.

My father's mother lived to nearly ninety in the farming community of McBain. My grandfather was a sturdy Frisian who took his role as head of the house with military seriousness. He was an aggressive lay theologian, lover, churchman, farmer, manager of his fifteen children, fourteen of whom survived childhood and thirteen to advanced old age. Grandmother was an incredibly joyful and resilient woman and a happy but not very mystical Christian. In her old age, after my grandfather had died and she was living alone, I asked her how it was that she was always able to keep such a sunny outlook through all the heated theological debates that swirled around her, all the changes in the church as pastors got fired and new ones came with all their human foibles, as the community went through the euphoria of the '20s, the poverty of the '30s, the anguish of the '40s, and the radical changes from the family farm to agribusiness in the '50s, through all the ups and downs of life and death.

Her answer was simple, definitive, and operationally oriented. She said, "Well, you know, it was not the theology and it was not the preaching. I lost my awe of preachers and theologians long before you became one. It was the hymns and the psalms." It was interesting to me and certainly not accidental that then she began to sing for me a hymn which is wholly operational in its orientation.

> I sought the Lord, and afterward I knew
> He moved my soul to seek him, seeking me.
> It was not I that found, O Savior true.
> No, I was found of Thee — of Thee.
> Thou didst reach forth Thy hand and mine enfold;
> I walked and sank not on the storm-vexed sea;
> 'Twas not so much that I on Thee took hold,
> As Thou, dear Lord, on me.
> I find, I walk, I love; but O the whole
> Of love is but my answer, Lord, to Thee!

For Thou wert long before-hand with my soul;
Always, always, Thou lovedst me.[8]

That is operational theology fashioned from the bottom up. It remains of great interest to me that only after those words rang through her soul did she follow it with another in somewhat the same cast, though of a slightly more transcendent and ethereal look.

Great is thy faithfulness, O God my Father;
There is no shadow of turning with thee;
Thou changest not, thy compassions, they fail not;
As thou hast been thou forever wilt be.
Summer and winter and springtime and harvest,
Sun, moon, and stars in their courses above
Join with all nature in manifold witness
To thy great faithfulness, mercy, and love.
Pardon for sin and a peace that endureth,
Thine own dear presence to cheer and to guide,
Strength for today and bright hope for tomorrow,
Blessings all mine, with ten thousand beside![9]

It is psycho-spiritually demonstrable, at the empirically observable, operational level that grace works and love heals. Those aspects of Scripture, therefore, which effect discernible operational change of a redemptive or constructive nature, in real human experience, have authority. They have the power to act and, therefore, the authority to claim that they should be taken seriously and revered. The rest does not. First, that authority must be demonstrably redemptive, able to effect comprehensive salvation in lost souls and broken lives; that is, effect change which enhances function on the psycho-spiritual and socio-political level. Then we have a right to accord it a higher kind of authority. Then we have a right to claim that it speaks for God since God is obviously into the enterprise of our healing. Those scriptures that are operationally effective may be seen to

8. George W. Chadwick, 1890, set by Seymour Swets in 1934 to *Finlandia* by Jean Sibelius, as published in the *Psalter Hymnal* (Grand Rapids: Publication Committee of the Christian Reformed Church Publishers, 1934).
9. Text by Thomas O. Chisholm, 1923; music by William M. Runyan, 1923, published in the *Psalter Hymnal* (Grand Rapids: CRC Publications, 1987).

have divine authority, transcendent dimensions, extra-human sources, and trans-personal value.

No sacred scripture has any inherent authority which stands out there in mythic splendor unless it has earned it from its operational effectiveness. Much of scripture has insinuated multi-forms of mayhem into human culture with its irrational violence at the very center. Some scripture from the Bible has changed our lives redemptively and surprised us by joy.

Of course, we must ask, "How can one sort out the framework of the biblical literature from the gospel's good news? How can one distinguish between the cultural-historical matrix which carries the message, on the one hand, and the word of grace, on the other?" There are those who fear that if we do not accord every word of the Bible a general magical status we cannot hold on to any of it as God's truth, or know God's authoritative word in Scripture at all. The biblicists have gotten away with that false claim too long. The answer is much simpler than it may seem. It is easy to sort out the human words from the revelatory and salvific words.

The thing to do is to stand in the middle of the refuse of human dysfunction and the rage of human suffering and from that vantage point reach with open heart and mind for the foot of the cross. It is easier to get a clear strong grip on it from there than from anywhere else in the world. There one can get into focus the unmistakable demonstration that God will go to any lengths to get out the word and to catch hold of our hands and hearts. When we have grasped it we will not hear so much the ancient chords of atonement but the operational thunder of one clear and single word. It is the word of grace — uncalculating, unconditional, unlimited grace; grace abounding to the most completely smashed of all humankind and operational in tangible steps and procedures which can change everything in life redemptively.

From that perspective, with both feet in the perplexities of human life, and both hands on the foot of the cross, it is possible to gaze backward down the corridors of Old Testament time and forward through the garden of the gospels and epistles and see quickly what it is therein that rings true to that vision of grace at the foot of the cross. What rings true is gospel. What doesn't isn't.

III. Conclusion

I claim, therefore, that there is a glorious future for Christianity. I claim the Bible is relevant to the sophisticated age of the new millennium. I claim that all of us dysfunctional humans are sick and need healing treatment. Borderlines are illustrative of all of us. I claim that for human beings who are diagnosed as suffering from Borderline Syndrome or other such disorders, treatment is available. It is one of the expressions of God's comprehensive grace, whether medical, psychological, or pastoral intervention. Calling them sinful does not help. I claim that for all human beings uncalculating, unconditional, and unlimited grace is given by our loving God who will catch hold of your hands and hearts and who constantly forgives our dysfunctions and frailty. I claim that this is the only way we will be healed and free.

I believe that the problem which has obstructed our conveying the radical message of grace more effectively and applying it comprehensively to the healing of the total person and human community has been a problem of misdiagnosis. We moralized, spiritualized, and trivialized human dysfunction as sin. Thus when we turned to the enterprise of healing, we mythologized God, spiritualized salvation, and trivialized God's redemptive intervention as a magical inner and hidden miracle. We hung round that picture the subtle notion that God's affirmation of us is conditional. That cut the tap root of people's capacity to perceive, grasp, and trust the radical, unconditional, universal, and applied operational nature of God's grace.

I claimed that if we are willing to take God seriously and trust God to operate in practical terms in our world to redeem and heal us, in keeping with the way God created human persons and intended human communities, we must do psycho-theology and we must do it from the bottom up. We must stand in the human condition of brokenness, understand it and speak its language thoroughly, make its idiom the idiom of our operations, and there listen for the central message of the Word from God, unbiased by the screen of irrelevant ancient metaphors. If we do, we will hear the clear and certain trumpet of untrammeled, unconditional, radical, and universal grace. We will discern readily from that vantage point how grace saves us operationally and comprehensively.

Is not the whole story really John Bunyan's allegory of Pilgrim Christian in his progress, with its operational, pastoral orientation, *desperate to heal humans;* rather than John Milton's Theodicy of idealistic mythology regarding Paradise Lost and Regained, *desperate to justify God?*

Whether we are sinners is, of course, an important question. But it is trival compared with the fact that we have a sickness unto death. It was undoubtedly this fact to which the former editorial cartoonist of the *Kansas City Star* alluded at his retirement dinner. After forty years of producing particularly caustic graphic commentary upon the fractures and dysfunctions of humankind, he was asked by the Master of Ceremonies to share a few thoughts on how he really felt about the human race. He rose and said simply, "I think we ought to be kind to it. It is the only one we've got." Apparently God feels the same way!

SALVATION FORMULAE IN THE CHURCH

I. Blame-Justification Equation

(ANXIETY/SHAME/GUILT/BLAME)

+

(JUSTICE/PENALTY/PUNISHMENT/EXPIATION)

=

(JUSTIFICATION/FORGIVENESS/RESTORATION/EQUILIBRIUM)

II. Grace-Wholeness Equation

(PAIN/SHAME/GUILT/ANXIETY)

+

(PASSION/COMPASSION/MERCY/GRACE)

=

(FORGIVENESS [and Other Therapies]/
AFFIRMATION/HEALING/ACTUALIZATION)

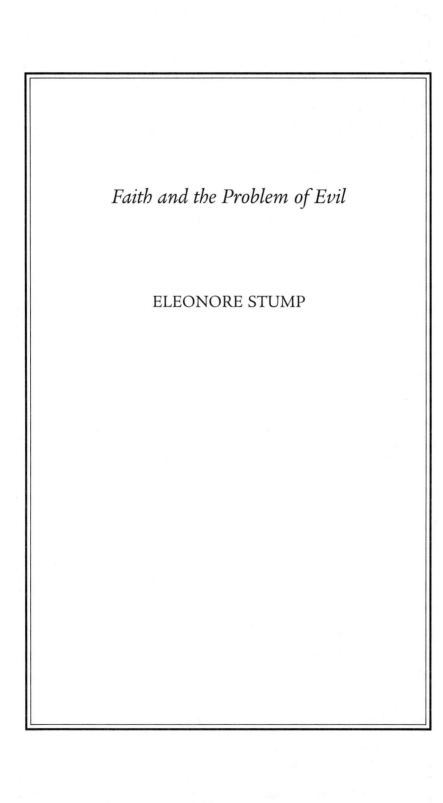

Faith and the Problem of Evil

ELEONORE STUMP

For Ted
in fletu solacium

Contents

Preface

The period in which I wrote these lectures was marked for me by a firestorm of grief. I wish I knew how to express thanks adequately to all the people who were good to me in that painful time. I am blessed in the people whose lives are interwoven with mine, and I am deeply grateful for all the warm, generous care and kindness given me by my family and friends, my students and colleagues, and the Christian community in which I live. I have dedicated the lectures to Father Theodore Vitali, whose wise counsel and great-hearted willingness to suffer with me walked me through the storm.

One or the other of these lectures, or of some precursor of either lecture, was given at Oberlin College, Princeton Theological Seminary, St. Louis University, the University of Helsinki, and Calvin College (where the Stob Lectures were presented). I am grateful to audiences at all these schools for their comments and questions. I have also had very useful discussion or written comments on one or the other lecture, or precursor of the lectures, from my friends Harry Frankfurt, Yehuda Gellman, Philip Quinn, and Howard Wettstein. I owe a special debt of gratitude to Al Plantinga and Nick Wolterstorff, whose mentoring friendship has meant a great deal to me and whose extensive comments and questions on earlier versions of the lectures were very helpful to me. Their own Stob Lectures set a standard of excellence for this series by which other Stob Lectures must be measured. Finally, I owe more than I can say to Norman Kretzmann. The Stob Lectures are the first thing I have written without him.

The line in the dedication comes from a medieval Latin poem which is a prayer to the Holy Spirit. This poem in its Latin form is one of the first prayers I knew and said. It expresses or at least implies what my own experience confirms, that consolation increases with affliction. I reproduce it here in my translation, for the sake of the reader, and in Latin, for my sake.

Veni, sancte spiritus,
Et emitte caelitus
Lucis tuae radium.
Veni, pater pauperum,
Veni, dator munerum,
Veni, lumen cordium.

Consolator optime,
Dulcis hospes animae,
Dulce refrigerium,
In labore requies,
In aestu temperies,
In fletu solacium,

O lux beatissima,
Reple cordis intima
tuorum fidelium.
Sine tuo nomine
Nihil est in homine,
Nihil est innoxium.

Lava quod est sordidum,
Riga quod est aridum,
Sana quod est saucium.
Flecte quod est rigidum,
Fove quod est frigidum,
Rege quod est devium.

Da tuis fidelibus,
in te confidentibus,
Sacrum septenarium.
Da virtutis meritum,
Da salutis exitum,
Da perenne gaudium.

Eleonore Stump

Come, Holy Spirit,
and send forth from heaven
the stream of your light.
Come, Father of the poor,
come, Giver of gifts,
come, Light of the heart.

Best of comforters,
sweet guest of the soul,
sweet healer,
rest in hardship,
relief in fire,
solace in sorrow,

O blessed light,
fill the inmost hearts
of those who trust in you.
Apart from you
man is nothing,
and everything is toxic.

Wash what is filthy;
water what is dry;
heal what is sick;
flex what is unyielding;
incandesce what is cold;
rule what is bent.

To those who trust in you,
who put their confidence in you,
give your sevenfold gifts.
Give the merit of virtue;
give salvation in the final hour;
give unending joy.

Second-Person Accounts and the Problem of Evil

Introduction

In my two lectures, I am going to address the difficult and much-discussed problem of evil, but I am going to address it in a Christian formulation, from a Christian point of view. This is not the usual way in which philosophers approach the problem of evil, but it seems to me the right way to proceed in the Stob Lectures. So in my two lectures, I want to ask and go some way towards answering this question: How are we as Christians to understand and respond to a God who could prevent our suffering but does not do so? I am going to address this question only indirectly in this lecture; in the next lecture, I will deal with it directly and try to give an answer to it.

But before I say anything at all about the problem of evil, I want to consider in some detail a preliminary question about methodology: how should we approach philosophical problems such as the problem of evil? What method should we use to think about them? I need to talk about this methodological issue because in these two lectures I want to support my general claims not only by philosophical argument, in the usual way, but also by an interpretation of biblical narratives. So I am going to begin by looking in some detail at a basic methodological issue in philosophy. Once I have done so, it will become apparent shortly what the connection between it and the problem of evil is.

First-Person and Third-Person Accounts

It has become customary in philosophy to distinguish between what is often called 'a third-person point of view' and 'a first-person point of view.' The difference is hard to define precisely but easy to illustrate; it is perhaps most notable in philosophy of mind.[1] When, from my first-person point of view, I observe the mind I know best, my own, I am aware of beliefs, doubts, questions, desires, inclinations, willings, and things of this sort. But if a neurologist were to examine me, what he would perceive from his third-person point of view is something very different. He would observe synapses, neurochemicals and their receptors, neurons, clumps of nuclei and bands of fibers, topological maps, and things of this sort. He would not see beliefs and desires. None of the things he finds from his third-person point of view are observable to me from my first-person point of view when I introspect; and what I find from my first-person point of view, beliefs and desires and the rest, is not apparent to the neurologist from his third-person point of view.

This split between the first-person and the third-person point of view has received considerable attention in philosophy of mind, but it is present, if less dramatic, in other areas of philosophy as well. There is some-

1. In this lecture, I distinguish not only among first-person, second-person, and third-person points of view, but also among the corresponding experiences and accounts. I have no neat and precise definitions for any of these, but, put roughly, what I have in mind is this. A first-person experience is an experience I have with some degree or other of conscious awareness and which I could have by myself. A first-person point of view is my reflection on or observation of my (real or imagined) first-person experience considered as a first-person experience (as distinct, for example, from considering that experience as a neurologist or some other third person might consider it). And a first-person account is my account to someone else of my reflection on or observation of my (real or imagined) first-person experience qua first-person experience. So, my wanting a cup of coffee when I am in a normal cognitive and conative condition is a first-person experience; I want the coffee, and the desire is a conscious desire in me. My conscious, introspective reflection on or observation of that conscious desire is a first-person point of view. I can have a conscious state without a conscious reflection on it or observation of it, as I do when I drive to work, conscious of the state of the road but focused intently on the news on the radio, so that I don't attend to the conscious visual states which guide my driving. And my explaining my desire considered as a first-person experience to someone else is a first-person account. Something roughly similar distinguishes experience, point of view, and account for the second- and third-person analogues.

thing at least analogous to it in philosophy of religion. Atheistic philosophers examining religious belief often suppose that such belief is irrational unless it is supported by sound arguments. But it is notable that believers, who consider religious belief from an insider's point of view — which is at least analogous to if not the same as a first-person point of view — very rarely base their belief on arguments. That is not because they have tried to find arguments and failed. That is because, from a first-person point of view or the point of view of an insider to religion, even looking for arguments can seem perplexingly misguided. Many religious believers have had at least on some occasion some sense of being in the presence of God, of feeling his love, sensing his forgiveness, recognizing him in the beauty of creation, or something else of this sort.[2] To such an insider to religion, to look for an argument that will justify belief in God's existence, of the sort that outsiders require, will seem just as odd as trying to find an argument to prove that you have beliefs and desires. You *know* you have beliefs and desires because you see them when you introspect. From your first-person or insider's point of view, an *argument* for the existence of beliefs and desires would be much weaker evidence than you already have. Similarly, for many religious believers who consider the existence of God from an insider's point of view or a first-person point of view, arguments for the existence of God seem not only unnecessary but even nugatory. Religious believers may not take themselves to have experienced anything as fancy as

2. It is no part of my distinctions among first-person, second-person, and third-person experiences, points of view, and accounts to suggest that there is opposition among these so that an agent who adopts one of these about something is thereby precluded from adopting any of the others. So, for example, someone who has first-person experiences of beliefs and desires might also consider even his own beliefs and desires from a third-person point of view, as a neurologist would. It is also possible to combine first-person, second-person, and third-person perspectives in an iterative fashion. For example, I might tell you about my introspective experiences of listening to music; then you would have a second-person experience of me which included my first-person account. Or I might introspect reflectively on my second-person experience of you, considering how I really felt about what you said. Then I would have a first-person point of view about a second-person experience. The perspective of the religious believers at issue in the text seems to me an iterated perspective of this sort. Religious believers can consider religion from a first-person point of view, where that point of view includes reflection on what they take to be their own second-person experiences connecting them in some fashion with the person of God. I am indebted to Al Plantinga for prompting me to consider this issue.

perceiving God, but they may nonetheless suppose that they are in contact with the person of God in such as way as to have some sense of him as a person or to be in some kind of Reidian sympathy with him.[3] On the other hand, of course, from the point of view of an outsider to religion, from the analogue in religion to a third-person point of view, the sense of religious believers that they perceive God in some direct or indirect way looks delusional, the product of inappropriate psychological conditions or regrettable social and economic forces.

Faced with this sort of split in philosophical issues between a first-person point of view and a third-person point of view, what are we to do? Some philosophers have tended to assume that the only legitimate procedure is to adopt the third-person point of view, the point of view of an outsider to the practices or states under consideration. So, for example, some philosophers of mind are notorious for arguing that the very concepts of belief and desire will have to be replaced with some neurological construct because there is no place for beliefs and desires in a scientific picture, a third-person or outsider's picture, of the mind.[4] But to many people, this seems a fairly extreme reaction to the discomfort generated by the split between the first-person and third-person points of view. On the other side, certain movements in philosophy of religion can be read as advocating the legitimacy of abandoning the third-person point of view. So, for example, the movement of Reformed epistemology argues that taking belief in God as a basic belief, a belief accepted without arguments, is rational. As religious believers, some people find in themselves a conviction that God exists, and they are rational to maintain this belief even in the absence of good arguments which confirm it. This is a position which legitimates belief held by insiders to a certain practice, those who have a first-person point of view with regard to religion. It does nothing to bridge the gap between the viewpoints of the believers and the unbelievers, however; and it has seemed to many who come to religion as outsiders or from a third-person point of view, to be a fairly extreme position, too.

Is there any alternative, however, to accepting either the first-person or the third-person point of view if there is a split between the two? In a re-

---

3. I am grateful to Al Plantinga for calling this point and the connection with Reid to my attention.

4. See, for example, Patricia Churchland, *Neurophilosophy: Toward a Unified Science of the Mind/Brain* (Cambridge, Mass.: MIT Press, 1986, 9th ed. 1996), pp. 395-99.

cent lecture, Avishai Margalit suggested that we should try bridging this gap by means of what Margalit called 'a second-person account.' I am not sure what Margalit himself had in mind; but I want to consider his suggestion carefully because, whether or not it is a panacea for this problem in all areas of philosophy, I think there is something to be said for Margalit's suggestion with regard to certain issues in philosophy of religion.

Second-Person Experience

To make use of Margalit's suggestion, we first have to understand it. What is a second-person account, and how is it to be distinguished from its first-person and third-person analogues? Put very roughly, a first-person account is a report of something from the point of view of *my* experience, a first-person experience. So it seems that a second-person account must be some kind of report of an experience suitably characterized as second-person from a second-person point of view. To understand what a second-person account is, then, we have to consider what a second-person experience is.

For purposes of this lecture, I will understand a second-person experience in this way. One person Aaron has a second-person experience of another person Nathan just in case

(1) Aaron is conscious of Nathan as a person (call the relation Aaron has to Nathan in this condition 'personal interaction'),

(2) Aaron's personal interaction with Nathan is of a direct and immediate sort,

and

(3) Nathan is conscious.

Condition 1 implies that Aaron does not have a second-person experience of Nathan if Aaron is dumped unconscious on top of Nathan; even if Nathan is conscious, it is necessary that Aaron be conscious as well.

Furthermore, if Aaron is conscious but not conscious of Nathan — say, because Nathan is hiding and Aaron doesn't know he is present — then Aaron doesn't have a second-person experience of Nathan. Condition 1 can be met, however, even if Aaron does not have perception of Nathan. It is possible for one person to be consciously aware of another without seeing, hearing, smelling, touching, or tasting that other person. For example, if

Aaron and Nathan are engaged in an animated conversation with one another which they conduct by means of smoke signals, Aaron has Nathan as an object of his consciousness, even if he doesn't perceive Nathan.

It is hard to know how to make this part of condition 1 precise. It is possible for two persons to make some sort of mind-to-mind contact even if neither of them perceives the other, so that one person's perception of another isn't necessary for his having a second-person experience of her. On the other hand, his just thinking of her in her absence does not count as his having a second-person experience of her even if in thinking about her he is conscious of her as a person in some sense. Second-person experience requires conscious contact with another person considered as a person; contact of that sort doesn't need perception, but it does take more than an image or a memory of a person.

Finally, the requirement that Aaron be conscious of Nathan as a person rules out cases of the sort made familiar to us from the literature on agnosia, where the agnosia patient is conscious and one of the objects of his consciousness is another person, but because of his agnosia he doesn't recognize the other person as a person; he takes her instead to be, say, a hat on a hat stand.[5] This requirement also rules out cases in which Aaron has conscious awareness only of some sub-personal part (say, an elbow) or sub-personal system (say, the circulatory system) of Nathan.

I take Aaron's personal interaction with Nathan to be mediated and indirect just in case Aaron has personal interaction with Nathan only in virtue of having personal interaction with a third person Monica. So condition 2 rules out cases of personal interaction which are mediated by third persons, but it does not rule out intermediaries which are machines or mechanical devices, such as glasses, telephones, and computers. If Aaron's only contact with Nathan is by computer, but if the computer contact between them meets the other conditions for second-person experience, then Aaron's computer contact with Nathan counts as a second-person experience. On the other hand, Aaron does not count as having a second-person experience of Nathan if Monica reports to Aaron something Nathan has said or done. In such a case, Nathan is conscious, and Aaron is conscious of

5. See the case which gives the title to Oliver Sacks's book *The Man Who Mistook His Wife for a Hat* (New York: Summit Books, 1985). For a helpful recent neurobiological study of agnosias, see Martha J. Farah, *Visual Agnosia* (Cambridge, Mass.: MIT Press, 1990).

Nathan as a person, in some sense; but this sort of consciousness of Nathan is insufficient to count as a second-person experience of Nathan because it is mediated by a third-person.

There are complications here. If Aaron reads a letter sent to him by Nathan, Aaron counts as having a second-person experience of Nathan on the conditions I have given. That remains the case even if Nathan dictated the letter to his secretary, since when Aaron reads the letter, Aaron does not have any personal interaction with the secretary. When he reads the letter, Aaron is not conscious of the secretary; or even if he is, it is not the case that he is conscious of Nathan only in virtue of being conscious of Nathan's secretary. But if the same message from Nathan to Aaron were delivered to Aaron orally by Nathan's secretary, then Aaron would not count as having a second-person experience of Nathan, because in that case Aaron's consciousness of the secretary mediates his consciousness of Nathan. This seems to me intuitively the right result.

On the other hand, however, suppose that Nathan's secretary delivers orally a message to Aaron, who gives the secretary a response, which the secretary delivers to Nathan, who in turn gives the secretary a message to deliver to Aaron, and so on. In such a case, is it still true to say that Aaron does not have a second-person experience of Nathan because condition 2 is violated? My intuitions are less clear in this case. It may be that getting the conditions for second-person experience precise and accurate is difficult or impossible to do; there may be boundary cases where adjudication regarding second-person experience could equally well go either way.

Finally, condition 3 requires that Nathan be conscious for Aaron to have a second-person experience of him. In certain fairy tales there is a girl in love with a prince who is prevented by magic from taking any notice of her. At some great price, she purchases the right to be present with him in the night, only to discover that her enemy has rendered him unconscious. As she laments through the night with the unconscious prince, the girl is keenly aware of the prince and aware of him as a person; she also has unmediated personal contact with him. But because he is unconscious, she has no second-person experience of him. So for one person, Aaron, to have a second-person experience of another person, Nathan, it is necessary that Nathan as well as Aaron be conscious. It is not necessary, however, that Nathan be conscious of Aaron. Polonius has a second-person experience of Hamlet when Polonius is hidden from Hamlet behind the arras, watching Hamlet interact with his mother.

This, then, is my bid at characterizing the notion of a second-person experience. It is an attempt to explicate what it is for one person to be conscious of another person as a person when that other person is functioning, however minimally, as a person. Even if it is only a rough and preliminary characterization, I think it is sufficient for present purposes.

On this characterization, it is clear that a second-person experience is different from a first-person experience. In a first-person experience, I am directly and immediately consciously aware of a person as a person, but that person is only myself. A second-person experience is also different from the sort of experience a neurologist has of his subject. It is possible for the neurologist to function as a neurologist when he has only a brain of some dead person in front of him. Or, even if his subject is living and conscious as well, the neurologist can practice neurology just by interacting with some part of that subject, recording electrical potentials from the skull, for example. A neurologist can therefore do his work without being conscious of his subject as a person. There are, of course, cases where it seems as if the neurologist is conscious of his subject as a person. For example, there are cases where it is crucial for the neurologist to talk to his subject in order for him to carry out his neurological work, as when the neurologist is trying to determine whether stimulation of a particular area of the brain affects language function. In such cases, I am inclined to say that the neurologist uses a second-person experience of his patient in order to get information relevant to the third-person neurological account he is trying to construct. So a second-person experience is different in character from a first-person or a third-person experience because it is necessary for a second-person experience, as it isn't for a first- or third-person experience, that you interact consciously and directly with another person who is conscious and present to you as a person, in one way or another.

Second-Person Accounts

But what is an account of such a second-person experience? Why think it differs from either a first-person or third-person account? In a first-person account I give a report about some first-person experience of mine. In the neurologist's third-person account, he gives a report about some feature or condition of someone else. What is there left for a second-person account to do? Why wouldn't a report of a second-person experience simply be one more first-person account — if I report the conscious states which I had while in the second-person experience[6] — or one more third-person account — if I report something about some other person which I observed during my contact with her?

If everything knowable in a second-person experience could be expressed in expository descriptions[7] of oneself or of the others with whom one interacts, then no doubt a second-person experience could be captured by first-person and third-person accounts, and there would be no room for anything that could be considered a second-person account.

But in fact there are some things we know in second-person experiences which are difficult or impossible to put in expository form at all.[8] What could that possibly be? a skeptical objector may ask. But, of course, if I give an answer to the skeptic's question, I will have an incoherent position: in answering the question, I will be presenting in expository prose what I said could not be presented that way. So is there another way of responding to the skeptical objector and showing that we learn something in a second-person experience which we can't express expositorily?

One way to answer the skeptic is by doing a thought experiment. Imagine someone — say, Mary — who from birth has been isolated by a mad scientist from contact with any other persons but who has had access to any and all information about the world as long as that information is only in the form of third-person accounts.[9] So, for example, Mary has available to

6. I am not here violating the explanation of first-person accounts given in footnote 1, because insofar as what is at issue is my conscious states, these are states I could have had during a hallucination of another person, when no other person was present; so the experience being reported in this first-person account is one I could have had by myself.

7. For purposes of this lecture, I take 'expository prose' to mean prose which does not constitute a story and which does not fall into some other genre of literature (such as certain sorts of poetry) that is story-like in its artistry.

8. I am not claiming that what makes second-person experiences different from first-person experiences is that only in second-person experiences is there something which can't be expressed in expository prose. In my view, part of what goes into at least some first-person experiences also can't be expressed expositorily, namely, what a conscious experience is like. My point here is rather that whatever is distinctive about a second-person experience is among the things that are not expressible expositorily.

9. I am here adapting an example from the literature in philosophy of mind which has been used to argue that qualia, the states one is in when one is conscious, can't be reduced to brain states. The example was originally introduced by Frank Jackson

her the best science texts for any of the sciences, from physics to sociology. She knows that there are other people in the world, and *(mirabile dictu)* she knows all that science can teach her about them. But she has never had any personal interactions of an unmediated and direct sort with another person. She has read descriptions of human faces, for example, but she has never been face-to-face with another conscious person. She has read books that describe the process of human communication, including the role of melody in speech and body language; but she has never had a conversation of any sort with anyone, and she has never participated in any way, even as a bystander, in anyone else's real or imagined conversation. In short, Mary has been kept from anything that could count as a second-person experience. And then suppose that Mary is finally rescued from her imprisonment and united for the first time with her mother who loves her deeply.

When Mary is first united with her mother, it seems indisputable that Mary will know things she did not know before, even if she knew everything about her mother which could be made available to her in expository prose, including her mother's psychological states.[10] To begin with, although

---

("Epiphenomenal Qualia," *Philosophical Quarterly* 32 (1982) 127-36), who constructed a thought-experiment involving a neuroscientist Mary who knows everything there is to know about the brain but who has had no perceptual experience of color; although she knows the neurobiology of color perception, she will learn something new when she first perceives color, Jackson argued. However we adjudicate the dispute in the philosophy of mind about qualia, Jackson's thought-experiment seems to me also to show something he didn't construct it to show, namely, that certain first-person experiences are not expressible in expository prose. That is why Jackson's Mary doesn't know qualia even though she has available to her a large scientific library. It isn't just that *neuroscience* books can't capture qualia. No expository books could. In my thought-experiment Mary comes to learn not the qualia associated with color perception but a particular sort of qualia or analogue to qualia which accompanies second-person experience.

10. Nicholas Wolterstorff has suggested to me in correspondence that if Mary had had the requisite sort of experience of personal interaction before her period of isolation, then it would have been possible to communicate to her in the expository prose of a third-person account what personal interaction with her mother would be like. On this view, the difficulty in communicating to Mary by a third-person account the nature of a second-person experience with her mother is just a function of Mary's innocence of second-person experiences. But I am inclined to think this diagnosis of Mary's difficulty is not correct. In ordinary circumstances involving persons socialized in the usual way, it remains true that when we meet a person for the first time, we learn something important we didn't know before, even if before the meeting we were given an excellent and detailed third-person account of that person.

Mary knows her mother loves her before she meets her, when she is united with her mother, Mary will learn what it is like to be loved. And this will be new for her, even if in her isolated state she had as complete a scientific description as possible of what a human being feels like when she senses that she is loved by someone else. Furthermore, it is clear that this is only the beginning. She will also know what it is like to be touched by someone else, to be surprised by someone else, to ascertain someone else's mood, to detect affect in the melody of someone else's voice, to match thought for thought in conversation, and so on. These will be things she learns, even if before she had access to excellent books on human psychology and communication.

The way in which I have formulated what Mary learns — what it is like to be touched by someone else, and so on — may suggest to someone that Mary learns things just about herself, and that she learns them in virtue of having new first-person experiences. It seems, then, that whatever Mary learns can be explained adequately in a first-person account. But this is clearly wrongheaded. Even if Mary does learn new things about herself, what will come as the major revelation to Mary is *her mother*. And even this way of putting what Mary learns is misleading, because it suggests that Mary's new knowledge can be expressed in a third-person description of her mother. But neither first-person nor third-person accounts will be adequate for Mary to describe what is new for her. What is new for her, what she learns, has to do with her personal interaction with another person. In her first direct and immediate experience with another human being, Mary's mind is opened to all that we learn and experience in face-to-face contact, the complex give-and-take of interpersonal interactions. Mary will be surprised by the nature of a second-person experience, no matter how good her science textbooks have been or how rich her isolated introspective experience may have been. The surprise makes two things clear: first, that she is learning something she didn't know before the personal interaction, and, second, that it isn't possible to teach her by means of expository prose (of the sort in the science books she has) what she comes to learn through personal interaction.

This thought experiment thus shows that there are things we come to know from our encounters with other people and that these things are difficult or impossible to describe from a third-person or a first-person point of view, because they are difficult or impossible to formulate in expository terms at all.[11]

11. In correspondence, Al Plantinga has suggested to me that I am here in fact ex-

(The well-known French philosopher Emmanuel Levinas insists that insightful philosophical thought and morally good living are possible only for a person who has vividly in front of him the face of the other.[12] Levinas's whole philosophy is marked by the emphasis on the importance of direct and immediate awareness of another person's face. Insofar as I understand Levinas's basic idea, it is the point I have been at pains to defend here, namely, that there is something to know in second-person experiences which can't be known in other ways. What Levinas adds to this idea is the insistence that what is known in this way is the most important and the most foundational of the things we know. If Levinas is even partly right about the importance of what we learn in second-person experiences and the inability of translating what we learn into first-person or third-person accounts, then analytic philosophy, which typically pays very little attention to second-person experiences, has something to learn from Levinas.)

So far I have argued that second-person experiences can't be reduced to first-person or third-person experiences without remainder; but I began this part of the discussion by asking what a second-person account might be, and my conclusion here might seem equivalent to the claim that a second-person account is impossible. If what we learn in second-person experiences is difficult or impossible to express in expository prose, how can any account of it be given at all?

In one sense, this point is right. There is no way to give an adequate expository account of a second-person experience. But it doesn't follow that no account of it is possible at all. While we cannot express the distinctive knowledge we gain in such an experience expositorily, we can do something to re-present the experience itself in such a way that we can share it

---

plaining in expository prose what it is that Mary learns, namely, what it is like to be loved by her mother, and so on. But that some sort of description of what Mary learns is possible doesn't mean that we can explain it adequately with an expository account. Consider, for example, that while it is possible to describe the experience of seeing red to a person who has been blind from birth by saying that when a sighted person sees a red object, she knows what it is like to see red, this description isn't an adequate explanation in expository prose of what the sighted person knows in knowing what it is like to see red.

12. I am grateful to Jonathan Malino, David Hartman, and the Hartman Institute for calling Levinas's work, and especially his superb Talmudic commentaries, to my attention.

with others who were not part of it.[13] This is generally what we do when we tell a story.[14] A story takes a real or imagined second-person experience and makes it available to a wider audience to share.[15] It does so by making it possible, to one degree or another, for a reader or listener to simulate what it would have been like for her if she had been a bystander in the second-person experience represented in the story.[16] That is, a story gives its reader some of what she would have had if she had had unmediated personal interaction with the characters in the story while they were conscious and interacting with each other, without actually making her part of the story itself, without her having to imagine or simulate the characters' having personal interaction with her. The re-presenting of a second-person experience in a story thus constitutes a second-person account. It is a report of a second-person experience which doesn't lose (at least doesn't lose entirely) the distinctively second-person character of the experience.

How much of what can be known in a second-person experience becomes available to others to learn by means of a story depends on the artistry of the story-teller. Harlequin romances no doubt give us something; the world's great literature, drama, and film give us much more. If in her isolation Mary had had available to her not only science books but also, for exam-

---

13. In this respect, a second-person experience differs from a first-person experience of the sort we have in perception. There is no way for me to convey to someone who has never seen colors what I know when I know what it is like to see red.

14. I am not here implying that the only function, or even the main function, of narratives (in one medium or another) is to convey real or imagined second-person experiences. My claim is just that much less is lost of a second-person experience in a narrative account than in a third-person account, ceteris paribus.

15. Someone might suppose that any information which could be captured and conveyed by a story could also be conveyed by an expository account. I have no good argument against this claim, for the very reasons I have been urging, namely, that we can't give an expository description of what *else* is contained in a story; but I think the claim is false. Consider, for example, some excellent and current biography of Samuel Johnson, such as Robert DeMaria's *The Life of Samuel Johnson: A Critical Biography* (Oxford: Blackwell, 1993), and compare it to the pastiche of stories in Boswell's *Life of Johnson,* and you see the point. There is a great deal to be learned about Johnson from DeMaria's *The Life of Samuel Johnson,* but Boswell's stories give you the man as the biography can't.

16. On the role of simulation in audience reaction to fiction, see, for example, Kenneth Walton, "Spelunking, Simulation, and Slime: On Being Moved by Fiction," in *Emotion and the Arts,* ed. Mette Jhorte and Sue Laver (New York: Oxford University Press, 1997). On simulation theory in general, see, for example, Martin Davies and Tony Stone, *Mental Simulation* (Oxford: Blackwell, 1995).

ple, the works of Eliot, Dickens, Tolstoy, Dostoyevsky, Angelou, and Achebe, or an array of the best movies and theatre productions, it is indisputable that her first experience with her mother would have been less of a surprise. (It is also perhaps worth pointing out in this connection that although Levinas is notable for his obscurity in his philosophical writings, which are attempts to give third-person philosophical accounts of the importance of the encounter with the face of the other, he is much clearer and more compelling in his Talmudic commentaries, where what is generally at issue is a narrative.)

Not every narrative is a second-person account. In general, narratives have interactions among people as their centerpiece, but there are stories in which the narrator relates experiences that include no people but himself. Jack London's story "To Build a Fire" is a story of this sort. Even stories such as "To Build a Fire," however, have this much of the second-person about them: in re-presenting for us what was originally only a first-person experience, they turn the first-person experience into something at least approaching a second-person experience insofar as the reader's experience of the character of the story is analogous to a second-person experience. The reader doesn't have direct and immediate contact with the story's character, of course. But the author's presentation of the character, if it is well done, makes that character available to us in somewhat the same way he would have been if he had in fact been directly and immediately present to us. The story thus contributes to our having and learning from something like a second-person experience. But the story still doesn't qualify as a second-person *account*, in the sense at issue here, because the story isn't presenting for others the interaction between the readers and the story's character.

It is also true that some forms of literature which don't count as stories in any medium can sometimes qualify as a second-person account. So, for example, some poems serve the same function as stories in portraying for us the interactions of persons;[17] and even some poems which have very few features of stories may still be successful in re-creating for us an image of one person's relations to others. So, for example, as I will discuss shortly, the poems which are God's speeches to Job present for the reader a picture of God's relations to his creatures, and the picture is vivid and lively enough to make it at least arguable that the poems are second-person ac-

---

17. And, of course, some poems, such as Homer's *Iliad* and *Odyssey* or Milton's *Paradise Lost*, are or at least include stories in an artistically complicated form.

counts, too. But the clearest examples of second-person accounts are stories (in one medium or another) involving more than one person.

Whether second-person accounts are useful in bridging the gap between first-person and third-person accounts, as Margalit thinks they will be, depends in my view on the nature of the particular gap. I have no confidence that second-person accounts will be a universal remedy,[18] but I do think that they have a special place in some areas of philosophy, including philosophy of religion. The major monotheisms take God to be a person, with a mind and a will, and it matters to many issues in philosophy of religion, perhaps especially to the problem of evil, that God is taken to be a person who has personal relations with created persons. Insofar as these personal relations make a difference to such issues as the problem of evil, narratives about God and his relations to human beings have a role to play in our philosophical and theological thinking about such issues. And, of course, it is noteworthy that the sacred texts of all three major monotheisms include not only divine laws and commands, but also narratives about God and human persons.

Because I want to highlight the importance of narratives in certain areas of philosophy, it is perhaps important to say explicitly that even in these areas of philosophy I don't think narratives supplant philosophical thought. Philosophical discussion apart from narratives is indispensable for thinking through contentious issues such as the problem of evil; straightforward philosophical investigation isn't rendered otiose by the usefulness of narrative any more than neurobiology is made superfluous by good novels. Narratives are an aid to thinking through certain philosophical issues; they are not a rival to philosophy itself.

With that caveat, I think that narratives representing second-person experiences which involve God's interactions with human persons are helpful in thinking about the problem of evil. Believers typically have available to them two main routes of accessing from a second-person point of view God's interactions with people. One comes from their own religious experience, which is (or is taken by believers to be) some sort of second-person experience of God. The other is the second-person accounts of God

18. Martha Nussbaum argues for the importance of narrative in philosophy in general but without giving much explanation of what narratives contribute that can't be provided by philosophy alone without narratives. See, for example, *The Fragility of Goodness. Luck and Ethics in Greek Tragedy and Philosophy* (Cambridge: Cambridge University Press, 1986, reprinted 1992), pp. 45-47.

and human persons in biblical narratives. Insofar as personal interactions make a difference to such issues as the problem of evil, stories about God and his relations to human beings of the sort we find in biblical narratives have a role to play in our philosophical and theological thinking about such issues.

Later I will say something about the relevance of a believer's own religious experience to her thought about the problem of evil. Now, however, I want to focus on biblical narratives. The classic biblical text having to do with the problem of evil is, of course, the book of Job; and with this much explanation of the role of stories in philosophy of religion, I want now to turn to the book of Job.

I should add that, for my purposes here, it does not matter whether we understand this narrative as historically true in every particular or constructed out of whole cloth by the biblical author, provided that we take the artistry of the storyteller to be good. George Eliot's *Mill on the Floss,* for example, is fictional throughout, but the portrayal of the main character of that novel, Maggie, is veridical, because Eliot is a great artist. Because Eliot's portrayal of Maggie is true to life, we can learn a great deal about how human persons relate to one another by the story of Maggie, even though without any doubt the story of Maggie is Eliot's invention. So in what follows I will have nothing to say one way or another about the historical accuracy of the biblical narratives. There are contexts in which the historical accuracy of biblical narratives matters very much, but this is not one of them.

The Anchor Bible Interpretation of the Book of Job

The book of Job has a complicated form. The heart of the book is a set of dialogues, but they are framed by a story about what God does both to Job and in interactions with others that crucially affect Job and cause him great suffering. The dialogues themselves consist in a heated debate about Job's suffering and God's role in it, so that the dialogues are a commentary on the story that frames them. But part of the dialogues is itself a conversation between God and Job, and so this part of the dialogues furthers the framing story because it consists in interaction between God and Job. In addition, in his part of this conversation, God re-presents for Job God's personal relations with his creatures. The divine speeches to Job consist in vivid descriptions of God's interactions with the non-human parts of his creation.

Consequently, there is an intricate set of nested second-person accounts in the book of Job. The description of God's personal relations with the non-human parts of his creation is contained within an account of God's conversation with Job, which is part of the dialogues commenting on God's relations with Job, which are themselves the subject of the text framing the dialogues. All of this taken together constitutes the story of God and Job.

And yet the book of Job is commonly treated as if it were little more than a philosophy treatise on the problem of evil. The details and intricacies of the narrative and its second-person context are neglected as unimportant or dismissed as uninteresting additions to the philosophically important debate in the dialogues. Furthermore, the debate in the dialogues is treated as an unsatisfactory philosophical discussion because it is taken to break off without a decisive conclusion regarding the problem of evil. The one thing Job wants, as he says over and over, is for God to explain to him why he suffers; and, on the common reading of Job, that is the one thing Job never gets from God.

The Anchor Bible commentary on Job is a good example of this sort of interpretation of Job, and I can show what I want to say about the book of Job more easily by taking the Anchor Bible as my foil.[19] Contrary to the common interpretation, I think that Job does get what he wants in this story, namely, an explanation of why he suffers. Consequently, I also think that the book of Job is helpful for thinking about *solutions* to the problem of evil, but only if it is read with careful attention to its character as a second-person account.

The Anchor Bible, on the other hand, supposes that the story of Job gives us no help with the problem of evil. The Anchor Bible commentator says,

"It has been generally assumed that the purpose of the book [of Job] is to give an answer to the issue with which it deals, the problem of divine justice or theodicy. This question is raised inevitably by any and every instance of seemingly unmerited or purposeless suffering, and especially the suffering of a righteous man. Job's case . . . poses the problem in the most striking possible way. A man of exemplary rectitude and piety is suddenly overwhelmed with disasters and loathsome disease. How can such a situa-

19. Marvin Pope, *Job*, The Anchor Bible (New York: Doubleday, 1965).

tion be reconciled with divine justice and benevolent providence? It must be admitted first and last that the Book of Job fails to give a clear and definitive answer to this question."[20] (footnote omitted)

The Anchor Bible quite rightly sees Job's reaction to his suffering as passionately defiant. The commentator says, "Job bluntly calls into question divine justice and providence";[21] his "bitter complaints and charges of injustice against God shock his pious friends who doggedly defend divine justice. . . ."[22] Job, on the other hand, "vehemently denies that he has sinned, at least not seriously enough to merit such misery as has been inflicted on him. Justice, he argues, often appears abortive in the world and for this God must be held responsible. Hence Job infers that God has no concern for justice or for human feelings. . . . [Job] wishes to argue his case with God, but he cannot find God nor force him to grant a fair hearing."[23]

On the Anchor Bible reading of the story Job recognizes God's power,[24] but in a series of vehement protests against God he calls into question God's goodness. Here, at any rate, I think the Anchor Bible has it right. Job's own passionate insistence on moral goodness in the governance of the world underlies his violent protests against God and his demands that God be called to account. Job's friends are shocked at what they take to be his blasphemy. They repeatedly point out to Job the contrast between Job's limitedness, on the one hand, and God's power and knowledge, on the other.[25] "God's greatness is beyond man's comprehension . . . ," the comforters say, and so, in their view, Job ought to appeal to God for mercy and forgiveness in order to be restored to God's favor.[26] But Job rejects the comforters' attitude with scorn. Job readily grants that God has power. What is at issue for Job is God's goodness. According to the Anchor Bible commentator, "[Job] charges God with vicious and unprovoked assaults. . . . He cries out for vindication. . . . God has afflicted him unjustly."[27] I agree entirely with the Anchor Bible on *this* score: Job will not submit to a God who is not good, no matter how powerful he is.

20. Ibid., p. lxxiii.
21. Ibid., p. xv.
22. Ibid., p. xxiii.
23. Ibid., p. lxxv.
24. Cf., e.g., p. lxxx.
25. Ibid., pp. xvii-xxii.
26. Ibid., p. xviii.
27. Ibid., p. xix.

Because Job makes such a powerful indictment of God, the Anchor Bible maintains that God's answer to Job, which comes in God's speeches near the end of the book, is "something of a surprise and . . . a disappointment. The issue, as Job had posed it, is completely ignored. No explanation or excuse is offered for Job's suffering. . . . Job had already expressed his awe and wonder at God's power. . . . He had questioned not divine omnipotence but [divine] justice and mercy. The complete evasion of the issue as Job had posed it must be the poet's oblique way of admitting that there is no satisfactory answer available to man. . . ."[28] The Anchor Bible commentator says, "The fundamental question [about suffering], If not for sin, why then? is completely ignored. . . . It is quite understandable that readers . . . are left with a feeling of chagrin at the seemingly magnificent irrelevance of much of the content of the divine speeches."[29] What Job called into question with so much passion and rebellion was God's goodness. But, on the interpretation of the Anchor Bible, the only attribute of God's on display in God's speeches to Job is God's power.[30]

So the picture the Anchor Bible paints is this. Job, an innocent man, suffers horribly at God's hands. In his suffering, Job acknowledges God's great power, but he complains bitterly about God's apparent lack of goodness. When God finally appears on the scene to answer Job's charge, however, all God talks to Job about is God's power. So, as the Anchor Bible reads the story, God simply fails to address Job's charge — and if that is right, then this part of the story certainly is both surprising and disappointing, as the Anchor Bible commentator says.

A Puzzle for the Anchor Bible Interpretation

But I myself think that there is something even more surprising and puzzling about the story as the Anchor Bible interprets it, and it is something the Anchor Bible commentator fails to comment on at all. What does Job do in the face of the disappointing high-handed description of God's power which he gets in God's speeches to him? On the view of the Anchor Bible, Job "answers with humble acknowledgment of God's omnipotence

28. Ibid., p. lxxx.
29. Ibid., p. lxxxi.
30. Ibid., p. 291, note 3b; cf. also p. 318, note 9b.

and his own ignorance;"[31] in the face of God's majestic declaration of his divine power, "Job repents and recants."[32] So on the Anchor Bible interpretation, Job not only takes back what he has been saying, but he also submits to God with a good deal of humility.

But isn't this a surprising response to find on Job's part? It seems to me so surprising as to call in question the fundamental conclusions of the Anchor Bible interpretation. Is it really credible that after all Job's passionate focus on goodness, after all his defiance of the power of God, he simply collapses into a heap of humility when the almighty ruler of the universe comes to talk to him and Job has impressed on him how really powerful God is? Are we to suppose that Job was a pompous windbag, willing to complain about the boss of the universe behind his back but utterly unable to stand up to him to his face? I don't see how anyone could read Job in this way. On this score, the Anchor Bible interpretation of the text seems to me thoroughly implausible.

Furthermore, the Anchor Bible interpretation can't account for the intensity with which Job repudiates his earlier accusations against God. After God's first speech, Job says, "Behold, I am vile" (40:4);[33] and after God's second speech, Job says, "I recant and repent in dust and ashes." (42:6) If the divine speeches have as their only function reiterating the power of God, which Job has already acknowledged when he was alienated from God and insisting on an explanation of his suffering, why do God's speeches have this effect on Job? Why do they produce so powerful a repentance of his earlier attitude towards God? He could, after all, submit to God with suitable deference without going so far.

The Anchor Bible interpretation thus gives us a serious incongruity in the character of Job. In the speeches to his friends, he is heedless of everything except goodness, and he is willing to confront even the power of God to get it. But in his response to God's speeches, on the Anchor Bible interpretation, Job just cringes in front of power. Now we can, of course, always chalk up an incongruity of this sort to the artistic incompetence of the author or editor of the narrative, though in this case it would be a fairly serious and dramatic incompetence. Even if the author or editor of the

31. Ibid., p. xxii.
32. Ibid., p. lxxx.
33. The Anchor Bible translates this line as "Lo, I am small"; the root meaning of the Hebrew word is to be contemptible or to be disgraced, so 'vile' seems better than 'small'.

book wanted Job to be submissive to God at the end of the book, there are ways to write the story more plausibly than simply to have the rebel turn at once into a lackey in the face of God's assertion of his power. Furthermore, impugning the competence of an author ought to be an interpretative strategy of last resort, to be employed when other attempts at explanation have failed. In this case, it is also a particularly lame strategy, because of the magnificent artistry which is readily recognizable in the rest of the book.

An Alternative Interpretation of the Divine Speeches

I am inclined to think that the problem in the Anchor Bible interpretation arises because the Anchor Bible commentator is oblivious to the fact that the divine speeches both are set in the context of second-person relations, in the story they are part of, and themselves constitute a second-person account, in their content.

Take, first of all, the content of the speeches. The Anchor Bible summarizes the divine speeches this way:

"Who is Job to speak out of ignorance? [God says, addressing Job]. What does [Job] know of the founding of the earth, the subjugation of the violent sea, the dawn of day, the depths of the infernal regions, the expanse of the earth, the abodes of light and darkness, the treasure houses of the snow and ice, the ordering of the constellations and the rains . . . ? Can Job provide food for the lion and the raven? Does he know the birth season of the wild goats, the habits of the wild ass? . . . Yahweh speaks to Job out of the storm and challenges him to show that he has divine powers."[34]

There is no question that the Anchor Bible commentator is right in thinking that these speeches of God's describe God's power; God's power and knowledge are undoubtedly a central theme in the divine speeches. But the commentator seems to me to miss an equally important feature of the speeches which is crucial for an adequate interpretation of Job's response to them.

Consider, for example, the beginning of God's first speech, which the Anchor Bible characterizes as describing the power of God in the founding of the earth. That description is correct as far as it goes, but it is seriously incomplete. Here is what God says to Job:

34. Ibid., p. xxii.

"Where were you when I founded the earth? Tell me, if you know so much. Who drafted its dimensions? Surely you know? Who stretched the line over it? On what are its sockets sunk, who laid its cornerstone, while the morning stars sang together, and all the sons of God rejoiced?"[35] (38:4-7)

As the Anchor Bible correctly maintains, these lines represent God as having the immense power to create the earth. But they also show God's role in a community which participates in God's creating by watching what he does and rejoicing in it. Furthermore, this community is not passive. It responds to what it sees God doing, and the response is communal, too: the morning stars sing together. When God creates the earth, then, he does not create alone. He shares his creating with a community of his creatures who rejoice together at his creating and sing, and clearly part of the point of the sharing is precisely to bring this joy to this community. Finally, it is important not to miss the parental imagery. The group that rejoices is the group of God's sons. From the beginning of creation, then, and from the start of the divine speeches God is portrayed as a parent. So what we see here in this part of the first divine speech is not just the metaphysical attributes of power and knowledge necessary for God's creation of the earth. We also see God as a person, in personal and parental relationships with his creatures, sharing what he has created with them and making them glad by doing so.

The Anchor Bible characterizes the next part of this divine speech as a description of God's subjugation of the sea. Now what God says in the part of the speech about the sea is this:

"Who shut the sea within doors, when it came gushing from the womb, when I made the cloud its garment, dark mist its swaddling bands,

---

35. I have used the Anchor Bible translation throughout, except where noted, for the sake of fairness, since I am disputing its interpretation of the text. In this case, I have departed from the Anchor Bible translation at two points. The Anchor Bible translates as 'gods' a Hebrew phrase which it acknowledges to mean literally 'sons of God.' Since the Anchor Bible translation thus obscures just what I think is interesting about this phrase, I have translated it more literally. I have also translated as 'rejoiced' what the Anchor Bible translator renders 'exulted,' but just because 'exult' can carry an array of connotations, such as gloating, for example, which don't seem warranted by the Hebrew. Finally, the Anchor Bible translator prints the text as if it were English poetry, in short broken lines beginning with words which are capitalized; but since there is no warrant in the Hebrew text for any such arrangement, I have simply omitted it.

when I put bounds upon it, set up bars and doors, saying, 'Thus far come, but no more. Here your wild waves halt'?" (38:8-11)

It is important not to be oblivious to the second-person account in these lines. In the first place, the imagery here depicts maternal interactions between God and the sea. The sea is created by coming forth from a womb, and God deals with the sea as a mother deals with her child: he wraps it in swaddling bands; he clothes it with a garment. The description of the creation of the sea is thus couched in the sort of language we would ordinarily use to tell the story of a mother and her new baby.

Furthermore, the relations between God and the sea are described as personal relations.[36] The Anchor Bible characterizes these lines as a description of God's subjugating the sea; but it is noteworthy that God controls the sea by *talking* to it. In fact, it's hard to see these lines as a description of a *subjugation*. God does not simply bend the sea to his will. He doesn't just wield his great power to decree what the nature and attributes of a sea must be. Almighty God could do so with an act of will alone, without making any utterances. Or if he wanted to determine what the sea did by an utterance, he could make an impersonal statement, addressed to no one in particular, of this sort: 'I decree that the sea will extend from here to there, but it will not extend any further.' Instead, what we get in the speech is a description of a personal interaction between God and the sea. God addresses the sea directly, and he addresses it as if the sea were a rambunctious and exuberant child of his, but nonetheless a child who can hear him, understand him, and respond to him. God brings the sea into conformity to his will by talking to the sea itself and explaining to it what it can and cannot do.

The remainder of God's speech describing the inanimate parts of his creation continues in the same way. In this part of his speech, God portrays inanimate created things as if they were children of his with whom he has a personal relationship and for whom he has a parental concern. Furthermore, he not only describes himself as talking to inanimate creatures, as he does in the section on the sea; he also describes these inanimate creatures as responding by talking to him.

36. These interactions don't count as personal, strictly speaking, on the interpretation of 'personal interaction' which I gave above, because they are interactions between God and creatures which are not themselves persons. But insofar as these non-human creatures are portrayed in personal terms in the divine speeches, God's relations with them are also portrayed as personal interactions.

"Did you ever command a morning?" he asks Job (38:12), and a little later he says, "Where is the way to light's dwelling, darkness, where [is] its abode, that you may guide it to its bourne, [and] show it the way to go home? . . . Who cleft a channel for the downpour, [or] a path for the thundershower, to bring rain on no-man's land, [on] the wilderness with no man in it, to sate the desolate desert, [and] make the thirsty land sprout verdure?" (38:19-20, 25-27); "Can you send lightning scurrying, to say to you, 'Here we are'?" (38:35)

Darkness and light have dwelling places, and God guides them there; even darkness and light get to their proper place in the world because God shows them the way home. God talks to the morning; and when he sends the lightning where it should go, the lightning talks to him.

The explicitly parental terminology continues here as well:

"Does the rain have a father?" God asks Job. "Who sired the dew drops? From whose womb comes the ice[?] The hoarfrost of heaven, who bore it . . . ?" (38:28-29)

These parts of the divine speeches constitute a second-person account. They are not a story, but they are story-like. They convey in the vivid sort of way a story would a picture, an impression, of God's entering into personal relations with all parts of his creation and of his dealing with his creatures in maternal ways. That impression is only strengthened in the next part of the speeches which constitutes a second-person account of God's dealings with animals.

Here what God tells Job shows not only God's power over the animals and his knowledge of their nature and ways, as the Anchor Bible holds, but also his great care for them. He hunts the prey for the lions, makes a home for the wild donkeys, and gives the hawks the wisdom necessary for flight. Even in the case of the ostrich, who is portrayed as an inept and foolish mother, deprived of wisdom by God, there is a loving note in the description; and the implication is that if the ostrich's eggs and children survive, it is because God does the mother's job for the ostrich mother. She forgets, God says to Job, that the eggs she leaves in the sand are easily crushed and are vulnerable to animals that pass by. There is a maternal note in the complaint that the ostrich *forgets*.[37] Who but God told her, or told her and reminded her, of what she is forgetting, and who but

---

37. The Anchor Bible translates the Hebrew word as 'heedless' rather than as 'forgets,' but its standard and root meaning is 'forgets.'

God preserves the eggs which the mother ostrich so forgetfully leaves vulnerable? (39:14-15)

Furthermore, the animals are portrayed as responding to God's care by relating to him personally. For example, the raven's young don't just cry when they are hungry; they cry to God. (38:41) Not only young and helpless animals but also powerful, fully-grown animals are described as having an intimate personal relation to God. "Will the buffalo deign to serve you?" God asks Job. "Will he stay beside your crib? Can you hold him in the furrow with rope? Will he harrow the valley after you? Can you rely on his great strength, can you leave your labor to him? Can you trust him to return and gather the grain of your threshing floor?" (39:9-11) The implication of these questions is that even if a human being such as Job couldn't have the close and trusting relationship with this fierce animal implied by the mention of all these activities characteristic of domesticated animals, God can and does.

The second of God's speeches to Job has to do with two great animals, behemoth and leviathan. Aquinas thought that behemoth is an elephant; some modern interpreters take it to be a hippopotamus; and the Anchor Bible takes it to be a mythological beast. There is a similar spread of opinion about leviathan. For my purposes here, it is enough to take behemoth and leviathan as great and impressive beasts of some sort, real or mythological, which are difficult or even impossible for human beings to tame. I'll refer to them just as behemoth and leviathan, with no attempt to take sides in the controversies about what exactly they are.

Some of the second speech is devoted to describing the strength of these beasts and the even more impressive power God has over them, including the power to capture or even to kill them. But there are also passages such as this: "Will [Leviathan] make long pleas to you, cajole you with tender words? Will he make a covenant with you, will you take him as [an] eternal slave? [Will you] [p]lay with him as with a bird,[38] leash him for your girls?" (41:3-5) For Job, the obvious answer to all these questions is "no." For God, on the other hand, the answer is clearly different. God has a close relationship with these great beasts, who not only talk to him with

---

38. The Anchor Bible translation is marked by a tone-deafness to the nuances of English which requires patience in the reader, but here the problem extends to grammar. I have changed the Anchor Bible's "Play with him like a bird" to "play with him as with a bird."

tender words but cajole him, plead with him, play with him, and make covenants with him.

It is a mistake, then, to characterize God's speeches as demonstrating nothing but God's power over creation. The speeches certainly do show God's power; but, equally importantly, they show God having personal interactions with all his creatures. He relates to everything he has made on a face-to-face basis, as it were; and in these personal interactions, God deals maternally with his creatures, from the sea and rain to the raven and the donkey and even the monstrous behemoth and leviathan. He brings them out of the womb, swaddles, feeds, and guides them, and even plays with them. Most importantly, he talks to them; and somehow, in some sense or other, they talk to him in return. These speeches thus show God as more than powerful; they show him as personally and intimately involved with his creation; they portray him as having a mother's care towards all his creatures, even the inanimate ones.

Explanations for Suffering

The divine speeches don't make claims about God's relations to creation. If they did, they would be a third-person account laying out some general theological claims. Instead, they constitute a second-person account which lets us participate, to some limited extent, in the perception of God's relation to inanimate things, plants, and animals. The speeches begin with a reference to the morning stars singing together and the sons of God rejoicing as they watch God's dealings with his creation. To some minimal degree, the speeches invite us to see what they saw. The implication is that if we see it, we also will be inclined to rejoice. What Job wanted was an explanation of God's relations with him, and he does get it, but in the form of a second-person account. He had demanded goodness. What he gets is what caused the sons of God not just to find God good but to rejoice in him and in his relations to his creatures.

But what exactly is this? For the reasons I gave above, I don't think that this question can be answered, or at least not answered without remainder. The question is a request that what is presented as a second-person account be translated into a third-person account, and I argued above that this could not be done without losing what is most important about the second-person account. Nonetheless, I want to say one thing which is in my view suggested by the second-person account of the relations between creator and creatures in the divine speeches.

The divine speeches suggest that God's relationship to all his creatures is personal, intimate, and parental or even maternal. Now a good mother will sometimes allow the children she loves to suffer — but only in case the suffering benefits the child who experiences the suffering, and benefits him in some way which couldn't have been equally well achieved without the suffering. A good mother, for example, wouldn't cause suffering to an innocent child[39] for the sole purpose of getting the dean of her college to learn a lesson. In the divine speeches, God is portrayed as giving the animals what they need because they need it — food for the baby birds who cry to him, prey for the young lions, help in mothering for the foolish ostrich. Nothing in the speeches suggests that God considers whether the hunger of the baby birds might be a good thing for the cats in their neighborhood. God doesn't think about whether their need and weakness might not be turned to good account for some other part of his creation, so that letting them stay hungry is justified by the good it produces elsewhere in the world. He just considers what will be good for them, and so he feeds them when they cry. And so there is not a claim but a suggestion, a picture, a portrayal, that leads us to think God operates on the principle I attributed to good mothers. This claim is not equivalent to the justly ridiculed Leibnizian principle that this is the best of all possible worlds in which everything that happens happens for the best. Rather, this is a point about one necessary condition for good mothering, namely, that, other things being equal, the benefit which justifies a mother in allowing some suffering to an innocent child of hers has to go to the child;[40] if she let her child suf-

---

39. To put this point precisely, it would have to be restricted to innocent, *unwilling* sufferers. In a previous paper, I have discussed the difference it makes to these issues if the sufferer in question has explicitly or implicitly, in virtue of a certain religious commitment, given consent to the suffering. See my "Providence and the Problem of Evil" in *Christian Theism and the Problems of Philosophy*, ed. Thomas Flint (Notre Dame, Ind.: University of Notre Dame Press, 1990), pp. 51-91. I am grateful to Al Plantinga for calling my attention to the need to make this point clear.

40. The ceteris paribus clause is necessary here because a good mother might be stuck with a choice only of evils, and the lesser of two evils might require letting her child suffer with no benefit accruing to him at all. For example, the mother might have to choose between alleviating a small suffering of her child's or a life-threatening suffering of some third person. In that case, she might let her child suffer without there being a benefit for the child. Whether this sort of dilemma results from the limits on human

fer for someone else's sake or for some abstract general good, to that extent she wouldn't count as a good mother.

Nothing in God's speeches to Job specifically describes God's relations with human beings, of course, but there is certainly a ready inference — both for Job and for readers of the book — from the way God deals with the rest of his creation to the way in which he deals with human persons. If God deals maternally with even the inanimate parts of his creation, if he seeks to produce good even for infant ravens, then a fortiori in his dealings with human beings God will operate in the same way, allowing their suffering only in case he can turn it to some good available to them.[41] If an innocent person suffers, then, it will be because a good God, a loving God involved face-to-face with his creatures, produces out of the suffering a good meant for that person which in the circumstances couldn't have been produced, or produced as well, without the suffering.[42] The inference to this

power or whether an omnipotent deity might also be in such a position is an issue that arises in connection with some attempts at theodicy.

41. There is, of course, an additional complication in the case of Job, because there God is at least actively collaborating in Job's suffering, not just allowing it. In other papers, I have discussed ways in which this feature of the story can be included in a theodicy. See my "Aquinas on the Sufferings of Job," in *Reasoned Faith*, ed. E. Stump (Ithaca, N.Y.: Cornell University Press, 1993), pp. 328-57; revised and reprinted in *The Problem of Evil*, ed. Daniel Howard-Snyder (Bloomington, Ind.: Indiana University Press, 1996). See also my "Saadya Gaon and the Problem of Evil," *Faith and Philosophy* 14 (1997) 523-49.

42. A standard objection at this point consists in pointing to some particularly horrible example of evil, such as the cases of the suffering of children described by Dostoyevsky's Ivan Karamazov or the Holocaust, and ask what good for the sufferers could possibly justify such suffering. Because I am here presenting and arguing for an interpretation of Job, rather than presenting and defending a particular theodicy, the objection is not germane to my enterprise. But it is perhaps important to say a word about it anyway. My interpretation of the divine speeches in Job can be taken as setting a condition for any successful theodicy. To be successful, a theodicy will have to show that any innocent suffering justifiably allowed by God has to benefit the sufferer primarily; it will not be successful if it maintains that the suffering of some innocent person is for the benefit of some other individual or group or that it contributes in some very general way to the goodness of creation as a whole. Whether or not such a condition has been met in any individual case of evil may in fact be impossible to tell, for reasons discussed at length in the literature; see, for example, the papers by William Alston, William Rowe, and Stephen Wykstra, in Daniel Howard-Snyder, *The Problem of Evil* (Bloomington, Ind.: Indiana University Press, 1996). In the case of the Holocaust, which is special if not unique in its evil, I would not want to engage in a philosophical discussion of the rea-

explanation about suffering is available to Job, as I said, but if I am right about second-person accounts, Job doesn't need to draw it, since in the second-person account of the divine speeches he has something epistemically stronger than this inference.

In addition, however, Job has another source of information about God's reasons for allowing him to suffer, and it is even more powerful than the second-person account in the divine speeches. It is the experience of God which he has while God is talking to him. The Anchor Bible, which doesn't see or doesn't accord much weight to the personal interactions described in God's speeches, also doesn't recognize the importance of the context in which the divine speeches are set. While God has been talking to Job, what is the relation between Job and God supposed to be? We don't have to speculate because Job explains it in his last lines to God. "I had heard of you by the hearing of the ear,"[43] Job says to God, "but now my own eye has seen you." (42:5) While God has been talking, Job has been seeing God. The communication between God and Job is thus face-to-face communication; in the course of the divine speeches, God has been somehow directly present to Job. The second-person account of the divine speeches to Job is thus set in the context of a second-person experience of God for Job.

When Job complained bitterly about the goodness of God, his charge wasn't just a metaphysical complaint raised for philosophical reasons. It was a personal complaint. Job's history before the start of his suffering is a history of trust in God and obedience to him, as Job makes clear in his speeches to the comforters. His protest against God in the dialogues thus at least includes a charge of betrayal of trust. But for this charge, a face-to-face encounter can make all the difference. To answer a mistaken charge of betrayal, a person who loves you can try to explain, or he can just face you and let you see *him*. If Job can see the face of God who loves his creatures as a mother loves her children, then he will see, or feel in some other way, that he is encompassed by that love also. So in the sight of God which Job has in his

sons which might possibly justify God in allowing such suffering even if I could think of any. It is enough for me that I am a member of the species that perpetrated this evil. For such evil, speech should fail. The only right response for philosophers and theologians as regards God and the Holocaust seems to me the response of Job: I will consider the vileness of human beings and lay my hand on my mouth and be silent.

43. I have rendered the Hebrew literally; the Anchor Bible has "I had heard of you by hearsay."

second-person experience of God in the course of the divine speeches to him, Job has another powerful response on God's part to Job's demand for an explanation. The sight of the face of a God whose mothering love is directed even towards rain and ravens is also an explanation of Job's suffering.

It is, of course, an explanation which is short on what we might think of as engineering or medical details. A child with aggressive leukemia who is suffering the pains of a bone marrow transplant may want to know from his mother why she doesn't help him and stop his suffering when she so clearly could, just by taking him out of the hospital. She could respond to that demand for an explanation with the details about the benefits of the transplant, a third-person, quasi-engineering medical account about the reconstruction of healthy bone marrow. She might share that medical account with her son in this way: "Well, see, you have a cancer which affects the blood, and the major blood products are produced by stem cells in the bone marrow. So what we are doing is removing some of your stem cells; the lab hunts through those till it finds some that aren't diseased, and it clones them, for eventual reinfusion. Then we inject you with a series of cytotoxic drugs which destroy the diseased stem cells in your bone marrow. Those drugs work because they target fast-growing cells. The cancer cells in your bone marrow are fast-growing; but so are your hair cells, the cells in the mucus membranes which line your mouth, your esophagus, and your gut. The cytotoxic drugs kill those, too. That's why you have sores in your mouth; that's why you're throwing up, and why you're constipated." And so on and on.

It might be that this is the right explanation for her son. But then again it might not be. There are circumstances in which third-person explanations of this sort are utterly inefficacious to comfort. That's why, for example, even after all the explanation needed to take away from you the impression you had that your friend had betrayed your trust, even when you do see for yourself that there was nothing hurtful there, the breach may not be healed for you until you make eye contact, clasp hands, get a hug, or in some other way make personal contact with your friend. The child undergoing a painful medical procedure may be more hurt by what he takes to be her abandonment of him, her apparent indifference to his pain and need, than by anything that is happening to his bones and mucus membranes. In that case, the best response to his need for an explanation — perhaps the only efficacious response — is to show him, with some second-person experience of her, that she loves him, that she would only let

526

him suffer in order to bring about some serious good for him which she couldn't get for him in any easier way.

The explanation that Job gets is of this second-person kind. What exactly the suffering effects in him, the medical or engineering details, aren't part of the explanation the divine speeches provide. But that they provide an explanation, and just the right kind of explanation for Job, is shown by Job's response. I began by asking how we could explain Job's subsiding into humility and acquiescence after all his defiance of God and his insistence on justice, if God's speeches to Job contain nothing but an assertion of God's power. What a closer look at the speeches makes clear is that this question rests on a false view of the content of the divine speeches and an obliviousness to their context. If we see the speeches in the way I have argued for, a second-person account set in the context of a second-person experience, showing Job the love of God, then we can understand better why Job reacts to them as he does.

Suppose you had been sure that the person who should love you the best had betrayed you, had abused your trust and used your vulnerability to him to cause you pain. Suppose that you've given vent to your anger and sense of betrayal in vehement speeches to his friends, or to anyone who will listen; suppose you've made these views known to him, too. And then two things happen. First, you are forcefully reminded, with a vivid second-person account, of the deeply loving character of your supposed betrayer and all the good he has done in the past. And, secondly, you see that powerful goodness and love directed towards you in his face. How would you feel? You might very well feel stricken, abashed, ashamed, and repentant — just the sort of emotions we find in Job. Job says, "Now my own eye has seen you," and he follows that line with this one: "So I recant and repent in dust and ashes" (42:6). Job wanted bare justice, but his face-to-face experience with God goes past justice to love.

Conclusion

Job does, then, have an explanation of his suffering; but it isn't of the sort that philosophers have been interested in when they considered theodicies, because it isn't a third-person account. A second-person experience can constitute a good explanation of a mistaken charge of betrayal for the person who has that experience, but it will be hard for him to use that experience to convince a third party, for just the reasons I gave when I was explaining why second-person accounts differ from third-person accounts. How Job knows what he knows — that his suffering is at the hands of a good and loving God — is hard to explain to someone who wasn't part of the same second-person experience. The best that can be done, as I argued above, is to turn that experience into a second-person account, of the sort we have in the story of God's conversation with Job. But stories aren't arguments; they can't compel a certain view of things as arguments can. Furthermore, they are much more likely to be persuasive to those who have had some experience of their own of the sort being described in the story. It is for that reason that people reveal themselves when they explain what novels they find moving.

Furthermore, what Job knows, that God loves him and didn't betray his trust, may not be what someone looking for a third-person account wants. It may be enough for the sick child, who has a shared history of loving relations with his mother, to know that she allows him to suffer only because she loves him. But an outsider who doesn't know the mother, who has no relation to her, may well want to know exactly what the connection between the suffering and the child's well-being is, before he is willing to grant that the mother is justified in allowing the child to suffer.

For both these reasons, the problem of evil presents itself differently to believers and to unbelievers. Believers come to the problem of evil with some sort of history of relations with the God they believe in. They can and they should draw on that history in reflections on suffering, in their own lives or in the lives of others. Very few religious believers can claim to have seen God, as Job did. But it is possible to have considerable intimate personal contact even with a person one has never seen, as, for example, people now sometimes do by means of the computer. In the shared history that such contact builds, there is a second-person experience that ought to make a difference to the way in which believers approach the problem of evil. Furthermore, the second-person accounts of God, the stories about God in Scripture, will be read differently by believers, who have their own religious experiences to draw on as they read them, from the way in which they are read by unbelievers, just as the second-person account in the divine speeches will strike Job differently from the way in which they strike an outsider.

So believers need not and should not think about the problem of evil in the same way unbelievers do, and a believer's resolution of the problem may be successful even if it isn't persuasive to non-believers. This is, in my view, one of the lessons of the book of Job, which we learn when we are sensitive to the nested second-person accounts which make up much of the book. And it helps to explain why contemporary academic accounts of the book take the form we find in the Anchor Bible commentary, which sees the book as raising a charge of injustice against God that is never answered, while a committed believer such as Thomas Aquinas reads the same texts as constituting a good explanation of the way in which a loving providence operates to govern the world.[44]

What a philosopher is naturally inclined to do at this point is to ask exactly how and why a believer is in a different position with regard to the problem of evil from that of a non-believer. Is a believer in a different epistemic position from a non-believer, and if so, in what respects, and why do those respects make a difference to the resolution of this problem? And why shouldn't a believer adopt the perspective of a non-believer in examining the problem of evil? Are there obligations to govern one's beliefs in certain ways; and if there are, what sort of obligations are they? And so on. These are good and important questions, but I am going to take up none of them. In my next lecture, I am going to examine what a believer's response to the problem of evil should be; but I am going to examine it in the spirit with which I began this lecture, in the conviction that there is an important role for second-person accounts in certain areas of philosophy. So I will look not at these philosophical issues, but at a biblical narrative, the binding of Isaac. Abraham is called the father of faith in consequence of his binding of Isaac. What is it that Abraham does in this story, and why does it constitute an expression of faith? What is the relation of faith to the problem of evil? To see the answers to these questions, we will have to look at the story of Abraham and Isaac as we looked at the book of Job, with attention to its nature as a second-person account of relations between a human person and God. When we have done so, the narrative will reveal itself to us in a new way, and what it shows us, I will argue, is a pattern for a believer's response to God in the face of suffering.

44. See my "Aquinas on the Sufferings of Job," op. cit.

SECOND LECTURE

Evil and the Nature of Faith

Introduction

In "Second-person Accounts and the Problem of Evil," I discussed the problem of evil in a preliminary way. I raised a methodological issue regarding philosophical problems such as the problem of evil, and I argued that at least sometimes an important role in their examination can be played by what I called (adapting a phrase from Avishai Margalit) 'a second-person account.' A second-person *experience* is the sort of experience I have when I have personal interaction of a direct and unmediated kind with another conscious person. A second-person *account* is a representing of such a second-person experience in a form which helps someone who was not part of that experience to simulate what it would have been like for him if he had been a bystander in it. I went on to argue that the book of Job is a second-person account of Job's interactions with God, and that God's speeches to Job are themselves a second-person account of God's interactions with his creatures. I tried to show that, contrary to common opinion, there is a theodicy in the book of Job but that it is in the form of a second-person account. Such a second-person account will have much more weight with believers than non-believers because, like Job, believers have their own second-person experiences of God, of one sort or another, to draw on. So, I argued in the last lecture, believers and non-believers will and should approach the problem of evil in different ways. Believers should bring to bear on the problem not only the usual array of philosophical and theological considerations but also their own religious experience of God and their interpretations of second-person accounts involving God, especially biblical narratives. To do so is to approach the problem of evil with the stance Job takes towards God at the end of the book.

530

In this lecture, I want to ask what difference it makes if we approach the problem of evil in this way.

Because I am going to talk about the problem of evil more directly in this lecture than in the last, it is important to ward off at the outset some possible misconceptions.

In the first place, because I will be discussing suffering in philosophical and theological ways, it is important to be reminded that nothing about this academic exercise ought to lessen our sensitivity to the pain of others or our determination to diminish it if and where we can. If reflection on suffering made us complacent about it, we would have gained the good of reflection at the cost of our humanity. To put the same point in a slightly different way, nothing in what I am going to say implies that suffering isn't really suffering. Whatever comforting context Christians may find for suffering, it remains a context for *suffering*.

Secondly, I want to draw attention to the form in which I am raising the problem of evil. I put the problem this way: If we draw on our experience as believers, how are we to understand and respond to a God who could prevent our suffering but does not do so? I am asking about our response as believers, and so I am not considering the problem in the standard way philosophers of religion do when they consider the problem as it is usually raised by unbelievers. In addition, I am asking about our response to God, and not about our response to people who suffer. For the purposes of this lecture it will be helpful for you to focus just on your own suffering, in order not to confuse the question I am asking with this very different question: how are we to understand and respond to the suffering of others? What is good and right for you to think to yourself about your suffering may be stupid and insensitive for you to say to someone else about her suffering.[1] This conclusion follows from the central role I am giving to second-person accounts in the explanation of the problem of evil. To the extent to which you do not

1. In my view, there are in fact instances of evil in the world with regard to which the only proper response is silence. In this connection, it is important for me to repeat a point I made in the first lecture. In the case of the Holocaust, which is special if not unique in its evil, I would not want to engage in a philosophical discussion of the reasons which might possibly justify God in allowing such suffering even if I could think of any. It is enough for me that I am a member of the species that perpetrated this evil. For such evil, speech should fail. The only right response for philosophers and theologians as regards God and the Holocaust seems to me the response of Job: I will consider the vileness of human beings and lay my hand on my mouth and be silent.

know someone else's story, you will not grasp the appropriate way for her to understand her suffering or God's role in it.

The answer to the question I *am* asking — how should we as believers understand and respond to a God who could prevent our suffering but does not do so? — has been given so often in the Christian tradition that it has become practically meaningless, and it is bound to strike you as deeply disappointing. The traditional answer is that in the face of our suffering we are to respond to God with faith.

I certainly don't intend to differ with the Christian tradition as regards the nature of the answer. But I do want to try to lessen the disappointment that the bare answer generates. As I promised in the first lecture, I am going to address the question of this lecture by turning for help to a second-person account, namely, the biblical story of the binding of Isaac.[2] Abraham is the father of faith, and he becomes the father of faith in virtue of his willingness to sacrifice Isaac at God's command. So if faith is the traditionally recommended response of Christians to suffering, we can consider in some detail what that response comes to by looking carefully at Abraham's actions as he becomes the father of faith. The second-person account of Abraham's interaction with God in the story of the binding of Isaac gives us insight into the nature of faith and so also into the nature of the right response of believers to suffering.

In what follows, I will examine the story of Abraham and Isaac at length, because I want to show a way of understanding that story which is different from some of the best-known interpretations of it. When I have made clear the interpretation I think is the right one, I will return to the problem of evil, to show what the story of Abraham and Isaac teaches us about faith as a response to suffering.

The story of Abraham's willingness to sacrifice his son figures prominently in all three major monotheisms;[3] and in the tradition I know best,

---

2. The discussion of the story of the binding of Isaac in this lecture is taken from a longer, unpublished study of the narrative. That study has benefited from helpful comments and criticisms by Harry Frankfurt, Yehuda Gellman, and Philip Quinn. Norman Kretzmann and I discussed the narrative for years, and his views were influential on my reading of the story. His own insightful analysis of it can be found in "Abraham, Isaac, and Euthyphro: God and the Basis of Morality," in *Hamartia. The Concept of Error in the Western Tradition. Essays in Honor of John Crossett*, ed. Donald Stump, James Arieti, Lloyd Gerson, and Eleonore Stump (New York: Edwin Mellen Press, 1983), pp. 27-50.

3. The son in question is Isaac for Judaism and Christianity, but Ishmael for Islam.

the Christian tradition, the story has been the source of endless discussion and commentary.[4] There are interesting and insightful interpretations of it by, for example, Origen, Augustine, Jerome, Aquinas, Nicholas of Lyra, Luther, Calvin, Kierkegaard, and hosts of others. It's not hard to see why the narrative commands this attention. The story itself is poignant: Abraham meekly going to sacrifice at God's command the beloved child of his old age. And it raises puzzling philosophical and theological questions. Why should God ask this sacrifice of Abraham, or why should he try Abraham as he does? And what is laudatory about Abraham's willingness to kill his own child? Why should Abraham's consent to destroy his son make him the father of faith?

Because Kierkegaard's reading of the story is as compelling as it is well-known, I will begin with a very rough summary of the basic conclusion of Kierkegaard's interpretation, as I see it. I make no pretensions to Kierkegaard scholarship, which is as contentious as the scholarship on any major figure in the history of philosophy; I am not attempting to contribute to that scholarship here, and I do not mean to adjudicate among any of the competing views regarding Kierkegaard's interpretation of this biblical narrative. But I can show more easily the interpretation of the story I want to offer if I take Kierkegaard as a foil, and Kierkegaard's interpretation is important for my purposes only insofar as it helps me bring out the salient features of the interpretation I argue for. So the reader who is primarily interested in Kierkegaard himself and who has his own strong views on how to interpret Kierkegaard correctly should take the next section of the lecture as presenting only a Kierkegaard-like interpretation.

---

4. There is, of course, extensive discussion of it in Islam and Judaism as well. For a translation of the Midrash Rabbah, see *Midrash Rabbah. Genesis*, vol. 1, trans. H. Freedman (London and New York: Soncino Press, 1983). For contemporary historical biblical study with considerable attention to rabbinic tradition, see Jon D. Levenson, *The Death and Resurrection of the Beloved Son* (New Haven: Yale University Press, 1993). I also learned a good deal from the excellent study by Jerome (Yehuda) Gellman, *The Fear, the Trembling, and the Fire: Kierkegaard and Hasidic Masters on the Binding of Isaac* (Lanham, Md.: University Press of America, 1994). I do not have the scholarly expertise to give even as much help as this in gaining access to the Islamic tradition of interpretation.

Kierkegaard's Interpretation of Abraham's Binding of Isaac

Kierkegaard thinks that we need to see Abraham and his faith in contrast to someone such as Agamemnon, who (in Kierkegaard's view) is a tragic hero but not a person of faith. A tragic hero such as Agamemnon "remains within the ethical," Kiekegaard says, but Abraham "overstepped the ethical entirely."[5] Agamemnon believed that the gods would not allow the winds to be favorable so that his army could sail to Troy unless he sacrificed his daughter to them; and he also believed that he had a moral duty to bring the army to Troy. So when Agamemnon sacrificed his daughter, he was within the bounds of the ethical, according to Kierkegaard, because he resigned his own dearest desires in order to fulfill his public responsibilities. Agamemnon, then, is faced with a difficult moral dilemma, but it is difficult for him just because it pits his desires and his duty to his daughter against his moral duty as leader of the army. When Agamemnon chooses his public duty over his daughter, Kierkegaard thinks, Agamemnon chooses what he sees as the lesser of two moral evils. Abraham, on the other hand, is a different case. Abraham is also caught in a dilemma, but it isn't a moral dilemma, on Kierkegaard's interpretation. In Abraham's case, there is no ethical principle which overrides the duty to his son. Instead, Kierkegaard thinks, Abraham was prepared to sacrifice Isaac "for God's sake, because God required this proof of his faith."[6] This attitude on Abraham's part is what Kierkegaard calls 'the teleological suspension of the ethical.' What is higher than ethical principles is Abraham's relationship to the person of God; and the demands of that relationship, which can't be codified in universal principles, take precedence over morality, on Kierkegaard's view. That is why there is a teleological suspension of the ethical in Abraham's case.

It looks therefore as if Kierkegaard understands the story of the binding of Isaac in this way. Morality imposes a requirement on Abraham, namely, that he not kill his son Isaac. But God's command also imposes a requirement. This isn't a moral requirement; if it were, Abraham's case would be assimilable to Agamemnon's. He would be subject to two conflicting moral requirements, of which one — namely, that imposed by

---

5. *Fear and Trembling,* trans. Walter Lowrie (Princeton: Princeton University Press, 1968), p. 69.

6. Ibid., p. 70.

God's command — would take precedence over the other. But Abraham is significantly different from Agamemnon in Kierkegaard's view, and the difference comes to this, that the requirement imposed by God's command isn't itself a moral requirement. Abraham is faced with two requirements, but one is moral and the other is religious. Since, however, the requirement imposed by God's command can't be overridden by anything and can itself override other obligations, what Abraham must do is consent to sacrifice his son. For Kierkegaard, Abraham's greatness consists in his willingness to suspend the ethical for the sake of obedience to God's command and his relationship to God.

Kierkegaard's explanation of the story leaves it perplexing in more than one respect. First, why would God try Abraham in this way? That is, why would a good God want to put his authority *against* morality, rather than with it? Given the constant emphasis of the biblical texts on the sinfulness of human beings, surely we aren't meant to suppose that the patriarch needed no encouragement and no improvement as regards morality but could go on to something greater instead. Second, why is Abraham's act supposed to make him the father of faith? In his willingness to submit ordinary morality to religious requirements he not only isn't unique but is even superseded. Jephthah was also willing to abrogate the prohibition against killing one's child for the sake of obedience to God; and, unlike Abraham, he actually did it.

Abraham, Isaac, Hagar and Ishmael

Kierkegaard's interpretation of the story of the binding of Isaac is insightful in many ways, but these difficulties with it seem to me sufficient to warrant rethinking the story as a whole. Kierkegaard is sensitive to the interaction between Isaac and Abraham, but like most commentators he pays little attention to the women in the story. In my view, however, it is important to read the story of the binding of Isaac in the context of other episodes in Abraham's life involving women and children. In fact, Abraham had three wives or concubines and eight sons, and the stories of these other wives and children are all useful for understanding the narrative about the binding of Isaac. In the interest of brevity, I will focus on just the most important of them, the expulsion of Hagar and Ishmael.

When it looks as if Sarah will never have children, she gives her maid

Hagar to Abraham, and Abraham has a son Ishmael by Hagar. Then, in her old age, when she is ninety and Abraham a hundred years old, Sarah does after all give birth to a son, whom Abraham names "Isaac." Ishmael is fourteen at the time of Isaac's birth. He has been Abraham's only child, his only son, for all these years; now he has a brother.

The story skips over Isaac's infancy and focuses directly on his weaning. When he was weaned, Abraham made a great feast, the story says. It is not clear how old Isaac was at the time of weaning; at least two or three years isn't an unreasonable speculation. If that is right, then Ishmael would have been at least sixteen or seventeen at the time. During the feast Ishmael does something — the Hebrew can be translated variously but has traditionally been understood as meaning that Ishmael was mocking Isaac. Whatever it is Ishmael is doing, Sarah sees him and blows up. She has been violent towards her rival Hagar in the past. Given her history, the wonder is not so much that she blows up now as that with a son of her own she has tolerated Abraham's other son for so long.

What would be appropriate punishment for a teenage boy who mocked a younger brother, if in fact the reading which assigns this much culpability to Ishmael is right? Take his car privileges away for a week, we might say — but then we are a soft-hearted, child-centered culture. Nineteenth-century British educators, made of sterner stuff, would perhaps have prescribed a beating. What does Sarah want? She wants him thrown out of the family together with his mother, never to return. There is no suggestion whatsoever that Hagar has been in any way unkind to Isaac, but the punishment Sarah envisages for Ishmael encompasses Hagar, too.

If the punishment Sarah had in mind were just banishment from the family, it would be a terrible evil. Ishmael is Abraham's son, and Hagar, his mother, has been a part of this complicated family for two decades or more. For years Abraham no doubt thought this boy would be his only child. Ishmael was his son, his only son, the son of his old age, for fourteen years before Isaac came. The bonds of trust and love between Abraham and the boy must have been powerful. For Abraham to throw the boy out is a horrible betrayal of the boy's trust towards his father, which can hardly be justified by whatever Sarah saw in his relations with Isaac at the party.

But what Sarah wants is considerably worse than this. In nineteenth-century Britain, sons thrown out by stern fathers were thrown into city life, where they might try to get their own living or sponge off friends or at nightmarish worst beg on street corners. But if Hagar and Ishmael are thrown out, they will be thrown out to the desert with all its perils. Being taken as slaves or chattel is the best that is likely to happen to them. If they aren't found and preyed on by others, their chance of surviving alone in the wilderness is small. In fact, as the story develops, it takes divine intervention just to keep them from dying of thirst. Throwing a woman and her child out into the desert without protection is the analogue of exposing unwanted infants. Perhaps it isn't identical to murder, but the difference doesn't seem to have much moral significance. If anything, what Sarah wants is in a sense worse than infanticide. At least, an infant hasn't built up trust in his father; the father's exposing him doesn't betray years of love and intimacy.

Clearly, Sarah isn't interested just in removing Hagar and Ishmael from the family. What Sarah wants is not the absence of her rival but revenge on her, and on her offspring, too. Her anger is murderous, and the depth of her passion is shown by that fact that she expresses it in a direct command to her husband: "cast out the bondwoman and her son." (21:10) This is not the direction the order of command usually flows in this patriarchal society.

That Abraham is willing to contemplate going along with Sarah at all is testimony to the virulence and implacability of her wrath. But even so, he can't bring himself to agree, no matter how wretched she makes him. "[T]he thing was very grievous in Abraham's sight on account of his son."[7] And so Abraham is caught between options each of which must seem unthinkable to him: on the one hand, holding out against his furious wife Sarah; on the other hand, agreeing to abandon and expose his son and the mother of his son. It should be clear that although he may be torn between these options, they don't constitute a moral dilemma for him. All morality is on one side; what the other side has to recommend is just domestic peace.

It is at this point that God comes to talk to Abraham. "Let it not be grievous in your sight because of the lad and because of your bondwoman," God says. "[I]n all that Sarah says to you, hearken to her voice."[8] So God breaks the deadlock, and he breaks it, very surprisingly, by siding

7. Genesis 21:11; for present purposes I am using the translation of Genesis in *The Pentateuch and Haftorahs,* ed. J. H. Hertz, second edition (London: Soncino Press, 1961), but I have modernized the English slightly.
8. Genesis 21:12.

with murderous Sarah. How can God tell Abraham to listen to his wife when what she wants is so evil? The answer to this question has two parts. First, although Sarah's intentions are evil, the result she wants, that only Isaac should count as Abraham's heir, is the result God has foreordained all along; and, secondly, God undertakes to guarantee not only Ishmael's safety but also his flourishing.[9] "[O]f the son of the bondwoman," God tells Abraham, "I will make a nation."[10]

If God promises to make Ishmael a nation, then God is promising that the boy won't die in the desert, where Sarah wants to abandon him. On the contrary, God is promising that Ishmael will become the progenitor of a whole people. So what Sarah sees as a way of abandoning and exposing Ishmael to likely death, God will turn into a way of making Ishmael something glorious. God's promise, then, relieves Abraham of the evil of conspiring to kill his son. It also relieves him, at least to a considerable extent, of the evil of betraying his son's trust — because he can tell Ishmael what God has said. He can explain that he is not acting in such a way as to bring about Ishmael's death or even his ruin, because God is guaranteeing Ishmael's thriving.[11]

It is clear, then, that God's message to Abraham makes all the difference. It is as if the place where the wicked stepmother wanted the father's son to be deserted should turn out to be the boarding school from which the society's leaders and rulers come. Abraham can explain this to his son, and in explaining it, Abraham will show not only God's love for Ishmael but also his own. So God's promise to make of Ishmael a great nation enables Abraham to go along with Sarah without being guilty of betraying

9. There is also the question, of course, about God's relations to Sarah. Insofar as he sides with Sarah when she is so thoroughly in the wrong, he might seem to fail her. God's relations with Sarah, however, and the details of Sarah's role in the story of Abraham and Isaac are outside the scope of this lecture. It is certainly worthwhile considering Sarah's acts, Sarah's beliefs and emotions, and Sarah's responses in the stories of Ishmael and of the binding of Isaac; but it isn't possible to examine everything in this short space. What is at issue in this lecture is just Abraham's faith in the binding of Isaac.

10. Genesis 21:13; see also 17:20 and 21:18, where the promise is to make out of Ishmael a great nation.

11. For the sake of brevity, I am leaving the dreadful injustice to Hagar to one side; but this much should probably be said. Given the nature of this society, insofar as God guarantees Ishmael's safety and flourishing, much of what constitutes Hagar's well-being is also safeguarded.

and destroying his son. Without God's promise, the action Sarah wants Abraham to engage in goes directly contrary to the strong moral concerns Abraham evinced even for total strangers in Sodom and Gomorrah, where he worried about the injustice of condemning the righteous with the wicked and killing those that were innocent. With God's promise Abraham can acquiesce to Sarah's demands without thereby betraying either his moral convictions or his son.

And so Abraham rises up early in the morning, gives Hagar and Ishmael a bottle of water and a loaf of bread, and sends them off to walk through the desert. In these circumstances, things go for the mother and son pretty much as one might have predicted: they wander aimlessly in the wilderness until the water is spent, without finding any shelter or protection, without finding any wells. After a while Hagar is sure they will die of thirst, and she goes some distance from her son, weeping as she goes, in order not to be a witness to his death. At that point, God intervenes. He helps Hagar find water, and he comforts her by repeating his promise: "I will make [Ishmael] a great nation."[12] The narrative closes this episode by saying that God was with the boy in the wilderness as he grew. In other words, in the story God fulfills the promise he made to Abraham.

Abraham and the Expulsion of Ishmael

It is important to see here that God's promise to Abraham enables Abraham to give in to Sarah without being guilty of a terrible moral wrong only in case God's promises are trustworthy, and in two senses. In order for God's speech to serve its beneficial functions, it must, first, be true that God keeps his promises; God must be good, unwilling to concur in the unjust punishment of the righteous or the killing of an innocent child. As the story of Hagar and Ishmael in the wilderness makes perfectly plain, God's promise is trustworthy in this sense. But, second, it must also be the case that Abraham believes God is good in these ways. If God's promises were reliable but Abraham didn't believe that they were, then Abraham would be guilty of a great evil in agreeing to Sarah's plan, even if (contrary to what Abraham believed) God made good on his word to care for Ishmael.

Furthermore, if Abraham is so much as double-minded about God's

12. Genesis 21:18.

539

goodness in this case, where the lives of Hagar and Ishmael are at stake, then he is facilely using God as an excuse to betray the trust of his son and to do a dreadful injustice to an innocent child and his mother. If Abraham accepts God's promise as an excuse to give in to Sarah without entirely and wholeheartedly believing that promise, it will be clear that he doesn't really believe in God's goodness; he will be supposing that God doesn't much mind being used as an accessory to serious evil. So it makes a great deal of difference what we suppose Abraham's psychological state was when he accepted God's promise.

The problem is that in difficult and complicated cases, where morality and self-interest are obviously on the same side, it is not easy for anyone to tell which is the main motivator for the action. When God tells Abraham to do what Sarah wants, God is decreeing that Abraham take the husband's easy way out of a conflict with a passionate and strong-willed wife: don't fight it; give in. Is Abraham doing what he does because he believes God is good and has the right of it, or is he doing it because it is a great relief not to have to try to withstand Sarah? Perhaps because in this case Abraham's self-interest and his perceived duty are on the same side, no clear and determinate answer can be given.

On the other hand, it is instructive to contrast Abraham's reaction to this promise of God's with other occasions on which Abraham talks with God. When the issue was the lives of total strangers, in Sodom and Gomorrah, Abraham bargained with God. But here, where what is at issue is the abandonment of the child who has been a part of his life for sixteen years or more, he attempts no negotiations with God. He might have asked God whether he couldn't guide Ishmael and his mother personally to a sheltering community or at least to some oasis. He might have asked whether he couldn't send an entourage of servants with Hagar to protect her, or whether at least he couldn't send her and the boy off with some herds and flocks to sustain them. When he sends away the sons of his concubine Keturah, years later, he sends them away with gifts.[13] This child, who was his only child for at least fourteen years, is dismissed with a bottle of water and a loaf of bread. When Abraham wants a wife for Isaac, he puts together an enticing array of jewelry and other gifts, and he provides a servant and animals to help bring her back. Hagar has no servants to protect her, no animals for speed and comfort, and no nest egg of gifts;

---

13. Genesis 25:6.

she is just sent off with her son, and virtually nothing else at all, to walk away from her home.

Furthermore, earlier on, when God made him a promise of biological offspring, Abraham asked for some divine confirmation of the truth of God's promise; how shall I know this is true? he asked. Here, where the life of his son is at stake, he asks for no sign. Without any negotiations, without any request for a sign of the truth of the promise, he just rises up early in the morning, hands Hagar and Ishmael some meager provisions, and sends them away.

Even given the reassurance of God's promise, there is something distressing about the readiness with which Abraham acquiesces in Sarah's demand to get rid of Hagar and Ishmael.

The Binding of Isaac

The last recorded occasion on which God comes to talk to Abraham is the episode of the binding of Isaac. The story begins by noting the lapse of time: "some time afterwards," or "it came to pass after these things."[14] How much afterwards? The only way to mark the time is by the description of Isaac. He is still young enough to be diffident and deferential towards his father. On the other hand, he is old enough to carry some distance up a mountain a load of wood big enough for him to lie down on. So it seems plausible to suppose that Isaac is somewhere in his teens, reasonably close, in other words, to the age Ishmael was when his father abandoned him in the desert.

At the outset of God's message is an elaborate identification of Isaac: "your son, your only son, Isaac, whom you love." The phrase 'your *only* son' is striking. If you had abandoned one of your two boys in the desert, would you be able to hear that phrase "only son" without wincing? And if the phrase came from the person who told you to go ahead and do it, wouldn't you wince all the more? And if the person who guaranteed the safety of your deserted son now uses the locution "only son," wouldn't you immediately think of the boy you abandoned and wonder in what sense Isaac was an only son? So the trial of Abraham comes at a time when Isaac is about the age Ishmael was when Abraham threw him out, and it begins by re-

14. Genesis 22:1.

minding us irresistibly of Ishmael in virtue of referring to Isaac as Abraham's only son.

The content of God's message is enough to turn a father's heart to stone: take the only son you have — that is, the only son you have left — and offer him up to me as a burnt offering. But here we should again be brought to think of the expulsion of Ishmael. Then God gave permission for Abraham to act in a way which, without divine intervention, seemed likely to bring about Ishmael's death. What made it morally permissible for Abraham to accept God's command to give in to Sarah and abandon Ishmael was that he had a promise from God that God would make Ishmael a great nation. That promise entails not only that Ishmael survive but also that he flourish. So if that promise is trustworthy, Ishmael can be left to himself in the wilderness without fear of harm coming to him, however reasonable it would otherwise seem to believe that he would die. It is only Abraham's belief in God's goodness and his belief in the trustworthiness of God's promise which kept Abraham on that occasion from committing a terrible wrong against his own child. Now God himself requires the death of Isaac. But, of course, as we know, Abraham also has a promise from God about Isaac: Isaac also is destined to be the source of a great nation.

If God is good and does not break his promises, then Isaac will have children, who will count as Abraham's descendants, inherit the land of Canaan, increase greatly in number, and include kings.[15] But when God tells Abraham to sacrifice Isaac, Isaac is still a boy, without children of his own. If Abraham ends Isaac's life now, God's promises about Isaac will be false, God won't be good, and his promises won't be trustworthy. And conversely, if God is good and his promises are trustworthy, then Isaac's life won't end now, however reasonable it seems from the human point of view to believe that sacrificing him will terminate his existence.

What should Abraham think? Abraham now has to confront in deadly earnest the fact that he was willing to abandon his first-born son in the desert on the strength of God's promise to make of him a great nation. From a human point of view, abandoning a child in the desert is very likely to kill him. But if God is good and keeps his promises, then Ishmael will not only live but even prosper in the desert. How God can bring that about is perhaps not clear in advance, but as God says to Abraham and as Abraham himself learns by experience in the conception and birth of

15. Cf. Genesis 15:4-5, 15:18, 17:4-16.

Isaac, lots of things which look impossible turn out to be not too difficult for God. And so Abraham turned Ishmael and Hagar out to wander in the wilderness, believing of himself that he was doing nothing immoral in the process.

But that was then, when his self-interest was strongly on the side of supposing that God would keep his promises. Now things are different. Doing what looks certain to bring about the death of Isaac is as strongly opposed to his self-interest as it could possibly be. If Abraham now demurs, if he now finds that it is unreasonable to believe both that he could act in a way extremely likely to bring about a child's death and yet the child could live, or if he now conceives a great doubt whether he can trust the promises of God, what will we think, looking back, on the way he dealt with Ishmael? Won't we think that his apparent trust in God then was a facile excuse for doing a great moral wrong because it made his life easier? Won't we suppose that he took God lightly, using God to rationalize his own actions when it suited him but doubting God and hanging back now when self-interest points the other way? And if he refuses to entrust Isaac to God's promises now, won't we be inclined to see his willingness to cast Ishmael out then as a monstrous act toward his own son, rendered all the more sleazy by being cloaked in the hypocrisy of religion?

In asking him to sacrifice Isaac, God is asking Abraham what he would have done in the case of Ishmael if self-interest and trust in God had been on opposites sides, instead of converging. In effect, God's command to sacrifice Isaac asks Abraham to decide what he would have done on that earlier occasion if it had been Isaac instead of Ishmael. Would he have believed God's promises in that case, or did it make a difference that the child whose life was at risk was Ishmael? If Abraham really believed that God could be trusted to make Ishmael survive and flourish when he sent him to walk into the desert with a bottle of water and a loaf of bread, doesn't he also have to trust God's promises with regard to Isaac?

And perhaps because Abraham was so ready to obey God's command to give in to Sarah, without any bargaining for Hagar and Ishmael, the trial here is particularly difficult for him. It is one thing to believe that God can make Ishmael survive in the desert. It is another thing to believe that God can make Isaac the ancestor of kings and great nations if he is sacrificed as a burnt offering. And the pain of the trial is also intense. In the case of Ishmael, Abraham exposed his son to the perils of the wilderness. In the case of Isaac, God is asking him to do the killing directly himself. If you were Ishmael, don't you suppose you might think Abraham had this trial coming, in all its difficulty and intensity?

Looking at the trial from Ishmael's point of view makes it seem like punishment. Looking at it from God's point of view makes it seem like a refining fire for Abraham. In the expulsion of Ishmael, Abraham's motives were mixed, so that there was perhaps no fact of the matter about whether Abraham acted out of trust in God's goodness or out of a self-interested desire to achieve domestic peace. The command to sacrifice Isaac pulls apart trust in God's goodness and self-interest. Abraham must now stake his hopes on God's goodness, or he must make clear that in the expulsion of Ishmael he was just using God as a means to a disgustingly wrong act, without supposing that God cared or took much notice of the wrongness of his action. So this trial refines Abraham; whichever way he acts, he will act out of unmixed motives this time. He will act either out of self-interest with suspicion towards God, or out of belief in God's goodness but in a way which seems to jeopardize what he loves best.

Abraham's Test

Abraham's options, then, are to refuse to participate in what he believes will bring about the death of his son, because he doesn't after all trust God's promises, or to be willing to sacrifice Isaac, believing that in so doing he will not be bringing about the death of his son because a trustworthy God has promised that Isaac will be the progenitor of a great nation. It is important to see that, contrary to Kierkegaard's view, on neither option is Abraham willing to murder his son, although on the second option he is doing what, humanly speaking, *would* end the child's life save for the power and promise of God.

Furthermore, contrary to Kierkegaard's view, there is no dilemma for Abraham here. Abraham ought to trust God with Isaac, not only because that is the right attitude to take towards God but also because he has already staked the life of one son on God's goodness. There is nonetheless a test for Abraham, and a painful one at that. As long as Abraham is human and loves his son, entrusting him to God in this way will cost Abraham a groaning.

And what does Abraham do? Just as in the case of the expulsion of Ishmael, in response to God's command Abraham rises up early in the morning to do what he was told. But, of course, this fact alone doesn't tell us whether Abraham passes the test.

To see whether Abraham passes the test, we need to be clear about what would constitute failing it. He will fail this test if he does not treat Isaac in the same way in which he treated Ishmael. In the case of Ishmael, he was morally justfied when he willed to act in ways which, humanly speaking, looked likely to kill his son, just in case he believed that God would keep his promises and God's promises entailed that Ishmael would live and flourish. He has similar promises about Isaac, and here, too, he is being asked to act in ways which, humanly speaking, seem sure to destroy the child. To treat the two cases in the same way, then, requires believing that even if he sacrifices Isaac, Isaac will live and flourish. Is there anything too difficult for God? So Abraham passes this test not in case he is willing to give up Isaac, as most commentators assume, but just in case he believes that in sacrificing Isaac, he is not bringing Isaac's life to an end. He passes the test only if he believes that in sacrificing Isaac he is *not* giving him up.

On this way of seeing the story, Abraham's line to the servants is not a polite fib. When Abraham tells them, "Abide here with the donkey, and I and the lad will go yonder; and we will worship, and come back to you,"[16] Abraham isn't saying something he believes to be false in order to keep the servants from growing suspicious. Rather, he believes it. Similarly, when he tells Isaac, "God Himself will provide the lamb for a burnt-offering, my son,"[17] he is not engaging in tender deception or unconsciously cruel irony, as he would have to be if he thought he were about to kill Isaac. He believes what he says. There is agony, though, if not irony, in these lines, because of what it takes to believe them. Think about a man mountain-climbing with his son, who finds that the only way to safety lies across a large crevasse. If he didn't believe his son could make it, he wouldn't ask him to leap. But he may be bathed in sweat, with years taken off his life, by the time the boy makes it over.

The impression given by Abraham's lines to the servants and to Isaac is confirmed when God comes to deliver his verdict: Abraham passes the test. What God says to Abraham, at the point at which Abraham has raised the knife over Isaac, is this: "Do not lay your hand on the lad, or do anything to him; for now I know that you are a God-fearing man, seeing you

16. Genesis 22:5.
17. Genesis 22:8.

have not withheld your son, your only son, from Me."[18] And this line seems right. If Abraham had refused to trust Isaac to God after having been willing to expel Ishmael on God's promise, Abraham would have been mocking rather than fearing God on the earlier occasion involving Ishmael, acting as if God didn't matter much or didn't care much about the death of innocent children. But until Abraham had to choose whether to trust Isaac to God or not, perhaps no one could have known whether Abraham feared God, because Abraham's motives in the case of Ishmael were confused and mixed together. God knows now, because the trial over Isaac has refined Abraham's character. Abraham has been willing to trust his son, his *only* son, to God. And so God says to him at the end, "because you have done this thing, and have not withheld your son, your only son, . . . in blessing I will bless you, and in multiplying I will multiply your seed as the stars of the heaven, and as the sand which is upon the sea-shore; and your seed shall possess the gate of his enemies; and in your seed shall all the nations of the earth be blessed; because you have hearkened to My voice."[19]

Abraham as the Father of Faith

If we read the story of the sacrifice of Isaac in this way, in the context of the narrative about the expulsion of Ishmael, we will be able to answer the questions which posed serious difficulties for Kierkegaard's view. The story of Ishmael makes it clear that there is a morally acceptable answer to the question why God should try Abraham and why the test should take the form it does. What is at issue is whether Abraham will believe in the goodness of God, in Isaac's case as well as in Ishmael's, and not whether Abraham will sacrifice anything, morality included, to obey God.

Furthermore, what is praiseworthy about Abraham isn't his readiness to do just anything, including killing his son, in order to obey God. As we saw in the beginning, if that were what was supposed to make Abraham specially admirable, he would have to take second place to Jephthah, who not only raised the knife over his child but brought it down as well. Jephthah supposed that God wanted the death of his daughter and would be severely displeased if he didn't get it; he believed that God and morality can be on

18. Genesis 22:12.
19. Genesis 22:16-18.

opposites sides. But in Abraham's case, it is his willingness to believe in God's moral goodness, even against exceedingly strong appearances to the contrary, that makes him the father of faith. When Abraham passes the test, he passes it just because he believes that God is good and will not betray his promises, so that sacrificing Isaac will not end Isaac's life.

Abraham's faith, then, is not a faith in the existence of God, or in the divinity of the being who commands the sacrifice of Isaac, or in a duty to obey God's commands, no matter what. Abraham has a belief in God's existence and power and in his own obligation to obey God even before he decides what to do about God's command to sacrifice Isaac. But he becomes the father of faith only with his decision to sacrifice Isaac. No amount of evidence of the existence of the deity would have produced faith of this sort in Abraham; it required a state of will and character also. So the story of Abraham and Isaac, interpreted in this way, helps us see the nature of faith. The faith that makes Abraham the father of faith is an acceptance of the moral goodness of God, including a belief that God would never break his promises, that he would never deal with people in hurtful and deceitful ways.

It is important to belabor this point a little because the claim that God is good is often eviscerated of content for us, just as the notion of faith itself is. Sometimes when some suffering soul is told that God is good, the line seems to mean just that God is indeed hurting her but that, unlike Job, she must not complain about it. Not just any way of believing that God is good counts as Abraham's sort of faith, however. Job's comforters also insisted to Job that God is good, and they thought Job should take whatever happened to him as good and right because God did it. But it is noteworthy that when God adjudicates the dispute between Job and the comforters, God comes down squarely on Job's side. It takes sacrifices and Job's prayers to keep the comforters from the wrath of God.

How, then, does the position of the comforters differ from the position I am ascribing to Abraham which makes Abraham the father of faith?

It is as if the comforters and Abraham came down on opposites sides of the Euthyphro dilemma.[20] "Does God will what he wills because it is

---

20. For a discussion of the story of the binding of Isaac in connection with the Euthyphro dilemma, see Norman Kretzmann, "Abraham, Isaac, and Euthyphro: God and the Basis of Morality," op. cit.; see also Eleonore Stump and Norman Kretzmann, "Absolute Simplicity," *Faith and Philosophy* 2 (1985) 353-82.

good?" Socrates asks Euthyphro, "or is what God wills good because God wills it?" For the comforters, whatever God wills is good just because it is God who wills it. So in deciding whether something that happens is good, on the comforters' view of it, we need first and foremost to consider the agency; if God is the agent of what happens, then we don't need to know anything further in order to know that what happens is good. But if Abraham took this attitude, he would be failing the test which the command to sacrifice Isaac sets him. As I argued above, he passes the test only in case he believes that God's promise regarding Isaac is trustworthy and that, contrary to all reasonable expectation, he will not end Isaac's life in sacrificing him. For Abraham, then, there is an objective standard of goodness which includes the obligation to keep promises, and God does what he does because it is really, truly, objectively good.

Abraham is the father of faith, then, because he manages to believe that God is good even while he goes to sacrifice his son at God's command. And to say this is not to say that Abraham is willing to call 'good' anything demanded by a deity. God promised Abraham that he would have descendants through Isaac; and if what God wills is objectively good, God cannot be a promise-breaker. Abraham is the father of faith because he believes God is good in this sense, and so he also believes God does not break his promises. Therefore, although Abraham clearly understands what it is to sacrifice a child, he nonetheless believes that if he obeys God's command to sacrifice Isaac, Isaac will go on to live, to flourish, and to have descendants. Abraham believes that if he consents to sacrifice what he wants most and loves best, his son — his only son — Isaac, because God wills him to do so, he will still have what he wants most and loves best, because God is good. This looks paradoxical, of course; but it is important to see that, as the story itself shows, it is not contradictory. This paradoxical-looking belief on Abraham's part turns out in the story to be entirely correct.

Faith and the Problem of Evil

At the outset of this lecture, I raised the question, "How should we as believers understand and respond to a God who could prevent our suffering but does not do so?" and I said that the traditional answer is the apparently bland and disappointing line, "with faith." The story of Abraham's binding of Isaac gives us a second-person account of the nature of faith which makes that traditional line considerably less bland and not at all disappointing, in my view.

In the interest of brevity, I will elucidate this point just by recommending to you a thought experiment. Think of some suffering in your own life which broke your heart. (The thought experiment works only for your own suffering, for the reasons that I gave at the outset of this lecture.) In our suffering, what we as Christians are inclined to believe is that God exists, that he is powerful, that he can arrange our lives as he likes, that he does not arrange them as we like, and that we have to accept it at his hand, with whatever patience we can muster, because he is God. This looks like faith, but it isn't, as the story of Abraham and Isaac makes clear. The faith of Abraham is believing that God is really good and so keeps his promises. Now think of the promises of God, not just those directly attributed to God in Scripture but also those that Scripture makes on behalf of God. Consider, for example, this one: "Delight yourself in the Lord, and he will give you the desires of your heart" (Psalm 37:4).

What difference would it have made to you in your suffering if, with Abraham-like faith, you had managed to believe that God could be trusted to keep this promise? It is important here not to empty the phrase 'the desires of your heart' of its meaning. It doesn't mean some great abstract good which you ought to want but don't. It means what it says: the desires of *your* heart; and some general good you don't want is not a desire of your heart.

But, you might think, God couldn't give a heartbroken person the desire of his heart; for someone to be heartbroken is just for him to have lost the desire of his heart. I grant it looks this way — but then the belief that God would fulfill his promise to Abraham must also have been difficult for Abraham as he was going to sacrifice his son. Difficult to accept is not the same as irrational, however. For Christians as for Abraham and for Job, religious experience, reason, and the testimony of authoritative narratives about God converge on the conclusion that God is good; and if he is good, then he does not break his promises.[21]

If you managed to hold this belief in your suffering, it would not take

---

21. In an unpublished essay, "Betrayal of Trust: Mary, Martha, and Lazarus," I have addressed in some detail the implausibility of the claim that God can fulfill the Psalm's promise even for the heartbroken who seem to have lost the desires of their heart.

away the pain of the suffering. How could it possibly? But there is an appropriate analogy with the pains a woman goes through in childbirth. Although it does not take anything away from her pain, it makes all the difference in the world to a woman in the throes of the pain of childbirth to feel the presence of someone who loves her and to believe that her pain will eventuate in a baby who is the desire of her heart.

For these reasons, I think the traditional Christian answer, that we are to respond to God with faith in the face of suffering, isn't bland and disappointing. On the contrary, I think it is tough, deep, and comforting.

Conclusion

I argued in the first lecture that Job's response to God after God's speeches is best understood as Job's having come to a conviction that God is good and loving. Job's attitude towards God in the face of his own suffering is thus faith of Abraham's sort. Furthermore, I also argued that when Job sees God in this way, he does have an explanation for his suffering. It isn't a theodicy of the standard sort which tries to show just exactly what good suffering produces and how it produces it, in order to show that God is justified in allowing that suffering.[22] But it is an explanation nonetheless. We may still want a theodicy, for one reason or another. Faith seeking understanding is a traditional Christian attitude, and a successful theodicy would in some respects increase the understanding of faith. But believers need not suppose that without a successful theodicy they have no explanation for suffering. Those who share Abraham's faith also have Job's explanation for suffering.

22. It is possible to have Abraham's sort of faith and also a theodicy of this sort. Abraham himself may have understood very well why God was putting him through his ordeal. But often we don't know what benefit is connected to some particular suffering or the connection between the suffering and whatever benefit there may be.